Tax Assurance

Editor: dr R. Russo

Tax Assurance

Nathan Andrews

Irene Burgers

Eelco van der Enden

Joost Engelmoer

Eveline Gerrits

Hans Gribnau

Richard Happé

Bas Herrijgers

Robbert Hoyng

Mark Kennedy

Elmer van Lienen

Edwin van Loon

Marieke Louwen

Jeltje van der Meer-Kooistra

Ronald Russo

Eric van der Stroom

Jan van Trigt

Robbert Veldhuizen

Arco van de Ven

Leen Wesdorp

Wolters Kluwer

When you have to be right

Deventer – 2015

Cover design: Hans Roenhorst, www.h2rplus.nl
ISBN 978 90 13 12782 9
ISBN 978 90 13 12783 6 (E-book)
NUR 826/611

© 2015, Wolters Kluwer

All rights in this publication are reserved by Wolters Kluwer. No part of this publication may be copied, stored in an automated database or made public in any way or any format whatsoever without the prior written permission of Wolters Kluwer.

To the extent the Dutch Copyright Act allows the making of photocopies, the statutory fee shall be payable to Stichting Reprorecht te Hoofddorp, The Netherlands (PO Box 3060, 2130 KB).

Although the publisher has made every effort to ensure the accuracy of the information contained in this publication, the authors, editors and Wolters Kluwer Nederland B.V. do not accept any liability for any omissions or inaccuracies in this publication or any effects thereof.

TABLE OF CONTENTS

Preface
(Peter Essers) / XVII

1. **Definition and overview**
   (Ronald Russo) / 1

2. **Internal control and risk management**
   (Arco van de Ven) / 5

2.1   Introduction / 5
2.2   Financial reporting and fraud / 5
2.3   The shift to internal control / 7
2.4   Standardization of internal control / 10
2.5   The COSO internal control framework 2013 / 11
2.6   From internal control to risk management / 15
2.7   Limitations and side effects / 17
2.8   Conclusion / 21

3. **Corporate Governance and Taxes**
   (Ronald Russo, Jan van Trigt) / 23

3.1   General introduction / 23
3.2   Corporate governance and tax / 23
3.2.1   Introduction / 23
3.2.2   Corporate Governance: OECD regulations / 25
3.2.3   Corporate Governance: country regulations / 26
3.2.3.1   Germany / 26
3.2.3.2   UK / 26
3.2.3.3   The Netherlands / 27
3.2.3.4   US / 27
3.2.3.5   Summary and concluding remarks on corporate governance codes / 27
3.2.4   Risk appetite and policy / 28
3.2.5   How to respond to tax scandals / 30
3.2.6   How to deal with taxes as a board / 35
3.2.6.1   The importance of an approved tax policy / 35
3.2.6.2   Companies internationally active / 36
3.2.6.3   Central or decentralized management approach / 36
3.2.6.4   Be prepared for the public domain / 37

3.2.6.5	Does tax planning add to shareholders value? / 38	
3.2.6.6	Tax planning requires good corporate governance / 39	
3.2.6.7	A balanced set of KPI's for management performance measurement / 40	
3.2.6.8	A vision on transparency / 41	
3.2.6.9	How to deal with taxes as a board: summary / 42	
3.3	Tax in external communications / 42	
3.3.1	Tax position in the commercial accounts/provision for uncertain tax positions / 42	
3.3.2	Tax in other external communications / 45	
3.4	Cooperative compliance / 47	
3.5	Concluding remarks / 47	

4. Ethics and International Tax Planning
(Richard Happé) / 49

4.1	Introduction / 49
4.2	The splendid isolation of tax is over / 51
4.3	Aggressive tax planning: the phenomenon / 53
4.4	Aggressive tax planning: the ideology / 55
4.5	Is ethics relevant to economic behaviour? / 57
4.6	Aggressive tax planning and ethics / 58
4.7	A topical example of indignation about aggressive tax behaviour / 59
4.8	Tax ethics for multinationals / 61
4.9	Law, ethics and social reality / 63
4.10	The compliance obligation and the spirit of the law / 64
4.11	The fair share obligation and international tax arbitrage / 66
4.12	Reputation and the Aristotelian virtues / 68
4.13	Conclusion / 70

5. A Tax Operating Model
(Robert Hoyng, Nathan Andrews, Marc Kennedy) / 73

5.1	Introduction / 73
5.2	Tax operating model / 77
5.2.1	Level 1: Effective / 79
5.2.2	Level 2: Efficient / 86
5.2.3	Level 3: Transparent / 96
5.2.4	Value added / 107
5.3	Transformation / 112
5.3.1	Data and Information / 121
5.3.2	Process and Policy / 123
5.3.3	Technology and Systems / 125
5.3.4	People and Organisation / 129
5.4	Conclusion / 131

6. Cooperative compliance: large businesses and compliance management
(Robbert Veldhuizen) / 135

6.1	Introduction / 135	
6.1.1	New Governance and Cooperative Compliance / 135	
6.1.2	Outline of this chapter / 138	
6.2	Cooperative compliance: the urgency for a new compliance strategy / 138	
6.2.1	Australia and New Zealand / 138	
6.2.2	The Netherlands / 139	
6.3	OECD: from 'Enhanced Relationship' to 'Cooperative Compliance' / 140	
6.4	The development of Horizontal Monitoring in the Netherlands / 143	
6.4.1	Introduction / 143	
6.4.2	Horizontalisation of society / 143	
6.4.3	Corporate Governance and Internal Control / 144	
6.4.4	Scientific theorisation and research on tax compliance and behaviour / 146	
6.5	Horizontal Monitoring in practice / 148	
6.5.1	Introduction / 148	
6.5.2	Horizontal Monitoring: how it started / 148	
6.5.3	Horizontal Monitoring of large businesses in practice / 150	
6.5.4	Evaluation of HM by the Commission Horizontal Monitoring / 153	
6.6	Compliance Management Systems in New Governance / 153	
6.6.1	Compliance Management Systems / 153	
6.6.2	Effectiveness of Compliance Management Systems / 156	
6.6.3	Standard Setting in the context of Compliance Management Systems / 158	
6.6.4	NTCA and TCF / 160	
6.7	Conclusion / 162	

7. Cooperative compliance: small and medium sized entities
(Bas Herrijgers) / 163

7.1	Introduction / 163	
7.2	Dutch landscape of small and medium sized companies / 164	
7.3	New ways of supervision for SMEs / 165	
7.4	Horizontal monitoring by SMEs / 168	
7.4.1	Compliance agreement discussions and concluding a compliance agreement / 168	
7.4.2	Applications for and reviews of entrepreneurs / 170	
7.4.3	Preliminary consultations / 170	
7.4.4	Filing and processing of compliance agreement tax returns / 171	
7.4.5	Audits of random samples of tax returns / 171	
7.4.6	Monitoring and evaluation of the compliance agreement / 171	
7.5	Meta-monitoring / 172	

7.6	The changing role of the tax service provider / 175	
7.7	Dutch horizontal monitoring in SME segment in international perspective / 176	
7.8	Opportunities and threats of horizontal monitoring in SME segment / 177	
7.9	Alternatives for horizontal monitoring in the SME segment / 179	
7.9.1	Pre-filled tax return / 179	
7.9.2	Outsourcing monitoring / 179	
7.9.3	Certification of Tax service providers / 180	
7.9.4	Managed audit / 180	
7.9.5	Tax Statement / 180	

8. Cooperative compliance: some procedural tax law issues
(Hans Gribnau) / 183

8.1	Introduction / 183
8.2	A very short introduction to Horizontal Monitoring / 186
8.2.1	An informal approach based on compliance risk management / 186
8.2.2	Conflicting and shared interests / 190
8.3	Horizontal Monitoring and procedural tax law / 194
8.3.1	Discretion and voluntary agreements / 194
8.3.2	Two techniques of levying taxes / 197
8.3.2.1	Levying by way of assessment / 198
8.3.2.2	Levying taxes by way of a tax return / 199
8.3.2.3	Evaluation / 200
8.3.3	Disclosure obligations, sanctions and legal protection / 201
8.3.3.1	Disclosure obligations / 201
8.3.3.2	Sanctions / 202
8.3.3.3	Right to objection and right of appeal / 204
8.3.3.4	Principles of proper administrative behaviour / 205
8.4	Horizontal Monitoring and the legal framework / 207
8.4.1	General remarks / 207
8.4.2	Proactively providing information / 208
8.4.3	Penalties / 209
8.4.4	Dispute resolution / 209
8.4.5	Principle of equality / 210
8.4.6	Fair play: agree to disagree / 212
8.5	Conclusion / 215

9. Tax Accounting
(Eveline Gerrits) / 217

9.1	Introduction / 217
9.2	Introduction of IAS 12 / 218
9.3	Current tax / 218
9.3.1	Recognition of current tax / 218
9.3.2	Measurement of current tax / 219

9.3.3	Reporting of current tax / 219	
9.4	Deferred tax / 220	
9.4.1	Temporary differences / 221	
9.4.1.1	The origination of temporary differences / 221	
9.4.1.2	Taxable and deductible temporary differences / 222	
9.4.1.3	Recognition of temporary differences / 223	
9.4.1.3.1	Exceptions to the recognition of temporary differences. / 224	
9.4.1.4	Investments in subsidiaries, branches, associated participations and interests in joint arrangements. / 228	
9.4.1.4.1	No deferred tax liability in respect of investments in subsidiaries / 229	
9.4.1.4.2	Recognition of deferred tax assets in respect of investments in subsidiaries / 230	
9.4.1.5	Recognition of deductible temporary differences / 230	
9.4.2	Unused tax losses and other unused tax credits / 232	
9.4.2.1	Recognition of unused tax losses and tax credits / 233	
9.4.3	Measurement of deferred tax / 233	
9.4.3.1	Discounting / 234	
9.4.4	Reporting of deferred tax / 234	
9.4.4.1	Changes to the carrying amount of deferred tax / 235	
9.5	The disclosure of information / 235	
9.5.1	Tax components / 235	
9.5.2	Tax recognized in equity or OCI / 237	
9.5.3	The effective tax rate reconciliation (ETR) / 237	
9.5.4	Changes to tax rates / 238	
9.5.5	Unrecognized deferred tax assets / 239	
9.5.6	Temporary differences related to investments in subsidiaries for which no deferred tax liability was recognized / 239	
9.5.7	Tax consequences of dividend distributions to shareholders / 239	
9.5.8	Movement schedule of deferred tax / 240	
9.5.9	Business combination / 240	
9.5.10	Recognized deferred tax assets in tax loss situations / 240	
9.5.11	Discontinued business operations / 241	
9.6	Presentation / 241	
9.6.1	Current tax / 241	
9.6.2	Deferred tax / 242	
9.7	Uncertain tax positions / 242	
9.7.1	Provisions dealt with in IAS 37 / 243	
9.7.2	Measurement under IAS 37 / 244	
9.7.3	Contingent liabilities / 247	
9.7.4	US GAAP, Accounting Standard Codification (ASC) 740 / 247	
9.7.4.1	Disclosure / 248	
9.8	VAT, payroll tax and social security contributions / 249	
9.8.1	Assets and liabilities / 250	
9.8.2	Provisions and liabilities / 250	
9.8.3	Contingent assets / 251	
9.8.4	Conclusion / 252	

9.9	Country-by Country-Reporting (CbCR) / 253	
9.9.1	Extractive Industry and CbCR / 253	
9.9.2	Credit institutions and investment firms / 254	
9.9.3	Base Erosion and Profit Shifting / 254	
9.9.4	Interaction with tax accounting / 255	

10. Payroll taxes 'in control'
(Elmer van Lienen, Marieke Louwen) / 257

10.1	Introduction / 257
10.2	Payroll taxes: introduction and key players / 258
10.2.1	Introduction / 258
10.2.2	Key players / 259
10.2.2.1	HR department / 259
10.2.2.2	Finance department / 260
10.2.2.3	Payroll department / 260
10.2.2.4	Tax department / 261
10.2.2.5	Legal department / 261
10.2.2.6	Fleet management department / 261
10.2.2.7	Marketing department / 261
10.2.2.8	Procurement department / 262
10.2.2.9	Global mobility department / 262
10.2.2.10	Payroll provider / 262
10.2.2.11	Internal audit / 263
10.2.2.12	The tax authorities / 263
10.2.2.13	Third parties / 263
10.2.2.14	Other / 264
10.2.3	Conclusion / 264
10.3	Risks and control / 264
10.3.1	Framework / 264
10.3.2	Inherent risks / 265
10.3.2.1	Payroll administration / 265
10.3.2.2	Payroll tax knowledge / 267
10.3.2.3	Communication / 267
10.3.2.4	Hiring new employees / 268
10.3.2.5	Firing/retiring employees / 269
10.3.2.6	HR and payroll mutations / 269
10.3.2.7	(Fixed) expenses / 269
10.3.2.8	Global mobility / 271
10.3.2.9	Hiring third parties / 272
10.3.2.10	Company car / 272
10.3.2.11	Benefits in kind / 273
10.3.2.12	Work related Cost Regulation / 273
10.3.3	Approach identifying payroll tax risks / 274
10.4	Monitoring/testing / 275
10.4.1	Appointed points of attention / 275

Table of Contents

10.4.2 Completeness / 277
10.5 Summary / 277

11. Specific issues indirect taxes
(Edwin van Loon) / 279

11.1 Introduction / 279
11.2 The impact of VAT / 279
11.2.1 General / 279
11.2.2 Finance / 280
11.2.3 IT and audit / 281
11.2.4 Internal audit / 282
11.2.5 The role of the tax administration / 283
11.3 Paradoxes and misunderstandings / 284
11.3.1 The paradox: 'VAT is paid by companies that are exempt from VAT' / 284
11.3.2 'VAT is not a cost' / 285
11.3.2.1 The European VAT GAP / 285
11.3.2.2 The 'VAT dogma' / 286
11.3.2.3 The tax assurance professional's response / 290
11.4 The (indirect) tax function's risk assessment function / 290
11.4.1 Introduction / 290
11.4.2 ITR: Inherent Tax Risk (ITR) / 291
11.4.3 OTR: Operational Tax Risks / 293
11.4.4 TCR: Tax Controls Risk / 294
11.4.5 TDR: Tax Detection Risk / 295
11.5 Indirect tax issues / 295
11.5.1 Introduction / 295
11.5.2 Direct debits and credits / 296
11.5.3 Foreign VAT / 297
11.5.4 Supplier/customer transactions / 299
11.5.5 Netting / 300
11.5.6 Bad debt accounting / 302
11.6 Conclusive remarks / 303

12. Specific issues corporate income taxes
(Eelco van der Enden, Eric van der Stroom) / 305

12.1 Introduction: Why is it difficult to manage CIT? / 305
12.2 The model / 306
12.2.1 Business and tax environment / 307
12.2.1.1 Tax strategy / 308
12.2.1.2 Tax roles and responsibilities / 309
12.2.1.3 Tax awareness / 310
12.2.1.4 Soft controls / 311
12.2.2 Business operations / 311
12.2.3 Tax operations / 314

12.2.3.1	CIT preparation and filing / 315	
12.2.3.2	CIT Accounting process / 316	
12.2.3.3	CIT assessment and payment / 317	
12.2.3.4	A possible CIT audit by Tax Authorities / 318	
12.2.4	Tax risk management / 320	
12.2.4.1	Main CIT risks / 321	
12.2.4.1.1	Tax technical risks / 321	
12.2.4.1.2	Risks relating to processes, people and systems / 326	
12.2.4.1.3	CIT preparation and filing / 326	
12.2.4.1.4	CIT Accounting process / 327	
12.2.4.1.5	CIT assessment and payment / 328	
12.2.4.1.6	A possible CIT audit by Tax Authorities / 328	
12.2.5	Monitoring and testing / 329	
12.2.5.1	Controls testing / 330	
12.2.5.2	Substantive testing / 330	
12.2.6	Tax Assurance / 331	
12.2.6.1	Internal Assurance / 331	
12.2.6.2	External Assurance / 332	
12.3	Concluding / 333	

13. Control Frameworks for Cross-Border Internal Transactions: the Tax perspective versus the Management Control perspective
(Irene Burgers, Jeltje van der Meer-Kooistra) / 335

13.1	Introduction / 335
13.2	The tax perspective / 340
13.2.1	Introduction / 340
13.2.2	Arm's length principle / 340
13.2.3	Codification in Art. 9 OECD Model and Art. 9 UN Model for intercompany transactions (parent-subsidiary) / 341
13.2.4	Codification in Art. 7 OECD Model and Art. 7 UN Model for intracompany transactions (PEs) / 342
13.2.5	Transfer Pricing Guidelines and Reports on the Allocation of Profits to Permanent Establishments / 343
13.2.6	Transfer Pricing Methods / 346
13.2.7	Documentation requirements / 350
13.2.8	OECD Transfer Pricing Risk Assessment Handbook / 352
13.2.9	Tax Control Framework / 353
13.3	The management control perspective / 354
13.3.1	Introduction / 354
13.3.2	Benefits of internal transactions: lower transaction costs / 354
13.3.3	Supporting the decision-making process / 355
13.3.4	Key elements of the management control framework of internal transactions / 357
13.4	Differences between the tax perspective and the management control perspective / 358

Table of Contents

13.4.1	Goal of the perspective: preventing double taxation and profit shifting versus influencing behaviour within the company / 358
13.4.2	Goal of the perspective: focus on significant transfer pricing risks versus risks in general / 359
13.4.3	Point of departure: legal entities versus organisational units / 360
13.4.4	Point of departure: country-by-country versus organisational unit-by-organisational unit / 360
13.4.5	Point of departure: transfer pricing documentation requirements that may differ from country to country versus transfer pricing documentation determined by the (group of) company(ies) / 361
13.4.6	Synergy effects versus transaction costs / 361
13.4.7	Aim of transfer pricing methods used: arm's length result versus desired degree of decentralisation / 361
13.4.8	Determination of costs: what costs would be used by third parties versus what costs would influence the behaviour of the transacting parties / 362
13.4.9	Bargaining as transfer pricing method / 363
13.4.10	Acceptance of simultaneous use of two or more transfer pricing methods / 363
13.4.11	Timing issues: 'no hindsight' versus 'making use of up-to-date information' / 364
13.4.12	Relation of transfer pricing systems with the overall Management Control System / 364
13.5	Consequences of using one framework for controlling internal transactions for both the tax perspective and the management control perspective / 364
13.6	Conclusions: one or two control frameworks of internal transactions? / 366

14. Audit of tax
(Leen Wesdorp) / 369

14.1	Introduction / 369
14.1.1	General purpose of an audit / 369
14.1.1.1	Objective of an auditor / 370
14.1.1.2	Reasonable Assurance / 370
14.1.2	Risk based methodology (audit risk model) / 371
14.1.2.1	Risks of material misstatement at the financial statement level / 372
14.1.2.2	Risk of material misstatement at the assertion level / 372
14.1.2.3	Risk assessment procedures / 372
14.1.3	High level summary of the audit process / 375
14.1.3.1	Planning and risk identification / 375
14.1.3.1.1	Determination Planning Materiality / 376
14.1.3.1.2	The perspectives and expectations of the users of the financial statements / 376
14.1.3.1.3	The appropriate measurement basis / 377
14.1.3.1.4	The appropriate percentage to apply to the measurement basis / 377

14.1.3.1.5   Determination Tolerable Error (TE) / 377
14.1.3.1.6   Determination SAD nominal amount / 378
14.1.3.1.7   Identification of significant accounts and disclosures and determination of relevant assertions / 378
14.1.3.2   Strategy and risk assessment / 380
14.1.3.2.1   The identification and understanding of the SCOT, SDP and FSCP, performing walkthroughs and testing of manual and IT controls / 380
14.1.3.2.2   Performing the combined risk assessment / 381
14.1.3.2.3   Designing test of controls including journal entry tests, substantive and general audit procedures / 385
14.1.3.2.4   Preparation of audit strategy memorandum / 386
14.1.3.3   Execution / 387
14.1.3.3.1   Execution of the test of controls / 387
14.1.3.3.2   Journal entry testing and fraud procedures. / 388
14.1.3.3.3   Performing substantive and general audit procedures / 388
14.1.3.4   Conclusion and reporting / 388
14.2   Application of the audit methodology to income taxes / 389
14.2.1   Specific characteristics of the income tax positions in the consolidated financial statements / 389
14.2.1.1   Introduction / 389
14.2.1.2   Jurisdictions and different frameworks and currencies / 390
14.2.1.3   Current income tax / 391
14.2.1.4   Deferred income tax / 392
14.2.1.5   Disclosure requirements and tax accounting tools / 393
14.2.1.6   Restatements procedures and income taxes / 394
14.2.1.7   Impact on inherent risk assessment / 395
14.2.2   Audit methodology and income taxes / 395
14.2.2.1   Planning and risk identification / 395
14.2.2.2   Strategy and risk assessment / 397
14.2.2.2.1   Combined risk assessment relating to income taxes / 398
14.2.2.2.2   Design of primary and other substantive audit procedures relating to income taxes / 399
14.2.2.3   Execution of the substantive procedures / 400
14.2.2.3.1   Testing of the reconciliation of US GAAP profit before tax to Local GAAP profit before tax to Taxable income / 400
14.2.2.3.2   Testing of the provision for current and deferred income taxes / 402
14.2.2.3.3   Testing the need for impairment of deferred tax assets / 403
14.2.2.3.4   Reviewing the movement of the current and deferred account balance from opening balance to ending balance / 405
14.2.2.3.5   Testing whether the provision for uncertain tax positions is in accordance with the US GAAP framework / 407
14.2.2.3.6   Testing the at arms' length nature of the intercompany transactions. / 409
14.2.2.3.7   Reconciling the current and deferred income tax balances from the trial balances to the financial statements including evaluation whether the income taxes are correctly classified / 411
14.2.2.3.8   Assessment tax effect of other audit adjustments / 411

Table of Contents

14.2.2.3.9	Testing whether the income tax disclosure notes meet the US GAAP requirement / 411
14.2.2.3.10	Obtain management representation relating to income taxes. / 412
14.2.2.3.11	Specific tax accounting topics at consolidated level / 412
14.2.2.4	Conclusions and reporting / 413
14.2.3	Summary and Conclusions / 414
14.3	Comparison with tax audits performed by Tax Authorities / 415
14.3.1	Level of materiality, tolerable error and nominal amount / 415
14.3.2	Nature of the audits / 416
14.3.3	Compensating effect of current and deferred taxes / 416
14.3.4	Liability for uncertain tax positions and current tax payable/receivable accounts / 417
14.3.5	Tax effect on compensating adjustments as a result of mutual agreement procedures / 417
14.3.6	Deferred tax positions / 418
14.3.7	Disclosure note requirements and communication regarding the operational effectiveness of the internal controls and audit differences / 418
14.3.8	Communication regarding the operational effectiveness of the internal controls and audit differences / 418

15. Tax audit
(Joost Engelmoer) / 419

15.1	Introduction / 419
15.2	Tax risk management process / 419
15.3	Tax audit related law and legislation / 421
15.4	Principles of the tax auditing approach / 422
15.4.1	Transaction model / 422
15.4.2	Audit layer model / 423
15.5	Traditional tax auditing approach / 425
15.5.1	Definition of tax audit / 425
15.6	Stages of a tax audit / 425
15.7	Pre-planning / 426
15.7.1	Gathering information about the company / 426
15.7.2	Preliminary risk analysis / 427
15.7.3	Materiality / 428
15.7.4	Critical internal processes / 428
15.7.5	Design of the AO/IC / 429
15.7.6	Existence of the AO/IC / 429
15.7.7	Residual risk for the management / 429
15.7.8	Preliminary audit tests / 430
15.7.9	Effectiveness of the AO/IC / 430
15.7.10	Residual risk for the tax auditor / 431
15.8	Completeness checks / 431
15.8.1	Minimum procedures / 432

XV

15.9	Accuracy checks / 432	
15.10	Overall evaluation / 433	
15.11	Tax audit and Tax Control Framework / 433	
15.11.1	Monitoring as a part of a Tax Control Framework / 433	
15.11.2	Reduction of completeness checks / 434	
15.11.3	Reduction of accuracy checks / 434	
15.12	Tax audit in relation to the external auditor and tax assurance provider / 437	
15.12.1	External auditor / 437	
15.12.2	Tax assurance provider / 437	
15.13	Tax audit and cooperative compliance or horizontal monitoring / 437	
15.13.1	Pre-planning / 438	
15.13.2	Preliminary consultations / 438	
15.13.3	Non-routine (tax) events / 438	
15.14	Conclusions / 438	

About the authors / 441

Preface

In 2008, representatives of the Ministry of Finance in the Netherlands and of the big four accounting firms asked the Fiscal Institute of Tilburg University to explore the possibilities of incorporating the subject of Tax Assurance in its educational master programs. Certainly, this was not an easy challenge since the topic of Tax Assurance is new and therefore largely unexplored on a scientific level. It is also by its very nature multi/disciplinary and can only be dealt with in an international comparative perspective.

In 2010, Tilburg University decided to implement a Tax Assurance program in its master Tax Economics. In 2011, we started with a profile Tax Assurance which was immediately a success. The profile consists of two electives (Tax Assurance I and II) plus extra requirements for the master thesis. Upon completing the profile, the student receives a reference on his or her grade list.

The program, coordinated by dr. Ronald Russo, is currently running for the fourth year. All aspects of Tax Assurance are treated in the lectures. Many disciplines are involved, such as accounting (internal control, tax accounting, audit), management, governance (legal, business and ethical aspects), tax policy (by companies and countries), formal tax aspects (relationship between tax authorities and companies). By inviting specialized guest lecturers of the tax authorities, tax advisors and (multinational) companies, students can get a firm theoretical and practical grip on the different subjects. In this way, the students get a balanced view of the problems involved. The program has been run successfully. But it has also led to much research output from the Fiscal Institute of Tilburg University. The most notable recent publication is this book on Tax Assurance. It is the first comprehensive publication on this subject both from a national and from an international perspective. Many guest lecturers and colleagues from the Fiscal Institute of Tilburg University as well as from other universities, tax firms and the tax administration have contributed to it. For all this, I would like to thank and congratulate the authors heartily. Especially, I would like to thank dr. Ronald Russo, who has also done the planning and editing of this book.

Professor dr. Peter Essers

Head of the Department of Tax Law of Tilburg Law School, January 2015

RONALD RUSSO

1. Definition and overview

Assurance is primarily an accounting and auditing term with a distinct meaning in those fields of practice, most commonly in relation to the commercial accounts of a company. It is not a common term in taxation, or at least it did not used to be. In the International Auditing and Assurance Standards, Handbook of international Quality Control, Auditing, Review, Other Assurance and Related Services Pronouncements, 2012, volume 1, p. 16, an Assurance engagement is defined as follows:

An engagement in which a practitioner expresses a conclusion
designed to enhance the degree of confidence of the intended users other than the
responsible party about the outcome of the evaluation or measurement of a subject
matter against criteria.

In a narrow perspective tax Assurance could be viewed as Assurance on the tax position in the commercial accounts, so that users of those accounts have more confidence in the correctness of it. In this book we view Tax Assurance in a wider context: in our view everything concerning the process of taxes in a company belongs to the field of Tax Assurance. Not just how taxes end up in the commercial accounts (tax accounting), but also (tax) risk management, internal control, management control, corporate governance, tax policy, relations with media, relations with tax authorities, ethical sides of taxation and audit are relevant for Tax Assurance in a broader sense and are therefore present in this book.

The different relevant sides of Tax Assurance as mentioned above are handled in different chapters, each by an author or authors who have expertise in that particular field. Most authors are also lecturer or guest lecturer in the Tax Assurance program of Tilburg University and publish on the topic regularly.

We start the overview of Tax Assurance by looking at processes in a company in general. Generally speaking every process in a company, especially if it may contain risks, must be managed and controlled by the management. These days control is usually effectuated by installing and maintaining systems that can provide such control (identify the risks involved and manage it following established policy). Chapter 2 of this book written by Arco van de Ven is therefore dedicated to risk management in general and the relationship with internal control systems. The history of risks and the reactions of companies and regulators are reviewed critically and illustrated with a look at frauds in the past and the recent past. The reaction primarily seems to focus on regulating: first the accounts, then the accountants and then the auditors. Whether this ultimately leads to more assurance, remains to be seen.

The characteristics of an internal control system are greatly influenced by the input, the choices made in the designing of it. The risk appetite of a company for instance determines how much risk a company is willing to take which in its turn (co) shapes the relevant procedures of the internal control system. This applies in general, but also specifically to taxes. The choices regarding the input of the control systems of a company are governed by their own rules and regulations and deal with the issue of how to manage a company. These regulations include the various corporate governance codes in various jurisdictions that, incidentally, all demand an internal control system as a prerequisite for good governance. Issues like 'tone at the top' and whether or not to have 'tax principles' are important issues that transcend traditional corporate governance debate and move into the field of ethical standards of behaviour. Therefore the fields of Corporate Governance and Ethics are dealt with in Chapters 3 written by Ronald Russo and Jan van Trigt and 4 written by Richard Happé respectively.

Combining the knowledge of risk management and internal control with corporate governance and ethics will lead to a system to control the risks within a company: a Business Control Framework. The part of this framework that deals with taxes is commonly referred to as the Tax Control Framework (TCF). In Chapter 5 Robbert Hoyng, Nathan Andrews and Mark Kennedy work out such a model: a tax operating model; they describe what a perfect system would look like or should at least entail. In this Chapter it becomes clear that the tax function must be linked to the other systems of the company, both with data and people. The influence of, for instance, new forms of information technology that enable new and better ways to store and use data is also apparent.

In Chapters 6, 7 and 8 an important element of Tax Assurance – the relationship between a company and the tax authorities – is looked at more closely. These chapters build on the previous chapters as the tax authorities themselves also use risk management techniques in applying their scarce resources to where they are most effective. The tax authorities can take the internal controls of a company into account in the choices they make. Since internal control is usually fundamentally different in large companies (where ownership and management are usually not in the same hands) and small and medium sized companies (where ownership and management usually are at least partly the same persons), the tax authorities in principle have a different approach for these categories of companies. Chapter 6 written by Robbert Veldhuizen is dedicated to large companies, whilst Chapter 7 written by Bas Herrijgers looks at small and medium sized companies. The concepts of horizontal monitoring, enhanced relationships and cooperative compliance as new ways for tax authorities to interact with companies are dealt with in detail for each category. In particular the position of intermediates in taxation (accountants and tax advisors) is viewed as they play a major part in the application of cooperative compliance for small and medium sized companies. The system of the Netherlands is viewed in more detail on this topic since it is the only jurisdiction where cooperative compliance actually works with small and medium sized companies.

In Chapter 8 some formal tax issues are discussed by Hans Gribnau, such as the principles of equality and fair play, procedural law and the legal boundaries of cooperative compliance systems. Cooperative compliance as such is not embedded in law as it is a way of supervision that commonly falls under the executive competence of the tax authorities. Apart from that: it is a relatively new strategy that has barely led to applicable case law. This can lead to uncertainty within companies regarding their exact tax liabilities and obligations, an undesirable situation for all parties involved. The main pitfalls and uncertainties are therefore dealt with in this chapter.

In Chapter 9 the result of risk management, internal control and the TCF for the commercial accounts is viewed in more detail by Eveline Gerrits: tax accounting. Tax accounting deals with the impact of taxes on the commercial accounts: the balance sheet, the profit and loss account and disclosures. Strictly speaking this is the field of accountants (ruled by accounting standards such as IAS 12), but the content of the issue is taxation, so this is an area where accountants and tax experts meet. This last statement is true for most aspects of Tax Assurance as many fields of expertise are needed to come to a reasonable level of assurance. In this chapter there is also room for the position of other taxes than corporate income tax (as they can also have significant impact in the commercial accounts), the relevant disclosures and new developments such as country by country reporting.

In Chapters 10, 11 and 12 the general content of the first chapters is applied to the three most important categories of taxes. The general set up as discussed in chapter 5 is now made more specific for different categories of taxes. To be in control of tax means something different for wage taxes than value added taxes or corporate income taxes. In practice the general TCF is often divided in specific frameworks for each category. These categories are therefore treated separately each in its own chapter. In Chapter 10 Elmer van Lienen and Marieke Louwen take the reader through the field of wage taxes and related contributions; they look at the specific challenges these taxes pose to be in control. An important issue here is that the controls for these taxes must be closely integrated with other functions of the company, especially the general pay roll function. The main risks for this category of taxes are also covered. In Chapter 11 the emphasis is laid by Edwin van Loon on indirect taxes and similarly as with wage related taxes the controls for indirect taxes must be coordinated with the other functions of the company such as sales and finance. As in the previous chapter the main risks specific for indirect taxes are viewed in more detail. In chapter 12 Eelco van der Ende and Eric van der Stroom tackle control on corporate income taxes that require yet other forms of coordination (primarily accounting and finance). The main risks are discussed and also ways to manage these risks are provided. From all contributions on specific tax categories it becomes clear how difficult it is to manage the complete field of taxation within a company. Another common observation is that they all require the tax function to be integrated into the rest of the company, although the focus of which parts are most essential can differ per category.

It gets even more difficult if a company tries to integrate controls for different purposes or risks. In Chapter 13 such an attempt is made by Irene Burgers and Jeltje van der Meer-Kooistra. They have chosen the subject of transfer pricing, perhaps the single greatest risk for multinational companies in the area of corporate income taxes. They look into control frameworks for transfer pricing and management control and research whether these frameworks could (to some extent) be integrated. Their conclusion is that to some extent, this is possible, but differences are most probably unavoidable. For instance: for taxation purposes the 'at arms's length' principle broadly speaking demands that within a multinational company the profits are allocated to affiliated companies as if they were unrelated parties each with their own profit. For management control purposes it might be useful to look at a company and its management just from a cost perspective and not a profit perspective. These two perspectives clash and are hard to reconcile.

The last chapters are dedicated to audit: the audit of taxes (in the process of finalizing the commercial accounts) in Chapter 14 written by Lees Wesdorp and the tax audit by the tax authorities in Chapter 15 written by Joost Engelmoer. The essences of audit are the same for both forms of audit and are dealt with in chapter 14. The remaining part of this chapter is dedicated to the process of auditing the tax paragraphs of the commercial accounts. In Chapter 15 the essences of audit from Chapter 14 are used to build up to the specifics of an audit by the tax authorities and especially its interaction with Tax Assurance. It is interesting to see that while both forms of audit are based upon the same principles they each have their own way of dealing with the problems presented.

The field of Tax Assurance is young and developing fast. New techniques in auditing and testing made possible by further developments in information technology will change the way in which control systems function. The international attention for and focus on tax avoidance is still growing and will lead to all sorts of new developments such as more detailed tax principles to which companies can be held accountable and more cooperation between different jurisdictions. With this book we hope to create more insight into the diverse field of Tax Assurance in the broad sense as we understand it.

ARCO VAN DE VEN

2. Internal control and risk management

2.1 Introduction

How do we know if our tax returns are filled in properly? Do we know if our company complies with the different tax rules and regulations? Could the reputation of our company be damaged if the tax strategy is a part of public debate? One possibility would be to let experts check these reports and decisions. However, expert knowledge on different tax issues alone does not give satisfactory answers to these questions. Scholars of internal control and risk management approach this question from another angle. Not only the expertise of the specific tax laws and regulations, but also the control of the tax processes determine the tax and related risks that companies face. Accountants and auditors have developed such a risk-based perspective to assert the reliability of the financial statement, which is used more and more to evaluate different types of enterprise risks. The purpose of this chapter is threefold. First an overview will be given of the development in the field of accounting and auditing to understand the underlying reasons of current internal control and risk management systems. Secondly, the content of internal control and risk management systems, often referred to as control frameworks, will be described and finally we will reflect on the side effects and limitations of these management systems.

2.2 Financial reporting and fraud

The development of risk management is a story of finding ways to prevent, detect and react on fraud[1]. The first Dutch accounting firm[2] was founded in 1883, a couple of years after the fraud and conviction of the prominent Dutch entrepreneur and politician Lodewijk Pincoffs. Public trust was shattered when it became known that the published profit of 2 million guilders was not a profit but a loss of 9.5 million guilders. These kinds of frauds led to regulation on financial reporting and boosted the development of the accounting profession worldwide. The Companies Acts of 1900

---

1   van de Ven, A.C.N. (2010) Chapter 2: Risk Management from an accounting perspective in M. van Daelen, C. van der Elst (2010) *Risk Management and Corporate Governance: Interconnections in Law, Accounting and Tax*, Cheltenham: Edward Elgar.
2   Bureel van Boekhouding Confidentia of Bernard Moret.

and 1907 in Britain enforced the publication and auditing of the balance sheets of public companies.[3] In the United States the Ivan Kreuger fraud raised a lot of attention. Reported earnings where overstated with more than 275 million dollars.[4] The *New York Times* published more than 300 articles in the years 1932 and 1933. US Congress wanted to protect investors against these types of fraud and the Security Act of 1933 and the Security and Exchange Act of 1934 prescribed mandatory disclosures of prospectuses and audit by an independent accountant of the financial statements. The Royal Mail case of 1931[5] made it clear that transparency without standards of how figures exactly should be made transparent could be problematic. British mail turned a loss of more than half a million pound sterling in 1926 into a profit by releasing a taxation reserve of £ 750,000. Shareholders where not made aware of what exactly drove the profit. The income statement was very condensed and covered up the release of the provision, it was hidden under income, which was labeled: 'Balance for the year, including dividends on shares in allied and other companies, adjustment of taxation re- serves, less depreciation of the fleet, etc.' The Chairman of the Board, Lord Kylsant, and the auditor, Harold Morland, were tried on charges of publishing false information.[6] Both men were acquitted, largely based on the testimony of Lord Plender, a former president of the Institute of Accountants of England and Wales (ICAEW). The main argument was that the reference to the 'adjustment of taxation reserves' was in accordance with best practice. The Royal Mail case stresses the importance of having accounting principles. The accounting profession discussed and developed these principles over the years. Following these principles financial reports must present a 'true and fair' view of the financial position and income of organizations. This development has lead to the founding of independent not-for-profit organizations responsible for issuing general accepted accounting principles like the Financial Accounting Standards Board (FASB) in the United States, Financial Reporting Council (FRC) in the United Kingdom and internationally the International Accounting Standards Board (IASB). Nowadays the audit opinion of accountants not only states that the financial statements present fairly the financial position, results and cash flows but also that they are in accordance with general accepted accounting principles.

So transparency, standards and audits were the mechanisms in these early days to fight fraudulent behavior. Companies had to disclose financial information and mandatory audits were held using general accepted accounting standards. The frauds however did not stop. The McKesson and Robbins case in 1939 led to the first audit standard. McKesson and Robbins looked like a financially healthy organization with revenues of $174 million, gross assets of $87 million and earnings of $3.6 million.[7]

---

[3] Camfferman, K. (1998), Perceptions of the royal mail case in the Netherlands, *Accounting & Business Research*, **29**, (1), pp. 43-55 (Camfferman 1998).
[4] Clikeman, P. M. (2009), *Called to account*, Routledge: New York (Clikeman 2009).
[5] Based on Camfferman 1998, p. 44.
[6] Camfferman 1998, p. 44.
[7] Baxter, W.T. (1999), McKesson & Robbins: a milestone in auditing, *Accounting, Business & Financial History*, **9**, (2), pp. 157-174 (Baxter 1999) p. 157.

Price Waterhouse & Co (PW), then the largest organization of public accountants,[8] had audited the financial statement and stated the accounts 'fairly present... the position of the combined companies'.[9] A Security and Exchange Committee (SEC) inquiry concluded that the revenues consisted of fictitious sales of over $18 million and non-existing assets of $9.1 million accounts receivables and of $10.1 million inventories in the balance sheet. The case shows that reconciliations of numbers on paper alone are not enough for an audit. The auditor has to check if the assets really exist, for example by being present at an inventory. Ultimately the McKesson and Robbins case led to the publication of the first audit statement. An audit had to include an inventory count and debtors should confirm to the auditors the amount of money due at year's end.[10] The development of new auditing standards is nowadays a highly institutionalized activity and the responsibility of the International Auditing and Assurance Standards Board (IAASB). The IAASB is an independent standard-setting body that issues International Standards on Auditing (ISAs).

2.3 The shift to internal control

The reactions on the different fraud cases so far do not directly link to internal control and risk management processes of the organizations. The way fraud is addressed is by regulating which information should be disclosed by organizations and standardization of what should be disclosed. To secure that companies complied with the regulation, reports had to be audited by independent accountants. Next to the increased transparency, accounting standardization and audits, there was a standardization of auditing practices to professionalize the way audits must be performed.

The McKesson and Robbins case also addressed the importance of internal control. The SEC commissioners in the McKesson and Robbins case reported that the PW should have checked the effectiveness of the internal controls.[11] Expert knowledge of the auditor alone is not sufficient to detect fraud and assure that reports are reliable. The way that the organization has structured his processes, the division of responsibilities and the checks and balances that are put in place helps auditors to assure that the information is reliable and that fraud is prevented or recognized in an early stage. Auditors therefore included the importance of internal controls in their audit methods. The risk that auditors fail to discover material misstatements in financial reports also depends on their assessment of the effectiveness of the internal controls of the organization.

Another fraud investigation highlighted the importance of internal control. In 1976 the SEC and subsequently the Senate Foreign Relations Committee investigated and acknowledged the accusation that more than 200 hundred large US companies had

---

8 Baxter 1999, p. 167.
9 Baxter 1999, p. 158.
10 Clikeman 2009, p. 40.
11 Baxter 1999, p. 171.

secret funds to pay foreign bribes. In the draft of the Foreign Corrupt Practice Act (FCPA) the California Representative John Moss proposed amendments to include that the board of directors had to review and approve the corporation's internal accounting controls and the requirement that an independent auditor would publicly attest that the internal controls were adequate to safeguard the assets of the company.[12] This was the first time that legislation was proposed to highlight the management responsibility of internal accounting controls and that an independent auditor should attest the effectiveness of these accounting controls. The amendments were rejected and it took a financial crisis and another accounting scandal to enforce internal control regulation.

The savings and loan crisis was until the financial crisis of 2007-2008 the largest financial disaster in the United States since the Great Depression.[13] Over the period of 1986-1995 more than a thousand lending institutions, thrifts, with total assets of over $500 billion collapsed.[14] According to Curry and Shibut[15] the savings and loan crisis has cost the taxpayers approximately $124 billion and the thrift industry another $29 billion as of end December 1999. Because of a guaranteed repayment of loans with a limit of $ 100,000, like in the financial crisis of 2007-2008, the taxpayer paid the majority of the losses. If banks could not repay the deposits of the clients a federal insurance by the Federal Deposit Insurance Corporation (FDIC) guaranteed the loans. The large losses led to a study of the underlying causes of the crisis. The United States General Accounting Office (USGAO)[16] reviewed 184 banks that failed in 1987. Their report highlighted internal control weaknesses.

> 'Of the internal control weaknesses federal regulators identified, those which contributed most significantly to the 184 bank failures were inadequate or imprudent loan policies (79%), inadequate supervision by the board of directors (49%), weak loan administration (42%), and poor loan documentation and inadequate credit analysis, over reliance on volatile funding sources (32%), the presence of a dominant figure (31%) an a failure to establish adequate loss allowances (29%).[17]

The USGAO concluded that mandatory management and audit report on internal control[18] could have prevented the crisis. The 1991 US Congress passed the Federal Deposit Insurance Corporation Improvement Act (FDCIA) to establish mandatory reporting and audits for federal deposit insurance corporations. Fifteen years after the amendments of representative John Ross there was legislation for a mandatory review and audit in internal control for banks and financial institutions.

---

12 Shapiro, B. and D. Matson (2008), 'Strategies of resistance to internal control regulation'. *Accounting, Organizations and Society, 33*, (2-3), pp. 199-228, (Shapiro, B. and D. Matson 2008), p. 214.
13 Curry, T., L. Shibut (2000), The cost of savings and loan crisis: truth and consequences, *FDIC Banking Review*, **13**, (2), pp. 26-32 (Curry, T. and L. Shibut 2000), p. 26.
14 Curry, T. and L. Shibut 2000, p. 33.
15 Curry, T. and L. Shibut 2000, p. 33.
16 United States General_Acounting_Ofice (1989), *Bank failures: Independent audits needed to strengthen internal control and bank management.* Report to the Congress of the US General Accounting Office: Washington, DC (US General Accounting Office 1989).
17 US General Accounting Office 1989, p 3.
18 Shapiro and Matson 2008, p. 220.

The FDCIA stresses the responsibility of management for financial statements and internal controls. Each insured depository institution according to the new regulation has to prepare:

> 'A report signed by the chief executive officer and the chief accounting or financial officer of the institution which contains –
> (A) a statement of the management's responsibilities for – (i) preparing financial statements (ii) establishing and maintaining an adequate internal control structure and procedures for financial reporting; and (iii) complying with the laws and regulations relating to safety and soundness which are designated by the Corporation or the appropriate Federal banking agency; and
> (B) an assessment, as of the end of the institution's most recent fiscal year, of – (i) the effectiveness of such internal control structure and procedures; and (ii) the institution's compliance with the laws and regulations relating to safety and soundness which are designated by the Corporation and the appropriate Federal banking agency.[19]'

An independent auditor should review the required report and assessment.

> '(1) IN GENERAL. –With respect to any internal control report required by subsection (b)(2) of any institution, the institution's independent public accountant shall attest to, and report separately on, the assertions of the institution's management contained in such report.
> (2) ATTESTATION REQUIREMENTS.–Any attestation pursuant to paragraph (1) shall be made in accordance with generally accepted standards for attestation engagements.[20]'

This legislation meant a shift from only transparency, standardization and audits on the external financial statements of organizations towards transparency and audits of the underlying internal organization and processes. How companies control the reliability of their financial statements also became important.

It took until 2002 before the obligation to report and audit internal control was introduced for a broader range of companies. During the Internet bubble and crisis of 2001 one of the largest organizations of the world, Enron, collapsed. Fortune Magazine named Enron six years in a row as the most innovative organization.[21] Enron reported revenues of more than one hundred billion dollar in 2000 and a net income of nearly one billion dollar.[22] Enron declared bankruptcy on 2 December 2001, a company with more than 11 billion dollars in shareholders' equity[23] and an annual statement signed off on February 23, 2001 by the auditors of Arthur Andersen.[24] The Enron bankruptcy shattered the trust of the public, politics and investors. Enron had inflated earnings by using market values and 'hid' liabilities off-balance by using special purpose entities. Eleven congressional committees researched different aspects and expert witnesses like SEC chairman Arthur Levitt pleaded for more severe

---

19 Public Law 102-242, 105 stat. 2242-2243.
20 Public Law 102-242, 105 stat. 2243.
21 Clikeman 2009, p. 245.
22 In millions revenues $100,789, net-income 979 – Enron Annual Report 2000, p. 1.
23 In millions $11,470 – Enron Annual Report 2000, p. 35.
24 Enron Annual Report, p. 30.

regulation, harsher penalties for fraud and a stringent oversight over public accountants.[25] The news and pictures of employees of Arthur Anderson shredding tons of paperwork shattered the reputation of Arthur Andersen, one of the oldest auditing firms in the US. Enron was not the only accounting scandal at the beginning of this century. Worldcom announced on June 25th, 2002 that their 2000-2002 earnings had to be restated for at least 3.8 billion dollars.[26] The news of Worldcom accelerated the decision making on new legislation. The senate approved the Sarbanes-Oxley (SOX) Act twenty days later on the 15th July 2002.[27]

The SOX-act,[28] which applies to listed companies in the United States of America, consists of several elements to prevent accounting scandals and fraud. More stringent oversight over public accountants is addressed. The Public Company Accounting Oversight Board is established, which is a kind of auditor for auditing firms. Regulation is formulated to safeguard the independence of auditors. The element of harsher penalties for fraud is also included, with the possibility of imprisonment for up to twenty years. And in line with the FIDC regulation the SOX act also includes articles on transparency and audit of internal control. Article 302 states that the CEO and CFO have to sign the financial report and have to present their conclusions of their assessment of internal control over financial reporting. They have to report significant deficiencies in the design or operation of internal controls, which adversely could affect the ability to record, process, summarize and report financial data. Article 404 describes the requirement that an independent auditor should attest and report on the internal control assessment that management has made.

2.4 Standardization of internal control

FIDC regulation and the Sarbanes-Oxley Act required transparency and an independent audit of internal control, but how exactly should internal control be evaluated? In other words: is there a standard way to evaluate internal control? The National Commission on Fraudulent Financial Reporting, also known as the Treadway Commission, after their chairman James C. Treadway, raised this question back in 1987. The American Institute of Certified Public Accountants (AICPA), the American Accounting Association (AAA), the Financial Executives Institute (FEI), the Institute of Internal Auditors (IIA), and the National Association of Accountants (NAA) sponsored this study on causal factors for reporting fraud and possible steps to reduce its incidence.[29] Their report recommended that the sponsoring organizations should cooperate in the development of additional integrated guidance on internal control.[30] The recommendation was followed and the Committee of Sponsoring Organizations of the Treadway Commission, COSO, over the years developed different frameworks for internal control and enterprise risk management. The COSO internal control

---

25 Clikeman 2009, p. 272.
26 Clikeman 2009, p. 273.
27 Clikeman 2009, p. 273
28 Public Law 107-204, July 30,2002.
29 Treadway Commission (1987), *Report of the National Commission on Fraudulent Financial Reporting*, New York: AICPA Inc.,Treadway Report, (Treadway Commission 1987), p. 1.
30 Treadway Commission 1987, p. 48.

framework is regarded as a best practice to describe and evaluate the internal control of companies. Tax control frameworks are almost always based on the COSO framework. The first COSO internal control framework was published in 1992 and republished with small adjustments in 1994. In 2013 a revised internal control framework was published which supersedes the earlier versions of 1992/1994.

2.5 The COSO internal control framework 2013

What is internal control? COSO defines it as follows: 'Internal control is a process, effected by an entity's board of directors, management, and other personnel, designed to provide reasonable assurance regarding the achievement of objectives relating to operations, reporting and compliance.'[31]

The definition points to different aspects, or objectives, of internal control. Internal control over (financial) reporting is distinguished from internal control related to the compliance with applicable laws and regulations, like specific tax regulation and from the internal control over effectiveness and efficiency of operations. Therefore the framework can be applied for very different purposes, like controlling sales processes, compliance of SOX-regulation or for the internal control of tax related activities and reports.

Next to distinguishing different objectives of internal control, the COSO framework could also be used at different organizational levels. For example, it could be used for the internal control of the tax function within the organization but also at enterprise level, for the organization as a whole.

The last and most important element of the COSO- framework is the introduction of five different components that according to COSO the system of internal control define. The components are: (1) the control environment, (2) risk assessment, (3) control activities, (4) information and communication and (5) monitoring activities.

The three different elements of COSO are represented in figure 1: the COSO cube. The columns of the cube represent the different objectives, the rows represent the different components and the third dimension reflects the possible different organizational levels.

---

31 Committee of Sponsoring Organizations of the Treadway Commission (COSO) (2013) *Internal Control – Integrated Framework – Framework and Appendices* , New York: AICPA Inc., May 2013 (COSO, 2013), p.1.

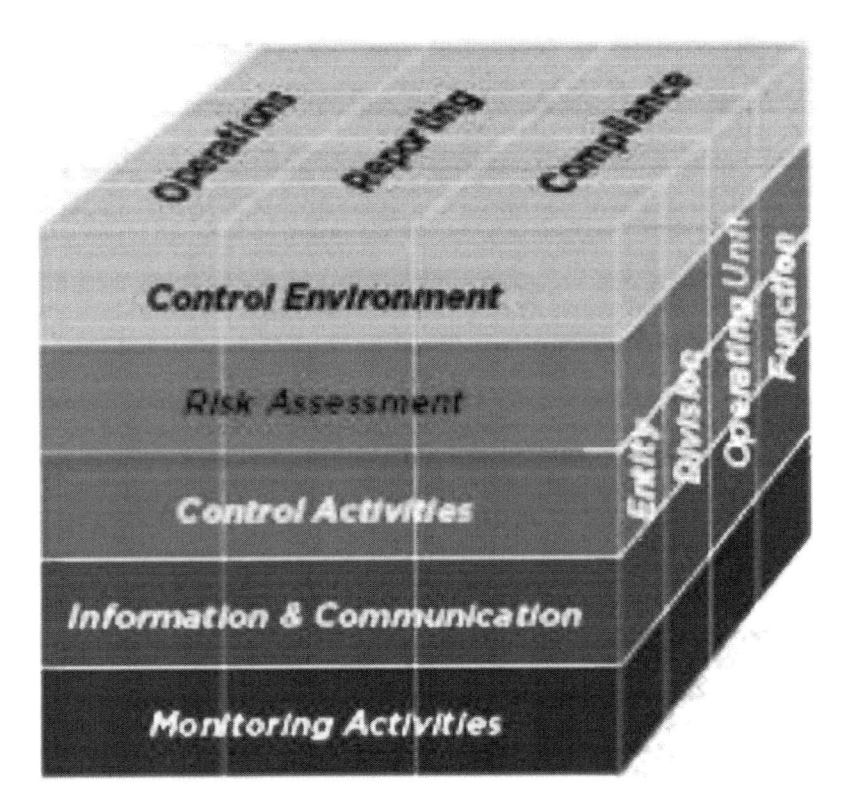

Figure 1. COSO cube 2013[32]

The COSO internal control framework describes each component and highlights the importance of the component for the purpose of internal control. Furthermore for each component principles are formulated, seventeen in total for all components. Each principle is elaborated by discussing the attributes of that principle. The components of the 1992/1994 COSO and 2013 COSO framework and also the content of the components have not changed much. The introduction of principles and attributes is new and helps to communicate the important elements of internal control in a more structured manner.

COSO Components and principles
When are we reasonably certain that the COSO objectives will be reached? This is the central question that has to be answered by evaluating different components of internal control. Formal controls are always mentioned when there are questions about the effectiveness of internal control. What did the members of the organization check? Were there enough checks and balances in the organization? Of course such

---

32 Committee of Sponsoring Organizations of the Treadway Commission (COSO) (2013) Internal Control – Integrated Framework – Executive Summary, New York: AICPA Inc., May 2013, p. 6.

formal controls are part of the COSO-framework and they are dealt with in the component control activities. However the COSO framework explicitly states that only formal controls will not give the desired assurance. The other components are also essential. The environment in which those formal controls operate is of utmost importance. The component control environment operates as a kind of foundation for the other components.

> 'Control Environment
> 1. The organization demonstrates a commitment to integrity and ethical values.
> 2. The board of directors demonstrates independence from management and exercises oversight of the development and performance of internal control.
> 3. Management establishes, with board oversight, structures, reporting lines, and appropriate authorities and responsibilities in the pursuit of objectives.
> 4. The organization demonstrates a commitment to attract, develop, and retain competent individuals in alignment with objectives.
> 5. The organization holds individuals accountable for their internal control responsibilities in the pursuit of objectives.[33,]

Figure 1. Principles relating to the Control Environment component.

The control environment determines if internal control is really taken serious in an organisation. Are decisions taken opportunistically or do ethical values and integrity prevail in situations where stakes are really high? And how is the tone at the top? Does the executive management team walk the walk, and talk the talk? These questions are all related to the principles discussed in the control environment.

Effective internal control hinges on the recognition of risks and following actions. Recognising possible future events that can threaten the accomplishment of objectives is an important element of risk management. The principles in the component risk assessment deal with systematically identifying risks and analysis of those risks to assess and determine if and how risks should be managed.

> 'Risk Assessment
> 6. The organization specifies objectives with sufficient clarity to enable the identification and assessment of risks relating to objectives.
> 7. The organization identifies risks to the achievement of its objectives across the entity and analyzes risks as a basis for determining how the risks should be managed.
> 8. The organization considers the potential for fraud in assessing risks to the achievement of objectives.
> 9. The organization identifies and assesses changes that could significantly impact the system of internal control.[34,]

In the component control activities the formal controls to mitigate the risk that are assessed are discussed. The principles address that control activities should be selected and developed that effectively mitigates the risks and that they are translated into policies and procedures. The role of general IT (information technology) controls

---

33 COSO 2013, p. 31.
34 COSO 2013, p. 59.

is highlighted in the 2013 COSO version. General controls are not application specific, but apply to all IT-systems in the organization. Why is the importance of IT general controls stressed so much? The mitigation of risks will to a very large extent be enforced by controls within software applications. For example, delivering a product bought on the Internet, could be only executed if the product is paid for in advance. Customers could be forced first to pay to complete the purchase, instead of paying when the goods are delivered. From the vendors viewpoint this is an effective measure to control the risks that clients will not pay. The effectiveness of these kinds of application controls depends on general IT-controls. The effectiveness depends more specifically on if and how these application controls have been tested. Do they work for all clients and all products; is there no possibility to sidestep the payment? Or after the testing: is it possible to change the application control in the software without the proper authorization? Therefore sound general IT controls are a necessary precondition for the effectiveness of application controls.

'Control Activities
10. The organization selects and develops control activities that contribute to the mitigation of risks to the achievement of objectives to acceptable levels.
11. The organization selects and develops general control activities over technology to support the achievement of objectives.
12. The organization deploys control activities through policies that establish what is expected and in procedures that put policies into action.[35,]

Information and communication play an important role in internal control processes. Responsible managers need relevant and high quality information to support the functioning of the other components of internal control. Not only should relevant and reliable information be present, the way it is communicated is also relevant. Information should flow downwards and upwards in the organization. Information that flows downwards is necessary to inform members of the organization on matters related to internal control, like the values of the organizations, important risks and relevant control activities. Information should also flow upwards regarding non-compliance on policies, regulation and controls. If control activities are not performed in an effective manner recognising control deficiencies and communicating these deficiencies in a timely manner could reduce possible negative consequences.

'Information and Communication
13. The organization obtains or generates and uses relevant, quality information to support the functioning of other components of internal control.
14. The organization internally communicates information, including objectives and responsibilities for internal control, necessary to support the functioning of internal control.
15. The organization communicates with external parties regarding matters affecting the functioning of internal control.[36,]

Setting up a system of internal control does not guarantee that internal control stays effective over the years. A changing environment could lead to new risks or to a

---
35 COSO 2013, p. 87.
36 COSO 2013, p. 105.

different assessment of the consequences. New leadership could impact the control environment and the effectiveness of control activities could change over time. The monitoring and adjustment of the different components of internal control is therefore necessary. The analysis, communication and corrective action of internal control deficiencies is the most important element of the monitoring component.

> 'Monitoring Activities
> 16. The organization selects, develops, and performs ongoing and/or separate evaluations to ascertain whether the components of internal control are present and functioning.
> 17. The organization evaluates and communicates internal control deficiencies in a timely manner to those parties responsible for taking corrective action, including senior management and the board of directors, as appropriate.[37]'

The COSO framework not only helps organizations to evaluate and improve their internal control. Also it offers a standard to make internal control transparent. Annual statements of publicly traded companies often contain of a paragraph on internal control and frequently the descriptions are structured by the components of the COSO framework. A side effect of the regulation that forces companies to focus on internal control is that COSO has become the standard on how to evaluate and report on internal control.

2.6 From internal control to risk management

The COSO internal control framework follows a risk-based perspective to discover what to do to ensure that operations will be performed in an effective and efficient manner, information will be reliable and laws and regulation will be complied to. Strategic choices are not a part of the scope of the analysis. Internal control regards strategy as something given that has to be implemented and controlled. Strategic choices and the level of risks companies are willing to accept do not play an important role in the discussed internal control framework. At an enterprise level organizations can decide in a very deliberate manner to pursue very risky strategies with possible high future returns. Continuity of organizations depends heavily on these kind of strategic choices.

The financial crisis of 2007/2008 reminded the world that unreliable reporting of organizations was not the only risk and certainly not the most important risk that could shatter trust in society. Risky financial products like sub-prime mortgages and credit default swaps combined with low solvency levels endangered the continuity of large financial institutions and led the world in turmoil. The financial system nearly collapsed after September 15th 2008 when Lehman Brothers filed for bankruptcy protection. The economy got into the worst financial crisis since the Great Depression of the 1930's. The International Monetary Fund (IMF) estimated write-downs that could reach a total of around $4 trillion.[38] Alan Greenspan, the chairman of the Federal

---

37 COSO 2013, p. 107.
38 IMF (2009) *Global Financial Stability Report – Responding to the Financial Crisis and Measuring Systemic Risk*, april 2009, World Economic and Financial Surveys, Washington DC: IMF, (IMF 2009), p. xv.

Reserve Board until 2006, estimated the global equity loss close to $50 trillion, the equivalent of four fifths of 2008 global GDP.[39]

The way organizations manage their strategic risk became an important element in corporate governance debates. COSO developed an enterprise risk management framework in 2004, often named COSO ERM or COSO II. COSO ERM is an extension of the discussed internal control frameworks of 1992/1994 and 2013. These internal control frameworks are included in the COSO ERM framework.

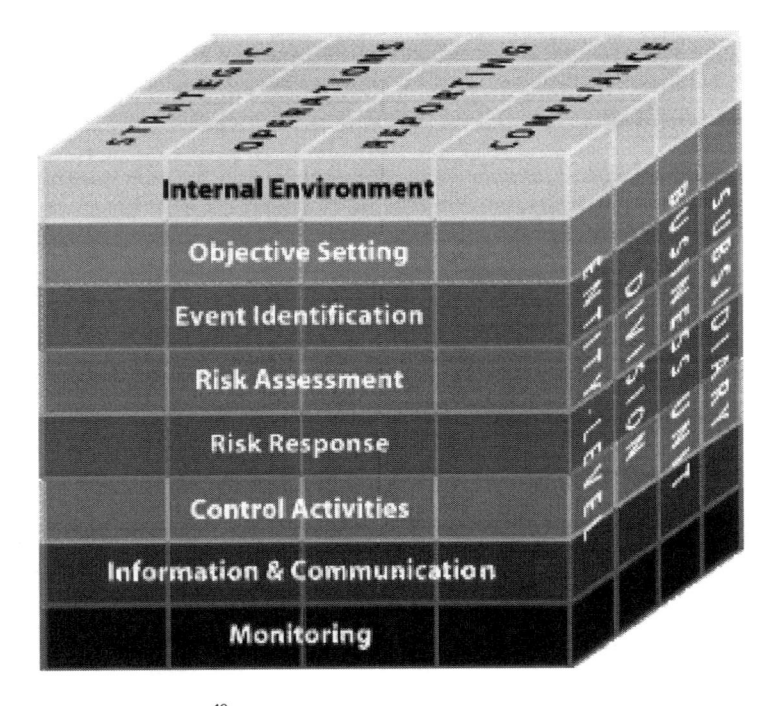

Figure 2. COSO ERM Cube[40]

The COSO-ERM framework has only changed on the following points:
1. Strategy is added as a new objective.
2. The component 'control environment' has been replaced by the component 'internal environment'.
3. The component 'risk management' is replaced by four components: ' objective setting', event identification', 'risk assessment' and risk response.

The focus on enterprise risks means that next to effectiveness and efficiency, doing things right, in COSO ERM the aspect of doing the right things is also addressed. From

---
39   Greenspan, A. (2013) *The Map and the Territory. Risk, Human Nature, and the Future of Forecasting.* London: Alan Lane, (Greenspan 2013), p. 38.
40   Committee of Sponsoring Organizations of the Treadway Commission (COSO) (2004) *Enterprise Risk Management– Integrated Framework – Framework December 2004 – Draft*, New York: AICPA Inc., (COSO 2004), p. 5

the different components three components: 1) monitoring, 2) information and communication and 3) control activities are also included. The component 'control environment' is renamed. Strategic choices depend heavily on the risk appetite of the organization. This element has been included in the 'internal environment' component of COSO-ERM and is not included in the 'control environment' component of the internal control framework. The most important difference between the two COSO frameworks is the elaboration of the component risk analysis. COSO-ERM includes components, which deal with the formulation of objectives and analysis of future events that could stand in the company's way for reaching those objectives. These two components form the input for the risk assessment. The COSO internal control framework just starts with the risk assessment and does not address how the risks have to be discovered. After the risk assessment COSO internal control addresses the mitigation of the risks with control activities. From a more strategic viewpoint other different responses are possible. If the risks are within the risk appetite of the organization the risks could be accepted as they are. If the risks are too large, the company could search for ways to avoid those risks and to alter their strategy. Another response could be to share the risk with other companies. Insurance and joint ventures are examples of this risk response to share the risk.

Although the COSO-ERM framework includes the COSO internal control framework a lot of organizations keep on working with the COSO internal control framework. The publication of the new internal control framework in 2013 confirms that for the control of 'operations', 'reporting' and 'compliance' objectives the COSO internal framework will not be replaced by COSO-ERM. The expectation is that companies will use the internal control framework for internal control over financial reporting and that companies will use the enterprise risk management framework for controlling risks related to strategy.

2.7 Limitations and side effects

Over the years attention to prevent frauds and other societal risks has shifted from transparency, standardization and audits of what should be reported towards transparency, standardization and audits of the system how organizations manage and control these risks. The COSO frameworks guide organizations to evaluate and improve their internal control and enterprise risk management processes. But will this prevent fraudulent reporting and new bankruptcy cases? And are there possible negative side effects?

Foreseeing risks
Is it possible to manage risk to such a high degree? Risks are events that possibly will take place in the future and lead to undesired negative consequences. As an Old Danish proverb states: 'it's difficult to make predictions, especially about the future'. Risks are not somewhere present, they have not occurred yet. Therefore risks are more perceptions than hard facts. Reading about the component risk analysis of the COSO method superficially one could get the impression that if two experts would perform the analysis they will end up with the same results. The difficulty to predict makes it rather unlikely that different experts will end up with the same risks. Risk

analysis is according to Beck about imagination and staging of risks.[41] The background and experience of the risk analysts determines the risks that will be analyzed. There is also an important cultural element. Before the 2007/2008 financial crisis there was a deep conviction that nothing like the Great Depression could happen again. Although the 2007/2008 crisis was not the first bank crisis in its kind, banks were not prepared. These types of risks could be foreseen, but unfortunately they were not. There are also uncertainties that are harder to assess and events that cannot be predicted. Taleb distinguishes so called 'black swans', highly improbable events with three characteristics: they are unpredictable, have a massive impact and after it has happened the desire to make it appear less random and more predictable than it was.[42] Black swans according to Taleb imply the inability to predict the course of history.[43] The disappointing fate of risk management could be that the most important risks are the ones we cannot predict.

Effectiveness of formal controls
Another limitation of internal control frameworks deals with limitations of formal controls. Risks are central to the COSO framework and controls are effective when they mitigate the risk to an acceptable level. The effectiveness of control therefore can only be assessed in combination with risks. The lack of a separation of duties does not automatically mean a control deficiency. It depends on the presence of other controls to mitigate the risks. A one-person bank would theoretically be possible if the process is totally automated with effective application controls and general controls.[44] Of course legislation in many countries makes this impossible, nowadays the presence of internal audit departments, a compliance officer and a chief risk officer is mandatory.

The combination of controls in relation to the specific risks determines the effectiveness of controls. Because of the variety of risks and the specific features of organizations, there exists no normative framework of effective controls that each and every organizations should implement. Different controls are possible not only for different risks but also for identical risks. This makes auditing difficult. There are no rules against which the controls can be checked. Formal controls are only part of the solution. As stated earlier formal controls alone cannot assure that the distinguished risks will be mitigated. The control environment stresses the importance of culture for the effectiveness of internal control. Does management intervene if rules and regulations are not followed, do they lead by example and are employees aware of the importance of controls? For the effectiveness of internal control these are important elements. But how can auditors assess the consequences of a lesser internal environment? It is much easier to check if formal controls are in place than to check if the culture is up to standard, and to what extent the existing culture endangers reaching the objectives of the organization. It is clear that such an assessment is much

---

41 Beck, U. (2009), *World at risk*, Polity Press: Cambridge, (Beck 2009), p. 12.
42 Taleb, N. N. (2007), *The black swan*, Random House: New York, (Taleb 2007), p. xvii-xviii
43 Taleb 2007, p. xx.
44 Leennaars, J.J.A. (1995) *De betekenis van Informatietechnologie voor de Bestuurlijke Informatieverzorging*, inaugural speech, Amsterdam: Vossiuspers, (Leennaars 1995).

Internal control and risk management 2.7

less objective than checking expense claims. Although COSO stresses the importance of 'soft' controls, in practice most of the attention is given to the more formal controls.

Level of assurance

Academic research shows that risk management is a complex phenomenon. Risk management is not only an instrument that can and maybe should be used in organizations but is also an element of the modern society we live in. Internal control/risk management is a societal phenomenon, which plays a very dominant role in our daily life. Beck states that we are living in a 'risk society'.[45] Power refers to the current society as the 'audit society'.[46] The adoption of frameworks like COSO depends not only on the possibilities to lower risks but also on the need of organizations to legitimize their actions. In the words of Power,

> 'it [risk management –Van de Ven] has much less to do with real dangers and opportunities than might be thought, and more to do with organizational accountability and legitimacy'.[47]

The legitimate action for regulators is to demand more transparency, issue standards and procedures and demand audits. The need to react decisively and send a signal to society could be of greater importance than the effectiveness of the proposed legislation. Romano concluded on the effectiveness of SOX back in 2005:

> 'An extensive empirical literature suggests that those mandates were seriously misconceived because they are not likely to improve audit quality or otherwise enhance firm performance and thereby benefit investors as Congress intended. In the frantic political environment in which SOX was enacted, legislators adopted proposals of policy entrepreneurs with neither careful consideration nor assimilation of the literature at odds with the policy prescriptions.'[48,]

The underlying assumption of SOX is that only an audit opinion regarding the financial statements is not enough. The annual statement of Enron of the year 2000 confirms this. As mentioned earlier the financial result over the year 2000 were very positive, revenues of over $100 billion and shareholders' equity of nearly $11.5 billion. Arthur Andersen gave the following opinion on February 23th 2001:

> 'In our opinion, the financial statements referred to above present fairly, in all material respects, the financial position of Enron Corp. and subsidiaries as of December 31, 2000 and 1999, and the results of their operations, cash flows and changes in shareholders' equity for each of the three years in the period ended December 31, 2000, in conformity with accounting principles generally accepted in the United States.'[49,]

Another assumption of the new Sarbanes-Oxley regulation is that mandatory reporting and auditing of internal control over financial reporting is necessary and more likely to prevent new accounting scandals. The new SOX-regulation therefore requires

---

45   Beck, U. (1992), *Risk society - towards a new modernity*, SAGE Publications: London, (Beck 1992).
46   Power, M. (1997) *The Audit Society*, Oxford University Press: Oxford, (Power 1997).
47   Power, M. (2007), *Organized uncertainty - designing a world of risk management*, Oxford University Press: Oxford (Power 2007), backcover.
48   Romano, R. (2005). Quack corporate governance. *Regulation, 28*(4), 36-44, (Romano 2005), p. 44.
49   Enron Annual Report 2000, p. 30.

an audited internal control statement. Surprisingly Enron Annual Statement 2000 includes such an opinion.

> ' We have examined management's assertion that the system of internal control of Enron Corp. (an Oregon corporation) and subsidiaries as of December 31, 2000, 1999 and 1998 was adequate to provide reasonable assurance as to the reliability of financial statements and the protection of assets from unauthorized acquisition, use or disposition, included in the accompanying report on Management's Responsibility for Financial Reporting. Management is responsible for maintaining effective internal control over the reliability of financial statements and the protection of assets against unauthorized acquisition, use or disposition. Our responsibility is to express an opinion on management's assertion based on our examination.
> Our examinations were made in accordance with attestation standards established by the American Institute of Certified Public Accountants and, accordingly, included obtaining an understanding of the system of internal control, testing and evaluating the design and operating effectiveness of the system of internal control and such other procedures as we considered necessary in the circumstances. We believe that our examinations provide a reasonable basis for our opinion. Because of inherent limitations in any system of internal control, errors or irregularities may occur and not be detected. Also, projections of any evaluation of the system of internal control to future periods are subject to the risk that the system of internal control may become inadequate because of changes in conditions, or that the degree of compliance with the policies or procedures may deteriorate. In our opinion, management's assertion that the system of internal control of Enron Corp. and its subsidiaries as of December 31, 2000, 1999 and 1998 was adequate to provide reasonable assurance as to the reliability of financial statements and the protection of assets from unauthorized acquisition, use or disposition is fairly stated, in all material respects, based upon current standards of control criteria. [50],

Enron had, on a voluntary basis, already a management assertion on internal control over financial reporting and Arthur Andersen audited this internal control assertion. The transparency and audit of the internal control systems at Enron did not prevent or signal in an early stage one of the biggest accounting scandals ever. Frameworks, like COSO, support management to evaluate and improve internal control and risk management, but proof is lacking that internal control audits will prevent accounting scandals in the future.

Side effects
Instruments like the COSO frameworks are not only used for reducing risks as stated earlier. A code of ethics can be used as a means to improve the internal environment, but it can also be used as a façade. The board of Enron also stressed the importance of ethics. In their 64 page code of ethics they stated that Enron has a reputation for fairness and honesty[51] and

> "Enron stands on the foundation of its Vision and Values. Every employee is educated about the company's Vision and Values and is expected to conduct business with other employees, partners, contractors, suppliers, vendors and customers keeping in mind respect, integrity, communication and excellence.[52]"

---

50 Enron Annual Report 2000, p.30.
51 Enron (2000), Code of Ethics, July 2000, retrieved on May 30, 2014 from *http://www.thesmokinggun.com/enron/enronethics1.html*, (Enron Code of Ethics 2000), p. 1.
52 Enron Code of Ethics 2000, p. 2.

Nowadays Enron stands for corruption and fraud. The term Enron Ethics is a new catchword for the ultimate contradiction between words and deeds.[53] The code of ethics was only used to create an image and it worked as a kind of façade. Reality was hidden behind their image of respect and integrity. It was certainly not used to improve the internal environment; it even helped to create an environment that put 'the bottom line ahead of ethical behavior and doing what's right[54]'

On a smaller scale applying risk management can also lead to the use of more and more formal controls. Even if these controls are not effective, they signal that the corporation takes enterprise risk management serious. These formal controls often replace the trust we have in expertise of people to perform the activities. Porter claims such a negative interaction between standardization and trust.[55] Trust is one of the important elements of the internal environment. Intrinsically motivated employees want to deliver high quality service and will be dedicated to limit negative consequences of possible risks. In the end more formal controls, especially the non-effective ones, can be disruptive.

Formal controls also trigger more checks and audits. When formal controls are present these controls also have to be enforced and employees have to prove compliance. A system of: tell me, show me, and prove me. Checking compliance of formal controls is more rule-based and therefore much easier than assessing the effectiveness of controls. If the weakest point of risk management is the internal environment and the effectiveness of controls then stressing compliance does not work. In the audit society however it sometimes looks like compliance is of greater importance than the effectiveness of controls.

2.8 Conclusion

Assurance of reliability of financial statements has been in the past and probably will be in the future an important societal issue. Accounting fraud over the years shattered public trust. The political reaction has been to enforce more transparency in the form of reports and disclosures, combined with detailed accounting standards and mandatory audits. The political intervention was not restricted to accounting standards and disclosures, but also towards auditors. Extensive auditing standards were developed and oversight of auditing firms was institutionalized. Auditors got their own auditor. The sharpened regulation did not prevent accounting irregularities like Enron and Worldcom in the beginning of this century.

To get more assurance the attention shifted from not only regulating what information should be disclosed and audited towards regulating the internal control processes. The COSO internal control and risk management frameworks describe elements that organizations have to address if they evaluate the internal control and risk management of their organization. Effective internal control and risk management depend heavily on the tone at the top and the culture within the organization.

---

53 Sims, R. R., & Brinkmann, J. (2003). Enron ethics (or: Culture matters more than codes). *Journal of Business Ethics, 45*, 243-256, (Sims, Brinkmann 2003), p. 243.
54 Sims, Brinkmann 2003. p. 243.
55 Porter, T. (1995), *Trust in numbers*, Princeton University Press: Princeton, NJ, (Porter 1995).

Formal controls alone will not offer reasonable assurance for reaching the organizational objectives.

Regulators have enforced that management asserts the internal control of their organization and that independent accountants audit the effectiveness of the internal control systems. With regard to tax assurance, these COSO control frameworks are often used as the basis for tax control frameworks in organizations. Evaluating internal control using a framework obviously enables management to improve internal control, however it has not stopped accounting shenanigans and frauds. Internal control and risk management have inherent limitations and will not give absolute certainty. Uncertainties and black swans are hard, maybe even impossible, to predict. There are no absolute norms what could be considered effective controls. In other words, the assessment that controls that are in place, within the control environment, shall lead to the behavior of employees that future negative consequences will be prevented, is subjective in nature.

Next to the limitations of internal control and risk management systems there are side effects. Risk management frameworks are also used as means to legitimize the organization. The extensive code of ethics of Enron is a sad example. If legitimization is the only objective this can lead to a form of Enron ethics, an ultimate contradiction between words and deeds. All the boxes of the framework are ticked, however the company could be out of control.

The new regulation of internal control assessment and audits also leads to more attention for compliance of formal controls. In the words of Power, we live in an audit society. Non-compliance, even of not so important controls, will lead to a loss of legitimacy. To manage this reputation risk attention shifts from the effectiveness of the system of risk management to compliance of the formal controls. These audits limit the risk of non-compliance, but do they also give a higher assurance that objectives will be reached? In other words: is auditing always the weakest link in risk management? The importance of the control and internal environment, risk analysis and the effectiveness of controls would defend spending more time and money to improve the internal environment, risk analysis and the effectiveness of controls and to lower the effort put into auditing the compliance of control activities.

RONALD RUSSO
JAN VAN TRIGT

3 Corporate Governance and Taxes

3.1 General introduction

In this chapter the influence of corporate governance on taxation will be viewed in more detail. Firstly we discuss the way corporate governance is handled in various codes and how it influences tax, including tax in the commercial accounts.[1] Thereafter the relationship between risk management/(tax)policy and corporate governance will be viewed more closely. We will give separate attention to the impact of tax scandals, how boards can approach their role in tax matters and aspects around tax in external communications including the provision for uncertain tax positions in the commercial accounts. Finally, we will look more closely at the influence of cooperative compliance on corporate governance and vice versa. We will end with a summary and concluding remarks.

3.2 Corporate governance and tax

3.2.1 Introduction

Corporate governance deals with how to run a company.[2] What good governance actually entails in detail is not always to be found in legal rules. In many jurisdictions sets of rules and principles have been brought together in a code by way of self-regulation. The reason often given for this solution is that legislation is rigid and not capable of adapting to the ever-changing business world.[3] On the other hand self-regulation cannot be enforced as easily as legislation. One of the principles of the

---

1 For a more specific view on the dutch situation see Ronald Russo, Corporate Governance en de (fiscale) jaarrekening. *Weekblad Fiscaal Recht 2013*, nummer 7007.
2 See for definitions the various Corporate Governance Codes (UK: Governance and the Code, Germany: Preamble, US: Foreword and Introduction, NL: Preamble, points 3 and 4), for a general approach the OECD Principles of Corporate Governance, Preamble. The Codes can be found on http://www.ecgi.org/codes/all_codes.php
3 See the UK Code under Comply or Explain, point 6 where it states that comply or explain is an alternative to a rules-based system.

codes is that companies have to 'comply or explain':[4] non-compliance to a voluntarily non-legislative code does not have the same effect as non-compliance to legislation (even if explained, non-compliance to legislation leads to punishment of some sort). This can be seen either as a pro or a con of self-regulation depending on your outlook. Companies usually see it as a positive element.[5] At the same time, in various jurisdictions, hybrid systems have grown. Good governance principles have been wholly or partly enacted into law.

The comply or explain principle has evolved to 'apply or explain'. In this concept it is assumed that the board is more actively involved than the word comply may suggest.[6]

One of the duties of the board of a company is to be accountable for its (financial) policies through a yearly report: the commercial accounts (also referred to as the financial statements). The financial accounts (made by the company) will usually be submitted (mandatory in most jurisdictions for companies exceeding a certain size) to an audit of an accountant who will report his findings as part of the commercial accounts. The commercial accounts have grown over the years as shown in chapter 2. They must comply with business law[7] (EU Standard 1 to 13[8]) and since 2005 the consolidated accounts of listed companies in the EU must comply with IFRS (insofar as they have been endorsed by the EC[9]).

Corporate governance codes have a great impact on the commercial accounts and the work and position of the auditor. Commercial accounts usually are to a large extent similar or at least form a starting point for the tax accounts. This depends on whether, in a jurisdiction, the tax accounts are formally linked to the commercial accounts. Even if there is no such formal link, there is usually a material link if for no other reason than that many basic data are highly similar if not identical for both sets of accounts (for instance wages paid, goods sold, etc.[10] Through the commercial accounts, corporate governance rules therefore indirectly influence the tax accounts. Apart from this indirect approach corporate governance rules sometimes address tax issues directly. In the next paragraphs we will look more closely at corporate

---

4   The OECD principles stress that the rules are not binding. The Dutch Corporate Governance Code explicitly states comply or explain in Preamble, point 4. The German Code states the same in its preamble. The UK Code has a separate chapter after the Preface called "Comply or explain". The US Code in the last paragraph of its Foreword and Introduction mentions (not literally) the comply or explain principle.
5   See for instance *De Toekomst van Toezicht*, nr 3, May 2013, a publication of Deloitte in which several companies express this view.
6   See M.E. King (2009). *King Code of governance for South Africa 2009*, chapter 3 The governance compliance framework. Institute of Directors in Southern Africa.
7   For an overview of a business law perspective on risk management see M. van Daelen (2012). *Riskmanagement en Corporate Governance*. Brugge: Die Keure, Chapter 3.
8   See P. van Schilfgaarde (2013). *Van de BV en de NV*. Ed. 16, edited by J. Winter & J.B. Wezeman. Deventer: Kluwer, p 456.
9   Regulation 1606/2002/EC concerning the application of international accounting standards, adopted on July 19th 2002 by the European Parliament and the Council.
10 See Peter Essers, Theo Raaijmakers, Ronald Russo, Pieter van der Schee, Leo van der Tas & Peter van der Zanden (2009). *The Influence of IAS/IFRS on the CCCTB, Tax Accounting, Disclosure, and Corporate Law Accounting Concepts – A Clash of Cultures*. EUCOTAX Series on European Taxation. Alphen a/d Rijn: Kluwer Law International. Chapter 2.

governance regulations, starting with the OECD regulations, followed by some specific country codes.

3.2.2 Corporate Governance: OECD regulations

Corporate Governance Codes usually contain principles and best practices on good governance. They regulate the relationship between the shareholders, the board of directors and the supervisory board (or non-executive board members). The role of other stakeholders is explicitly mentioned in paragraph IV of the OECD set up. Together these principles and regulations should clarify the conditions for and prerequisites of good governance.

The OECD has published principles of corporate governance to provide guidance as to which issues should be addressed in regulations concerning good governance. According to the OECD there are six principles:
- I. Ensuring the Basis for an Effective Corporate Governance Framework
- II. The Rights of Shareholders and Key ownership Functions
- III. The Equitable Treatment of Shareholders
- IV. The Role of Stakeholders in Corporate Governance
- V. Disclosure and Transparency
- VI. The Responsibilities of the Board

For the commercial accounts and tax planning and tax risk management, V and VI are most directly applicable and we will look at the key relevant elements of these principles more closely.

V. Disclosure and Transparency
The company should disclose material information on the financial and operating results of the company, the company objectives, foreseeable risk factors and governance structures and policies and the process by which they are implemented (V.A). Under V.B is stated that the information should be prepared and disclosed in accordance with high quality standards of accounting and financial and non-financial disclosure. Under V.C the annual audit is prescribed by an independent, competent and qualified auditor to provide external and objective assurance to the board and shareholders that the financial statements fairly represent the financial position and performance of the company in all material respects. The auditor should be accountable to the shareholders and owe a duty to the company to exercise due professional care in the conduct of the audit (V.D).

This principle is directly applicable to the commercial accounts: the board should disclose all information in accordance with accounting standards. The external auditor is positioned strongly: an audit should be performed by an independent auditor who is accountable to the shareholders. The issue of who appoints the auditor is not specifically mentioned.

VI. Responsibilities of the Board
The board must review and guide corporate strategy, major plans of action, risk policy, annual budgets and business plans, setting performance objectives, monitoring implementation and corporate performance and overseeing major capital ex-

penditures, acquisitions and divestitures (VI.D.1). Of particular interest is VI.D.7: ensuring the integrity of the corporation's accounting and financial reporting systems, including the independent auditor and that appropriate systems of control are in place, in particular systems for risk management, financial and operational control and compliance with the law and relevant standards.

This principle is also highly relevant for the commercial accounts. The board is responsible for the systems that lead to the commercial accounts: the internal organisation and control systems. Separately mentioned is the responsibility to comply with the law and relevant standards. This encompasses not only accounting law and standards but also tax law and standards.

In the next paragraph we will look in more detail as to whether the OECD principles have found their way into some national country codes.

3.2.3   Corporate Governance: country regulations

3.2.3.1   Germany

In the German Code the principles of the OECD are visible. Under 4 the responsibilities of the board are mentioned: compliance to law and internal guidelines (4.1.3.) and to implement risk management and control systems (4.1.4.). More detailed than the OECD model are the rules under 5 and 7 on the supervisory board. The supervisory board must appoint an audit committee that will supervise, amongst others, internal control and deals with the external auditor (7.2.2.). The position of the external auditor complies with the OECD model. The position of other stakeholders is specifically mentioned in point 4.1.1: the board must take their interests into account.

3.2.3.2   UK

The UK Code starts with the main principles (A to E). These principles are subsequently dealt with in more detail separately. The main principles are not the same as the OECD model. The most important ones are under A (leadership) and C (accountability). Under A.1 is stated that the board's role is to provide entrepreneurial leadership within a framework of prudent and effective controls that enables risks to be assessed and managed. Under C.1 is stated that the board should present a fair, balanced and understandable assessment of the company's position and prospects. C.2 specifically addresses internal control and risk management: the board must determine the nature and extent of the significant risks it is willing to take in achieving its strategic objectives. The board should maintain sound risk management and internal control systems. Under C.3 (audit committee and auditors) the board is required to establish formal and transparent arrangements for considering how they should apply the corporate reporting and risk management and internal control principles and for maintaining an appropriate relationship with the company's auditors. The audit committee must consist of independent non-executive directors and review, amongst others, the financial controls, internal controls and risk management systems. The audit committee should make recommendations to the board (to put to the shareholders for their approval at general meetings) for the appointment

Corporate Governance and Taxes 3.2.3

and terms of engagement and remuneration of the external auditor (C.3.1 and 2). As in the case of the German Code, the position of external auditor complies with the OECD model, but is not quite as strong (it 'makes recommendations' instead of in the German Code 'deals directly with'). Other stakeholders are not mentioned as such. In the Preface point 7, companies are encouraged to recognize the contribution made by other (than shareholders) providers of capital.

3.2.3.3 The Netherlands

Under the NL Code the board has to develop policies for the company and is required to control the risks involved through a risk management system (II, 1.4). The supervisory board has to supervise the policies and the control system (III, 5.4). The system has to be implemented and monitored. Tax is explicitly mentioned as an area on which the board should have a policy and the supervisory board must supervise. Tax is also one of the risks that should be controlled. The external auditor must be appointed by, in order, the general meeting of shareholders and then the supervisory board or the board. In the preamble it is clearly stated that in all decisions the board must weigh the interests of all stakeholders. The position of the external auditor complies with the OECD model but in practice is often not as strong, as the board often deals with the auditor and his remuneration.

3.2.3.4 US

In the US Code,[11] under II, the board is responsible for the reviewing, understanding and implementation of the company's strategic plans. It is also responsible for reviewing and understanding the company's risk assessment and overseeing the company's risk management process. The board should also oversee legal and ethical compliance and set the tone at the top. The audit committee is particularly responsible for the review of risk management, financial reporting, contacting the internal and external auditor. The audit committee also selects and retains the external auditor and must approve in advance the terms of the annual audit engagement. This is a strong position for the external auditor as he does not have any direct dealings with the board on these issues. As for the ethical and legal standards: the audit committee should oversee the policies, codes of conduct and mechanisms it has in place for employees to report compliance issues. Under IV it is stated that the company has the paramount duty to optimize long-term shareholder value. Other obligations to stakeholders (such as employees, suppliers), maintaining an effective compliance program and strong corporate governance practices and a reputation for civic responsibility are all part of this.

3.2.3.5 Summary and concluding remarks on corporate governance codes

From the paragraphs above the communal picture is that the corporate governance codes, amongst others, regulate the responsibilities of the board and supervisory

---

11 There are many US codes, we selected the Business Round Table version for this comparison.

board (or non-executive directors). The responsibilities include having and supervising the policies of the company and controlling the risks in the company. One of the issues to have a policy on is taxes (only explicitly so in the NL code). Taxes are also one of the risks to be controlled and managed and to be reported upon in the commercial accounts. All codes regulate the relationship between the company and the external auditor. The position of the auditor is strongest in the US Code. All codes also address ethical behaviour (corporate social responsibility) and compliance. They also consider other stakeholders than the shareholders, some stronger than others. One of these other stakeholders is the government in the form of tax authorities.

In an ideal world the tax position in the commercial accounts would be identical to the tax returns. There are however many possible difficulties to overcome in order to reach this ideal world, such as:
- The consolidated commercial accounts are based on international accounting principles such as IFRS or US GAAP.
- Tax accounts are limited to one jurisdiction.
- The commercial consolidation is usually different from the tax consolidation.
- The commercial accounts are usually produced very early in the subsequent year, tax accounts later (and so are open to restatements).
- Tax and commercial accounts use different materiality.
- Tax accounts usually have less (formal) room for explanatory notes.
- Tax accounts are influenced by tax incentives such as accelerated depreciation and R&D incentives.

Despite the differences, the commercial accounts form an important tool or starting point for the tax accounts. The tax accounts are in some ways directly influenced by the corporate governance codes, next to the indirect influence through the commercial accounts as mentioned in paragraph 3.2.1. The need to have risk management control systems and the need to comply with law and ethical standards have a direct impact on the tax function within a company. We will explore this impact in the next paragraphs.

3.2.4   Risk appetite and policy

As shown in paragraphs 3.2.2 and 3.2.3 the board has to manage the risks within the company. This is usually implemented using a risk management system such as COSO: a Business Control Framework.[12] This system has to be implemented and then monitored. The supervisory board (or non-executive board members) supervises this process. To manage and control the risks associated with taxation a Tax Control Framework (TCF) will have to be implemented, as part of the Business Control Framework. A TCF contains all procedures within the company pertaining to taxation. A TCF can be relatively simple: just procedures on filing the relevant tax returns and paying taxes due, but it can also encompass procedures on public relations or

---

12   For more information on COSO see chapter 2.

marketing to limit reputational risks as a result of tax policy. The TCF is very important for the commercial accounts because the external auditor and the tax authorities would like to rely on the internal control of the company.[13] For them to rely on the TCF the quality of it should be acceptable. The internal procedures leading up to the tax return must lead to acceptable tax returns (tax authorities) and be without material errors (external auditor). These requirements are not identical but they point in the same direction. To rely on the work done by the company or external auditor is based on the Layer Model (see chapters 2, 6 and 7). These Layers can be the internal registration by the company of the primary data, the internal audit and the external audit. If an external auditor or a tax auditor decides that a layer is reliable the audit will be limited to the system and not the underlying data (see chapters 14 and 15 for the audit of tax by an accountant and the tax authorities respectively).

As with any system, implementation of a TCF is just the first step. After implementation it will have to be actually applied by the relevant staff of the company and constantly monitored. The monitoring can lead to changes in the procedures, for instance if the laws change, the procedure might have to be amended accordingly. In practice proper monitoring is not always done. Enron is a good example: praised for its risk management system, it went under due to, amongst other factors, tax risks.[14]

In designing and implementing the TCF it is essential to know the basic assumptions and the policy of the board. One of the issues is the risk appetite of the board: which risks it is willing to take.[15] One can argue about whether this is an issue of ethics or economics. For instance: is considering the environment an ethical choice[16] or is it an economical choice in which long term effects and the effects on the public opinion are taken into account?[17] The different codes that have been viewed (although only the Dutch code explicitly for taxation) demand policy and risk management systems. In our opinion the board is required to have a policy on taxation that contains its basic assumptions, including the risk appetite. The TCF will be modelled in accordance with this policy.

Different policy choices lead to different TCF's. We will go from the premise that illegal structuring as a policy is not possible. The policy of a company might be somewhere on a point between both ends of the spectrum:

(a) We will search for and use all legal options to pay as little tax as possible worldwide.

Or

(b) We do not want any conflict regarding taxes and avoid using possibilities that contain a risk of disagreement with tax authorities.

---

13 See in more detail chapter 6 for large companies and chapter 7 for small and medium sized companies. For the latter who do not always have a satisfactory system of internal control the tax authorities can sometimes rely on the internal control of an intermediate (such as an accountant or tax advisor).
14 See A.C. van de Ven (2010). Riskmanagement from an accounting perspective. In: M. van Daelen & C. van der Elst (eds). *Risk management and corporate governance*. Cheltenham UK: Edward Elgar Publishing Limited, pp 34-36.
15 See chapter 5.2.1. on the role of the strategy of the company in the tax operating model.
16 For more detailed information on ethics we refer to chapter 4.
17 Essentially: internal or external motivation, see further chapter 4 on ethics.

These different policies with different risk appetites will have their impact on the content of the respective TCF's. In practice the policy will be more detailed and probably somewhere in the middle of both examples mentioned above. In this respect it is not surprising that the Dutch tax authorities in assessing companies for co-operative compliance place great emphasis on the 'tone at the top' (see further paragraph 3.1.4 on cooperative compliance). Their objective is to know the policy of the board and also what kind of behavior is deemed as acceptable within the company (tolerated, stimulated) by the board. The external auditor would like to know the policy for his own reasons. If the company has a more aggressive policy (more towards a), the likelihood of the tax position being challenged by the tax authorities is greater and the possibility of a provision for uncertain tax positions is higher (see paragraph 3.3.1 and 9.7).

3.2.5 How to respond to tax scandals

Bearing in mind everything that we mentioned on tax policy as part of the governance structure and risk management, it is possible that a company implemented a tax saving structure within (the letter of) the law of all countries involved. If the corporate governance failed it may well be that this structure was not based on policy of the board. The reason might be that there is no specific policy or that the application of the policy was not monitored properly. If this tax structure reaches media coverage it is well possible that the public in general and/or politicians become outraged. This has happened in a number of cases.[18] For instance Amazon,[19] Apple,[20] Google,[21] Starbucks,[22] IKEA[23] and Vodafone[24] were rightly or wrongly heavily criticized for their tax related issues. To assess this criticism a number of issues must be viewed/questions answered:

a. Did the company operate within the letter of the (tax)legislation?

We go from the premise that companies will, as a rule, only implement structures that are legal or, as a minimum, defendable in law. Anyway in this section we do not elaborate tax evasion and its consequences. Incidental illegal aspects cannot, certainly in an international context, be absolutely excluded. A TCF is designed to control the tax risks on a worldwide level and it is difficult to get the same level of control in all relevant jurisdictions.

The question is whether the responsibility of the board ends with the legality of the structure. One could state that the legislator in creating a law weighs all necessary

---

18 For general comments see http://www.theguardian.com/commentisfree/2012/oct/30/roll-call-corporate-rogues-tax and http://www.theguardian.com/business/2012/oct/21/multinational-firms-tax-ebay-ikea.
19 See n.n. (2013). Internet retailing: Tax in cyberspace. In: *The Economist*, may 4th, 2013.
20 See n.n. (2013). Companies and tax: Cook lightly grilled. In: *The Economist*, may 25th, 2013.
21 See House of Commons (UK), Committee of Public Accounts (2013). *Tax Avoidance–Google, Ninth Report of Session 2013–14*. London: The Stationery Office Limited.
22 See n.n. (2012). Corporate taxation: Wake up and smell the coffee. In: *The Economist*, december 15th, 2012.
23 See http://www.forbes.com/sites/leapfrogging/2011/01/20/corporate-taxes-the-chief-business-of-the-conquerors/.
24 See http://www.ft.com/cms/s/0/21f91f9c-d5fa-11e3-a017-00144feabdc0.html#ixzz33TGFyFZG.

circumstances. As the board is under the obligation to maximize share value one could even argue that it would be liable to the shareholders if it would not explore the limit of the possibilities of the law.[25]

We think that this issue depends on what the exact obligation of the board is: is it to maximize share value short term or long term? Which cost should be taken into account if a structure is put into place? Does it also entail the cost of maintenance of the structure or adaption if one of the legislators of the involved jurisdictions changes the relevant laws? An important development in this respect is the fact that exploring all legal possibilities is becoming increasingly "not done" on an international level. The OECD,[26] the EU[27] and the IMF[28] have all named aggressive tax structuring as undesirable. It is therefore probable that more and more anti-abuse regulations and international coordination will come into effect, making aggressive tax structuring more difficult, uncertain in its results and more expensive. Another matter is whether social and environmental costs have to be taken into account. The growing emphasis on corporate social responsibility suggests[29] that this will be increasingly the case.

The corporate governance codes have in common the fact that, in one way or another, all stakeholders have to be taken into account. As governments are also stakeholders we think that a board is under no obligation to explore the limitations of the legal rules. The importance of corporate social responsibility and the intentions of international institutions as described above suggest the same.

b. Did the company comply with the spirit of the legislation?

This question is altogether harder to answer. The spirit or essence of legislation is harder to ascertain than the actual wording of the legal texts. Within a set of well defined tax laws, complying with the spirit of the legislation is akin to paying a Fair Share.[30] Fair Share in the context of taxes means to pay taxes in a jurisdiction corresponding to the economic benefits that are enjoyed in that jurisdiction.[31] Fair Share is basically an issue for the legislator and not for individual companies or tax authorities.[32] The legislator in drafting the laws must weigh all aspects. Ideally, Fair Share and the letter of the legislation should amount to the same thing. Another matter in this respect is that tax legislation is often extremely complicated. This is largely caused by anti-abuse regulations that are amended every time a new loophole is discovered. This makes ascertaining the spirit of the law very difficult.

---

25   See R.S. Avi-Yonay (2008). Corporate Social Responsibility and Strategic Tax Behaviour. In: W. Schön (ed). *Tax and Corporate Governance.* Springer. p 184.
26   See http://www.oecd.org/ctp/aggressive/
27   See http://ec.europa.eu/taxation_customs/taxation/tax_fraud_evasion/index_en.htm
28   See n.n. (2014). *Spillovers in International Corporate taxation.* IMF Policy paper of May 9th, 2014. http://www.imf.org/external/pp/ppindex.aspx.
29   These issues are addressed in all Corporate Governance Codes I have viewed, see paragraph 3.1.2.3.5.
30   See chapter 4, in particular 4.8.
31   See R.H. Happé (2010). Belastingethiek: een kwestie van fair share. In: *Geschriften van de Vereniging voor Belastingwetenschap,* geschrift 243.
       R. Russo (2010). Riskmanagement in Taxation. In: M. van Daelen & C. van der Elst (eds). *Risk management and corporate governance.* Cheltenham UK: Edward Elgar Publishing Limited, p 180.
32   In chapter 4 the concept of Fair Share is dealt with in more detail.

Although Fair Share is not primarily directed towards individual companies it can be argued that aggressive tax planning (making use of a legal possibility that, had the legislator realized this in the drafting process, would have been forbidden) certainly does not lead to Fair Share and is therefore not good governance (unless all (long term) cost of the planning would be included, such as cost of planning and adapting in case the law is changed, cost of a challenge by the tax authorities, cost of reputation damage etc.). In practice this is not easy as many laws are very detailed and contain anti-abuse regulation upon anti-abuse regulation and exceptions upon exceptions so that it is difficult to establish aggressive tax planning from normal tax planning (for instance: avoiding double taxation).

Tax authorities must apply the law as it is and have no responsibility to demand companies to pay a Fair Share if this would exceed the requirements of the letter of the law. They can challenge schemes in court and if this does not lead to the desired result, they can demand no more. At most they have a responsibility towards the legislator to inform him of undesirable use of legislation. It is then up to the legislator to decide whether or not to amend the law.[33]

c. Are legislators themselves to blame (at least in part) that companies engage in aggressive tax planning schemes?

This is a somewhat difficult issue for a lot of governments. On the one hand they want companies to pay their Fair Share, on the other hand they compete with each other to lure companies to invest in their jurisdiction.[34] One aspect of making a jurisdiction attractive for investors is to offer tax benefits, low rates etc. This causes companies to organize their legal structure in such a way that they benefit maximally from the incentives offered. The borderline between aggressive tax planning and structuring a company to profit from incentives offered is very thin and sometimes impossible to distinguish.

Legislators have dual objectives that are difficult to reconcile: the ethical principal of Fair Share versus economic competition to attract investors. An example is The Netherlands. They have implemented efficient tax treaties with many jurisdictions based on the principle of the free flow of capital (originally for the benefit of domestic companies). It is also possible to obtain advance rulings on divers subjects when investing in The Netherlands. For international investors it can therefore be attractive to lead investments through a Dutch company that is eligible to Dutch treaty protection (usually: be entitled to lower or even no withholding taxes in another jurisdiction). To obtain that protection the investment company must have enough substance in The Netherlands to be classed as a Dutch company. To put it simply: a mere 'letterboxcompany' should not suffice. In The Netherlands the government has issued substance requirements but there is no great zeal to enforce these rules.[35] This

---

33 This is not always realised by politicians if they demand that tax authorities should apply Fair Share.
34 See for example the British Finance Minister as quoted by V. Houlder in *Financial Times*, June 28th 2012: 'The government is working to create the most competitive tax system in the G20 ....'.
35 For the substance rules see Resolution of the Dutch Finance Minister, published in *Vakstudie Nieuws*. July 26th, 2012, no 38.

double position is clear: the government wants companies to pay a Fair Share, but to attract investors it seems not to care that other jurisdictions collect less (withholding) taxes, thus running the risk that the company does not pay its Fair Share in that other jurisdiction.

Unlimited competition between States can lead to a rat race to the bottom, in terms of the tax rates as well as the determination of the taxable base. States would ultimately (theoretically) lose their income from taxation and the possibility to influence investment behaviour. To solve this matter it is inevitable, at least to some extent, to coordinate at an international level: this applies to the rates as well as to the allocation of incentives.

d. How do stakeholders feel about tax scandals?

This depends on the sort of stakeholder. Generally, shareholders are quite happy if a company reduces cost and taxes form a major cost for companies. If however the effective tax rate of a company is too low, they (through analysts) will wonder whether the company policy on taxes is too aggressive and will lead to higher cost later (for instance cost of tax lawyers if tax returns are challenged by tax authorities).

Probably the most direct negative influence of an aggressive tax policy is if this policy causes (potential) customers of the company product not to buy the product and so reduce turnover and shareholder value. Damage of reputation gets management and shareholders worried pretty quickly. The Starbucks case was a clear example of this mechanism.[36]

Other stakeholders might take a different view. Customers for instance can be critical on a company for its policy, but we wonder if the criticism will last if the company changes its policy in the desired direction and prices go up as a result of this change.

Governments as stakeholders are more likely to insist on non-aggressive tax policy, although this does not always apply.[37]

All in all it is difficult to judge the feeling of stakeholders towards tax scandals. They are likely to have different reactions and even the reaction of the most important stakeholder for the board, the shareholder, cannot always be accurately predicted. Anyway it is important that the company is prepared for media attention. Even under pressure of media attention the response or "no- comment" of the company needs to be balanced, well thought and "on strategy". This in itself means that the company needs good governance on its tax positions so that it can immediately decide how to respond to media attention. We refer also to paragraph 3.2.6.8 hereinafter.

---

[36] See the internet blogs in October 2012:
http://www.cityam.com/article/starbucks-suffers-more-nike-after-reputational-hits
http://yougov.co.uk/news/2012/10/25/starbucks-suffers-more-nike-after-reputational-hit/
[37] The Dutch railway company (the NS) is a separate limited company but all shares are owned by the Dutch government. This company entered into a tax structure with Ireland to limit Dutch corporate income tax. It caused a stir in the Dutch parliament when the media found out, see http://nos.nl/artikel/413312-ns-drukt-belasting-via-ierland.html.

e. The influence of the personal income tax position of (supervisory) board members

We mentioned already in paragraph 3.2.3.4 the importance of tone at the top in the US governance code. Equally, when the first report of COSO was issued in 1987, the Treadway Commission addressed the importance of the "tone at the top." It was, in fact, the first recommendation in that report:[38]

> "The tone set by top management–the corporate environment or culture within which financial reporting occurs–is the most important factor contributing to the integrity of the financial reporting process. Notwithstanding an impressive set of written rules and procedures, if the tone set by management is lax, fraudulent financial reporting is more likely to occur."

The COSO reports have evolved over the years. When in 2004 the COSO-ERM framework was published the importance of the Internal Environment was articulated as one of the eight components of Enterprise Risk Management: "The internal environment encompasses the tone of an organisation and sets the basis for how risk is viewed and addressed by an entity's people, including risk management philosophy and risk appetite, integrity and ethical values and the environment in which they operate."[39]

Regularly the concept of tone at the top is re-articulated. An interesting recent version is: *demonstrated seriousness from the top*.[40] The concept of tone at the top is sharpened. It is not only about communication but it has to be proven by clearly recognizable actions and behaviour of top management and the board of the company.

In order to ascertain the demonstrated seriousness from the top, the personal income tax returns of (supervisory) board members and management may also become relevant. The premise is then that if the personal tax return of a board member does not comply with regulations or could be classified as frivolous, or aggressive or even includes tax evasion the risk management of the company might have the same deficiencies. For instance, if a board member files frivolous tax returns or hides away certain facts and circumstances, how trustful could that person act if the company states in its tax policy that "the company should be open and transparent with the Revenue Services and provide all relevant information that is necessary for the Revenue Service to review possible tax risks?"[41]

Also from a reputational perspective individual income tax issues of board members and top management can substantially hurt the company when these issues come into the public domain. The company has therefore good reasons to review the individual tax returns of this group of individuals.

---

38 Committee of Sponsoring Organizations of the Treadway Commission (COSO) (1987). *Report of the National Commission on Fraudulent Financial Reporting*. October 1987, p 32.
39 Committee of Sponsoring Organizations of the Treadway Commission (COSO) (2004). *Enterprise Risk Management –Integrated Framework Executive Summary*. September 2004, page 3
40 Howard Sklar (October 2012): http://openairblog.com/why-im-not-using-tone-at-the-top-anymore
41 This language is from the model statement of seven tax principles offered by the Confederation of British Industry to its members. http://www.cbi.org.uk/media/2051390/statement_of_principles.pdf

We therefore believe that the individual tax returns of board members and top management of a company are key elements of trust, integrity and risk management. However, there are still many companies where a review of the individual income tax returns of board and/or key management members is not yet part of the Tax Control Framework. Sometimes that is because of deemed privacy reasons. Sometimes the company is simply not that far in the maturity of its tax control framework. We believe the deemed privacy reasons are not very valid. The management of tax processes of a company already traditionally includes the tax returns of expatriates since it is complex under treaties and different local legislations. How to address privacy concerns can be learned from that practice and in many situations a third party review of individual income tax returns can easily be organised.

It may, however, take some efforts to develop criteria to measure the level of compliance of a personal income tax return. Not every challenge by a tax authority will constitute undesirable behaviour. Nevertheless the involvement of personal behavior of board members could very well be a part of any future approach to the tone at the top.

With respect to the individual income tax position of board members and management, there is one aspect of legislation in the Netherlands that is worth being mentioned. Normally the Dutch Revenue Service has a confidentiality and non-disclosure obligation with respect to all tax matters. However, there is an exception to this rule for individuals engaged in the management of financial institutions. Where such an individual has an issue in his tax filings that triggers a certain degree of penalties, the Dutch Revenue Service is required to inform the authorities supervising the financial industry.[42] Such penalties from the tax authorities escalate further: the individual has to resign from his responsibilities since there is a rule that he is deemed not to be trustworthy any longer. This type of legislation clearly illustrates the importance of the personal tax behaviour of individuals with an impact on the company.

3.2.6 How to deal with taxes as a board

In view of everything we described before there is no easy answer to this question. There are however some directions visible of what actions to take and what actions should be avoided.

3.2.6.1 The importance of an approved tax policy

The first thing that springs to mind is that in our opinion it is no longer possible not to have an explicit tax policy as a board. Taxes are no longer the exclusive domain of specialists. They play an important role in determining the reputation of a company in society. The board is under the obligation to control the risks connected to taxation within the company and to manage the process of complying with the relevant rules and regulations. In our opinion this is not limited to filing the proper tax returns and

---

42 Art 4:10 WFT; Art 15 *Besluit Gedragstoezicht financiële ondernemingen Wft.*
    Art 67 AWR Art 43c *Uitvoeringsregeling AWR*

making sure that the taxes due are timely paid. It also comprises control of collateral damage, such as reputational damage. If a company implements a tax structure it should be part of the policy that (1) the board is aware of the structure and (2) can explain to the public why this structure was chosen. This will prevent that the board is taken by surprise if politicians or media, at a later stage, question the structure.

This aspect of tax policy should also be on the agenda of the supervisory board (or non-executive directors). The members of the supervisory board (or the audit committee as part of it) will have to supervise the existence of policy and form an opinion on the headlines of it. We believe that a (constructively) critical and active role in this respect is required: not only on the existence of the policy and its compliance with the aforementioned, but also on implementation and monitoring of it.

The tax policy should be an integral part of the overall management style and corporate behaviour. The demonstrated commitment of top management and board are an important aspect. That requires demonstrated seriousness from the top. We refer to paragraph 3.2.5 sub e.

3.2.6.2 Companies internationally active

A general point of concern in this respect is the structure of internationally active companies. The tax policy must be implemented through the whole group of companies and this can prove a challenge in tax matters on a local (foreign) level. Tax systems differ substantially between jurisdictions. The drafting of the TCF in these cases must be done in a detailed and precise way: allocate responsibilities clearly with the relevant functions and employees and clearly drafting the content of the responsibilities. A beautifully drafted TCF that is not used in practice provides no control at all. Since the TCF encompasses all tax related risks, this concerns not only corporate income tax but also wage taxes, value added taxes etc.

3.2.6.3 Central or decentralized management approach

An important aspect to consider in this perspective is the management vision with respect to 'centralization or decentralization'. On the European continent there has been, historically, quite a tradition of decentralized management of foreign subsidiaries. Operating subsidiaries usually have some room in which to act. Within the overall scope and strategy of the multinational company the board of a foreign subsidiary has substantial authority to act independently and the holding company reviews at a high level only and at a distance. In many cases there is no harmonized ERP system over the countries nor has the central head office access to the local bookkeeping or ERP system when business goes as usual. Flipside of this management concept is that the head office is not equipped for a strong central review of details. Moreover, in this tradition, tax is often recognized as 'a detail'. Typically the local CFO reports monthly on the main line items of the P&L and cash position. Tax is often not a main item or lacks any detail. Tax risks are normally hardly or rudimentarily reported.

These attributes of the decentralized management approach are also significant outside the tax environment of the company. The leading receiver upon corporate bankruptcies in the Netherlands recently gave the following answer to the question:

What topics should the supervisory board take care of? "In three quarters of all cases it is about bad management. Therefore it is key for supervisory board members to have adequate provision of information. Especially at foreign subsidiaries many things can go wrong. "it is difficult to get that at your fingertips."[43] This quote clearly illustrates an important weakness of the decentralized approach: Governance of tax struggles with the same weaknesses in the decentralized approach and in many instances it even makes an adequate tax governance practically impossible.

The decentralized approach can last for a long time in many countries with an exemption method on intra company dividends in the profit taxation. The Netherlands is such a country with a longstanding participation exemption on intra group dividends. In the concept of the exemption method it is, for the receiving holding company, quite simple to prepare a tax return. No complex details are needed on the underlying profit taxation on the earnings from which the dividends are distributed. This is contrary to a system with a credit method. Under the application of the credit method many details and insights are needed to prepare the tax returns of the dividend receiving holding company. Typically the exemption method on dividends facilitates the decentralized management approach in general and on tax management topics especially.

We conclude that an adequate tax risk management is quite vulnerable in a decentralized management approach. The board should be aware of this and implement additional checks and balances.

3.2.6.4 Be prepared for the public domain

In society as well as in politics taxes are more than ever on the agenda. Non-governmental organizations and media play an important role in this newly found attention to taxation.[44] Board and supervisory boards should take this into account when deciding upon the tax policy for the company. The possible impact of the policy on public opinion and politics should be part of the tax policy. The recent developments in international regulation (such as per country reporting,[45] see more detailed chapter 9.9), developments in society in general (corporate social responsibility, Global Reporting Guidelines by GRI[46]) and from the OECD and EU (such as the Base Erosion and Profit Shifting report[47]) all lead to more attention for the taxation aspects of business. The board, in drafting its policy, should be aware of these developments and proactively anticipate its impact.

---

43 Louis Deterink in an interview in *Het Financieele Dagblad*, May 30rd 2014 (in Dutch).
44 See for example n.n. (2014). *Business among friends. Why corporate tax dodgers are not yet losing sleep over global tax reform*. Oxfam Briefing Paper, May 2014, www.oxfam.org.
45 See http://www.oecd.org/ctp/tax-global/country_by_country_reporting-development_perspective.pdf.
46 See www.globalreporting.org/Pages/default.aspx.
47 In which amongst others country by country reporting has been incorporated as action 13 in the BEPS action plan, see http://www.oecd.org/ctp/BEPSActionPlan.pdf .

3.2.6.5 Does tax planning add to shareholders value?

Irrespective of all the attention on tax from a reputational and ethical perspective, the board should also keep a good eye on tax from a shareholders value perspective. As mentioned in paragraph 3.2.3.4 in the US governance code it is mentioned that the company has the paramount duty to optimize longterm shareholder value. Obviously, but less explicitly, this is also true for companies in all other countries as well. Consequently, an important strategic issue is: can tax planning add value? Is the company in the long term able to add value for shareholders through tax avoidance that transfers value from the states in which it operates to the company?

It is of key importance that the board sets the rules of the road for the company in this area. First step: is tax avoidance recognized as an area where value can be added? Second step: what is allowed according to its own ethical standards? And an important question within these rules of the road is: what degree of transparency should the company maintain towards the tax authorities and the public? Hereinafter we elaborate on these questions.

It is important for the board to pay sufficient attention to the question: is it possible to add value through tax planning? At first sight the answer could well be yes because there is a need for tax planning activities to avoid double taxation in a multinational environment since tax regimes of nations are not harmonized. Another argument can be found in the observation that nations compete deliberately against each other in the attractiveness of their tax legislation in order to attract international investments in their country. It goes without saying that a company needs tax planning should it want to benefit from this competition. This however does not mean aggressive tax planning is a must. It is important to also note that no company benefits from aggressive tax planning that will be corrected by tax authorities at a later stage because of poor interpretation of the law or bad execution of structuring.

In the summer of 2014 there has been some interest on the impact of tax planning by US companies. Not only in politics but also by investors and there is a growing attention for the impact and volume of tax planning. The *Financial Times* reviewed the accounts of 14 cash rich US technology and pharmaceutical companies.[48] The 14 companies cut their tax rate between 2004-2013 by an average of 7,7%. By the last year they were taxed at a rate of just 10%. A little more than 85% of this average tax reduction could be attributed to expanding foreign operations including in tax havens and low tax countries. The companies are exempt from reporting the deferred tax charge upon repatriation of the earnings back to the USA for as long as they can prove that the profits are indefinitely reinvested abroad. It is obvious that this type of tax planning has an enormous volume. And in addition there is empirical evidence that tax planning is good for stock price and lowers cost of debt.[49] These are obviously good arguments pro tax planning.

---

48 See Vanessa Houlder (2014). Taxing times ahead over offshore rules. In: *Financial Times*, June 13th 2014.
49 Desai & Dharmpala (2009). Corporate tax avoidance and firm value. In: *Review of Economics and Statistics*, August 2009, Vol. 91, No. 3, pp 537-546.

However, there are also indications to be more reluctant. As mentioned before the difference between tax planning and aggressive tax planning is difficult to make. The *Financial Times* cites an investor warning against complacency by pointing out that a quarter of the improvement in net margins had been achieved only by reducing the tax bills.[50] This indicates that such an achievement of net margins by tax planning is less valued than margin improvement in the core business.

3.2.6.6 Tax planning requires good corporate governance

In literature this has already been addressed in empirical research in 2005. The simple presumption that corporate tax avoidance represents a transfer of value from the state to shareholders does not appear to be validated in the data. In the full sample, tax avoidance does not lead to increases in firm value. There is a positive effect found for a subsample of firms that are identified as being well-governed while there is no significant effect for firms that are less well governed. The results are consistent with the hypothesis that the valuation of tax avoidance is a function of firm governance and, more broadly, with the point of view that tax avoidance and managerial efforts to divert value from shareholders are intertwined. From this it can be learned that the market values tax avoidance with scepticism given the complexities it introduces and this scepticism is only offset in the presence of high quality governance.[51]

This is an important observation for the management and supervision by the board of the tax planning activities. A company should critically review the potential value for its shareholders of tax planning activities and the quality of the corporate governance in itself determines the impact of tax planning on shareholders' value. Consequently, tax planning activities only add value when markets recognize good corporate governance of the company in the field of taxes. This means that boards should definitely keep a hawkish eye on the tax planning activities due to the requirements in the corporate governance codes they are subject to (see paragraph 3.2.3) but even more so because of the perception of markets! The same hawkish eye is needed on their governance of tax principles and processes. This is required in order to avoid that the benefits of tax avoidance are diverted from shareholders value to managers' remunerations, inefficiencies within the company hid by the tax benefits or are lost upon any challenge by tax authorities due to bad execution of the implemented tax planning ideas.

The agency issue is quite a tough topic to tackle for supervisory board members. Friese, Link and Mayer rightly addressed this subject at the beginning of their article 'Taxation and Corporate Governance – The State of the Art.'[52] They referred to Adam Smith who had already pointed out in 1776: "The directors of such companies however, being the managers rather of other people's money than of their own, it

---

50 See Vanessa Houlder (2014). Taxing times ahead over offshore rules. In: *Financial Times*, June 13th 2014.
51 Desai & Dharmapala (2005). *Corporate Tax Avoidance and Firm Value*. Cambridge MA: National Bureau of Economic Research. Working paper 11241.
52 Friese, Link & Mayer (2008). Taxation and Corporate Governance- The State of the Art. In: W. Schön (ed), *Tax and Corporate Governance*. Berlin/Heidelberg: Springer.

cannot be expected, that they should watch over it with the same vigilance with which the partners in a private co-partnery frequently watch over their own."

Where normally the head of tax reports to the CFO, a supervisory board member is, in principle in many situations, fully dependent on information from the CFO. That set up can hardly be recognized as good governance providing a good insight. The supervisory board member should strive for more information from other sources than from the CFO only. The external auditors could be such another source. However, in their regular attest work for the annual accounts, they only have a limited review on the tax position. Consequently, a pressing issue for a supervisory board member is to develop a good, in depth view on tax processes, tax planning and tax policies. This is especially valid for members of the audit committee. This requires a subtle play of powers and contacts between the executive and supervisory members of the board and the next layers of management and staff. The supervisory board members need their own sources of information that includes direct contact with the head of tax. This is a delicate play which is still, in many instances, not very much appreciated in more traditional environments.

3.2.6.7   A balanced set of KPI's for management performance measurement

The matter of adequate information is also depending on the set of KPI's for the management of the company. The better that framework the more trust supervisory board members may have in balanced outcomes of the implemented management structures. The set of KPI's should create a balanced framework of performance incentives for managers but fully aligned with the corporate objectives. This KPI framework should protect the company's reputation in society as well as with tax authorities. Tax matters should be handled effectively and efficiently within the company's ethical framework and still maintain a focus on managing the longterm tax burden. To put it succinctly: the KPI's for management are an important aspect of good governance of tax anyway.

There is some research on how boards communicate their governance. There are many variations on how this takes place. In a review of the FTSE100 2013 it is reported that ninety groups made certain disclosures on their tax related governance. From these ninety:
- 40 made partial reference, for instance mentioning that the audit committee had reviewed tax accounting judgment areas;
- 50 provided fuller details, setting out processes for setting and monitoring adherence to tax policies and strategies.[53]

We believe that it is fair to say that UK companies are more active in this field of communication than many others in other countries. We mentioned before that the board should set out the rules of the road. Such rules should determine what is

---

53   MacPherson & Kennedy (2014). *Responsible Tax: An Integrated approach to tax transparency*. London: Deloitte LLP.
http://www.deloitte.com/assets/Dcom-UnitedKingdom/Local%20Assets/Documents/Services/Tax/uk-tax-rt.pdf

allowed according to the company's own ethical standards. This is the road map on how to navigate in the ethical terrain surrounding tax. Part of this road map goes back to the fundamental beliefs of the company on how society should be organized. Should tax be minimal and government small or should the vision be more directed towards the social welfare state? Differences in vision have a fundamental impact on the tax policy of the company and its approach of tax law.[54] It is the board and only the board that is at the helm of the company on these matters and the board needs to be aware of this.

3.2.6.8   A vision on transparency

Another part of the ethical terrain is tax and transparency. We mentioned already: Transparency is a new trend. It was in 2009 that Anderson, De Grave and Moore wrote: 'A common complaint of many heads of tax is the transparency required by IFRS and US GAAP with respect to uncertain tax positions. The required disclosures in the financial statements are viewed as a road map that can be used by the tax authorities to identify areas of risk or uncertainty that they can then focus on in order to drive assessments.'[55] This relates to a key aspect of tax policy: is the company seeking value from the state in hiding facts and circumstances and interpretations? Can value be created from the risk of non detection?

Some five years later and the scene has changed quite a bit. Transparency is the trend in tax. New disclosure rules pull back the veil of tax secrecy and far more details will become publicly available or discretionally available for Revenue Services.[56] It is fair to say that irrespective of the developments in regulations, companies are takings steps voluntarily. The UK is a front-runner in this field. Reference can be made to the Statement of tax principles as published by the Confederation of British Industry (CBI) in May 2013. It says: "UK business should therefore be open and transparent with HMRC about their tax affairs and provide all relevant information that is necessary for HMRC to review possible tax risks."[57]

What can the company win by transparency? Research from 2002 indicates that the markets not always reward voluntarily disclosed information.[58] Consequently, the question to be transparent or not, is one the board should decide upon based on the values of the organisation, its position in society and the trends in regulation. These are matters that relate to the licence to operate in society. The board should articulate its tax transparency principles on the basis of its general position and relations in society.

---

54   For a broad overview: Michael Sandel (2009). *Justice. What is the right thing to do?* New York: Farar, Straus and Giroux.
55   Janet M. Anderson, Koen De Grave & Jennifer M. Moore (2010). Tax Accounting. In: Anuschka Bakker & Sander Kloosterhof (eds), *Tax Risk Management From risk to opportunity*. Amsterdam: IBFD. Chapter 3.
56   For an overview: Raquel Meyer (2013). *Tax Transparency Business Horizons* . 56, pp 543- 549.
57   CBI Statement of tax principles
     http://www.cbi.org.uk/media/2051390/statement_of_principles.pdf
58   J. Roonen & V. Yaari (2002). Incentives for voluntary disclosure. In: *Journal of Financial Markets*.

3.2.6.9 How to deal with taxes as a board: summary

If we summarize the aforementioned, the following topics are to be addressed by the board on the governance of tax matters:
- How to approach public and tax authorities: is value to be gained by hiding facts and circumstances and play with the risk of non-detection?
- How does the cost of tax impact the set of KPI's applicable for bonuses and performance indicators for management? Does the KPI framework provide for a balanced mechanism for adequate management of the tax affairs?
- How centralized or decentralized is the management reporting structure of the group of companies? Is the tax control framework embedded adequately in this reporting system?
- Does the tax policy strictly follow the tax rules of the country or does the company have a compass of its own? Is that compass more in the direction of a libertarian vision of small government and low tax or more in the direction of corporate social responsibility (tax is the price we pay for a civilisation and the company does not want to negotiate on a discount)?
- Tone at the top: Has the board and top management demonstrated commitment on the execution of the tax policy of the company? This also includes behaviour on their individual tax position.

Apart from the activities the board should undertake to deal with taxation issues, we find it strange that corporate governance regulations and regulators do not give more attention to the tax aspects of corporate governance. In the Netherlands the Monitoring Committee on Corporate Governance reports, for instance, on its activities but no activities on monitoring of tax policy are included nor mentioned.[59] This does not seem logical as many of the cases on taxes in the media have a Dutch edge to them.[60] Perhaps the explanation is that in the regular world of corporate governance there is no or not much attention to taxation, unjustly so in our view.

3.3 Tax in external communications

Hereinafter we discuss the uncertain tax positions in the annual accounts as well as other external publications about tax.

3.3.1 Tax position in the commercial accounts/provision for uncertain tax positions

The tax position in the commercial accounts includes the costs in the profit and loss account (actual as well as deferred), the tax assets and liabilities in the balance sheet and the disclosures in the notes. It is the domain of tax accounting to determine the exact amounts in the balance sheet and profit and loss account and the appropriate

---

59 See www.mccg.nl for the reports of the monitoring committee.
60 Most notable is Starbucks who has offered to pay extra corporate income tax in the UK and has decided to move its headquarters from The Netherlands to the UK.

wording in the notes, according to the applicable accounting principles (IFRS, US gaap or local gaap). We refer to chapter 9.7. In this section we would like to draw attention to two issues where tax accounting meets corporate governance.

The first issue is that in general, as with all costs and risks within the company corporate governance, rules imply that the process of taxes must be controlled through a risk management system. The numbers that form the basis for tax accounting (but also commercial accounting) are taken from the administrative system of the company. The internal control measures of the company should guarantee that these numbers are accurate. In some cases the determination of the numbers is subject to estimates: in general, for commercial accounting for instance, provisions or hedge accounting issues depend on estimates of future events. Specifically for tax accounting there are a number of estimates or uncertainties involved. Deductibility of (intercompany) interest, applicability of exemptions and acceptability of pricing in intercompany transactions, whether a permanent establishment is present or not, are examples of such uncertainties (which can be found in commercial accounts of listed companies under tax risks[61]).

In many boardrooms tax in the annual accounts is recognized as a technical matter which does not require specific attention. However, we believe that the contrary is true. Tax is a complex and difficult element in the annual accounts that requires sufficient attention from the highest levels. From research in the USA it can be learned that an adequate presentation of tax in the annual accounts is one of the most complicated subjects in financial reporting. Since the introduction of the SOx regulations, quoted companies in the USA must report to the SEC when they find material weaknesses in their internal controls. These SEC-disclosures are publicly available at the SEC site and provide for insights in the quality of the annual accounts. From analysis it can be learned that the disclosures of material weaknesses in the tax area are the number one category of disclosed material weaknesses.[62]

Next to material weaknesses, restatements of annual accounts also have to be reported publicly to the SEC. Recently, these restatements have been analyzed.[63] Some results of that analysis are important. Similarly to the material weaknesses, after 2006 the number and volume of restatements is declining. However, the decline has come to a standstill over the last few years. It has also become clear that tax topics are amongst the most important areas from which restatements originate.

In conclusion, from the situation in the USA it can be learned that the tax position in the annual commercial accounts is complex and difficult. It should therefore be recognized as an important topic on the agenda of the board and especially of the audit committee.

This brings us to the second issue: if a tax position is unclear, a provision for uncertain tax positions must be accounted for in the commercial accounts. This

---

61 See for instance the annual accounts 2013 of Unilever (*Strategic report*, p 39.) and Shell (*Business overview, Risk factors*, p 5).
62 N.n. (2011). *Material weaknesses and restatements. Is tax still in the hot seat?* Deloitte Development LLC. https://www.deloitte.com/assets/Dcom-UnitedStates/Local%20Assets/Documents/Tax/us_-tax_materialweaknesses_012011.pdf
63 N.n. (2012). Financial Restatements. A twelve year comparison. In: *Audit Analytics*. Sutton Massachusetts 2013.

provision (as with many provisions) may be initiated or is at least reviewed by the external auditor who is not convinced that the tax position presented by the company in a tax return will hold (ultimately) in court. The underlying analysis of the provision in the commercial accounts (and the explanatory notes) is very interesting for tax authorities. It indicates that the tax position of the company is a subject of potential discussion. The audit file of the external auditor could be an important source of efficiencies for tax authorities. This would contain the details of the provision and would save the tax authorities a lot of work. In the Netherlands the principle of fair play (introduced by the Supreme Court) forbids the tax authorities to look into correspondence of companies with their advisors (and the external auditor) if this contains specific advice or interpretation on their tax position.[64] The Dutch Accountants Association (NBA) has drafted a special working document (nr 1113) for its members on how to deal with requests from the tax authorities for the audit file.[65] The tax authorities have cooperated in this working document which functions adequately in practice. In the end however, it means that the Dutch Revenue only has access to very limited information from the files of the statutory auditor.

It is remarkable how prudent Dutch practice is under the application of the fair play jurisprudence. There is a high degree of respect for the privacy of the corporate taxpayer and this is quite contrary to the practice in the USA. Approximately at the same time as the publication of the working document on the fair play principles in the Netherlands, the IRS introduced a new disclosure: Schedule UTP.

The Schedule UTP (form 1120; Uncertain Tax Position Statement) requires the company to report annually to the IRS which uncertain tax positions have been included in filed tax returns.[66] There are two categories of uncertain tax positions:
- 'Any tax position taken on a return for which there is a reserve recorded in the audited financial statements; and
- A tax position for which no reserve was recorded because of the expectation to litigate the position if (i) the probability of settling with the IRS is less than 50%, (ii) the company intends to litigate, and (iii) the company is more likely than not to prevail on merits in litigation.'

In September 2010 with the introduction of Schedule UTP the IRS Commissioner held a speech to the American Bar Association.[67] The topic of his address was transparency and some quotes provide for a good insight into the reasoning behind the introduction of Schedule UTP.

"Guided by the fundamental principle that transparency is essential to achieving an effective and efficient self-assessment tax system."

"I also believe the concept of more transparency is consistent with our nation's historic framework of a voluntary compliance system."

---

64 Supreme Court September 29th, 2005, BNB 2006/21.
65 www.nba.nl/Vaktechniek/Tools/Praktijkhandleidingen
66 http://www.irs.gov/pub/irs-pdf/i1120utp.pdf
67 http://www.irs.gov/uac/Prepared-Remarks-of-IRS-Commissioner-Doug-Shulman-to-the-American-Bar-Association

"I believe that it helps achieve what most taxpayers and the IRS strive for and basically want:
- We want certainty regarding a taxpayer's tax obligations sooner rather than later;
- We want consistent treatment across taxpayers; and
- We want an efficient use of government and taxpayer resources by focusing on issues and taxpayers that pose the greatest risk of tax noncompliance."

The concept of Schedule UTP is precisely contrary to the fair play principle as defined by the Dutch Supreme Court. In the USA, the company should be transparent to the IRS in its uncertain tax positions in tax returns filed, while in the Netherlands the company has the right, based on corporate privacy, to limit the access of the Dutch Revenue to the same information.

In paragraph 3.1.2.6.8 we mentioned that already in 2009 there were quite a number of heads of tax who were reluctant about transparency and disclosures about tax in the annual accounts.[68] The trend towards transparency has, as already discussed developed since then. It is important to note that in 2011 research was published on how equity investors value the uncertain tax positions in the annual accounts. There maybe several pros and cons in their valuation.

Negatively:
- It may trigger additional authority scrutiny;
- Reputation damage: a poor corporate citizen behaviour.

Positively:
- Expected benefit of tax avoidance;
- Tax avoidance may also been recognized as a management culture that is eager to seek opportunities for the company.

The conclusion of the empirical research is as follows: investors positively value uncertain tax positions where the uncertainties regard permanent tax savings (instead of temporary differences). However, the positive relation was only found at well governed firms.[69] Again this demonstrates the great importance of good corporate governance.

In view of everything we have viewed so far, the tax position in the commercial accounts and certainly the provision for uncertain tax positions should in our opinion be specifically addressed in the tax policy of the company. The board should be aware of the differences in approach of Revenue Services in all the countries the organization is active in.

3.3.2 Tax in other external communications

It has been a trend since 2012 that companies provide more background information on the way they handle the tax matters. Certainly the media coverage of tax in the corporate world has been a reason for many companies to be more articulate. It is still early days to analyze these external communications thoroughly and there are hardly

---

68 See For a broad overview: Michael Sandel (2009). *Justice. What is the right thing to do?* New York: Farar, Straus and Giroux.
69 A. Knoester (2011). *Investor Valuation of Tax Avoidance Through Uncertain Tax Positions.* Seattle, Washington: Foster School of Business, University of Washington.

any guidelines regarding them. These documents carry a variety of titles: Our Approach to Tax, Tax Principles, Tax Risk Management Strategy, A Report on the Economic Contribution to Public Finances and Revenue Transparency are just a few examples. The volume of the documents vary significantly as well.

When reading these documents of a group of leading large companies the following can be written in summary. Companies are providing insight to the public in three areas:
- tax risk management and governance within the company;
- tax principles in tax planning and compliance;
- taxes paid.

On tax risk management and governance one can typically find the internal organisation of tax processes and responsibilities. A company may also provide insights into the relationship using such key documents as code of conducts, business principles, whistleblower process, approach of KPI's for management, role of local subsidiaries and the head office.

In the second category of the published documents matters are addressed on the topics that go to the heart of the way the company deals with tax planning and tax compliance. The seven tax principles as published by the Confederation of British Industry provide for a good insight into the sort of topics.[70]
1. The business rationale of tax planning.
2. The response to incentives and exemptions.
3. How to interpret tax law.
4. Engagement in the international dialogue on tax rules and need for change.
5. Transparency to Revenue Services.
6. Collaboration with Revenue Services to achieve early agreement on disputes.
7. How to deal with public understanding and trust.

The third area is on the 'taxes paid'. Initiatives from NGOs like EITI, Publish What You Pay and GRI have certainly influenced companies. However, it is fair to say that the big push for disclosure of details on a per country basis comes from legislative actions. The Dodd Frank act in the USA and the proposals from the EU are the first major steps towards per country reporting for certain industries. The OECD's BEPS programme provides for more generic legislation. However, on a voluntarily basis companies are still reluctant to make steps in this direction.

A fascinating aspect on taxes paid is that certain countries give public access to the details of the tax assessments of companies. Denmark is one such country. It is important to note that the concept of corporate privacy has different meanings in different countries and companies should be aware of these differences. Legislators can give a push to transparency in two ways: disclosure by the company or disclosure by the Revenue Service.

---

70 http://www.cbi.org.uk/media/2051390/statement_of_principles.pdf

3.4 Cooperative compliance

Cooperative compliance is treated mainly in chapters 6, 7 and 8. In this paragraph we merely point out some aspects related to corporate governance. One of the main characteristics of cooperative compliance is that it uses the layer model and aims to rely on the internal control measures of the company. As shown in this chapter, internal control is also a major part of corporate governance. The quality of the internal control determines the extent of trust that the tax authorities have in it and influences reduction of audit by them.

Another characteristic of cooperative compliance is that it is built on trust between the company and the tax authorities. The tone at the top of the company is very important in this respect as well as the way the internal controls are implemented, monitored and adapted. Under cooperative compliance the company and tax authorities share information proactively and this can have a major impact on, for instance, the commercial accounts. If the contact between the company and the tax authorities is easy and in real time (instead of years later during a tax audit), the expectation is that there will be less uncertain tax positions. This will strengthen the reliability and usability of the commercial accounts for the stakeholders.

To enter into cooperative compliance can be a very important step for a company in the management of its tax position and tax risks.[71] The decision whether or not to do so should therefore, in our opinion, be explicitly dealt with in the tax policy of the company.

3.5 Concluding remarks

Corporate Governance influences taxation in both a direct and an indirect way. The indirect influence is due to the impact of Corporate Governance on the commercial accounts (and the influence of commercial accounts on tax accounts). The direct influence stems from the paragraphs in Corporate Governance Codes that, albeit not always specifically, cover subjects that relate to taxation directly. The biggest influence of Corporate Governance on taxation stems from the emphasis on internal control, the policies of the board and the supervision of the supervisory board. The quality level of internal controls is important in the relationship between the company and the tax authorities. The higher this level is, the more the tax authorities will be able to rely on it and as a result adapt their audits. This can be beneficial for the company as a (tax) audit is usually a costly and time-consuming affair. Also the tax position in the commercial accounts can be presented with a greater level of certainty. The tax authorities are also becoming increasingly keener on the policies of the company regarding risk management, especially tax risks. This is also an important factor in the relationship between tax authorities and the company.

For companies, their boards and supervisory boards these developments mean that they will have to give more attention to taxation, especially as there is much public attention on taxation. They will have to concern themselves with the policy of

---

71 We are not implying that it is not possible to manage tax risks without cooperative compliance. It is however one way of handling the issue and of growing importance.

the company in the field of taxation and monitor this as well. They will have to be prepared for public attention on specific taxation aspects of the company (be able to explain why it was done in that way) or if that is not possible, limit the damage done.

Next to the reputational aspect there is also a need for good corporate governance of tax in order to add shareholders value through tax planning activities. From empirical research it can be learned that without good governance it is not possible to create shareholders' value from tax planning activities. Of course the board does not have to concern itself with the day-to-day management, but overseeing the policy and its implementation and monitoring should concern them. The time in which tax was a difficult issue best left to the tax director is definitely over.

RICHARD HAPPÉ

4. Ethics and International Tax Planning

4.1 Introduction

The international tax practice is at a crossroads. This is the result of the financial crisis, which also gave rise to a tax crisis. This chapter focuses on the debate about whether aggressive tax planning is morally acceptable. In the one corner we have the international business sector and the major tax advisory firms, and in the other corner we have governments and societies.

The central issue dividing both camps is easy to define. The first group believes that they are doing nothing legally wrong with their – often aggressive – tax planning. As Microsoft recently stated in its defence: "Microsoft adheres carefully to the laws and regulations of every country in which we operate."[1] The key accusation of governments (as opponents of aggressive tax planning) was best expressed by Margaret Hodge, a member of the UK House of Commons: "We're not accusing you of being illegal, we are accusing you of being immoral."[2]

The purpose of this chapter is twofold: its first objective is to provide insight into the moral aspects of aggressive tax planning. Its second objective is to present a framework for a morally responsible tax planning policy.

The first part of this chapter (4.2-4.7) will examine the morality of the views held by the business sector and those held by society at large. It will outline how the events of the last few years gave rise to this debate. Important societal events, such as the emergence of the information and internet age and the current crisis, appear to have played a major role in this. The aggressive tax planning phenomenon will then be placed in a wider perspective. The outcome is one in which the current debate appears to fit the mould of a classic discussion of the relationship between the market and society. In modern jargon: a discussion between a neoliberal and a moral view

---

1   See http://www.icij.org/project/luxembourg-leaks/new-leak-reveals-luxembourg-tax-deals-disney-koch-brothers-empire.
2   MP Margaret Hodge, Chair of the Public Accounts Committee, House of Commons, UK, during the hearings on Google, Amazon and Starbucks, November 2012. See http://www.bbc.com/news/business-20288077. See for another example par. 4.7.

of tax planning. The first part of the chapter concludes with a practical example: the inversion structure applied by U.S. companies.

The second part of the chapter (4.8-4.12) focuses on the multinational enterprise: what morally responsible considerations does a company need to take into account with regard to its tax planning? The point of departure is that a society can be typified for both businesses and citizens as a cooperative venture for mutual advantage. Against this background two moral obligations are then identified and elaborated on: the fair share obligation and the compliance obligation. Both obligations also appear to involve practical criteria, which the parties concerned – the board, the tax director and the advisor – can use as a guide in making morally responsible choices. This is followed by a discussion of the concept of 'business reputation' and the two ways in which this should be dealt with from a moral perspective. The second part of the chapter will conclude with a discussion on the importance of two Aristotelian virtues: the virtue of practical wisdom or prudence and that of self-restraint and temperance. Both are essential for the good corporate citizenship of a company.

An extensive discussion of the role played by governments needs to take place, but that is outside the confines of this chapter, where it is only discussed if it is relevant to the discussion on the moral position of the company. This means that two situations are only fleetingly discussed. This first situation is the unique political response of the G20 and OECD in particular. For the first time in history a globally coordinated approach has been adopted.[3] The OECD report 'Restoring fairness to the tax system', which was presented to the G20 in April 2013, does not mince words about its intention:

> "Leaders, civil society and everyday taxpayers are renewing demands for greater transparency and (…) changes to the international tax rules to restore fairness and integrity of their tax systems and the global financial systems more generally. The message is clear: all taxpayers must pay their fair share."[4]

In September 2014 the first set of reports and recommendations (deliverables) on the 'Action Plan on Base Erosion and Profit Shifting (BEPS)'[5] were published.[6] The vigour exuded by world leaders on this issue is unprecedented.[7]

Another issue not discussed in this chapter, but which needs to be debated, is the fact that many countries continue to adopt a more or less conciliatory approach towards aggressive tax planning.[8] The fact that the expression "the rat race to the

---

[3] Cf. Cees Peters, *The faltering legitimacy of international tax law*, Tilburg: University, 2013, about the need for improvement of the legitimacy of international tax law.
[4] OECD, *Restoring Fairness to the tax System*, p. 3, available on the following website http://www.oecd.org/tax/2013-OECD-SG-Report-to-G20-Heads-of-Government.pdf.
[5] http://www.oecd.org/ctp/BEPSActionPlan.pdf.
[6] http://www.oecd.org/ctp/beps-2014-deliverables.htm.
[7] This is also the case with regard to the international exchange of information. See for example the OECD agreements on Common Reporting Standards that 98 countries signed up to in October 2014 in Berlin and the earlier US FATCA legislation.
[8] Instrumental legislation, the participation exemption, treaty networks and the ruling practice are important reasons for including the Netherlands in tax planning structures.

bottom" is used in this context says it all.[9] A cautious general trend can be discerned in the fact that countries are prepared to take steps in the right direction, provided other countries are also willing to do so.[10] In this area, countries clearly need to show more determination in order to restore their tax competition to a more reasonable level.

Part One

4.2 The splendid isolation of tax is over[11]

The last few years has seen tax ethics takes centre stage. The fact that a large number of businesses are not prepared to pay their fair share has aroused a storm of indignation from politicians and the public. Why is it that precisely at this time we are witnessing an increase in the moral indignation aroused by aggressive tax planning? The initial answer to this question is directly related to the financial and economic crisis. The second answer relates to the information and internet revolutions.

Galbraith's cycle: the inventory of undiscovered embezzlement
The economic crisis has aroused a fierce moral debate about the business sector. That is not a coincidence. In his book on the 1929 stock market crash, John Kenneth Galbraith identified a link between economic crises and moral action. He spoke of 'an inventory of undiscovered embezzlement':

> "In good times people are relaxed, trusting, and money is plentiful. But even though money is plentiful, there are always many people who need more. Under these circumstances the rate of embezzlement grows, the rate of discovery falls off, and the bezzle increases rapidly. In depression all this is reversed. Money is watched with a narrow, suspicious eye. The man who handles it is assumed to be dishonest until he proves himself otherwise. Audits are penetrating and meticulous. Commercial morality is enormously improved. The bezzle shrinks."[12]

Galbraith's observation is clear. This cycle is also now clearly perceptible. In 2002 the Enron and Arthur Anderson scandals were harbingers of the looming crisis.[13] The US reacted with stringent accountancy legislation: the Sarbanes-Oxley Act. When Lehman Brothers went bankrupt in 2008 the crisis burst forth in earnest. The

---

9   Cf. for example J.A.G. van der Geld, 'Ethiek en multinationale ondernemingen', in: J.L.M. Gribnau (ed.), *Principieel belastingrecht* (Happé-bundel), Nijmegen, Wolff Legal Publishers, 2011, p. 54-55. L.G.M. Stevens, 'Alles wat rechtswaarde heeft is weerloos', in the Happé-bundel referred to above, p. 217-218. and R.H. Happé, 'Over een ethische motivatie om belasting te betalen', in: Th. Groeneveld and L.J.A. Pieterse (ed.), *Met oog voor detail* (Van den Berge-bundel), The Hague: Sdu Uitgevers, 2013, p. 148.
10 Cf. for example the report of the Netherlands Court of Audit (*Nederlandse Rekenkamer*): 'Belastingontwijking. Een verdiepend onderzoek naar belastingontwijking in relatie tot de fiscale regels en het verdragennetwerk', The Hague, 2014, p. 89.
11 See chapter 3.2.6. for the corporate governance aspects of this issue.
12 John Kenneth Galbraith, *The Great Crash 1929*, Boston/New York: Mariner Books, 2009 (1954), p. 133. Cf. in this respect Tomas Sedlacek, *Economics of Good and Evil*, Oxford: Oxford University Press, 2011, p. 322. (Dutch translation: Tomas Sedlacek, *De economie van goed en kwaad*, Schiedam: Sriptum, 2012, p. 371).
13 The fraud had often been aided by aggressive tax planning methods. Cf. for example Mihir Desai and Dhammika Dharmapala, 'Tax and Corporate Governance: An Economic Approach', in: Wolfgang Schön (ed.), *Tax and Corporate Governance*, Berlin-Heidelberg: Springer-Verlag, 2008, p. 13-21.

magnitude of the deceptions were mind-boggling.[14] There was major public and moral indignation about the enormity of the fraud. The public's basic trust in large financial companies in particular was severely put to the test. For example, in 2009 the G20 agreed to take action against tax havens under the motto 'the era of banking secrecy is over'.[15]

Although aggressive tax planning generally does not involve fraud, Galbraith's cycle is nevertheless discernible here. The heyday of aggressive tax planning, which enveloped the period up to the beginning of this century, has now also been followed by a tax crisis that arose as a result of the financial crisis. The media is increasingly bringing to light the aggressive tax structures used by multinationals,[16] while world leaders such as Barack Obama, David Cameron, Angela Merkel and Francois Hollande have made public their outrage at the fact that a large number of multinationals do not pay their fair share. The OECD/G20 BEPS Project is the most tangible consequence of the resulting moral outrage.

A cycle is characterised by the fact that one stage is continually followed by an earlier stage. There is an important reason to assume that the attention currently being paid to aggressive tax planning will not diminish once the economy has recovered: the information and internet revolutions.

Plato's ring of Gyges
The tax world is characterised by information asymmetry: he who possesses more information than others has an advantage that can be used or abused. In this respect, tax authorities find themselves continually on the back foot in comparison to multinationals. Their view of the whole structure and the linkage between the various parts is by definition limited. After all, a major part of aggressive tax planning covers different jurisdictions, while tax authorities are, in principle, restricted by national borders.

This gives large companies an information advantage over tax authorities and there is, in a sense, no reason for them to spontaneously extend a helping hand to the tax authorities. Wolfgang Schön observed, for example, that many businesses do not feel inclined to make life easier for tax authorities, unless requested.[17] After all, although a lack of transparency benefits large companies, it concomitantly disadvantages governments.[18]

In his *Republic*, the Greek philosopher Plato made a relevant observation about the link between information and moral behaviour. Plato writes about the mythical giant Gyges who has a ring that makes him invisible. Ethical considerations are therefore

---

14 Joseph Stiglitz, *Free Fall*, New York/London: W.W. Norton & Company, 2010, Ch. 6. (Dutch translation: *Vrije val*, Houten: Spectrum, 2010, p. 193).
15 See G20, *London Summit – Leaders' Statement*, 2 April 2009 available at http://www.oecd.org/g20/meetings/london/G20-Action-Plan-Recovery-Reform.pdf. Cf. also *The Guardian*, 'G20 declares door shut on tax havens', April 2, 2009.
16 Also NGOs, like SOMO, ActionAid and Tax Justice Network play an important role. Cf. for example H.T.P.M. van den Hurk, 'Starbucks versus the People', in: J.A.G. van der Geld and I.J.F.A. van Vijfeijken (ed.), *Rijkersbundel*, Tilburg: Tilburg University, 2013, p. 209-230.
17 According to Wolfgang Schön in Stefan Mayer, "Report of the discussion" in W. Schön (ed), *Tax and Corporate Governance*, Berlin-Heidelberg: Springer-Verlag, 2008, p. 67.
18 Also Joseph Stiglitz, *The Roaring Nineties*, New York: W.W. Norton & Company, 2003, p. 130.

foreign to him. He can enrich himself without having to worry about being caught.[19] The knowledge that no-one can or will discover would you've been up to appears to affect the moral component of our behaviour.

The last decades have seen a fundamental shift on the issue of transparency as a result of the rise of the information and internet society. The internet is where whistleblowers make all sorts of documents available to the public. In this sense, Wikileaks and the Snowden files heralded the beginning of a new era.

The world of aggressive tax planning was not forgotten. The aggressive tax structures used by companies are increasingly also being brought to light. The media play an important intermediary role between whistleblowers and the public. For some time now the Netherlands has had Publeaks, a collaboration between investigative journalists, where the public can safely and anonymously pass on confidential information to the media.[20] The scale of the Luxembourg Leaks of November 2014 was unprecedented. An anonymous source passed on 28,000 pages of tax documents to the International Consortium of Investigative Journalists (ICIJ). At the beginning of November, the established media in 28 countries subsequently published 548 rulings that PwC, on behalf of more than 340 multinationals, had concluded in Luxembourg during the period from 2002 to 2010. The media refers to aggressive tax planning on an industrial scale, also by Luxembourg.[21] Luxembourg Leaks 2 followed several weeks later with a new series of disclosures on the tax structures used by 35 multinationals in which EY, Deloitte and KPMG had also been involved.[22]

Two conclusions can be drawn from these developments. Firstly, the series of tax disclosures confirms that the emergence of the information and internet society means that multinationals must permanently take account of the fact that confidential information will be disclosed. Secondly, the risk of publication has also considerably increased the risk of reputation damage.

4.3 Aggressive tax planning: the phenomenon

Since the 1970s tax planning has undergone an explosive development. International tax consultancy has seen an impressive growth of expertise in the field of multinational tax planning. Keeping tax costs to a minimum is the major objective. John Braithwaite has pointed out that for years some of the largest enterprises in the United States paid little or no corporation tax.[23] Too high taxes are a sign that a company is performing poorly in this area.

---

19 Plato, *Republic*, Book II, p. 360.
20 See https://www.publeaks.nl.
21 This of course also applies to states. With regard to the heated discussions surrounding Jean-Claude Juncker, the former Prime Minister of Luxembourg, see for example 'Luxembourg tax files: how tiny state rubber-stamped tax avoidance on an industrial scale', *The Guardian*, November 11, 2014.
22 See http://www.icij.org/project/luxembourg-leaks.
23 John Braithwaite, *Markets in Vice, Markets in Virtue*, Oxford: Oxford University Press, 2005, pp. 20 and 161. See also John Pender, 'Counting the cost of globalisation: how companies keep tax low and stay within the law', in the *Financial Times*, 21 and 22 July 2004. Based on annual management reports, he demonstrates that the big multinationals effectively pay little or no tax on profit.

How do they succeed in paying little or no tax? An important part of the answer to that question is the fact that tax planning has become a form of *engineering*. The advice that tax lawyers from the large international advisory firms provide to their clients is based on an instrumental view of tax law. They regard tax law as an instrument to achieve the client's wishes, i.e. to pay as little tax as possible.[24]

The arsenal used to reduce the tax burden mainly consists of three types of structures. Firstly, there are the *fraus legis-* or *abuse of law* structures that push the limits of legislation. For tax engineers anything goes as long as the taxpayer complies with the letter of the law. The spirit of the law is of no importance.

Secondly, corporations often make use of the technique whereby deductions are transferred to countries with relatively high tax rates and profits are deposited in countries where rates are low. Tax havens are very often indispensable to this type of tax engineering.

Finally, and in combination with the aforementioned structures, is the third type: the 'hybrid mismatch arrangement'. The OECD defines this as:

> "A hybrid mismatch arrangement is an arrangement that exploits a difference in the tax treatment of an entity or instrument under the laws of two or more tax jurisdictions to produce a mismatch in tax outcomes where that mismatch has the effect of lowering the aggregate tax burden of the parties to the arrangement."[25]

These arrangements make use of hybrid entities, dual resident entities, hybrid instruments and hybrid transfers.[26] One of the most renowned examples is probably Google's 'Double Irish with a Dutch Sandwich' structure.[27] Edward Kleinbard shows how a structure like this "relies on deeply embedded global tax norms, and how it operates to disassociate taxable income from any connection with any location in which the value-adding activities that generated that income could plausibly be said to lie."[28] He speaks of "stateless income". Ronen Palan summarizes international tax planning as nothing other than "a plethora of accounting strategies aiming at exploiting legal loopholes that allow individuals and companies to shift residence without actually moving."[29]

In this way tax engineers are able to design structures which allow multinationals to substantially reduce their effective tax rate. On the one hand these structures have a tailor-made character: the individual structure is designed with mathematical precision and is tailor-made to fit the tax particularities of the countries involved and their mutual treaties. On the other hand this involves a mass-produced product.

---

24 Cf. in general Brian Z. Tamanaha, *Law as a Means to an End, Threat to the Rule of Law*, Cambridge: Cambridge University Press, 2006, p. 133-155. and Brian Z. Tamanaha, *The Perils of Pervasive Legal Instrumentalism*, Tilburg Law Lectures Series, Nijmegen: Wolff Legal Publishers, 2006, p. 53.
25 OECD, *Neutralizing the Effects of Hybrid Mismatch Arrangements*, 2014, p. 29. See http://www.oecd-ilibrary.org/taxation/neutralising-the-effects-of-hybrid-mismatch-arrangements_9789264218819-en.
26 For a description of these structures see OECD, *Hybrid Mismatch Arrangements: Tax Policy and Compliance Issues*, 2012, p. 7. See http://www.oecd.org/tax/exchange-of-tax-information/HYBRIDS_ENG_Final_October2012.pdf.
27 Cf. for example 'Double Irish With a Dutch Sandwich', *The New York Times*, 26 April 2012 or http://www.nytimes.com/interactive/2012/04/28/business/Double-Irish-With-A-Dutch-Sandwich.html?_r=0.
28 Edward D. Kleinbard, 'Stateless Income', *Florida Tax Review* (11) 2011, p. 708.
29 Ronen Palan, *The Offshore World: Sovereign Markets, Virtual Places, and Nomad Millionaires*, Ithaca and London: Cornell University Press, 2003, p. 84.

The 'tax structures market' is dominated by a limited number of players, including the Big Four: PricewaterhouseCoopers, Deloitte, EY and KPMG.[30]

It is no surprise that aggressive tax planning is extremely complicated.[31] This type of tax planning frequently leads to tax structures that taxpayers unschooled in tax cannot or can only just understand. Even qualified tax advisors often fail to understand the exact scope of these structures.[32] To quote the editorial board of the Harvard Law Review:

> "[These] tax shelters spot unusual interactions among various provisions in ways never contemplated – and sometimes in ways that few professionals fully understand. Tax shelters have become virtually impossible to define because of the myriad ways in which taxpayers may mix and match Code provisions to produce unintended – but technically legal – tax benefits."[33]

In this respect, tax law has become an engineering science: extremely complicated and incomprehensible to the non-initiated. From a moral perspective it is important that multinationals and their tax engineers are also unable or barely able to explain the applied structures to the non-initiated nor convince them that they are realistic.

4.4 Aggressive tax planning: the ideology

Economic justification: neoliberalism
Keeping the tax liability as low as possible is in line with the neoliberal ideology of the free market: business only has one goal and that is maximising profit. It must be as unrestricted as possible in achieving this. Milton Friedman, one of the famous economists of the Chicago School, rejects any form of social responsibility, provided the law is adhered to.[34] Businesses must play according to the rules of open and free competition, subject to the condition that they refrain from fraud or deceit.[35] It is not the task of business to take account of other – for example moral – considerations in their economic behaviour. As *homo economicus* they must let the rational choice model determine their actions: the attainment of the highest utility on the basis of a

---

30 Cf. for example John Braithwaite, *Markets in Vice, Markets in Virtue*, Oxford: Oxford University Press, 2005, p. 103.
31 P.J. Essers, 'International Tax Justice between Machiavelli and Habermas', *Bulletin for International Taxation*, February 2014, p. 57 points out that the expression 'aggressive tax planning' is difficult to define from a legal perspective. In this article, the expression is discussed from a moral and social perspective. Of particular importance for this expression is the fact that 'the meaning of a word is its use in the language'; Ludwig Wittgenstein, *Philosophical Investigations*, 43,. Oxford: Blackwell Paperback, 1976 (1953), p. 20.
32 Cf. Joseph Bankman, 'The New Market in Corporate Tax Shelters', 83 *Tax Notes* 1775, 1786-87, (1999): 'The more complicated tax shelters are created by a handful of top tax lawyers. It may be that only a few hundred other leading tax lawyers are capable of understanding and identifying such shelters in a timely fashion.'
33 Harvard Law Review, 'Governmental Attempts To Stem the Rising Tide of Corporate Tax Shelters', in: *Developments – Corporations and Society, Harvard Law Review*, Vol. 117:2169 (2003/2004), p. 2252.
34 Milton Friedman, 'The Social Responsibility of Business is to Increase Its Profits', *The New York Times Magazine*, September 13, 1970.
35 M. Friedman, 'The social responsibility of business is to increase its profits', in: T.I. White (ed.), *Business ethics: A philosophical reader*, Prentice Hall, Englewood Cliffs, NJ, 1993, p. 167.

mathematical approach. In a free market, businesses will therefore seek to maximise their profit, thereby simultaneously achieving the maximum benefit for society.[36]

According to this view, taxes are costs that must be kept to a minimum. There is also no room for motives other than economic ones in the field of tax.

Tax-legal justification: the freedom to choose the path of minimum cost
A second justification is used to defend how businesses deal with their tax position. Each taxpayer is allowed to give precedence to its self-interest in complying with its tax obligations. For example, from a Dutch perspective the tax court has long accepted the fact that the taxpayer is free to choose the most tax-efficient approach.[37] The Dutch legislator has also expressed itself in a similar manner. It has repeatedly argued that it is not the intention of the law (i.e., Wet Richtige Heffing) to prevent the normal use of permissible means of tax avoidance.[38]

A similar acknowledgement is found in many other countries. A common example quotes Lord Clyde, a UK judge:

> "No man in the country is under the smallest obligation, moral or other, so to arrange his legal relations to his business or property as to enable the Inland Revenue to put the largest possible shovel in his stores. (...) And the taxpayer is (...) entitled to be astute to prevent, so far as he honestly can, the depletion of his means by the Inland Revenue."[39]

The taxpayer does not however have unlimited freedom. The limit is reached once the law is abused. In the Netherlands this is especially the case where the court considers the doctrine of fraus legis to apply.[40] The unbridled pursuit of self-interest is therefore not legally permissible.

This has not however appeared to be a major deterrent for aggressive tax planning. An important reason is that the courts are bound by the law, even if they conclude that a particular structure abuses that law. Another limitation is that the courts must rule on the basis of national law and tax treaties. The law of other states is, in principle, outside its domain. Aggressive tax planning actually focuses on the application of law that is outside the courts' domain.[41]

---

36 For a critique of the ideological nature of neoliberalism see John Gray, *Black Mass*, London: Penguin Book, 2007, p. 84 and Hans Achterhuis, *De utopie van de vrije markt*, Lemniscaat, Rotterdam, 2010.
37 Supreme Court, 19 January 1994, *BNB* 1994/87. Also Tony Judt, *Ill Fares The Land*, London: Penguin, 2010. (Dutch translation: *Het land is moe*, Amsterdam/Antwerpen: Uitgeverij Contact, 2010).
38 Cf. Parliamentary Documents II, 1955/56, 4080, no. 5, p. 11. Cf. for example also Supreme Court 8 March 1961, *BNB* 1961/133, in which the Supreme Court refers to these and similar passages.
39 Lord Clyde, President of the Court of Session, in Ayrshire Pullman Motor Services v. Inland Revenue, (1929) 14 Tax Case 754. Cf. also Hoogendoorn in his commentary to Supreme Court judgement 23 August 1995, no. 29 251, BNB 1996/3, who also refers to a similar ruling by the Conseil d'Etat. On the United States of America see Marvin A. Chirelstein, 'Learned Hand's Contribution to the Law of Tax Avoidance', *Yale Law Journal*, (77) 1967-1968, p. 440.
40 Cf. for example Advocate General Verburg in the Opinion he issued for Supreme Court judgement 6 September 1995, no. 27 927, *BNB* 1996/4.
41 Cf. R.H. Happé, *Belastingethiek: een kwestie van fair share* (preadvies), in: Geschriften van de Vereniging voor Belastingwetenschap, No. 243, Deventer: Kluwer 2011, p. 32 and R.H. Happé, *Belastingrecht en de geest van de wet, Een pleidooi voor een beginsel-benadering in de wetgeving*, Tilburg: Tilburg University 2010, p. 29. This can also be found at https://www.tilburguniversity.edu/upload/de20e45d-a089-4ffc-8bff-fb99387b34ec_afscheidsrede.pdf.

Outcome: an ethics-free zone
The neoliberal view and the view that the unbridled pursuit of the path of minimum cost is justified would thus appear to converge. Aggressive tax planning fits the neoliberal mould. Multinationals that apply aggressive tax planning choose to operate in an ethics-free zone.[42]

4.5 Is ethics relevant to economic behaviour?

In his book *Supercapitalism* Robert Reich notes that: "Whether or not you agree with Friedman, companies under supercapitalism no longer have the discretion to be virtuous."[43] Reich thus chooses to take the view that ethics ultimately has nothing to do with the market.[44] Whether this view is correct was already being challenged at the beginning of the Enlightenment. The debate on it has a long history. The fiery polemics between Bernard Mandeville and Adam Smith are a classic example of this.

At the beginning of the 18th century Mandeville published his poem *The Fable of the Bees or Private Vices, Public Benefits*.[45] Even before Adam Smith mentioned the 'invisible hand' it was already detectable in Mandeville's poem. For Mandeville, man's economic behaviour is motivated by self-love and vanity. Other motives are put forward only to hide the fact that the vice of self-love is the true motive. Acting on the basis of self-love benefits society as a whole. To quote Mandeville:

"Thus every Part was full of Vice,
Yet the whole Mass a Paradise".

Adam Smith disputes this. Not as far as it concerns the 'invisible hand' of his *The Wealth of Nations*,[46] but as regards the vice of self-love being the only motive for behaviour. In his *The Theory of Moral Sentiments* Smith challenges Mandeville's view. Firstly, Smith regards self-love as a virtue not a vice; this places self-love in another context. Sometimes he speaks of self-love, at other times of self-interest or prudence. This virtue is beneficial for the welfare of the individual, but cannot be viewed separately from virtues that are beneficial for others, such as "humanity, justice, generosity, and public spirit".[47] Moral sentiments are thus central to Smith.

---

42   Cf. for this view H.K.C. Bakker, 'Fair share: wat moet ik er mee?', in: Th. Groeneveld en L.J.A. Pieterse (ed.), *Met oog voor detail* (Van den Berge-bundel), The Hague: Sdu Uitgevers 2013, p. 29-34, F.A. Engelen, De lotgevallen van Starbucks, Amazon en Google, *NTFR* 2013/158 and Otto Marres in: 'De Kwestie, Fair play vs. fair share' (discussion with Richard Happé), *Orde* (NOB), 2013, no. 1, p. 31.
43   Robert Reich, *Supercapitalism. The Battle for Democracy in an Age of Big Business*, London: Icon Books, 2009, p. 173.
44   Cf. also Cees Peters, *The faltering legitimacy of international tax law*, Tilburg: Tilburg University, 2013, p. 174-175.
45   Bernard Mandeville, *The Fable of the Bees: or Private Vices, Public Benefits*, Oxford: Clarendon Press, 1924 (oorspronkelijk 1723); Dutch edition: *De fabel van de bijen*, Rotterdam: Lemniscaat, 2008.
46   Adam Smith, *The Wealth of Nations Books I - III*, London: Penguin Books, 1999 edition.
47   Adam Smith, *The Theory of Moral Sentiments*, London: Penguin Books, 2009 edition, p.221.

In summary, this means that society and the market can survive without ethics, at least according to Bernard Mandeville. A free market by itself ensures a socially good result. In contrast, Adam Smith posits that humankind is not only motivated by self-interest but also by other virtues.[48] Hutcheson, a contemporary of Smith, also observed that Mandeville's vice of self-interest encourages distrust and thereby undermines the social character of society.[49]

The similarity between this 18th century debate and the discussions currently taking place is striking. Amartya Sen makes a comparison with the current crisis and points out in his Introduction to *The Theory of Moral Sentiments* that "the nature of the present economic crisis illustrates very clearly the need for departures from unmitigated and unrestrained self-seeking in order to have a decent society."[50] In line with Adam Smith and Hutcheson, Sen clearly challenges Reich's view that ethics has no place in the economy.

Stiglitz also points out that the balance between the market, government and society currently needs to be restored.[51] In reality, a separate system of rational economic choices and calculations that is divorced from societal relationships does not exist.[52] Such a unilateral approach, in which profit maximisation is the only goal, wrongly ignores the extent to which many businesses let non-economic motives such as trust and fairness guide them.[53] What is needed in the relationship between business and society are businesses with a well-considered self-interest that also take account of the interests of society.

4.6 Aggressive tax planning and ethics

The above makes clear what is wrong with aggressive tax planning: motives other than pure self-interest are wrongly ignored. Moreover, taxes have a feature that other business expenses do not: they are the remittance that has to be paid to the government as established by democratic laws. One could argue that taxes therefore give rise to a somewhat paradoxical situation. What is, in principle, meant as a contribution to state financing, is seen by business as a cost that must be kept to a

---

48 Cf. for example Gertrude Himmelfarb, *The Roads to Modernity. The British, French and American Enlightenments*, New York: Alfred A. Knopf, 2005, p. 31 and 36, and Tomas Sedlacek, *Economics of Good and Evil*, Oxford: Oxford University Press, 2011, Chapter 6 and 7. (Dutch translation: Tomas Sedlacek, *De economie van goed en kwaad*, Schiedam: Sriptum, 2012, Chapter 6 and 7).
49 Nicholas Phillipson, *Adam Smith. An Enlightened Life*, London: Penguin Books, 2010, p. 49.
50 See Amartya Sen, 'Introduction', in: Adam Smith, *The Theory of Moral Sentiments*, London: Penguin Books, 2009 edition, p. XI.
51 Cf. Joseph Stiglitz, *Free Fall*, New York/London: W.W. Norton & Company, 2010 Jan Tromp's interview with John Stiglitz in *de Volkskrant* of 6 February 2010. Also Hans Achterhuis, *De utopie van de vrije markt*, Rotterdam: Lemniscaat, 2010, p. 300.
52 Cf. also Hans Achterhuis, *De utopie van de vrije markt*, Rotterdam: Lemniscaat, 2010, p. 110.
53 Cf. also George A. Akerlof and Robert J. Schiller, *Animal Spirits*, Princeton/Oxford: Princeton University Press, 2009, p. 3, who place the *animal spirits* of Keynes in a current context. Cf. also Robert Skidelsky, *Keynes, The Return of the Master*, London: Penguin Books, 2010.

minimum.[54] Ingvar Kamprad, the founder and senior advisor of IKEA, responded as follows to the criticism of his company's aggressive tax planning: "We have always viewed taxes as a cost, equal to any other cost of doing business."[55] Such comments are in line with a neoliberal view of the market.

Tax advisors who design aggressive tax structures and businesses that apply these structures lose sight of the crucial link between taxes and society. The fundamental principle of taxes as a societal contribution is ignored, while the view that it is permissible for tax purposes to choose the path of minimum cost becomes an absolute truth. A 'marketisation of tax' occurs: the marketable product 'tax structure' is bought and sold as *the* instrument to ensure that no or almost no tax is paid.[56]

In this way aggressive tax planning eats away at the basic confidence society has in its institutions and shows a lack of respect for democratically established law. Those who make use of aggressive structures are behaving as free riders. They profit from what others contribute and from what society accomplishes for all citizens with these contributions.[57]

The relationship between respect for law and loyalty towards society, on the one hand, and profiting from public goods, on the other, was already described by the English philosopher, John Locke, in the seventeenth century:

> "And to this I say, that every man, that hath any possessions, or enjoyment, of any part of the dominions of any government, doth thereby give his tacit consent, and is as far forth obliged to obedience to the laws of that government, during such enjoyment, as any one under it; whether his possession be of land, to him and his heirs for ever, or a lodging only for a week; or whether it be barely travelling freely on the highway; and in effect, it reaches as far as the very being of any one within the territories of that government."[58]

4.7 A topical example of indignation about aggressive tax behaviour

'Inversion' troubles the U.S. Burger King, Medtronic and Abbvie are just a few examples of the growing number of large U.S. companies that have moved or intend to move their tax domicile abroad through the tax structure of inversion. In essence

---

54 Cf. for example Arne Friese, Simon Link and Stefan Mayer, 'Taxation and Corporate Governance – The State of the Art', in: W. Schön (ed), *Tax and Corporate Governance*, Berlin-Heidelberg: Springer-Verlag, 2008, p. 406 and critically Richard Happé, 'Book Review' (review of: W. Schön (ed), *Tax and Corporate Governance*, Berlin-Heidelberg: Springer-Verlag, 2008), *British Tax Review*, Issue 3, 2012, p. 361-362, Also R.H. Happé, 'Het tijdperk van splendid isolation voor de fiscaliteit ligt definitief achter ons' (book review), *WFR* 2012/6967, p. 1169.
55 *Financial Times*, January 27, 2011. The response of Kamprad and IKEA can also be found on http://www.ikea.com/at/de/about_ikea/newsitem/statement_Ingvar_Kamprad_comments.
56 Cf. Michael J. Sandel, *What Money Can't Buy: The Moral Limits to Markets*, New York: Farrar, Straus and Giroux, 2012. (Dutch translation: *Niet alles is te koop. De morele grenzen van marktwerking*, Utrecht: Uitgeverij Ten Have, 2012).
57 Cf. for example Tony Judt, *Ill Fares The Land*, London: Penguin, 2010, Chapter III. (Dutch translation: *Het land is moe*, Amsterdam/Antwerpen: Uitgeverij Contact, 2010, H. III, p. 71).
58 John Locke, *Second Treatise of Civil Government*, Ch. VIII, par. 119.

the structure is simple: the U.S. corporation becomes a subsidiary of a foreign parent corporation. The intent is also clear: the new parent company faces a lower tax rate and no tax on the company's foreign-source income.[59] Favourite countries for their new headquarters are Ireland, the UK and the Netherlands.[60]

In July 2014, in an unusually fiery speech at a technical college in Los Angeles, President Obama responded to this trend: "These companies are cherry-picking the rules, and it damages the country's finances." He continued: "It adds to the deficit. It sticks you with the tab to make up for what they are stashing offshore" and "I don't care if it's legal – it's wrong,"[61] Later on he said: "They're technically renouncing their U.S. citizenship, they're declaring their base someplace else even though most of their operations are here. You know some people are calling these companies 'corporate deserters'." He invoked "economic patriotism".[62]

Shortly before this, the Secretary of the Treasury Jacob Lew wrote a letter to one of the committees of the U.S. House of Representatives in which he described in more detail the need for this new sense of patriotism.

> "Recently announced transactions cover a wide range of industries including pharmaceuticals, retail, consumer, and manufacturing. The firms involved in these transactions still expect to benefit from their business location in the United States, with our protection of intellectual property rights, our support for research and development, our investment climate and our infrastructure, all funded by various levels of government. But these firms are attempting to avoid paying taxes here, notwithstanding the benefits they gain from being located in the United States."
>
> "What we need as a nation is a new sense of economic patriotism (...). We should not be providing support for corporations that seek to shift their profits overseas to avoid paying their fair share of taxes."[63]

The indignation of Obama and his Secretary of the Treasury is abundantly clear. It is important that this moral outrage has raised many questions, such as: Do companies take moral considerations into account when deciding whether to make use of aggressive tax structures such as inversion? How do the company's decision-makers view tax law? Do they regard it as an expression of a country's basic values[64] or simply as a bunch of rules? Do they pay attention to considerations of corporate citizenship, loyalty or fair share? And if so, to what extent, or if not, why are such considerations irrelevant for them? How do they see their role and place in the society in which they operate? More specifically: how do they see their social responsibility and is taxation an integral part of that? Part 2 deals with these and other questions.

---

59 Regarding the structure of inversion cf. Donald J. Marples and Jane G. Gravelle, 'Corporate Expatriation, Inversions, and Mergers: Tax Issues', Congressional Research Service, 27 May 2014 on: http://fas.org/sgp/crs/misc/R43568.pdf.
60 Cf. 'Irish, Dutch, UK law firms in tax inversion beauty contest in U.S.', *Reuters*, 24 July 2014 and 'Mylan wijkt via 'papieren transactie' uit naar Nederland', *FD* 30 July 2014.
61 See 'Obama Seeks to Close Loophole That Firms Use to Shield Profits Abroad', *The New York Times*, 25 July 2014. A similar reference was made by Margaret Hodge (quoted in par. 1).
62 See 'Obama presses to end corporate trick for evading taxes', *Reuters*, July 24, 2014.
63 See http://online.wsj.com/public/resources/documents/Treasuryletter071514.pdf.
64 Also Joseph Stiglitz, *The Roaring Nineties*, New York: W.W. Norton & Company, 2003, p. 177.

Part two

4.8 Tax ethics for multinationals

The change in attitude of governments and the public to aggressive tax planning has had a major impact on the tax world: the splendid isolation of tax is over. Politicians are increasingly expecting multinationals to pay their fair share, while other taxpayers increasingly feel that they are having to pay the tax that multinationals avoided paying. In light of this political and public indignation about aggressive tax planning, multinationals would be well-advised to rethink their tax policy from a moral perspective.

The starting point for this must be how multinationals view their position in the society in which they operate. Part one of this article made clear that cooperation and trust are of fundamental importance to a society. John Rawls, the most important political philosopher of the last century, describes a society therefore as "a cooperative venture for mutual advantage".[65]

This means that, in addition to the principal pursuit of self-interest, everyone can be asked to adapt their behaviour to take account of the interests of others and of the society of which they are a part. This is not only a question of pure rational self-interest. Man is also a social animal. This means that motives other than the rational pursuit of self-interest determine one's behaviour. People also allow themselves to be guided by motives such as respect and friendship or solidarity and altruism. Such motives, which take account of the legitimate interests of others, are the fundamental motives that drive human behaviour.[66]

This view of the cooperative character of society also makes clear what citizens expect from one another with regard to tax.[67] Everyone knows that there can be no modern state without taxes. Two fundamental moral obligations arise: the fair share obligation and the compliance obligation.[68]

The first obligation, the *fair share obligation*, asks each member of society to contribute their fair share to make possible and maintain the society of which they are a member. Citizens thus only make use of the public goods developed by a society. This is partly why citizens not only expect their fellow citizens to contribute their share, but they also know that their fellow citizens will expect the same of them.

---

65   John Rawls, *A Theory of Justice*, Oxford: Oxford University Press, 1972, p. 4. (Dutch translation: *Een theorie van rechtvaardigheid*, Rotterdam: Lemniscaat 2009, p. 52).
66   Cf. R.H. Happé, 'Over belastingheffing en ethiek. Enige politiek-filosofische verkenningen', in: D.A. Albregtse and P. Kavelaars (ed.), *Maatschappelijk heffen* (Stevens-bundel), Deventer: Kluwer 2006, p. 335.
67   A similar view can be found in Govert den Hartogh, *Mutual Expectations, A Conventionalist Theory of Law*, Dordrecht: Kluwer Law International, 2002, p. 93.
68   Cf. John Rawls, *A Theory of Justice*, Oxford: Oxford University Press, 1972, p. 48, (Dutch translation: *Een theorie van rechtvaardigheid*, Rotterdam: Lemniscaat 2009, p. 90.) about the notion of reflective equilibrium. It aims at a kind of integrity between convincing general principles and more specific and 'undeniable' judgments, like the two moral duties of fair share and compliance.

Without everyone's fair financial contribution, an ordered, let alone just, society is not possible. Citizens who shirk paying their contribution, profit from those that do not. To quote Den Hartogh: "the latter object to parasitic behaviour, precisely because it is parasitic behaviour."[69] This is also the accusation President Obama directed at multinationals that use inversion structures to evade paying tax in the US. These companies profit from the public goods that are financed by the taxes of others.[70] Apparently the fact that a "modern economy (...) would be impossible without the framework provided by government supported by taxes" does not apply to them.[71]

Then there is the compliance obligation: the obligation to comply with the democratically established rules of a society. This obligation is based on the fact that legally enforceable rules are necessary to ensure that everyone contributes their fair share to the society of which they are a part.[72] Without legally enforceable rules the *free rider* problem is inevitable. In our highly developed and complicated societies only a select few would continue to contribute in the knowledge that others will or can evade doing so.[73] This is not possible without legally enforceable rules.

> "It would be nice if everyone voluntarily contributed money for maintaining roads, running schools and post offices, and the hundreds of other functions of government. But few people would do so knowing that many others would pay nothing. Most people can be convinced that taxes for public works are desirable, provided that everyone pays. Thus government enforces payment of taxes."[74]

There is also a second ground for the moral compliance obligation. We also need rules to ensure that everyone contributes a specific and accordingly a *fair* share, which does justice to the principle of equality. The fair share obligation is too indeterminate and society too complicated to establish what everyone's contribution to society should be in a specific situation.[75] For this reason the compliance obligation is indispensable if an insight is to be gained into what everyone's contribution to society should be in a specific situation. To this extent, it is inevitable that tax law will determine how citizens pay their contribution to society.[76]

Thus the view that society is a cooperative venture with its accompanying two moral obligations of fair share and compliance provide a moral framework for acting

---

69 G.A. den Hartogh, 'Fiscale moraal en de moraal van de fiscus', WFR 1987/5772, p. 543.
70 See par. 4.7.
71 Stephen Holmes and Cass R. Sunstein, *Why Liberty Depends on Taxes*, New York/London: W.W. Norton & Company, 1999, p. 69 and Liam Murphy and Thomas Nagel, *The Myth of Ownership, Taxes and Justice*, Oxford: Oxford University Press, 2002, p. 8. Cf. also J.L.M. Gribnau, 'Fiscale ethiek in de Boardroom', *Vakblad Tax Assurance*, 2014/1.
72 It is also important that legal rules are democratically legitimised.
73 Cf. Peter Sloterdijk, *Die nehmende Hand und die gebende Seite*, Berlin: Suhrkamp, 2010 and R.H. Happé, 'Over een ethische motivatie om belasting te betalen', in: Th. Groeneveld en L.J.A. Pieterse (ed.), *Met oog voor detail* (Van den Berge-bundel), The Hague: Sdu Uitgevers 2013, p. 147.
74 William Poundstone, *Prisoner's Dilemma*, Anchor Books, New York, 1992, p. 127. Cf. also Tony Judt, *Ill Fares The Land*, London: Penguin, 2010, (Dutch translation: *Het land is moe*, Amsterdam/Antwerpen: Uitgeverij Contact, 2010, p. 204).
75 Cf. R.H. Happé, '*Belastingethiek: een kwestie van fair share* (preadvies)', in: Geschriften van de Vereniging voor Belastingwetenschap, No. 243, Deventer: Kluwer 2011, p. 9.
76 Tony Honoré, 'The Dependence of Morality on Law', *Oxford Journal of Legal Studies*, (13) 1993, p. 2: "Apart from law no one has a moral obligation to pay any particular amount of tax."

responsibly in the field of tax planning.[77,78] The theoretical and practical aspects of this framework will be explained in more detail below. What is in any event clear is that tax ethics principally acknowledges motives other than that of pure self-interest.

4.9 Law, ethics and social reality

In the regular legal practice moral considerations usually operate in the background. That is also the case in the tax practice. Legislation is usually relatively clear. In cases where the interpretation of a provision is disputed, it is the task of the courts to establish the law's intent. Insofar as social or moral considerations operate in the background, this occurs via the filter of legislation and case law. With regard to regular tax law, citizens and governments can suffice with taking the legal rules into account.

Citizens can and are therefore allowed to presume that by doing so they are not only meeting their legal but also their moral obligations.[79] By paying their tax liability, citizens are thus contributing their fair share to the financing of government expenditure. Empirical studies confirm this. Most citizens appear to meet their tax obligations better than would be expected if viewed from a rational individual perspective. Citizens are willing to make a substantial contribution in the public interest. As Erich Kirchler observes:

> "a large number of empirical studies (…) demonstrate that the majority of taxpayers are inherently honest and willing to pay their fair share. If taxpayers are unable to understand the complex tax law and seek help from tax practitioners, they do it with the goal of preparing a correct tax file rather than finding aggressive strategies to reduce their taxes within the legal scope."[80]

In this way, citizens show their cooperative, intrinsic motivation. Frey talks about a *citizenship contract* that is based on 'a mutual belief in good intentions'.[81] There appears to be a virtue of restraint against behaving as a *free rider*. This not only applies to ordinary citizens but also to businesses. The majority of taxpayers have an intrinsic willingness – a tax morale – to abide by the law and contribute their fair share accordingly.[82] This allows taxpayers to maintain their trust in one another that everyone will contribute their share. Trust breeds trust.

Many large companies have also shown that they have a positive attitude. In this context, the Dutch cooperative compliance Horizontal Monitoring model is worth mentioning: the Dutch tax authorities and multinationals conclude a covenant based on mutual trust, which lays down that both parties will take account of each other's

---

77 Cf. in general Govert den Hartogh, *Mutual Expectations, A Conventionalist Theory of Law*, Dordrecht: Kluwer Law International, 2002, p. 102.
78 Cf. S.A. Stevens, 'De fair share plicht van landen en ondernemingen', *TFO* 2014/131, p. 67.
79 Cf. R.H. Happé, *Belastingrecht en de geest van de wet, Een pleidooi voor een beginsel-benadering in de wetgeving* (valedictory speech), Tilburg: Tilburg University 2010, p. 9.
80 Erich Kirchler, *The Economic Psychology of Tax Behaviour*, Cambridge: Cambridge University Press, 2007, p. 167.
81 Bruno S. Frey, 'Flexible citizenship for a global society', *Politics, Philosophy & Economics* (2) 2003, p. 101 and 106.
82 Bruno S. Frey and Benno Torgler, 'Tax morale and conditional cooperation', *Journal of Comparative Economics* (35) 2007, p. 140. In a more general sense: Tom R. Tyler, *Why people obey the law*, Princeton: Princeton University Press 2006.

interests.[83] Similar developments are occurring at the international level where governments and large companies are striving for an enhanced relationship.[84] Trust breeds trust also applies here.

In opposition to this is the group of companies that design and apply the aggressive tax planning structures.[85] These companies are the modern-day free riders. With their aggressive tax planning they take advantage of the aspects of tax law that are indefensible. Their aim is to back out of making a normal tax contribution to the society in which they operate. Their aggressive structures with which they 'play the tax system' are aimed at paying as little tax as possible.

Multinationals that do not contribute their fair share eat away at the fundamental confidence society has in its institutions. More than ever before the current public and political debate has made clear that multinationals do not operate in an ethics-free zone as regards their aggressive tax planning. Society is becoming more vocal in its demand that large companies be more disposed towards cooperation. These large companies would be well-advised to take this public outrage seriously and to choose to conduct themselves not only as good corporate citizens but also as good corporate taxpayers.

The following part of this article will examine what the moral obligations of compliance and fair share mean for a socially responsible tax policy.[86] More is at stake than reputation alone.

4.10 The compliance obligation and the spirit of the law

A common argument put forward by taxpayers that are called to account on aggressive tax planning is that they are acting strictly in accordance with the tax laws. What is wrong with this response is its moral aspect: they seek aspects of the law that are indefensible. Doreen McBarnet observes that these taxpayers show "a mindset in which to comply with the letter but defeat the spirit of the law is deemed clever and legitimate." [87]

---

83 Cf. for example The Dutch Tax and Customs Administration, *Horizontal monitoring within the medium to very large businesses segment*, 2010 at http://download.belastingdienst.nl/belastingdienst/docs/horizontal_monitoring_very_large_businesses_dv4061z1pleng.pdf and Commissie Stevens, *Fiscaal toezicht op maat*, Den Haag, 2012, at http://download.belastingdienst.nl/belastingdienst/docs/fiscaal_tz_op_maat_tz0151z1fd.pdf. Also R.H. Happé, 'Multinationals, Enforcement Covenants and Fair Share', *Intertax*, Volume 35, Issue 10, (2007), p. 537-547 and T.W.M. Poolen, 'Horizontalisering van het toezicht: veranderingen in de verhoudingen', in: J.L.M. Gribnau (ed.), *Principieel belastingrecht* (Happé-bundel), Nijmegen, Wolff Legal Publishers, 2011, p. 173-183.
84 Cf. for example OECD, *Co-operative Compliance: A Framework. From Enhanced Relationship to Co-operative Compliance*, OECD Publishing, 2013.
85 Cf. R.H. Happé, *Belastingethiek: een kwestie van fair share* (preadvies), in: Geschriften van de Vereniging voor Belastingwetenschap, No. 243, Deventer: Kluwer 2011, p. 28.
86 For a discussion of the tax and moral obligations within a Corporate Social Responsibility framework see R.H. Happé, *Belastingethiek: een kwestie van fair share* (preadvies), in: Geschriften van de Vereniging voor Belastingwetenschap, No. 243, Deventer: Kluwer 2011, p. 56-58.
87 Doreen McBarnet, 'After Enron will 'Whiter Than White Collar Crime' Still Wash?', *British Journal of Criminology* 46(6) 2006, p. 1104.

One should, of course, be able to expect that the legislator will produce legislation of a high quality.[88] It is nevertheless a fact of life that perfect legislation is an unattainable ideal. There is an indefensible side to law. As Aristotle taught with regard to this:

> "for the error (of the law) is in the law nor in the legislator but in the nature of the thing, since the matter of practical affairs is of this kind from the start."[89]

All legislators are aware of this. Anthony Kronman expressed it as follows:

> "Of course, no one can anticipate all the cases to which a statute may one day apply. The later history of even the most carefully drafted statute is bound to contain some surprises."[90]

Situations will always arise that cannot be classified neatly under a literal interpretation of the law, but which should nevertheless belong there as regards their intent. The opposite is also possible: situations that can be covered by a literal interpretation of the law, but that are not in keeping with the spirit of the law. Generally, it is the responsibility of the legislator to keep its legislation up-to-date.[91]

The tax engineer goes even further. He makes use of these inevitable deficiencies in the law. He deliberately opts to create a structure that is in accordance with the letter of the law but which ignores the spirit of the law.[92] This is precisely where his expertise lies. He knows as no other not only the history and purpose of the law, but also the spirit of the law. On the basis of this knowledge he constructs, in a way not foreseen by the legislator, a tax structure that will achieve the maximum reduction in the tax burden.[93] In short: the tax engineer knows that the structure will realize a result not intended by the legislator.

In this way the actions of the tax planner are at odds with the moral compliance obligation. The rationale for this obligation can be found as far back as Aristotle:[94]

> one should not apply structures that would have been reason for the legislator – had it been aware of them at the time the law was being drafted – to formulate the law differently.[95]

---

88 In this respect, it would also be advisable for governments to stop with their often bad and ill-considered instrumental legislation. See in this regard the closing sentences of par. 1.
89 Aristoteles, *Ethica Nicomachea*, V.14, 1137 b. (translation W.D. Ross). See also the translation of the edition of the Historische Uitgeverij: Groningen, 1999, p. 170.
90 Anthony T. Kronman, *The Lost Lawyer*, Cambridge (Massachusetts) & London: The Belknap Press of Harvard University Press, 1993, p. 361.
91 However, the legislator is often too lax in closing loopholes. Inaction by the legislator can, in time, be regarded as an implicit form of lawmaking. Cf. also S.A. Stevens, 'Maatschappelijke ondernemingen en ethiek: heeft de overheid een voorbeeldrol?', in: J.L.M. Gribnau (ed.), *Principieel belastingrecht* (Happé-bundel), Nijmegen, Wolff Legal Publishers, 2011, p. 228-230.
92 The legal instrumentalism of the tax engineer is discussed in par. 3.
93 Added to this is the fact that, in practice, these structures regularly go unnoticed by the tax authorities. Paragraph 2 explains how Gyges' ring works.
94 Aristoteles, *Ethica Nicomachea*, V.14, 1137 b.
95 Cf. Richard Happé, *Belastingrecht en de geest van de wet*, (valedictory speech), Tilburg: Tilburg University, 2011, p. 46.

In this context, the compliance obligation requires restraint as regards what is technically possible. John Rawls expresses the same concept as follows:

> "We have a natural duty of civility not to invoke the faults of social arrangements as a too ready excuse for not complying with them, nor to exploit inevitable loopholes in the rules to advance our interests. The duty of civility imposes a due acceptance of the defects of institutions and a certain restraint in taking advantage of them."[96]

The moral compliance obligation demands an Aristotelian restraint, which asks the tax planner to stay within the spirit of the law and not to seek the outer limit of the law. While it is precisely this tax and legal expertise that enables him to devise an aggressive structure that is contrary to the spirit of the law, it also enables him to devise a tax structure that is in accordance with it.[97] The compliance obligation also enables the Board of a multinational to ask the right question of its tax director and its tax advisor: will we remain within the spirit of the law with this structure?[98]

4.11 The fair share obligation and international tax arbitrage

The fair share obligation has long played a central role in international tax law. This concerns the generally acknowledged responsibility by states to avoid double taxation. An extensive network of tax treaties and national regulations must prevent taxpayers from having to pay double taxation because the same income is taxed by more than one country. Reuven Avi-Yonah has pointed out that this network of rules forms a more or less coherent international tax system. One of the key basic norms of this system is the *single tax principle*. This principle is part of customary international law: "law that results from a general and consistent practice of states followed by them from a sense of legal obligation."[99] Avi-Yonah describes the principle as follows: "income should be taxed once – not more and not less."

One of the fundamental principles of international tax law is thus encapsulated: income must only be taxed once, not more and not less. This also advances the level playing field, not only between internationally operating businesses themselves, but also between businesses that only operate nationally.[100]

The connection between the ethical fair share concept and this fundamental principle of international tax law is evident: businesses must not be forced to pay double their fair share in more than one country.

---

96 John Rawls, *A Theory of Justice*, Oxford: Oxford University Press, 1972, p. 355. (Dutch translation: John Rawls, *Een theorie van rechtvaardigheid*, Rotterdam: Lemniscaat, 2009, p. 369).
97 Cf. in this respect also Daniel N. Shaviro, *Corporate Tax Shelters in a Global Economy*, Washington D.C: The AEI Press, 2004, p. 25.
98 Cf. R. Russo, 'Corporate Governance en de (fiscale) jaarrekening', WFR 2013/7007, p. 829, remarks that it is often also a matter of common sense and policy.
99 Reuven S. Avi-Yonah, 'Tax Competition, Tax Arbitrage and the International Tax Regime', *Bulletin for International Taxation*, 2007, p. 130. In addition to the single tax principle he also distinguishes the benefit principle.
100 Cf. in this respect A.J. van den Tempel, *Corporation tax and individual income tax in the European Communities*, Series Studies – Competition – Approximation of Legislation, No. 15, Brussels, 1970. Also C. van Raad, *Nondiscrimination in International Tax Law*, Kluwer, Deventer, 1986, p. 256-263.

Viewed from the above perspective, international tax arbitrage is the polar opposite of the avoidance of double taxation. The rules of international tax law, together with national tax rules, are used by internationally operating taxpayers in ways not intended: they are not intended to avoid double taxation but to realize zero taxation.[101] Joseph Stiglitz concluded that the problem with tax arbitrage is not double taxation but zero taxation.[102] A simple example is the double dip structure. David Rosenbloom has summed up the essence of such a structure rather picturesquely: "One airplane, two owners, two sets of deductions."[103] More complicated are the hybrid mismatch arrangements referred to previously.[104]

These structures ultimately all have a simple purpose: substantially reducing the effective tax burden. The recent revelations culminating for the moment in the Lux Leaks have made clear how widespread aggressive tax planning by multinationals is, as well as its scale.[105]

What all these structures have in common is that countries are included as links in a chain that is only – or virtually only – intended to enable companies to profit from the possibilities to reduce their tax burden. Not only the notorious tax havens of the Bahamas, Guernsey and the Netherlands Antilles, but also countries such as Luxembourg, the Netherlands and Ireland are attractive options for multinationals and their tax engineers in this respect.

A picture emerges from this of multinationals that approach tax law from a purely instrumental perspective. These multinationals choose to regard national and international rules as a bunch of rules which can help them to obtain the maximum tax benefit possible.[106] As such, they are completely in line with the neoliberal view of profit maximisation. The fair share concept has absolutely no value for them.

It is important to note that some multinationals also challenge aggressive avoidance behaviour. A number of them prefer to show restraint in this respect in the various countries in which they operate. This can be achieved by respecting the moral norm of a fair share. The single tax principle that is based on the fair share obligation points the way: avoid no tax if single tax is economically appropriate.[107]

From a moral perspective, it is essential that the multinational itself be fully aware of what motivates it to adopt a specific avoidance structure: are activities that are

---

101 Cf. R.H. Happé, 'Belastingethiek vraagt om regels ter voorkoming van 'geen belasting'', WFR 2006/6654, p. 41-42.
102 Joseph Stiglitz, *The Roaring Nineties*, New York: W.W. Norton & Company, 2003, p. 329.
103 H. David Rosenbloom, 'The David R. Tillinghast lecture: International tax arbitrage and the international tax system', *Tax law review*, vol. 53, 2000, p. 142.
104 See par. 4.3.
105 See par. 4.2.
106 Cf. also Doreen McBarnet, 'Corporate social responsibility beyond law, through law, for law: the new corporate accountability', in: Doreen McBarnet, Aurora Voiculescu and Tom Campbell (eds.), *The New Corporate Accountability*, Cambridge: Cambridge University Press, 2007, p. 49-50.
107 Cf. in this respect also *BEPS 2014 Deliverables*, available at http://www.oecd.org/ctp/beps-2014-deliverables.htm. One of the proposals put forward by the OECD in this report is to use legislation to combat hybrid mismatch arrangements. The single tax principle and the fair share concept are clearly discernible in the proposals.

economically relevant to the company the reason, or is it the tax benefit?[108] As tax advisor Urs Landolf observed about fair share: "Artificial constructs without lasting economic justification are, even if formally they can possibly be captured by fiscal legislation, not good tax planning."[109]

Adopting an appropriate restraint with regard to tax planning should be the joint responsibility of the tax director and the Board of the company.[110] A properly functioning tax risk management is important in this respect.[111] After all, if the Board places too much emphasis on reducing the effective tax rate they risk the tax director feeling compelled to resort to aggressive tax planning.

4.12 Reputation and the Aristotelian virtues

It has been said before: multinationals are not separate from society. The last few years has shown that negative publicity about aggressive tax planning can considerably damage reputations. One of the best known examples of this concerns Starbucks UK that received a lot of very negative publicity at the end of 2012, because although it had been making profits for years it had only paid a minimal amount of corporate income tax. [112]

A recent publication by EY "Bridging the divide, Tax risk and controversy survey" addresses the issue of reputational risk. EY concluded that businesses are exposed to a greatly increased risk with regard to their reputation. The news media and policymakers are paying much more attention to company tax conduct. "The survey results illustrate just how rapidly reputation risk has become a key concern. Eighty-nine percent of the largest companies say they are somewhat or significantly concerned."[113] Reputational risk is a factor that can only be ignored at one's own economic peril.[114] Other publications also make the connection with ethics. For example in 2004 KPMG recommended:

> "Boards should recognize, when overseeing the design and monitoring of tax strategies and policies, that contemporary debates about governance, corporate social responsibility and ethics

---

108 Cf. in a similar vein Henderson, Global Investors, *Responsible Tax*, p. 6, who points out that a number of companies maintain the principle that tax structures must be related to the 'real world activities of the organization's underlying business'.
109 Urs Landolf, 'Tax and corporate responsibility', *International Tax Review* (29) 2006, p. 9. Can also be found at http://www.pwc.com/en_MT/mt/publications/assets/tax-management-in-companies-06.pdf.
110 Cf. in the same vein Reuven Avi-Yonah, 'Corporate Social Responsibility and Strategic Tax Behavior', in: Wolfgang Schön (ed.), *Tax and Corporate Governance*, Berlin Heidelberg: Springer-Verlag, 2008, p. 184.
111 Cf. Robert van der Laan, 'Managing the TaxValueChain', *International Tax Review* (29) 2006, p. 4. This can also be found at http://www.pwc.com/en_MT/mt/publications/assets/tax-management-in-companies-06.pdf.
112 For more on this see Richard Happé, 'Tax in the Boardroom van Starbucks', *WFR* 2012/6981, p. 1666-1667, which reports on a fictional Board meeting about the damaged reputation of Starbucks.
113 http://www.ey.com/Publication/vwLUAssets/EY-2014-tax-risk-and-controversy-survey-highlights/$FILE/EY-2014-tax-risk-and-controversy-survey-highlights.pdf.
114 Reputation is discussed in R.J.M. Jeurissen (ed.), *Bedrijfsethiek een goede zaak*, Assen: Van Gorcum, 2009, p. 110-112.

mean that even legal tax-minimization activity can generate reputational liabilities that can destroy shareholder value."[115]

These publications from the tax advisory world raise the question whether and to what extent moral considerations play a role in managing reputational damage. It can be inferred from the abovementioned publications that the economic dimension appears to be decisive for a large group of companies. In their view, they cannot be accused of aggressive tax planning. After all, it is the responsibility of the legislator to set limits by means of legislation if it objects to the conduct of taxpayers.

When it comes to reputational risk, these companies are guided by an extrinsic motivation arising from a fear of reputational damage. At the core of this are purely egoistic calculations,[116] which are in line with a neoliberal view of the market. Of course these calculations can result in these companies exhibiting greater restraint in their tax planning in order to reduce reputational risk. The continuing revelations of late make clear how real this risk is.[117]

For the other group of companies, the moral dimension is given prominence alongside the economic dimension. These companies are also guided by an intrinsic motivation arising from a desire to be a respectful member of society. This motivation clearly involves a moral perspective, whereby the fair share principle can act as a framework to ensure that the right choices are made.[118]

The recent statements by two opinion leaders from the tax advisory world reflect the different approaches adopted with regard to the reputational factor. On the one hand there is Steve Varley, chairman of EY UK, whose clients include Google and Apple, who said: "We'll carry on as before ... Parliament should legislate if they want a different outcome. I don't think it's up to us to get embroiled in politics", while on the other hand there is Dennis Nally, chairman of the international arm of PwC, who, when asked if tax advice has a moral dimension, answered: "I think it does (...). It is not only what companies could do but what should they do."[119]

However, is it practical for multinationals and their tax advisors who adhere to a neoliberal vision to continue to think in either/or terms? In practice, there is often a variety of motives driving people – and companies – to act as they do. It is important that companies recognise the moral aspects of the choices that need to be made.

In this article we have seen that these aspects are first of all related to the fact that aggressive tax planning harms other members of society who not only have to pay the tax that companies avoid paying, but whose fundamental confidence in society's institutions is damaged by the actions of these companies. Secondly, companies must realise that others – politicians and society – place the choices companies make

---

115 See KPMG, 'Tax in the Boardroom' at http://www.kpmg.com.au/aci/docs/tax-boardroom.pdf.
116 Bruno S. Frey, 'Flexible citizenship for a global society', *Politics, Philosophy & Economics* (2) 2003, p. 101 and 106.
117 Cf. for example Arne Friese, Simon Link and Stefan Mayer, 'Taxation and Corporate Governance – The State of the Art', in: W. Schön (ed), *Tax and Corporate Governance*, Berlin-Heidelberg: Springer-Verlag, 2008, p. 417.
118 With regard to this debate cf. Arjo van Eijsden, 'The Relationship between Corporate Responsibility and Tax: Unknown and Unloved', *EC Tax Review*, 2013/1, p. 56-61.
119 See 'Tax advice has moral aspect, says PwC chairman', *Financial Times*, 7 October 2014.

with regard to their tax planning in a moral context.[120] Reputational damage reflects this fact.

This ultimately brings us to an Aristotelian virtue ethics. The good entrepreneur should embody two virtues. The first is to have *practical wisdom* to take a good decision in a specific situation. This requires the ability to distinguish the morally relevant aspects of a situation and to respond appropriately with regard to others.

The second virtue is that of self-restraint and temperance. The fair share obligation and the compliance obligation act here as a guide to exercising social temperance. They serve as a corrective to the unbridled pursuit of a multinational's self-interest. In this, the good entrepreneur has a moral 'tax compass' that enables him to reconcile the self-interest of the company with the legitimate interests of the society and the members of that society. Thus, taking Aristotle's Doctrine of the Mean[121] seriously is simply well-considered self-interest.

4.13 Conclusion

This chapter has examined the moral aspects of aggressive tax planning. The first part of the article established that there is a tax crisis: politicians and society are fiercely indignant about the fact that multinationals use tax structures for large-scale tax avoidance. Multinationals generally regard this criticism as misplaced; after all they adhere to tax legislation.

This was followed by a discussion about aggressive tax planning being in line with a neoliberal view of the market: taxes as an expense that must be kept to a minimum. This corresponds to an instrumental view of law where the economy and tax law are ethics-free zones. That this debate is not new is attested to by the fact that the relevance of moral motives for economic behaviour was already being fiercely debated in the 18th century. The discussion between Bernard de Mandeville and Adam Smith is renowned; a discussion that regularly recurs in the current debate about the economy. The first part of this chapter concluded with a current example: the inversion structure, which in the US has led to hostile reactions from politicians, academics and society.

In part two the contours of a tax ethic for multinationals were outlined. The point of departure was Rawls' view of society as 'a cooperative venture for mutual advantage'. Two moral obligations for the tax field were subsequently discussed. The first obligation – the compliance obligation – expects taxpayers to adhere to the spirit of the law. One should not wish to profit from the inevitable loopholes in the law.

The second obligation – the fair share obligation – asks each member of society to contribute their fair share. What this obligation means for international tax arbitrage was examined. The latter involves making use of the mismatches between different legal systems with the aim being 'no tax' instead of 'single tax'. The moral fair share obligation simply asks for a single tax.

---

120 Companies and tax advisors often argue that the criticism levelled at them is extremely biased and inaccurate. See the above-mentioned report by EY.
121 Cf. for example Aristotle, *Ethica Nicomachea*, 1119 a 10.

Both obligations do not demand a contribution that is more than that expected by law. They do, however, ask that a legal choice be made which takes both obligations seriously.

Finally, it was emphasised that a good entrepreneur must embody the virtues of practical wisdom and self-restraint and temperance. The first virtue enables the good entrepreneur to also take all the moral aspects of a specific tax planning situation into account, such as both of the moral tax obligations, and to act with integrity with regard to others in this. The second virtue is that of self-restraint and temperance. The fair share obligation and the compliance obligation can also provide guidance in this respect. Both obligations share the same message: avoid aggressive tax planning.

Thus the good entrepreneur also has a moral 'tax compass' that enables him to reconcile the self-interest of the company with the legitimate interests of the society. Unbridled self-interest is thereby exchanged for well-considered self-interest.

ROBBERT HOYNG
NATHAN ANDREWS
MARK KENNEDY[2]

5. A Tax Operating Model[1]
building a World Class Tax Function

5.1 Introduction

The tax landscape has changed and continues to evolve. The economy has increased our focus on public finances and the need to collect taxes. Action groups and media campaigns have, in some jurisdictions, targeted large companies and applied pressure to them to demonstrate their contribution to society through tax and to justify the way in which they conduct their tax affairs. Boards are taking more interest in tax outcomes and demanding more of the tax function. By "tax function" we mean those accountable or responsible for managing taxes in a group. Typically a group tax department would be a leading player in the tax function, but would be in concert with others in the business such as finance and HR.

It is not just scrutiny from society and the media alone that has applied pressure to Tax functions. Tax authorities, so often resource-constrained, are increasingly adopting risk-based approaches that seek to focus their attention on those organisations that present the greatest risk to tax collection. In doing so, tax authorities are placing more pressure on organisations that are considered less risky to self-evaluate and steward their own tax practices.

Adding to the picture is an increased focus on businesses to reduce cost, improve margins and find efficiencies: tax has a key role to play in this area. More than ever before, the tax function is under pressure to add value by, for example, streamlining processes or planning.

---

1 This chapter is based on the information available at July 1, 2014.
2 The authors like to express their gratitude to all those who provided support, talked things over, read, wrote, offered comments, allowed us to quote their remarks and assisted in the editing, proofreading and design. We would like to thank especially from:
Deloitte Netherlands: Niels Bloklander, Jeroen Boerman, Chris Kinders, Marvin de Ridder and Marco van der Meer
Deloitte US: Emily Van Vleet and Peter Sweeney
Deloitte UK: Kimberley Macdonald, James Paul and Ben Woodfield

Many organisations use these drivers for change as an opportunity to change the way they "do tax". Some make minor adjustments, for example recruiting resource or outsourcing. Others go much further creating efficiencies of process, embracing risk management methodologies and using technology to free up the people in the tax function to do what they do best – add value. Some even aim to lead in their field, using new operating models and embracing leading-edge best practice to get the most from their teams. They seek to be world class. This chapter explores what it means to have a "world class tax function" and how organisations might build and improve their tax management capabilities as part of a strategic change.

Why is tax a key management challenge?
Tax is a technical subject that, historically, has not been well understood by those outside of the tax department. A lack of comprehension of day-to-day activities and subject matter has meant that the interaction between the wider business and the traditional tax department has not always been at the required level. Tax has often been brought to the project table late in the day or, in some cases, too late to consider the impact resulting in lost opportunities, diminished results as well as regulatory or legal expenses, fines and penalties. Bridging the gap can be challenging.

Adding to insufficient interaction with the business is the fact that tax activities don't neatly fit within a single department. Instead, elements of the tax process are carried out by many other parts of the business, often with little or no tax training or experience, making it much harder to control. For example, accounts payable staff enter invoices into financial systems and make a decision about the VAT consequences of a transaction. Similarly, HR staff may implement a new reward scheme that has tax consequences without involving those with tax knowledge.

Tax in large organisations is also often characterised by the involvement of multiple jurisdictions, insufficiently detailed data and archaic systems that were not set up to support the growing demands placed on tax functions.

The technical difficulty of tax, its pervasive nature in the business and the complex (and often outdated) infrastructure has provided a key management challenge for those in a stewardship role. For effective tax management, the business and those doing tax need to appreciate and engage in a new way of thinking about tax and embrace new operating models.

Tax operating model
A tax operating model is the way in which a tax function's tax activities, people, processes and infrastructure are organised to allow an organisation to comply with tax laws and regulation while achieving its own strategic aims. For a tax operating model to be successful it must be effective, efficient and transparent. These themes are introduced below and will be explored in more detail throughout this chapter.

A Tax Operating Model 5.1

Effective
To manage taxes effectively, a business' commercial strategy and policies must clearly inform the direction and goals of the tax function i.e. the tax strategy. The tax strategy must be recognised by the Board, have full organisational support and should also be supported by an underlying tax policy and governance statements which provide clear guidance on the parameters within which tax activity takes place. A tax function can, after all, only be truly effective when it knows what it is trying to achieve.

Given that tax activity can be so wide-reaching in an organisation (for example, with the involvement of finance, HR, legal etc. in the end-to-end process) defining clear roles, responsibilities and accountabilities for specific activities as well as ensuring they are recognised by those tasked with the activity is vital for success.

But, what is success? How does the tax function know when it has achieved effectiveness? What is the tax cash out? These questions can only be properly answered if the tax function has considered methods of measurement. The tax department and those that carry out tax activities must have considered and logical key performance indicators that can be assessed periodically and concluded upon.

Efficient
Carrying out the right activities as defined by the tax strategy and policy is only part of the picture. To be successful, a tax function needs to make the best uses of its resources. It therefore requires the appropriate processes and infrastructure to be able to support its activities.

The tax function must be able to manage risk appropriately (by identifying risks, designing controls to mitigate the risk and testing controls for effectiveness) to limit unexpected surprises and have a plan of action should events materialise.

The tax function needs to have the right people in the right places to manage the key tax risks. This is not just about ensuring that tax staff have the right knowledge. In the largest organisations, the tax function spans multiple jurisdictions with local variations in tax requirements. Key to appropriate tax risk management is to ensure that these jurisdictions are well considered and that the organisational model is appropriate for the risk that they present.

Tax functions also need appropriately detailed data to be able to calculate tax liabilities accurately and timely information to influence and contribute to tax-impacting business decisions. Standardised processes as well as tax-sensitised financial systems are key to this. Streamlining the provision of data will also play a role. All too often tax data is contained in multiple systems that are not only poorly maintained but also unable to communicate with each other leading to duplicated effort and sometimes conflicting data.

Efficiency, like effectiveness, also needs to be monitored. We are increasingly seeing internal audit and third parties helping businesses to test whether or not the standards they have introduced as part of their infrastructure, for example the controls designed to mitigate risks, are being upheld.

Transparent
Each business will have different demands for tax information from different people. Increasingly there will be interest from the wider business, from the Board wanting updates on ETR, key tax risk and tax strategy through to its employees caring about corporate tax policy. There may also be external pressure from suppliers, customers and external regulators including the tax authorities. The key is for organisations to recognise their range of stakeholders and manage the flow of tax information to them whilst making sure that all messages are consistent and that there is confidence in all the data and commentary provided. Businesses are increasingly considering how to provide assurance around their tax commentary with many engaging internal audit services to test both their underlying processes and numbers.

Adding value
Whilst having an effective and efficient operating model for managing tax compliance and reporting is a key component of the tax function, adding value to the business is still an important aim. This could, for instance, be in the form of maintaining a steady effective tax rate. The options available to a tax department for creating value are many and varied. Key is evaluating the options proactively and systematically whilst delivering against the tax strategy, and managing stakeholder expectations.

In making tax decisions in the current tax environment consideration should be given to many factors, including but certainly not limited to the tax technical analysis, and the outcomes should both reflect the overall risk appetite of the business and be consistent with a balanced view of the needs of its stakeholders.

Increasingly, therefore, businesses are considering and documenting their tax risk appetite as part of their Board endorsed tax policy, giving their tax function both a licence to operate in certain situations and a structured and fully supported escalation framework for key tax decisions.

Data analytics is also an increasingly important focus for tax departments, both in terms of analysing options and also allowing organisations to use tax data in new ways to make smarter decisions, improve performance and drive the strategy.

Going further
It is an appetite for adopting new methods, such as data analytics, and embracing new delivery models, practices and ways of thinking that allows a tax function to move from good to world-class. Those that are using the drivers for change in the current landscape to reassess how and why they do things are those that are able to capitalise on the efficiencies and benefits that are available.

Imagine, for example, a Tax function that doesn't just have standard processes but has integrated workflow tools that support them and can provide a real-time global picture of the organisation's tax status. Or imagine a Tax function that has not just sensitised its ERP system for tax but has developed automated validations and exception reports, has centralised access rights to tools and has a tax portal. The shift from good to world class isn't easy but the benefits are considerable and organisations are realising that those benefits are available to them.

This chapter considers the key themes that we have introduced in this section in more depth and illustrates what a world-class tax function really looks like, the challenges faced by organisations and benefits that can be achieved.

In the next section, we will discuss the key characteristics of the operating model of a world class tax function which adds value and is effective, efficient and transparent.

5.2 Tax operating model

A tax management framework

A framework that incorporates the tax department's key processes and enablers can help define ways to drive value. A framework should combine the key tax processes and value drivers, as well as key enablers that affect those value drivers. Striking the right balance with respect to value drivers is critical, as is prioritising the enablers appropriately. Many companies tend to focus more on processes and people. But accomplishing more with less requires highly functioning systems and technology that can deliver the right data and information.

The framework is a simple way to deconstruct complex tax operations from record to report, and enables tax executives to assess, prioritise, and explore opportunities for tax to add value through efficiencies, risk mitigation, and better planning.

Understand value drivers. In global organisations, decisions must be weighed in the light of tax value drivers that link to broader corporate objectives. Any action should create value in one or more of those areas.
Engage the business to improve data flow and processes. Organising work streams by functional area can help focus the process improvements necessary to achieve the targeted value drivers.
Leverage enablers. Four primary enablers are critical to a high-performing tax function: 1) people and organisation, 2) process and policy, 3) technology and systems, and 4) data and information.

Tax Operating Model

Groups that achieve the right balance between risk and control are likely to have a clearly thought-through and implemented tax operating model (below)

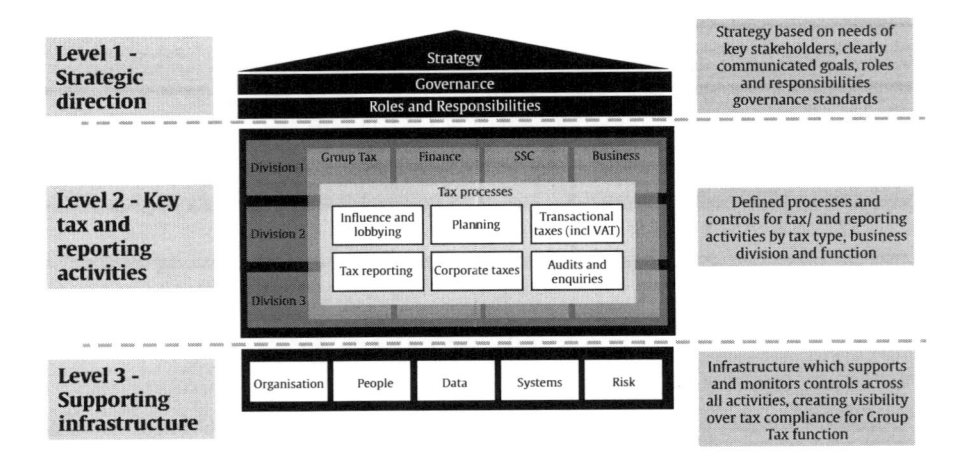

Level 1 - Strategic direction
- Strategy
- Governance
- Roles and Responsibilities

Strategy based on needs of key stakeholders, clearly communicated goals, roles and responsibilities governance standards

Level 2 - Key tax and reporting activities

Division 1	Group Tax	Finance	SSC	Business
Division 2	Tax processes: Influence and lobbying	Planning	Transactional taxes (incl VAT)	
Division 3	Tax reporting	Corporate taxes	Audits and enquiries	

Defined processes and controls for tax/ and reporting activities by tax type, business division and function

Level 3 - Supporting infrastructure
- Organisation
- People
- Data
- Systems
- Risk

Infrastructure which supports and monitors controls across all activities, creating visibility over tax compliance for Group Tax function

The people within the tax function, the tools and resources provided to them, and how they are deployed figure significantly in the tax function's ability to add value to the organisation. Solid processes and policies enable people to use systems and technologies consistently and effectively. Systems and technology are required to capture, store, and maintain the integrity of data. And data is the foundation for tax and finance decisions.

Building a world class tax function requires a sound tax control framework

The ultimate goal of a tax control framework is to build a tax function within an organisation that is effective, efficient and transparent.

Effective:	Do we do the right things?
Efficient:	Do we do the things right?
Transparent:	Do we have proper control and accountability information?

These attributes will be used to drill down into the various components which combine in a world class tax function, starting with effective – do we do the right things?

5.2.1 Level 1: Effective

The tax function should support and contribute to the organisation's overall strategy. In the area of tax planning, it is essential to understand the overall strategy. Spending time on tax planning is only worthwhile if it contributes to the strategic objectives.

The tax department's effectiveness relies on a comprehensive global tax strategy and a detailed implementation plan. Executives should assess their existing tax department strategy and map it against the organisation's business strategy. Areas to consider include risk tolerance which tax must reflect, management of intellectual property and other critical assets, the impact of product and service flows on the global cash flow and tax positions, which activities are core to the department's effectiveness, and which could be out- or co-sourced.

Organisations are expecting their tax function to bring more operational and strategic value to the business. Yet the growth in regulations to be addressed with diminished headcount and resources makes it difficult for tax departments to meet those expectations without creating unwelcome risk.

The ways in which companies organise their tax functions vary significantly
Review the tax function's effectiveness in light of the group's tax strategy and operating model: what are the department's objectives and how does the model facilitate their achievement?

Understanding the goals of the organisation allows us to determine the efficiency with which their tax function is meeting these objectives, assessed in terms of:

People – organisational structure, reporting lines, performance measurement, stakeholders etc.
Processes – methods used for compliance and reporting, tax planning activity etc.
Systems – use of technology as part of defined processes.

While reviews tend to focus on "People" this is intrinsically linked to processes and systems.

Assessing stakeholders' needs and the way in which the tax function is meeting them is key to determining its effectiveness. The first stage is to identify and prioritise relevant stakeholders and their requirements. Once stakeholders and their needs have been identified and prioritised, assess the extent to which their needs are being met. This requires data on which to base the analysis.

Strategy

Tax strategy
Tax strategy is intimately linked to an organisation's vision, mission and strategy. Vision describes the reason for the company's existence. Mission is the activities the company will undertake in pursuit of its vision. Strategy is about how these activities are executed and tax strategy defines the tax function's contribution to the overall goals of the organisation and the context for all tax activity.

Establish a vision, mission and strategy

Sample

	Behaviors	Definitions
Vision A Tax Organization seen by all [Company] executives as a strategically oriented business partner recognized for pro-activity, quality and responsiveness of its tax services for the company and customers.	Leads strategically	• Link Tax Organization goals to corporate goals and risk management objectives • Focus tax resources on strategic activities
	Builds alignment	• Align Tax and business purpose for strategies, initiatives, and cutomer products • Align compliance, audit and planning activities
	Communicates directly	• Provide proactive, value adding customer service • Initiate formal and productive regular and ad hoc staff meetings
Mission Build a Tax Organization driven by standardized and integrated data, processes and technologies and risk management methodologies that enable broadly skilled individuals to collaboratively focus on quality and value adding activities, including customer value.	Drives performance	• Assign workload by skill sets • Standardize and integrate process and technology
	Collaborates	• Integrate process, data and technology with business partners • Capture and share knowledge across tax functions
	Energizes others	• Adopt positive attitude of leadership in word and deed • Enhance involvement in new and challenging projects
Strategy Develop a Tax Organization whose performance is driven by core [Company] behaviors.	Develops others	• Provide opportunities to expand technical and managerial skill sets • Focus on balancing workload requirements with career goals

Historically, tax departments have been separate and functioned on the side lines of the organisation taking care of compliance and tax accounting. From a financial perspective, the tax department has always been regarded as a cost centre charged with delivering services to the organisation at minimal cost rather than a profit or investment centre which is measured against sales and ROI. To become an investment centre, the tax department should formulate a fiscal strategy, execute it effectively and clearly communicate its priorities to other departments. By doing this, the tax department becomes a business partner in the decision making process sitting within an interdisciplinary tax function where it is involved with other parts of the organisation and offers tax expertise which adds value.

The tax strategy component of the TCF comprise goals, communication and involvement, organisational life cycle, regulation, and tax governance and social responsibility.

Goals
Organisational goals are either qualitative or quantitative:
Qualitative goals relate to continuity of operations, transparency, ability to provide information, and good corporate citizenship.
Quantitative goals will vary but ultimately relate to earnings per share (EPS), tax cash flows and the effective tax rate (ETR).

The changing role of the tax executive
The need for tax departments to elevate and expand their role in the business isn't new, but the demands being placed on them are, both in type and intensity. Mandates from CFOs and other important stakeholders across the business that are driving this shift include:

Expand the tax department's role and focus
The current environment requires tax professionals to learn about the broader business and how tax considerations integrate into its decision making and approach to risk management. The tax department can help lead strategic initiatives in which tax cost is a major decision factor.

Become a stronger partner to the broader business
Companies continually refine their business structures and CFOs often lead the associated transformation. Tax executives are well positioned to work with CFOs and business unit leaders in their decision-making processes by clearly articulating why tax matters and identifying areas where potentially significant value can be gained by taking a tax-aligned approach.

Be ever more effective, efficient and transparent
Business model transformations are typically followed by refinements to the operating model – i.e. roles, responsibilities, processes, technology, data, and sourcing strategies across the organisation. CFOs expect the tax function to continue performing its traditional tax planning, compliance, and risk management duties, but do so in a more sustainable and efficient manner through processes and technology to better leverage their people and data.

Add value and communicate effectively

Senior stakeholders all benefit from clearly presented insights into tax issues – in language they understand and in the context of business issues to which they can relate. Tax executives must communicate the value the tax function is generating for the business, how tax executives are building sustainable tax processes around compliance and reporting, how tax personnel leverage technologies used by the rest of the finance function, and the succession plan for critical tax professionals.

Roles and Responsibilities

Industries and geographies are key in defining the shape of the tax function, but reference should always be made to a company's tax strategy, risk tolerance and alignment of the organisational structure to meet the overall goals of the business/department.

Tax function models adopt various organisational structures that incorporate the multiple responsibilities of a tax department and may allocate those responsibilities on a geographic basis, on a business line basis or a matrix approach that includes all dimensions. RACI (Responsible, Accountable, Consulted, Informed) matrices can help to address a preferred model as they set out who within the business is expected to fulfil specific tax objectives or obligations.

Activities	Responsibility				
	SFS	Regional SFS Leader	Global Tax	Statutory Director	External Advisers
Corporate Tax Return					
Provision of tax templates	R		A		R'
Extracting all of the data necessary for the tax return (in tax templates)	R		A		
Data reconciliations	R		A		
Preparation of tax returns	R		ACI		R'
First review of tax returns	R		ACI		R'
Second tax review of tax returns			RA		
Internal sign-off of tax returns			RA		
Signing of tax returns			RA	R	
Submission of tax returns	R		RA		R'^
Producing book to tax adjustments for each entity	R		A		R'
Reconciliation (true up) of accounting tax figures to return tax figure	R		A		R'
Review of local reconciliation (true up) of accounting tax figures to return tax figure			RA		
Preparing all other corporate tax calculations	R		A		R'
Tax Payments					
Extracting all of the data necessary for local tax payments	R		A		
Preparation of tax payment calculation	R		A		R'
Review of tax payment calculations			RA		
Signing of tax payment calculations			RA	I	
Submissions of tax payment	R		A		

Responsible: This individual owns the activity or project
Accountable: The individual to whom R is accountable, who signs off work before it is effective
Consulted: Individuals with information or capabilities necessary for completion of the work
Informed: Individuals who must be notified of results but need not be consulted.

Measurement

The tax function and tax executive are likely to be given specific performance targets to assess their success. It is clearly beneficial for the tax executive and other tax leaders to drive these.

Measures for when a tax function needs to become more efficient might include:
- Value added – average cost per hour worked vs. average cash saved per hour worked
- Scalability – increase in tasks processed per person year on year
- Organisational effectiveness – total tax workload vs. tax core competency workload
- Strategic contribution – business partner feedback, contribution to strategic planning, understanding business operations, proactive tax services delivered at all corporate levels
- Cost efficiency – declining tax department budget as percent of worldwide revenue, year on year reduction in average cost per hour per tax reporting task
- Operational effectiveness – shorter close cycles year on year due to increasing integration of accounting and tax people, data, processes, and technology.

Managing change to produce results

Building a world class tax function depends on the ability to move the department along the value and performance axes (see below) through more informed stakeholder decision making.

Embed quality	Drive value and performance
• Strong financial reporting • Maintained tax rules • Visibility of tax positions and risks • Data quality and information sharing • Process transparency and documentation • Record retention	• Paying the right tax • Data for better planning • Information for stakeholders • Leading practice performance • Providing analysis for business decisions
Manage total cost of tax	Enhance the tax talent pool
• Process simplification and standardization • Automation • Maintenance of tax process and tools • Lower audit adjustments and penalties	• Foundation to align tax organization • Clearer accountability • Transparent performance measurement • Focus on analysis, not administration • Balance of workforce numbers and skills

(Vertical axis: Performance; Horizontal axis: Value)

A carefully crafted change management process can help accomplish this with tactics including:
- Review of known and potential risks e.g. corporate culture, change-resistant personnel, and negative past experiences with change, and development of strategies to address them.
- Working with affected personnel to build understanding and support for proposed changes.

- Regular meetings to introduce intent, define process methods and roles, and status updates to discuss findings and potential improvements.
- Surveys, confidential interviews, workshops, and other techniques to identify issues early so they can be addressed.
- Team members with strong interpersonal skills and experience in the tax operation change process who are sensitive to the unique reactions of personnel and their need for individual coaching.

Measuring performance to track results

Most CFOs gauge tax department performance on process efficiency, cost-effectiveness of operations, quality of results, and value added. These areas are important because they are broad enough that a non-tax executive can understand and appreciate the underlying metrics and compare them to other departments for which they are responsible. Importantly, CFOs usually say they don't expect anyone to be perfect; they're simply looking for evidence that tax leaders know where they are, where they need to be, and that they have a reasonable plan for closing the gap. A well-conceived performance measurement process can help in building that perception.

Performance measurement

Effective performance measurement involves implementing a standardised and repeatable process which is embedded in the tax operation's management process and incorporates several elements:

Setting tax department goals aligned with company-wide goals that adapt as priorities change.
Establishing a performance baseline against which progress can be measured.
Defining key performance indicators to evaluate the tax function and get ideas for improvements.
Identifying leading practices and tailoring them to fit the characteristics of the industry and culture.
Implementing improvement initiatives, prioritised to prevent overload in a project plan with deliverables, flexibility, change activities, and an empowered and experienced project manager.
Executing the measurement process and sharing the results achieved.

Various tools can help this process. One is a simple spreadsheet that captures how the people in the department spend their time. After accounting for time off, training, and other administrative time, it divides an individual's remaining hours by tax/function (rows) and activity (columns). While these allocations are estimated, this tool can help establish more precise measures over time.

Sustaining organisational performance

Tax leadership can sustain the department's performance over time by tracking it continuously in each element of tax operations. The table gives some specific metrics for the four measures used by CFOs. Each tax department must select those that fit best and translate their results into the four general categories for effective reporting at the business executive level.

Tax department performance measurement: Sample leading practices/metrics

Cost effective	Process efficient	High quality	Value adding
Responsibilities require tax core competence	Processes are standardized across all tax functions	High level or specific skills are accessible when needed	Tax function goals are aligned with corporate and business unit
Resource focused on key, relevant tasks	Processes and data are integrated in the tax and accounting functions	High level or specifically skilled staff are not overburdened	Tax provides on site support to business units for both tactical and strategic issues
Organization designed to handle change	Processes are automated where appropriate	Review steps are appropriate for specific tasks	Tax planning balances innovation and risk
Workforce numbers and skills are balanced	Documentation is effective and managed for easy access	Communication is effective across all tax functions	Business leaders are fully aware of tax positions and risks
Workload distributed to appropriate skill levels	Knowledge is captured and managed for leverage	Succession planning and short-term backup are in place	Tax "value" is defined with business leaders, ROI is monitored
Performance measures are tied to goals and monitored	Workflow is managed to prevent surprises	Continuous training is required for all staff	Tax processes are documented with appropriate "controls"

Pre- vs. post-tax measurement

Pre-tax measurement is the most common financial tax performance measurement. This is an area for which control and responsibility typically lie with tax executives, but gathering data from foreign operations can be difficult as can getting business unit leaders' attention to below-the-line taxes.

Post-tax measures tend to attract the attention and cooperation of business unit executives – sometimes at the cost of control and disruptive participation in tax strategy and execution by all stakeholders. These measures may make sense globally but not locally, or vice versa; thus, they may require more focus on communication and "customer service" in order to explain positions and discuss alternatives. In the worst case, they may prompt a local unit to rely on local advisors and take actions that benefit the local entity at the cost of the organisation. Nevertheless, post-tax measures can drive greater tax efficiency by improving quality, risk management, and the value delivered by the tax department.

A first step in improving tax processes is to undertake a current state analysis of the tax function through benchmarking and tax risk profiling to better understand the current state of the function and identify where the tax function wants to be in the future. Some organisations use benchmarks to identify gaps.

The use of benchmarks helps to define an end-state – where the tax function wants to get to over time. Organisations that plan ahead in this way set up overarching systems that benefit multiple tax processes. This requires formalisation of how the tax function should operate. These tax objectives should cover every aspect of tax management such as:
- reducing the resources spent on compliance by a specific percentage or volume over a specified period of time;
- reducing the tax financial close process to a specified duration;
- allocating specific resources to specific areas such as tax-effective business planning; and
- improving standardisation and consistency to enhance tax governance processes.

Having examined the effectiveness of world class tax functions and the steps that can be taken to get and stay there, we now turn to efficiency – do we do the things right?

5.2.2 Level 2: Efficient

The tax function must be organised to achieve strategic goals as efficiently as possible. It must consider what resources are necessary to deliver the strategy, taking account of location, outsourcing, co-sourcing and budget. The tax function should be an integral part of the organisation, so that the control framework for tax can leverage the organisation's existing control measures. Finally, the tax function should address what supporting tools can promote efficiency through system integration and automation of daily processes.

Data

One of the biggest challenges for tax departments today is maintaining and being able to quickly retrieve critical, tax-relevant data and documents for example for tax authorities during examinations. Improved tax data management can strengthen audit defence activities, streamline tax compliance and reporting, and support tax planning.

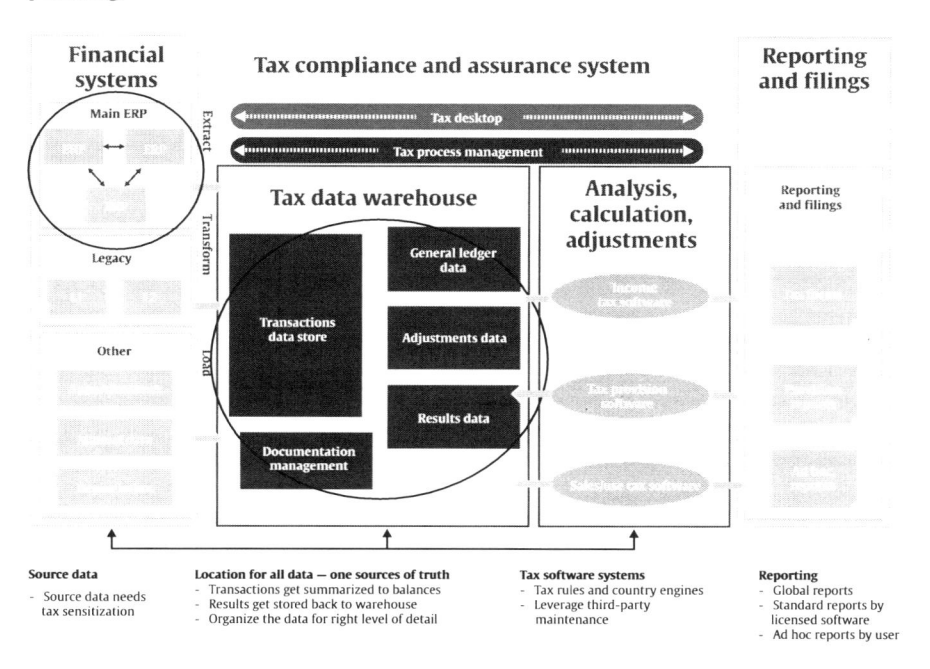

Financial systems	Tax compliance and assurance system		Reporting and filings
Main ERP (Extract) Legacy (Transform) Other (Load)	**Tax data warehouse** Transactions data store General ledger data Adjustments data Results data Documentation management	**Analysis, calculation, adjustments** Income tax software Tax provision software Other tax software	Reporting and filings
Source data - Source data needs tax sensitization	**Location for all data – one sources of truth** - Transactions get summarized to balances - Results get stored back to warehouse - Organize the data for right level of detail	**Tax software systems** - Tax rules and country engines - Leverage third-party maintenance	**Reporting** - Global reports - Standard reports by licensed software - Ad hoc reports by user

Tax data management and the record-to-report process

Two elements of the record-to-report process are particularly relevant to tax data management: tax data captured within the ERP systems (circled on the left of the diagram) and tax-sensitised data stored for computation and adjustments by other systems (circled in the centre).

Within the data store, tax-sensitised data from enterprise systems resides with data derived from downstream systems such as provision, compliance, and speciality tax software. In some cases, all of this data is centralised – perhaps in a data warehouse. More commonly, though, the data resides in a variety of tax data stores that are accessed using workflow or process management tools.

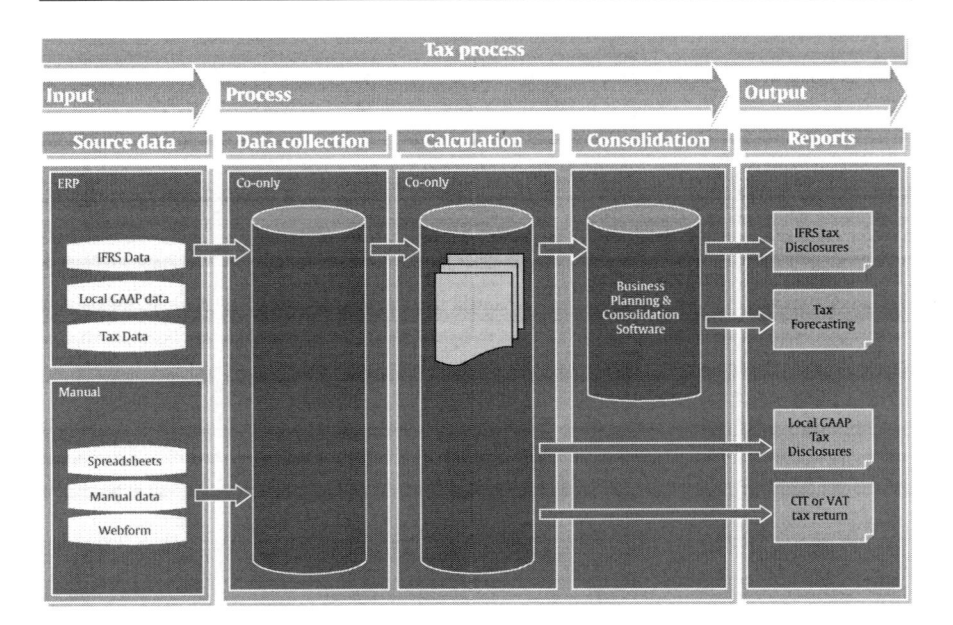

Tax process

Input → **Process** → **Output**

| Source data | Data collection | Calculation | Consolidation | Reports |

- Source data: ERP (IFRS Data, Local GAAP data, Tax Data); Manual (Spreadsheets, Manual data, Webform)
- Data collection: Co-only
- Calculation: Co-only
- Consolidation: Business Planning & Consolidation Software
- Reports: IFRS tax Disclosures, Tax Forecasting, Local GAAP Tax Disclosures, CIT or VAT tax return

Tax processes: any "Input" > "Process" > "Output" e.g. preparing a tax return, determining the correct VAT rate or calculating wage taxes.

Source data collection: source data (transactional, reporting-based or non-financial) required in a tax process can come from various sources and be extracted in a structured way directly from an ERP system. Unstructured data can be collected separately and enrich the structured data.

Calculation(s): Using tax logic to process source data so that it can be entered in a tax return or included in another calculation.

Consolidation: Data calculated on an entity level may not be sufficient. It may need to be aggregated and certain (intercompany) eliminations performed to get to a usable data set.

Report(s): Calculated data needs to be presented in a certain format for compliance purposes, or to be user-accessible. Reports range from a single number to complex and detailed e.g. a tax return.

Data extraction and collection: Issues and available tools

Most tax departments wrestle with data collection for tax purposes. One of the most significant challenges is a lack of understanding. Businesses often don't understand tax data requirements, while tax departments have a limited understanding of business issues or transactions because they are focused on compliance, do not have regular touch points, or are not involved in transactions or initiatives that impact their operations, such as a financial system design or implementation.

Another common issue is that core information required by the tax function resides outside a structured system; for example, on someone's hard drive. Or, it resides in non-tax-sensitised systems such as international accounting systems and data collection processes that are designed for the locale and don't consider the provision process. These situations require significant work to collect and convert information into a usable format for tax processes. Tax departments often have to sift a lot of non-relevant data to locate the information they need. It is not uncommon to have multiple instances of the same data; for example, in provision, compliance, and audit work papers.

Processes and Standardisation
For tax departments, the record-to-report cycle involves several distinct "mega processes": compliance, cash management, estimates and extensions, provisions, controversy management, and tax planning. In many organisations, the group responsible for each mega process operates in a "silo" using internally designed tools which are typically not connected across tax mega processes – much less with other corporate functions. As a result, data moves across these mega processes manually limiting opportunities to capitalise on synergies and efficiencies across functional areas. It can also create compliance risks if the environment has a limited audit trail, fewer control points, and inconsistent management reporting and capabilities.

The integrated tax lifecycle
Tax seen as a lifecycle incorporates standardised processes, shared data, and the tools to deliver an integrated view of tax reporting. This approach eliminates tax process silos, streamlines data usage across multiple tax processes, helps manage risk of errors in financial and tax compliance reporting, and enables multi-scenario forecasting and analysis.

Integrated tax lifecycle

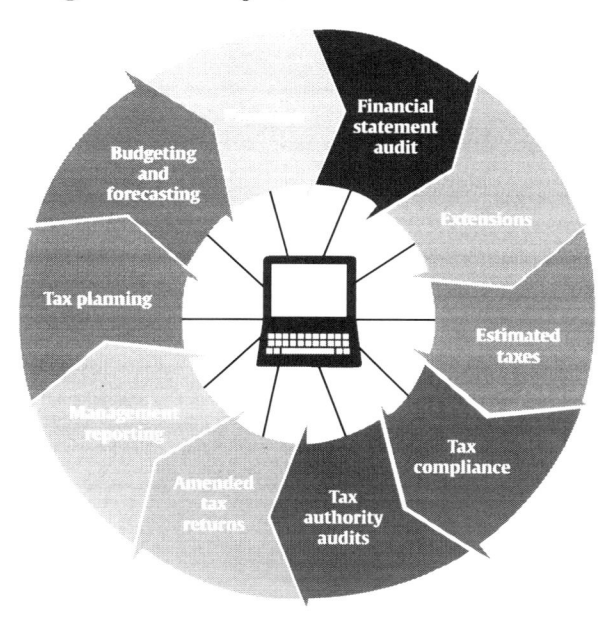

Tax process improvement: the challenge
For many companies, tax planning and compliance – sometimes under the umbrella of the finance function – are supported by a sprawling array of resources, processes, and systems especially if they are involved in mergers and acquisitions (M&A). Keeping up with compliance obligations can leave these expansive organisations little time or resources to refine their tax operations.

Focus on the upside
Automating and standardising processes can transform the efficiency of compliance and reporting, open up new possibilities for how tax compliance and reporting are executed as well as where and how tax resources are organised. For example, some tax resources can be co-located in shared service centres to maximise efficiency and improvement gains from creating centres of excellence under one "roof". Outsourcing, co-sourcing and offshoring are equally applicable to tax.

The benefits of automation and standardisation are best shown by comparing how companies operate their tax reporting and compliance today and how those adopting greater automation are achieving a more efficient, timely and effective process. For many organisations, in-country finance directors retain responsibility for preparing the local tax pack in readiness for filing a return. Typically, this is a largely manual process with information extracted from financial systems and re-purposed for tax locally before submission to an adviser who generates and submits the tax return. Some companies are beginning to use shared services centres to remove some of the burden from local finance directors, reducing the complexity of what is presently a multi-staged process.

Others are poised to go further. Automation is helping them to evolve a seamless process in which data flows directly from the financial system into the appropriate points in the tax return. A "review-ready" return can then be assessed by suitably trained resources in a shared service centre before local filing. For this approach to be feasible an appropriate ERP system needs to be in place – which is likely at present to be restricted to a company's larger territories – as well as tax return software. This sort of automation can and should support the tax provision process as well.

Standardisation
Standardisation, if implemented and utilised correctly, can be a very useful tool to mitigate risk in the financial reporting of income taxes. Checklists can be used as a means of facilitating a minimum level of completeness of an income tax provision calculation, for example, listing the main issues to consider or a checklist that indicates the schedules to be completed and supporting documentation to be provided. Standardised tax packs create a familiar platform on which figures can be consistently input and reported period after period. Standardisation is also useful for review purposes where the reviewer does not need to spend time and brainpower becoming familiar with different tax packages and the way in which the packages calculate or present the final information requested based on the particular

preferences of the preparer. The risks associated with standardisation are discussed under risk management below.

Structure: Tax Organisation and Resources

The challenge
When elevating the tax function to a more strategic level, questions may arise about whether to keep certain activities in-house or outsource them. Should they stay within business units or be centralised in shared services centres? What are the risks and rewards of onshore versus offshore centres?

These decisions gain complexity in the context of broader enterprise strategies, especially M&A, restructuring, downsizing, carve-outs, or the sale of a business unit, subsidiary, or product line. Often the tax department is the last to learn about such activities, but first to be held accountable for missed deadlines or failure to comply with regulations it may not have known applied.

Many larger businesses have deployed ERP systems to automate transaction processing and financial data collection, analysis, and reporting. Although the information in these systems is critical to all tax planning and reporting activities, many were configured and implemented without appropriate tax department input so a significant amount of information is not tax-sensitised.

There can be far-reaching tax implications to how ERP systems are purchased, leased, located, and configured. Few companies consider these implications up front when they can provide the greatest benefit to the organisation. The increasing integration of performance management applications into ERP platforms is providing organisations and their tax department's new ways to monitor, measure, and manage business performance.

Organisational Characteristics
Forward-thinking tax leaders are designing their departments to evolve continuously and at the proper pace to sustain performance and minimise the disruption of sudden dramatic change.
In general, tax department organisation design should promote:
- High levels of coordination between and within units,
- Efficient work flow,
- Responsive decision making,
- Retention of top performers, and
- High levels of customer satisfaction.

Sample tax organisation design characteristics may include:

Characteristics	Definition
Skill development	The tax department values tax technical skill development and wants long term tax technical growth for its people
Quality within tax accounting	The tax department provides information for financial statement disclosure that is timely, accurate, and thoroughly analyzed, and is supported by strong internal controls
Collaboration / communication	The tax department communicates and collaborates effectively and efficiently among the tax areas of compliance, planning, tax accounting and controversy. Tax also communicates and collaborates effectively with other areas in the organization such as treasury, finance, and IT
Retention	Tax department employees have long term job satisfaction resulting in low turnover and high retention
Knowledge management	The tax department "knows" what it knows and effectively utilizes the skill sets of its employees and captures, stores, and organizes knowledge in a way that is accessible for all to utilize
Facilitates continuous process & technological improvements	The tax department continually recognizes and implements improvements in process and technology in order to refine deliverable and work better, faster, and smarter
Manages fluctuation in work flow	The tax department recognizes peaks and valleys in workload throughout the year and has a flexible staffing model which enables it to dedicate additional resources to key areas during peak times
Management capability	The tax department has management who is engaged with its people and effective in managing day to day activities, strategic planning, and who also acts as the face of tax while communicating key metrics to senior management, the board, and the audit committee
Flexibility for growth and strategic initiatives	The tax department has the resources and the knowledge to react quickly to growth opportunities and is able to provide tax advice, risks, opportunities to support strategic initiatives of the business

Organising resources efficiently, balancing tax compliance, quality of reporting and planning

Most companies organise tax department resources according to functional area – national, international, indirect, tax provision, compliance etc – with little sharing of resources. Some combine resources under a common manager, but retain separate staffing due to the differing schedule and/or nature of the work. More recently some companies have reorganised tax compliance and provision personnel as they search for an optimal allocation of resources for these areas. In many cases though the two functions still have separate teams.

How best to organise tax department resources will depend on factors such as company size, workload type, and industry. A clear definition of workload (type, volume, timing, and complexity) and the organisation's existing technology, dataflow and processes should help determine the number of tax professionals and skills needed. Factors such as industry and company size will influence the division of the tax labour pool across tax functions and tax activities. While efficiency is certainly an objective, it should not compromise the organisation's ability to perform effective tax planning. Short-term tax planning and reporting is now as important as long-term tax planning.

In a large, complex environment, it is more difficult for the tax function to see everything that is happening within the business and to react accordingly, especially when there are overseas operations. The larger the enterprise the more appropriate it will be to organise tax resources by business unit and align them to the business unit's areas of focus. Organising by business unit can foster a proper understanding of the company's operations and environment. The number of tax professionals per business unit depends on the related tax issues and the quantity and complexity of data requirements. Typically the 80/20 rule will apply in which 80 percent of the effects come from 20 percent of the causes.

A functional structure facilitates development and application of specific tax knowledge and experience. But, given peaks and troughs in workload, it can result in suboptimal efficiency. Instead, pooling resources across tax functions can help leaders adjust resources more efficiently to fill specific needs. This approach may require more cross-training and planning of resources but it can be the fastest way to leverage resources effectively and provide adequate focus on planning. The success of a pooled staff structure often hinges on the manager's own tax technical knowledge and ability to manage a team whilst ensuring the tax function has the right tax processes and technology in place. Technology applications can improve efficiency by alleviating staff of time-consuming or manual processes, but software applications can take longer to produce the benefits and return.

Another common question is how to allocate responsibilities between the tax and accounting functions. Studies estimate that approximately 40 percent of tax compliance work is gathering and assembling accounting information, so this should either be transferred to accounting to utilise tax resources more effectively or tax must work with accounting to develop alternative solutions. These typically involve combining in-house effort and sub-contracting elements of the work externally either to contract personnel or full co-sourcing (see graphic). In addition most companies should take steps to produce truly tax-sensitised data from the start. Doing so can reduce the time required to gather and assemble information – for both functions – and enable an organisation to use its resources for more productive planning exercises.

	In-house service delivery	External service delivery	
	Captive	Contract personnel ("loan staffing," "resource augmentation")	Outsourcing ("cosourcing")
Characteristics	• Work is performed by the company's own employees • Company takes full responsibility for filings	• Provider professionals work under corporate tax's direct supervision • Provider personnel are typically used to fill a specific staffing need on a temporary basis • Company has complete control and visibility over the preparation process • The company takes full responsibility for all filings • Provider personnel do not sign returns	• Provider professionals work under varying levels of corporate tax supervision • Company has varying levels of control and visibility over the preparation process, as specified in agreed-upon statements of work and service-level agreements • Each party takes responsibility for work performed by its professionals • Provider is typically considered a paid preparer with respect to its work product • Provider personnel often sign returns as a paid preparer to represent the provider • Contracts are typically longer-term than in most contract personnel agreements
Considerations	• Company retains full control over process and outcomes • Greater potential for long-term savings than external service delivery models (due to the absence of provider margin cost) • Typically requires greater initial investment and longer time to return on investment (ROI) than external service delivery arrangements • Talent-related costs may erode wage arbitrage savings • Requires a significant amount of support from the U.S. tax department	• Company gains access to resources while retaining full control over process and outcomes • Generally costs less than many outsourcing arrangements • Company must provide supervisory professionals • Provider personnel typically must remain offshore to drive the desired savings, requiring proficiency in virtual work practices and/or the presence of corporate supervisors in the offshore location • If used only during busy seasons, a provider may be unable to guarantee year-to-year continuity of personnel • Limited availability of service providers with capable offshore resources that offer a contract personnel model	• Company can choose its level of control over process • Company gains access to provider's tax knowledge base • Requires less corporate tax supervision than a captive or contract personnel model
Under what circumstances might this option be appropriate?	• Leaders are not comfortable with outsourcing tax • Company has an extremely large volume of U.S. income tax work (enough for approximately 50 or more full-time employees) • Company has extensive experience in managing offshore captive operations • Leaders are willing to accept a relatively large up-front investment as well as a relatively long time to ROI	• Company needs to quickly increase capacity for a non-recurring project • Company has operation(s) in the preferred offshore location that can accommodate U.S. tax professionals to provide on-site supervision • The company and the provider are both highly proficient in remote collaboration	• Company has few in-house tax resources to supervise offshore staff • Company looking for a smaller initial investment and/or a shorter time to ROI than would be feasible with a captive • Company lacks the volume of U.S. income tax work to support approximately 50 full-time offshore tax professionals • Company plans to outsource as an interim approach while developing a captive tax capability

Tax departments are being asked to work harder and smarter. Efforts to increase efficiencies, such as shared service centres, offshoring, or co-sourcing can help but bring their own challenges and costs can vary. Establishing and maintaining a shared service centre involves extensive process change, documentation, technology, and people including highly skilled internal reviewers. Co-sourcing also involves these costs and the transition work to create and maintain the infrastructure. In addition, executives should use care that tax operations stay close to the business.

Recently organisations have explored offshoring certain administrative tax activities. Companies that have been successful often start with indirect taxes as these involve repeated processes, a relatively constant workload, and heavy reliance on data. While some have used offshoring successfully, it can be difficult to establish and carries risks: lack of proximity to the business is magnified when tax practitioners work in another country, and additional training may be required to embed knowledge and experience of HQ country tax law. Companies using outsourcing or offshoring often expect to be able to use resources interchangeably to handle multiple responsibilities, but this assumes the teams have the required technical experience.

When considering offshoring, one of the most important factors is the size of the tax department. In a large tax department with many process-oriented roles it may be feasible to take certain roles offshore for efficiency purposes. However, many tax departments are not large enough to do this. Offshoring capitalises on economies of scale, but these are scarce if the tax team is only 10 strong. An option for such companies is to integrate with larger offshore finance operations and have finance supervise the tax roles. This arrangement will require added coordination to make sure it truly supports tax objectives.

The pros and cons of shared services and offshoring
Shared service centres can improve efficiency and alleviate administrative burdens. In addition, personnel in shared service centres are often closer to data sources which can help when performing tax compliance or provision activities. On the other hand, shared service centres are typically further removed from the business and so less aware of changes occurring in it. To retain its ability to plan, an organisation might consider putting some compliance activities in a shared service centre for efficiency and keeping planning activities in proximity to the business.

Shared service environments assume that resources are interchangeable which may require more training given the technical nature of tax activities. If the shared service centre is not in the same physical location as related finance functions, tax leaders may need to focus on communication and relationship building to enhance staff access to the data and information they need.

Information Technology
As the legal and regulatory environment evolves, the role of technology grows more important in the tax function. Companies installing an ERP or consolidation system often overlook the tax-related functionality now built into these systems, as well as the impact of these systems on the tax department. In many cases the tax function and system implementers may be unaware of the tax capabilities. Software companies have been adding tax functionality and increased reporting capabilities, especially in the area of tax accounting, indirect taxes and transfer pricing. Tax-specific systems have been greatly enhanced, as well, providing a variety of methods to automate and reduce the spreadsheet-based processes that can introduce risk into tax accounting, compliance and reporting.

There are at least three good reasons why tax executives should be strategically involved with major business IT initiatives, such as ERP projects. First, tax departments are generally the largest consumers of financial data within their organisations; therefore, it is critical that IT systems capture most, if not all, tax data requirements. In addition, lack of appropriate data raises the risk of financial reporting as well as tax compliance errors. Finally, as tax is often the largest expense item after cost of sales, tax involvement could mean significant benefits in the form of lower operating costs, reduced risk, and enhanced tax planning. Despite these compelling reasons, the tax function is often not involved when planning for transformative IT initiatives. That must change.

In fact, the tax function has a lot to gain from involvement in technology- and data-driven business initiatives. These initiatives can produce source data that is tax-aligned, able to be used by all tax disciplines, and transparent through to the transaction level; all features that reduce the need for the tax function to collect, format, and manipulate accounting data. From a technology and systems perspective, these initiatives can help automate non-core tax activities, embed planning decisions in the technology, and integrate tax systems where appropriate.

The final "leg" of a world class tax function which is a value-adding partner to the business is transparency – do we have proper control and accountability information?

5.2.3 Level 3: Transparent

Transparency applies to the tax function on various levels and is relevant both within the business as well as externally.

The requirements of tax management and reporting have changed fundamentally, and the demand for transparency and clarity in tax communication will continue to increase.

For effective transparency your company needs a strategy for explaining its tax position based on who is interested and what they want to know. These days it is safe to assume that everyone from the tax authorities to members of the public consider themselves to be stakeholders in your company. They will have varying expectations as to what you disclose and otherwise communicate about your tax affairs. Tax compliance and disclosures have the potential to make or mar reputations and brands, so you need a robust, effective communication policy with board approval and oversight.

Start with your context – the regulatory and commercial environment in which you operate, the jurisdictions and fiscal regimes to which you are subject, your investment and business cycles. You need robust internal tax management processes to be able to explain your tax profile with figures of taxes paid and taxes borne.

Corporate social responsibility (CSR)
Like it or not companies nowadays are expected to act as responsible citizens. At the heart of CSR lies the notion that companies should contribute to society which includes paying tax. CSR means more than compliance – have you acted in a spirit of citizenship?

External stakeholders

1. *The financial community*
The financial community wants to understand the current tax charge, the cash tax position and, importantly, the reasons for any differences between the two. The current tax position, risks and uncertainties need to be communicated simply. There is a growing trend for analysts to ask about the potential impact of prospective tax law change – and so awareness of the changing environment, forecasting, scenario planning and impact assessments is of increasing importance.

2. *Employees, customers, suppliers and broader society*
It is important to monitor developments in the public's view of your tax position; clear communication reinforces positive popular sentiment and may strengthen brand value.

Accountability
Popular stakeholders have been pressing for multinationals to report country by country (CbCR) to understand the tax contribution per country. This is now on the international agenda and it is only a matter of time before it is mandatory.

3. *The tax authorities*
This traditional tax stakeholder is looking at all your communications. The increasing effectiveness of the tax information exchange (TIEA) regime, together with other information sharing methods mean that your global tax messaging will be open to review and reinforces the need for consistency.

4. *Regulators*
The OECD's Base Erosion and Profit Shifting (BEPS) action plan to address Transfer Pricing manipulation, the Extractive Industries Transparency Initiative, the Dodd-Frank Act in the US and the EU Capital Requirements Directive IV all demonstrate the extent to which tax is no longer limited to business and tax authority relationships, but is a significant strategic business issue.

Making and explaining your case
You need to have the right information readily available and confidence in your communications which relies on the right supporting processes and controls. Steps to make and explain your case:
1) Design and deliver an integrated approach to tax communication which satisfies all stakeholders and allows the business to manage the public disclosure of its tax management approach as efficiently as possible.
2) Gather the information you need to communications: understanding the people, processes and systems required and how they should work together to provide robust, high quality financial and tax information.
3) Recognise the range of stakeholders, actively manage the information flow to them and deliver consistent messages to all of them.

Managing behaviour
It is increasingly common to have an over-arching tax policy. The policy needs to be owned by the business, recognised and approved at board level and understood by all those in the business who touch tax in one way or another.

Your working tax policy should have:
- Active board level involvement in setting, approving and reviewing the tax policy.
- CSR or similar (non-finance and tax) teams involved sufficiently to ensure consistency with broader CSR objectives.
- Regular board level oversight of tax policy.
- Regular reviews of tax policy.
- 'Extraordinary' reviews of tax policy triggered when new material risks emerge.

You should communicate how the tax policy works, how it supports the strategy of the business and how it fits with, and is appropriate for, the aims and ambitions of the business.

Internal stakeholders
There are several internal stakeholders that have an interest in the tax affairs of the organization. Examples are: CFO, CEO, board of directors, CSR teams and public relations. It is important to be able to communicate the different aspects of the tax strategy and tax positions in a clear, consistent and transparent way to these stakeholders. Further, roles and responsibilities should be transparent bearing in mind that the tax function is broader than just the tax department. Each person with a role in the tax function should understand their own and other's responsibilities. Furthermore, when carrying out the tax function, each decision should be transparent

A Tax Operating Model 5.2.3

as to its impact on the tax strategy – not only for the desired result, but also for the impact of other possible outcomes of the decision.

Tax Assurance (Insight, Analysis, Follow-up)
The tax function is not just the tax department. For example, the M&A department of an organisation has a role, even if only to inform the tax department that an acquisition is being considered. The whole organisation needs to understand this principle. It is tempting to approach the tax control framework from the view point of the tax department, but this runs the risk that the perception of the roles and responsibilities of tax differs between the business and the tax department. If this is not addressed, all relevant tax opportunities and risks may not be considered. Interpretation of the tax law is seldom a source of tax risk. In most cases, risks are triggered either by not realising that tax may play a role in a transaction ("insight") or that an issue although spotted is not correctly addressed. This is often the result of incorrect factual information ("analysis") or incorrect follow up ("follow-up") of the tax technical advice given as illustrated below:

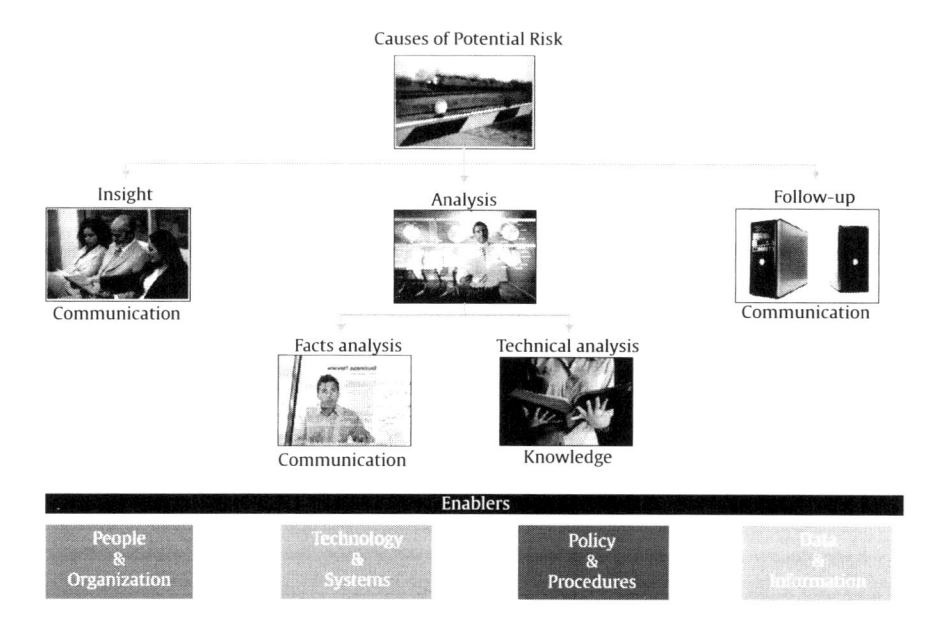

Causes of Potential Risk

Insight — Communication

Analysis
- Facts analysis — Communication
- Technical analysis — Knowledge

Follow-up — Communication

Enablers: People & Organization | Technology & Systems | Policy & Procedures | Data & Information

Clearly, communication is a key component in avoiding risks; making sure that the relevant people understand the issue, the facts, what is needed to resolve the issue and, most importantly, who takes ownership.

Common areas of tax-related financial reporting risk
Management estimates:
- valuation allowances;
- uncertain tax positions;

- administrative practices; and
- indefinite reversal criteria.

Other financial reporting risks:
- changes in laws or rates;
- distinguishing a change in estimate from correction of an error;
- subsequent events;
- acquisition accounting; and
- interim reporting (discrete versus effective tax rate).

To mitigate these risks tax must have a seat at the table and integrate with the business, becoming a player in companywide risk management efforts. Tax executives must verify the business strategy and its tax alignment to manage tax risks and opportunities arising outside of tax.

In practical terms, a risk intelligent tax executive must:
- ensure that tax compliance and financial reporting risks are well understood, updated, and addressed through appropriate controls and processes throughout the enterprise, while managing operational and cash-flow risks (such as not paying more tax than necessary);
- proactively seek out, analyse and understand which business decisions throughout the enterprise have significant tax implications; and
- bring the analysis of tax risk to the business units, corporate executives and boards in a way that helps them make better business decisions.

By fulfilling these expectations, the risk intelligent tax executive helps the business adopt a holistic view of tax and related risks; both unrewarded (nothing is gained from taking the risk) and rewarded (provides value if risk is managed well). A risk intelligent tax executive understands that decision making without proper tax input is a fast track to missed opportunities, so they actively collaborate with the business to secure tax savings that may help fund strategic projects, embrace opportunities to address tax risk, for instance, by evaluating internal audit and SOX 404 internal control findings.

Implicit in these expectations is a close working relationship between the tax executive and the CFO. In many organisations tax executives report directly to the CFO, making the CFO's support a prerequisite for the success of a risk intelligent approach to tax.

Transactional risk
Tax impacts almost every transaction in an enterprise from the sale of goods to M&A. Transactional risk is the risk associated with applying current tax laws and regulations to a particular transaction.

The tax risks associated with repetitive transactions are typically handled through technology and processes. Risk can emerge if tax is not appropriately represented in the implementation of new technologies or the development of new processes within the enterprise. For example, as an enterprise undertakes the implementation of an ERP system, the tax function should be involved during the planning and implementation stages of the project. If appropriately represented, the tax function is sure to have access to "tax-sensitised" data for planning, calculating and reporting purposes, which will allow tax processes to be streamlined.

Another area of transactional tax risk relates to non-recurring transactions, such as acquisitions. If the tax function is not appropriately involved in the planning and execution of an acquisition, a profitable transaction on paper may be loss making after tax is accounted for. Tax executives must be cognisant of business strategies and be plugged into the decision and planning process to determine that tax effects of transactions are considered before they occur.

Reputational risk
The tax function cannot make a positive impact on the company's reputation. Tax professionals strive to pay what is due under the tax laws and regulations, no more and no less. If a tax position is too aggressive, or is thought to cross a line by the public at large, the reputation of an organisation may be damaged. Where a lack of tax controls has led to a material weakness or restatement for financial reporting purposes, a company's reputation can be adversely affected.

The existence of a material weakness depends only on the reasonable possibility of a material misstatement. However, a restatement is a common indicator of the presence of a material weakness. When an entity reassesses its internal controls over financial reporting during the restatement process, it often realises that a material weakness most likely led to the restatement. Although income tax accounting can be complex, many errors are caused by carelessness or factors such as poor coordination between an entity's tax and financial reporting or other departments. For many entities, the core information required by tax departments often resides outside of a structured system or in "non-standard" tools (e.g. a spreadsheet).

Leading practices for managing income tax accounting issues and reducing the risk of tax-related material weaknesses and restatements include ongoing training, beginning the tax provision process early, working effectively with other departments (particularly financial reporting) and reviewing processes regularly for efficiency and effectiveness. Some tax technologies reduce the need for manual manipulation of data and reduce reliance on manual controls, which may lower the risk of a material misstatement in the financial statements.

Standardisation including the use of checklists can also make a contribution as has already been discussed. However, there is risk in the use of standardisation. The same standard checklists and tax packs that can help to promote efficiency and consistency should not be relied upon as a comprehensive set of instructions or assumed to represent a perfect template free of exceptions. Standardisation cannot compensate for lack of technical knowledge and experience: a local controller with minimal knowledge of accounting for income taxes is likely to only consider the items on the checklist and input the minimum required fields in a template if there is no understanding of the purpose or the end result. There is no comfort that all issues have been considered and that an overall "sense check" has been performed. As local tax personnel are often not fully competent in accounting for income taxes, standardisation reinforced with ongoing training can be a powerful tool to improve the quality of income tax accounting across an organisation.

Tax Risk Management

Introduction
Multinational companies remain focused on managing the risk associated with non-local taxes for foreign entities. The CFO increasingly expects that corporate tax executives will manage the tax organisation globally. This includes:
- keeping current with tax laws and changes as they occur;
- improving controls over tax financial reporting requirements;
- managing the global tax audit activity;
- determining that compliance with tax requirements occurs in every jurisdiction;
- providing access to proper expertise in each jurisdiction (e.g. HQ GAAP to local GAAP adjustments, and technical skill and knowledge about accounting for income taxes); and
- accurately reporting global tax accounts by jurisdiction.

While expected to manage these risks, the tax executive is also expected to understand and contain the associated costs in these locations. Often, this is despite having limited:
- control over overseas headcount;
- direct control over the global tax budget;
- understanding about where the work is done (i.e. in-house versus outsourced);
- understanding of the scope of services provided by external resources for specific fees; and
- knowledge of the cost of the tax services.

The demand for increased focus on financial reporting is one key driver of this trend, coupled with a demand for improved transparency by investors, shareholders and management alike. Accounting for income taxes is a complex area and the source of many tax-related material weaknesses and restatements. Add to that the need to determine worldwide audit exposure for financial reporting purposes, and it becomes apparent that HQ tax executives should find better and more efficient methods for monitoring and impacting tax activity globally.

Enterprise risk management trends
The perceived failure of risk management practices to stave off economic downturn has led to dramatic non-tax regulatory changes that are fuelling changes in how companies measure, manage and report risks. For example:

- Boards are more active in risk governance, audit committee interest in tax matters is increasing and tax presentations to the audit committee are on the rise.
- Risk management teams are struggling to understand and manage the drivers of reputation risk, including perceptions regarding tax and good corporate citizenship.
- Companies are linking strategic planning with risk management, and tax is expected to be part of those processes.
- Chief Risk Officers, Chief Tax Risk Officers and Chief Compliance Officers are becoming more common.
- Compliance risk, including tax compliance risk, is developing into an enterprise issue.
- Company-wide risk committees are pushing risk management tools into business units and functions, including tax.
- Risk management technology is maturing and being embedded further into company processes, and tax processes are more often in scope.
- Internal audit departments are expanding their reach beyond SOX controls and increasingly reviewing tax departments.

Risk intelligence maturity model

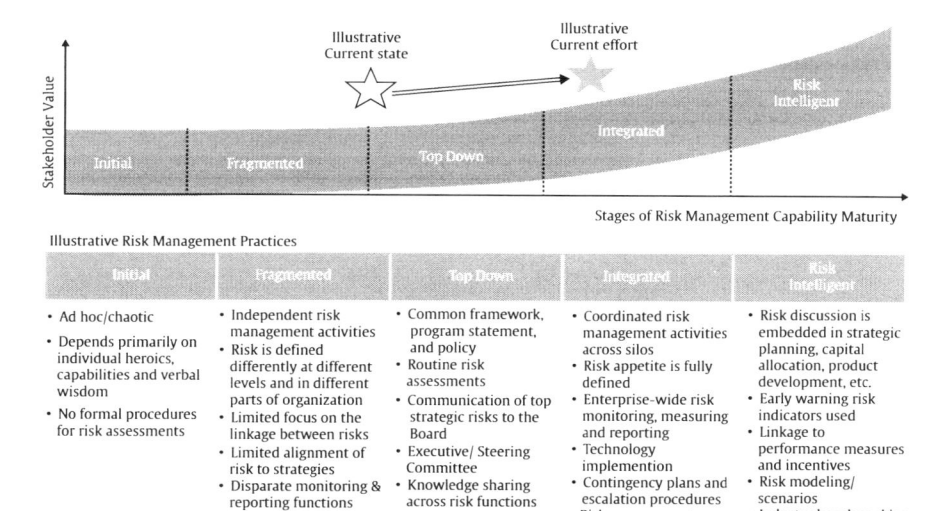

Illustrative Risk Management Practices

Initial	Fragmented	Top Down	Integrated	Risk Intelligent
• Ad hoc/chaotic • Depends primarily on individual heroics, capabilities and verbal wisdom • No formal procedures for risk assessments	• Independent risk management activities • Risk is defined differently at different levels and in different parts of organization • Limited focus on the linkage between risks • Limited alignment of risk to strategies • Disparate monitoring & reporting functions	• Common framework, program statement, and policy • Routine risk assessments • Communication of top strategic risks to the Board • Executive/ Steering Committee • Knowledge sharing across risk functions • Awareness activities • Formal risk consulting • Dedicated team	• Coordinated risk management activities across silos • Risk appetite is fully defined • Enterprise-wide risk monitoring, measuring and reporting • Technology implementation • Contingency plans and escalation procedures • Risk management traning	• Risk discussion is embedded in strategic planning, capital allocation, product development, etc. • Early warning risk indicators used • Linkage to performance measures and incentives • Risk modeling/scenarios • Industry benchmarking used regularly

As a result, tax risks and opportunities are increasingly included as companies discuss the potential cumulative and cascading effects of risk events, and tax departments are looking for new ways to understand, explain and manage tax risks and tax risk interdependencies.

Tax risk management in the global environment
The resourcing of global tax functions appears to vary significantly from company to company, but outside HQ there are often inconsistent levels of in-house tax expertise.

The structure has usually evolved rather than been designed and is determined by historical precedent, the presence of in-house tax expertise in certain countries, the approach of the local finance controllers and local relationships with external tax advisors. Consequently, ensuring there is sufficient expertise is rarely a straightforward choice between in-house or outsourcing, and hybrid models prevail. Responsibility for taxes is also company-specific, but it is not uncommon for the tax or controller organisation of the foreign affiliate to have dotted-line reporting responsibility to the HQ tax executive so that appropriate information can be collected for tax accounting and group compliance processes.

Dealing with the global complexity of tax
One way to understand global tax reporting requirements is to perform a global operational control assessment focused on the following four specific areas of tax in the foreign locations:

Understanding global filing requirements: to gain an understanding of the global tax operations, tax executives need to gain visibility into the activities being performed in relevant countries. This starts with the tax executive contacting the local country tax director or controller. The resulting conversation should reveal:
- the compliance and reporting requirements in the local country;
- the responsible party for performing the activity (internal or external resource);
- and the cost of the activities.

Once this baseline is determined, the HQ tax executive is in a position to gather further information.

Understanding processes: from a tax compliance perspective, the HQ tax executive needs to understand who has responsibility for compliance activities in each jurisdiction and who, within the enterprise, decides on which outside providers to use, when applicable, and who reviews and signs off on the compliance work and returns. The tax executive should also determine whether appropriate records are maintained of tax filings and calculations in addition to learning how the local organisation tracks the tax filings and payments. An assessment of the skills of those providing information and computations and the quality of service providers is also important.

Tracking transactions: the HQ tax executive must get comfortable with the tax provision data received from foreign affiliates. Tracking significant tax planning projects and foreign acquisitions or transactions around the world can help confirm that the tax provision is appropriately reported and adequate controls are in place. It is also important to determine who is performing the work and what training and experience they have. Accounting for income taxes capabilities from both an HQ and an international perspective is critically important.

Tracking foreign tax controversy: discussions with tax authorities should involve personnel with the appropriate skills and technical knowledge. Inaccurate reporting to the HQ tax function of uncertain tax positions can create significant financial reporting risk. Understanding how to track and account for settlements, and accurately report the consequences is an often overlooked aspect of controversy management.

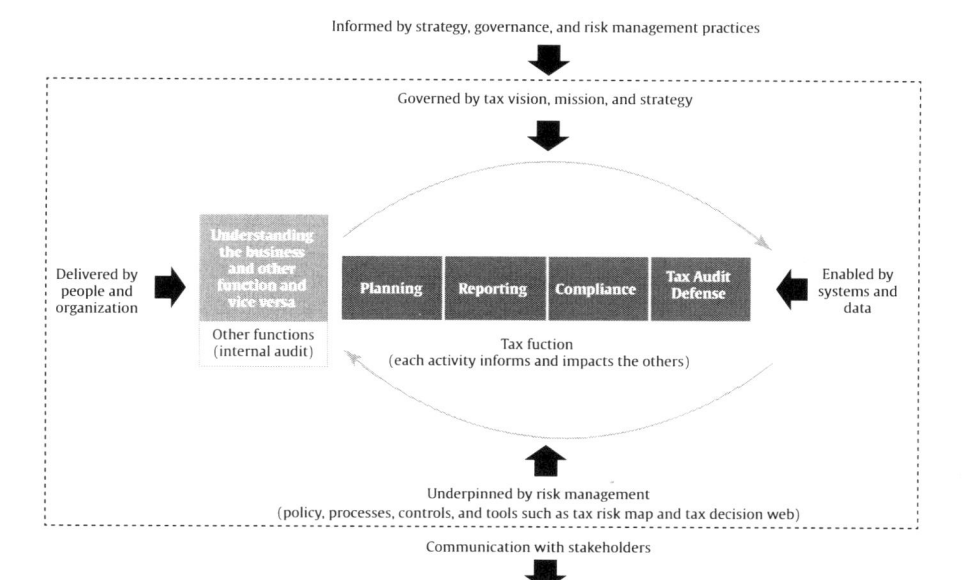

Informed by strategy, governance, and risk management practices

Governed by tax vision, mission, and strategy

Delivered by people and organization

Understanding the business and other function and vice versa

Planning | Reporting | Compliance | Tax Audit Defense

Enabled by systems and data

Other functions (internal audit)

Tax fuction
(each activity informs and impacts the others)

Underpinned by risk management
(policy, processes, controls, and tools such as tax risk map and tax decision web)

Communication with stakeholders

Performing a process, controls and skills assessment is the first step to understanding the risks that foreign operations pose to an enterprise. Once this groundwork is performed, the tax executive can make informed decisions on how to manage the risk, what policies and procedures to put in place and what additional actions are needed to strengthen controls. One of the benefits from the assessment is to strengthen relationships with foreign tax resources. The process also reveals how tax compliance is managed in each jurisdiction which can affect cost and quality of delivery.

Communication

Communication and business partnering
To make the tax function work as an integrated part of the organisation, all parties need to change the way they involve the tax function in the organisation's primary activities. The tax department should organise itself to create stronger connections with the rest of the organisation and consider the value it adds bearing in mind where the organisation is in its life cycle.

Considering the tax function as an integral part of the organisation will help to identify tax risks at an earlier stage so that they can be taken into account during regular decision making processes. The tax function as an integral part of the organisation is, besides involvement, about communication between departments. Communicating business issues to the tax function during commercial decision making improves the process as a whole. Often risks can be identified early which otherwise could have a high impact on the business case. This requires the tax function to become a strategic business partner, providing management with adequate information. Furthermore, the tax function should proactively suggest where value could be added. By transforming itself into a strategic partner, the tax function will add more value and have a more prominent role in the organisation.

Effective business partnering elements include;
- Understanding key business drivers.
  - Proactive communications on business transactions, operations, and plans.
  - Minimise fire-drills/ ad-hoc data requests and projects.
  - Drive effective planning for local operating taxes as part of selling, general and administrative expenses spend in local countries.
- Communications and collaboration.
  - Planning and coordinating tax process schedules with business partners so tax data needs can be better anticipated and business partners can have more time to respond.
  - Training on why the data is needed and how it is used.
  - Providing the right level of training on key tax topics that are important to the business partners.

Tax function processes to enable collaboration and effective day-to-day operations
To support their tax compliance and planning responsibilities, tax departments should have effective communication, information-sharing and measurement processes across functional areas. Information-sharing and communication are similar, but different concepts. Information-sharing helps team members have timely access to the data and information they need to perform their jobs. Constant and regular communication provides team members the context they need to use the information and to perform their responsibilities according to expectations.

Communication and information-sharing are particularly important when teams are based in multiple locations or when they include individuals outside the department such as consultants who do not work on site every day. There are many tools and technologies available that enable groups to work together in real time, without being in a common location. These include workflow tools, document management systems, dashboards, electronic work papers, and portals.

Measurement is essential to building a cohesive team focused on common goals. If a tax department establishes common measures across groups, then individual members of those groups are more likely to assist others and work together to achieve the desired outcomes. It is important to use care in setting measures as they can drive both good and bad behaviour.

The tax function which is effective, efficient and transparent is well placed to add value to the business as a whole through planning and, increasingly, tax data analytics.

5.2.4 Value added

Planning
Tax complexity offers opportunities to explore potential tax savings and address corporate tax compliance risks. Almost every business decision has a tax consequence, so an organisation should consider the related tax impact as early as possible in the planning stage. Having the resources, time and skills in place to implement the planning is often one of the largest hurdles tax departments face. Some of the areas of opportunity that a tax executive should evaluate and prioritise include:

Structuring: Legal structure can significantly affect an entities tax exposure. Tax credits, deductions, and apportionment rules must all be taken into consideration. An effective tax executive will assess whether a proposed substantive business structure is tax efficient, while also being mindful of the financial reporting impact and the tax risks encountered.

Transaction planning: The structuring of business transactions can have a variety of different and sometimes unexpected tax results. The tax consequences of business transactions and alignment with strategic planning require adequately skilled and experienced resources to support transaction planning. Facilitating well-reasoned decisions during the transaction process can be critical to enhancing a company's tax position and elevates the stature of a tax department.

Credits and incentives: Many countries offer tax credits and other incentives for activities such as making new investments, job creation or retention, or doing research. These credits and incentives should be taken into account for tax planning.

Common challenges
- Ignoring the enhanced value tax can deliver.
- Leaving potential tax planning savings on the table.

- Failing to take into account the tax implications of everyday business decisions.
- Implementing technology which cannot track details necessary for tax planning and compliance.
- Accessing data, implementing effective controls, and creating tax-aligned systems.
- Developing the organisation's ability to identify and respond to changes in laws when enacted.
- Communicating the tax vision to the CEO, board, analysts, and throughout the enterprise.

Data Management & Analytics

Data management and analytics provides increased transparency into an organisation's data and provides the management of the organization with critical business-planning data. These tools can also reduce the amount of time the tax department spends collecting and manipulating source data for tax accounting and reporting purposes and allows for more time spent on critical analysis and high level reviews.

Tax authority record storage requirements create another set of risks for tax departments. These include notices of inadequate records, accuracy-related civil penalties, criminal penalties for wilful failure, and lack of evidence to support tax filing positions. The risks can be greater for companies that have implemented ERP systems that may not provide for automatic extraction of data in a format consistent with local tax authority record requirements.

With structured, centralised tax data management tax-related personnel and processes across the enterprise use common data residing in a central repository or user interface. This repository aggregates information from different sources into a meaningful management report or dashboard. In this way, the data used for tax purposes can be continually monitored and managed throughout the tax data life cycle. This approach provides the stability, scalability, and reduced risk that is often lacking and associated with interconnected spreadsheets.

Tax authorities are increasingly using data analytics to drive their tax enforcement efforts. Businesses that lack their own analytics capabilities are at a significant disadvantage. Tax data analytics can be used for compliance and to gain valuable insights into tax department performance and other tax-related activities across the enterprise for strategic business planning purposes.

Through tax analytics organisations can analyse data to identify patterns, uncover anomalies, and create value. Tax analytics can help an organisation perform tax benchmarking, trend analysis, and predictive analysis to gain deeper insights into tax processes and profiles using tax data tools to access and analyse all types of tax data, as well as management of the master tax data and automation of the manual integration between systems.

Analytics allows tax executives to change mind-set from "what I need to do" to "what I need to know," based on the premise that data is the foundation for tax and finance decisions. Technology is required to capture, store, and maintain the integrity of this data. Solid processes and policies enable the consistent and efficient use of data so it can be harnessed by the business.

The information and withholding process typically involves large amounts of data. There are numerous tools available that enable analysis of data from disparate sources, linking various data sets for a more complete picture and reconciling data for greater accuracy. In addition, they offer capabilities for customising numerous tests, based on the need to discover anomalies in data, such as payment and contract information. These tools can be customised for specific tasks and configured to e.g. analyse vendor data to review withholding and reporting compliance. These types of tools can help turn static information into data that can flow from one system to the next.

A tax IT roadmap for the future
The diagram below offers an example of an IT roadmap for the tax function that is thinking strategically and positioning itself well to deal with the current and future challenges of the record-to-report process. On the left are tax-aligned enterprise systems that extract, transform, and load data into a well-structured tax technology platform. In addition to the traditional tax compliance and provision software, there are new tools available to help tax functions manage workflow, including tax portals. These systems can be integrated to drive a very smooth reporting process.

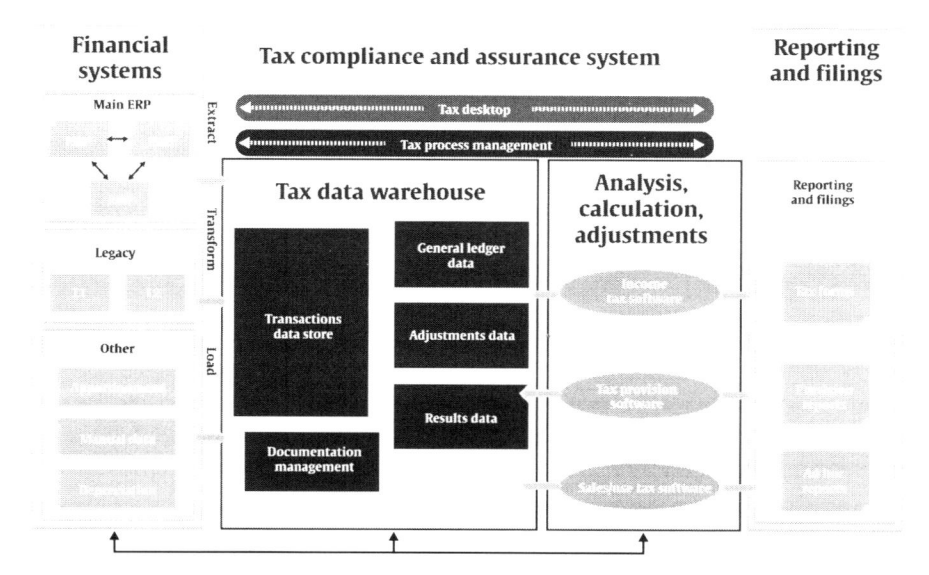

Leveraging data analytics
Today most organisations are "drowning" in data but need to be able to make sense of it in a short timeframe. Data analytics is a means of supplying decision makers with relevant data so that they can make more informed decisions. In practical terms, data analytics covers large populations of data rather than samples and draws data from

multiple systems and data sources, extracting useful information to provide objective, factual results. It is used to supplement or replace other procedures, such as observation, inquiry or sampling – in effect, improving our ability to identify trends, risks, and anomalies.

Several trends are driving new approaches to analytics. They emphasise a relentless demand for improved performance and more disciplined risk and information management. These include:
- Exponential growth in data volumes and technology capacity.
- Regulatory demands for deeper insight into risk, exposure, and public responsiveness.
- Remaining competitive and growing profitably which depends on meeting customers' needs.
- The complexity of new data sources, including e-mail, social media, or sensor-enabled facilities.
- The need to process unprecedented amounts of information in order to uncover hidden patterns that may otherwise go undetected.

How does tax fit into this environment? Companies must have a proactive audit defence, run efficient tax operations, produce accurate reporting and tax accruals, and be SOX compliant. Data analytics can help on all counts.

A practical approach to tax data analytics
Over the past two decades, companies have invested heavily in origination and servicing systems to streamline their processes. This has resulted in a significant increase in organised data, as well as a shift in focus toward analysing information to improve performance. The tax function mind-set is changing from "doing" to "knowing".

Advanced analytics enable tax to do things that operational reporting typically did not, including:
- Looking forward rather than back to predict rather than just understand.
- Discovering and simulating rather than "slicing and dicing".
- Modelling changes that could happen if facts change and circumstances change.
- Improving information rather than just analysing it.
- Using key performance predictors (KPPs) rather than just KPIs.

The exhibit illustrates how tax data analytics leverages "hidden" data. With indirect tax, most of the master data required comes from transactions owned by other processes. Interactive tax data analytics allows the tax executive, for example, to access all of the "hidden" data and apply predefined rules in order to detect potential risks or opportunities and test indirect tax calculations.

A Tax Operating Model 5.2.4

Example of tax data analytics approach

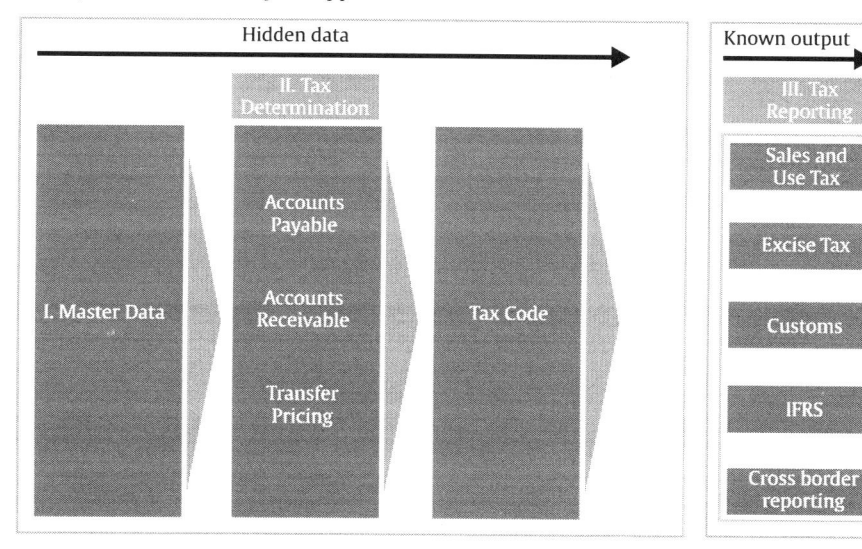

```
Hidden data →                           Known output →

                II. Tax                      III. Tax
             Determination                  Reporting

                                           Sales and
                                            Use Tax
              Accounts
              Payable                      Excise Tax

              Accounts
I. Master Data   Receivable   Tax Code     Customs

              Transfer
              Pricing                       IFRS

                                          Cross border
                                           reporting
```

Applying analytics to the overall process enables the extraction of data from the tax software database and automation of the analysis to determine whether the system is producing the results as designed based upon user inputs. After collecting and mapping data into the analytics tool, a tax analyst gets a high-level snapshot of possible coding errors – for example, incorrect, missing, or generic values – in a variety of data groupings, such as vendor, company code, and jurisdiction.

A data analysis and monitoring tool also allows tax departments to prepare for potential audits more effectively. In fact, continuous monitoring may help transform an indirect tax department from reactive audit defence to proactive error remediation. In addition, tax data analytics may help:
- Communicate to the business the benefit of correcting data errors.
- Reduce time spent on manual data analysis activities – often significantly.
- Remediate data entry errors proactively and prevent them from happening in the future.

There are many tools available to facilitate data collection. While it may be tempting to add applications to address specific data collection needs, it is better to increase the functionality of source systems already at the tax department's disposal that can be deployed on a large scale, consolidate data from diverse general ledger systems and locations, and provide tax-sensitised trial balance data.

Eliminating manual manipulation of data is one benefit of technology. To the extent data can be formatted and structured in a financial system, the greater the efficiency and mitigation of risk. Many provisioning systems perform this type of data transformation each time they import data from a financial system. In addition, they can automatically import data when it is available and/or allow users to import data on an as-needed or scheduled basis.

Internet-based tools can facilitate accurate data collection with simple, step-by-step data-gathering processes – providing workflow automation and other benefits. In addition, these tools produce real-time reports and often have document management capabilities that enable individuals, such as foreign controllers, to attach documents to complete the audit trail. Together, these capabilities may allow tax departments to replace foreign data collection packages.

Data collection leading practices
Understanding data requirements – those of the tax department and the enterprise as a whole – is the foundation for designing solutions that produce the information needed for tax calculations. Other data collection leading practices include:
- Using distributive technology such as portals and business management tools where possible.
- Using the same tool/functionality as corporate accounting.
- Using web-based technology that allows access to data any time, from any location.
- Confirming that users enter/import data only once.
- Automating imports of book/GAAP data and tying it to target balances.
- Calculating local country and currency, as well as HQ GAAP and provisions via multiple ledgers.

A tax function that is effective, efficient and transparent and which adds value to the business is well-placed to undergo the transformation to become a world class tax function.

5.3 Transformation

Transformation means making fundamental changes in how business is conducted in order to help cope with a shift in market environment by making employees more productive, processes more efficient while less costly, and the business as a whole more competitive.

Transformation for tax executives
Transformation has been a pervasive theme in the business world for many years, enabled by the emergence of enterprise resource planning (ERP) systems. Successful initiatives in areas such as manufacturing and supply chain, human resources, sales and marketing, customer relationship management, and, of course, finance and accounting show how the effective application of organisational design, process improvement, and enabling technology can improve efficiency and performance while driving value for the business.

While these significant transformations took place, the tax department was often relegated to the sidelines or completely overlooked as a "black box" of arcane rules and requirements. But when so many business stakeholders are demanding more from the tax function it's time for tax executives to change that paradigm: deep tax department involvement is essential. Tax executives need to be at the table, influencing enterprise-wide business decisions. Visionary tax leaders use transformation projects to significantly improve their own tax operations.

With a clear view of how the tax function's role can evolve and expand, and the commitment of the CFO and tax executives, something big can happen. The tax function can enhance operational efficiency at a global level and contribute significantly to decision-making across the business. Its operations can become more transparent to CFOs and other senior executives, from performance and risk management perspectives, in much the same way other business functions have become in the past decade or two. And, importantly, tax executives and other tax specialists – especially those willing to develop a broader understanding of the business and play leadership roles in the transformation – should be able to build eminence within the business and lay the foundation for career growth in the future as the business reaps the rewards of the transformation.

The path to tax department transformation is challenging, but tax experts are helping companies navigate the changes – both already seen and not yet visible. A Tax Function Assessment Framework is essential to helping tax executives deconstruct complex tax functions from record to report. Analysing a tax department's people, process, technology, and data elements, allows executives to assess, prioritise, and explore improvement opportunities. Practical benefits of a framework include process efficiencies, cost savings, and effective resource deployment. Strategic benefits include more time for adding value to the business and the data necessary for informed decision making.

Compared to other corporate departments the tax function has historically been slow to adopt technology and process management. Tax technology adoption lies on a continuum, with more advanced and integrated solutions increasing the value that tax can offer to the business:

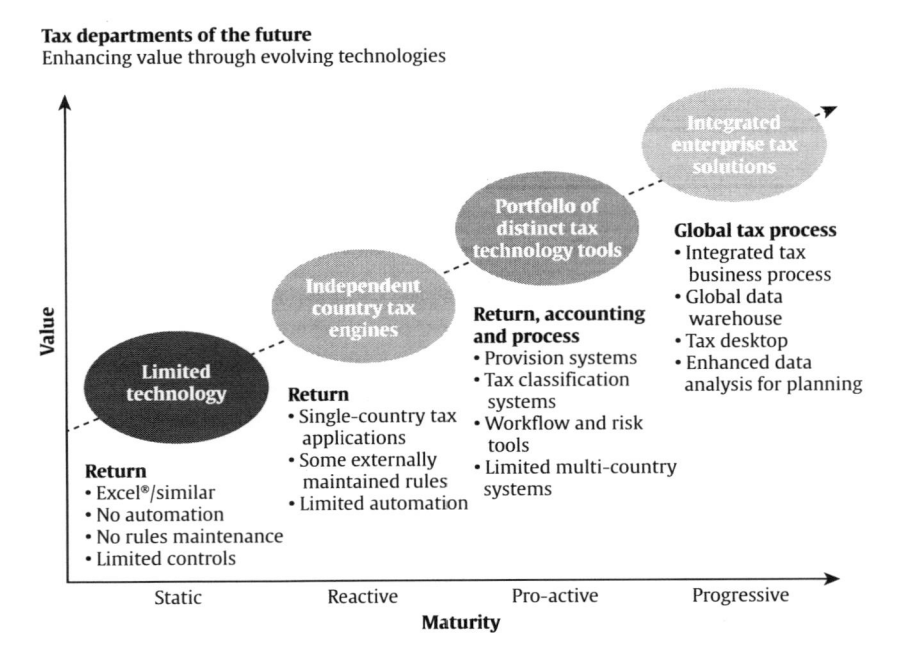

Tax departments of the future
Enhancing value through evolving technologies

A diagram plots Value (y-axis) against Maturity (x-axis: Static, Reactive, Pro-active, Progressive) showing five stages:

- **Limited technology** (Static)
  Return
  - Excel®/similar
  - No automation
  - No rules maintenance
  - Limited controls

- **Independent country tax engines** (Reactive)
  Return
  - Single-country tax applications
  - Some externally maintained rules
  - Limited automation

- **Portfolio of distinct tax technology tools** (Pro-active)
  Return, accounting and process
  - Provision systems
  - Tax classification systems
  - Workflow and risk tools
  - Limited multi-country systems

- **Integrated enterprise tax solutions** (Progressive)
  Global tax process
  - Integrated tax business process
  - Global data warehouse
  - Tax desktop
  - Enhanced data analysis for planning

Many tax departments fall toward the bottom left of the diagram above – in the "static" state with little or no automation and largely manual controls. Tax departments in the "reactive" state use single-country tax engines, which are more effective at addressing country-specific compliance issues but still offer little or no automation and interactivity with other tools. The "proactive" model emphasises use of tax-specific technologies, such as compliance and provision software. More often than not, though, these remain largely stand-alone systems with little or no interaction with other systems. On the right is the world class tax function with integrated processes and technologies, centralised data, and embedded controls, providing better visibility to management and consistent reporting and other outputs throughout the tax lifecycle.

To move from left to right tax departments should develop a solid foundation based on:
- People and organisation. Personnel have the right tools and training, clearly defined and communicated career paths, and operate under a common vision and strategy.
- Processes and policies. Processes are enabled by data and a comprehensive technology vision, facilitating cross-discipline interaction. Tax policies are aligned with the function's strategy.
- Technology and systems. Non-core tax activities are automated and planning decisions are embedded in the tax technology. Tax systems are integrated where appropriate.

- Data and information. Common data is captured, stored, and used across tax disciplines. The complicated challenge of tax-sensitised enterprise source data has been overcome.

Critical success factors for tax transformation from static to progressive
1. Joint ownership – by finance and tax of the business and technology effort
2. Clear goals – clarify cost reduction, control, and business value added goals, and their priority
3. Be pragmatic – set bold targets, but recognise organisations cannot change overnight
4. Visioning – time-limited visioning at the beginning helps set the scope for all subsequent activity
5. Embed change management – the approach to change must be tailored to the impacted parties
6. Data – effective solutions rely on understanding data flows, fragmentation and transformation
7. Run project as steady state – how the project runs sets post-transformation expectations.

The desired outcome of transformation is a high-performing tax department. A high-performing tax department spends less time and resources on tax compliance, planning, reporting, and risk management, thereby freeing time to deliver strategic support and more value to the broader organisation. Becoming a high-performing tax department is essential to sustainable transformation so the tax department is ready for anything.

Transformation driving change
Expanding the role of the Tax Function

Traditional Role

| The company's tax and finance profile | Planning
Reduce global tax burden & enhance cash flow | Reporting
Comply with reporting obligations | Managing
Operate within an appropriate risk framework |

Emerging Additional Expectations

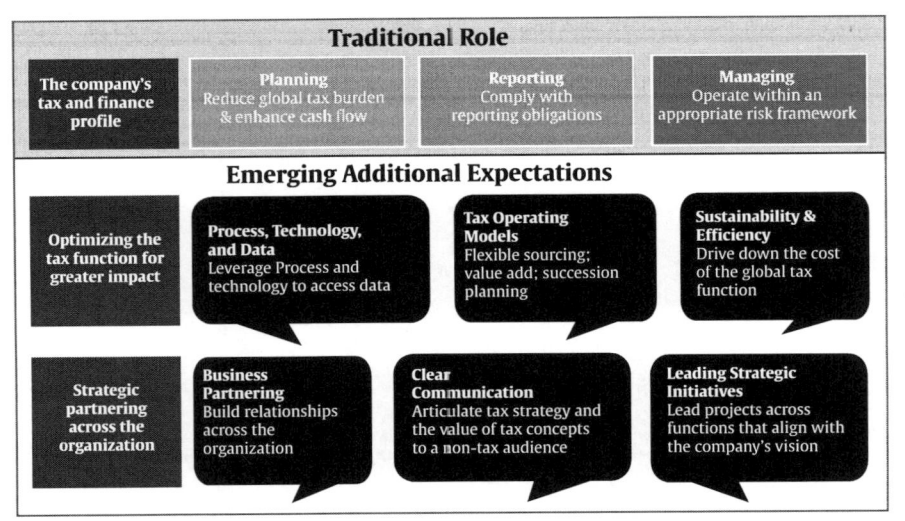

| Optimizing the tax function for greater impact | **Process, Technology, and Data**
Leverage Process and technology to access data | **Tax Operating Models**
Flexible sourcing; value add; succession planning | **Sustainability & Efficiency**
Drive down the cost of the global tax function |
| Strategic partnering across the organization | **Business Partnering**
Build relationships across the organization | **Clear Communication**
Articulate tax strategy and the value of tax concepts to a non-tax audience | **Leading Strategic Initiatives**
Lead projects across functions that align with the company's vision |

Expanding the role of the Tax Function
Enhancing the tax function for greater impact

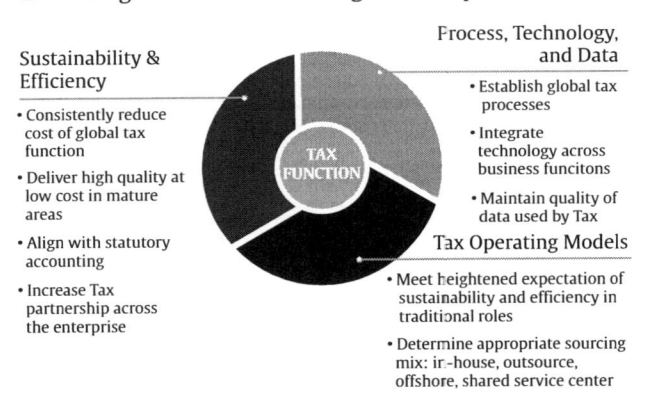

Sustainability & Efficiency
- Consistently reduce cost of global tax function
- Deliver high quality at low cost in mature areas
- Align with statutory accounting
- Increase Tax partnership across the enterprise

Process, Technology, and Data
- Establish global tax processes
- Integrate technology across business funcitons
- Maintain quality of data used by Tax

Tax Operating Models
- Meet heightened expectation of sustainability and efficiency in traditional roles
- Determine appropriate sourcing mix: in-house, outsource, offshore, shared service center

Expanding the role of the Tax Function
Strategic partnering across the organization

Business Partnering — Operating models and expanded responsibilities for Tax require close collaboration with every facet of the business

Clear Communication — Articulating a confident, concise and compelling value proposition for an integrated and well-funded Tax and risk management function

Leading Strategic Initiatives — When tax savings or risk management are important success factors, the Tax Executive is well positioned to lead

The three largest benefits of the tax function transformation as described above are generally considered to be:
- Enhanced business partnering across the organisation (ie greater alignment between the tax and finance departments)
- Enhanced ability to reach strategic and financial goals
- Sustainability and efficiency of the tax function through cost savings.

And the risks of a successful transformation taking place have been identified as:
- Inadequate funding
- Lack of buy-in from the department and stakeholders
- Competing priorities between business functions
- Lack of measurable return on investment
- Insufficient knowledge of and integration with the business.

Trends in tax transformation
Comprehensive transformation

Trends in tax transformation
Transformation defined by focus area

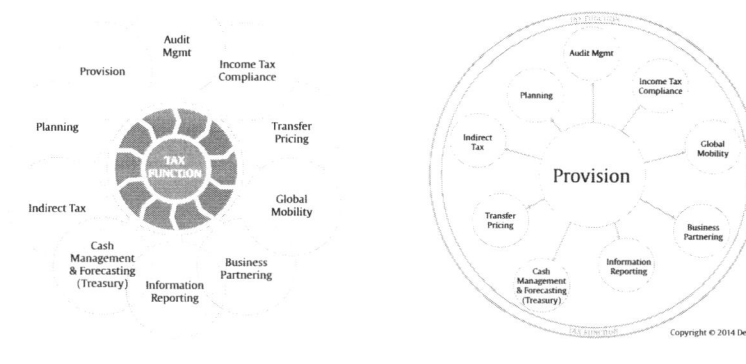

Copyright © 2014 Deloitte De

With comprehensive transformation the whole tax function is transformed, whereas transformation defined by focus area is more limited. Organisations might choose for a transformation by focus area instead of a comprehensive transformation because of (acute) internal pressure, changes in legislation, or budget constraints.

The right-hand graphic gives an example of transformation focused on Provision which affects areas such as audit management, income tax compliance, and information reporting.

Any transformation is enabled by People, Technology, Process and Data which impact value being driven into direct and indirect tax and provisioning as illustrated below.

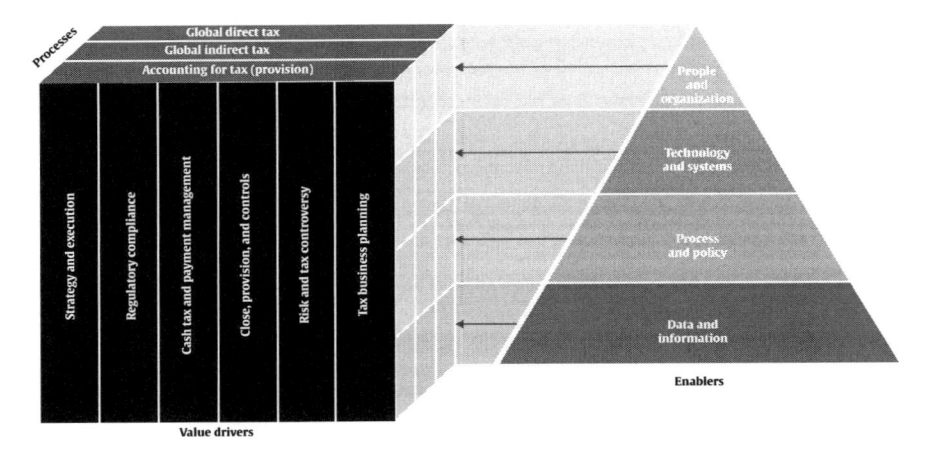

- People and organisation. A sophisticated tax function's personnel have the right tools and training. They have clearly defined and communicated career paths. They operate under a common vision and strategy.
- Technology and systems. A mature tax function has automated non-core tax activities and embedded planning decisions in its tax technology. Its tax systems are integrated where appropriate.
- Processes and policies. In a mature tax function, processes are enabled by data and a comprehensive technology vision, and they facilitate cross-discipline interaction. Tax policies are well aligned with the function's strategic intent.
- Data and information. The ability to capture, store, and use common data across tax disciplines is the foundation from which improvements are derived. The key to an effective data layer – tax-sensitised enterprise source data – sounds simple, but achieving it is among the most complicated challenges for tax functions today.

Tax function assessment framework
The strength of the enablers determines the amount of time available for tax staff to focus on important matters which utilise their skills rather than monitoring

deadlines. Enablers should include those within tax as well as those used by business partners, for example:
- Technology – Are you producing the right reports and data at the right level? Is your technology fully integrated within the tax function and with the stakeholder functions? Have you automated communications, performance, and risk management processes?
- Processes – Are your processes integrated across tax types and activities? Are you able to identify and address operational issues, and are you coordinating with stakeholders to define responsibilities for addressing them? Are your controls formally managed and enforced?
- Data – Are you getting the data you need in the right electronic format and at the right time?

People "get it done" by leveraging workload and enablers. To achieve its long term vision the tax function should have a core team with strong leadership, management, and communication skills, and with clear role definitions, succession plans, training plans, and performance measures.

Transformation places significant demands on finance and tax leaders. Taking a structured approach to the process helps smooth transition, identify issues as they arise, and capitalises on opportunities along the way. Important elements of such an approach include:

Planning
Align tax department and business objectives.
Understand the goals of the business and what it will look like in five years. Identify how the tax department can help the business achieve its objectives and set goals and direction accordingly. This aligns the tax department with the broader business and helps make the business case for investment and change.

Envision the future-state tax department.
With business and tax goals in view, consider the people, process, and technology strategy that the tax department will need, including: information and analysis the business should have; the likely scope of the regulatory landscape that will need to be addressed; and the skills and experience tax department professionals will need to address regulatory and business requirements. If business goals are transformative, the tax department's evolution will need to be as well.

Create a roadmap.
Understand current tax department capabilities, areas of underperformance, and tendency to focus on activities that are not strategic to the function and overall organisation to determine what it will take to reach the new vision. The transformation could take three to five years, so prioritise the initiatives and use early improvements in efficiency to fund or make the business case for future investment.

Execution

Enhance and streamline tax processes.
Create greater efficiency through technology-enabled processes – a key element of transformation is to free up tax professionals' time so they can address emerging needs and provide strategic value to the business. Early opportunities for process improvement should be those that involve multiple handoffs, long cycle times, support from multiple tools, and quality or risk issues.

Evaluate enabling tools and technologies.
No one-size-fits-all technology solutions exist, so consider tools that are compatible with existing ERP platforms and other vital business systems to facilitate integration with minimal enhancement. Analysing data will be just as important as reporting on it, so look for systems and tools that provide broad analytics capabilities, from identifying data anomalies to modelling various planning scenarios.

Design new organisational models.
Explore the roles, responsibilities, and skills the tax department might need to support the vision. Besides tax and accounting backgrounds, consider other types of experience that can support business collaboration and teaming, including project management, technologists, mathematics (e.g. decision sciences), and finance. This exercise can identify training needs for existing tax personnel who might take on new roles, as well as a recruiting effort to locate external resources, if needed.

Communication

Measure results.
Formalise the strategy by developing an effective set of key performance indicators. It takes time and resources to track progress, measure and communicate results but it is an important step. Helping the management of the organization understand the transformation journey and the impact it is having will create better transparency and leadership alignment, and build continued support and confidence.

Support the change.
The changes implemented will be new to the tax department, and the rest of the business. Dedicate time to creating a plan that generates awareness inside and outside the tax department of the vision and new capabilities the department can offer. Within the tax department, set clear expectations and align performance management systems as needed.

The following sections explore the contribution that the key enablers make to the transformation process.

5.3.1 Data and Information

In a world class tax function enterprise source data is tax-aligned, common data is used by tax disciplines and data is transparent through to the transaction level including adjustments made during close processes.

ERPs and tax data management: High-level plan

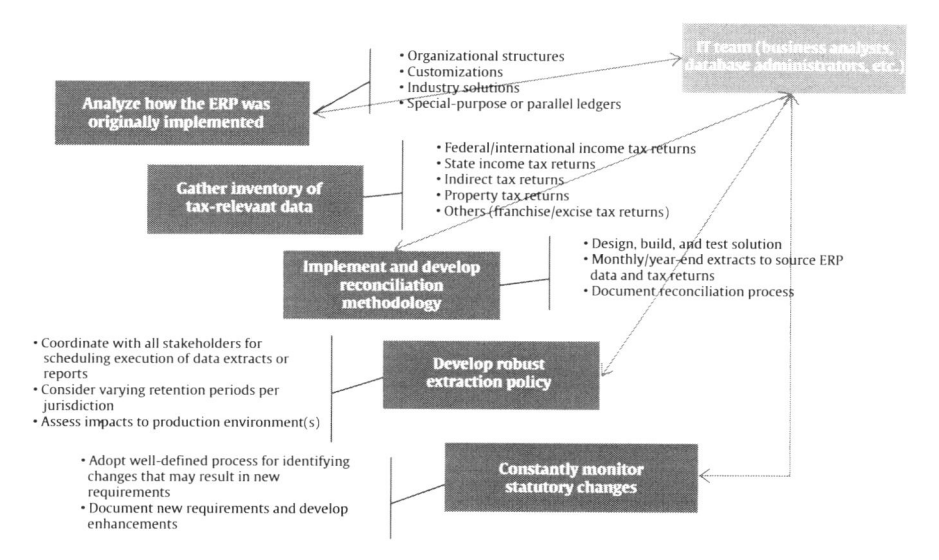

[Diagram: Flowchart showing the following boxes and annotations]

- **Analyze how the ERP was originally implemented**
  - Organizational structures
  - Customizations
  - Industry solutions
  - Special-purpose or parallel ledgers
  - → **IT team (business analysts, database administrators, etc.)**

- **Gather inventory of tax-relevant data**
  - Federal/international income tax returns
  - State income tax returns
  - Indirect tax returns
  - Property tax returns
  - Others (franchise/excise tax returns)

- **Implement and develop reconciliation methodology**
  - Design, build, and test solution
  - Monthly/year-end extracts to source ERP data and tax returns
  - Document reconciliation process

- **Develop robust extraction policy**
  - Coordinate with all stakeholders for scheduling execution of data extracts or reports
  - Consider varying retention periods per jurisdiction
  - Assess impacts to production environment(s)

- **Constantly monitor statutory changes**
  - Adopt well-defined process for identifying changes that may result in new requirements
  - Document new requirements and develop enhancements

"Garbage in, garbage out" is as true for tax as other data. Many tax leaders cite data collection and processes for extracting information from ERP systems and converting it into a legal entity format that the tax function requires, as one of their biggest challenges. Without the right data in the right format, everything else – technology, processes, and people – cannot perform as expected.

Blueprinting: Improving and accelerating data collection
"Blueprinting" maps out a strategy for improved data collection which gathers tax department requirements, finds and brings together common data attributes, and accelerates data collection.

Blueprinting is a specific part of technology solution design. It produces a list of detailed data requirements and describes how each tax data requirement will be enabled or designed into a technology or process solution. In addition, blueprinting aids development teams, providing implementers with a possible high-level working solution that involves a change in business process, configuration, or master data. It also spells out reporting and/or extract requirements and provides a detailed analysis and clear definition of tax business requirements at a data element level that the implementation team can use to configure the new system. Finally, it identifies which tax business processes must be redesigned and automated using new system functionality.

Data integration and analytics
Many companies have already tax-aligned their enterprise source data from their ERP systems and other business software, configuring those systems so the source data is "tax-sensitised", managing the master tax data and automating manual integration between systems. With structured centralised tax data management, tax-related personnel and processes across the enterprise use common data residing in a central repository or user interface, aggregating information from different sources into a meaningful management report or dashboard. In this way, the data used for tax purposes can be continually monitored and managed throughout the tax data life cycle. In addition, the data can provide key metrics and analytics used to manage the operations of the tax department and to identify cash savings.

Data collection
A perennial struggle for tax professionals is the collection of tax data. Typically obtained from a multitude of sources and in a variety of formats, tax data collection is often a manual, time-consuming, and potentially error-prone process. It also can be difficult to manage, track, and validate tax-sensitive information. World class tax functions develop and implement tools for the timely collection, consolidation, and validation of tax data in an automated and controlled fashion.

Data and information
When a company implements an ERP system, consolidation tool, planning tool or tax software, the inherent complexity of today's tax requirements requires careful planning and integration of multiple systems across multiple corporate functions. The factors that need to be considered with regard to the complexity of the tax data to be captured and maintained by these systems include:
- the jurisdiction imposing the tax;
- the basis for the tax (profits, transactions, etc.);
- components of the tax base;
- dependencies amongst multiple systems; and
- reporting requirements.

Tax calculations and subsequent reporting generally rely on data generated outside the tax function. The tax department does not control the source data required to comply with the tax laws and regulations. In addition, employees across all facets of the business are unknowingly driving tax decisions. The risk of the tax function not "owning" the data can be managed if, during any system implementation, the tax department works with IT and stakeholders to enable efficient tax data collection by identifying the detailed tax data requirements and by designing and building an ERP approach to capture those requirements.

Operational data archiving versus tax record retention
Archiving is the process of moving data from a "live" system or database to another storage medium. Companies archive data for a variety of reasons, but most commonly to enhance system performance. Archiving can also ease system management by reducing maintenance frequency.

Data archiving typically involves only business-complete transactions, which can present issues with reconciliation, and the data may not be easily accessed once archived. Although there are some standard ERP retrieval tools that enable access to archived data, users in many environments may still require assistance from the IT department to access the data they need for audit support.

Tax record retention for financial data relies on a completely different concept. Unlike archiving, it doesn't take data out of the production database; rather, it is the process of extracting an exact copy of the tax-relevant financial information from the ERP to meet statutory and regulatory tax record retention requirements.

A tax record retention solution should be implemented before archiving to make sure the taxpayer has reconciled transactional data readily available to support audits and that the organisation does not have to waste time searching for and reconciling archived (and potentially incomplete) data once tax authorities issue information requests. Once that tax record retention solution is in place, it is important to monitor any tax-relevant changes made to the ERP system, such as new fields or new tables, because those ERP changes may result in necessary modifications to the extract solution.

5.3.2 Process and Policy

The prevalence of silo-based tax mega-processes has already been described. The big challenge is taking these silos and turning them so that they lend themselves to multiple uses and reuses – that is, sharing of data across multiple processes. Tax operations can then be viewed as a lifecycle with standardised processes, shared data, and the tools to deliver an integrated view of tax reporting.

Process
In a mature tax function, processes are enabled by data and a comprehensive technology vision, and they facilitate cross-discipline interaction. Tax policies are well aligned with the function's strategic intent. In the future state tax process:
- Processes are standardised across tax functions.
- Processes and data are integrated in the tax function and with the accounting/finance functions.
- Processes are automated where appropriate.
- Documentation is effective and managed for easy access.
- Knowledge is captured and leveraged.
- Tax processes are enabled by data and technology vision.
- Tax processes facilitate cross-discipline interaction.
- Tax policies align with organisational strategy and goals.

Global integration
Many tax departments have worked hard to locally integrate their data, processes, technology, and personnel with those of the finance function and other corporate and

business unit functional areas. But globalisation requires new – and more extensive – integration efforts across disparate and geographically dispersed business units. This is easier said than done, as offshore business units are not usually under the direct control of the HQ executives driving these integration initiatives. In addition, complexities and frequent changes in accounting methods and tax types make it more difficult to achieve global integration at the granular data element or tax process levels. To make progress in this area, it is important to accomplish first standardisation and integration at a higher level. Steps such as developing a global standard controller's manual and chart of accounts, conducting training on specific topics, and holding pre- and post-close meetings with accounting staff are all effective ways to initiate integration across geographies.

Reviewing process and policy

Tax departments are challenged to customise processes and controls that meet many different tax compliance and reporting objectives while adding value to the organisation. When reviewing tax processes and policies for improvement, tax functions should consider:
- compliance with corporate policy on process controls, SOX and documentation requirements;
- management of time required to meet accelerated reporting requirements and to avoid delaying the financial close process;
- integration with financial systems and an enhanced tax-sensitive chart of accounts;
- enhancement of the financial reporting consolidation systems to leverage consolidation and data collection tools;
- management of risk by reducing reliance on spreadsheets to support tax compliance and financial reporting processes;
- deployment to operating units of consistent pre-populated audit-ready work papers to streamline data collection;
- management of risk and control points using a single system and database for tax compliance, provision, estimates, forecasting and planning;
- expansion of tax work papers to include both current activity and balance sheet validation;
- execution of tax planning and other activities to add value to the organisation;
- management of the time and effort needed to complete compliance activities while increasing the quality, accuracy and accountability of information;
- delivery of quality tax advice and tax planning in a fast-paced, global environment; and
- communication, collaboration and coordination across the tax and financial reporting functions.

Taking these issues into account both helps manage operational risks associated with tax reporting and compliance, and can help tax executives to become strategic partners to the business.

A Tax Operating Model 5.3.3

Issues
What business problem are you trying to solve?

Applied Analytics

Data Management

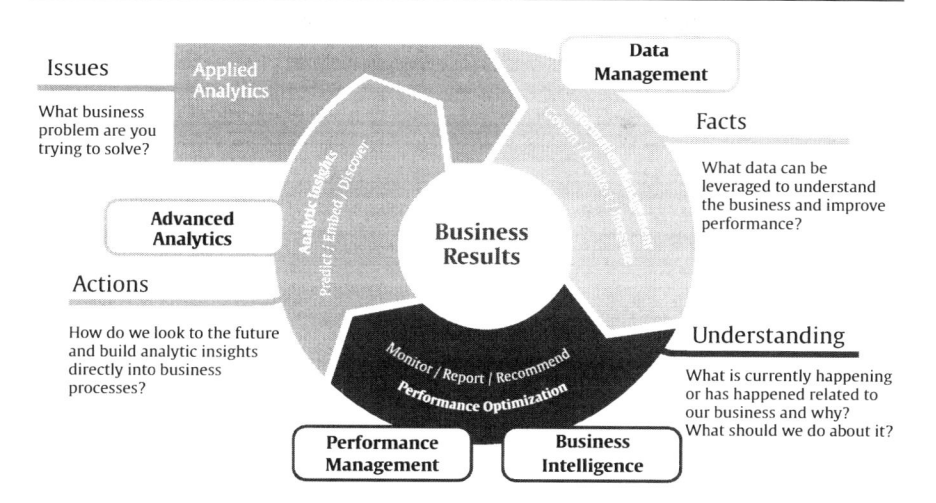

Facts
What data can be leveraged to understand the business and improve performance?

Advanced Analytics

Business Results

Actions
How do we look to the future and build analytic insights directly into business processes?

Understanding
What is currently happening or has happened related to our business and why? What should we do about it?

Performance Management

Business Intelligence

Many organisations are mapping their end-to-end processes and the systems that support them. Such process maps should highlight the volume and value of transactions flowing through different elements of the process and key interfaces between different processes and systems. These exercises help businesses identify areas of key tax risk and how they are currently controlled. Documentation of the process is particularly important where tax activities are undertaken by non-tax specialists, either because the activity is diffused throughout the organisation (as is frequently the case with indirect tax reporting) or has been moved into a shared services environment.

Maintaining the quality of tax compliance in these circumstances is paramount and less reliance can be placed on the informal understanding of a closely knit tax team as perhaps was the case in the past. Tax authorities are often keen to carry out this kind of work to build their understanding of large corporate processes and systems, and this is particularly true where they see tax compliance activities moving into shared services centres. As a rule, many companies are uncomfortable providing this kind of access to tax authorities in the absence of a formal enquiry and so would rather share their own documentation to provide the necessary assurance.

Organisations which can convince their stakeholders (including tax authorities) that their tax systems and processes are robust will be able to communicate their tax risk more confidently, and will be better placed to cope in a constantly changing regulatory and risk environment through greater certainty, improved efficiencies and a stronger basis to defend tax planning and reporting.

5.3.3 *Technology and Systems*

Leveraging technology
New technology tools can help companies enhance global governance by improving areas such as document and knowledge management, data management and storage, communication, resource planning, workflow, and quality controls. A common tax

desktop can provide authorised users with instant access to information and data, and enable them to take actions without having to understand the detailed procedures on how to compile information or transfer it to the correct computer applications for processing. This can be a significant benefit for individuals who have to manage or govern globally.

Innovative approaches are evolving to automate tax calculations ranging from R&D credit calculations and tax provision computations to transfer pricing analysis, compliance activities, and technology-enabled tax basis balance sheet assessment, development, and reporting.

Successful implementation and use of these tools requires sustained focus by a champion with the commitment, authority, and time to guide the project. Keeping this focus means correctly prioritising the project in the minds of all stakeholders, establishing a common understanding of importance and expected benefits, and being clear on the interdependence of roles and responsibilities. Typical activities include:

Process mapping and redesign: prior to any changes in ERP or tax technology, review existing compliance, planning, and tax accounting processes to identify a more efficient and value-driven future state set of processes.

Software selection and implementation: decide which provision and compliance software may best fit the organisation's objectives and requirements, implementing new systems, or re-implementing ones that were installed inadequately or that are not performing in accordance with expectations.

Tax-efficient implementation: assess, research, and implement opportunities for potential tax savings directly and indirectly related to the ERP and tax technology implementation, including tax credits and deductions, training incentives, transfer pricing, VAT, and other savings opportunities.

Data identification: this is the process of identifying data specifications via interviews, analyzing existing data structures and preparing documentation with the end-result of having applications information that answers data questions such as how departments use data. For taxes this is the identification, documentation and communication of ERP data requirements for a wide range of taxes for example direct and indirect taxes; tax depreciation, property, payroll taxes; and transfer pricing.

Data interfaces: developing interface requirements that can dramatically decrease a tax department's need to manipulate data used by tax, and define the conversion requirements for tax data so legacy-based tax information is properly loaded and maintained in the legacy systems.

Configuration: incorporating tax and legal-entity reporting needs into ERP and tax technologies through configuration while managing the impact on underlying business processes.

A Tax Operating Model 5.3.3

Enhancing value through evolving technologies

The tax function's adoption and use of technology is evolving from a static environment with almost no automation, limited controls, and no real rules maintenance to a very progressive environment with processes that are highly integrated into the overall business. Most tax functions today fall somewhere in the middle.

A world class tax function will develop highly integrated processes that break down silos in favour of an integrated "lifecycle" approach that:
- Includes a high degree of integration between tax accounting and tax compliance.
- Uses tax-sensitised data for multiple purposes.
- Leverages technology-enabled processes and standardised work papers across all legal entities.

Various forces are converging to move tax operations in this direction. The most significant are the increasing sophistication of technology and governments requiring electronic data submission.

A world class tax function from a technology perspective

Data from the core financial systems and consolidation tools feeds the central components of the tax technology solution, a data store, and an integrated calculation engine. Above this are the central process management tools, including workflow engines, document management tools, dashboards, and tax portals. On the right are the outputs: consistent, accurate reporting and filings.

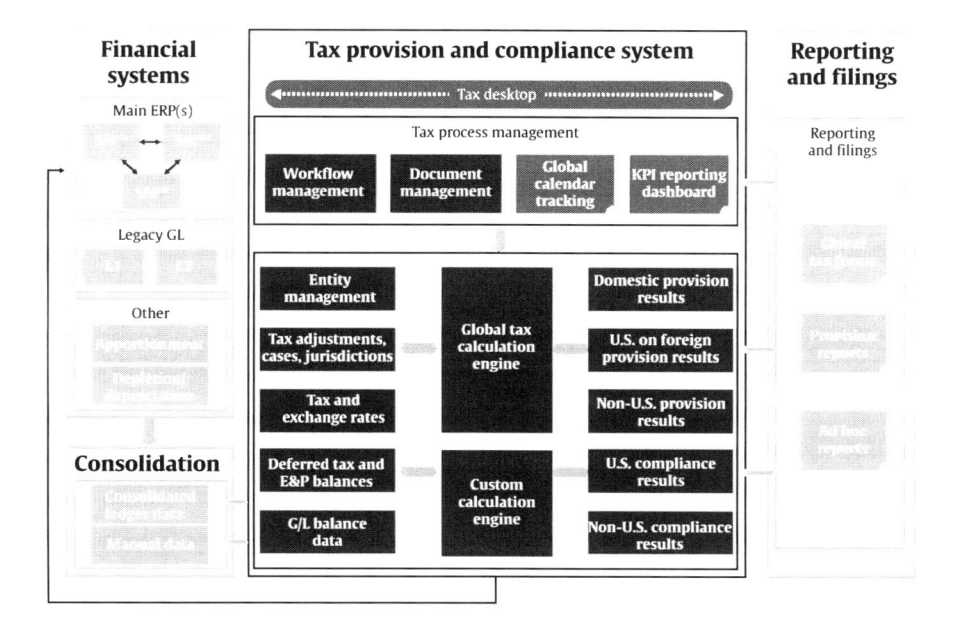

Available technology
There are three primary categories of available technologies: tax point solutions, stand-alone solutions, and enterprise-level solutions. Tax point solutions provide a good starting point; for some users, they may serve as a longer-term solution. These products typically have "manual" workflows, so individuals still have to check off tasks to indicate process status. They also offer document management capabilities, as well as a "tax-friendly" user interface. Standalone solutions on the other hand typically address particular capabilities and can plug into just about any environment. Some products are closely associated with an organisation's ERP, are typically used for substantial organisational workflows and may or may not be able to extend into the tax function depending on configuration and organisational willingness.

These technologies have expanded the possibilities for integrating the tax function across processes. They are more tax-friendly, intuitive, and business-oriented than past solutions. Many organisations use these tools to manage complex processes with accompanying internal know-how.

A tax department that embraces new technologies and fully utilises their capabilities is on the way to being a world class tax function and playing a more strategic role in the enterprise.

Tax technology
Many tax systems are available to assist corporations in complying with global tax provision and compliance obligations. Both technology and processes have matured over time. Historically, many tax systems were maintained in spreadsheets and related documentation. As organisations gain access to better data and financial systems interfaces, it is easier to implement technology to enable the management of tax risk from an operational and strategic perspective.

Tax Technology Landscape

Company systems installed on company hardware to collate the transactions as they occur:
- **Business Systems** are the basic nominal general ledger (GL) system, but can be adapted to produce tax data efficiently.
- **Transaction Data Storage** stores data which drives the financial systems. In some countries there is a requirement to keep records of compliance with more than one accounting standard and these tools are used for this purpose.
- **Tax Determination** software can extract data as required to meet indirect tax requirements or to control mark-ups on intercompany transactions to ensure compliance with tax policies.
- **Global Provisioning** tools are used to take data from financial systems and produce current tax and deferred tax numbers at both company and group level and, where necessary, adjust local numbers to meet different accounting standards at group reporting level.

Add-on tools which can be either integrated or used stand-alone for return or information filing:
- **Tax Return** systems deal with corporate tax and, in some countries, VAT.
- **Accounts Production** software takes GL figures and produces hard copy, iXBRL or XBRL tagged accounts. These can be integrated with financial systems or stand-alone.
- **Disclosure Management** generates reports from software systems in whatever format is required. These tools are used to produce consolidated accounts, but could also be used to generate any standard report required by tax authorities.
- **Master Data Management** automatically standardises master data and links source data to specific outputs without the need for any manual intervention.

Tools used to interrogate data systems for audit or tax planning purposes:
- **Transfer Pricing** software assesses transfer pricing parameters and assists in the production of transfer pricing documentation.
- **Tax Audit Management** software keeps a central record of tax audit / investigations into individual company tax positions.
- **Record Retention** systems search records and delete ones outside a retention period.
- **Scenario Planning** software plots profits, interest, royalties etc. and tax payable on a company and country basis and assesses if changing location will affect the tax position.

Knowledge sharing and retention software:
- **Document management and storage** is the central repository for electronic data.
- **Data analytics** software are interrogation tools which can be used defensively to find non-tax compliant irregularities or to obtain "sound" data to enable tax decisions.
- **Knowledge systems** are third party tax technical resources.
- **Process Management** systems are used for the management of the tax process.
- **Portals** are used as a common access point to disparate underlying systems.

5.3.4 People and Organisation

Whilst technology has an important role to play, a team with the right combination of skills is fundamental to successfully transforming the tax function to a world class operation.

As many organizations have discovered in change initiatives, transformation is often complex, and it's almost always difficult. from a technology standpoint alone, challenges can arise in implementing tax functionality akin to those that plagued ERP implementations, such as unclear requirements, unrealistic expectations, user adoption issues, and hidden costs and delays.

Finance and tax leaders could encounter a belief within their organizations, and perhaps their own minds, that tax technology is a "silver bullet" that will solve many issues. But realizing the benefits of transformation will most likely require process and organizational redesign, as well as technology implementation and even culture change.

These diverse elements will demand more than tax or technology experience alone to translate new requirements into defined roles, responsibilities, processes, workflow, and governance and controls. A tax transformation team will need to possess a combination of skills:

- Industry and business-specific knowledge so tax transformation aligns with broader finance function and enterprise objectives.
- Tax technical expertise to devise new ways of gathering, analyzing, and using tax information.
- ERP and tax technology experience for tying together the other elements through the underlying data and systems.
- Change management skills to encourage adoption of changes resulting from the transformation, guide and support necessary training to support adoption, and effectively communicate throughout the transition period.
- A team with this combination of skills = Successful Transformation

In the context of this type of cross-functional team, technologists certainly will be instrumental in configuring systems, developing interfaces, and connecting tax applications to the broader enterprise systems. But tax-technical specialists will be vital for verifying that relevant, accurate tax information is being collected and used appropriately across the dimensions of tax planning, compliance, reporting, and analytics.

A world class tax function is viewed as a strategic partner in the enterprise operating under a common vision and strategy. Its personnel are equipped with leading tools and training and career paths are clearly defined and communicated.

Tax leaders, people and organisation

By looking at a tax organisation broadly and focusing on how each professional does their work, use of available tools and the quality of the data they access fosters a risk intelligent tax organisation. Areas of tax leadership focus should include:

- An operating model that properly balances workload among corporate and business unit financial reporting departments, internal tax resources and strategic business partners.
- An organisational model that provides for productivity, quality and value with the ability to scale rapidly as the business changes.
- Employing the right number of people, with the right skills, focused on the right work and giving them clear goals, roles and training.
- Locating staff in the right places to support tax and business processes.
- Avoiding knowledge being concentrated in one person through documentation and training.
- Managing operations and communicating issues within the tax function and with other stakeholders.

Forward-thinking tax leaders are designing their departments to evolve continuously and at the proper pace to sustain performance and reduce the disruption of sudden dramatic change. Keys to success in this effort include:

- Looking broadly across tax and corporate operations that may affect tax performance.
- Linking with ongoing corporate initiatives involving structure, product mix, and customers and suppliers; upcoming information technology projects; and/or the use of shared services, offshoring, or centres of excellence.
- Building in the ability to adjust staffing models to changing realities.

- Attracting, growing, utilising, and retaining good people, especially in core positions.

People are the ones who "get it done" by leveraging workload and enablers. The tax function should have a strong core team, composed of positions critical to achieving its vision over the long term – a team with strong leadership, management, and communication skills, and with clear role definitions, succession plans, training plans, and performance measures. Other considerations for building a strong resource team include:
- Work environment and location.
- Balanced workload.
- Scalable organisational model.
- Clear goals, roles, training, and succession plans.
- Documentation and cross-training.
- Short-term skill set backup and long-term succession planning.

Finally, one of the most common perception issues cited by non-tax stakeholders is that tax professionals are not good business partners or communicators. This can be due to anything from the ability to simplify and translate complex topics into "business language" to mutual understanding and appreciation of schedules. Effectively, business partnering is the key to managing performance expectations. It relies on a carefully conceived communication plan that is tailored to each business partner; for example, how and when you partner with a business unit leader will be different than your partnership approach for the CFO.

5.4 Conclusion

Ultimately, a world class tax function produces results in four areas: effectiveness, efficiency, transparency, and added value. The table below summarises benefits in each of these areas, with particular areas of importance highlighted in bold. The table can be used as a diagnostic to assess areas in which a business's tax function is world class and areas in which work is needed to bring it to that level.

World class tax functions are:

Effective	Efficient	Transparent	Value adding
Responsibilities require tax core competencies	Processes are standardised across tax functions	**Roles and responsibilities are understood by all in the tax function**	Tax function goals are aligned with corporate and business function goals
Resources are focused on critical, relevant tasks	Processes and data are integrated in the tax function and with the accounting/finance functions	Tax risks are widely understood so they can be managed	**Tax planning is part of strategic business discussions and balances opportunities and risks**
Organisation is designed to handle change	Processes are automated where appropriate	**Communication is at the heart of tax risk management**	Tax provides on-site support to business units for tactical and strategic issues
Workforce numbers and skills are balanced	Documentation is effective and managed for easy access	Tax executives have a seat at the decision-making table	Business leaders are aware of tax positions and compliance risks
Workload is distributed to appropriate skill levels	Knowledge is captured and leveraged	**Tax understands and is privy to business decisions with a tax implication**	Tax "value" is defined with business leaders using common and agreed-upon metrics
Performance measures are tied to goals and are monitored	**Workflow is managed to prevent surprises**	Tax function goals are articulated and measured	**Tax processes are documented with appropriate controls**

Your world class tax function, harnesses people and organization, using their expertise to leverage technology and systems to best effect, so that robust and reliable data can reflect the group's tax policy and processes. These are the fundamental building blocks which together enable a tax function which is effective, efficient and transparent and which consequently adds value to the group and its stakeholders.

This publication contains general information only and Deloitte -meaning any member firm of Deloitte Touche Tohmatsu Limited, a UK private company limited by guarantee and its respective subsidiaries and affiliates, their predecessors, successors and assignees, all partners, associate partners, principles, members, owners, directors, employees-, is not, by means of this publication, rendering accounting, business, financial, investment, legal, tax, or other professional advice or services. This publication is not a substitute for such professional advice or services, nor should it be used as a basis for any decision or action that may affect your business. Before making any decision or taking any action that may affect your business, you should consult a qualified professional advisor. Deloitte, its affiliates and related entities, shall not be responsible for any loss sustained by any person who relies on this publication.

Copyright © 2015 Deloitte. All rights reserved.

ROBBERT VELDHUIZEN

6. Cooperative compliance: large businesses and compliance management

6.1 Introduction

6.1.1 New Governance and Cooperative Compliance

Worldwide, governments and regulators are restructuring, developing and implementing regulatory models with the objective to be more effective. *'Supervisory capacity in the broadest sense, including that of external auditors, to detect non-compliance is limited and often not timely'.*[1] Revenue bodies are facing a big challenge to oversee and monitor a still growing population of taxpayers while on-going budget cuts affect their capacity. Next to limited resources, citizens, companies and NGOs frequently criticise the performance of government, regulators and also tax administrations. Finally, societies are dynamic and consequently the requirements for government and government agencies change over time. Revenue bodies must respond to the changing environment and be as proactive as possible and are forced to make choices in allocating limited resources. These dynamics lead to new enforcement and compliance strategies.

Happé describes this changing environment for, and the response of, the Netherlands Tax and Customs Administration (NTCA)[2] Until the end of the 1980s the NTCA tried to maintain a 100% Philosophy - meaning that all filed tax returns were assessed. In the 1990s, due to economic growth, the population of taxpayers in the Netherlands grew significantly and so the NTCA needed a tool to allocate the capacity and implemented a Risk Management approach. The idea was to identify the high-risk taxpayers where tax inspectors were needed to enforce the law. In the beginning of the new century the NTCA developed a compliance strategy referred to as Horizontal Monitoring (HM). The basic idea of HM is to identify the low risk taxpayers, those who are willing and able to be compliant with tax law and regulations. The NTCA concludes covenants with these taxpayers with the objective of encouraging and fostering their internal

---

[1] Power, M. (2007). *Organized Uncertainty, Designing a world of risk management*. New York: Oxford University Press, p. 40.
[2] Happé, R.H. (2008). Multinationals, Enforcement Covenants and Fair Share. In: Freedman, J. (ed.), *Beyond Boundaries, Developing Approaches to Tax Avoidance and Tax Risk Management*. Oxford University, Centre for Business Taxation, p. 162, see also chapter 4.2 and 4.3.

compliance motivations. In the covenant, the taxpayer and the NTCA agree to collaborate based on trust, mutual understanding and transparency. The covenant also reinforces the responsibility of the taxpayer for his own compliance. So from the perspective of risk, the main difference between the risk management programme and the horizontal monitoring programme is that the NTCA, identifies the low-risk taxpayers who are co-operative and transparent. These low-risk taxpayers need less attention and so the resources can be deployed for taxpayers who are not co-operative and transparent.

Ford and Condon describe approaches like this as New Governance.[3] In the literature, they argue, there is broad agreement on several elements central to new regulatory approaches:
a) a more collaborative relationship between the state and regulated entities;
b) placing responsibility on organisations for their own compliance and fostering or engaging authentic compliance-supporting internal motivations;
c) giving regulated entities greater autonomy to design their own internal processes to meet broadly defined outcomes;
d) problem solving and experimenting (learning by doing).

Revenue bodies around the world are re-thinking and re-inventing their enforcement strategy in order to become more effective unless decreasing capacity. Reports on studies of the Forum on Tax Administration (FTA) of the Organisation of Economic Development and Cooperation (OECD) give some insight on these developments and can be related to the elements of new governance as recognised by Ford and Condon. When it comes to *(a) a more collaborative relationship between the state and regulated entities* the 2008 FTA report the '*Study into the Role of Tax Intermediaries*' is a good example.[4] Based on this report, the FTA encourages revenue bodies to establish a relationship with large taxpayers based on trust and co-operation to fight aggressive tax planning - the so-called 'enhanced relationship'. The report discusses which strategies revenue bodies can follow to prevent and fight aggressive tax planning. The FTA states all revenue bodies need robust strategies in this area. The analysis in the report is as follows.[5]

'*As advisers, tax intermediaries play a vital role in all tax systems, helping taxpayers understand and comply with their tax obligations in an increasingly complex world. But some of them are also designers and promoters of aggressive tax planning, a role that has a negative impact on tax systems.*'

'*Tax intermediaries represent the supply side of aggressive tax planning, but large corporate taxpayers, tax intermediaries' clients, set their own strategies for tax-risk*

---

3 Ford, C. & Condon, M. (2011). Introduction to 'New Governance and the Business Organization', *Law & Policy*, Volume 33, Issue 4, October 2011, p. 450.
4 Organization for Economic Co-operation and Development (OECD) (2008a). *Study into the role of tax intermediaries*. Fourth meeting of the OECD forum on tax administration, 10-11 January 2008, South Africa. http://www.oecd.org/dataoecd/28/34/39882938.pdf
5 OECD (2008a). *Supra* note 4, p. 5.

management and determine their own appetites for tax risk. They are the ones who decide whether to adopt particular planning opportunities. Taxpayers represent the demand side of aggressive tax planning.'

The report 'therefore considers the tripartite relationship between revenue bodies, taxpayers and tax intermediaries' and concludes 'that there is significant scope to influence the demand side – at least in relation to large corporate taxpayers.'

The conclusions and recommendations in the report were discussed during the fourth meeting of the FTA in Cape Town in 2008 and confirmed in The Cape Town Communiqué.[6] This study was followed by the report 'Co-operative Compliance: A Framework' in 2013.[7] Next to element (a) *a more collaborative relationship*, this report takes the elements (b) *placing responsibility on organisations for their own compliance and fostering or engaging authentic compliance-supporting internal motivations* and (c) *giving regulated entities greater autonomy to design their own internal processes to meet broadly defined outcomes* into account.

In the report *cooperative compliance* is characterised as 'Transparency in exchange for certainty'.[8] This '*cannot exist without the disclosure of tax risks and the underlying frameworks provide assurance that these risks surface*'.[9] With *the underlying frameworks*, the report refers to the risk management and internal control frameworks that large taxpayers do have in place in order to control their business in the broadest sense. The report suggests these frameworks can be used to improve tax risk management and internal control. '*Corporate boards should adopt tax risk management strategies to ensure that the financial, regulatory and reputational risks are fully identified and evaluated. The commitment of business to co-operate, to be transparent and to be tax compliant should be reflected in its risk management systems, structures and policies.*'[10]

The suggestion that risk management and internal control frameworks can be helpful in the compliance strategies of regulators is an important element in new governance. It reveals the belief that private actors, like taxpayers, can be 'moralised', 'responsibilised' or 'socialised' *by requiring them to implement internal compliance systems.*[11] This goes together with the belief that the results of these compliance management systems can be re-used by the tax administration to help them to aim their limited

---

6   Organization for Economic Co-operation and Development (OECD) (2008b). *Cape Town communiqué*. Fourth meeting of the OECD forum on tax administration, 10-11 January 2008, South Africa. http://www.oecd.org/dataoecd/26/43/39886621.pdf
7   Organization for Economic Co-operation and Development (OECD) (2013). *Co-operative Compliance: A Framework, from enhanced relationship to co-operative compliance*. OECD Publishing. http://dx.doi.org/10.1787/9789264200852-en
8   OECD (2013). *Supra* note 7, p. 29.
9   OECD (2013). *Supra* note 7, p. 57.
10 OECD (2013). *Supra* note 7, p. 57.
11 Parker, C. & Gilad, S. (2011). Internal corporate compliance management systems: structure, culture and agency. In: Parker, C. & Lehmann Nielsen, V. (ed.), *Explaining Compliance: Business Responses to Regulation*. Cheltenham, UK: Edward Elgar Publishing Ltd, p. 170-195.

capacity in a more effective and efficient way. Power argues *'This reflects a broad shift in regulatory preference from ex post discovery of norm violation to ex ante anticipation and to prevention and self-discovery via internal systems of compliance which secure organizational conformity'.*[12] This broad shift is not undisputed. I will touch on this in the next sections.

6.1.2 Outline of this chapter

In this chapter I elaborate on the developments of new compliance strategies and new governance in the tax world. The Horizontal Monitoring case in the Netherlands will be used as an illustration of this recent development. The outline of the rest of this chapter will be as follows.

- Section 6.2 starts with a short overview of the origins of cooperative compliance. The urgency for revenue bodies to develop new tax compliance strategies will be explained using the experiences in Australia, New Zealand and the Netherlands.
- In section 6.3, the studies of the OECD mentioned above will be discussed in more depth. This discussion gives some insight into the response of the OECD on the urgency for revenue bodies to change their enforcement and compliance strategies.
- In section 6.4, I explain the developments in the Netherlands leading to the development of the Horizontal Monitoring strategy by the NTCA.
- In section 6.5, I explain the implementation in practise of Horizontal Monitoring of large businesses.
- In section 6.6, I discuss the role of compliance management systems, or internal control systems, in regulatory strategies in general, and in tax compliance strategies in particular, in more depth.
- In section 6.7 I draw some conclusions

6.2 Cooperative compliance: the urgency for a new compliance strategy

6.2.1 Australia and New Zealand

In the Introduction, I mentioned the limited resources as one of the main drivers for revenue bodies to re-think their enforcement strategies. Next to limited resources, government and regulators, in several countries, are facing the discontent of their citizens. Job & Honaker report accusations to the Internal Revenue Service (IRS) in the United States for being *'rude, abusive or unhelpful and offering poor and deteriorating service'*.[13] The Australian Tax Office (ATO) and the New Zealand Inland Revenue (NZIR) are confronted with more or less the same issues and of *'being out of touch and of compromising the integrity of the tax system'.*[14] These perceptions of the communities

---

12 Power (2007). *Supra* note 1, p. 38.
13 Job, J. & Honaker, D. (2003). Short-term experience with Responsive Regulation in the Australian Taxation Office. In: Braithwaite, V. (ed.), *Taxing Democracy: Understanding Tax Avoidance and Evasion*. Aldershot, UK: Ashgate Publishing.

in Australia and New Zealand led to questions about the organisational cultures, the regulation and enforcement methods, and the traditional command-and-control methods of the ATO and NZIR.[15]

In the late 1990s, to reinforce legitimacy, the ATO and NZIR started programmes to reform organisational culture and to (re-)design and implement new and additional enforcement methods.[16] These programmes were based on cooperative compliance models grounded on the responsive regulation theory developed in the early 1990s.[17] In short, *'this model seeks to promote voluntary compliance with Australia's taxation laws by tailoring the administrative treatment of taxpayers in accordance with the individual taxpayer's tax compliance posture'*.[18]

The goals of the ATO compliance model were to:
a) understand taxpayer behaviour;
b) build co-operative relationships with the community;
c) encourage and support compliance;
d) introduce a range of sanctions, escalating in severity and known to taxpayers, so that difficulties could be settled before costs became too great for both parties;
e) reduce time of the handling of complaints of procedural injustice; and
f) implement the Taxpayers' Charter.[19]

6.2.2 The Netherlands

In the beginning of the 21st century, the NTCA was criticised by Dutch society and politicians. Large businesses, industrial organisations and tax advisory bodies were unsatisfied with the way the NTCA was organised and enforced tax law and regulations.[20] The NTCA was blamed for distrusting taxpayers, inefficient tax assessments and audits, large backlogs (a backlog of 7 years was no exception), and 'fishing expeditions'. Above this these organisations and also politicians had the opinion the NTCA acted too formalistic. The tax inspectors had little discretion because of the

---

14 Job, J., Stout, A. & Smith, R. (2007). Culture Change in Three Taxation Administrations: From Command-and-Control to Responsive Regulation. *Law and Policy* 2984-101.
15 Job (2007). *Supra* note 14.
16 Job (2007). *Supra* note 14.
17 See for an academic overview: Braithwaite, V. (ed.), *Taxing Democracy: Understanding Tax Avoidance and Evasion*. Aldershot, UK: Ashgate Publishing.
See also policy documents of the ATO and NZIR, for example:
Australian Taxation Office (1998) *Improving Tax Compliance in the Cash Economy*. Canberra: Commonwealth of Australia.
New Zealand Inland Revenue (2003) *The Way Forward – Achievements and Future Direction 2003 Onwards*. Wellington: Inland Revenue.
18 Burton, M., (2007). Responsive Regulation and the Uncertainty of Tax Law – Time to Reconsider the Commissioner's Model of Cooperative Compliance? *Journal of Tax Research* (2007) vol. 5, no. 1, p. 71-104.
19 Job (2007). *Supra* note 14.
20 Poolen ,Th.W.M. (2012). 'Horizontaal toezicht vanuit het perspectief van de Belastingdienst'. *TFO* 2009/101 (in Dutch), p. 16-17, Committee Horizontal Monitoring Tax and Customs Administration (2012). *Tax supervision – Made to measure: Flexible when possible, strict where necessary*. The Hague, June 2012, p. 26.

power of back office knowledge groups. Important questions needed to be answered by these knowledge groups to which taxpayers had no access.

At the same time it appeared that the NTCA had made agreements against the law ('contra legem') with certain industries and groups of taxpayers, referred to as 'fiscale vrijplaatsen' (tax refuges). This contra legem regulation was explained using two main reasons.[21] First, the industries (coffee shops (shops where soft drugs are legally sold), call shops, illegal employment agencies) and groups of taxpayers (trailer parks) were perceived to be closely related to criminal activities. Enforcement by the NTCA had led to the intimidation and threats of violence towards its inspectors. The conclusion of the State Secretary for Finance[22] was to call for greater co-operation with other regulators and enforcers (like the municipalities) and, because of the violence threat, the police.[23]

A second reason is the perceived tension between the law and real life. 'No judicial system can stand without solutions to reduce the tension between law and reality'.[24] In this context, street level tax enforcers sometimes tried to find practical solutions to secure the levy and collection of tax.

These issues forced the State Secretary and the NTCA to develop and implement new and more effective compliance strategies. They came up with the Horizontal Monitoring programme. The foundations and practice of this programme is discussed in sections 6.4 and 6.5.

6.3 OECD: from 'Enhanced Relationship' to 'Cooperative Compliance'

In the introductory paragraph, I mentioned the 2008 report of the FTA (OECD) on the *Study into the Role of Tax Intermediaries*.[25] The study focused on innovative ways to address aggressive tax planning by large taxpayers and tax advisors. This report suggested the tax advisor to be the supply side of aggressive tax planning and large tax payers the demand side. The report suggested there is significant scope for influencing the demand side. Risk management by revenue bodies is advised to be an essential tool in addressing the demand side. Risk assessment would allow revenue bodies '*to assess the risk presented by taxpayers or groups of taxpayers and allocate resources to respond to these risks*'. Subsequently, the report argues: '*Risk management relies on information, which makes it important to encourage disclosure from taxpayers*'.[26]

---

21 State Secretary for Finance (2004). *Letter to The Dutch House of Representatives, June 3, 2004*, Kamerstukken II, 2003-2004 29 643, no. 2.
22 In the Netherlands, the State Secretary for Finance is politically responsible for the Tax and Customs Administration.
23 State Secretary for Finance (2004). *Supra* note 21, p. 4.
24 State Secretary for Finance (2004). *Supra* note 21, p. 4.
25 OECD (2008a). *Supra* note 4.
26 OECD (2008a). *Supra* note 4, p. 4.

To encourage disclosure, the 2008 Study suggests large corporate taxpayers, tax advisors and revenue bodies engage in a relationship based on co-operation and trust. The report describes a conceptual framework for this so called *'enhanced relationship'* approach. The organising principles of this conceptual framework are *trust* and *co-operation* and it anticipates disclosure beyond statutory obligations.[27]

The framework is built on seven pillars:
- 'Revenue bodies need to operate using the following five attributes when dealing with all taxpayers: understanding based on commercial awareness; impartiality; proportionality; openness (disclosure and transparency) and responsiveness.
- In dealing with revenue bodies, taxpayers providing disclosure and transparency'.[28]

In 2013 the FTA published a study of the practical implementation by revenue bodies of the ideas suggested in the 2008 study.[29] In this study, the conceptual framework of an *'enhanced relationship'* was renamed *'cooperative compliance'* because this term describes more accurately the objective (compliance) and the conceptual (co-operation) ideas. Based on a survey among 24 member countries of the Large Business Network (LBN) of the FTA, the report concluded that a cooperative compliance model had been developed and/or implemented by all the 24 countries.[30] Early adopters of the cooperative compliance model were the revenue bodies of Ireland (2005), the Netherlands (2005, Horizontal Monitoring), USA (2005, Compliance Assurance Program), Australia (2011, Annual Compliance Agreement), South Africa (2004, Taxpayers Engagement Strategy) and the UK (2006, Large Business Strategy including a customer relationship management model and a Tax Compliance Risk Management framework).

The 2013 study elaborates on the *disclosure and transparency* to be provided by the taxpayer in dealing with revenue bodies. Openness (*disclosure and transparency*) is mentioned as the most important characteristic. 'Cooperative compliance approaches can best be characterised as "Transparency in exchange for certainty"'.[31] To stress the importance of disclosure and transparency, the 2013 study refers to the OECD Report *Tackling Aggressive Tax Planning through Improved Transparency and Disclosure*:

'A system which starts with the upfront disclosure of such information not only allows for quicker dispute resolution and improved legal certainty, but also holds the potential for significant reduction in costs through better allocation of resources for both governments and taxpayers.'[32]

---

27 OECD (2008a). *Supra* note 4, p. 34.
28 OECD (2008a). *Supra* note 4, p. 13 and 35.
29 OECD (2013). *Supra* note 7.
30 OECD (2013). *Supra* note 7, p. 22.
31 OECD (2013). *Supra* note 7, p. 29.
32 Organization for Economic Co-operation and Development OECD (2011). *Tackling Aggressive Tax Planning through improved Transparency and Disclosure*. Paris: OECD, www.oecd.org/ctp/exchange-of-tax-information/48322860.pdf

The survey indicates that different countries make different choices when adopting the cooperative compliance model regarding mandatory or voluntary disclosure. Several countries have enacted general disclosure rules in regard to tax shelter or tax avoidance schemes.[33] In this respect, the 2013 study also refers to the emergence of Corporate Governance legislation. *'The existence of visible and reliable systems of tax governance provides more assurance that the taxpayer is able and willing to meet the required standard of disclosure and transparency. In this respect a (tax) risk management control system or Tax Control Framework (TCF) is an important tool'*.[34] The 2008 Study reveals what a revenue body should expect from a taxpayer in terms of disclosure and transparency:[35]

- *'Disclosure goes beyond information taxpayers are statutorily[36] obliged to provide. It should include any information necessary for the revenue body to undertake a fully informed risk assessment. This includes any transaction or position where there is a material degree of tax uncertainty or unpredictability, or where the revenue body has indicated publicly that the matter is of particular concern from a policy standpoint and will, therefore, be scrutinised.*
- *Transparency is the ongoing framework within which individual acts of disclosure take place. It describes the manner in which the parties to an enhanced relationship approach tax issues which give rise to a material degree of risk or uncertainty (or may give rise to such a degree of risk or uncertainty in the future).'*

In summary, expectations of disclosure and transparency for large corporate taxpayers are to:[37]

- *'volunteer information where they see potential for a significant difference of interpretation between them and the revenue body that may lead to a significantly different tax result; and*
- *provide comprehensive responses so that the revenue body can understand the significance of issues, deploy appropriate resources and reach the right tax conclusions.'*

The 2013 Study explains how the disclosure and transparency can be achieved by the tax payer:[38] *'the taxpayer will have to have in place systems of internal control that ensure that the returns submitted to the revenue body are accurate and that transactions or positions giving rise to material tax uncertainty are disclosed. This is the Tax Control Framework (TCF)... The importance of the TCF in the current context is that it can be assessed objectively by the revenue body as part of its risk assessment process. The existence of an effective TCF, coupled with a taxpayer's explicit willingness to meet the

---

33 OECD (2013). *Supra* note 7, p. 33.
34 OECD (2013). *Supra* note 7, p. 30.
35 OECD (2013). *Supra* note 7, p. 36.
36 Referring to (general) tax laws and regulation on the obligation of taxpayers to provide information to the revenue body or tax administration.
37 OECD (2013). *Supra* note 7, p. 37.
38 OECD (2013). *Supra* note 7, p. 35-36.

requirements of disclosure and transparency that go beyond their statutory obligations, provide an objective and rational basis for different treatment. The revenue body can place a justified reliance on the tax returns it receives from taxpayers who meet the requirements and can be confident that material tax risks and uncertainties will be brought to its attention. In cases where the TCF is inadequate and/or the taxpayer is not prepared to provide more information than is strictly required by statute, revenue bodies necessarily have to use a different and more intrusive approach to ascertain what tax risks may be present in the case.'

6.4 The development of Horizontal Monitoring in the Netherlands

6.4.1 Introduction

In 2005 the NTCA started to develop and implement a new compliance strategy. The Horizontal Monitoring (HM) programme was at the core of this strategy.[39] The State Secretary for Finance noted the need for the NTCA to differentiate in its supervision and enforcement approach. On the one hand, he noticed the urgency to provide adequate supervision and strong enforcement, without diminishing the quality of service. On the other hand, he recognised a need to reinforce the responsibility of citizens and businesses to comply with the law and regulations. This distinction demands the development of a new enforcement approach: the reinforcement of personal responsibility of regulated entities demands new enforcement concepts like HM.[40]

With this, the NTCA not only responded to criticism by the public and politicians - in the presentation of its new strategy, the NTCA mentioned developments in Dutch society, the global business community and in behavioural and regulatory science, as important drivers for the new strategy. For the NTCA, three developments were of major importance for implementing a new compliance strategy:
1. Horizontalisation of society.
2. The growing importance of internal control and risk management in Corporate Governance.
3. Scientific theorisation and research on compliance behaviour and the effects on different enforcement strategies.

6.4.2 Horizontalisation of society

In 2002, the Netherlands Scientific Council for Government Policy published the report 'The Future of The National Constitutional State'.[41,42] The council recognised

---

39 In Dutch, the procedure is called 'Horizontaal Toezicht'. The official translation, given by the NTCA is Horizontal Monitoring. For explanatory reasons Horizontal Supervision is mentioned as an alternative translation.
40 State Secretary for Finance (2004). *Supra* note 21, p. 3.
41 Wetenschappelijke Raad voor het Regeringsbeleid (2002). *De Toekomst van de Nationale Rechtstaat, Rapporten aan de Regering no. 63.* Den Haag: Sdu Uitgevers http://www.wrr.nl/fileadmin/nl/publicaties/PDF-Rapporten/De_toekomst_van_de_nationale_rechtsstaat.pdf

globalisation/internationalisation, individualisation of citizens and computerisation as three major developments in society and analyses the consequences for the public. The Council made recommendations for a better balance of responsibility between the government and its citizens. Government and society share the public space from where social problems need to be solved. Public tasks should be increasingly shared with private actors, like businesses. The Council calls this sharing 'horizontalisation' and expects private actors to take some responsibility. Such a development demands an open, flexible, responsive and collaborative way of regulation with different kinds of meta-regulation by government.

This observation by the Council was adopted by the government in the Netherlands and incorporated into government policies on regulation. The government's vision on supervision was published in two documents in 2001 and 2005.[43]

'The Government and society need to appreciate, more than in the past, that the government is neither willing nor able to bear all risks. The control of risks and prevention of errors is a joint duty of both government and society'.[44]

The NTCA used the idea of horizontalisation in the re-orientation of the enforcement strategy. In the 2008-2012 Business Plan, the NTCA concluded: 'The NTCA uses Horizontal Monitoring in the business tax collections, next to traditional ways of supervision and enforcement. This choice is based on the perception that most businesses and organisations will and may take their (social) responsibility seriously'.[45]

6.4.3 Corporate Governance and Internal Control

Due to the book-keeping scandals over the past decade, followed by the credit crunch in 2008, 'Corporate Governance' became an issue of major importance for businesses. Many countries promulgated strict laws and regulations to compel businesses to be transparent and report statements on the quality and adequacy of the internal control over financial reporting.[46] Tax is an important issue in financial reporting. The financial reporting standards and related interpretations under IFRS,[47] US

---

42 Scientific Council for Government Policy (2002). *The Future of the National Constitutional State, Reports to the Government nr. 63, Translation of the extensive summary of the Council's report De Toekomst van de Nationale Rechtstaat.* Den Haag: Sdu Uitgevers. http://www.wrr.nl/fileadmin/en/publicaties/PDF-Rapporten/The_Future_Of_The_National_Constiutional_State.pdf
43 *De Kaderstellende visie op toezicht,* Parliamentary Documents II 2000/01, 27 831, no. 1; *Minder last, meer effect, zes principes van goed toezicht,* Parliamentary Documents II 2005/06, 27 831, no. 15, p. 10.
44 *Minder last, meer effect, zes principes van goed toezicht,* annex to Parliamentary Documents II 2005/06, 27 831, no. 15, p. 9.
45 NTCA, Business Plan 2008-2012, p. 21, http://www.rijksoverheid.nl/documenten-en-publicaties/kamerstukken/2008/11/11/bedrijfsplan-belastingdienst-2008-2012.html
46 E.g. US Sarbanes Oxley Act of 2002. https://www.sec.gov/about/laws/soa2002.pdf
47 International Financial Reporting Standards (IFRS): International Accounting Standard 12 (IAS 12): Income Taxes.

GAAP[48] or any local GAAP are detailed and complex and so is tax law. This means tax is a high risk in financial reporting and tax risk management and tax accounting are becoming increasingly more important to mitigate this risk.[49, 50]

Gleason et al. reports 'Of the nearly 1,000 company-year reports indicating material weaknesses in internal controls (both account-specific and company-level) in SEC filings included in the Audit Analytics database as of June 2007, more than one-third reflect income tax-related weaknesses. The prevalence of weak internal controls in the income tax area likely reflects the high degree of complexity and judgment required in income tax reporting coupled with a lack of adequate documentation of the tax reporting function'.[51]

Questions about good business governance emerged in the Netherlands ever since the Dutch United East India Company[52] was established as the first chartered company in the world in 1602. Since then many book keeping scandals, frauds and bankruptcies occurred, to which government and regulators consequently responded with increasing and stricter laws and regulation. For a short overview on these developments I refer to Cools[53] and Hoogendoorn.[54]

In the beginning, the regulation was mostly aimed at financial reporting. Since the 1990s the object of regulation was extended to internal control, enterprise risk management and, since the first decade of this century, Corporate Governance.[55] A notorious example of the law in this field is the Sarbanes Oxley act in the US, focusing on internal control over financial reporting. It is well known because of its high demands for transparency and responsibility by management of organisations and the impact on organisational operations and reporting.[56] Another example of such regulation is the so-called Corporate Governance Code.[57] In the Netherlands e.g.,

---

48 US Generally Accepted Accounting Principles: Accounting Standards Codification 740 and FASB Interpretation no. 48, Accounting for Uncertainty in Income Taxes (FIN 48).
49 Anderson, J.M., De Grave, K. & Moore, J.M. (2010). Tax Accounting.
    In: Bakker, A. & Kloosterhof, S. (ed.), *Tax Risk Management, From Risk to Opportunity*. Amsterdam: IBFD, p.74.
50 Elgood, T., Fulton, T. & Schutzman, M.D. (2008). *Tax Function Effectiveness*. Chicago: PriceWaterhouseCoopers, CCH, p. 23-3.
51 Gleason, C., Pincus, M. & Olhoft Rego, S. (2011). *Material Weaknesses in Tax-Related Internal Controls and Earnings Management*, Working Paper 1 December 2011, p.6, http://papers.ssrn.com/sol3/papers.cfm?abstract_id=1509765
52 In Dutch: *Vereenigde Oost-Indische Compagnie*, VOC.
53 Cools, K. (1993). *Controle is goed, vertrouwen nog beter; over bestuurders en corporate governance*. Assen: Van Gorcum.
54 Hoogendoorn, M.N. (1993). *Het belang van de jaarrekening; interactie tussen gebruikers, verschaffers en controleurs*. Schoonhoven: Academic Service.
55 Power (2007). *Supra* note 1.
56 Sarbanes-Oxley Act of 2002. *Supra* note 46, Section 404 of this Act requires management to assess internal controls over financial reporting and report on this in each annual report and *each registered public accounting firm that prepares or issues the audit report for the issuer shall attest to, and report on, the assessment made by the management of the issuer.*
57 In the Netherlands: Monitoring Commissie Corporate Governance (2008). *Nederlandse Corporate Governance Code*: www.corpgov.nl

Corporate Governance is not regulated by law but by a code.[58] Companies need to comply to this code or explain the reason why they don't (comply or explain).

Van Leeuwen & Wallage have made an analysis of the law and regulation on Corporate Governance in the US, UK, European Union and the Netherlands.[59] They conclude that the evaluation of the effectiveness of internal control systems is a major issue in all assessed regulation. There are differences in the required scope of internal control, method of evaluation and reporting (the 'in control statement'). In all jurisdictions, management is considered to be responsible for an adequate internal control system. This responsibility includes the evaluation of and reporting on the effectiveness of internal controls.[60]

Emphasising the responsibility of management for effective internal control, the evaluation and the reporting (transparency) in Corporate Governance is in line with the observations supporting horizontalisation and HM.

As a consequence of the government adopting the recommendations of the Scientific Council, other regulators started programmes on horizontal monitoring too.[61] For example, the Independent Post and Telecommunication Authority (OPTA) and the Netherlands Food and Consumer Product Safety Authority (NVWA). These regulators are also referring to Corporate Governance regulation as support in regulation and enforcement of compliance.[62]

6.4.4 Scientific theorisation and research on tax compliance and behaviour

Tax compliance has long been studied from an economic perspective only. The 'rational decision theory' was most often used to explain the degree of tax compliance by taxpayers. This economic approach has had a major influence on the design of tax systems all over the world. More recent research shows that this approach needs to be revised, with more attention being paid to the behavioural approach. Kirchler et al. argues *'Purely economic factors such as audit rates and fines have shown inconsistent*

---

58 Monitoring Commissie Corporate Governance Code, 2008, *supra* note 57.
59 Leeuwen, O.C. van & Wallage, Ph. (2007). De zoektocht naar meer transparantie. *Maandblad voor Accountancy en Bedrijfseconomie*, jg. *81*, no. 10, pp. 469-479.
60 E.g. Sarbanes-Oxley Act of 2002, *supra* note 46, section 404, p. 116 STAT. 789: *'The Commission shall prescribe rules requiring each annual report (...) to contain an internal control report, which shall:*
    1) *State the responsibility of management for establishing and maintaining an adequate internal control structure and procedures for financial reporting; and*
    2) *Contain an assessment, as of the end of the most recent fiscal year of the issuer, of the effectiveness of the internal control structure and procedures of the issuer for financial reporting.'*
    In the Dutch Corporate Governance Code this obligation is regulated in Section II.1.4, http://commissiecorporategovernance.nl/download/?id=609
61 Ottow, A (2009). *Enforcement by regulators through self-regulation and compliance programs*. Draft Paper for Discussion Purposes, ACLE Conference 'To Enforce or Comply: Incentives Inside Corporations and Agencies' 5-6 March 2009.
62 Opta (2008). *Visie op toezicht en handhaving*, maart: http://www.opta.nl/download/Visie+op+toezicht+en+handhaving+2008.pdf
    Voedsel- en Waren Autoriteit (2005). *Zicht op toezicht. Effectief toezicht houden, hoe doe je dat?*: www.vwa.nl/portal/page?_pageid=119,1639724&_dad=portal&_schema=PORTAL

effects on tax compliance, for various reasons. First, the assumption that taxpayers are trying to avoid taxes whenever it pays must be doubted. Many studies show that a vast majority of citizens are willing to pay taxes. Second, most taxpayers seem to take the legitimacy of the tax system for granted. They believe in the overarching objectives of the government and pay their share without considering possibilities to avoid or to evade taxes'.[63]

James and Alley analyse tax compliance using these different approaches:
'Tax compliance is a complex subject with broad implications. There are two main approaches - the economic and the behavioural, used to encourage taxpayers to comply with the taxation system. The economic approach, usually confined to penalties, may be necessary to enforce compliance by those taxpayers who would otherwise refuse to discharge their obligations as citizens. However, there are dangers in using such an approach more widely. It is suggested that taxation is a means to an end and an unnecessarily harsh enforcement regime, such as that which appears to have been used in some countries, detracts from the whole exercise of raising money for the public benefit. Furthermore, such harshness can reduce the willingness of otherwise responsible citizens to comply with what may then be perceived as an unjust system. There is a clear need to strike the right balance in encouraging voluntary compliance as well as deterring wilful non-compliance. Despite the limitations of its approach and the intuitive appeal of the wider behavioural approach, the economic approach still has a place in tax compliance as it is reasonable to assume that, to a greater or lesser degree, financial considerations do influence taxpayer behaviour, for example, the maximisation of shareholder wealth in corporations'.[64]

This broadening of the discussion on tax compliance has been a major influence on tax policy makers. It is one of the supporting developments for tax administrations to rethink their tax compliance strategies. In 2010 the OECD published an 'Information Note' on the topic of taxpayer behaviour with the objective 'to describe current knowledge on taxpayer compliance behaviour in order to assist countries in their effort to cost effectively influence taxpayer behaviour to improve compliance'.[65]

Very interesting theorisation and research on the balance between the economic and the behavioural approach has been carried out by Erich Kirchler. In his framework, the 'Slippery Slope Framework', tax compliance is jointly influenced by two major factors: the power of tax authorities and the trust in tax authorities, and their interactions.[66]

---

63 Kirchler, E., Hoelzl, E. & Wahl, I. (2008). Enforced versus voluntary tax compliance: The "slippery slope" framework. *Journal of Economic Psychology, 29* (2008) 210–225, p. 211.
64 James, S. & Alley, C. (2002). Tax compliance, self-assessment and tax administration. *Journal of finance and management in public services, 2, 27-42*, p 38.
65 Organization for Economic Co-operation and Development (OECD) (2010). *Understanding and Influencing Taxpayers' Compliance Behaviour*. Information Note
    November 2010, http://www.oecd.org/tax/administration/46274793.pdf
66 Kirchler, E. (2007). *The economic psychology of tax behaviour*. Cambridge: Cambridge University Press.

6.5 Horizontal Monitoring in practice

6.5.1 Introduction

Horizontal Monitoring can be defined as a form of social non-governmental control, aiming for the improvement of product and service quality within certain professional groups or industries.[67] Professional codes, certification and hallmarks are possible ways to support this type of control.

The goals of HM are: (a) improving compliance; (b) improving service level for business; (c) working in real time; (d) providing certainty in advance; (e) reducing the administrative burden. HM starts with the assumption that the regulatee is willing to comply with laws and regulations.

6.5.2 Horizontal Monitoring: how it started

The starting point of the HM approach of the NTCA is that all taxpayers (businesses and private individuals) are personally responsible/accountable for complying with applicable laws and regulations. This concept of compliance, advocated by the Dutch Scientific Council for Government Policy, has had a major influence on the development of the Tax Compliance Model in the Netherlands. The Council concludes that because of globalisation, individualisation and computerisation the relationship between the state and its citizens changes. Individualisation leads to normative emancipation of citizens regarding the creation of public interests. Citizens will not only manifest themselves as voters or native but also as customer and co-creators of policy.[68]

In April 2005 the State Secretary introduced the concept of HM to the Dutch parliament.[69] HM is about (a) mutual trust between taxpayer and the NTCA; (b) clearer marking of the responsibilities and possibilities of both parties to enforce the law; (c) confirm and comply with mutual agreements. Its purpose is to equalise the relationship and the communication between citizen and government. Horizontal monitoring fits into the recent developments in society and acknowledges that law enforcement in a changing society needs to use the knowledge within that society. For supervision, enforcement and managerial purposes, the NTCA divides the total population of taxpayers into three target groups (a) large enterprises; (b) small and medium sized enterprises (SME's); (c) individuals. The State Secretary, for each target group, presented a number of possible applications of HM.

---

67 Dutch Ministry of Justice (2006). *De 'Tafel van Elf' een veelzijdig instrument*. Den Haag: Expertisecentrum Rechtspleging en Rechtshandhaving, p. 16. http://www.hetccv.nl/binaries/content/assets/ccv/dossiers/Nalevingsexpertise/Programmatisch+handhaven/Tafel_van_elf_2006.pdf
68 WRR (2002). *Supra* note 41 and 42.
69 State Secretary for Finance (2005). Letter of 8 April 2005 to the House of Representatives, Parliamentary Documents II 2004/2005, 29 643, no. 4, p. 1.

In the same letter the State Secretary announced a pilot project in which the HM-concept was applied to 20 large enterprises, mainly companies listed on the Amsterdam Stock Exchange. At board level, voluntary compliance agreements[70] were concluded. In 2006 the number of participants in the pilot was increased to include another 20 large enterprises. On the request of the Senate of the Dutch Parliament, an anonymous version of the compliance agreement was published.[71] The characteristics of the compliance agreement are:
a) voluntary (gentlemen's) agreement on the relationship, the co-operation and the supervision;
b) inclusion of all taxes and tax collection and if relevant customs;
c) within the boundaries of the law, tax policy and jurisprudence;
d) no additional rights nor obligations;
e) underpinned by the core values of HM mutual trust, understanding and transparency.

The compliance agreement can best be seen as a gentlemen's agreement because no additional rights or obligations are in the agreement. The main reason for concluding the agreement is to foster and improve the co-operation, in tax supervision, between the taxpayer and the NTCA.

In 2008 the NTCA gives the following additional explanation on HM (translated): '*The starting point is that tax supervision is worked on as a joint responsibility of all partners in the tax chain* (the tax chain is not explained, but what is meant is the chain from taxpayer via tax intermediaries to the tax administration RV). *The core values for the collaboration are mutual trust, respecting mutual interests and transparency. The purpose of the collaboration is to try to solve problems as much in advance as possible and prevent duplication of compliance activities in the tax chain. In this approach the taxpayer will get certainly more timely and less time consuming assessment afterwards. By increasing the legal certainty and decreasing the administrative burden, the NTCA want to contribute in a positive way to the (fiscal) business climate*'.

'*The NTCA seeks for opportunities to collaborate with taxpayers, industry organisations, advisors, auditors and administrative software developers with the objective to minimise the burden of supervision and to maximise the voluntary compliance*'.[72]

Part of HM is the transparency by taxpayers on potential disputes making it possible to deal with these issues in real time, close to the moment they occur. This will decrease the administrative burden and increase the certainty on these tax positions. Solving problems in real time is, in general, less time consuming and will possibly

---

70 Compliance agreements are also called Enforcement Covenants. In this paper the term compliance agreement will be used.
71 http://download.belastingdienst.nl/belastingdienst/docs/standaardtekst_individueel_convenant_dv4111z4ed.pdf
   English translation: http://download.belastingdienst.nl/belastingdienst/docs/individual_compliance_agreementincl_customs_dv4111z3edeng.pdf
72 NTCA. Business Plan 2008-2012, *supra* note 45, p. 34.

contribute to the legitimacy of the tax administration. Legitimacy and morality are values that matter when it comes to compliance. Tyler[73] argues people obey rules when they view these rules as being more legitimate and they obey them when the rules accord with their personal views about what is right or wrong.

Furthermore, when people see legal authorities exercising their authority in just ways, they are more likely to indicate that the laws themselves are consistent with their moral values. In other words, procedural justice facilitates the belief that laws are morally appropriate. Procedural justice can be fostered or improved if the tax administration adheres to the basics of HM - trust, understanding and transparency.

To support the implementation of HM the NTCA published guidelines, for use by taxpayers and tax inspectors, on how to execute HM. For HM, with the SMEs, a guideline was published in 2011.[74] For large businesses the first guideline was published in 2010.[75] In 2013 a totally revised Guideline on the 'Supervision of Large Businesses' was published.[76] In these guidelines the process of HM for SMEs and large businesses is explained. The guiding principles are the same for both SMEs and Large Business (see above for the characteristics of the compliance agreement). As already mentioned, HM is based on trust, mutual understanding and transparency - the objective is to improve compliance by co-operation and in exchange for transparency the taxpayer will get certainty on tax positions in real time.

6.5.3 Horizontal Monitoring of large businesses in practice

The process of HM for large businesses consists of a number of steps. These steps are thoroughly explained in the Guideline and in the remaining part of this section, I will discuss some of these steps.

The process starts with the HM meeting.[77] The objective of this meeting is to explore the feasibility of horizontal monitoring (the horizontal monitoring meeting). It is held between the senior management of the taxpayer and the NTCA. If both parties conclude HM to be feasible, the Compliance Scan[78] will be executed.

The objective of the compliance scan is to carry out a joint assessment with the organisation to review, in more depth, the feasibility of horizontal monitoring. *The compliance scan is carried out by interviewing a number of the organisation's key officers.*

---

73   Tyler, T. (2007). *Psychology and the Design of Legal Institutions*, Tilburg Law Lectures Series, Montesquieu seminars volume 3. Nijmegen: WLP, p. 6.
74   NTCA (2011). *Leidraad Horizontaal Toezicht MKB Fiscaal dienstverleners*. Only available in Dutch. http://download.belastingdienst.nl/belastingdienst/docs/leidraad_horizo_toezicht_fiscaal_dienst-verl_dv4071z1pl.pdf
75   No longer available.
76   NTCA (2013). *Supervision Large Businesses in the Netherlands*. http://download.belastingdienst.nl/belastingdienst/docs/supervision_large_business_in_netherlands_dv4231z1fdeng.pdf
77   NTCA (2013). *Supra* note 76, p. 14.
78   NTCA (2013). *Supra* note 76, p. 17.

These interviews yield information for the determination, in consultation with the organisation, of the feasibility of horizontal monitoring and the need for further agreements, where relevant, to be included in the process. A discussion of the mutual expectations of the further steps in the horizontal monitoring process lays the foundations for appropriate co-operation.'[79]

The compliance scan is completed with internal consultations on the feasibility of HM by the NTCA staff: *'the most important issue to be given consideration during these consultations is the question as to whether the NTCA´s officers have gained the impression that the organisation is willing to gain tax control (in the longer term) and is transparent about tax issues, or that their earlier impression that this is the case has been established.'*[80]

In a closing meeting of the compliance scan, the NTCA will discuss its impressions with the board of the taxpayer. In this meeting, both the taxpayer and the NTCA need to decide on the feasibility of HM and any further steps. If both parties decide to continue with HM, the next step is the settlement of pending issues: *'the objective is to settle as many pending issues as possible before the conclusion of the compliance agreement. When this is not feasible then the account management team and the organisation reach procedural agreements.'*

'Pending tax issues are understood as tax issues or collection issues that are known to the organisation and NTCA at the start of the horizontal monitoring process. These are issues that impede working in real time and can frustrate flexible co-operation and which, consequently, need to be settled.'[81]

Both parties, of course, are obliged to settle the pending issues within the boundaries of applicable law, regulations and jurisprudence. The last step in this process is concluding the compliance agreement: *'the NTCA and the organisation will have jointly reviewed the feasibility of horizontal monitoring during the horizontal monitoring meeting, experiences in managing the individual account and the compliance scan. Both parties have now obtained a clear insight into the horizontal monitoring process, the division of their responsibilities and their mutual expectations. The organisation will have stated that it is both willing and able to comply with and continue to comply with the horizontal monitoring principles. The horizontal monitoring relationship can now be laid down in a compliance agreement.'*[82]

The compliance agreement is standardised.[83] The idea behind a standard agreement is to treat all large business in HM equally. The compliance agreement with large business is evaluated biannually and with very large businesses annually. This

---

79   NTCA (2013). *Supra* note 76, p. 17.
80   NTCA (2013). *Supra* note 76, p. 19.
81   NTCA (2013). *Supra* note 76, p. 22.
82   NTCA (2013). *Supra* note 76, p. 24.
83   Compliance Agreement. *Supra* note 71.

evaluation is a permanent element of the horizontal monitoring relationship. The guideline elaborates on other issues such as preliminary consultations, tax collection and tax adjustments and penalties. I will skip these issues and refer you for further explanation to the guideline. However, I will discuss one more important issue: the adjustment of supervision in HM and the transparency of the NTCA on the Strategic Treatment Plan.

The basic assumption in HM is that, because the large business agreed to be transparent on relevant tax issues, ex post supervision actions by the NTCA, for example, audits on tax returns, can be limited to a minimum of reality checks. This will help to deploy the limited capacity of the Tax Administration in the most effective way and reduce the administrative burden for taxpayers. To do this, it is important for the taxpayer and the tax administration to be confident that all relevant tax issues will be raised by the tax risk management and control procedures of the taxpayer. As already mentioned, the OECD argues: *'the existence of visible and reliable systems of tax governance provides more assurance that the taxpayer is able and willing to meet the required standard of disclosure and transparency. In this respect a (tax) risk management control system or Tax Control Framework (TCF) is an important tool.'*[84]

At the start of the first pilot of HM involving large businesses, the State Secretary of Finance emphasised the basic assumption of HM: 'that compliance agreement will be concluded with enterprises that have their 'tax control framework' in place, referring to IFRS-standards and the US Sarbanes-Oxley act'.[85]

The term 'tax control framework' (TCF) was, until that moment, unknown in the fiscal vocabulary in the Netherlands. In March 2008, the NTCA published an internal document to clarify the meaning of TCF and to explain how the TCF will be used in the supervision and enforcement activities of the NTCA.[86] The NTCA describes a TCF as an integral part of a company's Business or Internal Control Framework (BCF or ICF) specifically focusing on businesses' tax processes. In this document, HM and the TCF have been explained clarified referring to international developments in Corporate Governance. As I have mentioned before, one aspect of Corporate Governance is to maintain a sound and effective system of Internal Control.[87] The NTCA emphasised that all businesses, participating in HM or not, need to have implemented an internal control framework to meet the demands of Corporate Governance legislation and regulation and with that tax law and regulations.[88] An adequate Internal Control Framework gives the NTCA the opportunity to deploy staff efficiently by re-using business data, results of control procedures and internal audits etc., executed by the

---

84 OECD (2013). *Supra* note 7, p. 30.
85 State Secretary for Finance (2006). Letter of 9 June 2006 to the Senate of the Parliament of the Netherlands, nr. DGB06-3312.
86 Netherlands Tax and Customs Administration (2008). *Tax Control Framework, Van risicogericht naar "in control": het werk verandert.* Kennisgroep ZGO, Werkgroep TCF, maart 2009.
87 Power (2007). *Supra* note 1, p 35.
88 Section 52 of the General Tax Law (Algemene Wet inzake Rijksbelastingen) in the Netherlands, see Chapter 8.3 on more formal issues in Dutch tax law.

business itself, for supervision purposes. And of course this will help to limit the administrative burden. In the next paragraph I will elaborate on the use of internal control and compliance management systems in tax supervision and enforcements by revenue bodies.

The way the supervision is adjusted is laid down by the NTCA in the Strategic Treatment Plan of the large business. When the large business participates in HM and has signed the compliance agreement, this plan is then shared by the NTCA with that large business.

The NTCA uses the HM strategy not only for large businesses. The NTCA applies the strategy on SMEs too. The practise with SEMs is out of the scope of this chapter. For an in-depth discussion I refer to chapter 7 of this book.

6.5.4 Evaluation of HM by the Commission Horizontal Monitoring

The State Secretary of Finance appointed the Commission Horizontal Monitoring (Commission) on November 10, 2011. The Commission was given the assignment to evaluate HM, to give an opinion on the policy change, to implement this new approach, to signal bottlenecks and vulnerabilities in regard to its approach and to recommend and propose future developments and ways to measure the effectiveness of this approach.

The commission reported on June 21, 2012.[89] In general, the commission concluded positively on HM - that HM is, based on the study of the commission, to be considered a legal way of tax supervision. But the commission also asked questions and made 20 recommendations on, for example, guiding principles for the TCF, deployment of HM with SMEs and the effectiveness of the approach and how to measure the effectiveness. The State Secretary of Finance promised to adopt these recommendations.

6.6 Compliance Management Systems in New Governance

6.6.1 Compliance Management Systems

The emergence of the cooperative compliance models, like HM, has much to do with the rise of trust, as an organising principle, in modern societies. Power reports 'a *growth of agency relationships whereby agents are entrusted with custody and discretion over the management of the assets of other people'*, suggesting the necessity of creating trust between agent and principle and to rely on the representation of the one to the other.[90]

---

89 Committee Horizontal Monitoring Tax and Customs Administration (2012). *Tax supervision – Made to measure: Flexible when possible, strict where necessary*. The Hague, June 2012.
90 Power, M. (2007). *Supra* note 1, p. 39.

However, in many regulatory strategies, the freedom given by the regulator (trust and greater autonomy) is counterbalanced by mandatory compliance management, internal control or risk management systems. Shamir puts the focus on the objective of regulators and policymakers: *'private regulation schemes or new governance approaches attempts to 'moralise', 'responsibilise' or 'socialise' commercial actors by requiring them to implement internal compliance systems.'*[91]

Scholars advocating new governance approaches do suggest that *'it ought to be possible to empirically identify internal management structures, decision making processes, employee training and other practices that can effectively prevent misconduct in corporations. Moreover, it has been suggested that it should be possible to design government or voluntary regulatory programmes that would force or encourage corporations to self-regulate by putting in place these corporate compliance management systems.'*[92]

This type of regulation is known as 'meta-regulation' because it attempts to regulate self-regulation.[93] Other terms that are used are 'management based -', 'systems-based-', 'principles-based -', 'process -' and 'process-oriented -' regulation.[94]

Strategies like these are also referred to as 'enforced self-regulation'.[95] In enforced self-regulation, the focus of the regulator is shifting to control of control. Power puts it like this: *'in place of direct surveillance, an impossible pure transparency, the regulatory process 'observes' in first instance the conditions under which trust is supported, that is, the norms of behaviour to which organisational agents are held to account by their own managerial commitment to self-regulation'.*[96] This trend of enforced self-regulation has been observed in the regulation of health and safety, food safety, financial markets, environmental,[97] rail regulation, sustainable forestry, toxic chemical reduction and trades practices.[98] Braithwaite observed this phenomenon in the context of tax: *'the next level of interference might be called enforced self-regulation. Taxpayers have responsibility for correcting their own mistakes, but a mechanism is in place to ensure they do so, and to provide feedback to indicate whether or not the taxpayers' compliance plan is sound.'*[99]

---

91 Shamir, R. (2010). Capitalism, Governance, and Authority. *The Case of Corporate Social Responsibility, Annual Review of Law and Social Sci*ence, 6, 531-553.
92 Parker, C. & Gilad, S. (2011). *Supra* note 11, p. 170.
93 Parker, C. (2007). Meta-Regulation: Legal Accountability for Corporate Social Responsibility, In: McBarnet, D., Voiculescu, A. & Campbell, T. (ed.).*The New Corporate Accountability: Corporate Social Responsibility and the Law.* Cambridge: Cambridge University Press, pp. 207-237.
94 Coglianese, C. & Lazar, D. (2003). Management-Based Regulation: Prescribing Private Management to Achieve Public Goals. *Law and Society Review (37)* 691-730.
95 Ayres, I. & Braithwaite, J. (1992). *Responsive Regulation: Transcending the Deregulation Debate.* Oxford: Oxford University Press.
96 Power (2007). *Supra* note 1, p. 40.
97 Parker and Gilad (2011). *Supra* note 11.
98 Gunningham, N. & Sinclair, D. (2009). Organizational Trust and the Limits of Management-Based Regulation. *Law and Society Review, (43)*, 4, 865-900.
99 Braithwaite, V. (2002). A New Approach to Tax Compliance, In: Braithwaite, V. (ed.), *Taxing Democracy.* Aldershot, England: Ashgate Publishing Ltd, p. 4.

The policy intention is to have regulatory institutions whose role is confined to mandate and monitor firms' self-evaluation, design and management of their operations, governance and controls, resulting in a better performance, more effective and efficient performance of regulators.[100] Power argues: *'this reflects a broad shift in regulatory preference from ex post discovery of norm violation to ex ante anticipation and to prevention and self-discovery via internal systems of compliance which secure organisational conformity.'*[101]

The focus on compliance management systems in new governance approaches looks paradoxical in relation to its organising principle - trust. Power tries to explain this paradox with the following reasoning:

The rise of trust-based relationships *'drives a demand for new guardians of trust who can explicitly balance incentives for principals to take risks with those of agents to engage in deviant behaviour.'*

The demand for trust creates corresponding demands for evidence: *'internal control systems and related public disclosures, such as financial statements and internal control statements, have been transformed into the material representation or proxy for trusting organisations and their leaders.'*[102]

However, the need for evidence or control is not for accountability reasons only. Nooteboom argues that there is an important link between trust and control: *'for expectations between organisations to be met there must be trust in both people and the organisation, and the connection between them lies in roles people play and positions they take up in the organisation, as specified in internal control systems;* and: *External control requires internal control to ensure that personal conduct is in line with what organisational trust requires.'*[103]

So it seems like trust and the need for control go together in new governance approaches such as cooperative compliance and HM. Based on the assumption that the control systems relate/contribute to the level of trust in the self-enforcement capabilities of the regulated entities and, with that, to the level of compliance, these systems play a pivotal role in new governance. However, because of a lack of theorisation and empirical evidence, this assumption is questioned and criticised. In the next section I will elaborate on this.

---

100 Parker & Gilad (2011). *Supra* note 11.
101 Power (2007). *Supra* note 1, p. 38.
102 Power (2007). *Supra* note 1, p. 39.
103 Nooteboom, B. (2004). *Management control in inter-organizational relationships*, p. 3. http://www.bartnooteboom.nl/site/img/klanten/250/Management_control_in_inter-organizational_relationships.pdf.

6.6.2 Effectiveness of Compliance Management Systems

The assumption that businesses can be 'moralised', 'responsibilised' or 'socialised' by requiring them to implement internal compliance systems can also be recognised in most of the Corporate Governance regulation that has been developed since the beginning of the century. Because of major corporate failures and book-keeping scandals, regulators all over the world brought in strict Corporate Governance laws and regulation, emphasising the importance of internal control.[104] Most Corporate Governance regulation refers to the Commission of Sponsoring Organisations (COSO) Internal Control Framework as a good practice for internal control. COSO developed a globally acknowledged 'best practice' for internal control and risk management.[105] COSO's definition of internal control includes the assumption that control systems can contribute to compliance with laws and regulation:[106]

Internal control is a process, effected by an entity's board of directors, management and other personnel, designed to provide reasonable assurance regarding the achievement of objectives in the following categories:
- *Effectiveness and efficiency of operations*
- *Reliability of financial reporting*
- *Compliance with applicable laws and regulations*

The definition raises the question of how the objectives in the different categories relate to each other. Do the objectives go together, are they aligned, or do objectives compete with each other? It is plausible to assume that mandated compliance norms are possibly not aligned with voluntary effectiveness and efficiency norms. How does the process of internal control provide reasonable assurance that possibly competing objectives in the different categories can be achieved simultaneously?

Power argues that internal control systems are designed and implemented with the objective to facilitate core business processes in an organisation. Mobilisation of internal control as a regulatory resource suggests that there is no distinction between the norms that are governmentally mandated by laws, and regulation and norms that are mandated by management and those used by agents in operation: *'this neo-liberal compliance ideal anticipates a potential where the traditional 'problem of compliance' no longer exists because regulatory and business goals are perfectly aligned. That this ideal is not an empirical reality, and principal agent models reminds us that it is not aligned with theory either, should not detract from its broad discursive status as an aspiration or telos of regulation.'*[107]

---

104 Illustrative examples are the Sarbanes-Oxley act in the USA and Corporate Governance Codes like the Dutch Corporate Governance Code in the Netherlands, *supra* note 46, 56 and 57.
105 COSO (1992). *Internal Control – Integrated Framework*; COSO (2004). *Enterprise Risk Management*, COSO (2103) *Internal Control – Integrated Framework*. www.coso.org
106 COSO (1992). *Internal Control – Integrated Framework*, www.coso.org
107 Power (2007). *Supra* note 1, p. 41.

Power is not alone in questioning the rationale of the mobilisation of internal control as a regulatory resource. Huisman et al. conducted a review on the academic literature relating to the compliance of businesses. Based on this study, he questions the eagerness with which policymakers are adapting new regulatory strategies like self-regulation, reputation sanctioning, and enforcement based on risk profiling, because there is little empirical substantiation.[108]

In line with Power, Parker and Gilad argue: *'research shows that the implementation of compliance management systems often does not and cannot achieve idealistic policy purposes'*.[109] Referring to relevant research, Parker and Gilad come to the following reasoning:
- Compliance management systems are implemented *for the purposes of external impression management or 'window dressing' without making the necessary substantive changes to achieve external policy goals.*
- Differences in risk appetite of corporate managements and regulators. *Corporate managers are generally motivated to accept greater risks of non-compliance than regulators might expect, and to define certain things as compliant that regulators might prefer to see as non-compliant.*
- *This suggests that compliance systems will often be designed to manage risk and to set up grounds for management to negotiate with regulators that they have tried to do the right thing, rather than the compliance system being designed purely to eliminate non-compliance.*
- *Finally, even if corporate managements genuinely want to prevent non-compliance, it may be just too difficult and resource intensive for most managers to work out what effective compliance requires in each and every set of circumstances.*

Parker and Nielsen used survey style research to measure the extent to which adoption of formal compliance systems and top management commitment to substantive compliance values shape the daily management of compliance issues.[110, 111] Their *'data certainly demonstrate that formal compliance systems provide no easy formula for changing the everyday habits and practices of corporate managers and employees in relation to compliance issues. Rather, compliance management in practice is something that combines management, resources, values, and formal compliance management systems'.*[112] They recommend further research to test how the combination of formal systems, good management, and values influences actual compliance outcomes – how corporate managers and employees actually behave and whether they violate the law or not.

---

108 Huisman, W. & Beukelman, A. (2007). *Invloeden op regelnaleving door bedrijven, Inzichten uit wetenschappelijk onderzoek.* Den Haag: Boom Juridische Uitgevers, p. 43.
109 Parker & Gilad (2011). *Supra* note 11.
110 Parker, C. & Lehmann Nielsen, V. (2009). Corporate Compliance Systems: Could They Make Any Difference? *Administration & Society, Volume 41,* Number 1, March 2009 p. 3-37.
111 Parker and Nielsen conducted a survey of top management representatives from 1000 large Australian business in relation to their compliance with competition and consumer protection law.
112 Parker & Nielsen (2009). *Supra* note 110, p. 28.

Gunningham reports in a similar way. Based on empirical research in the mining industry, he reports that, in that specific meta-regulation arrangement with an emphasis on management-based regulation, commitment at the corporate level does not necessarily percolate down to individual facilities: *'the claim that management based regulation – or meta regulation more broadly – can overcome many of the traditional challenges of regulating complex organisations is overstated.'* (p. 35)[113]

6.6.3 Standard Setting in the context of Compliance Management Systems

When it comes to standard setting in the context of new governance, Ford and Condon[114] suggest that the regulated entity is primarily responsible for its own compliance and that this responsibility goes together with a greater autonomy to design their own internal processes to meet broadly defined outcomes. Gunningham elaborates on the issue of standard setting in the context of self-regulatory strategies and argues in line with Ford and Condon: *'in contrast to traditional prescriptive standards (which tell duty holders precisely what measures to take) or to performance standards (which specify outcomes or the desired level of performance), this approach involves firms developing their own process and management system standards, and developing internal planning and management practices designed to achieve regulatory or corporate goals.'*[115]

In the Netherlands, standard setting, in the context of the TCF, is being discussed. Van der Enden and Oenema advocate a supervision framework that they describe as regulated self-control. The core of their proposal is a system in which the NTCA stops auditing the tax returns if the TCF of the business meets the standards set by the NTCA or in the law. [116] They argue that the NTCA is reticent when it comes to standard setting even though the Commission Horizontal Monitoring recommended the NTCA to consider standard setting.[117]

Besides the fact that standard setting doesn't fit with the organising principles of new governance and cooperative compliance, it can be doubted that standard setting will help taxpayers become more compliant e.g. research conducted on the effectiveness of the regulation of Corporate Governance in laws and codes doesn't support this idea. Cools reports, based on the study of 60 academic publications, that laws and codes did not lead to the improvement of business results. Furthermore, he concluded there is no convincing proof that Corporate Governance helps businesses to reduce incidents or frauds.[118] Paape reports in a similar way – no matter whether rules were voluntary

---

113 Gunningham & Sinclair (2009). *Supra* note 98, p 35.
114 Ford & Condon (2011). *Supra* note 3.
115 Gunninham & Sinclair (2009). *Supra* note 97.
116 Enden, E. van der & Oenema, M. (2013). Horizontaal toezicht 2.0 Gereguleerde zelfcontrole. Een derde tak aan de fiscale toezichts- en handhavingsboom, *Weekblad Fiscaal Recht* 2013/430.
117 Committee Horizontal Monitoring Tax and Customs Administration (2012). *Supra* note 89.
118 Cools, K. (2006). *Controle is goed, vertrouwen nog beter; over bestuurders en corporate governance.* Assen: Van Gorcum, p. 24 e.s.

or mandatory, scandals persisted. He concludes that there still seems to be room for improvement.[119]

McBarnett analyses the problem with laws and how they provoke cooperative compliance.[120] And so does Baldwin:

'As far as transparency is concerned, regulators will also face two contradictary demands. On the one hand their regulatees and advisors (often accountancy firms) will demand that discretions are reduced and that regimes are made open, predictable and consistent with the rule of law. They will accordingly, demand the promulgation of guiding rules. On the other, the same individuals may complain that the regulatory rules they face are to over-restrictive and strangling enterprise. They will, in addition, seek to take advantages of key weakness of precise rules – their vulnerability to circumventing by those who can side step the rules with "creative compliance" on the advice of astute advisors (often accountancy firms).'[121]

Van Elk, Poelmann and Veldhuizen argue that the reticence of the NTCA actually helped support the placement of the responsibility on to the taxpayers and the tax intermediaries for their own compliance and to design their own solutions and frameworks to use in their accounting system, business and tax control framework.[122] Furthermore they argue, with reference to the General Tax Law, the standard for the TCF is that it needs to meet the needs of the business.[123] This 'open standard' for the TCF is accompanied by a standard for the tax returns to be filed by the businesses. This standard is called the 'acceptable tax return'. The TCF is a precondition to file complete, correct and timely tax returns and to pay tax debt timely. The NTCA considers a tax return acceptable when it meets all legal requirements and is free of material errors. How the NTCA operationalises the standard of the acceptable tax return is explained in a memo on the Tax Audit Approach of the NTCA.[124] The concept of the acceptable tax return is exemplified as follows:

'It should be noted that the 'acceptable tax return' is not an autonomous legal concept. The relevant legislation and regulations prescribe the requirements to be met by taxpayers in their tax returns. Taxpayers are under the obligation to and bear the responsibility for

---

119 Paape, L (2008). 'In control' verklaringen: gebakken lucht of een te koesteren fenomeen? Oratie, Nyenrode Business Universiteit, p. 12 e.s. http://www.nyenrode.nl/FacultyResearch/research/Documents/Inaugural%20lectures/paape_inaugural_lecture.pdf
120 McBarnet, D.J. (2003). When compliance is not the solution but the problem: from changes in law to changes in attitude. In: Braithwaite, V. (ed) *Taxing Democracy: Understanding Tax Avoidance and Evasion*. Aldershot, UK: Ashgate Publishing.
121 Baldwin, R. (2000). *'Is Regulation Right'?* Discussion paper, published by the Centre for Analysis of Risk and Regulation van de London School of Economics and Political Science, London, www.eprintslse.ac.uk/35976/1/IsRegulationRight.pdf.
122 Elk, M.A.C. van, Poelmann, E. & Veldhuizen, R.J. (2013). De zekerheid van een goede administratie, *Tijdschrift voor Formeel Belastingrecht*, nr. 6/7 Oktober 2013, p.19-25.
123 Algemene wet inzake Rijksbelastingen, art 52 lid 1, Kamerstukken II, 1988-1989, 21 287, nr. 3.
124 Netherlands Tax and Customs Administration (2013). *Controleaanpak Belastingdienst (CAB). De CAB en zijn modellen toegepast in toezicht*. http://download.belastingdienst.nl/belastingdienst/docs/cab_dv4221z1fd.pdf.

complying with the legislation and regulations when they prepare and file their tax returns. The 'acceptable tax return' term is of importance to the NTCA's supervision. The 'acceptable' term gives shape to the requirement for the efficient and effective carrying out of the legislation and regulations as specified in the standing mandate issued to the Tax and Customs.'

6.6.4 NTCA and TCF

In order to make tax supervision efficient and effective (reducing the administrative burden), the NTCA re-uses the organisational compliance or internal control systems of the business. The NTCA refers to this principle using a model called the 'layer-model', figure 6.1.[125] The NTCA explains the concept of the layer-model as follows.

'Efficiency' and 'effectiveness' imply that the NTCA will make selections in the division and deployment of the Administration's (supervisory) capacity. It is neither feasible nor necessary for the NTCA to audit all issues. The NTCA provides customised supervision. The CAB supports this on the basis of the following two principles:
1. *The audit evidence must be appropriate: sufficient quantitative and qualitative audit evidence must be obtained in a structured manner to base opinion on the acceptability of the tax return. Consequently, the precise quantity of audit work/activities is carried out to substantiate the conclusion.*
2. *The audit evidence does not need to be limited solely to the information auditors collect from their personal tests: the layer model shows how they can use audit evidence already collected by others. The auditor makes as much use as possible of the information-, internal control- and monitoring systems of the organisation itself and of the audit- and monitoring activities already performed by the organisation and third parties, such as financial auditors.*

---

125 Kloosterman, H.H.W (1991). Schillenmodel. *De Accountant, jg. 97,* no. 7, maart, pp. 403-406/ and adapted:
Netherlands Tax and Customs Administration (2013). *Supra* note 124, figure 2, p. 7.

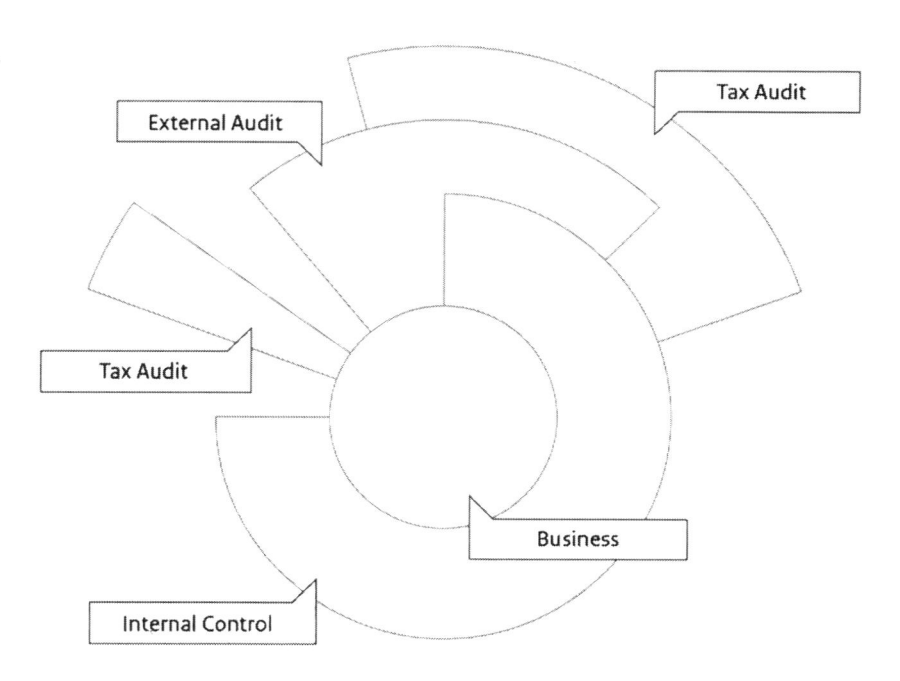

Figure 6.1. The NTCA layer-model

The model shows the different layers of control, assessment and (internal/external) audit around the business processes. From the point of view of the NTCA, the outer layer is the tax assessment/audit. This perspective makes it possible to re-use the activities performed in the inner layers. Tan et al. calls this principle the 'piggy-back' principle.[126] The re-use of internal controls is a generally accepted principle in the regulation of financial audits.[127]

This principle is very powerful in the design of an effective and efficient compliance strategy under the condition that the re-used controls in the inner layers are adequate. This needs to be determined by tests of controls. By using this model the NTCA is capable of adapting the supervision activities, like assessments and audits, to the compliance and control characteristics of the specific taxpayer and prevent duplications of activities. By adapting the supervision strategy based on the evidence of the adequacy of the TCF, the Tax Audit Approach of the NTCA probably provides a way to overcome the discussed problems with the compliance management systems above.

---

126 Tan, Y.-H., Bjorn-Andersen, N., Klein, S. & Rukanova, B. (eds.) (2011). *Accelarating Global Supply Chains with IT-Innovation*. Berlin-Heidelberg: Springer-Verlag, p. 21.
127 International Auditing and Assurance Standards Board (IAASB) (2009). *International Standards on Auditing (ISA) 315 "Identifying and Assessing the Risks of Material Misstatement through Understanding the Entity and Its Environment" and ISA 330 "The Auditor's Responses to Assessed Risks"* (section 7).

6.7 Conclusion

In this chapter I discussed the emergence of New Governance and Cooperative compliance in the tax world. I started with the global picture in sections 6.2 and 6.3. In sections 6.4 and 6.5 I focused on the Horizontal Monitoring strategy developed by the NTCA and its implementation in practice. The basic assumption in the New Governance strategies, like Cooperative compliance, is that compliance of businesses can be improved by 'moralising', 'responsibilising' or 'socialising' them. For this reason the strategies are said to be built on trust and transparency. All parties involved, like businesses, revenue bodies and governments, need a level of comfort or assurance when it comes to the effectiveness of the new strategies. So it can be said that the demand for trust creates corresponding demands for evidence. It is advocated by policy makers and academics that compliance management systems or internal control systems, like the tax control framework, can deliver the evidence needed. In section 6.6 I discuss this assumption. My conclusion is that this assumption is not undisputed by theorists. My second conclusion is there is little empirical evidence supporting this assumption. Nevertheless, this assumption feeds the aspiration of policy makers and regulators, facing the challenge to balance high demands and diminishing resources, leading to a certain eagerness, with which the new regulatory strategies are adapted. My third conclusion would be that more empirical research, with the objective to gain a better understanding of the effectiveness of new governance and compliance management systems for both regulators as regulatees in general and, more specific, in the tax world, is urgently needed.

BAS HERRIJGERS

7. Cooperative compliance: small and medium sized entities

7.1   Introduction

The subject of Chapter 6 is horizontal monitoring/cooperative compliance with large businesses. In this Chapter, the subject will be horizontal monitoring/cooperative compliance with small and medium sized companies (SME). It must be clear that there are considerable differences between the two - differences in terms of quantity, in example the amount of entrepreneurs, these will be discussed in section 7.2. The fact that most large businesses have a two tier board, and a separation of board and ownership, results in the National Tax and Customs Administration (NTCA) not being the only stakeholder that depends upon reliable figures. With SME this is different. It is often the case that the owner is also the director and even the most important employee.

Besides the NTCA and the bank, there are less to no other stakeholders to the annual reports. These corporate governance aspects are the subject of Chapter 3. As a result of all these differences, it makes sense that the NTCA has chosen a different form of supervision regarding SME. In this Chapter, the supervision tailored to SME will be discussed in section 7.3, 7.4 and 7.5.

There is also a difference in the role of the tax service provider or tax adviser (TSP). Most of the large businesses have an 'in house' basic tax awareness and knowledge and use the tax adviser mostly for specific issues. SME generally don't have this basic tax level knowledge in house. For tax related matters they rely on their TSP. The role of the TSP for SME is changing in relation to the horizontal monitoring program by the NTCA. This will be discussed in section 7.6. Dutch horizontal monitoring program from an international perspective will be discussed in section 7.7. In section 7.8 the threats and opportunities of horizontal monitoring will be discussed. This Chapter will be concluded with some alternative forms of supervision relating to horizontal monitoring in section 7.9.

7.2 Dutch landscape of small and medium sized companies

SME contributes a substantial part of the total turnover in the Dutch economy. In 2011, the total turnover was € 932 billion.[1] €495 billion of this came from SME.[2] This is a larger portion than that coming from Large Businesses. However, the total contribution in taxes shows a different picture with Large Businesses contributing more than 60% of the total tax revenues.[3] The characteristic difference between the two is clear when we look at the number of companies that make up this turnover and contribution in taxes. NTCA mentions that there are around 1,500,000 entrepreneurs in the SME segment.[4] The number of very large and medium large companies in 2011 amounted to 12.500 jointly.[5] So less than 1% of companies contribute over 60% of the total tax revenue.

The NTCA has to make choices to achieve its goal.[6] These choices depend upon decisions at a political level. Politicians decide priorities and allocate resources to the NTCA.[7] In 2011, the NTCA had a total staffing level of 29,011 FTEs.[8] In 2012 the staffing level decreased to 28,454 FTEs.[9] 7,735 FTEs of the total staff was assigned to the supervision of businesses. These 7,735 can be allocated as follows: 1,846 FTEs to the Large Businesses segment and 5,889 FTEs to the SME segment.[10]

The figures above show that, in the Large Businesses segment, 0,15 FTE per organisation was available for supervision in 2012.[11] In the SME segment, 0,004 FTE was available for supervision per organisation.[12] Given the differences between these two segments in terms of corporate governance, contribution to tax revenues, the number of organisations and the available staffing level of the NTCA, it must be clear that supervision can be identical in theory only. I would hereby like to refer to Chapter 2 about Risk management. The chosen method of horizontal monitoring in the Large

---

1 Kerngegevens MKB 2012/2013, *MKB & Ondernemerschap in zakformaat*, 2013, p. 6. (only available in Dutch).
2 Kerngegevens MKB 2012/2013, *MKB & Ondernemerschap in zakformaat*, 2013, p. 6.(only available in Dutch).
3 Committee Horizontal Monitoring Tax and Customs Administration (2012). *Tax Supervision made to measure*, p. 36.
4 Committee Horizontal Monitoring Tax and Customs Administration (2012). *Tax Supervision made to measure*, p. 36.
5 Committee Horizontal Monitoring Tax and Customs Administration (2012). *Tax Supervision made to measure*, p. 36.
6 The mission of the NTCA is to efficiently and effectively collect the amount of tax due by maintaining and improving voluntary compliance of taxpayers and by acting repressively to those who are not complying voluntarily. http://www.oecd.org/tax/administration/43241144.pdf.
7 The NTCA has had to deal with a hiring freeze extended until 2013. From 2013 is invested in monitoring capacity. Almelo, L. van, (2013). De Belastingdienst komt naar je toe. *Het Register*, april 2013, nr. 2, p. 16 (only available in Dutch).
8 Belastingdienst (2012). *Beheersverslag 2011*, p. 80 (only available in Dutch).
9 Committee Horizontal Monitoring Tax and Customs Administration (2012). *Tax Supervision made to measure*, p. 83.
10 Committee Horizontal Monitoring Tax and Customs Administration (2012). *Tax Supervision made to measure*, p. 83.
11 1.836 FTE / 12,500 organisations = 0.15FTE per organisation.
12 5.889 FTE / 1,500,000 organisations = .004 FTE per organisation.

Businesses segment, as discussed in Chapter 6, by compliance agreements is not practically possible within the SME segment.[13] The NTCA performs a two-track policy in horizontal monitoring.[14] One track focuses on individual account management for large businesses and another on the non-individual account management for SME.[15] This second track of horizontal monitoring, as a part of modified supervision, will be discussed in the next sections.

7.3   New ways of supervision for SMEs

The SME segment contains approximately 1.5 million entrepreneurs.[16] Considering the amount of entrepreneurs and the staff numbers available for supervision, the NTCA has searched, and continues to search, for forms of supervision that make the monitoring process as effective and efficient as possible. The NTCA has divided the SME segment into: SME with employees (including self-employed with employees), start-ups (companies in the first three years of the company's existence) and sole proprietors (self-employed).[17] All of these entrepreneurs fall within the scope for new ways of supervision.

The NTCA has searched for co-operation with other parties outside the government for new forms of supervision. Presently, the NTCA does this in three ways:
1. Co-operation with the software industry focused on creating a reliable chain from administrative record to tax return.[18]
2. Co-operation with sectoral organisations to resolve specific sectoral tax issues in advance.
3. Co-operation with TSPs focused on the quality of tax returns.

In the first method the NTCA approaches parties that develop software such as accounting and cash register (POS) software.[19] The NTCA wants to create a situation in which it evaluates the software before the developer brings it to the market. For POS systems in 2011, the label reliable POS system was developed. The organisation behind the label has defined a set of norms for cash register systems that any system must meet in order to carry the label.[20]

---

13   Poolen, Th. W. M. (2009). Horizontaal toezicht vanuit het perspectief van de Belastingdienst. *Tijdschrift Fiscaal Ondernemingsrecht*, 2009/16, p. 20.
14   Hel, L. van der, & Pheijffer, M. (2012). Evaluatie horizontaal toezicht: fiscaal toezicht op maat. *Maandblad voor Accountancy en Bedrijfseconomie*, October 2012 (only available in Dutch).
15   Hel, L. van der, & Pheijffer, M. (2012). Evaluatie horizontaal toezicht: fiscaal toezicht op maat. *Maandblad voor Accountancy en Bedrijfseconomie*, October 2012 (only available in Dutch).
16   Committee Horizontal Monitoring Tax and Customs Administration (2012). *Tax Supervision made to measure*, p. 36.
17   Committee Horizontal Monitoring Tax and Customs Administration (2012). *Tax Supervision made to measure*, p. 34.
18   Belastingdienst (2012). *Programma Horizontaal Toezicht MKB*. Jaarverslag 2011, p. 3 (only available in Dutch).
19   Belastingdienst, (2007). *Bedrijfsplan Belastingdienst 2008-2012*, p. 22 (only available in Dutch).
20   Belastingdienst (2012). *Programma Horizontaal Toezicht MKB*. Jaarverslag 2011, p. 7 (only available in Dutch).

In addition to approaching software developers, the NTCA also approaches sectoral organisations and their members. These approaches are initiated to solve specific sectoral tax issues. This can result in establishing a compliance agreement with the sectoral organisation. If this sectoral organisation is not capable of monitoring as to whether their members comply with the agreement, a consultation can be agreed upon instead. Currently, there are compliance agreements or consultations with 15 sectoral organisations ranging from the mussel farming industry and the taxi industry to music venues. The members of these sectoral organisation are not automatically covered by the agreement, but have to join separately.

The first and second new forms of modified supervision are not considered to be horizontal monitoring because the covenant partners cannot be held responsible for the acceptability of the tax return and/or to carry out monitoring activities.[21] The third new form of supervision is different. This form - the co-operation with TSPs - can be called horizontal monitoring within the SME segment.

The NTCA has put considerable effort into the co-operation with TSPs.[22] The OECD also believes that there is potential for a form of enhanced relationship between TSPs and the Tax Administrations.[23] The role of the TSP is described by the OECD as follows: 'tax intermediaries play a vital role in all tax systems, helping taxpayers understand and comply with their tax obligations in an increasingly complex world'.[24] In this co-operation with TSPs the NTCA concludes compliance agreements with umbrella organisations of TSPs or individual TSPs. For this, a standard compliance agreement is available. This standard compliance agreement contains the principles of horizontal monitoring.[25] By the end of 2013, 89,000 entrepreneurs, through TSPs, participated in a horizontal monitoring agreement in the SME segment.[26]

The choice for the TSP is a logical one. The TSP has traditionally been the link between the tax authorities and the entrepreneur. Research also shows that the use of a TSP influences tax compliance of taxpayers.[27] One of the behavioural drivers of TSPs is the client and legal responsibilities they have.[28] Through a compliance agreement the TSPs and the NTCA enter into a relationship with mutual responsibilities.

With this relationship, the NTCA has a great source of potential participants for horizontal monitoring amounting to around 600,000 entrepreneurs. These entrepreneurs

---

21 Committee Horizontal Monitoring Tax and Customs Administration (2012). *Tax Supervision made to measure*, p. 24.
22 Klein Sprokkelhorst, A., 'Het is de kunst om de relatie met de buitenwereld aan te gaan.' Kors Kool over horizontaal toezicht, Belasting magazine, december 2009, blz. 8 – 9. (only available in Dutch).
23 OECD (2008). *Study into the role of tax intermediaries*, p.44. Paris: OECD.
24 OECD(2008). *Study into the role of tax intermediaries*, p.5. Paris: OECD.
25 Horizontal monitoring is based on the principles of mutual trust, understanding and transparency.
26 http://www.rijksbegroting.nl/2013/verantwoording/jaarverslag,kst195482_7.html.
27 Klepper S., Mazur, M., & Nagin, D. (1991). Expert Intermediaries and legal compliance: the case of tax preparers. *Journal of Law & Economics*, vol. XXXIV, April 1991, p. 228.
28 OECD (2008). *Study into the role of tax intermediaries*, p.5.

belong to the sub segment SME+. This sub segment contains two categories of SMEs: SMEs with employees, and self-employed with employees.

The target is to have 100,000 participating entrepreneurs by late 2014.[29] The long term aim of the NTCA is to have a total of 210,000 participating SMEs.[30] There is a leading role for the TSP in achieving this target.

The role of the TSP varies widely per entrepreneur. It can be that the entire process is taken care of – from preparing the administration to delivering the tax return. In other cases, only the tax return is provided. The exact role of the TSP in horizontal monitoring is further set out in section 7.4.

These three new ways of supervision fit into the Tax Audit layer model that the NTCA uses in its audit strategy.

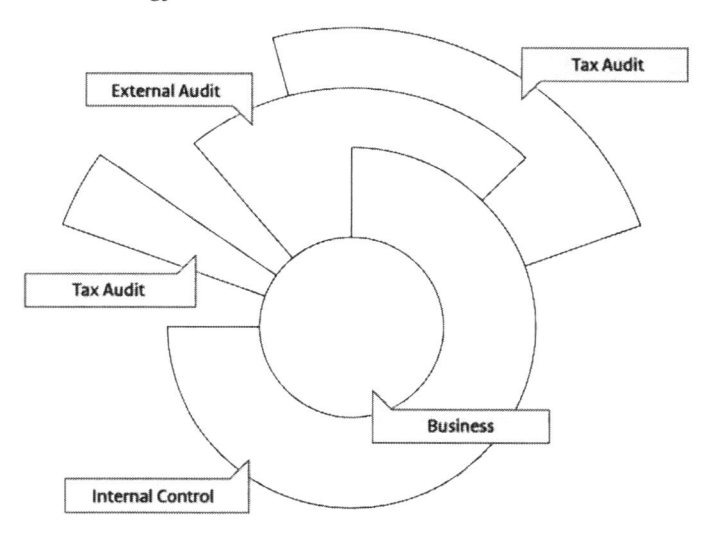

Figure 7.1. Layer model[31]

The use of one or more new ways of supervision for an entrepreneur in the SME segment will result in the strengthening of one or more layers. This has an impact on the NTCA supervision layer. The use of one or more of these new ways of supervision will have the effect of diluting this particular layer. Co-operation with TSPs ensures better quality of tax returns. This causes a reinforcement of the external control layer. It will also have an impact on the layers of internal controls and the primary processes as the TSP detects inaccuracies at the front of the process. But it also improves the processes of the TSPs themselves. Co-operation with sectoral organisations may, depending on the nature of the co-operation, strengthen different layers - primary

---

29 http://www.rijksbegroting.nl/2014/voorbereiding/begroting,kst186724_10.html.
30 Belastingdienst (2012). *Programma Horizontaal Toezicht MKB*. Jaarverslag 2011, p. 4 (only available in Dutch).
31 Netherlands Tax and Customs Administration, (2014). Audit Approach, p. 7.

processes, internal control and internal audit. The co-operation with software developers ensures a strengthening of the internal control layer.

7.4 Horizontal monitoring by SMEs

A compliance agreement between the NTCA and the TSP implies an agreement on attitude, behaviour and processes.[32] This is the basis for the relationship between the TSP and the NTCA. As with an individual compliance agreement, it is expressed that parties will be transparent, trustful and understanding. The goal is that the parties define their processes in a way that the tax return is good enough to accept without any form of supervision from the NTCA except for meta-monitoring.[33] This creates a so-called 'compliance agreement chain'. Entrepreneur, TSP and the NTCA together form this chain.

The NTCA recognises in this form of horizontal monitoring, the following six steps:
1. Compliance agreement discussions and concluding a compliance agreement.
2. Applications for and reviews of entrepreneurs.
3. Preliminary consultations.
4. Filing and processing of compliance agreement tax returns.
5. Audits of random samples of tax returns.
6. Monitoring and evaluation of the compliance agreement.[34]

These steps are explained below.

7.4.1 Compliance agreement discussions and concluding a compliance agreement

In the process to conclude a compliance agreement, various points are discussed beforehand. The first set of meetings often has an introductory character. Particularly in the first meeting, the NTCA has an important role in setting out the objective of horizontal monitoring and the method of horizontal monitoring. These discussions give the relationship more form and substance. The NTCA addresses, at a minimum, the following issues in the discussions after the introductory phase:
- the tone at the top: what is the TSP's attitude towards co-operation with the NTCA, and is the TSP prepared to enter into a relationship based on transparency, understanding and trust?;
- an explanation of the key concepts and principles of horizontal monitoring, in particular the concept of the acceptable tax return;
- the responsibilities and expectations of each party;
- the TSP's quality assurance system;

---

32 Belastingdienst, (2008). *Horizontaal toezicht – Samenwerken vanuit vertrouwen*, p. 4 (only available in Dutch).
33 Dijk, F.J.H. van, (2009). 'Compliance', TCF en convenanten. *Tax Assurance in beeld 5 – Tax Assurance Essays III*, Nyenrode, p. 154 (only available in Dutch).
34 Netherlands Tax and Custom administration (2012). *Guide Horizontal Monitoring SME*, p. 9.

- the fact that horizontal monitoring is targeted at the large majority of the TSP's clients and a discussion of the TSP's implementation plan (or the joint implementation plan);
- the approach the TSP and NTCA adopt to the dissemination of the concept of horizontal monitoring in their respective organisations;
- an outline of the 6 steps involved in the horizontal monitoring process, in particular the preliminary consultations and meta-monitoring;
- experiences with current or recent NTCA contacts.[35]

Besides building a relationship through a number of meetings, the NTCA also forms an image of the quality and professionalism of the TSP. This is done through the inspection and discussion of a number of client files, with the TSP.

An adequate quality assurance system contains measures that focus on processes concerning:
- verifying the reliability of the inputs (information received by the TSP from the entrepreneur);
- supplementing or adding the information to arrive at a compliance agreement tax return.[36]

In addition, the NTCA have issued a number of benchmarks which show the professional level of the TSP:
- the office management's responsibility for the quality.
- the implementation of (internal) professional ethics standards.
- the acceptance of clients and the continuation of assignments.
- experience and expertise.
- the quality assurance system:
  - client acceptance;
  - risk policy;
  - work programs;
  - documentation;
  - peer consultations and reviews;
  - specific tax advice;
  - tax affairs department;
- quality control.[37]

During the review of the client files and the discussion about these files, the NTCA examines whether these benchmarks have been met.

---

35 Netherlands Tax and Custom administration (2012). *Guide Horizontal Monitoring SME*, p. 11.
36 Netherlands' Tax and Custom administration (2012). *Guide Horizontal Monitoring SME*, p. 12.
37 Netherlands' Tax and Custom administration (2012). *Guide Horizontal Monitoring SME*, p. 12.

7.4.2 Applications for and reviews of entrepreneurs

When the compliance agreement has been concluded, the process of the registration of entrepreneurs begins. During this phase the NTCA carries out a marginal review. This review contains the following issues:
- does the entrepreneur belong to a sector which the NTCA excludes from horizontal monitoring?[38]
- is the entrepreneur known in the NTCA files under the same name?
- is there a current heightened attention to the entrepreneur at the NTCA?
- are there tax payment arrears which are associated with reluctance?
- are there current supervision activities?

7.4.3 Preliminary consultations

Preliminary consultations are an important element of horizontal monitoring as they provide assurance in advance and contribute to the quality of the tax returns. Prior to submitting a tax return, relevant tax issues may arise. Consultation about these issues ensures that the tax return provided through the TSP does not contain surprises for the NTCA. Either the issue is solved in the preliminary consultation or brought before a judge (agree to disagree). In the process of preliminary consultation the TSP is responsible for the completeness and accuracy of the facts presented. The NTCA does not perform independent additional research.

Preliminary consultations are not exclusive for participants of horizontal monitoring. But in horizontal monitoring parties agree to always have a preliminary consultation at the moment they expect a relevant tax issue may arise.

Conducting preliminary consultation strengthens the relationship. The NTCA describes this as follows: 'preliminary consultations contribute to the enhancement of the relationship and increase trust: the preliminary consultations give the parties an insight into each other's professionalism and intentions, as well as their approach to the quality of the products and service.'[39]

The Swiss tax authorities also give taxpayers or tax advisers the possibility of preliminary consultations - with positive results - 'by agreeing to discuss the matter, the tax authorities create a positive climate in which the relationship between the parties can develop favourably on a long term basis.'[40]

---

38 NTCA mentioned specific sectors that are excluded for horizontal monitoring. They are characterised as 'havens', i.e. coffee shops, the prostitution sector or mobile home sites. Netherlands' Tax and Custom administration (2012). *Guide Horizontal Monitoring SME*, p. 4.
39 Netherlands' Tax and Custom administration (2012). *Guide Horizontal Monitoring SME*, p. 18.
40 Bugnon M., (2012). Horizontal Treatment – New Forms and Experiences of Achieving Enhanced Relationship between Tax Administrations, Taxpayers and Tax Intermediaries: The Swiss Approach – With a Focus on the Ruling Practice. *Tax Tribune 28*, p. 177.

7.4.4 Filing and processing of compliance agreement tax returns

A TSP files two sorts of tax returns: tax returns of entrepreneurs who joined the horizontal monitoring program - the so-called compliance tax returns - and tax returns from entrepreneurs who have not joined the horizontal monitoring program.

The compliance agreement tax returns are acceptable tax returns. An acceptable tax return is a tax return that complies with requirements imposed by the legislation and regulations and is free of material misstatements.[41] It is up to the TSP to generate tax returns that meet the standards. In the opinion of the NTCA, this is up to the professionalism of the TSP.[42]

The NTCA processes the submitted compliance agreement tax returns without an audit. In other words, it is a 'no touch' situation. Except under the following conditions:
- the tax return includes technical inaccuracies (for example, parts of the declaration are damaged or fields are filled with the wrong kind of characters).
- the tax return contains inconsistencies (for example, total counts do not fit).
- the tax return contains information that differs from what can be expected in a way accuracy of the tax return should be doubted (for example, a company with a normal yearly turnover of € 100,000 files a tax return with a turnover of € 100 Million).

7.4.5 Audits of random samples of tax returns

To validate the horizontal monitoring process, compliance agreement tax returns are included in the random audit program.[43] In 2011, a maximum of 1% of the total number of filed compliance agreement tax returns have been selected in this random sample.

These compliance agreement tax returns are audited by the NTCA in accordance with the Tax Audit Approach (CAB). This subject is elaborated upon in section 7.5 and the audit itself in Chapter 15

7.4.6 Monitoring and evaluation of the compliance agreement

Periodically, the NTCA and TSP discuss their experiences relating to horizontal monitoring. In this way, input is given to the learning circle (figure 7.2).

---

41 In practice, the acceptable tax return term causes confusion as the terminology employed by the 'legal sector' and the 'audit sector' is not consistent. In this chapter we use the term as described. Further information about the acceptable tax return can be found in NTCA: Audit Approach. Netherlands Tax and Customs Administration (2014). Audit Approach, p. 3.
42 Netherlands' Tax and Custom administration (2011). *Guide Horizontal Monitoring SME*, p. 9.
43 The NTCA audits every year 1% of the total businesses. These businesses are selected at random. This is one of the forms of supervision. It's also working as an internal control mechanism which gives information about the effectiveness of the other ways of supervision.

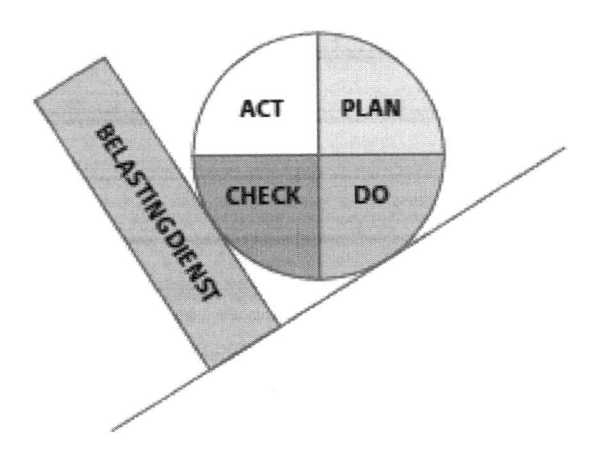

Figure 7.2 Horizontal monitoring learning cycle

Compliance agreements are made to optimise the relationship and the process of horizontal monitoring. It is not just about the tax return as such. This is part of the overall monitoring, but the monitoring is also about issues such as tax return behaviour, the process of preliminary consultation, the time needed to generate tax returns, the payment behaviour of participating entrepreneurs and the manner of implementation of meta-monitoring.

The roles of the NTCA and the TSP in the learning circle depend on the type of action to be taken. However, the NTCA's aim is to ensure that the learning circle will only move forward.

7.5 Meta-monitoring

In horizontal monitoring in the SME segment the NTCA uses meta-monitoring. Meta-monitoring can be defined as 'monitoring which is based on relying on the monitoring results of others'.[44] In this case, the monitoring is related to the quality assurance system and the execution of procedures and quality controls of the TSP.

The audit of a random sample of tax returns is part of the process of meta – monitoring by the NTCA. The inclusion in horizontal monitoring results in the participating entrepreneurs no longer being involved in regular monitoring. Supervision based on risk assessment no longer takes place. Participating organisations are also no longer involved in national and regional NTCA supervision actions.[45] The only form of supervision is meta-monitoring.

---

44 Algemene Rekenkamer (2007). *Horizontale vormen van verantwoording en interne vormen van toezicht*, p.2. (only available in Dutch).

45 In principle, these tax returns are not involved in actions. However, these tax returns may be involved when an action adresses aspects that the tax service providers can not assess or only to a limited extent. Netherlands' Tax and Custom administration (2011). *Guide Horizontal Monitoring SME*, p.10.

Through meta-monitoring, the NTCA tests whether the compliance agreement tax returns are indeed acceptable. Based on the meta-monitoring, the NTCA examines where the quality of the tax returns needs further improvement. This information is of value to the TSP to optimise its processes and quality assurance system.

Meta-monitoring consists of several elements: preliminary consultations and other contacts with the TSP. However, the real evaluation moment is the audit of compliance agreement tax returns. These audits prove whether the processes and quality assurance system of the TSP delivers compliance agreement tax returns which are acceptable.

The amount of work that the NTCA will have to invest in an audit depends on the quality of the compliance agreement tax return. A compliance agreement tax return that is included in the meta-monitoring should be audited in accordance with the CAB.[46] The CAB allows for a reliance on the work of third parties. This is the primary approach to perform an audit.

The audit will start with understanding the business and conditional controls.[47] This will result in a risk analysis of the business based on the available information. Appropriate audit measures are determined by seeking a combination of system oriented tests and substantive tests that will result in an audit that is as effective and efficient as possible.[48] Part of these appropriate audit measures is to compare the risk analysis with the file of the TSP. Based on this risk analysis, the work of the TSP is reviewed. The NTCA reviews whether the work performed to generate the tax return had the necessary level and depth. If this is the case, the NTCA limits it's audit to peruse this information. Where there are considered to be elements lacking in the work performed by the TSP, the NTCA will carry out additional control activities conducted by the entrepreneur in order to obtain sufficient quantitative and qualitative audit evidence to approve the acceptability of the compliance agreement tax return.[49]

---

46 Netherlands' Tax and Custom administration (2011). *Guide Horizontal Monitoring SME*, p.22.
47 Netherlands Tax and Customs Administration (2014). Audit Approach, p. 18.
48 Netherlands Tax and Customs Administration (2014). Audit Approach, p. 19.
49 Netherlands Tax and Customs Administration (2014). Audit Approach, p. 4.

```
              ┌─────────┐
              │    ↑    │
   Fiscus     │    │    │
              │    ↓    │
              ├─────────┤
              │    ↑    │
   Adviseur   │    │    │
              │    ↓    │
              ├─────────┤
              │    ↑    │
   Ondernemer │    │    │
              │    ↓    │
              └─────────┘
```

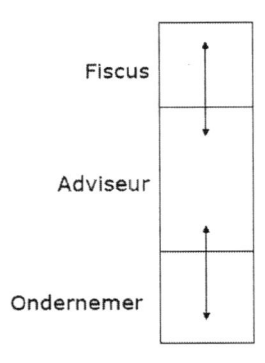

Figure 7.3 Communicating vessels in the process of validated tax return

In figure 7.3, the dividing of labour in the situation of meta-monitoring to come to a validated compliance agreement tax return is shown. The total column represents the validated compliance agreement tax return. The column is divided into three segments that can be considered as communicating vessels.

The quality of the accounting and internal control of the entrepreneur (ondernemer) indicates the starting position in order to achieve an acceptable tax return. The level of the controls determines the quantity of work that the TSP (adviseur) has to perform in order to achieve a tax return that meets the requirements of an acceptable tax return. The amount of work relating to meta-monitoring that the NTCA (Fiscus) has to perform varies according to the quantity and quality of the work already performed by the entrepreneur and TSP.[50]

Meta-monitoring can result in four kinds of actions:
1. The audited tax returns were acceptable. No action is needed and the TSP can continue its process in the same way.
2. The audited tax returns were acceptable, but the files of the TSP are not complete. Possibly, some documents that were used, were not documented. Another option is that some actions were performed but not documented. On the basis of these lapses, the NTCA and the TSP discuss how to bring the client file to the needed minimum level.
3. The audited tax returns were not acceptable. The tax returns contain a material error. The TSP has to ascertain whether this tax return is the only case or that other tax returns he prepared, maybe even for other clients, also contain this error. In both situations the TSP has to correct the error in the specific tax return(s). Afterwards, the NTCA and the TSP have to discuss how to improve the process of the TSP so that these errors will not occur in the future. The relationship could be

---

50 The amount of work for the NTCA can vary within the same tax service provider. For example, one client uses a certified cash register and the other client doesn't. This will reflect on the amount of work that the NTCA has to perform to come to a validated compliance agreement tax return.

damaged in this situation - but the actions taken to repair this situation, and to improve the process for the future, can diminish the damage caused.
4. The audited tax return was not acceptable. The tax returns contain material errors, or even fraud, that was known by the TSP. The relationship between the NTCA and the TSP will have suffered serious damage. The NTCA will usually have only one option open - ending the compliance agreement. This can cause reputational damage for the TSP and the NTCA. For the clients it will mean that they will be included in the regular ways of supervision.

7.6 The changing role of the tax service provider

The TSP for SMEs has traditionally been a trustee of the SME entrepreneur (see figure 7.4). Within horizontal monitoring in the SME segment, the role of the TSP changes (see figure 7.5).

NTCA

Entrepreneur   **Tax Service Provider**

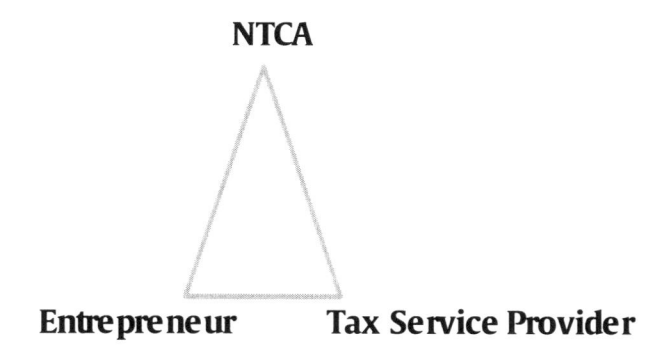

Figure 7.4 Traditional role of tax service provider

NTCA

Tax Service Provider

Entrepreneur

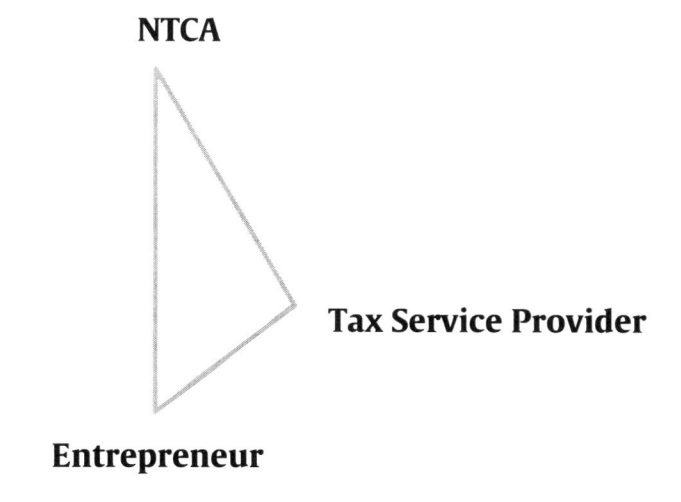

Figure 7.5 Role of tax service provider under horizontal monitoring

The TSP, through its quality assurance system, adds value to the tax return of the entrepreneur. Through the compliance agreement, the TSP also has a responsibility towards the NTCA. This is a change in its role – the TSP no longer only serves his client but also the NTCA.

Whether this change of responsibility results in a change in the relationship between the TSP and the entrepreneur is not clear at this point in time. Fact is that the roles in the relationship can become more complicated.[51]

The changing role also brings another kind of pressure to bear on the TSP. It is the TSP that is responsible for the registration of entrepreneurs under the compliance agreement. The TSP is not required to register all its clients. It is even questionable as to whether a TSP is able to do so. After all, the TSP will not have built the same kind of relationship with each client. There may be very different legitimate reasons for a TSP to refuse a client to join his compliance agreement. For example, the client is new to his office, or there are special circumstances such as a merger or change of shareholders. However, under TSPs, the fear exists that they implicitly express an opinion on the reliability of the entrepreneurs to whom they refuse access to any compliance agreement - and that the TSP might be held liable for the damage to his client.

This decision, of allowing a client to join the agreement, is more than the use of the quality assurance system of the TSP. Also the client has an role he has to choose for horizontal monitoring. For the registration of clients the TSP has to make a decision based solely on his client knowledge. This client knowledge consists of two elements: explicit client knowledge that is documented in his client files, and implicit client knowledge that is not documented, but which the TSP has gained during the course of the relationship. This makes the choice even harder. There is no set of rules or principles that describe which client can join and which one cannot.[52]

7.7 Dutch horizontal monitoring in SME segment in international perspective

The committee that reviewed horizontal monitoring has concluded that in 2011 the NTCA was far ahead internationally in regard to its horizontal monitoring in the SME segment.[53] Slovenian tax authorities, at the end of 2011, were discussing the possibility

---

51   Committee Horizontal Monitoring Tax and Customs Administration (2012). *Tax Supervision made to measure*, p. 93.
52   Except for the specific mentioned sectors that are characterised as 'havens', i.e. coffee shops, the prostitution sector or mobile home sites. Netherlands' Tax and Custom administration (2012). *Guide Horizontal Monitoring SME*, p. 4.
53   Committee Horizontal Monitoring Tax and Customs Administration (2012). *Tax Supervision made to measure*, p. 124.

of implementing the Dutch method and started a pilot program in 2013.[54] Other tax administrations in Europe are also looking for other forms of enhanced relationships with SMEs. This is something the Forum of Tax Administrations has targeted with a specific project which is being led by Norway.[55] Also the tax administration of Poland is looking for ways to implement cooperative compliance in the SME segment. Both view the formalised co-operation with SMEs through industrial associations, tax advisors and accountant associations as the most significant option.[56]

7.8 Opportunities and threats of horizontal monitoring in SME segment

The chosen method in which the NTCA assumes that the TSP submits acceptable tax returns creates a different role for the TSP. The NTCA should ensure that this changing role does not become a threat to the method.

The way an SME entrepreneur joins horizontal monitoring via the compliance agreement of his TSP does not automatically ensure that the benefits for the Large Business segment also applies to the SME segment. The NTCA and the TSP must invest in clarifying the benefits for the SME entrepreneur.[57]

In addition to this, the TSP possibly will have to do more work in order to achieve acceptable tax returns than was the case in the past. This has the possible consequence of the administrative burden for the entrepreneur increasing rather than decreasing.[58] This potential increase of the administrative burden poses a threat to the method. Identifying and providing tangible benefits ensure that this threat can be mitigated.

The horizontal monitoring committee has mentioned the following advantages of horizontal monitoring in the SME segment based on the NTCA business case:
- A larger number of acceptable tax returns were filed.
- Participating SMEs had fewer objections and appeals.
- A higher percentage of enterprises in the SME segment make use of the service of a TSP.
- The NTCA staff exhibit an improved client oriented attitude and behaviour.
- The efficiency and effectiveness of supervision is improved.
- The percentage of appeals is reduced.

---

54 The only other known country that perhaps tried to copy the Dutch way of horizontal monitoring in the SME segment is Slovenia. Sinkovec, D. (2012). Practical Experience in Implementing the Horizontal Monitoring Pilot Project in Slovenia. *Tax Tribune 28*, p. 175. Jackowska-Polewczak, A. (2014). *Engaging and involving SMEs and their Intermediaries in Tax Administration Process*, Tax Tribune, vol. 30, p. 37.
55 Saint-Amans, P. (2014). New Ways of Ensuring Tax Compliance – A perspective from the OECD. *Tax Tribune 30*, p. 120.
56 Jackowska-Polewczak, A. (2014). *Engaging and involving SMEs and their Intermediaries in Tax Administration Process*, Tax Tribune, vol. 30, p. 37.
57 Committee Horizontal Monitoring Tax and Customs Administration (2012). *Tax Supervision made to measure*, p. 116.
58 Committee Horizontal Monitoring Tax and Customs Administration (2012). *Tax Supervision made to measure*, p. 124.

- Enterprises in the SME segment receive greater and earlier certainty.
- Businesses place greater trust in the NTCA.
- The market recognisability of TSPs who have concluded a compliance agreement is increased.
- The internal control of participating SMEs has improved.
- The administrative burden imposed on participating SMEs is reduced.
- The self-sufficiency of enterprises in the SME segment is increased.[59]

One threat to horizontal monitoring in the SME segment is the risk that firms participating in horizontal monitoring have more dealings with the NTCA than before. This threat is reinforced by the fact that the TSP has started with registering entrepreneurs for horizontal monitoring who have an administration of a high level. These entrepreneurs mostly have a history of less contact with the NTCA.

A maximum of 1% of the compliance agreements is included in the random audit program.[60] Of the total population of SME entrepreneurs, the NTCA yearly selects an amount of tax returns for the random audit program. In total, the NTCA performed 36,700 audits in the SME segment in 2011.[61] Besides the random audit program, this also contains all the forms of selection that lead to an audit.

However, the number of audits has been decreasing. This has been happening ever since 2009 even though the number of companies has increased.[62] The risk therefore exists that the advantages of the procedure is being lost as a result of the reducing density control. Research also shows that the audit rate has an influence on tax compliance.[63] The NTCA has anticipated this by recruiting new staff (in 2013 and 2014) to strengthen the supervision. One of the goals for 2014 is described as follows: 'the number of audits of entrepreneurs who are not joining the horizontal monitoring program will be increased compared to the level of 2012.'[64]

The Committee stated that the administrative burden imposed on participating SMEs has been reduced. The advantages have already been described. However, international research also shows that the administrative burden for SMEs, as a result of compliance costs, are 5 to 6 times higher than for large businesses (in percentage of sales).[65] Also, the tax compliance costs are significantly higher for SMEs.[66]

---

59 Committee Horizontal Monitoring Tax and Customs Administration (2012). *Tax Supervision made to measure*, p. 71.
60 Netherlands' Tax and Custom administration (2012). *Guide Horizontal Monitoring SME*, p.22.
61 Belastingdienst, (2012). *Beheersverslag 2011*, p. 18.
62 Belastingdienst (2012). *Beheersverslag 2011* (only available in Dutch).
63 Klepper S., Mazur, M. & Nagin, D. (1991). Expert Intermediaries and legal compliance: the case of tax preparers. *Journal of Law & Economics*, vol. XXXIV, April 1991, p. 208.
64 http://www.rijksbegroting.nl/2014/voorbereiding/begroting,kst186724_10.html.
65 Pope, J. (2001). Estimating and Alleviating the Goods and Services Tax Compliance Cost Burden Upon Small Business. *Revenue Law Journal, Vol. 11*: Iss. 1, Article 2.
66 OECD (2009). *Taxation of SMES – key issues and policy considerations*. No. 18, p. 119. Paris: OECD.

Horizontal monitoring for SMEs already shows measurable results. Participating entrepreneurs pay 8% more on time since their participation in a compliance agreement.[67]

The report of the committee has led to the conclusion that horizontal monitoring for SMEs results in a significantly more efficient use of the available staffing level within the NTCA. The 2011 figures show that the horizontal monitoring approximated cost almost as much capacity as the regular supervision. However, if we look at the staffing level of 2012, and the increasing number of participating entrepreneurs, we notice that the NTCA horizontal monitoring method is more effective.[68]

7.9 Alternatives for horizontal monitoring in the SME segment

The NTCA has opted for an approach to the SME segment by concluding compliance agreements with TSPs. However, there are other possible options for modified supervision.

7.9.1 Pre-filled tax return

In the Netherlands the concept of the pre-filled tax return is already implemented and expanded in the income tax. Individuals can download their data in the tax return. They only have to check and supplement the data if needed. These days, data such as corporate income, bank account balances, interest paid and mortgage debt is already pre-filled. It is conceivable that this could also occur for the corporate income tax returns of entrepreneurs. Bank balances of entrepreneurs are known to the NTCA. In addition, payroll taxes and sales taxes can be filled in together with the corresponding revenue and expense accounts. In the future, additional information could be added. For example, costs related to customs, insurance costs, costs for gas, water and electricity.

7.9.2 Outsourcing monitoring

The most radical option is to outsource the monitoring of SMEs. In this case, a market participant would be made responsible for monitoring the SME entrepreneur. This type of supervision would not be unique. In some states of the US, the tax authorities have the power to hire external contractors to perform audits.[69] In 1996, 200 sales and use tax audits were performed by external contractors.[70]

---

67 http://www.rijksbegroting.nl/2013/verantwoording/jaarverslag,kst195482_7.html.
68 Committee Horizontal Monitoring Tax and Customs Administration (2012). *Tax Supervision made to measure*, p. 83.
69 State of Florida Department of Revenue Rules (1992). *Transmittal Memorandum*, 12-25, Contract Auditing Rules.
70 Murray (1997). *The Sales Tax in the 21st Century*, p. 101-109.

7.9.3 Certification of Tax service providers

Another option is certifying TSPs. The difference with outsourcing is that the tax authorities maintain their rights to perform supervision. The TSP doesn't perform the audit in the name of the tax authorities. This procedure is also not unique. For example, Turkey has the 'Sworn in Certified Public Accountants of Turkey'. These auditors may approve financial and tax statements and they have the same rights as an auditor of the tax authorities. The Turkish tax authorities have a form of supervision that is akin to the Netherlands' meta-monitoring of the submitted tax returns.[71]

In Australia, TSPs can be certified by the 'Tax Agent Services Act'. This act has its own procedures in which the requirements and responsibilities for the TSP are described.[72]

In Florida in the US, a certification program exists. TSPs can follow, under the supervision of the tax authorities, a Certified Audit Program.[73] This allows certified public accountants to attain the power to perform tax audits. Entrepreneurs who choose a qualified CPA to file and audit a tax return will not be audited by the tax authorities unless in exceptional circumstances.[74]

7.9.4 Managed audit

Several states in the US have a so-called Managed Audit Program.[75] This managed audit is only used when dealing with the sales-and-use tax. The managed audit implies that the entrepreneur TSP performs a tax audit and enters into an agreement with the tax authorities. This agreement defines the scope of the audit, the procedures to be followed, audit techniques to be used, the elements that should be audited and the time frame for the audit. The tax authorities always retain the right to audit the tax returns. The same way of working could also be used for the corporate tax income return.

7.9.5 Tax Statement

Another possibility is to introduce a separate tax statement. This statement could be attached to the tax return as in a control statement in financial statements. A TSP can add this statement to the tax return. A guideline, in which the norms for such a statement would be defined, will have to be drawn up. For example, these guidelines could follow the existing accounting regulations, to which tax elements

---

71 Ucar, M. (1999). Accountancy Profession in Turkey. *Journal of Qafqaz University*, Year 1999, Volume II, Number II.
72 http://www.taxinstitute.com.au/EFF3D96E-5056-BE14-1224B5069BBBC262.
73 Florida Statutes 2008, Section 213.285, Certified Audits.
74 Florida Department of Revenue (2008). *Certified Audit Program*, GT-s800065, R. 08/09.
75 By illustration the follow states:
   - New Mexico, http://www.tax.state.nm.us/pubs/FYI-404.pdf.
   - Washington, http://dor.wa.gov/content/doingbusiness/Audits/doingBus_MgdAudit.aspx. Ohio, http://www.das.ohio.gov/LinkClick.aspx?fileticket=JYjp2auBFy4%3D&tabid=144.
   - California, http://www.boe.ca.gov/pdf/pub53.pdf.

could be added. These additions would have to be a mix of principle and rule based regulations. The TSP would not have to be certified, especially for the tax statement, but would have to follow the code of conduct of his professional organisation. The tax statement makes it possible for the tax authorities to reduce supervision to meta-monitoring.[76]

---

76 Herrijgers, S.A.A. (2010). De belastingverklaring: het assuranceproduct van de toekomst: een onderzoek naar de mogelijkheid tot implementatie van de belastingverklaring binnen horizontaal toezicht. Engelmoer, J.J. (2010). *Belastingverklaring een nieuw fenomeen in een nieuw vakgebied.* (only available in Dutch).

HANS GRIBNAU

8. Cooperative compliance: some procedural tax law issues*

8.1 Introduction

Cooperative compliance aims for effective and legitimate tax enforcement. This co-operation between taxpayer and tax administration takes place in the context of a particular power relationship. The particular form of power involved in tax enforcement accounts for the conditions, characteristics and boundaries of cooperative compliance in tax matters.

What kind of power is at stake? Legal asymmetry is a pervasive feature of the relationship between revenue bodies and taxpayers as revenue bodies have considerable unilateral powers to determine the mutual legal relationship, in particular the tax liability of the taxpayer. No wonder, because taxes are a compulsory financial contribution to the combined costs of society. Tax payments to the treasury provide the state with financial means to sustain society, for example by providing public goods. Hence, levying tax is a form of exercising power, establishing the compulsory financial contribution of the taxpayer and ensuring the payment of the amounts due.

The tax administration has unilateral powers, laid down in the law, to restrict the taxpayer's liberty. These powers partially compensate for the 'information asymmetry' with regard to the facts relevant to determine taxpayer's tax liability. The legal asymmetry in this tax relationship seems to be a far cry from co-operation and trust, for the exercise of unilateral (coercive) powers seems not to sit well with voluntary co-operation. Co-operation however, is not limited to legal relationships voluntarily entered into such as contractual relationships. Co-operation is also important in asymmetric relationships: tax administrations cannot fulfil their tasks without a considerable degree of compliance, which in its turn is difficult to achieve in the long term without co-operation and trust. Both are essential to another important value in taxation: (legal) certainty.[1] Enforcing compliance is time-consuming, costly and requires a lot of staff. The Netherlands Tax and Customs Administration (NTCA) therefore has adopted a dual approach. It has opted for Horizontal Monitoring as a

---

* The author wishes to thank Ronald Russo for his comments on a previous draft of this paper.

means to enhance taxpayers' voluntary co-operation, supplementing the traditional deterrence approach. Voluntary compliance evidently contributes to an easier and more efficient application of tax law.

The concept of 'Horizontal Monitoring', the Dutch model of cooperative compliance, symbolises a kind of 'horizontalisation' in the tax relationship – co-operation on a more equal footing than in the traditional command and control model. Moreover, Horizontal Monitoring implies a form of de-juridification, for example, by giving more prominence to social norms such as trust, fair play, respect, reciprocity and shared responsibility in the interaction between tax administration and taxpayers rather than legal norms. It is important to see that here de-juridification also means debating positions with regard to the legal consequences of actions as early as possible rather than after tax returns have been filed (in which legal positions are taken). This exchange and debating of opposing views should take place prior to the filing of the tax return and the assessment, when parties have not yet committed themselves to a legal position. This timing often makes a flexible response to disagreement possible.[2] Horizontal Monitoring must be seen as supplementary to traditional, vertical supervision, whereby the authorities check whether taxpayers comply with tax law using their unilateral enforcement powers such as the power to invoke disclosure requirements, audits and sanctions (like (administrative) penalties and reversal of the burden of the proof) coercive measures with respect to tax collection and fraud investigations. This traditional, vertical form of supervision is repressive, not trust-based and it concerns regards taxpayers who are not transparent. Both approaches are possible within the existing legal framework as NTCA has discretion with regard to the allocation of its scarce resources.

However, the legal framework imposes certain boundaries on both approaches. In this chapter, I will deal with some of the legal boundaries to Horizontal Monitoring. Moreover, the legal framework may have unintended effects such as juridification and antagonistic interaction which may go against its intended aim of legitimate and efficient tax collection and may be an impediment to co-operation and problem-solving. An informal approach like Horizontal Monitoring may enhance the same goals and values. Of course, this approach has to fit in with the legal framework but the point is that an informal approach is about co-operation rather than about competencies, obligations and rights.

The key values and concepts relating to Horizontal Monitoring are trust, transparency and mutual understanding – all related to fair play. These concepts are linked to the concept of legitimacy which comprises the moral and normative aspects of power relationships.[3] Legitimacy is 'the property that a rule or an authority has when others feel obligated to defer voluntarily to that rule or authority'.[4] For those who are

---

1 Soler Roch, M.T. (2012). Tax Administration versus Taxpayer – A New Deal? *World Tax Journal*, October 2012, p. 282 ff, p. 288. Briefly, the main reason is that the lack of trust means uncertainty and uncertainty increases the risk – in this case, the tax risk both for the Tax Administration and for the taxpayer.
2 Gribnau, H. (2007). Soft Law and Taxation: The Case of the Netherlands. *Legisprudence*, 3, 291-326. See at p. 312-325.

subordinated to power, legitimate exercise of this power is crucial to a sense of obligation. Legitimate exercise of power provides grounds for the obligation for those subject to power to support and co-operate with its holders. Legitimacy is important for what authorities' power can be used to achieve. According to the political scientist Beetham, it is significant 'for the degree of co-operation and quality of performance that the powerful can secure from the subordinate.'[5] Consequently, NTCA's legitimate exercise of power over taxpayers enhances voluntary compliance.

The most basic aspect of legitimacy is that power is acquired and exercised in conformity with established rules.[6] This is the principle of legality: government action should have a legal, namely statutory basis (see 8.4). With regard to Horizontal Monitoring these rules are to be found in the statutory framework which determines the enforcement powers of the tax administration. Moreover, and this is the second aspect, these rules should be justifiable in terms of shared beliefs. In the context of Horizontal Monitoring an important belief is embodied by the value of fair play. This value and other values are central to the concept of procedural justice which is about fair treatment. Important factors are 'voice', respectful treatment and adequate explanations. Voice is the belief that the taxpayer has an opportunity to present his/her case and that the tax authorities give consideration to his/her views. Moreover, it is important that the taxpayer has the feeling that they are being treated with respect in the course of the interaction. Thirdly, perceived fairness increases when taxpayers believe that the process and decision have been adequately explained. The social-psychological concept of procedural justice is better tailored to the particular kind of interaction in this fiscal relationship rather than a more general political theoretical perspective on legitimacy.[7] I will not elaborate on this social-psychological concept in this context. It suffices to say that an informal approach such as Horizontal Monitoring enhances procedural justice – as will become clear.

A third aspect or level of legitimacy involves the evidence of consent on the part of the subordinate. Actions, such as the concluding of agreements, express this consent and will introduce a moral component into the power relationship and 'create a normative commitment on the part of those engaging in them', according to Beetham.[8] With respect to Horizontal Monitoring, concluding a compliance agreement may be viewed as evidence of consent on the part of the taxpayer. Of course, the final goal is the

---

3   Beetham, D. (1991). *The Legitimation of Power*, Atlantic Highlands: Humanities Press International, p. 25.
4   Tyler, T.R. & Y.J. Huo (2002). *Trust in the Law: Encouraging Public Cooperation with the Police and Courts*. New York: Russell Sage Foundation, p. 101 drawing upon the work of Beetham and others.
5   Beetham, D. (1991). *The Legitimation of Power*, Atlantic Highlands: Humanities Press International, p. 29. Of course, legitimacy is also important to remain 'in power'.
6   Beetham, D. (1991). *The Legitimation of Power*, Atlantic Highlands: Humanities Press International, p. 16.
7   Steenbergen, A.K.J.M. van (2013). *Legitimiteit en fiscale rechtshandhaving, juridische en sociaalwetenschappelijke aspecten*. Utrecht: Belastingdienst. It shows that some aspects – beliefs and values – of procedural justice are entrenched in legal principles which are standards of behaviour for the NTCA; see also below § 5.3.3.4 and § 5.4.6.
8   Beetham, D. (1991). *The Legitimation of Power*, Atlantic Highlands: Humanities Press International, p. 18.

efficient and legitimate levying of taxes by way of voluntary compliance leading to the payment of the right amount of tax at the right time.

This chapter is structured as follows. Firstly, the basic characteristics of Horizontal Monitoring will be briefly summarised with a view to procedural tax aspects. Then, an overview will be presented of the normal legal framework which determines NTCA's enforcement powers and taxpayers' obligations. Thirdly, some aspects of the statutes and legal principles in force will be elaborated upon because, at first sight, the Horizontal Monitoring approach might seem to be at variance with these aspects of the legal framework. This is followed by some conclusions.

8.2 A very short introduction to Horizontal Monitoring

Here I will point out some features of Horizontal Monitoring which are relevant from a legal point of view.[9] Horizontal Monitoring as a soft law instrument is based on trust, transparency and mutual understanding.[10] It is a fairly new governance method which is meant to enhance compliance by other than strict control-and-punishment – relying on trust rather than on power.[11] It is a supplement to the traditional form of vertical supervision. On the one hand, it will be shown that this informal cooperative compliance approach is based on a compliance risk management strategy which enables NTCA to differentiate between taxpayers who are not compliant and taxpayers who are willing to comply. The voluntary compliance of the latter is partly the basis and partly the effect of the trust-based co-operative relationship which is an important feature of Horizontal Monitoring (8.2.1). On the other hand, it will appear that NTCA and taxpayers have shared interests without denying there are also conflicting interests. A company engages in Horizontal Monitoring because of the shared interests in combination with its willingness to comply. The existing legal framework allows for this approach as well as for the use of coercive powers within a command-and-control enforcement approach in case taxpayers lack a willingness to comply (vertical supervision, 8.2.2).

8.2.1 An informal approach based on compliance risk management

Compliance is defined as citizens and businesses satisfying four basic tax obligations: 'to register for tax purposes; to file tax returns on time (i.e. by the date stipulated in the law) or at all; to correctly report tax liabilities (including as withholding agents);

---

9   Horizontal monitoring for large companies and small and medium sized companies is dealt with primarily in chapters 6 and 7 respectively.
10 Cf. Van der Hel-van Dijk, L. & Pheijffer, M. (2012). A Tailor-Made Approach to Fiscal Supervision: An Evaluation of Horizontal Monitoring. *Bulletin for International Taxation*, Vol. 66, No. 10.
11 Trust increases and power decreases voluntary compliance, whereas power increases and trust decreases enforced compliance; Wahl, I., Kastlunger B., Kirchler & Hoelzl, E. (2010). Trust in Authorities and Power to Enforce Tax Compliance: An Empirical Analysis of the "slippery slope" framework. *Law and Policy*, 32, No. 4, p. 383–406.

and to pay taxes on time (i.e. by the date stipulated in the law)'.[12] However, the term 'compliance' is ambiguous, for apart from taxpayers' actual behaviour, the concept of compliance may also regard taxpayers' attitude and their willingness to fulfill their tax obligations.[13] A cooperative compliance approach should lead to less audits and legal proceedings, both costly enforcement instruments, thus resulting in efficiency gains. The tax administration introduced this component of its compliance strategy in order to support and strengthen the willingness of taxpayers to observe their statutory obligations.[14] Thus, NTCA tries to increase not only compliance but also voluntary compliance.

Of course, there are many legal obligations which taxpayers have to comply with. In this regard, they do not have any choice. Nonetheless, taxpayers can be divided into compliant taxpayers who fulfil their tax obligations and non-compliant taxpayers who are not willing to fulfil their tax obligations. Moreover, compliant taxpayers are compliant because they fear repressive measures of the tax administration or because they are intrinsically motivated to fulfil their tax obligations. The compliance of the latter group of taxpayers may be described as 'voluntary'.[15] NTCA's behaviour influences voluntary compliance. Tax authorities have become aware of the necessity of fair treatment of taxpayers considering them as 'equal partners', sometimes even as customers.[16] And rightly so, for nowadays taxpayers expect tax administrations to be engaging and helpful.

In this way, the tax administration may influence taxpayers' behaviour as the tax administration and taxpayers react on each other's actions. The tax administration's compliance strategy may enhance compliance by taking into account – and acting accordingly – the causes of non-compliant behaviour of taxpayers ranging from lack of knowledge to fraud (responsive regulation). However, as just stated, the concept of compliance regards taxpayers' actual behaviour as well as their attitude. NTCA can also enhance taxpayers' intrinsic motivation (voluntary compliance). Therefore, a carefully designed compliance strategy may lead to a change in the taxpayers'

---

12   OECD (2008). *Monitoring Taxpayers' Compliance: A Practical Guide Based on Revenue Body Experience*, Paris: OECD, p. 9. Cf. OECD (2013). *Co-operative Compliance: A Framework: From Enhanced Relationship to Co-operative Compliance*, Paris: OECD, p. 16: 'compliance leading to payment of the right amount of tax at the right time'.
13   Cf. European Commission (2010). *Compliance Risk Management Guide for Tax Administrations*, p. 5, relating this willingness to the obligations of 'registering, filing, correct declaration of the tax return and payment of the tax due.' http://ec.europa.eu/taxation_customs/resources/documents/common/publications/info_docs/taxation/risk_managt_guide_en.pdf.
14   See Van Kommer, V. & Alink, M. (2009). *The Dutch Approach: Description of the Dutch Tax and Customs Administration*, Second Revised Edition, Amsterdam: IBFD, p. 11 ff.
15   Cf. Seer, R. (2013). Voluntary Compliance. *Bulletin for International Taxation*, Vol. 67, No. 11, p. 584-590, at p. 584 who argues that because the idea of voluntary compliance is linked to a self-assessment tax system the '"voluntary" tax compliance systems are better described as state-controlled self-regulation tax systems.'
16   Kirchler, E. & Hoelzl, E. (2006). Modelling Taxpayers' Behaviour as a Function of Interaction between Tax Authorities and Taxpayers. In: Elffers, H. e.o. (eds), *Managing and Maintaining Compliance*, The Hague: Boom Legal Publishers; Kirchler, E. (2007). *The Economic Psychology of Tax Behaviour*, Cambridge: Cambridge University Press; p. 176-181.

attitude. Compliance may increase as a 'service-based' approach enhances a co-operative atmosphere of mutual trust and voluntary co-operation.[17] However, it may have another effect as well. It may not only influence taxpayers' attitude but may also lead to a change of taxpayers' behaviour. Delivering good customer service, information, education and advice makes it simpler for taxpayers to comply.[18] When taxpayers' knowledge of the often extremely complex tax laws is improved, a better understanding of obligations under tax law may improve their actual compliance (better filing of tax returns). In this way, the tax administration addresses impediments to compliance. As a result, unintentional non-compliance behaviour is reduced.[19]

The tax administration therefore employs risk management to allocate the available scarce resources to high taxpayer-service and high-risk areas.[20] Taxpayers are classified according to their degree of observed compliance or non-compliance by performing an initial risk assessment. The resulting risk profile of the taxpayer determines the intensity of the monitoring by the tax administration. The European Commission defines compliance risk management as follows: 'a systematic process in which a revenue body makes substantiated choices on which interventions could be used to effectively stimulate compliance and prevent non-compliance, based on the knowledge of the behaviour of all taxpayers and related to the available capacity'.[21] This shows that risk management aims at enhancing the responsiveness of regulation – contributing to the legitimacy of the tax administration. NTCA gears its supervision to taxpayers' attitude and behaviour. It does not only target non-compliance, as 'compliance risk management strategies should also benefit the taxpayers who are willing and able to comply'.[22] The reward for the complying taxpayer is less supervision and therefore a lower administrative burden. The resulting reduction in compliance costs is a serious incentive to comply. The tax administration can use the capacity made available by reduced vertical supervision to deal with other, less compliant, taxpayers.

---

17 Kirchler, E. (2007). *The Economic Psychology of Tax Behaviour*, Cambridge: Cambridge University Press.
    Gangl, K., Muehlbacher, S., Groot, M. de, Goslinga, S., Hofmann, E., Kogler, C., Antonides, G. & Kirchler, E. (2013). "How Can I Help You?" Perceived Service Orientation of Tax Authorities and Tax Compliance. *FinanzArchiv* 69, p. 487-510.
18 Bentley, D. (1998). Definitions and Developments. In: Bentley, D. (ed.), *Taxpayers' Rights: An International Perspective*, Gold Coast: Bond University, p. 43.
19 McKerchar, M. (2001). *The Impact of Complexity upon Tax Compliance: A study of Australian Personal Taxpayers*, Sidney: Australian Tax Research Foundation.
20 Bentley, D. (1998). Definitions and Developments. In: Bentley, D. (ed.), *Taxpayers' Rights: An International Perspective*, Gold Coast: Bond University, p. 11 and Seer, R. (2013). Voluntary Compliance. *Bulletin for International Taxation*, Vol. 67, No. 11, p. 585-586.
21 European Commission (2010). *Compliance Risk Management Guide for Tax Administrations*, p. 9. Note the process-oriented perspective, which is a key feature of governance, cf. Morgan, B. & Yeung, K. (2007). *An Introduction to Law and Regulation: Text and Materials*, Cambridge: Cambridge University Press, p. 186: 'compliance is an elaborate concept, one better seen as a process rather than a condition.'
22 OECD (2013). *Co-operative Compliance: A Framework: From Enhanced Relationship to Co-operative Compliance*, Paris: OECD, p. 41.

Co-operation based on mutual respect and trust is the crux of this compliance strategy.[23] Of course, it is about justifiable, reasonable trust among the tax administration and taxpayers rather than naïve trust.[24] Respect is another important value, which in turn demands empathy on the side of the tax officials. An empathetic approach 'increases the taxpayers' respect for the tax agency and inclination to cooperate and reduces the risks of misunderstanding'.[25] This informal approach is embedded in a – more traditional – vertical monitoring framework which entails the use of extensive unilateral powers which NTCA can use to enforce compliance.[26] Deterrence relies on gaining compliance through the power of legal authorities to sanction people.[27] Deterrence, however, is of limited utility for tax compliance as 'enforcement cannot play the deterrence role expected in compliance models for the majority of taxpayers'.[28] The Committee Horizontal Monitoring Tax and Customs Administration (named after its chairman: 'Stevens Committee'), which evaluated developments relating to Horizontal Monitoring at the request of the Minister of Finance, rightly points at developments in socio-psychology which have shown that 'inspection frequencies and the imposition of sanctions do not exhibit a marked correlation with the degree of compliance'.[29] Psychological research shows that compliance is determined by intrinsic motives (encompassing personal and social standards), extrinsic stimuli and the opportunities available for compliance and non-compliance. Hence, government supervision can exert an influence on taxpayer's behaviour, for example by means of persuasiveness and the enhancement of mutual trust. These psychological research findings account for the fact that the NTCA annually measures by way of the 'Tax Monitor' the norms and values which indicate taxpayers' attitude towards the payment and evasion of taxes.[30] Thus, this survey tool is used to monitor the degree of voluntary compliance, i.e. the willingness to comply.

---

23   Cf. OECD (2007). *Tax Intermediaries Study Working Paper 6 – The Enhanced Relationship*, Paris: OECD, p. 3: 'Fundamental to the long-term success of the enhanced relationship is the establishment and maintenance of trust amongst all the parties'.
24   Stevens Committee (2012). *Tax supervision – Made to Measure: Flexible When Possible, Strict Where Necessary*, The Hague: Ministry of Finance, http://www.ifa.nl/Document/Publicaties/Enhanced%20Relationship%20Project/tax_supervision_made_to_measure_tz0151z1fdeng.pdf', p. 20.
25   Höglund, M. & Nöjd, S. (2014). Professional Communication of the Tax Authorities. *Intertax* Vol. 42, 8/9, p. 496-508, at p. 501.
26   Power is often defined as the capacity to influence another person's behaviour in a certain direction. This can be done by reward or punishment; cf. Höglund, M. & Nöjd, S. (2014). Professional Communication of the Tax Authorities. *Intertax* Vol. 42, 8/9, p. 500.
27   Tyler, T.R. & Y.J. Huo (2002). *Trust in the Law: Encouraging Public Cooperation with the Police and Courts.* New York: Russell Sage Foundation, p. 204.
28   Scholz, J.T. (1998). Trust, Taxes, and Compliance. In: Braithwaite, V. & Levi, M. (eds.), *Trust and Governance.* New York: Russell Sage Foundation, p. 147. Cf. Frey, B. (2003). Deterrence and Tax Morale in the European Union. *European Review*, 11, p. 385-406.
29   Stevens Committee (2012). *Tax supervision – Made to Measure: Flexible When Possible, Strict Where Necessary*, The Hague: Ministry of Finance, http://www.ifa.nl/Document/Publicaties/Enhanced%20Relationship%20Project/tax_supervision_made_to_measure_tz0151z1fdeng.pdf, p. 21.
30   Van Kommer, V. & Alink, M. (2009). *The Dutch Approach: Description of the Dutch Tax and Customs Administration*, Second Revised Edition, Amsterdam: IBFD, p. 118-121. This monitoring focuses also on effect indicators – tax return behaviour, fill-out behaviour and payment behaviour – which illustrate the extent to which taxpayers comply with the tax rules voluntarily.

An informal approach aims at stimulating voluntary compliance. The willingness to co-operate is embodied in compliance agreement (covenants) concluded between tax administration and taxpayers. These covenants express the importance of mutual trust between the taxpayer and the tax administration, clear articulation of each party's responsibilities and means of enforcing the law and the establishment of and compliance with reciprocal arrangements.[31] The enforcement covenants have quite an informal character – expressing parties' mutual intentions to co-operate. The reciprocal commitment is deliberately not exhaustively fleshed out in obligations and sanctions. A rule based contract or agreement would be counterproductive in an approach aimed at de-juridification.

8.2.2 Conflicting and shared interests

An informal and service-based approach puts underlying relations and communication between government and citizens on a more equal footing, communication being all important to prevent misunderstanding and trench warfare of parties who perceive one another as enemies. This is in line with the more general idea that communication-based and consensual-based techniques are important tools to secure compliance. A kind of informal 'proceduralisation' by way of a semi-permanent dialogue takes places which ascribes 'a critical role to deliberative, participatory procedures'.[32] Vertical supervision is reduced and in return the company undertakes to provide transparency. Taxpayers are required not only to report all actions that involve tax risks but also to disclose their views about the legal consequences of such actions – including, therefore, the positions taken by them.[33] Hence, they are required to go beyond compliance with their statutory reporting obligations. Tax inspectors for their part share their specific monitoring strategy for the company concerned and will take a stance on company planned actions and their tax consequences.[34] In this way it is transparent about its response to taxpayers' actions.[35] NTCA will also provide

---

31 Of course, trust is also a major value for and within an administrative body, such as the tax administration itself; cf. Sobis, I. & De Vries, M.S. (2011). The Social Psychology Perspective on Values and Virtues. In: De Vries, M.S. & Kim, P.S. (eds.), *Value and Virtue in Public Administration: A Comparative Perspective*, Basingstoke/New York: Palgrave, p. 98-114.
32 Morgan, B. & Yeung, K. (2007). *An Introduction to Law and Regulation: Text and Materials*, Cambridge: Cambridge University Press, p. 141.
33 OECD (2013). *Co-operative Compliance: a Framework: from enhanced relationships to co-operative compliance*, Paris: OECD, p. 20-21: Mandatory disclosure rules are impartial but, like most rules, can be circumvented. Voluntary disclosure rules can complement mandatory disclosure regimes but raise different issues. They clearly require the taxpayer to agree to go beyond compliance with their statutory reporting obligations.
34 See the internal HM-guidelines (*Leidraden*) issued by the tax administration to guarantee uniform treatment with regard to cooperative compliance – enhancing equal treatment and legal certainty.
35 Transparency is of general importance in the interactions between tax administration and taxpayers. See Waller, V. (2007). The Challenge of Institutional Integrity in Responsive Regulation: Field Inspections by the Australian Taxation Office. *Law & Policy* Vol. 29, No. 1, p. 67-83, who shows that the lack of transparency about field officers' purposes when conducting an 'unannounced registration integrity check' ('walk-in') undermines trust and confidence in the tax office as well as some taxpayers' perceptions of procedural fairness. 'In other words, it has the perverse effect of ultimately undermining compliance'. (p. 81)

information on its interpretation of new legal rules. In the case of these kind of issues taxpayers may expect a prompt response, for a good working relationship demands 'working in the present' with real time problem solving. Thus, the tax administration meets taxpayers' needs for legal certainty (with regard to tax positions) and predictable behaviour. The voluntary reporting of tax structures goes beyond the taxpayer's actual statutory obligations according to which the taxpayer is only obliged to provide proper factual information. Moreover, the taxpayer has to provide assurance that the information and returns submitted are both accurate and complete by setting up a Tax Control Framework (TCF). By way of a TCF of sufficient quality the taxpayer gives the tax administration a strong indication about the degree he is in control.[36] Hence it is a means to provide transparency.[37] As a result of this voluntary compliance the tax inspector will in principle follow tax returns that are filed under a covenant agreement (apart from random audits of tax returns). Thus, he can rely on the tax return which the TCF 'produces'. An adequate TCF enhances taxpayer's trustworthiness on which the tax inspector reacts with following his tax return, therefore trusting in the taxpayer.

These enforcement covenants try to do justice to the occasionally conflicting interests of the two actors while acknowledging the shared interests. Their co-operation is conditional upon some form of reciprocity – a basic requirement for any kind of co-operation. The interests of the (corporate) taxpayer lie first and foremost in reducing uncertainty. Less audits, for example, mean reduced administrative burdens. Field audits, which takes place on the firm's premises, tend to be time-consuming and costly – for both taxpayers and NTCA. Besides, there is the inquisitorial nature of auditing: the taxpayer is under the obligation to provide data and information on request and make available the complete financial administrative records and data carriers for audit. Furthermore, auditing to examine the accuracy of the information declared by taxpayers in their tax returns is essentially retrospective. It often takes place after the taxpayer has filed a tax return and thus has declared its tax position. On the basis of this declared tax position, the company has established its annual report which usually has been made public. The tax inspector checks the tax return followed by sending a notice of assessment to the taxpayer. The verification process, however, may lead to adjustments. The tax inspector may use his legal powers to revise and reassess the tax debt declared by the taxpayer. Consequently, tax auditing may result in additional payments to be made and retrospective changes in the company's tax liabilities – sometimes after time-consuming and costly litigation. They may lead to adjustments in the company's next annual commercial accounts. The mere possibility of retrospective changes results in uncertainty which, understandably, is not very

---

36 Van Kommer, V. & Alink, M. (2009). *The Dutch Approach: Description of the Dutch Tax and Customs Administration*, Second Revised Edition, Amsterdam: IBFD, p. 114.
37 A TCF is an instrument of internal controls, specifically showing the tax aspects of an enterprise. NTCA requires large companies to have a TCF in order to conclude an enforcement covenant. A TCF must be designed in such a way that financial administrative processes of these (large) business produce a tax return which complies with the legal requirements. Cf. Bronzewska, K & E. van der Enden, E. (2014). Tax Control Framework – A Conceptual Approach: The Six Nuances of Good Tax Governance. *Bulletin for International Taxation*, p. 635-640.

appealing to companies.[38] Financial restatements appear to have a negative impact on a company's reputation.[39] No wonder as companies prefer obtaining legal certainty in advance. Of course, achieving certainty with regard to the tax consequences of actions is also important from the perspective of a company's tax risk management which is a critical factor of good corporate governance.[40] Thus the indeterminacy of tax laws, giving rise to uncertainty around their interpretation, partially accounts for company's need of tax risk management.[41] The broader meaning of tax risk management is, in the wording of the OECD, that it 'will allow the enterprise to not only act as a good corporate citizen but also to effectively manage tax risk, which can serve to avoid major financial, regulatory and reputation risk for an enterprise.'[42]

Thus, corporate taxpayers and the tax administration both reduce uncertainty. Trust, reasonableness and fairness play a cardinal role in this voluntary engagement based on a mutually beneficial co-operation. Furthermore, the use of this informal enforcement technique shows that the aim of securing compliance does not necessarily lead to (more) juridification of the taxpayer/tax administration relationship.

Of course, both tax administration and taxpayers have to stay within the legal framework (see below, 8.3). Enforcement covenants should not influence the company's total tax liability. The tax administration, therefore, has a special obligation to guarantee such important procedural values as impartiality, equality, accountability, transparency and publicity. However, the legal framework does not only provide rules to determine and calculate the tax consequences of all kinds of actions but also the procedural rules to establish and formalise the tax liability. Procedural law consists of competencies, rights and obligations of both taxpayers and tax administration. The tax administration is not allowed to exceed its competence. Taxpayers have to perform their duties but they are not obliged to go beyond their legal obligations. However, as will be shown, they may voluntarily go beyond their legal obligations.

---

38 Gribnau, H. (2007). Soft Law and Taxation: The Case of the Netherlands. *Legisprudence*, 3, 291-326, p. 322-323.
39 Gertsen, F.H.M. (2013). *Riding a Tiger without Being Eaten: How Companies and Analysts Tame Financial Restatements and Influence Corporate Reputation*, Rotterdam: Erasmus Universiteit (Ph.D. Thesis) diss., p. 68.
40 For the relationship between tax and good corporate governance, see Cf. Bronzewska, K & E. van der Enden, E. (2014). Tax Control Framework – A Conceptual Approach: The Six Nuances of Good Tax Governance. *Bulletin for International Taxation*, p.636-637.
41 In the post-Enron era with new regulations (Sarbanes Oxley 2002) established in the USA, the accounting and reporting of corporate income tax has received increased scrutiny by all kinds of stakeholders. Consequently, increased attention is being given to tax risks by company management. Mulligan, E. & Oats, L. (2009). Tax Risk Management: Evidence from the United States. *British Tax Review* 6, p. 680-703 find that concerns with reputation both within the organization and as perceived by the 'public' is very important. They point out that the media play a particularly striking role in this respect.
42 OECD (2011). *OECD Guidelines for Multinational Enterprises*, Paris: OECD, p. 61. The OECD connects internal control to ethics and compliance. Cf. OECD (2014). *Principles of Corporate Governance – Draft for Public Comment*, Paris: OECD, p. 33: '117. Companies are also well advised to establish and ensure the effectiveness of internal controls, ethics, and compliance programmes or measures [whereas] compliance must also relate to other laws and regulations, as well as relevant international agreements, such as those covering securities, competition, taxation (...)'.

Taxpayers may for example provide the NTCA with more information than they are legally obliged to. They also may provide the NTCA semi-voluntarily with information, namely in an early stage so that the NTCA does not need to invoke its statutory powers to request that information. This obligation is established in the HM-covenant.

Thus, the tax administration and taxpayers not only have to comply with substantive tax law but also stay within the framework of procedural (tax) law. The procedural (tax) laws comprise all kinds of obligations and, in case of non-compliance, sanctions. In other words, the tax administration can shift to classical command and control regulation in case of non-compliant taxpayers. The tax administration, therefore, does not abandon classical enforcement mechanisms (vertical supervision) but puts them on hold. Enforcement of tax law cannot do without a measure of deterrence – even if it is lying in the background – after all.[43] Rightly so, because not enforcing the law in case non-compliant taxpayers would go at the expense of the equal treatment of taxpayers and their trust in NTCA.

On the one hand, therefore, NTCA will respond to trustworthy compliant taxpayers by showing trust (voluntary compliance).[44] On the other hand, NTCA will use its coercive powers to enforce non-compliant taxpayers to comply with their legal obligations (enforced compliance). Hence, trust and coercion are closely related in this horizontal approach to compliance and governance. No law can do without the backing of an effective enforcement agency. Coercing non-compliant taxpayers to comply with their obligations also supports compliant taxpayers. An enforcement strategy that ineffectively deals with free riders undermines voluntary compliance which accounts for the need of vertical supervision in order to restore compliant taxpayers' trust. Without vertical supervision voluntary compliance would decline. However, the tax administration cannot exclusively rely on its coercive powers to achieve taxpayers' compliance. To be effective, an agency should not try to deter each citizen from breaking the law but should instead try 'to provide a basis for trust by ensuring that untrustworthy citizens will be made to obey the law'.[45]

After this brief presentation of some basic features a brief overview will be given of some relevant features of the existing legal framework. Afterwards, Horizontal Monitoring will be evaluated from a legal point of view.

---

43 See Shaw, J., Slemrod, J. & Whiting, J. (2010). Administration and Compliance. In: *Dimensions of Tax Design: The Mirrlees Review*, Edited by Institute for Fiscal Studies (IFS), Oxford: Oxford University Press, p. 1115 ff. Cf. Hasseldine, J. (1999/2000). Using Persuasive Communications to Increase Compliance: What Experimental Research has (and has not) Told Us. *Australian Tax Forum*, 15, p. 227-242: who concludes from a review of empirical research that both formal legal sanctions and alternative mechanisms have some effect. However, 'deciding which alternative is most effective, and what enforcement strategy should be used when, remains a difficult decision parameter for government and tax agencies' (p. 238).
44 Cf. Braithwaite, V. Responsive Regulation and Taxation: Introduction. *Law & Policy*, Vol. 29 No. 1, who argues in favour of responsive regulation in contradistinction to 'regulatory formalism' in order to influence citizens' commitment to pay tax.
45 Scholz, J.T. (1998). Trust, Taxes, and Compliance. In: Braithwaite, V. & Levi, M. (eds.), *Trust and Governance*. New York: Russell Sage Foundation, p. 163. He adds that the long trust-based compliance cannot do without trust in the broader set of political institutions.

8.3 Horizontal Monitoring and procedural tax law

8.3.1 Discretion and voluntary agreements

Horizontal Monitoring takes place within the normal legal framework which determines NTCA's enforcement powers and the rights and obligations of taxpayers such as of companies.[46] Statutory law, for example, provides for the power of NTCA to demand a transfer of information which is in the hands of taxpayers – information needed to assess taxpayers' compliance with the tax rules. More generally, 'all cooperative compliance approaches operate within the boundaries of law and regulations'.[47] Therefore, a closer look at the existing Dutch legal framework is needed.

With regard to the procedural law framework, it is important to note the applicability of general administrative law in the field of tax law. General administrative law is the *lex generalis* and administrative tax law is the *lex specialis*. Tax law is part of administrative law, so the General Administrative Law Act (*Algemene wet bestuursrecht*; GALA) applies. This statute contains the uniform law of administrative procedure which applies to tax procedure. However, with regard to tax, some provisions in the General Taxes Act (*Algemene Wet inzake Rijksbelastingen*; GTA) contain exceptions – in favour of the tax administration.[48] These exceptions have decreased in the past ten years.

Here, the question to be answered is whether the law leaves the tax administration room at all for a cooperative compliance strategy such as Horizontal Monitoring. Has the NTCA any discretion in this sense? Galligan points to the fact that administrative officials make decisions in the 'absence of previously fixed, relatively clear and binding legal standards'. In his view, this discretionary power is generally thought of as impossible to eliminate due to the 'vagaries of language, the diversity of circumstances and the indeterminacy of official purposes'. He goes on to explain that these reasons do not account for the notion of discretion in a stronger sense as 'an express grant of power conferred upon officials where determination of the standards according to which power is to be exercised is left largely to them'.[49] Consequently,

---

46 In this respect the principle of legality is deemed to constitute an obstacle in some jurisdictions. Cf. Italy which will issue a new legislative decree containing detailed regulations necessary for a formal introduction of a co-operative compliance approach. See Van der Enden, E. & Bronzewska, K. (2014). The Concept of Cooperative Compliance. *Bulletin for International Taxation*, p. 568-572.
47 OECD (2013). *Co-operative Compliance: A Framework: From Enhanced Relationship to Co-operative Compliance*, Paris: OECD, p. 31. It is added 'that countries formalising the approach have mostly not needed to change existing laws and regulations.'
48 Especially Artt. 25 and 26 GTA.
49 Galligan, D.J. (1986). *Discretionary powers: A Legal Study of Official Discretion*. Oxford: Clarendon Press, p. 1. More specifically, a distinction can be made between norms that confer discretionary powers and vague norms which indicate a standard or guideline for the use of administrative power – although not a very precise standard or guideline for this use of power. Furthermore, the Dutch tax legislator often introduces deliberately vague norms which are called 'open norms.' Open norms are a species of the genus vague norms. Open norms belong to the domain of the courts which have to specify the content and scope of the open norm. Cf. Gribnau, H. (2010). Netherlands. In: Dourado, A.P. (ed.), *Separation of Powers in Tax Law*, Amsterdam: IBFD, p. 145-175, at p. 149-153.

the rule-giver consciously leaves officials a scope of assessment in the course of the decision. In short, discretion involves the official's power to choose standards for action, a choice which is made unilaterally, and 'the power to choose is conferred or legitimated by law'.[50] It is useful to distinguish discretion with regard to substantive tax law and discretion with regard to procedural tax law. NTCA, for example, has discretion with regard to the treatment of offenders as the legal provisions do not exactly determine the amount of the penalty in case of violation of a statutory obligation. With regard to substantive tax law, Dutch tax officials have considerably less discretion due to the great weight of the principle of legality.

With regard to procedural tax law the situation is slightly different. There are many (relatively) clear and fixed legal rules which bind the tax administration and its officials. Nonetheless, the tax administration has discretion with regard to enhancing and enforcing compliance. The legal framework leaves the tax administration room to decide how to deploy its (scarce) resources. There are no specific rules in this regard. The law does not dictate for example the intensity and frequency of audits, who should be audited or when, etc. As shown above, risk management allocates the available scarce resources to high taxpayer-service and high-risk taxpayers (see 8.2.1). Thus, the law does indeed leave the tax administration room for an informal cooperative compliance strategy. NTCA may base its enforcement strategy on trust and gear it in accordance to the nature and intensity of trust in (groups of) taxpayers. In this respect, a taxpayer's past performance may be a reason for a differentiated treatment in the sense of delivering (extra/quick) service and providing certainty on its tax position. Of course, a differentiated treatment should not amount to paying less tax. This kind of preferential treatment would violate the principle of equality. In short, Horizontal Monitoring concerns the process not the result (output).

In the following, some important characteristics, rules and principles of Dutch procedural tax law will be dealt with.[51] They account for, on the one hand, some undesirable consequences such as a time lag in dealing with disagreements and, on the other hand, the (legal) conditions within which Horizontal Monitoring takes place.

In the Horizontal Monitoring approach the reciprocal engagement to co-operate is somehow formalised in a voluntary agreement between tax administration and taxpayer. This compliance agreement (enforcement covenant) expresses parties' intention to co-operate. On the one hand, the covenant-partners assume a commitment to perform to the best of their abilities, for example with regard to an effective

---

50   Bell, J. (1992). Discretionary Decision-Making: A Jurisprudential View. In: Hawkins, K. (ed.), *The Uses of Discretion*. Oxford: Clarendon Press, p. 92 Cf. Dabner J. (2012). Constraints on the 'Enhanced Relationship' Model – What Really Shapes the Relationship Between the Tax Administrator and Tax Intermediaries in Australasia and the United Kingdom. [2012] *British Tax Review* 4, p. 541, 546. Apart from legal aspects there may be ethical aspects to the exercise of discretion, see Garofalo, C. (2011). Governance and Values in Contemporary Public Service. In: De Vries, M.S. & Kim, P.S. (eds.), *Value and Virtue in Public Administration: A Comparative Perspective*. Basingstoke/New York: Palgrave, p. 25-26.
51   For an elaborate treatment of these procedural tax law aspects, see Oenema, M. (2014). *De formeelrechtelijke aspecten van horizontaal toezicht in belastingzaken*, Deventer: Kluwer.

and efficient method of working.[52] These are 'soft' obligations which are a feature of a gentlemen's agreement.[53] This kind of commitment looks similar to a soft law instrument because it is not legally binding but nevertheless may have certain – indirect – legal effects that are aimed at and may produce practical effects'.[54] On the other hand, there are more 'hard' obligations which can be legally enforced. The taxpayer agrees to bear the responsibility of having an adequate framework of internal and external controls (TCF) and to 'proactively' report all actions that involve tax risks and to disclose their views about the legal consequences of such actions.

From a public law perspective, it is an agreement with regard to the way that the tax administration will use its powers, though not with regard to the content of an assessment or another administrative decision but the way it intends to use its supervisory discretion.[55] It is about the way the tax administration will exercise its supervisory powers which it will gear to the taxpayer's system of internal and external control. But NTCA will also deliver quick service, e.g. with regard to the payment of tax refunds and the taking of a stance on the tax consequences of a taxpayer's actions. This follows from NTCA's commitment to a good working relationship with real time problem solving. Hence, a covenant essentially sets out the way tax administration and a (corporate) taxpayer will interact albeit with some obligations.

In order to understand the advantages of Horizontal Monitoring the usual processes of assessment and contestation of assessments will be set out as well as the obligations of the taxpayers and the sanctions in case of non-compliance. The formal regulations account for some inherent characteristics and drawbacks of the traditional interaction between tax administration and taxpayers.

---

52 The Stevens Committee (2012), *Tax supervision – Made to Measure: Flexible When Possible, Strict Where Necessary*, The Hague: Ministry of Finance, http://www.ifa.nl/Document/Publicaties/Enhanced%20Relationship%20Project/tax_supervision_made_to_measure_tz0151z1fdeng.pdf, p. 96, uses the term 'working and behavioural agreements'.
53 Cf. Oenema, M.E. & Van der Enden, E.M.E. (2013). De kracht van het convenant. WFR p. 545 ff; Russo, R. (2013). Privaatrechtelijke aspecten van het convenant in het kader van Horizontaal Toezicht. *Vakblad Tax Assurance*, 2 and Oenema, M. (2014). *De formeelrechtelijke aspecten van horizontaal toezicht in belastingzaken*, Deventer: Kluwer, p. 96.
54 Senden, L. (2005). Soft Law, Self-regulation and Co-Regulation in European Law: Where Do They Meet? *Electronic Journal of Comparative Law*, Vol. 9.1, <http://www.ejcl.org/>, p. 17, last accessed 22 October 2014; cf. Senden, L. (2004). *Soft Law in European Community Law: Its Relationship to Legislation*, Oxford: Hart Publishing and Gribnau, H. (2007). Soft Law and Taxation: The Case of the Netherlands. *Legisprudence*, 3, p. 291-326.
55 This is unlike a 'fiscal compromise' in which tax inspector and a taxpayer reach a compromise concerning the fact and the application of the (tax) law on these facts; cf. Sommerhalder, R. & Pechler, E. (1998). Protection of Taxpayers' Rights in the Netherlands. In: Bentley, D. (ed.), *Taxpayers' Rights: An International Perspective*, Gold Coast: Bond University, p. 321 and Gordon, R. (1996). Law of Tax Administration and Procedure. In: Thuronyi, V. (ed.), *Tax Law Design and Drafting*. International Monetary Fund, p. 10: 'To further efficiency, throughout the dispute-settlement process the tax authority should be allowed discretion to settle issues of controversy with the taxpayer.'

8.3.2 Two techniques of levying taxes

Firstly I will set out the two different ways in which taxes are levied with their main features. These features account for different procedural law consequences. It will appear that the statutory provisions embody an approach to the interaction and information exchange at a time when early legal certainty is becoming more important to companies. The legal framework of these techniques to establish the tax liability has drawbacks not fully envisaged and appreciated at the time of their introduction. Horizontal Monitoring offers a solution for some of these drawbacks

In the Netherlands, taxes are mainly levied by way of assessment or by way of a tax return (self-assessment).[56] These two techniques determine the tax inspector's possibilities of correcting incorrect assessments. Both techniques are based on the idea that the tax inspector, at a certain point, checks the tax return filed by the taxpayer and may impose an additional assessment. He may do this during the five years after the end of the relevant tax year. This means that the tax administration remains passive until it receives a tax return. Hence, disputes on errors and positions taken in the tax return may occur and be discussed long after the end of the relevant tax year. Consequently, the taxpayer has to wait several years before he has certainty on his tax liability. Moreover, he has to pay statutory interest over additional amount of tax due and he runs the risk of – sometimes severe – sanctions in case of an incorrect tax return. Therefore, the stakes are high in case of disputes and disagreements on legal matters which then easily transform into ('relational') conflicts – at the expense of a good working relationship. This is an undesirable state of affairs.

No wonder that many tax administrations and taxpayers recognise that they have a shared interest in minimizing and quickly resolving tax disputes. Moreover, as Owens maintains, they both recognise that 'this requires focusing not just on one particular issue but on the whole process by which they can avoid disputes'. This requires, in turn, engaging taxpayers early on in the process of policy formulation and implementation. It also requires 'identifying and discussing issues before they become problems. It requires pre-filing resolutions'.[57]

This is clearly a plea for shared responsibility for the right assessment of tax liabilities. To establish its merits it is useful to elaborate on the two (main) techniques which, in the Netherlands, are used to levy taxes. This will show a few drawbacks to these two techniques which almost call for a more real time supplement such as provided by Horizontal Monitoring.

---

56 Customs are levied according to a third technique, comparable to the first technique, which will not be dealt with here.
57 Owens, J. (2013). The Role of Tax Administrations in the Current Political Climate. *Bulletin for International Taxation*, Vol. 67, No. 3, p. 156-160, at p. 160. He refers to the Netherlands' horizontal monitoring programme.

8.3.2.1 Levying by way of assessment

The first technique, levying by way of assessment, is for example used to assess the personal and corporate income tax liability. The process consists of two phases: the taxpayer files a tax return, after which the assessment by the tax authorities takes place.[58] The taxpayer must file a tax return within the time period set by the tax inspector if the latter has sent a request for filing a tax return to the taxpayer (Article 9, par. 1 General Taxation Act). Then, the tax administration, i.e. the tax inspector, checks the tax return (reasonably carefully), informs the taxpayer about mistakes in the tax return and asks the taxpayer for a reaction. After having received the taxpayer's reaction, the tax inspector gives notice of assessment and gives him information about the differences between the tax return and the tax assessment – if appropriate. In short, the tax inspector assesses the return against the law and corrects it if he or she notices that it differs in any way from the law. In the final tax assessment the amount of tax due is formalised and a taxpayer obtains (more) certainty about his tax position – his tax liability. Note that the tax inspector has to act and he has to impose an assessment before the taxpayer has any (formal/legal) obligation to pay. The inspector's assessment is constitutive of this obligation. Here, the responsibility for the assessment lies with the tax inspector – unlike in a system of self-assessment in which the taxpayer determines tax owed.

If the tax inspector has not formalised the amount of tax due correctly in the ('final'[59]) tax assessment, he can impose an additional tax assessment if certain conditions are met. The temporal condition is that it should be imposed within five years after the end of the relevant tax year. The general idea behind these conditions is that the tax inspector, being responsible for the assessment, has to check the tax return reasonably carefully before imposing an assessment. In principle, an additional tax assessment may only be imposed if there is a so-called 'new fact', a fact unknown to the tax inspector at the time of the assessment. In case of a new fact, new information has become available to the Dutch tax inspector after he has imposed the tax assessment. This can for example be the case when a tax audit results in new information. This condition of a 'new fact' is meant to preclude the imposition of an additional tax assessment in case of the tax inspector changing his mind with regard to the appreciation and understanding of the law or the relevant facts (including some mistakes with regard to processing relevant information). Hence, no additional tax assessment is possible when he discovers a mistake made by himself or other officials working in the tax administration, or in case of information that the tax inspector should have known at the time he issued the final tax assessment. There are a number of exemptions to this 'new fact' condition, for example in the case when the taxpayer has filed a return 'in bad faith'. Another exemption is a mistake made by the tax inspector which was (very) obvious to the taxpayer, e.g. a slip of the pen, a typo or a

---

58 Even if no income tax return is filed, the tax office can issue an 'ex-officio assessment', which is then based on an estimated amount of taxable income; Art. 11 GTA.
59 With regard to personal and corporate income tax, a preliminary tax assessment, often based on the taxable amount of previous years, often precedes the final assessment.

miscalculation. An additional tax assessment can also be imposed if the taxpayer should have reasonably known that the issued final tax assessment was incorrect because of mistakes caused by the tax administration's ICT-processes and the like.[60] The crux however, is that the taxpayer can derive a measure of certainty or trust on the assessment by the tax inspector. Only if the tax inspector has imposed an assessment with reasonable care may he intrude on taxpayer's (legal) certainty by imposing an additional tax assessment as will be shown in the next section. This is different from the other assessment technique.

To conclude, the possibility of an additional tax assessment involves lack of certainty of the taxpayer with regard to his tax liability. He may then incur further compliance costs such as the costs of the necessary expertise to establish the material and formal correctness of the additional tax assessment. Within the Horizontal Monitoring approach however, taxpayers provide the tax inspector pro-actively with information and differing views with regard to the qualification and the interpretation of law are discussed preferably before the filing of tax returns. Moreover, the taxpayer gives the tax administration assurance that his tax return will be acceptable – which implies that the tax inspector – in principle – does not need to check it. Hence he will impose an assessment according to the tax return filed.[61] Of course, this greatly enhances taxpayers' legal certainty.

8.3.2.2 Levying taxes by way of a tax return

The second technique consists of levying taxes by a tax return. Examples of taxes levied according to this technique are VAT and wage taxes. Here, no tax assessment is imposed by the tax inspector because the taxpayer can be relied upon for a correct assessment (self-assessment). The formalisation of the amount of tax due is not done by the tax inspector but by the taxpayer himself who is deemed to be competent and knowledgeable with regard to tax law. Hence, in the first instance, the taxpayer rather than the tax inspector bears the responsibility for the (correct) assessment. However, in case the correct amount of tax is not assessed and paid, which may be discovered in a field audit, the tax inspector can impose an additional tax assessment. As no tax assessment has been imposed by the tax inspector before, there are less conditions to be met for imposing an additional tax assessment for taxes levied by a tax return, compared to taxes levied by a tax assessment. No new fact is required. The temporal condition is the same, an additional tax assessment should be imposed within five years after the end of the relevant tax year.

Again, the possibility of an additional tax assessment involves lack of certainty of the taxpayer with regard to his tax liability. He may then incur further compliance costs,

---

60 In these last cases the temporal condition is two years instead of the regular five years after the final tax assessment has been imposed.
61 Thus with regard to taxpayers observing the horizontal monitoring approach, this first technique of levying taxes is informally evolving into the second technique (by way of a tax return), though the formal demand of new fact is still applicable. This informal shift stays within the existing legal framework; the statutory provisions have not changed.

such as the costs of the necessary expertise to establish the material and formal correctness of the additional tax assessment. However, taxpayers who engage in Horizontal Monitoring provide the tax inspector pro-actively with information. Like covenant partners within the framework of the first technique, they try to create consensus on the legal consequences of their actions preferably before the filing of tax returns and similarly payments of the amounts due. The tax inspector, in its turn, pro-actively communicates his opinion about the legal consequences of taxpayers actions. In this way they are clearly more certain about the tax inspectors' reaction on their tax return.

8.3.2.3 Evaluation

The tax code differentiates between two levying techniques for different kinds of taxpayers. These techniques are aimed at distinguishing between taxpayers who differ with regard to their level of tax knowledge and therefore, their ability to file a correct tax return. Taxpayers who lack tax expertise cannot be relied upon to file a correct tax return and therefore their returns need to be checked by the tax inspector who formalises the amount of tax due. In this way, the main difference between these two techniques is the distribution of the responsibility for the assessment. In case of levying taxes by way of a tax return, taxpayers, for example companies, are supposed to have expertise of tax law, which can be relied upon, and therefore they bear the responsibility for the assessment. The different distribution of the responsibility also accounts for the different conditions to be met by the tax administration for imposing an additional tax assessment. Both techniques have in common the fact that the tax inspector, in general, only appears on the scene after a tax return is filed. His activities are essentially backward looking, for the taxable events haven taken place. The taxpayer has taken a position on their legal merits in his tax return – which he often cannot easily change. Hence, the taxpayer lacks certainty as to whether the tax return will be accepted or corrected by the tax inspector – which has to be reported in the annual commercial accounts in case of major uncertainties. However, there is not only the risk of additional assessments (increased with statutory interest) but also of (administrative) penalties in the case of incorrect tax returns. Disputes about these additional assessments and accompanying sanctions may give rise to prolonged conflicts with the tax administration and become time-consuming, expensive legal procedures. These conflicts are also burdensome and costly for the tax administration. Again, taxpayers and the tax administration have a common interest to discuss diverging positions and solve disputes at an early stage in which both parties are often (still) able to respond flexibly to problems which arise. Early problem solving may offer the taxpayer legal certainty at the time in which he needs it.

Early problem solving is a main feature of Horizontal Monitoring. Taxpayers provide the tax administration pro-actively with information. The tax administration in turn is transparent about the application of the law. Moreover, taxpayers and the tax administration deliberate on differing views with regard to the legal consequences of taxpayers actions – enhancing taxpayers' legal certainty.

8.3.3 Disclosure obligations, sanctions and legal protection

8.3.3.1 Disclosure obligations

As stated in the introduction, legal asymmetry characterises the legal relationship between taxpayer and tax administration. The Netherlands Tax and Customs Administration has very broad statutory powers to unilaterally determine this legal relationship. The power to (re)assess is one of these powers but there are other powers for the purpose of a right assessment. Information gathering powers, for example, enable the tax authorities to request information needed for the assessment – information which is available to the taxpayer and/or third parties such as employers, banks and insurance companies (to compensating for information asymmetry).

In order to facilitate the levying of taxes the legal framework confers all kinds of powers to the tax administration and obligations to the taxpayers. For the sake of legal protection of the taxpayers the tax code also contains taxpayers' rights – for example, the right to object and appeal. Both powers and rights constitute boundaries within which the tax administration has to enforce the tax law. I will first deal with the tax administration's enforcement powers and the correlating taxpayers' obligations. I will proceed with the sanctions the tax administration can impose when taxpayers do not meet these obligations. I continue with a sketch of the rights to object and to appeal. This section will close with a subsection on legal principles which offer (additional) legal protection.

The tax administration depends on information available to the taxpayer (information asymmetry). Without this information it is often hard to check the taxpayer's tax return. However, not all taxpayers are eager to provide the necessary information. Therefore the tax administration has very broad powers with regard to the taxpayer. There are the many obligations of the taxpayer: to file a tax return, to provide data and information and documents that may be relevant in arriving at a tax assessment etc. Thus, the tax inspector has the competence to obtain information which is relevant for tax purposes. In the first instance, he collects this information by way of the tax return filed by the taxpayer. The law requires the taxpayer to file a tax return which provides the requested data unreservedly in a correct and clear manner as well as timely (Art. 8 GTA). In this way, he discloses the information needed for assessment. Moreover, NTCA has auditing powers in order to examine the accuracy of the information provided by taxpayers.[62] If necessary, the inspector can collect additional information from the taxpayer by (specifically) asking for it (Art. 47 GTA).

---

62 Alink, M. and Van Kommer, V. (2000). *Handbook for Tax Administrations: Organizational Structure and Management of Tax Administrations*, The Hague: Ministry of Finance, p. 94. Cf. Gordon, R. (1996). Law of Tax Administration and Procedure. In: Thuronyi, V. (ed.), *Tax Law Design and Drafting*. International Monetary Fund, p. 16, referring to USA Internal Revenue Code § 7605: 'taxpayers should have the right to have audits held at a reasonable time, in a reasonable place, and within reasonable limits'; and Höglund, M. & Nöjd, S. (2014). Professional Communication of the Tax Authorities. *Intertax* Vol. 42, 8/9, p. 501, who quote from the Swedish Tax Procedure Act: 'Tax audits should take place in conjunction with the auditee and in a way that does not interfere with business operations'.

Hence, the obligations of the taxpayer can be divided into primary and secondary obligations. The primary obligation is the duty to submit a tax return. If no tax return is filed the tax inspector may draw up an estimated assessment (Art. 11 GTA). The duty to submit a tax return can be fulfilled by filing the tax form (invitation) supplied by the tax administration.

The secondary obligations of the taxpayer concern (additional) information with regard to his tax position which the tax administration needs for the assessment. The taxpayer has to provide data and information on request; he has to make available books, documents and other data carriers for audit etc. Moreover companies have to keep a proper financial administration and taxpayers have to provide the requested data in a correct and clear manner and within a reasonable period of time. All this regards information which may be relevant for the assessment by the tax inspector.

8.3.3.2   Sanctions

In certain circumstances the tax inspector can fine a taxpayer. This is a far-reaching (statutory) power attributed to the tax inspector – which often causes great annoyance with taxpayers. In the Netherlands omission penalties and offence penalties can be distinguished between each other.[63] The difference between these two types of administrative penalties is that omission penalties can be imposed without any intent (gross negligence or purpose) on the part of the taxpayer, whereas offence penalties cannot be imposed without this subjective component. The NTCA can impose an omission penalty if a taxpayer fails to meet one or more of its tax obligations (Artt. 67a – 67cb GTA). For example, when an employer has filed a tax return but fails to pay the payroll taxes in time or in full the NTCA can impose an administrative penalty of 3% of the amount not paid in time or still outstanding, with a minimum of € 50 and a maximum of € 4,920 (Art. 67c GTA). If the employer does not file a return or does not file a return in time then he will receive an administrative penalty of € 61 (Art. 67b GTA).[64] Unlike omission penalties, offence penalties relate to the punishment of more serious offences which involve gross negligence or intention (Artt. 67cc – 67fa GTA). Such an offence penalty will be imposed for example, if the taxpayer has *willfully* not filed a tax return or filed an incorrect or incomplete tax return (Art. 67d GTA). With regard to taxes levied by a tax assessment, the penalty imposed amounts to that not exceeding 100% of that of the assessment. However, a penalty of 100% only occurs in exceptional cases, whereby for example the taxpayer on purpose and systematically did not file his tax returns. Here, the tax inspector has discretionary powers which is regulated by policy rules. Moreover, the tax inspector should act in conformity with the principle of proportionality (cf. Art. 3:4 GALA). Therefore, he has to verify whether or not the (amount of) penalty is in proportion to the specific facts and circumstances

---

63   If even a criminal offence is committed, the taxpayer is liable to a term of imprisonment or a fine for a certain amount. Chapter IX GTA (Artt. 68 – 88 GTA).
64   The NTCA can impose higher administrative fines in exceptional situations, for example, the recurrent failure to either file returns or file returns in time, file correct and complete returns, or make the associated payments or make the payments in time (Art. 22a, section 7 of the Decree on Administrative Fines Tax Administration (*Besluit Bestuurlijke Boeten Belastingdienst*).

of the case – which is monitored by the courts using the same principle of proportionality.[65]

The taxpayer may not fulfill obligations such as to file the required tax return, to answer specific questions from the NTCA or his record keeping obligation. A taxpayer may incur a sanction in a case where these obligations are not met. An important and far-reaching sanction, besides a penalty, of not fulfilling these obligations is the reversal of the burden of proof to the taxpayer (Art. 25, para. 3 and Art. 27e GTA).[66] In this case, statutory law holds that the burden of proof shifts (completely) to the taxpayer. The tax inspector estimates the amount of taxpayer's income and, if the taxpayer disagrees, he has to prove that this ex officio estimated income is incorrect.[67] Moreover, the taxpayer has to demonstrate convincingly the incorrectness of all the disputed elements of the assessment instead of making it plausible.[68]

Hence, if the tax administration is convinced that a company has not fulfilled a statutory obligation, such as its record keeping obligations, leading to changes in the tax liability and possibly (heavy) penalties, the company faces a serious problem because this will lead to amendments in its most recent accounts. These mistakes or incorrect statements have to be corrected in the next annual financial statement/ report.

Of course, it would be far easier to debate the quality of the financial administration before a tax return is filed – at a stage where there is no sanction like the reversal of the burden of proof hanging like a sword of Damocles over the company. This a clear advantage of real-time scrutiny, an important feature of Horizontal Monitoring. More generally, these legal obligations regard (additional) information to be disclosed on request which leaves room for voluntary, 'proactive' disclosure for co-operative taxpayers who do not want to 'play the audit lottery' as is the case with Horizontal Monitoring. Proactive disclosure allows for the possibility of timely discussion of information (preceding the file of the tax return) and correction of shortcomings in the way the accounts are kept; thus diminishing the probability of sanctions. This goes all the more for companies with an adequate TCF in place, for they are designed in such a way that the accounting processes produce a tax return which complies with the legal requirements.

---

[65] Furthermore, a term of imprisonment or a fine of a certain amount can be imposed in case the taxpayer commits a serious offence or crime. Here, these criminal offences will be left aside (see chapter IX GTA).

[66] Cf. Koopman, R.J. & Dwarkasing, R. (2013). The Netherlands. In: Meussen, G. (ed.), *The Burden of Proof in Tax Law*, (EATLP 2010), Amsterdam 2013, p. 189-203. The reversal of the burden of proof is not applicable in case of a tax penalty.

[67] The proof of the negative elements of the taxable income as deductible expenses and allowances remains with the taxpayer. With respect to these elements there is no shift of the burden of proof.

[68] Cf. Van Eijsden, A. & Meussen, G.T.K. (2010). Netherlands. In: Lang, M. et. al. (eds.), *Procedural Rules in Tax Law in the Context of European Union and Domestic Law* (Eucotax Series on European Taxation, volume 27), Alphen aan den Rijn: Kluwer Law International, p. 451.

8.3.3.3 Right to objection and right of appeal[69]

Above, some of the unilateral, often far-reaching powers of the tax administration were dealt with. These powers are kept in check by taxpayers' rights. The tax code provides taxpayers with means to contest assessments and other acts of the tax administration. Thus the tax administration's exercise of power is curbed. Disagreements and conflicts between NTCA and taxpayers are decided by impartial judges.

Taxpayers can appeal to an independent judge.[70] However, before lodging an appeal with the court the taxpayer has to make an objection to the tax inspector.[71] Without an objection, no appeal is possible. With regard to the possibility of any objection and therefore any appeal, the General Taxes Act deviates from GALA. The GALA is organised around the concept of administrative decision (*beschikking*) which implies that an interested citizen can object to an administrative decision by way of lodging a written notice (*bezwaarschrift*).[72] However, in tax law it is not possible to lodge a notice of objection to every administrative decision given by the tax inspector which impacts the legal position of the taxpayer. Filing a notice of objection is only possible if the assessment or (other kind of) administrative decision is specifically mentioned in tax statutes (see Art. 26 GTA).[73] This 'closed system of legal remedies' is an important feature of legal protection in Dutch tax law. No objection can be raised to decisions or actions of the tax administration unless explicitly stated in the law.[74]

The objection procedure is an 'administrative phase' which implies a possible revision of the assessment rule. Within six weeks of the date of the assessment the taxpayer may file a notice of objection with the inspector. As a rule, if a taxpayer lodges an objection, tax collection is suspended. However, the financial consequences are limited because the taxpayer or the tax administration has to pay interest depending on which of the two parties is successful. The objection must be sent to the tax administration that made the disputed assessment (itself). There is a regulation that provides for a hearing of the taxpayer at his request.[75] In most cases, the taxpayer will be heard. Unfortunately, there is no sanction for the tax inspector if he refuses to apply the obligation to hear the taxpayer. Officially, a different person from the one who raised the assessment must treat the objection but, in practice, this regulation is often ignored.

---

69 Cf. Happé, R.H. & Gribnau, J.L.M. (2007). Constitutional Limits to Taxation in a Democratic State: The Dutch Experience. *Michigan State Journal of International Law*, 15, 2, p. 417-459.
70 See also Sommerhalder, R. & Pechler, E. (1998). Protection of Taxpayers' Rights in the Netherlands. In: Bentley, D. (ed.), *Taxpayers' Rights: An International Perspective*, Gold Coast: Bond University, p. 310 ff.
71 Art. 8:1 read in conjunction with Art. 7:1 GALA.
72 Seerden, R. & Stroink, F. (2007). Administrative Law in the Netherlands. In: Seerden, R. (ed.), *Administrative Law of the European Union, its Member States and the United States*, Antwerp/ Oxford: Intersentia, p. 170.
73 An assessment is a kind of administrative decision.
74 Van Eijsden, A. & Meussen, G.T.K. (2010). Netherlands. In: Lang, M. et. al. (eds.), *Procedural Rules in Tax Law in the Context of European Union and Domestic Law* (Eucotax Series on European Taxation, volume 27), Alphen aan den Rijn: Kluwer Law International, p. 428.
75 Art. 25, para 1 of the General Tax Act read in combination with Art. 7:2 GALA.

The taxpayer may appeal to a District Court against any decision over an objection. The Dutch adjudication in tax law is conducted by independent and impartial judges. The right to a fair trial includes these and other demands and is laid down in Art. 6 of the European Convention on Human Rights. The judges of the Tax Divisions of the courts have specific expertise in the field of taxation. The Tax Division is part of the Administrative Division in the District Courts (*rechtbanken*). All seventeen District Courts have a tax division but only five of them are competent for state taxes. All courts are competent for the provincial, municipal, and water board taxes. They have territorial jurisdiction. These courts of first instance deal with questions of fact and of law. The term for appeal is six weeks and the taxpayers have to pay court fees.

Judgments of the administrative court, in first instance, may be appealed to the Tax Division of the Courts of Appeal (*gerechtshoven* – there are five Courts of Appeal, which have territorial jurisdiction). Both the taxpayer and the tax inspector may appeal to the Court of Appeal. Like the courts of first instance, these courts deal with questions of fact and the law.

Both the taxpayer and the tax inspector may appeal to the Supreme Court (*Hoge Raad*) against a decision of a Court of Appeal. This appeal in cassation may be lodged with the Tax Division of the court of cassation, the Supreme Court. Note that the Supreme Court makes judgements based solely on the law, not the facts. Here, the Advocate General has a right to state his opinion on the case.

Though there are some legal possibilities to accelerate the process,[76] in general the objection and appeal procedure may be time-consuming and costly while the result is uncertain. Even a taxpayer who is (almost) perfectly sure of his position knows that the actual outcome of a legal procedure is never completely predictable. Hence, to opt for objection and even appeal is often not a very efficient way of resolving disputes about the facts of the case at hand and its tax consequences and other (relational) conflicts between taxpayer and tax inspector.

8.3.3.4   Principles of proper administrative behaviour

The legal framework does not only consist of statutory law but also of unwritten law. The NTCA is an administrative authority and is bound by Netherlands tax law, the judicial interpretation of the law (i.e. case law) and by instructions from the government (by way of policy rules[77]). Traditionally, the principle of legality has limited the scope of this interference demanding a legal basis for government action such as the levying of taxes. The principle of legality thus demands that NTCA's actions must have a statutory basis. The exercise of powers by the NTCA is also bound by unwritten legal

---

76 With regard to the objection procedure, see Art. 7:1 GALA. With regard to the appeal procedure, see Art. 8:52 GALA and with regard to the appeal to the Supreme Court, see Art. 28, par. 3 GTA.
77 These policy or administrative rules do not bind the taxpayer nor the judiciary; see Gribnau, H. (2007). Soft Law and Taxation: The Case of the Netherlands. *Legisprudence*, 3, p. 301-308 and Gribnau, H. (2014). Not argued from but prayed to. Who's afraid of legal principles? *eJournal of Tax Research*, Vol. 12, No. 1, pp. 185 – 217, at p. 209-210.

standards that are called 'the principles of proper administrative behaviour' (*algemene beginselen van behoorlijk bestuur*; also referred to as 'principles of proper administration').

These principles of proper administrative behaviour offer legal protection to the citizen. They comprise procedural norms but also substantive norms and provide extra legal protection to taxpayers in addition to the protection embodied by statute law. In a way, they compensate for the failure of parliament to exercise adequate control over the government and the tax administration. The diminished legal certainty, legal equality of tax legislation and the ever growing power of the NTCA – which is reflected in a growing number of obligations for taxpayers – are counterbalanced.[78]

Hence, in the Netherlands the NTCA has to comply with principles of proper administrative behaviour. Most of these principles are developed in case law. They are partly codified in the General Administrative Law Act and partly still (unwritten) case law.[79] The most important and well developed principles of good administration in tax law are the principle of honouring legitimate expectations and the principle of equality (see 8.4.5). Other principles include the principle of fair play (see 8.4.6), of 'justification' (giving the grounds for the decision), of proportionality and the prohibition of the misuse of power (*détournement de pouvoir*).

To illustrate the importance of these principles we will take a closer look at the principle of honouring legitimate expectations. Nowadays, most citizens do not have extensive knowledge of tax legislation in force and depend on communications by the NTCA. The NTCA, for example, may provide general information to a taxpayer or taxpayers in general by way of policy rules (for example on its website) but may also promise a taxpayer that it will apply the tax law in a certain way. Given this importance of policy rules and other communications, the question is whether citizens can rely on them. The principle of honouring legitimate expectations may in exceptional situations justify a deviation from the strict application of the legislation (the principle of legality, therefore).

When will legitimate expectations be honoured? Suppose the NTCA promises a taxpayer to apply the tax law in a certain way. The Supreme Court decides that the expectations raised by a promise must be honoured if four criteria are (all) met: (a) the taxpayer has the impression that the tax inspector is taking a certain position concerning the application of the tax law; (b) the taxpayer has informed the tax inspector of all relevant facts and circumstances of his or her case; (c) the taxpayer may reasonably think that the promise is in line with the spirit of the law, and (d) the

---

78 Gribnau, H. (2010). Netherlands. In: Dourado, A.P. (ed.), *Separation of Powers in Tax Law*, Amsterdam: IBFD, p. 160.
79 Seerden, R. & Stroink, F. (2007). Administrative Law in the Netherlands. In: Seerden, R. (ed.), *Administrative Law of the European Union, its Member States and the United States*, Antwerp/ Oxford: Intersentia, p. 178-181.

tax inspector is competent to deal with the taxpayer.[80] In this case, the tax inspector has to deviate from the otherwise applicable legislative provision. In these criteria a balanced approach can be observed. For example, if the taxpayer is in bad faith, criterion (c) is not met, the principle of legality prevails.[81]

8.4 Horizontal Monitoring and the legal framework

8.4.1 General remarks

In sketching the legal framework, some aspects of Horizontal Monitoring have already been dealt with. Now some other aspects will be discussed. Horizontal Monitoring is, ultimately, embedded in a vertical monitoring framework. If a taxpayer does not behave in the spirit of the covenant, the NTCA may make use of in-depth audits, (administrative) penalties, investigations, under certain circumstances terminate the agreement, etc. How does Horizontal Monitoring relate to the legal framework, i.e., the statutory competences of NTCA, the statutory rights and obligations of the taxpayer and the principles of proper administrative behaviour?

The State Secretary Finance states: 'Upon concluding a covenant, arrangements are made about settling the past, thus increasing legal certainty. Another aim is to have tax inspectors take a stance on companies' future actions and their tax consequences. This is also possible because as yet unsettled 'problems of past years' no longer constitute an impediment to taking a stance. This is based on the premise that the law is applied and that no more or less favourable stances are taken. Another premise is that companies report actions that have a bearing on tax openly and in good time'.[82]

Thus, in the context of Horizontal Monitoring, the implementation of this compliance approach has to be performed within the framework of the statutory law, case law and policy (rules). The tax administration will not deviate from the law in force. First of all, this implies that taxpayers are free to choose whether they engage voluntarily in Horizontal Monitoring or not. There is no statutory provision to be observed which obliges taxpayers to participate in this governance method. So they have a choice, even when they are faced with the prospect of (more) field audits – which as such, may imply a certain pressure to opt for Horizontal Monitoring.[83]

Of course, once taxpayers seriously engage in a HM-relationship and conclude a covenant, they should comply with it wholeheartedly but they may terminate the

---

80 Supreme Court, 26 September 1979, no. 19 250, BNB 1979/311.
81 Happé, R. & Pauwels, M. (2011). Balancing of Powers in Dutch Tax Law: General Overview and Recent Developments. In: Evans, C. et. al. (eds.), *The Delicate Balance: Tax, Discretion and the Rule of Law*. Amsterdam: IBFD, p. 237-245, at p. 246.
82 *Parliamentary Documents II*, 2005-2006, 30 300 IXB, no. 40, p. 13.
83 The tax inspector who accordingly tells the taxpayer that he may face more field audits is not guilty of misuse of power. Cf. report 2012/021 of the Dutch ombudsman; www.nationaleombudsman.nl/rapporten/2013/021?aresult=198.

Horizontal Monitoring relationship when they are not satisfied (opt-out).[84] This may seem self-evident but it is not. First, engaging voluntarily in Horizontal Monitoring requires a significant investment from taxpayers.[85] A taxpayer who opts-out of a covenant therefore has to face a loss on that investment. Secondly, taxpayers who intend to terminate the Horizontal Monitoring relationship may fear unfair treatment by the NTCA and they may be afraid of an increase of distrust and, as a result, NTCA increasing its vertical monitoring. Thirdly, they may fear that terminating a covenant may go at the expense of their reputation, for enforcement covenants are sometimes viewed as a warranty of quality by stakeholders – for example as part of the company's Corporate Social Responsibility policy. Consequently, even in the absence of legal impediments, finishing the Horizontal Monitoring relationship is not all that free or straightforward.[86]

In the following part, some more legal issues will be dealt with although it will not be an exhaustive overview.

8.4.2 Proactively providing information

Within the framework of a HM-covenant, uncertain positions should be put to the inspector as quickly as possible so that the NTCA can take a stance. This includes issues on which disagreement with the NTCA can arise, for example, because of a difference in interpretation of facts or the law. Taxpayers are required not only to report all actions that involve tax risks but also to disclose their views about the legal consequences of such actions and the positions taken by them.

The information requested by the NTCA stays within the legal framework. As shown above there are a number of statutory obligations to provide information. The difference however, is that the voluntarily concluded covenant demands taxpayers to provide information in advance and proactively. This early disclosure makes real-time scrutiny and resolution of issues possible. Moreover, the taxpayer is requested to give his own view on the legal consequences of the tax position taken in order to enable the tax inspector to provide assurance.[87] Here, taxpayers voluntarily agree by covenant to go beyond their statutory obligations.

The general principles of proper administrative behaviour set boundaries for information to be requested on the basis of the statutory obligations. Here, the 'fair play principle' is relevant. This principle does not allow the tax authorities to request a letter containing tax advice or similar documents (e.g. a due diligence report). Nonetheless, a taxpayer may do this voluntarily. This also goes for taxpayers operating

---

84 Of course, the tax inspector can also terminate the Horizontal Monitoring relationship (opt-out).
85 For example, costs related to the communication with NTCA about the quality of the TCF. The costs of setting up a TCF will be made any way because a TCF is a value in itself for a company.
86 An issue may therefore be an indemnification in case the tax administration decides to terminate the covenant.
87 This aspect of transparency is explained in the published internal HM-guidelines.

within the framework of a HM-covenant. Again, a HM-covenant requires the taxpayer to fulfill statutory obligations proactively and he may voluntarily go beyond compliance with regard to these obligations by handing over to the tax administration letters containing tax advice or similar documents.

8.4.3 Penalties

As shown above, in certain circumstances the tax inspector can impose omission penalties and offence penalties (see 8.3.3.2). With regard to these penalties, the tax inspector has discretionary power which is regulated by policy rules. The tax inspector should also respect the principle of proportionality. Hence, he has to take into account the specific facts and circumstances of the case.

Covenant parties are expected to respond to mistakes with mutual understanding and willing to discuss the cause of a mistake to prevent reoccurrence. Therefore, in principle the NTCA's approach should be a willingness to discuss 'causes' and 'measures' rather than eagerness to impose penalties. This relates to the trust basis of the relationship, as the Stevens Committee rightly points out. 'The rigid invocation of penalty provisions – which are usually invoked in the event of intended or culpable negligence – in situations of this nature cannot be reconciled with a relationship based on trust'.[88]

Thus, a covenant may make a difference – depending on the particular specific facts and circumstances of the case. In the case where a company readily adjusts its internal control system after a mistake is discovered (in order to avoid future mistakes), the tax inspector takes this willingness to comply into account.[89] Therefore the penalty may be mitigated. Even so, for a taxpayer who does not keep to an HM-engagement, for example, because his internal control system is inadequately implemented, the penalty may not be mitigated (or even worse).[90] Hence, a differentiated treatment is in conformity with the principle of proportionality. Of course, just engaging in Horizontal Monitoring is not a sufficient condition; the taxpayer should show evidence of his trustworthiness, for example, by having a tax control framework in place.

8.4.4 Dispute resolution

At various stages of the Horizontal Monitoring process, (i) on concluding a covenant, (ii) during the execution of the covenant and (iii) at termination, the question can be

---

88 Stevens Committee (2012). *Tax supervision – Made to Measure: Flexible When Possible, Strict Where Necessary*, The Hague: Ministry of Finance, http://www.ifa.nl/Document/Publicaties/Enhanced%20Relationship%20Project/tax_supervision_made_to_measure_tz0151z1fdeng.pdf, p. 97.
89 According to the internal HM-guidelines the same goes for taxpayers without a HM-agreement who are willing to comply.
90 Cf. the decision of the Court of Rotterdam of 24 October 2013 (ECLI:NL:RBROT:2013:8216) with regard to the case of KPN which was fined by the Netherlands Authority for Consumers and Markets because of inadequate implementation of the agreed upon compliance programme. The Court determined the fine to be € 29,6 billion.

raised whether the distinction between participants and non-participants is in accordance with the principle of equality. On these points, the Stevens Committee formulated some recommendations to resolve some of the issues raised against Horizontal Monitoring but it detected no major legal flaws. Instead, the Committee argued that the concept of Horizontal Monitoring is based on mutual trust and issues should not be resolved in a legal context.

Although the Committee's opinion can be supported, there is still a certain reticence amongst legal scholars when it comes to the legal issues raised by Horizontal Monitoring. Given the particular nature of this trust-based relationship, it could be argued that important decisions with respect to Horizontal Monitoring (e.g. the rejection and denunciation of a covenant) should be brought within the scope of judicial review. Because of the Netherlands' 'closed system of legal remedies', disputes with regard to these decisions are not admissible in (tax) court.[91] However, judicial review of NTCA's decisions within the HM-framework implies juridification. The legal process has a logic of its own which may go at the expense of the trust-based relationship which Horizontal Monitoring – itself a form of de-juridification – aims for (see 8.1). The recommendation of the Stevens Committee to resort to mediation in these cases, therefore, deserves a more in-depth analysis.[92] Such a dispute resolving instrument focused on restoring trust contributes to a greater confidence in the concept of Horizontal Monitoring.

8.4.5 *Principle of equality*

In terms of outcome, Horizontal Monitoring should not lead to differences compared to other types of monitoring, more specifically vertical monitoring; neither a more stringent treatment nor a more lenient treatment (see 8.4.1). Covenants cannot be seen as a way to pay less tax than is due according to the law.[93] Horizontal Monitoring is about interaction between taxpayers and tax authorities rather than distribution of the tax burden (distributive justice). Only the monitoring process, the road to any outcome, varies. As stated above, the tax administration has discretion with regard to the way it fulfills its tasks and deploys its resources – in the most cost effective manner. The principle of equality requires treating like cases alike and unlike cases (accordingly) differently. Thus, it does not mean that every taxpayer has to be treated in exactly the same way. However, any differences of treatment should be rationally justified. Treating cases differently, therefore, should only be justified because of

---

91   A taxpayer may be of the opinion that the refusal for admission to a compliance agreement is based on incorrect grounds – think of the conditions attached to participation. According to the committee the 'decision on the need for judicial reviews of these cases is a political decision'; Stevens (2012) Committee, p. 98.
92   For an in-depth analysis of mediation and tax disputes, see Van Hout, M.B.A (2013). *Mens, maatschappij en mediation in het belastingrecht* [Man, Society and Mediation in Tax Law], Den Haag: Sdu Uitgevers.
93   Because the 'Enhanced Relationship' terminology earlier adopted by the OECD may unintentionally have given the impression that an enhancement of the relationship involves some benefit in violation of the equality of outcomes. OECD (2013), p. 47-48. The term 'Co-operative Compliance' is deemed to be more appropriate.

objective differences in the circumstances of the cases in question. Hence, the decision to audit a taxpayer, for example, 'does not require that every taxpayer should be subject to an audit'.[94] So, NTCA may opt for different enforcement strategies with regard to co-operative or compliant taxpayers on the one hand and non-co-operative or non-compliant taxpayers on the other. NTCA can apply a horizontal approach based on real-time scrutiny, early disclosure and resolution of issues to compliant taxpayers and a more traditional (vertical) approach based on traditional audit or enquiry to non-compliant taxpayers. Taxpayers' willingness to comply is the objective justification to enter into a HM-covenant.[95] Again, this differentiated treatment should not lead to a different, more favourable outcome in terms of tax payable by a taxpayer. Therefore, the principle of equality is (theoretically, at least) not at stake when Horizontal Monitoring is applied.[96] Moreover, the principle of equality is served by NTCA's HM-guidelines to guarantee uniform treatment.

Horizontal Monitoring is important for the NTCA. It is therefore important that covenants are concluded. Of course, some companies will have hesitations about engaging in Horizontal Monitoring. A little encouragement by way of a favour might help them to reconsider. The tax inspector might be tempted not to delve too deeply into the past in order to evade difficult discussions about tax positions taken in the past. Consciously not correcting incorrectly filed tax returns implies a favourable and therefore unequal treatment of taxpayers, in which case the principle of equality would be violated.[97] In other words, the Tax and Customs Administration 'would be prepared to incur a loss' on the settlement of (disputes regarding) past tax years when this resulted in the conclusion of an agreement – which 'could be indicative of preferential treatment in recruiting participation in horizontal monitoring'.[98] The Stevens Committee's discussions and the information it received, however, have not revealed any solid evidence to substantiate the conclusion that preferential treatment has been an issue.

---

94 OECD (2013). *Co-operative Compliance: A Framework: From Enhanced Relationship to Co-operative Compliance*, Paris: OECD, p. 45.
95 A taxpayer may be willing to comply and to co-operate on a trust basis but not wanting to enter in a HM-covenant. According to the internal HM-guidelines, in this case tax administration and the taxpayer can co-operate to conform to the covenant; however, without the obligation of an adequate TCF for the taxpayer and without (regularly) strategic consultation.
96 Stevens Committee (2010). *A Tailor-Made Approach to Fiscal Supervision (Fiscaal toezicht op maat)*. http://www.ifa.nl/Document/Publicaties/Enhanced%20Relationship%20Project/tax_supervision_-made_to_measure_tz0151z1fdeng.pdf, p. 96; cf. OECD (2013). *Co-operative Compliance: A Framework: From Enhanced Relationship to Co-operative Compliance*, Paris: OECD, p. 45-46. Cf. Parliamentary Documents II, 2004-2005, 29 800, no. 2. Cf. OECD (2013). *Co-operative Compliance: A Framework: From Enhanced Relationship to Co-operative Compliance*, Paris: OECD, p. 45-48.
97 Cf. OECD (2013). *Co-operative Compliance: A Framework: From Enhanced Relationship to Co-operative Compliance*, Paris: OECD, p. 51.
98 Stevens Committee (2012). *Tax supervision – Made to Measure: Flexible When Possible, Strict Where Necessary*, The Hague: Ministry of Finance, p. 50. Nonetheless, the Committee argues that a procedure drawn up for the settlement of those past tax issues at the time of horizontal monitoring's implementation would have been desirable. That would have enabled a broader verifiable consideration of interests. The Committee then concludes: 'This could be achieved by increasing the transparency of the Tax and Customs Administration's existing procedure'.

There may be another cause for unequal treatment. The NTCA performs its duties on the basis of trust in and understanding of the position of individual taxpayers. The HM-relationship is aimed at co-operation and trust. However, NTCA's staff (tax inspectors) risks losing its ability to form objective opinions.[99] The Stevens Committee emphasises that a loss of a professional critical attitude is a risk of Horizontal Monitoring. This risk is referred to as the 'risk of attachment' – also known as the 'risk of regulatory capture'. The Committee advocates an adequate policy to diminish these risks, for example, the rotation of staff, reviews of the quality of files or the separation of duties.[100] The importance of a good working relationship and striving for mutual understanding, therefore, should not be lost at the expense of a professional critical attitude.[101] The OECD rightly stresses the importance of providing assurance to external stakeholders ('wider society') about the impartiality and professional qualities of the tax administration. 'Failure to maintain a professional critical attitude could have a damaging effect on overall confidence in revenue bodies'.[102]

8.4.6 Fair play: agree to disagree

Compliance agreements (covenants) are concluded with taxpayers who are willing to comply voluntarily in a transparent trust-relationship with NTCA. But how about a taxpayer who takes a (favourable) position which the NTCA disagrees with? Can the NTCA tell the taxpayer that such a position is threatening the trust relationship and should not be taken by a taxpayer participating in Horizontal Monitoring? Or even, that taking such a position is a reason to terminate the covenant? In my opinion, the principle of fair play disqualifies the tax inspector from 'threatening' to terminate a covenant in this case.

Of course, it is possible that parties to the covenant come to the conclusion that they (continue to) disagree on the position that the taxpayer has taken. In this case, they

---

99 For the conflicting demands often faced by field officers who do not want to fail to detect non-compliance nor to alienate the taxpayer, see Waller, V. (2007). The Challenge of Institutional Integrity in Responsive Regulation: Field Inspections by the Australian Taxation Office. *Law & Policy* Vol. 29, No. 1, p. 67-83. Cf. the retirement of Dave Hartnett, Permanent Secretary at HMRC, after he was criticised for agreeing a number of 'sweetheart deals' with major companies including Vodafone and Goldman Sachs in the UK. See James, M. (2013). Cutting a Good Deal – UK Uncut, Goldman Sachs and the Challenge to Administrative Discretion. *Journal of Applied Accounting Research* Vol. 14, No. 4, p. 248-267.
100 Stevens Committee (2012). *Tax supervision – Made to Measure: Flexible When Possible, Strict Where Necessary*, The Hague: Ministry of Finance. http://www.ifa.nl/Document/Publicaties/Enhanced%20Relationship%20Project/tax_supervision_made_to_measure_tz0151z1fdeng.pdf, p. 51 Cf. Dabner J. (2012). Constraints on the 'Enhanced Relationship' Model – What Really Shapes the Relationship Between the Tax Administrator and Tax Intermediaries in Australasia and the United Kingdom. [2012] *British Tax Review* 4, p. 532.
101 Cf. Garofalo, C. (2011). Governance and Values in Contemporary Public Service. In: De Vries, M.S. & Kim, P.S. (eds.), *Value and Virtue in Public Administration: A Comparative Perspective*. Basingstoke/New York: Palgrave, p. 25, who points at 'the pervasive tendency in public organizations toward conflict avoidance.'
102 OECD (2013). *Co-operative Compliance: A Framework: From Enhanced Relationship to Co-operative Compliance*, Paris: OECD, p. 65. The report also deals with aspects of internal governance of co-operative compliance programmes within revenue bodies, see p. 71.

'agree to disagree' which has no impact on their HM-relationship; the disagreement only concerns the tax return – without further impact on the relationship.[103] This fits well with the OECD's observation that there must be 'scope for taxpayers and revenue bodies to have genuine differences of opinion about the proper tax treatment of some transactions, even within the framework of a co-operative relationship'.[104] A covenant tax return may therefore include a position which can be reasonably advocated and which differs from the position of the tax inspector provided that arrangements between parties are made about this position in the phase prior to the tax return. The taxpayer should be open and transparent about its position. So, within the framework of a HM-covenant, such a position should be put to the inspector so that the NTCA is informed before the tax return is filed. The tax inspector should be consulted with all issues raised in the future on which the tax inspector might have a diverging point of view. Full disclosure is required when taxpayers take a position in the tax return that is contrary to the view of NTCA. Again, this is an obligation voluntarily entered into as a part of the HM transparency dimension.

But how about a taxpayer engaging in tax avoidance? He may be completely transparent, providing the tax inspector with all the information needed to assess the taxpayer's position and therefore acting trustworthily. But still, a tax inspector might believe that the taxpayer is not paying his 'fair share', he is not acting in accordance with the 'spirit of the law'. Therefore, the tax inspector may think that the taxpayer is non-compliant while the taxpayer may feel forced to be over compliant. This is a moral issue. Is this a reason not to conclude a covenant with taxpayers looking for the most profitable route or, if a covenant is already concluded, to terminate the covenant? The answer is 'no'.[105] Taxpayers may arrange their tax affairs as they wish. They may engage in tax planning and structuring as long as they remain within the limits of the law and are transparent about their tax position(s). Some taxpayers may want to contribute a 'fair share', others may want to pay as little as possible (staying within the law).[106] If a taxpayer is completely transparent, disclosing the relevant issues to the tax inspector before filing his tax return, this is no reason to

---

103 According to the internal HM-guidelines the company has to make such a tax return identifiable. Cf. OECD (2013). *Co-operative Compliance: A Framework: From Enhanced Relationship to Co-operative Compliance*, Paris: OECD, p. 52: 'This principle provides flexibility and the possibility to go to court without jeopardising the relationship. The revenue body and taxpayer will jointly present the case to the court.'
104 OECD (2013). *Co-operative Compliance: A Framework: From Enhanced Relationship to Co-operative Compliance*, Paris: OECD, p. 50.
105 Cf. OECD (2013). *Co-operative Compliance: A Framework: From Enhanced Relationship to Co-operative Compliance*, Paris: OECD, p. 49: 'When interpreting what is 'the spirit of the law', the guideline for the revenue body should be the same within co-operative compliance as in an ordinary audit. It is critical to make clear there are neither advantages nor disadvantages in these aspects within co-operative compliance'. Cf. Poolen, T.W.M. (2011). Horizontalisering van het toezicht: veranderingen in de verhoudingen. In: Gribnau, H. (ed.), *Principieel belastingrecht. Liber Amicorum Richard Happé*. Nijmegen: Wolf Legal Publishers, p. 173-183, at p. 179-180.
106 See Gribnau, H. (2015). CSR and Tax Planning: Not by Rules Alone. *Social & Legal Studies*, June 2015, forthcoming.

terminate a HM-covenant. The principle of fair play does not allow the tax inspector to terminate the covenant. Nonetheless, NTCA may well give its opinion in a case where a company engages in aggressive tax planning (which is within the letter of the law but against the spirit of the law). In my opinion, this should be done with restraint and respect for the company's motives and circumstances, all the more so because companies may arrange their tax affairs to achieve a favourable tax treatment as long as they stay within the legal boundaries. In this respect, NTCA should not put pressure on a company and moral preaching is fundamentally forbidden; all the more because of the legal asymmetry inherent to this relationship.

An exception may exist, however, when taxpayers consciously explore the boundaries of the tax law. Then the HM-basis of trust will evaporate.[107] This kind of 'frontier exploration' occurs when the inspector has previously taken a position on the presented case, the taxpayer disagrees and then tries to make the case acceptable to the tax inspector by repeatedly (slightly) modifying the case. Furthermore, if a taxpayer makes continuous use of aggressive tax planning structures, repressive enforcement will be deployed. The Minister of Finance made a clear statement: 'Taxpayers who have concluded a compliance agreement are expected to refrain from continually seeking the limits of the relevant tax legislation'.[108] In a context of trust, mutual understanding and transparency, it is important that taxpayers' (and NTCA's) behaviour and attitude is regularly discussed. Part of the discussion should be companies' tax planning policy. To enhance mutual understanding, impressions and opinions will be exchanged. NTCA will voice its opinion on it in order to understand the companies' point of view. Without this exchange of experiences, views and ideas, NTCA can hardly reach the conclusion that a company is continually seeking the limits of the relevant tax legislation. Inevitably, moral views and ideas will also be voiced because there is no hard line between law and morality.

An indirect effect of the co-operative working relationship based on trust and openness could be that taxpayers become less willing to minimise their tax liability and are therefore more willing to pay their fair share. Some tax advisers have observed such a change in some of their clients' attitudes.[109] As shown above, trust, transparency and mutual understanding are key values in the informal co-operative relationship. In other words, fair play in a broader sense – that is what it's all about. In this way, a company's fair play towards NTCA, in a trust relationship which is about its tax liability, may spill over into fair play with regard to that tax liability itself. Hence, the perceived fair play in the interaction between taxpayers and tax authorities (procedural justice) may make a company less eager to maximise its use of tax-

---

107 Cf. Stevens Committee (2012). *Tax supervision – Made to Measure: Flexible When Possible, Strict Where Necessary*, The Hague: Ministry of Finance, http://www.ifa.nl/Document/Publicaties/Enhanced%20Relationship%20Project/tax_supervision_made_to_measure_tz0151z1fdeng.pdf, p. 39.
108 *Letter from the Minister of Finance of 1 July 2010*, No. DGB2010/2996U, p. 3 (translation taken from the Stevens Committee (2012), p. 39). Cf. the internal HM-guidelines and OECD (2013), p. 48.
109 Cf. Bobeldijk, A.C.P. (2011). *Invloeden op de vennootschapsbelasting*, Breukelen: Nyenrode Business University, p. 16, who provides some examples.

efficient arrangements and accept a certain tax burden as given. Thus, procedural justice may influence the outcome, i.e. the tax liability (distributive justice).[110]

8.5 Conclusion

In this chapter, some procedural law aspects have been discussed in the context of Horizontal Monitoring, the Dutch cooperative compliance model. The leading idea is that collaborative and trust based relationships between taxpayers and tax administrations are nowadays indispensable to ensure taxpayers' voluntary compliance, which in turn is vital to an efficient and legitimate enforcement of tax law. Horizontal Monitoring embodies a more informal approach to this legal relationship. It is based on the awareness that an exclusive (legal) focus on competencies, obligations and rights of, and tax administrations and taxpayers respectively, often goes at the expense of timely problem-solving and of meeting important needs and interests of the taxpayers. For such an elaborate and complex legal system framework there are often unintended results, viz. juridification and antagonistic interaction. In practice, parties become too easily entrenched in legal arguments. It goes without saying that few tax administrations and taxpayers benefit from such trench warfare.

An informal approach is about co-operation rather than about competencies, obligations and rights, without neglecting the legal framework in force. In a co-operative relationship based on trust, transparency and mutual understanding, there is a willingness to go beyond compliance with regard to procedural law requirements (disclosure etcetera). Hence, the informal approach accounts for an important shift within the framework of the statutory techniques of the levying of taxes. The interaction between NTCA and taxpayer occurs early: information is exchanged proactively and diverging views on legal consequences are debated early in order to establish agreement or disagreement.

This approach is focused on the temporal dimension of these obligations, viz. proactive disclosure but is also about being beyond compliance with statutory obligations, in the sense that the taxpayer provides NTCA with more information than he is obliged to do.

Several sanctions are possible in a case where a taxpayer does not meet his statutory obligations. Here, the co-operative and compliant attitude of a company that engages in Horizontal Monitoring demands that the NTCA be willing to discuss the causes of mistakes and to take measures to prevent their future occurrence rather than an eagerness to impose penalties. The rigid invocation of penalty provisions cannot be reconciled with a HM-relationship based on trust.

---

110 However, the Stevens Committee (2012), p. 79 points out that NTCA was unable to provide any information on 'the implementation of and development in the number of tax-efficient arrangements in the Very Large Businesses/Medium-Sized Businesses segments. This is complicated by the lack of a uniform definition of "a tax-efficient structure".'

With regard to disputes about entering or terminating covenants and the fulfillment of obligations engaged in by the HM-covenant, there is a need of a kind of informal dispute resolution mechanism. Here, the usual way – the legal process – will probably result in legal trench warfare and enhance distrust, whereas a soft law instrument is more in line with the aim of de-juridification and informal problem solving.

Principles of proper administrative behaviour provide for important legal protection beyond the statutory framework. The principle of equality may seem to be at risk because a distinction is made between covenant partners and taxpayers without covenant. The distinction involves a different treatment in the sense of informal versus a formal approach. This should, however, not lead to a preferential treatment of covenant companies. According to the Stevens Committee, there is no solid evidence of preferential treatment. Even so, NTCA must keep a keen awareness of the risk of regulatory capture which demands an adequate policy.

Another principle, the principle of fair play, accounts for the possibility that NTCA and a company 'agree to disagree' without impacting on their HM-relationship. Moreover, taxpayers may engage in tax planning as they wish, as long as they remain within the limits of the law. NTCA does not require the condition of paying a fair share. However, a company which continually seeks the limits of the relevant tax legislation, for instance by using structures through tax havens, undermines the HM-basis of trust. But the reverse may also be the case. An indirect effect of a fair play co-operative relationship based on trust and openness could be that taxpayers take the idea of paying their fair share more seriously. Fair play in an informal working relationship with NTCA may spill over to fair play towards the treasury (state) and, therefore, society – i.e. paying a fair share. In the end, a conceptual distinction between these two forms of fair play is useful but it should not obscure the link between these two forms of fairness.

To conclude, like all new phenomena, Horizontal Monitoring still has to mature, partially because it is not codified in statutory rules. Moreover, there is no case law yet, unsurprisingly because such an informal, soft approach is meant to de-juridify the relationship between NTCA and taxpayers. Horizontal Monitoring is a type of responsive regulation based on the behaviour and attitude of companies towards compliance. In this trust-based relationship NTCA takes companies' needs for legal certainty and transparency seriously. Nowadays most companies want a good working relationship with real time problem solving. To my mind, therefore, trust and fair play are indispensable for legitimate enforcement of tax law – its legitimacy being even more important than cost-efficiency. Of course, NTCA should respond to companies who are not willing to comply by (proportionally) using its traditional vertical enforcement power.

EVELINE GERRITS

9 Tax Accounting

9.1 Introduction

Tax accounting is concerned with the tax position in the annual financial statements, more specifically, the corporate income tax position reflected in the annual financial statements. In recent years, the tax position has come under increasing scrutiny. I believe that the increased focus on the tax position in the annual financial statements was initially a response to United States SOx legislation.[1] Briefly put, this legislation – introduced in 2002 and mandatory for companies listed on a US stock exchange – requires that the financial statements state that the company is "in control" of the significant balance sheet items in the financial statements. As a rule, income tax is a significant item in the financial statements. Consequently, businesses were required to set up a proven internal control system for income taxes. As a result of the SOx legislation, auditors have also increasingly shifted their focus to the corporate income tax in the financial statements. This focus is not limited to businesses listed on a US stock exchange, but now also encompasses other listed businesses. In addition, since the financial crisis of 2008 deferred tax assets have been subject to extra scrutiny by accountants. Public interest in company income tax positions has also increased. The public is interested in the tax morality displayed by these companies – Starbucks, for example – and partly as a result of this heightened interest, all sorts of initiatives on country-by-country reporting (CbCR) have been developed. One of the requirements of CbCR is that companies state the amount of income tax paid in the countries where they operate. I will briefly discuss the several initiatives in this respect in section 9.9.

The reporting requirements on income tax have been included in numerous financial statement reporting guidelines. With regard to the Netherlands, the income tax requirements are set out in Chapter 9 of Book 2 of the Dutch Civil Code and the Guidelines for Annual Reporting RJ 272; for companies reporting under US GAAP, the income tax requirements are set out in ASC 740, while the IAS 12 guidelines contain the income tax requirements for companies reporting under IFRS.

This contribution deals with the reporting requirements as set out in IAS 12. The following sections explain the basic concepts of tax accounting, indicating when and

---

1 Refer to Sarbanes Oxley Act (SOx-legislation): https://www.google.nl/url?url=https://www.sec.gov/about/laws/soa2002.pdf&rct=j&frm=1&q=&esrc=s&sa=U&ei=5I26U_HLA6Wc0QW17I HQCw&ved=0CBoQFjAB&usg=AFQjCNFWvkMO6GFYEyuyNqwTXz4mrHldGQ

how (deferred) tax assets and liabilities must be recognized, measured and accounted for in the annual financial statements, as well as setting out exactly what must be disclosed in the annual financial statements as regards income tax. For the most part, RJ 272 and ASC 740 correspond to IAS 12. However, ASC 740 differs significantly with regard to uncertain tax positions. These differences are dealt with in the section 9.7. For completeness I will also discuss the accounting treatment of other taxes, like value added tax (VAT) and payroll taxes with in section 9.8.

9.2 Introduction of IAS 12

IAS 12 is the IFRS accounting standard stipulating how income tax should be accounted for in the annual financial statements. Income tax is defined as domestic and foreign taxes that are based on taxable profits.[2] VAT is, for example, not levied on the profit for tax purposes, but on transactions and is not covered by this definition. IAS 12 stipulates that income taxes include withholding taxes, which are payable to the tax authorities by a subsidiary, associated participation or joint arrangement on distributions made to the reporting entity. There are numerous reasons why the qualification 'income tax' is important with regard to how they are accounted for in the annual financial statements. Income tax is accounted for under the 'tax' line in the income statement. Other taxes are accounted for as part of the operating result. In addition, a income tax asset is under circumstances subject to different reporting requirements than that of a non-income tax asset (see section 9.8).

Income tax not only refers to the tax that is directly payable to, or recoverable from, the tax authorities (current tax), but also to the income tax that is eventually payable or recoverable (deferred tax) in future periods. IAS 12 addresses both concepts. Current tax is dealt with in the next section, after which deferred tax will be addressed.

9.3 Current tax

A noteworthy feature of IAS 12 is the fact that only a handful of paragraphs deal with current tax; the greater part of the guidelines deal with deferred tax.

Current tax is defined as the amount of tax that is payable or recoverable on the taxable profit or loss in current and prior periods.[3]

9.3.1 Recognition of current tax

Current tax related to the current period or earlier periods is recognized as a liability on the balance sheet. This liability is subsequently reduced by the amount a company has already paid with regard to these periods.[4] For example, a company may already have paid tax by way of a provisional assessment. If the provisional payments exceed

---

2 IAS 12.2
3 IAS 12.5
4 IAS 12.12

Tax Accounting

the amount payable, an asset on the balance sheet – i.e. a claim on the tax authorities – arises. In the event of a tax loss, some countries allow this loss to be carried back to earlier profit years, whereby the tax paid in a preceding year is reduced and consequently the company has a claim on the tax authorities.[5] This claim is also recognized as an asset on the balance sheet under current taxes.

9.3.2 Measurement of current tax

Current tax is stated at the amount the company expects to pay to (or recovers from) tax authorities. This takes account of 'substantively enacted' rates.[6] 'Substantively enacted' means that *substantive* rates must be taken into account, even if the formal legislative process has not yet been completed. With regard to, for example, the Netherlands, this means that the relevant legislation must have been approved by the Upper Chamber of the Dutch Parliament;[7] subsequent actions – the King signing the legislation into law and publication in the Bulletin of Acts and Decrees (*Staatsblad*) – are purely formal actions. Although the legislation is not yet official, from a substantive perspective there is nothing to hinder the introduction of the tax rate. Which tax rate applies to the measurement of the current tax asset will in most cases be apparent. It is seldom the case that the current tax rate or the tax rate for earlier years is changed during the course of a year. What does need to be taken into account is the fact that under some tax regimes different tax rates apply to different types of profit. For example, some countries tax capital gains at a different rate to that of operating profit. Besides that, there are also tax regimes where a higher or lower rate applies if the profits are distributed as dividends to shareholders. IAS 12 stipulates that current tax must be stated at the tax rate that applies to profit that has not been distributed.[8]

9.3.3 Reporting of current tax

Current tax will often lead to a tax expense in the financial statements. Current tax income arises where there is a tax loss that can be carried back to an earlier year. As a general rule, tax expense or income are accounted for in the profit or loss account.[9] The only exception is if the underlying transaction or event from which the tax expense or income arises is not accounted for in the profit or loss account, but is included directly in the equity or accounted for as 'other comprehensive income' ("OCI").[10] OCI is a special component of equity, which takes account of unrecognized results, such as a revaluation reserve for real estate that has been remeasured.[11] At the time the tax on such a remeasurement is immediately payable under the applicable tax regime, the accompanying current tax expense is deducted from the revaluation reserve.

---

5   IAS 12.13
6   IAS 12.46
7   Co-legislating organ
8   IAS 12.52A
9   IAS 12.58
10 IAS 12.57 and IAS 12.58(a)
11 IAS 12.62(a)

Issuing costs are an example of an underlying transaction that is accounted for directly as equity. For financial reporting purposes, issuing costs are deducted from equity; for tax purposes, they are generally directly deductible. The accompanying tax income is subsequently also accounted for as equity.

9.4 Deferred tax

Deferred tax relates to tax that is payable to or can be recovered from the tax authorities in the future. IAS 12 does not contain such a literal definition, but this is implied from the definitions of deferred tax discussed below.

Unlike the scant treatment afforded current tax in IAS 12, deferred tax is dealt with extensively in the IAS 12 guidelines. Firstly, deferred tax liabilities and deferred tax assets are defined. Deferred tax liabilities are defined as amounts that are payable in the future on taxable temporary differences.[12]

Deferred tax assets are defined as amounts recoverable in the future as a result of deductible temporary differences and the carry forward of unused tax losses and/or unused tax credits.[13]

This is followed by a definition of temporary differences. Temporary differences are defined as differences between the carrying amount of a asset or a liability for financial reporting purposes and their tax bases.[14] IAS 12 uses the balance sheet liability approach. Under this approach, the point of departure for evaluating any tax effects is the carrying amount of the assets and liabilities on the balance sheet. Assets and liabilities are included on the balance sheet with the expectation that these values will be realized. Future tax effects (with respect to the temporary difference) must subsequently be taken into account with the point of departure being the fact that the carrying amounts will be realized.

A taxable temporary difference is a temporary difference that will lead to a taxable amount in a future period when the taxable profit or loss is determined when the carrying amount of the balance sheet asset or liability is realized. A deductible temporary difference is an amount that can be deducted in the future from the taxable profit or loss when the carrying amount of the balance sheet asset or liability is realized.[15] For a more detailed explanation of temporary differences I refer to Section 9.4.1.2.

In Section 9.4.1 I will address how temporary differences arise and I will subsequently explain when the resulting deferred tax assets and liabilities must be recognized on the balance sheet. In Section 9.4.2 I will discuss the issues of unused tax losses and tax credits. The last issues dealt with in this section is the way in which deferred tax assets and liabilities should be measured (Section 9.4.3) and reported (Section 9.4.4).

---

12 IAS 12.5
13 IAS 12.5
14 IAS 12.5
15 IAS 12.5

9.4.1 Temporary differences

In this Section the origination of temporary differences will be explained. Subsequently the recognition and the exceptions to recognition will be addressed.

9.4.1.1 The origination of temporary differences

As a result of the balance sheet liability approach adopted by IAS 12, temporary differences arise as soon as there is a difference between the carrying amount for financial reporting purposes (also referred to as the carrying amount in this Section) of an asset or a liability and its carrying amount for tax purposes (the tax base). The carrying amount for financial reporting purposes is the amount recognized in the annual financial statements pursuant to another IFRS guideline. IAS 12 has its own definition of the tax base of an asset or a liability. As a rule, the tax base is the amount attributed to that asset or liability for tax purposes.[16] However, for tax purposes separate financial statement are not always prepared in all countries. Besides that the amounts included in the tax return do not always reflect the tax base, which is used in IAS 12 to determine the amount of the temporary differences. I can imagine this is the reason why the IASB has included its own definition of tax base in IAS 12.

The tax base of an asset is defined as the amount that, for tax purposes, can be deducted from all the taxable economic benefits flowing to an entity once it realizes the carrying amount of an asset. However, if these economic benefits are not taxable, the tax base of the asset is the same as its carrying amount.[17] As a result of the balance sheet liability approach, IAS 12 only deals with temporary differences; it completely ignores 'permanent differences'. Costs that are, for example, non-deductible for tax purposes do not result in a difference between the carrying amount and the tax base, which means that from a balance sheet perspective this difference does not have to be defined as a permanent difference. And by subsequently stating that the tax base is equal to the carrying amount in those cases where the economic benefits are not taxable, IAS 12 has made the use of 'permanent differences' redundant for assets that will never result in a tax payment or tax deduction. This definition could prove problematic in cases where the carrying amount is nil. After all, in that case no taxable economic benefits arise upon realization of the carrying amount. For such situations, it is explicitly stated that even if assets have not been recognized on the balance sheet for financial reporting purposes, the tax base is the amount that the tax authorities are prepared to accept as deductible in a future period.[18]

---

16 IAS 12.5
17 IAS 12.7
18 IAS 12.9, e.g. R&D costs are immediately expensed for book purposes, but can be deducted in future periods for tax purposes. This will lead to a deferred tax asset.

The tax base of a liability is defined as the carrying amount less each amount that will be deductible for tax purposes in the future in respect of that liability.[19] This definition is somewhat confusing, but an example may help to clarify matters.

Assume that a guarantee provision for financial reporting purposes of 100 has been included on the balance sheet. If this provision is not permissible for tax purposes, the expenses can only be deducted from the taxable profit at the time the costs are incurred. If the definition contained in IAS 12 is applied, this means that the tax base is the same as the carrying amount less the amount that will be deductible for tax purposes in the future. In the future, 100 will be tax deductible, which results in a carrying amount for tax purposes of nil, i.e. 100 less 100.

The definition of a liability is different if revenue is received in advance. In that case, the definition is: in the case of revenue received in advance, the tax base of the resulting liability is the same as the carrying amount less any amount of the revenue that will not be taxable in future periods.[20] An example will also serve to explain this definition.

Assume that for financial reporting purposes, rent of 100 is received in advance, but that for tax purposes the rent received is taxed on a cash basis. According to the definition, the tax base is the same as the carrying amount of 100 less any future non-taxable amounts. As the rent has already been taxed on a cash basis for tax purposes, the amount of 100 will no longer be taxed and the carrying amount for tax purposes is therefore nil, i.e. 100 less 100.

9.4.1.2   Taxable and deductible temporary differences

As stated in the previous section, temporary differences arise when there is a difference between the carrying amount and the tax base. A temporary difference that results in a future tax payment is recognized as a deferred tax liability. A temporary difference that results in a future deduction when determining the taxable profit is recognized as a deferred tax asset.

From a balance sheet perspective, this means that where the carrying amount of an asset exceeds the carrying amount for tax purposes, the result is a deferred tax liability. After all, at the time the carrying amount is realized, the taxable deduction will be less than the income for financial reporting purposes, which means that tax is payable on the difference. The reverse scenario – the tax base of an asset exceeds the carrying amount – results in a deferred tax asset. In this situation the deduction exceeds the income for financial reporting purposes, which arises as a result of the carrying amount having been realized.

With regards to a liability, a carrying amount that is higher than the tax base will result in a deferred tax asset. At the time this carrying amount of a liability is deducted – for example, as a result of incurred costs that reduce the carrying amount of the provision – the costs can be deducted from the taxable profit. The reverse

---

19   IAS 12.8
20   IAS 12.8

scenario – the tax base of a liability exceeds the carrying amount – results in a deferred tax liability. From the perspective of the balance sheet liability approach adopted by IAS 12, this means that at the time a liability with a carrying amount of, for example, 100 is realized, for which the tax base exceeded the carrying amount and amounts to, for example, 120, the surplus of 20 will be taxable in a future period.

The above can be represented as follows:

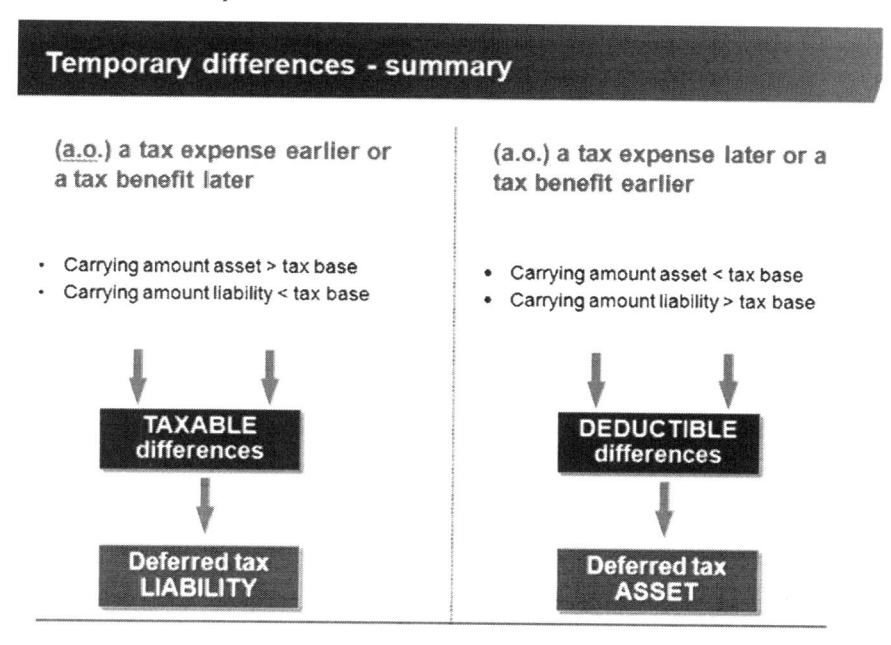

Temporary differences - summary

(a.o.) a tax expense earlier or a tax benefit later	(a.o.) a tax expense later or a tax benefit earlier
• Carrying amount asset > tax base • Carrying amount liability < tax base	• Carrying amount asset < tax base • Carrying amount liability > tax base
↓ ↓	↓ ↓
TAXABLE differences	**DEDUCTIBLE differences**
↓	↓
Deferred tax LIABILITY	**Deferred tax ASSET**

9.4.1.3 Recognition of temporary differences

According to IAS 12, the general rule is that taxable temporary differences must always be recognized on the balance sheet as a deferred tax liability.[21] The general rule for deductible temporary differences is that they must be recognized as a deferred tax asset to the extent that it is probable that taxable profit is available to allow the deferred asset to be realized.[22] Just when the latter would be the case will be dealt with under Section 9.4.1.5. This section deals with the exceptions to the abovementioned general rule.

---

21 IAS 12.15
22 IAS 12. 24

9.4.1.3.1 Exceptions to the recognition of temporary differences.

There are two exceptions to the general rule that deferred tax assets or tax liabilities[23] resulting from temporary differences must be recognized on the balance sheet. These exceptions relate to:
i. the initial recognition of goodwill; and
ii. the initial recognition of an asset or liability that meets certain conditions.

There is also a special provision on the recognition of taxable temporary differences related to measurement differences between the carrying amount and the tax base with respect to investments in subsidiaries, branches, associated participations and interests in joint arrangements. This special provision is explained in Section 9.4.1.4. The current section will deal with the two abovementioned exceptions.

Re i) The initial recognition of goodwill
IAS 12.15 prohibits the recognition of a deferred tax liability if the carrying amount of the initial recognition of goodwill differs from the tax base. According to IAS 12.21, this relates to goodwill arising from a business combination. IFRS 3 provides a definition of business combination. A business combination is defined as a transaction (or other event) by which an acquiring party gains control of one or more businesses.[24] A business is defined as consisting of resources and the processes applied to these resources in order to achieve production.[25] Resources, processes and production are subsequently defined. In practice, companies must determine whether there is a business combination or whether the transaction qualifies as an asset acquisition.[26] If it is not a business combination, the transaction is effectively treated as a 'normal' asset acquisition to which the rules for the business combination do not apply.

The business combination contained in IFRS 3 is based on the principle that the acquired identifiable assets and the transferred liabilities are recognized and stated at their fair value.[27] The difference between the price and the net balance of the identifiable assets and the transferred liabilities is then the goodwill.[28] If this is a negative difference, then there is badwill, which must be directly accounted for as a gain in profit or loss.[29] This produces an opening balance sheet that must be included in the consolidated financial statements. In the separate financial statements of the acquired company the carrying amount of the assets and liabilities remain the same and are not stated on the basis of their fair value.

IFRS 3.24 requires the deferred tax assets and tax liabilities arising from the business combination to be recognized and stated in accordance with IAS 12. IAS 12.19 states

---

23 The recognition of a deferred tax asset must, however, always meet the conditions described in Section 9.4.1.5.
24 IFRS 3 Appendix A
25 IFRS 3 B7
26 IFRS 3.3
27 IFRS 3.10 and 3.18
28 IFRS 3.32 and IAS 12.21
29 IFRS 3.34

that temporary differences can arise as the result of a business combination. For example, a share deal can change the carrying amounts, but not the tax base because the assets and liabilities for tax purposes are not stated at their fair value. If, for example, this results in a carrying amount of an asset being stated at a higher amount, while the tax base remains unchanged, a taxable temporary difference arises that leads to a deferred tax liability. IAS 12.66 states that this deferred tax liability is an identifiable liability, which as a result of the abovementioned computation method for determining goodwill, affects the amount of goodwill. Shortly said, the goodwill is the difference between the price paid and the net balance of the identifiable assets and liabilities (measured at fair value). Since deferred tax assets and liabilities are also identifiable assets and liabilities, these amounts consequently affect the amount of goodwill the entity recognizes. This means that a deferred tax liability (asset) will increase (decrease) the goodwill for the same amount. For tax purposes, a share deal does not give rise to goodwill under most tax regimes, and therefore the tax base is nil. Consequently a temporary difference also arises with regard to the goodwill for the difference between the carrying amount of for example 100 and the tax base of nil. However, IAS 12.15 prohibits the recognition of a deferred tax liability in respect of the temporary difference arising from the initial recognition of goodwill. The rationale behind this is that the goodwill is measured as a residual and the recognition of the deferred tax liability would increase the carrying amount of goodwill.[30] A simplified example can clarifies this method.

Example

Entity A buys the shares of entity B for 100.000.
    Entity B has equity of 60.000, which is invested in property. The tax base of the property also amounts to 60.000. The fair value of the property amounts 70.000 and 20.000 is attributable to a client portfolio. Assume that this transaction is classified as a business combination.

Question: What would be the opening balance of this acquisition?

Step 1: commercial balance sheet without deferred tax liabilities

Property	70.000	equity	100.000
Client portfolio	20.000		
Goodwill	10.000		

---

30   IAS 12.21

Step 2: calculation of deferred tax

Tax base:

Property	60.000
Client portfolio	0
Goodwill	0

Deferred tax liabilities:

property: 25%*10.000 (70.000-/-60.000)= 2.500

client portfolio: 25%*20.000 (20.000-/-0)= 5.000

Step 3: adjustment to goodwill for the deferred tax liabilities

Commercial balance sheet

Property	70.000	equity	100.000
Client portfolio	20.000	deferred tax liability	7.500
Goodwill	17.500		

Later reductions in the goodwill for financial reporting purposes that was non-deductible for tax purposes, reduce the unrecognized deferred tax liability. This reduction is also regarded as arising from the initial recognition of goodwill and therefore not recognized.[31]

On the other hand in the situation the goodwill is regarded as deductible for tax purposes no temporary difference arises, because in that situation the carrying amount and tax base will often be the same and consequently the difference is nil. In that situation any reduction in the goodwill for tax purposes (for example, due to amortization of the tax base) will result in the recognition of a deferred tax liability,[32] as this deferred tax liability did not arise from the initial recognition of the goodwill. At the time the transaction took place a deferred tax liability had not been recognized, but this was due to the absence of a temporary difference.

As stated above IAS 12 does not permit to recognize a deferred tax *liability* with respect to the initial recognition of goodwill. For the sake of completeness, please note that it is required to recognize a deferred tax *asset* at the initial recognition of goodwill. This means that where the goodwill's tax base exceeds its carrying amount, the company will recognize a deferred tax asset that has to be credited against the goodwill according to the general rule.

---

31 IAS 12.21A
32 IAS 12.21B

Re ii) the initial recognition of an asset or liability

The second exception provided for by IAS 12 refers to a company's initial recognition of an asset or liability on its balance sheet, whereby the tax base of an asset of liability differs from its carrying amount. In that case, the general rule is that a deferred tax asset or deferred tax liability must be recognized. However, IAS 12 prohibits the recognition of a deferred tax asset or deferred tax liability if the transaction (i) is not a business combination; and (ii) it does not affect the accounting profit nor the taxable profit at the time the transaction took place.[33] The first condition relates to the matters discussed in the previous section under i). In the case of a business combination, a deferred tax liability or deferred tax asset *must* be recognized for all temporary differences arising from the measurement of assets and liabilities. The deferred tax is subsequently adjusted against the amount of goodwill.[34]

The second condition is that the transaction must not affect the accounting profit or the taxable profit at the time it took place. As soon as the difference between the carrying amount and the tax base arises from a transaction which affects the accounting profit or the taxable profit, the temporary difference is caused by other factors. For example, if a difference arises as a result of the fact that expenses are recognized directly (at the moment of the transaction) for tax purposes and not for financial reporting purposes, the resulting deferred tax liability must be recognized with regard to this taxable temporary difference. The exception with respect to the initial recognition relates to temporary differences that are present at the time a transaction takes place, but which, at the same time, do *not* result in a difference between the accounting profit of the taxable profit. IAS 12[35] illustrates this with the following example: an asset is purchased at a cost of 1000, of which the depreciation is non-deductible for tax purposes. Any capital gain upon disposal of the asset would not be taxable, nor would a capital loss be deductible. The income from this asset is taxable, which invalidates the rule that the tax base equals the carrying amount for financial purposes.[36] The tax base amounts to nil, because, for tax purposes, at the time of realization no amounts can be deducted against the taxable profit. Without this exception, the entity would have to recognize a deferred tax liability at the initial recognition of the asset. The carrying amount of the asset would subsequently have to be increased by the amount of the deferred tax liability. However this action would increase the difference between the carrying amount and the tax base (which is stated at nil) and as a consequence the deferred tax liability must once again be adjusted. The prohibition on the recognition of deferred tax avoids this reconciliation process. IAS 12 justifies the prohibition on recognizing a deferred tax liability by arguing that such adjustments make the financial statements less transparent.[37]

---

33 IAS 12. 15
34 No deferred tax liability is subsequently recognized on the goodwill itself as discussed under i)
35 IAS 12.22
36 Please refer to the definition of the carrying amount for tax purposes of a balance sheet asset given in Section 9.4.1.1.
37 IAS 12. 22(c)

9.4.1.4 Investments in subsidiaries, branches, associated participations and interests in joint arrangements.

Temporary differences can also arise if the carrying amount of investments in subsidiaries, branches, associated participations and interests in joint arrangements (hereafter referred to jointly as "investments in subsidiaries") differ from the tax base of these investment. These types of temporary differences are also referred to as 'outside basis differences', i.e. the temporary differences are *not* the difference between the carrying amount and tax base of the assets and liabilities of the entity *itself*, but the difference between the carrying amount and the tax bases of the investment in subsidiaries at the level of the parent company. The general rule that applies to these differences is, once again, that deferred tax must be recognized. An exception to this rule is made for deferred tax liabilities, provided certain conditions are met. I discuss this exception in Section 9.4.1.4.1. The recognition of a deferred tax asset is, however, subject to additional conditions. These are discussed in 9.4.1.4.2.

In the present section I address the possible causes for temporary differences between the carrying amount for financial reporting purposes and the tax base of investments in subsidiaries, as well as their background. IAS 12.38 states that the tax base of these investments is often at cost, while the carrying amount is generally based on the equity method. Briefly put, the equity method recognizes the investment at cost (including the goodwill), which subsequently increases the carrying amount by the share of the profit or loss of the subsidiary.[38, 39] It goes on to list a number of potential causes for the differences between the carrying amount and the tax base.

Differences can arise, for example, from:
1. The existence of undistributed profits
2. Foreign exchange differences
3. Write-downs of the carrying amount

Re 1. Undistributed profits
For financial reporting purposes, the investments in subsidiaries recognized in the consolidated financial statements are generally stated according to the equity method.[40] IAS 12 assumes that, for tax purposes, the investments in subsidiaries are, on the whole, stated at cost. As soon as the subsidiary realizes a profit, the carrying amount will increase, while the tax base will remain unchanged. A temporary difference then arises for which, in principle, a deferred tax liability must be recognized. However, according to the definition of tax base (see Section 9.4.1.1), the tax base equals the carrying amount in those situations where the economic benefits of the asset are not taxed. This will often be the case in the Netherlands due to the

---

38 IAS 28.10 and IAS 28.3
39 If the subsidiary is included in the consolidation, this means that the carrying amounts of the investment will be the investor's share in the net assets including goodwill. This is the same amount as the amount under the equity method.
40 IAS 28.16.

participation exemption, which results in the tax base being the same as the carrying amount and therefore no temporary difference arises.

However, this is not the case if, for example, the subsidiary's state of residence applies withholding tax on the profit distributions made by the subsidiary. From the perspective of the parent company, the profits are taxed at the time they are distributed, which means the tax base is not the same as the carrying amount, because the economic benefits are taxed and consequently a temporary difference may arise. This temporary difference arises at the moment the subsidiary reports a profit that has not yet been distributed to the parent company. As stated this increases the carrying amount, while the tax base remains unchanged. A deferred tax liability must be recognized for this temporary difference.

The carrying amount of the investment in the subsidiary will decrease by the same amount at the time the profit is distributed to the parent company, which will bring it in line with the tax base again. The gross distribution is deducted from the carrying amount at the time of the profit distribution, with the net distribution being debited against the deferred tax liability and on the current account (or cash balance). This ensures that the tax effects of the still to be distributed profits are taken into account for financial reporting purposes at the same time that these profits are reporting in the profit and loss.

Re 2. Foreign exchange differences
The subsidiary and the parent company may use different currencies, whereby a temporary difference can arise as a result of changes in the foreign exchange rate used by the subsidiary. In this situation, it is also important to determine whether the income from the investments in the subsidiary is taxable or exempt for tax purposes. After all, if the income is not taxable, the tax base will be the same as the carrying amount, which means that no temporary difference will arise.

Re 3. Write-downs
A temporary difference can also arise as a result of subsidiary being written down for financial reporting purposes, while being stated at cost for tax purposes. This will result in a carrying amount that is lower than the tax base. The general rule for such temporary differences is that a deferred tax asset must be recognized. The temporary difference that arises in this situation, only arises if the income from an investment in a subsidiary is taxed. Otherwise the tax base will be the same as the carrying amount as a result of the IAS 12 definition of the tax base. However, unlike a deferred tax liability, the recognition of a deferred tax asset is subject to additional requirements (see Section 9.4.1.5). Furthermore, in this specific situation there is an additional condition (see Section 9.4.1.4.2).

9.4.1.4.1 No deferred tax liability in respect of investments in subsidiaries

IAS 12.39 states that deferred tax liabilities do not have to be recognized if the following two conditions are met:

1. the parent company can control the timing of the reversal of the temporary difference; and
2. the temporary difference will probably *not* be reversed in the foreseeable future.

These conditions are best illustrated by the situation where the parent company is able to determine the dividend policy of the subsidiary and the company is not intending to distribute dividends in the foreseeable future.[41] As soon as these conditions are met, the company does not have to recognize a deferred tax liability. However, it must state in the notes to the financial statements the amount of the temporary difference for which no deferred tax liability has been recognized (see Section 9.5.6).

9.4.1.4.2 Recognition of deferred tax assets in respect of investments in subsidiaries

As indicated above, a temporary difference can arise where a write down of a subsidiary has taken place for financial reporting purposes, while the measurement for tax purposes is at cost. In this situation, a deferred tax asset can only be recognized if the following two conditions are met:[42]
1. the temporary difference will probably be reversed in the foreseeable future; and
2. there will probably be sufficient taxable profit available against which the temporary difference can be deducted.

The second condition applies to all deductible temporary differences. This condition is discussed in Section 9.4.1.5. The first condition is an additional condition that only applies to deductible temporary differences in respect of investments in subsidiaries; it is not stipulated for other deductible temporary differences. In my view, the reason for this additional condition is a consequence of the fact that multiple actions are often required before a temporary difference is actually realized, for example, accounting for a liquidation loss. In the Netherlands, taking into account a liquidation loss is subject to various conditions. In the case of a liquidation loss, a deferred tax asset will only be recognized once it has become probable that the company is intending to liquidate the subsidiary in the foreseeable future and also if condition 2 has been met.

9.4.1.5   Recognition of deductible temporary differences

As stated in Section 9.4.1.3, a deferred tax liability must always be recognized for a taxable temporary difference (exceptions excluded). In principle, deductible temporary differences lead to deferred tax assets. However, IAS 12 places additional conditions on the recognition of a deferred tax asset. In general, IAS 12 states that a deferred tax asset can only be recognized on the balance sheet if it is probable that sufficient profit for tax purposes will be available to ensure the actual realization of

---

41   In practice, 'foreseeable future' is defined as 12- 24 months.
42   IAS 12.44

the deduction.[43] The term probable is not defined in IAS 12, however IFRS 5[44] gives a definition of the term probable, which means more likely than not, in other words a possibility of more than 50%.

IAS 12 sets out in three steps how to determine whether there is sufficient taxable profit available. In short, these steps are:
a. there are sufficient *taxable* temporary differences available, which will reverse in the same period as the deductible temporary differences;[45]
b. there is sufficient taxable profit available in the relevant period; and[46]
c. tax planning opportunities are available to the company that will create sufficient taxable profit in the relevant period.[47]

Re (a) Reversal of deferred tax liabilities
Taxable temporary differences always result in the recognition of a deferred tax liability. IAS 12 subsequently states that it is probable that sufficient taxable profit will be available if the deferred tax liabilities on the balance sheet are taxable in the same future period as the deferred tax assets lead to a deduction. At that time, the deferred tax assets and the deferred tax liabilities cancel each other out. The rules with respect to carry back or carry forward of tax losses in the relevant country must subsequently be taken into account, whereby a deferred tax asset that results in a deduction in year 1 is also canceled out by the taxable profit as a result of the reversal of a deferred tax liability in a later or earlier year, as long as this last year falls within the carry back or carry forward period of the particular country. In the above analysis, it is irrelevant whether the company expects to realize any taxable profits or losses. The rationale for this may be that a company that only reports tax losses consequently does not pay tax anyway on the reversal of the taxable temporary differences.

Re (b) Taxable profit
If there are not sufficient deferred tax liabilities, attributable to the same period as the deferred tax assets, it needs to be determined whether there is still enough taxable profit available to realize the deductible temporary differences. The amount of taxable profit is, first's instance, dependent on the anticipated accounting profit from which the company will subsequently have to determine the taxable profit, thereby taking into account the differences between the accounting profit and the taxable profit. These differences are, first and foremost, the income or costs that are, for tax purposes, neither taxed nor deductible. In addition, there is the accounting profit that will *not yet* be taxed for tax purposes, for example, because it has not yet been realized. Such a temporary difference will reduce the taxable profit and will once again lead to a deferred tax liability in the future period. The reversal of the newly created deferred tax liability will have to be taken into account when determining the

---

43 IAS 12.24
44 IFRS 5 Annex A
45 IAS 12.28
46 IAS 12.29
47 IAS 12.29 and IAS 12.30

profit for tax purposes in subsequent years. Although this will result in a lower taxable profit in the year in which the income is not taxed, the taxable profit will be higher than the accounting profit in the subsequent year (or years). On the other hand, there may be costs for accounting that can only be claimed as an expense for tax purposes in later years. Eliminating these costs for tax purposes will result in a higher taxable profit. This newly created deductible temporary difference will itself require an assessment of whether there will be sufficient taxable profit in the years following the creation of the difference, so that a deferred tax asset can be recognized. According to IAS 12, the latter – a future deductible temporary difference – *cannot* be taken into account when determining the future taxable profit, because this would, in effect, require a continuous evaluation of the possibility of recognizing newly created deductible temporary differences on the balance sheet.

Re (c) Planning opportunities
If the options described under (a) and (b) do not result in sufficient taxable profit, the company may take tax planning opportunities into account. This tax planning must enable the company to create profit for tax purposes in the relevant period. IAS 12 illustrates this point by way of a few examples, such as deferring the claim for certain deductions from the taxable profit, or taking advantage of a sale and lease back transaction. IAS 12 describes tax planning opportunities as actions which enable the company to generate taxable income within a certain period. In my view, this simply means that the tax planning can still be awaiting implementation. After all, action will only be taken in the year that sufficient profit for tax purposes actually needs to be generated. It can be inferred from the requirement regarding the probability of sufficient taxable profit being present against which the temporary differences can be deducted, that there must be more than a 50% chance that the tax planning opportunities can actually be implemented and that they will also have the desired effect. The assessment of the probability of the tax planning creating sufficient taxable profit is the responsibility of the management of the entity and can be supported by an opinion from a tax lawyer or a ruling from the tax authorities.

9.4.2 *Unused tax losses and other unused tax credits*

In addition to deductible temporary differences, deferred tax assets can also arise as a result of tax losses, which have not yet been settled with the tax authorities. A loss that can be carried back to an earlier year with taxable profit is not treated as an unused tax loss. As stated under 9.3.1 above, a tax asset that is the result of a loss carry-back must be recognized as a current tax asset on the balance sheet. Unused tax losses refer to tax losses that could be set off against future taxable profits: the carry forward of unused tax losses. A deferred tax asset can also arise as a result of the fact that tax credits have not yet led to a tax refund. An illustration of such a situation as it applies in the Netherlands is where a permanent establishment realizes profit for which double tax relief is available (this double tax relief was available up until January 1, 2012). However, if the Dutch company has negative worldwide income, the double tax relief cannot be utilized. It can only be claimed once the company starts making a taxable profit.

9.4.2.1 Recognition of unused tax losses and tax credits

The recognition of unused tax losses and tax credits is, in principle, subject to the same rules as those applying to the recognition of deferred tax assets arising as a result of deductible temporary differences (see Section 9.4.1.5).[48] However, according to IAS 12 the existence of unused tax losses is a strong indication that no taxable profit will be available in the future.[49] For this reason, a company that has reported tax losses in the recent past,[50] may only recognize the deferred tax assets arising from tax losses or tax credits to the extent that deferred tax liabilities are present or to the extent that there is convincing evidence that sufficient taxable profit will be available against which the tax losses or tax credits can be set off.[51] In addition to the rules referred to in Section 9.4.1.5, IAS 12 also states that the following must be taken into account when determining whether it is probable that sufficient taxable profit will be available:[52]

1. Whether there are sufficient deferred tax liabilities that will result in taxable profit in the periods before the expiration of the tax losses or tax credits.
2. Whether it is probable that the entity will have sufficient taxable profit available against which the tax losses and tax credits can be set off.
3. Whether the tax losses are a result of specific circumstances that are unlikely to recur in the future.
4. Whether there the company can take advantage of tax planning opportunities to create taxable profit in the period during which the tax losses or tax credits can be utilized.

The criteria listed under 1, 2 and 4 are, in effect, the same criteria as those for deferred tax assets arising from deductible temporary differences (see Section 9.4.1.5). Only criterion 3 is new.

For the sake of completeness, please note that in the case of tax losses, the more stringent rules – like the convincing evidence – for the recognition of deferred tax assets also apply to deferred tax assets arising from deductible temporary differences.[53]

9.4.3 Measurement of deferred tax

Deferred tax assets and deferred tax liabilities are measured at the tax rate that is expected to apply at the time the asset is realized or the liability is settled.[54] As is the case with current tax, this is the rate that has been substantively enacted in law at the end of the reporting period (see Section 9.3.2). To determine the tax rate at which

---

48 IAS 12.34 and IAS 12.35
49 IAS 12.35
50 In practice 'recent past' is defined as the current and immediately preceding year, which is also stated in the disclosure note (refer to Section 9.5.10)
51 IAS 12.35
52 IAS 12.36
53 IAS 12.31
54 IAS 12.47

deferred tax assets and deferred tax liabilities must be recognized, a company must establish, with the aid of reversal schedules, in which period the deferred tax asset or deferred tax liability will be realized or settled. This is particularly important in the event different tax rates are applicable for different years.

Furthermore as noted in Section 9.3.2, in some countries different tax rates apply to different types of tax profits, for example, a tax rate other than the general tax rate may apply to certain capital gains. In such situations IAS 12 states that the company must take account of the manner in which it expects to settle the deferred tax asset or deferred tax liability. IAS 12 also states that in determining the tax base, a company must take account of the manner in which it expects to realize the carrying amount of the asset or settle the liability.[55] IAS 12 is referring here to the fact that in some jurisdictions the cost of a balance sheet asset is fully deductible if it is actively used by the company, but that it is not deductible at the time it is sold.[56]

9.4.3.1 Discounting

According to IAS 12 deferred tax assets and deferred tax liabilities shall not be discounted.[57] This is because the timing of the reversal of temporary differences requires detailed scheduling. IAS 12 argues that such an analysis is highly complex and impractical, which means that it would be inappropriate to demand that the deferred tax assets and tax liabilities must be recognized at their discounted value. IAS 12 goes on to state that it would also be inappropriate to allow a company the option of discounting, because in that situation the deferred tax assets and deferred tax liabilities of different companies would not be comparable.[58] While I understand this reasoning, I believe it is not entirely in line with the intent of the guidelines. After all, in determining whether to recognize deferred tax assets (see Section 9.4.15) and which tax rate to apply to deferred tax assets and tax liabilities (see Section 9.4.3), a company must determine, to the extent possible, when the temporary differences will be reversed.

9.4.4 Reporting of deferred tax

As is the case with current tax, the general rule for deferred tax is that it must included in the profit or loss for the period;[59] the only exception being if the tax arises from an item that is not accounted for in the profit or loss for the period. This is the case if the underlying item has been accounted for directly in the equity or as OCI[60] (see Section 9.3.3). Available-for-sale financial assets are an example of an item that is accounted for under OCI. For financial reporting purposes, these financial assets are

---

55 IAS 12.51 and IAS 12.51A
56 There are two exceptions to the general rule with regard to tax rates and the determination of the tax carrying amount based on expected realization. The exceptions relate to real estate and are not dealt with here.
57 IAS 12.53
58 IAS 12.54
59 IAS 12.58
60 IAS 12.58(a)

stated at their fair value and changes to the fair value are accounted for in the revaluation reserve. In many jurisdictions these unrealized results are not included in the taxable profit. For tax purposes the financial assets are often stated at cost or at cost or their lower market value. Consequently the difference between the carrying amount and the tax base can result in a deferred tax asset or a deferred tax liability. The adjustment to the deferred tax – as well as the transaction or event itself – must also subsequently be accounted for in the revaluation reserve.

Deferred tax arising from a business combination is also not accounted for on the income statement, as set out in Section 9.4.1.3.1.[61]

9.4.4.1 Changes to the carrying amount of deferred tax

Sometimes the amount of deferred tax can change, despite the fact that the amount of the temporary differences remains the same. IAS 12 uses three examples to illustrate this point: i) a change in the tax rate or an change to tax law, ii) a reassessment of the recoverability of the deferred tax asset, and iii) a change in management's expectations of the manner in which the temporary difference will be realized. As a general rule, the change in the deferred tax will subsequently be accounted for in profit or loss, unless the initial deferred tax was accounted for via the equity or OCI.[62] This is also referred to as backwards tracing.[63]

9.5 The disclosure of information

An important part of IAS 12 is the mandatory notes to the financial statements. In this section, I indicate which mandatory disclosures are prescribed by IAS 12. The notes cover both current and deferred taxes.

9.5.1 Tax components

The notes to the annual financial statements must disclose the most important components of the tax expenses and income. The intention is to provide insight into the composition of the amount of current and deferred taxes. IAS 12 provides a list of examples of current and deferred taxes. The following components are listed as examples of current taxes:
- The current tax for the current period;[64]
- The current tax for prior periods;[65]
- The amount of current tax that was reduced as a result of the utilization of unrecognized deferred tax assets,[66] for example, tax losses, tax credits, or deductible temporary differences. Many tax regimes allow a company to set off, subject to conditions, the losses it still has available from previous years against the tax

---

61 IAS 12.58(b)
62 IAS 12.60
63 Under US GAAP (ASC 740) this change is accounted for on the income statement.
64 IAS 12.80a
65 IAS 12.80b
66 IAS 12.80e

profit in the current year, which results in a reduction of the current tax. As explained in Section 9.4.1.5 a deferred tax asset resulting from a tax loss can only be recognized if it is probable that the entity has future taxable profit available against which the tax loss can be utilised. If a deferred tax asset was not recognized for this tax loss, IAS 12[67] recommends disclosing this component of the current tax.

The latter two examples will also automatically disclose why the statutory tax deviates from the effective tax rate. This is explained in Section 9.5.3.

The following are components of deferred tax:
- The deferred tax arising from the origination and reversal of temporary differences;[68]
- The amount of deferred tax relating to changes to the tax rate or tax laws;[69]
- The amount of the deferred tax benefits arising from recognizing, at a later date, a deferred tax asset arising from a tax loss, a tax credit or a deductible temporary difference that was initially not recognized.[70]
- Deferred tax as a result of the write-down (or the reversal of earlier write-down) of a deferred tax asset in accordance with paragraph 56 of IAS 12. IAS 12.56 requires that the deferred tax asset is assessed at the end of each period. If it is no longer probable that the deferred tax asset will be realized, then the carrying amount of the asset must be reduced. The reduction will be reversed at the time it becomes probable again that sufficient taxable profit is available.[71]

The last three examples will also automatically disclose why the statutory tax deviates from the effective tax. This is explained in Section 9.5.3.

It is noteworthy that IAS 12 does not list changes to preceding years as a component of deferred tax, although they are listed in relation to current tax. In those cases where the current tax with regard to a prior year is increased or reduced as a result of a temporary difference, the deferred tax will be adjusted accordingly. I expect that the reason this component is not listed separately for deferred tax is because IAS 12 regards this as deferred tax that has arisen in the current period as a result of an adjustment to the current tax for earlier periods, for example, as a result of filing a tax return. However from my experience companies also report changes from earlier periods in respect of deferred tax.

It is also noteworthy that this list makes no mention of the release or inclusion of a potential provision for uncertain tax positions. In section 9.7 we will see that IAS 12 completely ignores uncertain tax positions.

67　I use 'recommend', because IAS12.80 states with regard to the provision of information that the tax burden 'may' comprise these components.
68　IAS 12.80(c)
69　IAS 12.80(d)
70　IAS 12.80(f)
71　IAS 12.80(g)

9.5.2 Tax recognized in equity or OCI

The notes to the financial statements must disclose how much tax has been recognized in equity or in OCI.[72] This assumes that the overall amount of taxes recognized in equity or in OCI must be disclosed, although the amount does not have to be split into current and deferred tax. However, the specific OCI component to which the tax relates must be identified.

9.5.3 The effective tax rate reconciliation (ETR)

The tax expense (or income) in the financial statements comprises the total amount of current and deferred taxes. The effective tax rate is defined as the amount of current tax and the amount of deferred tax that is recognized in profit or loss divided by the accounting profit before tax.[73] The effective tax (the aggregate current and deferred tax) will generally differ from the statutory tax. The statutory tax is simply subsumed by multiplying the accounting profit before tax by the statutory rate. The differences between the two amounts must be disclosed in the notes to the financial statements.[74] This reconciliation may be expressed in percentages or as tax amounts.

The statutory rate can be the rate applied in the country where the head office is established or an aggregate of the statutory rates of the various countries where the company is resident. The aggregate statutory rate is arrived at by i) multiplying the accounting profit before tax by the statutory rates applying in the relevant jurisdictions and ii) dividing the outcome of i) by the consolidated accounting profit before tax. In the first situation, the foreign tax rate will affect the ETR, because the rate used is that of the country where the head office is established. Whether the statutory rate for the head office or an aggregate statutory rate is used depends on the company's organizational structure and the jurisdictions in which results are realized. Whatever the choice, the ultimate effect must be that the applied rate provides the most meaningful information to the users of the financial statements.[75]

Differences between the statutory and effective tax rate can arise because income components are not taxed or costs are not deductible for example, but also because the tax expense (or income) in prior periods have been adjusted. The utilization of losses that were not recognized on the balance sheet resulting in a reduced current tax liability can also be a reason for the effective rate differing from the statutory rate. The last two examples – prior periods that have been adjusted and the utilization of unrecognized tax losses – are also listed as components of current tax (see Section 5.1) that could be disclosed in order to clarify the composition of current taxes. The adjustments with regard to prior periods directly affect the effective tax (compared to the statutory tax), because the profit affected by these adjustments is not part of the

---

72 IAS 12.81(a) and (b)
73 IAS 12.86
74 IAS 12.81c
75 IAS 12.85

accounting profit before tax for the current year. The reduction in the current tax as a result of the utilization of unrecognized deferred tax assets also results in a difference between the effective and statutory tax, as there is no corresponding write-off of the deferred tax asset, because this asset was not recognized on the balance sheet. This will result in an effective tax that is lower than would be expected based on the statutory rate.

As mentioned in Section 9.5.1 IAS 12 is silent with respect to uncertain tax position. The increase or decrease of a provision for uncertain tax positions will also affect the ETR. From my experience companies often include increases or decreases in such a provision as a prior year adjustment in the ETR. When the increase in such a provision relates to uncertain tax positions of the current period the increase is often included in for example non deductible costs or any other applicable item.

In addition to the abovementioned causes, such as tax exempt income, non-deductible costs, etc., which have an effect on current tax, various aspects of deferred tax can also affect the specification of the difference between the statutory and effective tax rate. These are, more specifically, the same aspects that are listed as components of deferred tax (see Section 9.5.1), such as changes to tax rates, the recognizing of previously unrecognized deferred tax assets and the write-off of previously recognized deferred tax assets. There are also other causes not explicitly referred to in IAS 12, such as not directly recognizing deferred tax assets. IAS 12 does not list the latter as a component, because it does not lead to deferred tax. This situation often occurs in practice and is partly the reason for the effective tax rate being higher than anticipated on the basis of the statutory tax rate. For the sake of completeness, please note that the originating or reversal of temporary differences – one of the most important components of deferred tax – must never affect the relationship between effective and statutory tax. This is due to the fact that deferred tax cannot be discounted, whereby the reduction or increase in the current tax resulting from a temporary difference is directly compensated for by a respective equivalent increase or reduction in the deferred tax. Any rate changes for future years or unrecognized deferred tax assets can then, for example, affect the amount of deferred tax, but this is not due to the origination or reversal of a temporary difference.

9.5.4 Changes to tax rates

The notes to the financial statements must disclose which tax rates have changed in relation to prior periods. This relates to the statutory rates in the jurisdictions where the company operates and can be meaningful for both current and deferred tax. For example, changes to the statutory rate can explain why this rate or the aggregate statutory rate differs from the preceding year's statutory rate or aggregate statutory rate. Changes to a statutory rate can also affect the amount of deferred tax (see Section 9.4.4.1).

9.5.5 Unrecognized deferred tax assets

The notes to the financial statements must disclose the amount of deductible temporary differences, unused tax losses and unused tax credits for which a deferred tax asset was *not* recognized in the financial statements. The expiry date of the amounts not recognized on the balance sheet must also be disclosed.[76] Deductible temporary differences do not have an expiry date as may be the case with tax losses, but the period within which these temporary differences will have to be deducted against the future taxable profit is usually obvious. Stating an expiry date provides the user of the financial statements with information about the possibility that the unrecognized deferred tax assets could lead to a deduction in the future. The same could apply to the settlement of deductible temporary differences. As such, I find it remarkable that IAS 12 only addresses the issue of the *expiry dates* of unrecognized deferred tax assets.

9.5.6 Temporary differences related to investments in subsidiaries for which no deferred tax liability was recognized

In Section 9.4.1.4 the fact is discussed that a deferred tax liability must always be recognized in those cases where the carrying amount of investments in subsidiaries exceeds the tax base of these investments, unless two conditions are met. As previously explained, these conditions refer to the situation where the company can determine when to settle the temporary difference and that the temporary difference will probably not be settled in the foreseeable future. However, as soon as the conditions are met and no deferred tax liability is accordingly recognized, IAS 12 requires that the amount of the temporary difference for which a deferred tax liability was *not* recognized is disclosed in the financial statements. It is not required to disclose the tax amount of the temporary differences, but only the amount of the temporary differences. IAS 12 gives as reason for this that it is often not possible in practice to calculate the amount of the unrecognized tax liability. However, if it is feasible in practice, companies are encouraged to disclose the amount of deferred tax liabilities.

9.5.7 Tax consequences of dividend distributions to shareholders[77]

As previously mentioned in Section 9.3.2, some countries tax profit that is distributed to shareholders at a different rate from that applying to undistributed profit. In determining the rate at which (deferred) tax assets and (deferred) tax liabilities must be recognized, the fact that the profit will be distributed as dividend must be ignored. However, the financial statements must disclose the nature and the amount of the potential income tax consequences that would result from distributing the profit as dividend.

---

76 IAS 12.81(e)
77 IAS 12.82A

9.5.8 Movement schedule of deferred tax

IAS 12 requires a statement of deferred tax to be included in the financial statements.[78] The statement must disclose the balance sheet items to which the deferred tax relates, for both the opening and closing balance, as well as the amount of deferred tax that relates to tax losses and tax credits. This statement should be in line with the company's balance sheet items, such as property, plant and equipment, financial instruments, provisions, etc. If, for example, a plant is depreciated at an accelerated rate for tax purposes but at a normal rate for financial reporting purposes, then the deferred tax will relate to the property, plant and equipment item.

IAS 12 also requires disclosure of how much of the change between the opening and closing balance has been recognized in profit or loss. The amount of deferred tax recognized in profit or loss must be listed *per item*. In practice, many companies provide a detailed statement of the change between the opening and closing balances of the deferred tax, which often states – besides the amount recognized in profit or loss, how much deferred tax has been recognized in equity or in OCI and how much deferred tax was created or settled as a result of divestment/investment.

9.5.9 Business combination

The principle of business combinations is discussed in Section 9.4.1.3.1. A business combination could give a company cause to adjust its own deferred tax asset. In that case, IAS 12 requires that the amount of the change to the recognized deferred tax asset as a result of the business combination to be disclosed.[79] This can be illustrated for the Netherlands by the following example: a company that once again starts realizing taxable profit as a result of a business combination, whereby losses that could not previously be set off can be set off in the new situation.

Furthermore with regard to deferred tax benefits *acquired* as a result of the business combination, if they are not recognized on the acquisition date, but are recognized *after* the acquisition date, a description of the event or change in circumstances must be given for this.[80] This relates to the deferred tax asset of the acquired company and will often be the result of an information backlog at the acquiring company.

9.5.10 Recognized deferred tax assets in tax loss situations[81]

In section 9.4.2.1 I explained that a company must have additional convincing evidence to support the recognition of a deferred tax asset in cases where a tax loss has been incurred in the current or preceding period. For these situations, IAS 12 requires the disclosure of the amount of the deferred tax assets that have been recognized on the balance sheet. This applies to both deferred tax assets arising from

---

78 IAS 12.81(g)
79 IAS 12.81(j)
80 IAS 12.81(k)
81 IAS 12.82

Tax Accounting

deductible temporary differences and deferred tax assets arising from tax losses and unused tax credits. The amounts that must be disclosed are only those that are recognized on top of the amounts, which are recognized because there are sufficient taxable temporary differences which are settled in the appropriate period (refer to Section 9.4.1.5 step a and 9.4.2.1). IAS 12 also requires that the nature of the evidence will be described in the financial statements. In my opinion, this requires disclosure of the grounds on which the company based its decision to recognize deferred tax assets on the balance sheet in this situation.

9.5.11 Discontinued business operations[82]

The tax expense related to the discontinuance of business operations must be disclosed in the financial statements. Not only the tax expense resulting from the discontinuance must be disclosed, but also the tax on the profit or loss realized by the normal activity of the discontinued operation.

9.6 Presentation

Another important issue is the manner in which the (deferred) tax assets and tax liabilities should be presented in the financial statements. In this section I will discuss if these assets and liabilities should be recognized separately on the balance sheet (debit and credit) or should they be set off against one another.

9.6.1 Current tax

IAS 12.71 states that current tax assets and current tax liabilities must be offset if
a) there is a legally enforceable right to offset the recognized amounts; and
b) the intention is to settle the liability on a net basis or to realize the asset and settle the liability simultaneously.

In short, these conditions mean that current tax assets and liabilities must be offset on the balance sheet if there is a legally enforceable right to make net payments to the tax authorities. This is usually the case if this concerns the same taxpayer and the same tax authorities. However, in some jurisdictions[83] taxpayers are entitled to offset tax assets and tax liabilities against one another, but this is not mandatory. In such situations, condition b – the intention to settle on a net basis – must be met.

It is important to take account of the fact that current tax assets and current tax liabilities *must* be offset against one another as soon as the conditions are met.

---

82 IAS 12.81(h)
83 For example, pursuant to the "group relief" system in the United Kingdom, losses *can* be transferred, in the year in which they were incurred, to one or more other group companies with which the transferring company is affiliated either directly or indirectly through a shareholding of at least 75%.

9.6.2 Deferred tax

IAS 12.74 states that deferred tax assets and tax liabilities must be offset if
a) the company has a legally enforceable right to set off current tax assets against current tax liabilities; and
b) the deferred tax assets and tax liabilities relate to taxes levied by the same taxation authority on i) the same taxable entity or ii) different taxable entities that either intend to settle the current tax assets and current tax liabilities on a net basis, or intend to realize the deferred tax assets in the same period as that in which the deferred tax liabilities are realized.

Briefly put, this means that the deferred tax assets and deferred tax liabilities must be offset against one another if the company is entitled to set off the current tax assets against the current tax liabilities.[84] This must involve the same taxable entity and the income tax must be levied by the same taxation authority. If this does not involve the same taxable entity, recognition on a net basis must nevertheless take place if the different taxable entities intend to set off the current tax. As soon as the last condition is not met, the company is obliged to offset deferred tax assets and deferred tax liabilities if the company intends to settle the deferred tax assets and tax liabilities in the same future period.

There is no obligation to draw up detailed schedules to establish whether the deferred tax assets and tax liabilities were settled in the same period, as long as a taxpayer has the right (and if applicable also the intention) to settle the current tax assets and current tax liabilities. A company will only have to draw up detailed schedules in those situations where it can opt to set off the current tax assets against the current tax liabilities, but subsequently chooses not to do so.

This means that in the Netherlands, for example, both current and deferred tax assets and tax liabilities must be set off against one another in the case of a fiscal unity. A fiscal unity is regarded as one taxable entity and the current tax assets and tax liabilities of the various entities in the fiscal unity are mandatory set off.

9.7 Uncertain tax positions

In Section 9.5.1 I stated that uncertain tax positions are not explicitly referred to in IAS 12. Consequently, the expression 'uncertain tax position' is not defined. I believe that a useful definition of the expression 'uncertain tax position' would be:

"Positions taken (or to be taken) by the company in its tax return, which can be disputed by the tax authorities."

In many cases, an uncertain tax position will affect the amount of current tax. In some situations, an uncertain tax position can, however, affect deferred tax, for example,

---

84 Again an election cannot be made if the abovementioned conditions are met, in that situation the company is obliged to sett of the deferred tax assets and deferred tax liabilities

because the uncertain tax position reduces the tax loss for which a deferred tax asset was recognized. It is also possible that a deferred tax asset arising from a deductible temporary difference may not be deductible. As soon as it is clear that the deduction in its entirety is not permissible, the deferred tax asset will have to be adjusted. Another situation that could arise is where a deduction is not accepted in a certain year, but is accepted in a subsequent year. In that case, the uncertain tax position will increase the current tax liability, but will also increase the deferred tax asset for the same amount (provided the future tax rate is the same).

In practice, various methods are available under IFRS to establish whether an uncertain tax position exists. IAS 12 does not refer to uncertain tax positions, but IAS 12.46 does state that current tax liabilities (and current tax assets) must be measured at the amount expected to be paid to (or refunded by) the tax authorities on the basis of tax rates and tax law that have been substantively enacted.[85] However, it is often quite complicated to determine which amount will ultimately be paid to the tax authorities. The IAS 37 guidelines deal with the recognition of a provision. Although IAS 37 states that uncertain tax positions fall outside its scope, in practice the methods described in IAS 37 are followed when determining the size of the uncertain tax position. This use of IAS 37 is substantiated by IAS 8, which states that in the absence of specific IFRS guidance on a transaction, management must judiciously devise a basis for the financial reporting. IAS 8.11 states that in doing so management must consider a) the IFRS requirements that deal with similar or related questions and b) the definitions, recognition criteria and measurement concepts for assets, liabilities, income and expenses in the IFRS Conceptual Framework. As mentioned previously, IAS 37 deals with the recognition and measurement of provisions and on the basis of IAS 8.11(1) many companies follow this valuation method.

9.7.1 Provisions dealt with in IAS 37

IAS 37 deals with provisions, contingent liabilities and contingent assets. I will discuss the contingent liabilities in Section 9.7.3. The contingent assets are briefly discussed in Section 9.7.2.

A provision must be recognized if:[86]
1. An entity has a present obligation (legal or constructive) as a result of a past event;
2. It is probable that an outflow of resources embodying economic benefits will be required in order to settle the obligation; and
3. A reliable estimate can be made of the amount of the obligation.

An uncertain tax position will usually meet condition 1. A company is obliged to pay tax on the grounds of various corporate income tax laws in the relevant countries. Even if the obligation to file a tax return has not yet been officially enforced, the company must take account of the fact that it must pay tax with respect to the

---

85 Cf. Section 9.3.2
86 IAS 37.14

expected taxable profit. Furthermore, this obligation is generally closely related to past events. Condition 2 is more difficult to assess and, in my view, is directly related to the measurement of the liability. The text of IAS 37.23 indicates that the recognition of an obligation in any case requires there to be more than a 50% probability that an outflow of funds will take place. As soon as the probability that this will occur falls below 50%, the less likely it is that an outflow of funds will take place and a provision must not be recognized. This means that not every provision has to be recognized, because it must first be established that there is more than a 50% probability that an outflow of funds will take place. The third condition also relates to the measurement of the obligation, i.e. a provision must not be recognized if the obligation cannot be measured with sufficient reliability.

9.7.2 Measurement under IAS 37

IAS 37 states that the amount that must be recognized as a provision must be the best estimate of the expenditure required to settle the current obligation,[87] and that this estimate is dependent on the circumstances. Where the provision to be measured encompasses a large number of items, the obligation must be estimated by weighting all possible outcomes by their associated probabilities. IAS 37 refers to this as the expected value. This makes the provision dependent on the various percentages the company uses to estimate the size of its loss.[88] If the company estimates that there is a 70% probability of a loss of a given amount, then a provision must be recognized for 70% of this amount. In the situation where an individual obligation must be measured, IAS 37 states that the individual most likely outcome could be the best estimate of the obligation, but that the company must also take other possible outcomes into account if these outcomes are for the most part higher or lower than the most likely outcome.[89] The latter will be the case if, for example, the most likely outcome is 40%, while there is a probability that the amount of the obligation may turn out to be 35% or 25% higher than the amount associated with the 40% probability. While the most likely outcome is the amount associated with the 40% probability, a higher amount must be recognized for the obligation in this case, as there is an overall 60% probability that the outflow of funds will exceed 40%. To explain in figures:

Assume that a company has recognized a tax asset of 4000 in its tax return. The company expects that the tax authority will dispute this tax asset and estimates the probability that eventually tax will have to be paid as:

Probability	Amount
40%	1500
35%	3000
25%	4000

---

87 IAS 37.36
88 IAS 37.39
89 IAS 37.40

Although the most likely outcome is that 1500 will have to be paid, there is a 75% probability that 3000 or more will have to be paid. According to IAS 37, the amount of the provision cannot be 1500, but must be recognized at a higher amount. There is a 75% cumulative probability that 3000 will have to be paid. In this example, the provision will have to be 3000, not 1500. In Section 7.4 it is discussed that this method is quite similar to the method prescribed by US GAAP, which is also based on cumulative probabilities.

In my view, an uncertain tax position must be assessed as if it were an individual obligation and the company must consequently recognize the most likely outcome. This will often lead to either the entire amount of the obligation being recognized or no obligation being recognized, because tax disputes do not always lend themselves to compromise. However, consultation with the taxation authorities is increasingly becoming standard procedure, which has changed the 'all or nothing' approach of the past with an outcome that is somewhere 'in between'. In this situation, the company will use the expected outcome of the consultation process as its most likely outcome.

As IAS 12 does not prescribe which method should be used to determine uncertain tax positions, this has led to various methods being used in practice to estimate the provision. In addition to the method based on the most likely outcome, some companies use a variant of the expected value method. Under this method, the obligation is estimated by multiplying the possibilities by the expected payments. This results in an obligation also being recognized for amounts of which there is a less than 50% probability of their being an outflow of funds. Estimating the probability that the tax position reported in the tax return is tenable remains a difficult proposition, whereby the use of the expected value method could be a good alternative. Especially where large amounts are involved, it is difficult not to recognize a provision at all as soon as there is a 51% probability that the tax position will prove tenable. There is, after all, still a 49% probability that the tax position will lead to a significant outflow of funds.

Another interesting question is whether, in examining if a provision arising from an uncertain tax position should be recognized, a company should not first ask itself whether it is even possible to recognize a tax asset on the balance sheet. IAS 37 then goes on to discuss contingent assets, thereby stating that a asset may only be recognized on the balance sheet if it is virtually certain that this will result in an inflow of funds. 'Virtually certain' is interpreted in practice as 90-95% certainty[90]. This 'virtually certain' criterion appears to conflict with IAS 12, because IAS 12 uses the probability criterion for (deferred) tax assets, which translates to a more than 50% probability.

As indicated, many companies calculate the provision for uncertain tax positions in line with the IAS 37 recognition and measurement guidelines, for which a 50%

---

90 International GAAP 2014 EY, volume 2, page 1738 (>95%), and https://www.pwc.ch/user_content/editor/files/publ_life/pwc_ifrs_challenges.pdf (reference to IFRS companies using the 95%-criterion, PWC), and agig.de/53-1.pdf (KPMG, reference is made to 90%)

probability criterion applies. Under this approach, a potential deduction is, in fact, treated as a reduction of the total debt to the taxation authorities, and the question whether a tax asset is allowed to be recognized becomes irrelevant. A similar question was recently presented to the IFRS Interpretations Committee of the IASB. The interpretations Committee was asked to clarify the recognition of a tax asset in the situation in which tax laws require an entity to make an immediate payment when a tax examination results in an additional charge, even if the entity intends to appeal against the additional charge. The staff of the IFRS foundation drafted an interpretation for this.[91] The main conclusion of this draft interpretation is that current tax assets (and liabilities) are within the scope of IAS 12 and not within the scope of IAS 37. Consequently the draft interpretations concludes that it is not appropriate to apply a virtually certain criterion to the recognition of a current tax asset, because in that situation the amount of tax expenses would be depending on the timing of the prepayment of an uncertain tax amount. In the draft interpretation it is noted that IAS 12.12 states that a current tax asset is recognized if the amount of cash paid (which is a certain amount) exceeds the amount of tax expected to be due (which is an uncertain amount). In the draft interpretation it is also noted that IAS 12.14 gives guidance with respect to recognition of a current tax asset in circumstances that a tax loss is used to recover current tax from a previous period. The recognition criterion for that situation is the probability criterion. In the July 2014 meeting of the Interpretations Committee[92] the committee decided that there is sufficient guidance in IAS 12 regarding this issue and remove it from the agenda. In the same meeting the Interpretations Committee noted that one of the principal issues in respect of uncertain tax positions is how to measure related assets and liabilities. As a consequence the Committee asked the staff to analyze how detection risk and probability should be reflected in the measurement of tax assets and liabilities in such situations. This staff paper has been prepared in September 2014 and it appears that the staff prefers shortly said an expected value method (in the situation that the uncertainty is high) and that an entity should assume that the tax authorities will examine the amounts reported to them and have full knowledge of all relevant information[93]. The Interpretation Committee decided in the September meeting[94] to proceed with this project, subject to further analysis and deliberations and asked the staff to prepare a proposal with respect to the scope of the project, the unit of account for measurement of uncertain tax positions and the possible approach. Although the Interpretation Committee agreed on the view of the detection risk, at this stage it is still uncertain what the outcome of this project will be.

---

91 http://www.ifrs.org/Current-Projects/IFRIC-Projects/Pages/IFRIC-activities.aspx. Work in progress=> Income Taxes: Threshold of recognition of an asset in the situation in which the tax position is uncertain, discussions and papers, ref 3A
92 IFRIC Update July 2014, http://media.ifrs.org/2014/IFRIC/July/IFRIC-Update-July-2014.pdf
93 http://www.ifrs.org/Current-Projects/IFRIC-Projects/Pages/IFRIC-activities.aspx. Work in progress=> Income Taxes: Threshold of recognition of an asset in the situation in which the tax position is uncertain, discussions and papers, ref 4
94 IFRIC Update September 2014, http://media.ifrs.org/2014/IFRIC/September/IFRIC-Update-September-2014.pdf

9.7.3 Contingent liabilities

IAS 12 does not require disclosure of uncertain tax positions. As previously stated,[95] this is the reason why companies often record adjustments in the provision for uncertain tax positions under the item 'Adjustments to prior years' in the effective tax rate reconciliation. As soon as the provision for uncertain tax positions relates to a transaction in the current period, the amount of the provision will often be included in the 'non-deductible expenses' item. IAS 12 does, however, refer to IAS 37 when dealing with contingent assets and liabilities. According to IAS 12.88, a company must disclose all tax-related contingent assets and contingent liabilities in accordance with IAS 37. Contingent assets were briefly discussed in the preceding section. According to IAS 37,[96] a contingent liability is present if a present obligation arises from a past event, but for which:
1. It is unlikely (= less than a 50% probability) that an outflow of resources embodying economic benefits will be required in order to settle the obligation; or
2. No reliable estimate can be made of the amount of the obligation.

Companies must disclose detailed information on their contingent liabilities in the financial statements. IAS 37.86 states that a brief description must be given of the contingent liability, which includes (if practicable) i) an estimate of the financial consequences; ii) an indication of the uncertainties relating to the amount of any outflow; and iii) the possibility of reimbursement.

The above information does not have to be disclosed if the likelihood that there will be an outflow of funds is remote. 'Remote' is usually defined as less than 5-10%[97] probability.

9.7.4 US GAAP, Accounting Standard Codification (ASC) 740

ASC 740 is the US GAAP standard that deals with the treatment of income tax. Unlike IAS 12, ASC 740 (formerly FAS 109 and Fin 48) contains extensive rules on uncertain tax positions. In 2006, the Financial Accounting Standards Board issued an FASB interpretation – FIN 48 – that deals with the computation and disclosure of uncertain tax positions. This interpretation has now been included in its entirety in ASC 740. In this Section, we will briefly discuss the most important features of this regulation.

According to ASC 740, a separate provision must be recognized for uncertain tax positions and denoted as a "liability for unrecognized tax benefits".[98] To determine the amount of this liability, ASC 740 requires a two-step approach to be taken.

---

95 Section 9.5.3
96 IAS 37.13 (b) (ii)
97 International GAAP 2014 EY, volume 2, page 1738 (<5%), and K agig.de/53-1.pdf (KPMG, reference is made to 10%)
98 ASC 740-10-25-16

The first step determines whether the tax position taken of will be taken in the tax return meets the recognition threshold. This requires the company to examine the tax position on its technical merits to determine whether it is "more likely than not"[99] that the position will be sustained upon examination. The term "more likely than not" means that there is more than a 50% probability that the position taken is tenable. This examination must include a technical analysis, whereby management must examine whether the probabilities that a tax audit, which may lead to legal proceedings, will find that the tax position is tenable is more than 50% and that the tax position will actually result in the inflow of funds. This examination must be based on tax law and regulations and must not take account of the outcome of consultations with the taxation authorities, for example. It is explicitly stated that this examination must be based on the assumption that the taxation authorities are aware of all the facts and circumstances. As soon as the recognition threshold is not met, a liability for the unrecognized tax benefits must be reported for the full amount of the obligation.

The second step involves the valuation of the tax position. In this step, the company determines for which amount there is a more than 50% probability that an inflow of funds will be realized as a result of the tax position.[100] This is based on the cumulative probabilities at the time that no one amount exceeds 50%. ASC 740 illustrates the above by the following example:

Possible outcome	Individual probability of occurring	Cumulative probability of occurring
USD 100	5%	5%
USD 80	25%	30%
USD 60	25%	55%
USD 50	20%	75%
USD 40	10%	85%
USD 20	10%	95%
USD -	5%	100%

In this situation, there is more than a 50% probability that the minimum amount received will be USD 60. The liability for unrecognized tax benefits will be USD 10, assuming a tax rate of 25%.

9.7.4.1 Disclosure

ASC 740 contains numerous disclosure requirements; one of the most important being the amount of the opening and closing balance sheets and the associated adjustments. The adjustments must be specified under the following items:[101]

---

99 ASC 740-10-25-6
100 ASC 740-10-30-7
101 ASC 740-10-50-15A

1. Adjustments as a result of an increase or decrease in the tax positions of earlier years.
2. Adjustments as a result of an increase or decrease in the tax positions of the current year.
3. A reduction in the liability as a result of its settlement with the tax authorities.
4. Release as a result of the expiry of the period within which the tax authorities can impose additional assessments.

In addition to this computational disclosure, a host of other qualitative disclosures are also required, such as the possible impact on the effective rate, outstanding years and information on penalties and interest.

9.8 VAT, payroll tax and social security contributions

VAT and payroll tax do not fall under the definition of 'income tax' and therefore IAS 12 does not apply to them. In this Section I describe how VAT and payroll tax and social security contributions should be recognized in the annual financial statements and according to which IFRS standards. Every business must, to a greater or lesser extent, remit VAT on the goods or services it supplies. In addition, the entity can recover the tax that it was charged – depending on the use to which the goods or services were put – from the tax authorities. These more or less standard transactions result in either a tax asset from or a tax liability to the tax authorities. VAT is often a so called intermediary item, to the extent that it can be recovered, and will not result in an expense on the income statement.

However, there are also other situations (non-standard transactions) where the recoverable or remittable VAT may result in a balance sheet item in the financial statements. For example, although a entity may have reclaimed VAT, it may nevertheless believe that there is a good chance that the tax authorities may reverse the deductible item. Another example is that an entity may defer recognizing a tax asset from the tax authorities in its return, such as the recoverable VAT on bad debts.

In addition, entities must remit payroll tax and social security contributions on reimbursements and on items that have been made available to employees. Both the employee and the entity must pay a share of the payroll tax and social security contributions. In both cases, this results in a tax liability to the tax authorities with the costs being accounted for on the income statement. The amount of payroll tax and social security contributions may be disputed by the tax authorities, resulting in the creation of a provision. It may also be the case that an entity remits the payroll tax and social security contributions, but subsequently files a notice of objection against its own return, because it does not believe that it should have had to remit these payments.[102] Consequently, the entity may have a tax asset on the tax authorities.

---

102 An example of this is the Dutch 16% crisis levy on excessive salaries.

In Sections 9.8.1 through 9.8.3 I outline the standards that apply to the reporting of assets and liabilities arising from various transactions and events in the area of VAT and payroll tax and social security contributions.

9.8.1 Assets and liabilities

There are no separate IFRS standards for assets and liabilities. Most assets and liabilities fall under the definition of IAS 39, the standard which deals with financial instruments. The definition of a financial instrument requires an agreement to be present. However, assets and liabilities relating to VAT, payroll tax and social security contributions do not arise from an agreement, but are the result of legislation, which means that IAS 39 does not apply. In Section 9.7, I discussed IAS 37, the standard dealing with provisions, contingent liabilities and contingent assets. 'Normal' (i.e. present) liabilities and assets are not specifically dealt with in the standard. I will therefore first address the definitions of assets and liabilities as included in the IFRS Conceptual Framework.

An asset is defined as:[103] a resource controlled by the entity as a result of past events and from which future economic benefits are expected to flow to the entity.

A liability is defined as: a present obligation of the entity arising from past events, the settlement of which is expected to result in an outflow from the entity of resources embodying economic benefits.[104]

Once an asset or liability meets these definitions, the circumstances under which an asset or liability must be recognized on the balance sheet need to determined. According to the Conceptual Framework, both the asset and the liability must be recognized on the balance sheet if it is probable that they will result in an inflow (asset) to the business or an outflow (liability) from the business of resources embodying economic benefits. Furthermore, it must be possible to make a reliable estimate of this inflow or outflow of resources.[105]

The question that subsequently arises is what 'probable' actually means. Does it refer to a probability of 50% or 70% or possibly even higher, e.g. 90%? The Conceptual Framework does not define 'probable', although IAS 37 does set out what is meant by it.

9.8.2 Provisions and liabilities

IAS 37 uses the same definition of liability as that found in the Conceptual Framework.[106] It also states that a provision differs from other types of liabilities in that a

---

103 IFRS Conceptual Framework 4.4 (a)
104 IFRS Conceptual Framework 4.4 (b)
105 IFRS Conceptual Framework 4.38
106 IAS 37.10

provision is a liability of uncertain timing or amount.[107] The conditions under which a provision must be recognized on the balance sheet are then discussed (I dealt with this in Section 9.7). These conditions are :[108]
a) An entity has a present obligation (legal or constructive) as a result of a past event;
b) It is probable that an outflow of resources embodying economic benefits will be required in order to settle the obligation; and
c) A reliable estimate can be made of the amount of the obligation.

These conditions for the recognition of a provision on the balance sheet are the same as the definition of a liability and the recognition criteria contained in the Conceptual Framework (see Section 8.1). IAS 37 then goes on to explain that what is actually meant by 'probable' is 'more likely than not',[109] which implies that there must be a more than 50% probability of an outflow of resources. In explaining 'probable', reference is made to the situation where a *liability* must be recognized on the balance sheet; a provision is not specifically referred to. A liability or provision must therefore be recognized on the balance sheet if there is a more than 50% probability of an outflow of resources. 'Normal' liabilities do not give rise to uncertainty about whether there will be an outflow of resources. Only if uncertainty exists, will a provision need to be created.

This means that an entity must evaluate whether discussions with the tax authorities about non-remitted VAT, payroll tax and social security contributions, and/or VAT that has been deducted and deductions on remittable payroll tax and social security contributions could increase the probability of an outflow of resources to more than 50%.

Discussion with the tax authorities can also lead to the creation of a contingent liability. As indicated in Section 9.7.3, a contingent liability arises if no reliable estimate of the obligation can be made or if there is a less than 50% probability of the outflow of resources. Various disclosure requirements apply to contingent liabilities. These requirements are outlined in Section 9.7.3.

9.8.3 Contingent assets

In Section 9.7.2 I briefly addressed contingent assets. A contingent asset is defined as: a possible asset that arises from past events and whose existence will be confirmed only by the occurrence or non-occurrence of one or more uncertain future events not wholly within the control of the entity.[110] A contingent asset is *not* recognized on the balance sheet, unless it is virtually certain that it will generate income. 'Virtually certain' is interpreted in practice as 90-95% certainty. In those situations where an inflow of economic resources is probable (more than a 50% probability), the business

---

107 IAS 37.10 and 11
108 IAS 37.14
109 IAS 37.23 explicitly states that the interpretation of this term only applies to this standard.
110 IAS 37.10

must provide a brief description of the nature of the contingent asset and an estimate of the financial consequences. This means that the interpretation of 'probable' as it relates to the recognition of an *asset* – including a VAT receivable or a payroll tax and social security contributions claim on the tax authorities – differs from the interpretation applied to it when recognizing a liability. As asset is only recognized if it is virtually certain – i.e. there is more than a 90-95% probability – that there will be an inflow of economic resources, while the recognition of a liability requires only a more than 50% probability.

Consequently, any claims that an entity may have on the tax authorities in respect of VAT or payroll tax and social security contributions will not be able to be promptly recognized on the balance sheet. In my opinion, this is an important difference with the recognition of income tax assets. The point of departure of IAS 12 for the recognition of deferred tax assets is the probability criterion. Although not explicitly referred to in relation to current income tax assets, this criterion is, in practice, applied often to them.[111]

9.8.4 Conclusion

IFRS does not have a specific standard for the recognition of assets from and liabilities to the tax authorities with regard to VAT, payroll tax and social security contributions. The Conceptual Framework defines assets and liabilities and states that an asset or a liability must be recognized on the balance sheet if it is probable that they will result in an inflow or outflow of economic resources to or from the business. IAS 37 subsequently explains how 'probable' should be interpreted. What this means for assets is that it is must be virtually certain that they will lead to an inflow of economic resources. For liabilities it must be 'more likely than not' that there will be an outflow of economic resources. The impact of these standards on businesses is that they will need to evaluate whether any discussions to be held with the tax authorities will have a more than 50% probability of resulting in a liability to the tax authorities. If a business believes it has a claim on the tax authorities, it will however have to evaluate whether there is more than a 90-95% probability of an inflow of resources. In my opinion, this difference in interpretation means that the important factor in any discussions on the same issue is whether or not a business has already deducted an amount in its return. If the business has already deducted the amount, but this is disputed by the tax authorities, the business will need to evaluate whether there is a more than 50% probability of having to repay this deduction. However, if the business has not yet deducted the amount, but intends to file a notice of objection against its own return in order to reclaim the deduction, the evaluation will have to take account of the 90-95% criterion. This difference in interpretation is also noted by the IASB with respect to income tax positions (see Section 9.7.3). The IASB[112] stated that the

---

111 As mentioned in Section 7.3., questions have been raised with the IASB.
112 http://www.ifrs.org/Current-Projects/IFRIC-Projects/Pages/IFRIC-activities.aspx. Work in progress=> Income Taxes: Threshold of recognition of an asset in the situation in which the tax position is uncertain=> agenda ref 3 July 2014, paragraph 15

recognition requirements should not depend on the timing and manner of settlement of the liability with respect to income tax. In my view it would be consistent to use the same interpretation for assets and liabilities regarding other taxes, like VAT and payroll taxes. Another important difference with the accounting treatment of income taxes relate to the disclosures. A provision with respect VAT and payroll taxes falls within IAS 37. IAS 37 requires extensive disclosures with respect to each class of provision. As income taxes fall withing IAS 12, no disclosures regarding uncertain tax positions are required.

9.9 Country-by Country-Reporting (CbCR)

In this chapter I will discuss the main features of Country-by-Country Reporting (CbCR). CbCR focuses on the amount of income tax paid in relation to turnover, number of employees and the nature of activities per country. In response to CbCR, several initiatives have been launched against the increasing call for more transparency in the tax position of large businesses. Organizations such as the Tax Justice Network have developed initiatives on this, because they believe that CbCR will eventually lead to a fairer system of taxation of multinationals. These initiatives and their interaction with tax accounting are discussed below.

9.9.1 Extractive Industry and CbCR

One of the first voluntary initiatives was the Extractive Industries Transparancy Initiative (EITI) launched in 2003. EITI focuses on using transparency to mitigate a negative impact, including corruption, for countries rich in natural resources, such as oil, gas and mining. According to EITI, these countries tend to under-perform economically, have a higher incidence of conflict and suffer from poor governance.[113] EITI emphasizes the need for transparency, accountability and good governance[114] with regard to the use of natural resources and payments to governments. Countries that implement these standards will have to disclose how much they receive from extractive companies and the extractive companies are, in turn, obliged to disclose the payments they make to governments. This disclosure includes all manner of payments to governments such as production entitlements, profits taxes, royalties, dividends, bonuses, license fees and other significant payments.[115]

In 2013, the EU introduced two directives, both containing CbCR regulations. The Member States must implement the directives – the Accounting Directive[116] and the Transparency Directive[117] – in 2015 and they apply to financial years starting on or after January 1, 2016. The Accounting Directive applies to EU public interest entities and large EU undertakings registered in the European Economic Area (EEA) that are

---

113 https://eiti.org/eiti/benefits and the standard, articles of association (Article2.2)
114 https://eiti.org/document/standard
115 https://eiti.org/document/standard, Article 4.1
116 http://eur-lex.europa.eu/LexUriServ/LexUriServ.do?uri=OJ:L:2013:182:0019:0076:EN:PDF (Directive 2013/34/EU)
117 http://eur-lex.europa.eu/legal-content/EN/ALL/?uri=CELEX:32013L0050 (Directive 2013/50/EU)

active in the extractive industry or the logging of primary forests. The Transparency Directive applies to all companies in the extractive or logging sectors, regardless of their size and their country of establishment, that are listed on recognized stock exchanges in the EU. The objective is to help governments of resource-rich countries implement the EITI principles and criteria and to provide accountability for the payments they receive as well as making them more transparent.[118] The disclosure requirements are more or less the same as those of EITI.[119]

On September 29, 2014, the Council of the European Union announced that the findings of a Commission report to be delivered by July 21, 2018 could make it necessary to require large undertakings in all sectors to produce a country-by-country report containing on the profit taxes paid in each Member State and third country.[120]

Furthermore, the Dodd-Frank Act also applies to SEC registered companies. This Act requires more or less the same disclosures as the EITI.

9.9.2 Credit institutions and investment firms

In 2013, the EU introduced the Capital Requirements Directive IV (CRD IV),[121] which applies to credit institutions and investment firms. This legislation is applicable to financial years from 2014 onward and disclosures must be audited.[122] The Directive had to be implemented by Member States no later than December 31, 2013. In short, the Directive applies to all credit institutions and investment firms established in the EEA.[123] The objective is to regain the trust of the public through transparency and the disclosure of taxes paid and subsidies received.[124] The disclosure requires information per country with respect to activities, turnover, number of employees, profit or loss before tax, tax on profit or loss and public subsidies received.

9.9.3 Base Erosion and Profit Shifting

The OECD has released 15 Action Plans on Base Erosion and Profit Shifting (BEPS). Action Plan 13 deals with transfer pricing and CbCR.[125] In September 2014, the OECD launched the final Action Plan. The objectives of Action Plan 13 are to ensure that taxpayers give proper consideration to transfer pricing requirements, provide tax

---

118 Accounting Directive 2013/34/EU, Articles 44 and 45 and the Transparency Directive 2013/50/EU Articles 7 and 8
119 Accounting Directive 2013/34/EU, Chapter 10 and Transparency Directive 2013/50/EU Article 6
120 Council of the European Union, Press release September 29, 2014 (ST 13606/14) on new transparency rules on social responsibility for big companies.
121 http://eur-lex.europa.eu/legal-content/EN/TXT/?uri=CELEX:32013L0036 (Directive 2013/36/EU)
122 Directive 2013/36/EU article 89.4, furthermore global systematically important institutions should report the profit before tax, tax on profit or loss, and subsidies to the European Commission on July 1 of any year. The EC will treat this information as strictly confidential (article 89.3).
123 Directive 2013/36/EU, article 89: it applies to institutions.The term "institution" is defined by Article 4(1)(3) of the Credit Requirements Regulation (CRR, regulation 575/2013) as a "credit institution" or "investment firm", and each of these terms is further defined in Article 4(1) and (2).
124 Article 52 of the Directive 2013/36/EU
125 http://www.oecd-ilibrary.org/taxation/guidance-on-transfer-pricing-documentation-and-country-by-country-reporting_9789264219236-en

administrations with the information necessary to conduct an informed transfer pricing risk assessment and thoroughly audit the transfer pricing practices.[126] Chapter C.3 discusses CbCR. C.3.25 states that the CbCR report will be helpful for high-level transfer pricing risk assessment purposes and may also be used by tax administrations when evaluating other BEPS-related risks. With regard to CbCR, businesses are required to disclose information with respect to revenues, profit or loss before income tax, income tax paid, income tax accrued, stated capital, accumulated earnings, number of employees and tangible assets and the main business activities per tax jurisdiction.[127]

This information should be disclosed to the tax authorities, not to the public.

9.9.4 Interaction with tax accounting

The CbCR requirement regarding the extractive industry and BEPS Action Plan 13 are fairly clear on how income taxes paid should be disclosed in the CbCR templates. CRD IV, however, refers to "taxes on profit or loss" and not specifically to "taxes paid". As CRD IV is an EU Directive, it must be implemented by the Member States. This has as consequence, that there are varying interpretations of what is meant by "taxes on profit or loss". For example, the Netherlands interprets "taxes on profit or loss" as referring to the financial statements, which are often based on IFRS and more specifically on IAS 12.[128] This means that businesses must disclose both the current and the deferred tax as recognized in the income statement and not the income taxes paid. The UK, on the other hand, interprets it as income taxes paid.[129] Under BEPS, CbCR refers to income taxes paid and current tax expenses accrued.[130] The above illustrates the varying interpretations being applied under the same directive and also the different requirements contained in the different CbCR initiatives.

IAS 12 does not refer to income taxes paid, but IAS 7 does. IAS 7 deals with the cash flow statement and requires disclosure of cash flows arising from taxes on income.[131] On a consolidated basis, the payments (or receipts) of income taxes are disclosed in the financial statements. It should also be noted that while IAS 12 does not require the opening balance of income tax receivables or payables to be reconciled with the closing balance of income tax receivables or payables, such a reconciliation is more or less required for deferred taxes (refer to Section 5.8). In my opinion, it would be helpful for interpretation purposes if such a reconciliation is required on a consolidated and on a country-by-country basis for current tax. Such a reconciliation should explain the difference between the opening and closing balances of income tax

---

126 BEPS Action Plan 13 part B, objectives of transfer pricing documentation requirements
127 BEPS Action Plan 13 Annex III
128 Decree of September 25, 2014, nr 26867, Article 3.e
129 https://www.gov.uk/government/publications/capital-requirements-country-by-country-reporting-regulations-2013-guidance/capital-requirements-country-by-country-reporting-regulations-2013-guidance
130 BEPS Action Plan 13, specific instructions for Annex III
131 IAS 7.35

receivables or payables and should include current income taxes accrued in the income statement, recognized in equity and other comprehensive income and recognized through investment or divestment. Such a reconciliation should not increase the administrative burden, as I believe that these kind of reconciliations are already necessary to ensure that the consolidated cash payments or receipts are accurate and complete.

I believe that a current tax reconciliation together with a comprehensive reconciliation of the deferred taxes would give a complete view of the tax position in the individual countries, as it would make clear whether companies can or shall defer taxes based on local legislation and whether they will pay income tax in the future or in fact "pay" the income tax with (recognized) tax losses. Such a reconciliation will be more helpful for the public to interpret the income tax position of the company than the sole disclosure of the income tax paid per country.

ELMER VAN LIENEN
MARIEKE LOUWEN

10. Payroll taxes 'in control'

10.1 Introduction

Most people identify taxes with corporate income tax, in particular when discussing the tax control framework. However, payroll taxes are one of the major forms of taxes in terms of tax revenues for the government. Therefore this chapter will focus on this particular type of tax and will discuss how a payroll taxes control framework can be set up.

Since the official introduction (2006, in the Netherlands) of horizontal monitoring and cooperative compliance, this new way of monitoring and implementation of the law has received considerable attention. In particular the formulated starting point that covenants will only be entered into with tax payers who have a tax control framework (or have the intention to build one) has led to a different approach to taxes. Since then several publications have described what a tax control framework should look like. In virtually all cases, they conclude that the tax control framework should be an integral part of the risk management system (business control framework) which is present within the organisation to control the risks within the regular business processes. Many companies have based their control systems on the model that has been developed by the Committee of Sponsoring Organisations of the Treadway Commission (hereafter: COSO).[1] A tax control framework can be an integral part of the internal control system of the organisation based on the components as defined by COSO.

How does this work out regarding payroll taxes? What is the minimum standard for a payroll taxes control framework? The answers to these questions are provided in this chapter, which starts with the premise that the goal of the organisation is to comply with laws and regulations. Herewith, support from higher management is crucial. When higher management does not support this then the goal of becoming 'in control' is virtually impossible. The entire process to get *and* remain in control is a

---

1   http://www.coso.org/, see chapter 2 for more detail on COSO.

long lasting process. Based on the components of COSO a payroll taxes control framework can be defined as follows: a framework based on which identified risks for payroll taxes purposes are determined and controlled and which monitoring is applied to the correct process of the control methods. Keeping up to date with respect to changes in the law and knowledge and communication is recorded separately.

This chapter is set up as follows: before discussing 'to become in control' for payroll tax purposes, we will set out 'in a nut shell' how payroll taxes work and who the key players are. The number of key players provides an indication of the complexity in the controlling of payroll tax risks. We discuss thereafter the most common payroll risks and the control measures which can be taken 'to become in control'. After discussing these topics, we will discuss the monitoring and testing of these control measures in order to implement the learning cycle and to ensure compliance. Finally, we will provide a conclusion and a high-level summary of this chapter.

Please note that the principles and the methodology as discussed in this chapter are common for most countries and therefore can be applied internationally. However, reference is made to the Dutch legislation and the examples included in this chapter are mainly from a Dutch payroll tax perspective.

10.2 Payroll taxes: introduction and key players

10.2.1 Introduction

Payroll taxes are taxes that, in principle, are levied from the employee. However, the employer is responsible for the withholding of these levies and the payment to the tax authorities by means of the periodical payroll taxes return. When payroll taxes are not withheld correctly then, in practice, the tax authorities will first impose a retrospective wage tax assessment on the employer. The object of the payroll taxes is in principle the wage of the employee, including all other kinds of benefits provided by the employer to the employee such as holiday allowance, bonuses, stock options, thirteenth month, allowances, gift vouchers, company owned products etc. Depending on the conditions as included in the tax laws, a wage component can be regarded as taxable wage.

Payroll taxes are filed by means of a periodical electronic payroll taxes return (most commonly on a monthly or four weekly basis). Often the payroll department is responsible for the payroll taxes return. This department receives the payroll mutations every period and processes the payroll, so that the payroll taxes return can be filed with the tax authorities. Most of the time the payroll department is part of the finance or HR department but it can also be (partly) outsourced to an external payroll provider. Many organisations have the view that payroll taxes risks are limited to the risks in the payroll administration leading to statements such as: "My accountant already checked the payroll taxes; We have outsourced the payroll taxes to an external provider and we have very experienced payroll administrators within our organisation." The underlying thought is that, when the payroll department (internal as well as external) is responsible for the payment and filing of the payroll taxes returns, they are 'in control' and the risks with respect to payroll taxes are limited. This view may be too narrow-minded. Of course the payroll administration is of importance in order to file an acceptable payroll taxes return. However, it is our experience that most risks for payroll taxes are not within the process of the payroll administration but in several common processes within the organisation which have influence on but are not limited to the payroll department.

Payroll mutations are provided by several departments within the organisation. The allocation of these responsibilities differs per organisation. The payroll taxes risks therefore relate mainly to payroll mutations that are *not* provided to the payroll department based on the processes. This, for instance, involves allowances and benefits that are paid out to employees on a net basis and are not included in the payroll administration. If they should have been included in the payroll and the taxes are not withheld, an incorrect tax return has been filed. To control these kinds of risks the organisation has to implement several control measures in the common processes for which different departments are responsible. Firstly we discuss which key players have an influence on the payroll tax position of an organisation.

10.2.2 Key players

The most important departments responsible for processes concerning payroll taxes are HR and finance. However, we can define more key players who can provide payroll mutations, payments or have a role in the payroll taxes processes. This will be explained in more detail below. Of course, it depends on the size of the organisation as to whether or not some key players can actually be defined.

10.2.2.1 HR department

Amongst other things, the HR department is responsible for the hiring, firing and retiring of employees as well as for drafting the labour conditions. It is important for an HR department to be in control of the hiring process and the retiring process. In these processes risks occur from a payroll taxes perspective. The HR department manages the applicable labour conditions of the individual employee during the employment. At the beginning of an employment various labour conditions are granted to the employee. The information then has to be processed as a mutation into the payroll administration. In addition, the various labour conditions can change and employees can decide during the employment to make use of a new labour condition or can be granted new benefits. This means that various mutations have to be processed for the individual employee during his employment. Within the responsibility of developing new labour conditions the HR department will have to bear in mind the possible tax consequences. Therefore, it is important to analyse the tax consequences of the employee handbook or manual, but also to verify the tax consequences of individuals as well as collective labour agreements.

The HR department makes use of a HR system to include all information concerning employees such as the personal data, benefits, education etc. We recommend interfacing this HR system with the payroll system. For example, when an employee moves to another house the controls have to be implemented that allow for tax-free travel expense allowances to be adjusted. Another example is when the employee is sick. The HR department is responsible for including this information in the HR system and to consult a health and wellness specialist but also to take a look at the benefits which can no longer be provided tax-free after a certain period, such as the fixed expense allowance, the internet allowance etc.The HR department is very important, indeed a key player in the payroll taxes processes. As a result, it is important that within this department a certain level of knowledge is available with regard to these taxes.

10.2.2.2   Finance department

The finance department is responsible for the cash flow between the employer and the employee and for paying the salaries to the employees. In addition, the finance department is responsible for the actual payment of the taxes to the tax authorities. The Controller or CFO signs off the periodical payroll taxes return before it is digitally sent to the tax authorities. After the filing of the payroll taxes return, the taxes will have to be paid to the tax authorities. To avoid penalties and such, it is very important to implement a process which ensures the payment is done correctly and within the obligatory time frames.

The process regarding expense claims is also often placed under the responsibility of the finance department. The employee has to provide the expense claim (automatically or by using a manual form), including the receipts, to the finance department. The expense claim will usually have to be approved by the direct manager and (for example) the HR department. The completed expense claim will then be processed by the finance department which usually has ultimate responsibility to decide whether or not it can be paid out without the levy of taxes. Therefore up to date tax knowledge is required.

In practice we see that the hiring of third parties (for example self-employed persons or hiring personnel via hiring agencies) is also a responsibility of the finance department. The finance department has to verify whether or not the hired person(s) needs to be included in the payroll. In this respect, mitigation measures can be taken to minimize the payroll taxes risks which the finance department has to be aware of.

10.2.2.3   Payroll department

Companies with a certain number of employees have designated staff whose main function is to process the payroll. Depending on the agreements made with the external payroll provider (if any), the payroll department is responsible for including the salaries and other benefits in the payroll system; keeping the payroll system up to date; processing the individual pay slips and year end statements; reconciling the payroll system with the finance system; answering queries of employees etc. Furthermore, the payroll department is (or should be) a conversation partner for HR to discuss the tax consequences of employee benefits. The payroll department is the link between the HR department and the finance department.

10.2.2.4 Tax department

Tax departments generally tend to focus on corporate income and value added taxes. However, the tax department can have a role in the payroll taxes processes for tax technical back-up. A tax department has an important role in identifying tax changes and discussing these changes with the other departments involved in the payroll taxes process. However, in practice we see that the tax department is not the department that has the ultimate responsibility in this matter.

10.2.2.5 Legal department

The role of the legal department is similar to the role of the tax department as described in paragraph 7.2.2.4. However, the legal department can also have an important role in noticing tax risks when it is involved in the settling of agreements with employees or with third parties.

10.2.2.6 Fleet management department

Fleet management is involved in the ordering and handling of company cars as well as the contacts with the lease companies etc. Having the disposal of a company car can – unless they are used for business matters only - be regarded as a taxable benefit for payroll taxes purposes. Pool cars also have tax consequences unless specific conditions are met. The administration of the company cars and the pool cars lies with fleet management which also determines the tax value of the car. This may therefore have an influence on the payroll taxes processes.

10.2.2.7 Marketing department

Companies are generally not aware of the influence that the marketing department might have on the payroll taxes process. The marketing department may provide gifts to employees such as clothes or company products. The marketing department is often unaware of the fact that these gifts may qualify as a taxable benefit in kind so they must become aware of the tax consequences of providing these gifts. The process should be designed in such a way that this department informs the payroll department that gifts have been provided, so that the latter can decide whether or not the gifts should be included in the payroll.

Marketing departments often grant benefits to non-employees. In principle, the granting of these benefits does not have consequences for payroll taxes. However in practice there is the possibility to withhold a final lump sum tax levy with the consequence that the non-employee does not need to include the benefit in his personal income tax return.

10.2.2.8 Procurement department

The procurement department is involved in the ordering of products and services for employees, for example laptops or tablets. Such benefits may well have payroll taxes consequences and therefore the procurement department should inform the payroll department when products have been ordered so that the payroll taxes consequences can be analysed.

The procurement department is also involved in the ordering of services such as the hiring of third parties. To avoid these being regarded as employees for payroll taxes purposes or that the organisation becomes liable for their payroll taxes position, a process should be designed whereby checks are automatically carried out. The procurement department should be aware of these risks and have a role in signaling them.

10.2.2.9 Global mobility department

The global mobility department is responsible for the global mobility processes within the organisation which means that they are involved in the short term or long term assignments of employees. The employees can come to the country in which the organisation is established (impats) or can be sent to a foreign country (expats). The payroll taxes (and personal income tax) consequences of the individual assignees must be analysed and carried out in a correct manner. Furthermore, all benefits (and expenses) of the assignees must be assessed on payroll taxes consequences. The global mobility department is the key department in this important process which influences the local payroll but can also lead to payroll obligations in foreign companies. Due to the need for a specific knowledge of international tax and social security rules it is important to have well-trained and experienced people working for this department.

10.2.2.10 Payroll provider

The payroll provider is responsible for proper payroll processing within the organisation. Based on the service level agreement, different kinds of services can be bought. This varies from only providing the payroll software (including updates) up to outsourcing the whole payroll. It is very important to ensure that the tasks and responsibilities between the organisation and the payroll provider are clear. If not, there is a risk that payroll related tasks are not picked up by any party at all. There are several payroll providers who each may have a different focus (dependent on the size of the organisation, the sector of the organisation, whether or not the organisation is globally working etc). The organisation needs to decide in advance what the expectations of the services of the payroll provider are. However, the ultimate responsibility always remains (from a tax legal point of view) with the employer.

A payroll provider can obtain an ISAE 3402 statement[2] which gives a qualification with respect to the internal processes and the level of control by the payroll provider. Such a statement can be issued by an auditing organisation (reference is made to paragraph 7.3.2.1).

10.2.2.11 Internal audit

The internal audit team can be involved in the testing of the payroll tax processes. This will be discussed in paragraph 10.4 in more detail. Most international organisations have an internal audit team, which verifies whether or not the organisation complies with the internal processes and regulations. We recommend companies who have an internal audit team to consider including the internal audit team in the tax control framework to test the payroll tax processes.

10.2.2.12 The tax authorities

The tax authorities can also influence the payroll tax processes of an organisation. There are possibilities to agree on advanced tax rulings with respect to payroll tax related matters. These advanced tax rulings may influence the processes and the controls that the organisation implements. The tax authorities can decide to reduce their level of auditing based on the level of control of the organisation and the processes that are implemented. From our point of view, having a strong relationship with the tax authorities based on transparency and trust is crucial.

10.2.2.13 Third parties

There are also third parties other than the payroll provider and the tax authorities which have an influence on the payroll tax processes. They include the lease company, insurance company, pension provider etc. These companies provide services to the organisation in relation to a specific benefit for the employees. Suppliers of the organisation may also provide benefits to the employees. These benefits may qualify as 'wage of a third party' which results in a withholding duty for the organisation (the employer).

Another important third party is the employment agency from which the organisation (temporary) can hire employees. To minimise payroll tax liabilities for the organisation, we recommend hiring employees of certified employment agencies only. In the Netherlands a so-called NEN 4400-01 (for Dutch employment agencies) or NEN 4400-02 (for foreign employment agencies) certificates are issued by the Stichting Normering Arbeid (hereafter: SNA).[3] Before issuing such a certificate (and also periodically after the certificate is issued) the SNA performs several checks, such as whether the payroll taxes are withheld and paid to the tax authorities and whether

---

2 http://www.isae3402.nl/payroll
3 http://www.normeringarbeid.nl/default.aspx

the identification requirements with respect to the employees are met etc. Consequently, contracting a certified employment agency can minimise some of the payroll tax risks.

10.2.2.14 Other

Below we identify other parties which may have an influence on the payroll tax process of an organisation. Trade unions for example may influence the specific employment benefits. When a collective labour agreement is applicable, it may be mandatory for an organisation to provide a certain level of employment benefits. The same is applicable when the organisation has an Employees Council which has to be consulted when the employment benefits change on a company level.[4]

Foreign entities of the organisation may also influence employee benefits. The headquarters of a multinational established in another country may decide that the employees should be granted a specific benefit regardless of the tax consequences. These benefits will have to be included in the payroll of the organisation as they will be regarded as taxable wage provided by the organisation. To maintain an accurate and complete payroll, a process should be designed to ensure the organisation is always informed when certain benefits are granted. For example, employee stock option plans provided and arranged by the holding company need to be included in the payroll of the specific organisation.[5]

10.2.3 Conclusion

In any process in which a payroll tax risk occurs, several of the discussed key players are often involved. To ensure maintaining 'in control' of payroll taxes risks, it is of great importance in the transition process from one key player to the other key player to have a clear understanding of the roles and responsibilities.

How payroll taxes in main lines are organised and which key players are involved differs per organisation. Every organisation, however, has to look further than the payroll administration to determine whether it is 'in control' of payroll tax.

10.3 Risks and control

10.3.1 Framework

An organisation should have the objective of complying with laws and regulations in the field of payroll tax and based on this, file an acceptable payroll tax return. To achieve this objective the first step is to map out the most important inherent risks. Inherent risks are risks that can occur within the organisation; this is without taking into account any control measures already in place. At a later stage it will be

---

4 http://www.rijksoverheid.nl/onderwerpen/ondernemingsraad/rechten-ondernemingsraad
5 Decision of the Supreme Court, 1 November 2000, BNB 2001/82.

determined how the organisation is in control of these inherent risks. With respect to the remaining risks, additional control measures can be taken depending on the level of control that the organisation wants to achieve.

In practice, various inherent risks arise at all organisations that are considered as an employer (withholding agent). Therefore it may not be necessary to perform an extensive analysis to determine whether these inherent risks arise at the organisation. These inherent risks should, in all circumstances, be included in the payroll tax control framework. Furthermore, there are inherent risks that only arise within a specific type of organisation. With respect to these specific risks, an additional analysis will have to be made.

10.3.2 Inherent risks

We identify the inherent risks that are most applicable to the majority of international operating organisations with employees. The most important inherent risks arising in almost every organisation relate to:
- Payroll administration
- Payroll tax knowledge
- Communication (given the large number of key players involved)
- Hiring new employees
- Firing/retiring of employees
- HR and payroll mutations
- Expenses
- Global mobility
- Hiring third parties
- Company car
- Wages in kind
- Work related Cost Regulation (specific legislation for the Netherlands)

Once it has been determined which of the above risks may exist, a framework can be created (with a focus on the identified risks) on which the organisation can become 'in control' of payroll taxes.

In the following paragraphs the focus will be made on the most important inherent payroll taxes risks. The various possibilities to maintain control of several inherent payroll taxes risks will be discussed. Such possibilities are based on practical experiences of professionals in the field. Of course there is a possibility that these measures may not be suitable for every organisation.

10.3.2.1 Payroll administration

As previously mentioned, in order to be in control of payroll tax, merely analysing risks that arise within the process of the payroll administration is not sufficient. This does not however, mean that the processes relating to the payroll administration are not an essential part of the payroll tax control framework.

During the execution process of the monthly (or four weekly) activities within the payroll administration, the following (most important) inherent risks usually arise:
- Incorrect input of mutations within the payroll administration
- Incorrect processing of the periodical mutations through the system
- Incorrect processing of the payroll administration data in the financial administration
- Incorrect parameters in the payroll administration system
- Filing of the payroll taxes return is not in time
- Payment of payroll tax is not in time

Companies have often outsourced (part of) the activities (with respect to the payroll administration process) to an external party. This external party often takes over the processing the monthly mutations in the system. It provides the output such as pay slips and cumulative wage tax statements and often takes care of sending the payroll taxes return to the tax authorities. These external parties also make sure that the non-company specific parameters in the payroll administration are up to date. The employer-specific parameters are provided and processed by the external party such as the Statement Employment continuation fund (Werkhervattingskas). By outsourcing (part) of the payroll administration, several inherent risks can be controlled depending on the quality of the input provided by the external party. The company can request an ISAE 3402 Type 2-statement from the external party. With such a statement an external accountant states that the services provided by the external party can be trusted and that the external party is in control in relation to the processing of the payroll administration.

The ISAE 3402 Type 2-statement provides a degree of assurance that the external party is in control of the processes. This does not mean however, that the company is not responsible for the correct processing. The company must therefore implement control measures in the payroll administration process. These control measures also have to be implemented in relation to the part of the process that is outsourced and for which an ISAE 3402 Type 2-statement is available.

To prevent the input relating to mutations from being processed incorrectly, the most thorough control measures must be implemented. The input should be verified and recorded. This way the process can be tested as to whether it has been followed. Furthermore, the organisation must perform a check on the output. Practical experience shows that the organisation must perform an annual check on the parameters that the external party have used.

To ensure the most effective organised payroll administration process it is of great importance that a process description is in place and that the checks are recorded. To determine the correctness of the journal entries it is important to reconcile the financial administration and the payroll administration on a monthly or at least a quarterly basis. This reconciliation is often the starting point of a 'vertical audit' by the tax authorities. IT-controls can be part of this process.

When an organisation is in control of the most important of the inherent risks relating to the payroll administration process, an in-depth analysis has to be performed. Next to the aforementioned inherent risks, *additional* risks can occur on a more detailed level such as incorrect use of the period and table on an individual level, incorrect use of several bases and an incorrect use of the cafeteria system (salary sacrifice system). On a more detailed level the organisation can 'cross its t's and dot its i's' by means of an in-depth analysis in the processing of 'difficult' pay slips.

If the organisation uses a payroll provider with no ISAE 3402 or an ISAE 3402 Type 1 statement the process in the framework must include additional checks and validation to ensure the same level of comfort as the ISAE 3402 Type 2 statement.

10.3.2.2 Payroll tax knowledge

An inherent risk in the area of payroll tax is that the employees involved in payroll taxes processes have insufficient payroll tax knowledge.

Within organisations a number of departments are involved in the process of payroll tax, as described in chapter 2. Many departments deal with payroll tax although they are not always aware of this. The knowledge of employees needs to be enhanced in this area. This will result in awareness from the employees' perspective that activities may have payroll tax consequences. Furthermore, the employees can point out risks and opportunities, which is not to say that all employees should become payroll tax specialists. It is necessary however that at least one department within the organisation has specific knowledge of payroll tax and this should have the overall responsibility for payroll tax purposes. This department may make use of an external advisor to support them. This department can be the single point of contact with the tax authorities.

A way to enhance the knowledge of the employees involved is to provide periodical payroll tax training, provided by internal or external specialists. Furthermore, annual training can be organised for the employees involved to discuss changes in law, regulations and possible changes in labour conditions. Such training can be provided in the form of e-learning.

10.3.2.3 Communication

Another risk related to payroll tax (due to the various number of key players) is a lack of communication between departments resulting in tax possibilities and risks not being identified such as changes in law, case law, mergers and such like. The lack of communication can also take place on a department level.

It is not easy to determine the degree of control with respect to the 'soft' inherent risks (in particular the lack of communication). Such risks mainly depend on human behaviour. Furthermore, it is difficult to determine the overall effect of a 'soft' control.

The roles and responsibilities in the area of payroll tax must first be determined and recorded. In addition to a clear definition of roles and responsibilities it is important that there is communication between managers of the departments involved. Organisations must therefore set up a regular meeting (e.g. once a month) between the departments involved to discuss all developments in the area of payroll tax and record the actions discussed during the meeting. During this meeting changes in law and regulations and case law can be discussed. In addition to this meeting one department must be responsible for keeping track of changes. Clearly defined arrangements have to be drafted concerning communication regarding changes in law and regulation. Which departments should be informed with respect to changes in the area of payroll tax?

These arrangements should be recorded in process descriptions to ensure that roles and responsibilities are clear. Clear arrangements need to be made with respect to implementing new labour conditions or adjusting labour conditions. The HR department has to present new labour conditions to the department that is responsible for payroll tax before it can be implemented or granted to an employee to determine possible payroll tax consequences. The department that is responsible can determine possible consequences. Should the payroll tax knowledge not be sufficient, an external advisor or the tax authorities can be contacted. It is important that the communication with the tax authorities is centralised within the organisation.

10.3.2.4 Hiring new employees

'Hire-to-fire/retire' refers to the lifecycle of an employee within an organisation. An employee starts his employment and works within the organisation during which period mutations arise and finally the employee will leave the organisation. From this lifecycle the HR department provides mutations to the payroll administration. The responsibility to assess the tax consequences of these mutations differs per organisation. It is often not clear who is responsible for this assessment. When the HR department is responsible, the employees of the payroll department can act as a back-up. It is important that an organisation is in control of the HR processes as mentioned in the payroll tax control framework. Every mutation must be approved by a person other than the person who enters the mutation and the approval must be recorded. IT-systems can play an important role in this respect. The processes must be recorded in process descriptions that pay specific attention to taxes. Next to the common controls of the hire-to-fire processes, several specific inherent risks related to payroll tax occur which require special attention.

When an employee starts his employment, the identity of this person must be determined based on a valid and correct identification document *before* the actual start of employment. The organisation has to make a copy of the identification document which must be recorded at the personnel or payroll administration. Furthermore, the organisation has to request and record a wage tax declaration ('Opgaaf gegevens voor de loonheffingen') that is signed by the employee. When the conditions have not been met, a so-called anonymous rate can be applied. The anonymous rate means that the organisation has to withhold the maximum tax rate of 52% for the employees concerned. Furthermore, all employee insurance premiums are due without a threshold and franchise. A checklist can be drafted to support the HR department in which the conditions are included relating to the identification document that have to be met. Furthermore, a checklist can be drafted that is used by HR at the start of employment in which the fiscal obligations are included, such as making a copy of the identification document as well as receiving a signed wage tax declaration. The checklist must be signed by an HR employee as well as an employee from management at the start of every employment.

10.3.2.5 Firing/retiring employees

From a control perspective it is essential that the organisation designs a process for firing and retiring of employees. In the case of a firing an employee is often granted a severance package. Based on the facts and circumstances the tax consequences can be assessed and processed in payroll in a correct manner. There can be substantial tax consequences and subsequent financials risks when the severance package is processed and taxed incorrectly.

When employees have worked for an organisation in different countries special attention is required regarding the allocation and taxability of severance packages. It requires thorough knowledge to ensure compliance of the payroll tax return. These specific inherent risks must be part of a payroll control framework.

10.3.2.6 HR and payroll mutations

A specific process must be designed relating to the large volume of mutations between HR and payroll departments. In most international organisations different IT systems are used, for example Workday and Peoplesoft for HR and SAP for payroll processing. It is essential that mutations between these systems are processed without errors.

To transfer mutations between the IT systems an interface is used. In the framework a procedure must be included to validate the quality of the interface and ensure complete and accurate transfer of information.

10.3.2.7 (Fixed) expenses

A top risk area regarding payroll tax risks is related to expenses and fixed expense allowances which have to be mapped per individual organisation.

When an organisation grants a fixed expense allowance to the employees or provides the employees with the possibility to claim expenses, the following risks could arise:
- The fixed expense allowance should have been considered as a taxable wage component and as a result the organisation still has to withhold and pay the payroll tax.

– The expense claims have wrongly been paid net based on laws and regulations. The most important issue in this respect is that the expense claim is also part of the fixed expense allowance.

Based on the *Wet op de loonbelasting 1964* (Dutch payroll taxes Act 1964) the nature and extent of the fixed expense allowance has to be specified per item. This means that the allowance needs to be divided into separate items and the amounts for the separate items need to be stated. In practice this means that in almost all cases the employees will have to collect the receipts for a period of at least three months. The tax authorities may require such a costs analysis. When the basis of the fixed expense allowance is not specified, the organisation runs the risk that the fixed expense allowances should have been treated as taxable wage. Based on the number of employees granted a fixed expense allowance this can lead to substantial retroactive wage tax assessments including penalties and interest. The organisation can remain in control of this risk by means of a costs analysis to substantiate the fixed expense allowances and agree on a settlement agreement with the tax authorities. Furthermore, within the organisation somebody must be appointed who monitors that the settlement agreement with the tax authorities does not expire. This person must also inform the HR-department that the organisation has agreed on a settlement agreement with the tax authorities. In this way the HR-department can process the correct fixed expense allowances when an employee starts his employment or changes position within the organisation.

To control the potential risk that expenses are incorrectly paid net, the first important control measure is to draft an expense policy which includes the costs for which an employee can make an expense claim, so that confusion will be prevented. This does not however mean that all costs mentioned in the expense policy can be reimbursed net. In this policy, the costs made for business purposes which the organisation wants to reimburse are stated. It is possible that the employer considers several costs as business costs although, if based on the *Wet op de loonbelasting 1964*, these costs cannot be reimbursed net. An example is laundry costs during business travel. Laundry costs for clothes that are not 'working clothes' based on Dutch tax laws and regulation cannot be reimbursed net. An employer often makes the mistake of reimbursing these costs net. This has to be pointed out when monitoring the expense claims.

How the expense claims are monitored differs per organisation. In practice the expense claims are often not checked after the authorisation by management. Because management usually does not bear in mind the possible payroll tax consequences of an expense claim, the organisation cannot be considered to be in control. Therefore a specific department (possibly the finance department) must also be responsible for the monitoring of expense claims. This is beneficial for the organisation because the knowledge will be centralised within one department. This department must be supported by the higher management of the organisation because this department must have the possibility of addressing a wrongly authorised expense claim to the management (that authorised the expense claim). A wrongly authorised expense claim by higher management must also be addressed at the higher management level.

An expense claim must be checked based on the expense claim policy which should constitute/include a check on the following:
- *Authorisation* to determine whether the expenses are authorised by the management.
- *Business purpose* to determine whether costs such as lunches, dinners or parking costs were made for business purposes. The business purpose must be stated on the expense claim.
- *Receipt.* The original receipt must be enclosed with the expense claim to determine whether the costs were actually made and when the costs were made.
- *Tax.* It has to be determined whether the costs are taxable and whether payroll tax has to be withheld. When the expense claim is (partially) taxable, the payroll administration has to be informed in order to process the expense claim in the payroll tax return.
- *Conjunction with fixed expense allowance (this check is also part of the point of attention as mentioned above):* to determine for every individual expense claim whether the expense claim is not part of the fixed expense allowance of the employee.

The points of attention mentioned above have to be included in a checklist which will be applied to every individual expense claim. This checklist has to be signed by the person who checked the expense claim. When monitoring the expense claims it can be determined whether the process has been followed when the checklists are signed.

Some of the aforementioned points of attention can be included in an IT-system. There are IT-systems in which an expense claim cannot be processed without the authorisation of the management or the presence of a business purpose. Furthermore the IT-system can check whether the expense claim is in conjunction with a fixed expense allowance. When this is all available within an organisation the expense claims will not have to be checked individually by a separate department. Then it has to be checked whether the process of the IT-system works correctly and testing can be focussed on this.

The complete process with regard to the expense claims must be laid down in a process description which describes the payroll tax risks and accompanying control measures.

10.3.2.8 Global mobility

Increasingly, companies are looking for talent in countries other than where the organisation is based causing an increase of global mobility. This applies to both talent coming to the Netherlands and talent being assigned to another entity outside the Netherlands. Specific stakeholders are involved in this process which makes this area a top risk for payroll tax.

Even for organisations with only small numbers of expats and impats the risks can be significant. Therefore it is very important that this topic is included in the tax control framework. Tax policies are frequently designed and processed outside of the Netherlands, for example by a global mobility department. In the framework all relevant stakeholders must be identified and included. The roles and responsibilities must be explicitly laid down and monitoring and testing is crucial to validate if the data are accurate and complete. Internal audit could be an important party to monitor and test the processed wages. When errors occur the organisation needs to determine what the cause of this error was and take immediate actions to avoid it from happening in the future.

10.3.2.9 Hiring third parties

The following inherent risks in the area of hiring these parties occur at withholding agents:
- The employer hires third parties and may be liable for payroll tax if the third party is not able to fulfil the financial payments for payroll tax.
- The information provided by a third party (for example a lease company) is incorrect and incomplete. This information is used by the employer to process the payroll tax return. As a consequence the organisation files an incorrect payroll tax return.
- The third party is not a self-employed person, but this party is considered an employee for which the organisation should withhold payroll taxes.

For the first risk the organisation has the possibility to mitigate the payroll tax risks by paying part of the amount to third parties on blocked accounts or directly to the (Dutch) tax authorities.

With respect to the second risk the organisation should analyse, in detail, how information is transferred between the different parties and IT systems. The withholding agent will always be held liable or accountable for payroll tax should the information used by the third party be incomplete and/or incorrect. Therefore the withholding agent should include processes to validate the information of third parties. Specifically in the payroll, separate processes are crucial and essential in order to guarantee a high quality for the payroll tax return.

For the last risk the organisation may set up a process to ensure the individual applies for a statement (VAR verklaring) from the tax authorities in which it is decided whether the individual is considered a self-employed person and not an employee. We note that several conditions apply and that the organisation should ensure that all the checks are performed including the validation of the identity document.

10.3.2.10 Company car

The company car is considered taxable wage for payroll tax when the employee uses the car for business as well as private matters. The potential payroll tax risk related to

Payroll taxes 'in control' 10.3.2

the company car is an incorrect tax withholding which is processed in the payroll tax return.

Companies regularly have an agreement with a third party (lease car company) to purchase the company car on behalf of the employer. This third party provides information about the company car to the employer. The employer is obliged to include this information in the payroll. Several risks may occur in this respect. The information from the lease car company could be incomplete or incorrect. The information provided by the lease car company needs to be transferred to another party (the payroll provider). Errors often occur during the transfer of information.

As its consequences are included in the payroll tax this is considered a high risk for the employer.

10.3.2.11 Benefits in kind

A payroll tax risk occurs when benefits in kind are granted to employees and the value of the wages in kind are considered taxable for payroll tax and are not included in the payroll tax return.

Employees may (also) benefit from the activities of the company when the company produces or sells products to customers. In some industries the employees need to wear the brand of the company thus being encouraged to act as an ambassador. However, the payroll tax risks with respect to these company owned products need to be identified.

Employees are regularly attracted to the brand of the employer and therefore apply for a job. This may lead to a large volume of employee sales within the company. If there is an amount taxable per transaction the financial risk for the employer is considered significant. Therefore the risk must be taken into consideration in the tax control framework for the payroll tax part.

10.3.2.12 Work related Cost Regulation

The inherent risk in the area of the Work related Cost Regulation (hereinafter: WCR) is that the (financial and payroll) administrations are both incomplete and inaccurate thereby preventing the organisation from complying with Dutch payroll tax. The organisation may not file a correct payroll tax return when this risk occurs.

Given the many key players involved we consider the WCR as one of the top risk areas for Dutch payroll tax. As of January 1, 2011 new legislation entered into force: the WCR or 'Werkkostenregeling'. The level of detail of the old regulation caused many complaints from Dutch employers and therefore the WCR has been introduced by the Ministry of Finance with a less complex set of conditions. The WCR provides employers a general budget of 1.2% (2015) of the organisation's taxable salaries to spend (column 14 of the payroll) on tax-free reimbursements and benefits in kind for employees.

If the WCR budget is exceeded, not including certain costs such as specific exemptions and intermediary costs, the employer, in principle, has to pay an employer's tax levy of 80% on the excess amount. As the final levy is an employer tax levy, it is a gross percentage of the single tax rate of 44,50% (a weighted average of the Dutch tax burden).

In case the budget is not fully used there are possibilities to provide employees with tax free extras. This is only possible as far as this tax-free extra benefit is 'common'. This requirement (for being 'common') will be further developed by the tax authorities and case law, depending on how this works out in practice,

Reimbursements and benefits to employees which are not exempt or do not qualify as intermediary costs will fill the budget unless the organisation specifically appoints the compensation or benefit. There are many ways to value a compensation or benefit: the actual value, a fixed value or a nil assessment.

To comply with this legislation the organisation needs to analyse in depth the impact on the Finance, HR and payroll administrations. International companies specifically face challenges to ensure a complete and accurate payroll tax return.[6] Given the relevance of this legislation for payroll tax this topic needs to be included in the tax control framework.

10.3.3 Approach identifying payroll tax risks

Next to the inherent risks which occur at all aforementioned withholding agents, every organisation has their own specific inherent risks. An important phase in developing a payroll tax control framework is mapping and thereafter controlling the most important organisation specific payroll tax risks. We recommend to start with the top risk areas in which the most important payroll tax risks are determined based on a risk based analysis. We also recommend deciding on the number of risks included. It is impossible to draft control measures for dozens of risks and in addition ensure that they are all monitored and tested.

There are several possibilities to perform a risk analysis but most take the existing control measures as a starting point. The results of the risk analysis provide an overview of the remaining risks. Starting with a description of the risks that can occur within the organisation, without taking into account the already existing control measures, creates a correct view of the most important inherent risks.

---

6   https://www.nba.nl/Documents/Mkb/NEMACC/Knelpunten%20in%20de%20werkkostenregeling.pdf

In the process to determine the organisation's specific inherent risks the following approaches are possible:
- An analysis by the payroll tax specialist. By combining knowledge of the organisation with knowledge of payroll tax the most important payroll tax risks can be determined. The payroll tax specialist will often be an external advisor. This is not necessary when sufficient knowledge is available within the organisation. Internal formulated company specific inherent risks can also be verified afterwards with an external advisor or the tax authorities.
- An analysis of the (financial) administration. An organisation can identify risks based on an analysis of the administration. The most important risk areas can be determined based on the costs made by the organisation. Of course it is important to have sufficient knowledge of payroll tax. Take the case for when the analysis shows that substantial amounts are paid for the hiring of third parties on a yearly basis. Then it would make sense to consider this issue as a top risk area and control the inherent risks in this respect by means of the payroll tax control framework.

The above mentioned possibilities are not limitative and every organisation can complete the analysis in its own way. The organisation has to conclude whether the results of the risk analysis concern inherent risks or remaining risks. When the top risk areas have been determined the organisation can analyse the control measures already in place for these top risks. Determining the already existing control measures will show the remaining risks.

10.4 Monitoring/testing

The next step after the risk analysis and determining and adjusting the control measures is monitoring. Monitoring can be described as 'the course of supervision with respect to the correct working of control measures'. The results of monitoring can be used to optimise the working of the control measures regarding the inherent risks in the appointed points of attention. Furthermore, the internal control process can be extended by means of monitoring. Potential additional risks that may arise during the monitoring can be included in the payroll tax control framework depending on the level of ambition with respect to be in control of the organization and the materiality of the risk for the organization.[7]

10.4.1 Appointed points of attention

'Monitoring' of inherent risks with respect to the appointed points of attention can be performed in several ways. The testing can take place based on output by means of a statistical sample check.[8] But the organisation can also make use of system controls in which case it does not check the output but instead checks the system that produces

---

[7] http://download.belastingdienst.nl/belastingdienst/docs/leidraad_horizo_toezicht_fiscaal_dienstverl_dv4071z1pl.pdf
[8] http://www.aicpa.org/Research/Standards/AuditAttest/DownloadableDocuments/AU-00350.pdf

the output. The system is the underlying processes and procedures that have the objective of complying with tax laws and regulations.

A combination of both testing methods is the preferred way to be in control. By using both testing methods both the source and output of potential errors are assessed.

Examples of fixed expense allowances and expense claims are further set out below. The risk that fixed expense allowances and expense claims are not taxed can be mitigated when the following specific control measures have been designed:
- The organisation has a settlement agreement with the tax authorities with respect to the fixed expense allowance.
- A checklist is designed and applied to every expense claim. Based on the checklist it needs to be verified whether the authorisation, the receipt, the business purpose, the tax consequences and the conjunction with the fixed expense allowance is assessed and / or available.

Settlement agreements with the tax authorities often expire after three or five years. It has to be checked (every three or five year's period) whether a new settlement agreement with the tax authorities is available with respect to this control measure and this has to be included in the test plan. It must also be flagged within the organization that after two and a half or four and a half year the organization contacts the tax authorities to prepare and agree a new settlement agreement. Next to the settlement agreement it has to be determined whether or not the fixed expense allowance is paid out to the correct employees. The pay slip, for example, of a random selection of employees with a fixed expense allowance can be checked on the correct amount of the fixed expense allowance in relation to the position of the employee.

A sample check can be used to determine whether a signed checklist accompanies the expense claims. During the testing it is determined whether the system has worked correctly. However, just the testing of the signed checklist is not sufficient. It then has to be determined whether the checklist has been applied correctly and that the employee who performed the check signed the checklist. When the organisation is more in control the output control can be decreased to a minimum and is it therefore sufficient to test the system. The testing will be increased when major changes occur such as changes in work force, tax laws and regulations or when the process is adjusted.

When it has been established that expense claims are paid wrongly, the error made in the process has to be determined. Depending on the nature of the error, measures have to be taken of which the communication with the employees involved is the most important. This learning cycle has to be documented correctly. Being 'in control' means not only that everything is settled in a sufficient way but also to make it visible based on the test results. This leads to a change from testing based on output to testing based on the system.

10.4.2 Completeness

Not all potential risks relating to payroll tax have been included in the paragraph regarding the inherent risks (paragraph 10.3.2). Instead, it serves as a starting point to design the payroll tax control framework. When the most important risks are managed, the framework can be extended to other risks. Monitoring can be used to determine the additional risks for payroll tax. Furthermore, it has to be determined regularly as to whether the organisation might be exposed to new/unidentified risks.

10.5 Summary

In this chapter we have explained how a payroll tax control framework should be designed. The first step is to appoint the key players within the organisation. The roles and responsibilities of these key players have to be clear, especially when more than one key player is responsible for the process. When the key players are clear, the payroll tax control framework can be drafted in which the most important payroll tax risks of the organisation are included. The process regarding the payroll administration is an important point of attention within the payroll tax control framework, regardless of the payroll tax risks that occur in regular organisation processes. The control measures already in place of all inherent risks have to be determined and additional control measures can be implemented with respect to potential remaining risks.

'Monitoring' is an important part of the payroll tax control framework. Based on the monitoring and testing results it can be verified whether existing control measures concerning the risks are actually working. Based on the conclusions of the 'monitoring' the control measures can be optimised. There are several possibilities to make up the control phase. In this phase it is important to look beyond the risks regarding the appointed points of attention. The control phase is particularly relevant to determine other risks in the payroll tax area for which control measures can also be determined. In this way intention, existence and operating of the payroll tax control framework can be optimised and control measures can be adjusted in accordance with the system.

EDWIN VAN LOON

11. Specific issues indirect taxes

11.1 Introduction

In this chapter I will discuss a variety of issues in the area of Value Added Tax (hereinafter VAT) that are impacting indirect tax assurance levels within both the tax functions and finance functions. VAT related assurance issues arise for a variety of reasons originating from a wide range of root causes.

Before discussing some of the most common root causes, I will provide a brief impact analysis of indirect tax on corporate functions (11.2), a few of the most common known paradoxes and dogmas in VAT (11.3), the VAT risk assessment function (11.4) and some specific tax assurance issues (11.5).

After reading this chapter, I expect the readers to understand some of the paradoxes of VAT and the financial impact that poor VAT accounting and VAT reporting may have on assurance levels in general. I also hope that you will understand some of the complexities, pitfalls and do's and don'ts of VAT assurance.

11.2 The impact of VAT

11.2.1 General

VAT impacts almost every business process. In general, almost every business process executed is hit by VAT, since all transactions executed are subject to VAT or at least 'relevant' for VAT accounting, VAT reporting and VAT compliance. A business that sells a service or a product must issue an invoice to the recipient of the supplied service or the supplied good and is therefore obliged to meet VAT invoicing requirements. Customers, for example, expect that suppliers provide clear descriptions of the products purchased, the correct calculation of the net purchase price, and a correct application and calculation of the VAT rules etc.

Finance functions, warehousing functions, sales and purchase functions, accounting and reporting functions are therefore all impacted by VAT legislation and VAT compliance rules.

Failing to understand the need for connectivity of VAT functions with business operations is one of the biggest threats to acceptable compliance levels.

In this chapter I will discuss the VAT risk assessment function that will illustrate how impacting factors can be distinguished and how they influence the twenty first century VAT function.

Indirect taxes/VAT have an impact on many internal and external roles, functions and stakeholders of a company. Since an impact listing will never be complete, I will discuss a few of the most important internal roles and functions and the role of one external stakeholder, the tax administration.

11.2.2   Finance

The finance function is often the function to which more than the day to day financial recording of business operations is delegated. Often, sub-functions within the finance functions are created for master data management; monitoring accounts receivable reporting including aging reports and bad debt provisioning, accounts payable, payment execution, time and expenses recording etc.

Next to the recording of these operations, the compilation and filing of VAT returns is often also a finance function's responsibility.

In an international business environment, VAT rate changes for services and product categories sold, changes in 'country of delivery' addresses, legislative changes and/or the opening of a new store in both foreign EU Member State countries as well as non EU countries – all of these events will have some sort of impact on VAT accounting, VAT recording and VAT compliance.

Two practice examples illustrating the impact of a 'minor'(?) operational change or events:
1. *Company A is a subsidiary of a US based trading company. US Headquarters decided to move its European Distribution Centre from Rotterdam (the Netherlands) to Antwerp(Belgium). Both the tax function and the finance function in the US were unaware of the fact that Antwerp was not located in the Netherlands. As a result, all the invoices with respect to deliveries from the new Antwerp distribution centre to Dutch and Belgium customers were invoiced wrongly, the VAT returns filed in Belgium and the Netherlands failed to comply and many customers refused to pay the incorrect invoices.*[1]
2. *A US company is distributing goods that are sold via a website and purchased by European consumers via a European distribution centre In Brussels. The company has hired a UK VAT specialist, but he/she was not aware of the sales volumes sold per country.*

---

1   Without a 'VAT Invoice Requirements'- proof purchase invoice VAT cannot be reclaimed.

Since neither the finance function nor the tax function were familiar with the VAT concept of distance sales provisions that demands companies to register as a VAT entrepreneur in a EU member state when business to consumer sales volumes exceed sales volumes threshold, and at the same time failed to recognise (increasing) sales volumes per country in Europe, the company was exposed to major VAT claims and penalties in a variety of European countries.

11.2.3 IT and audit

An IT specialist is *not* a finance specialist or a tax specialist. The IT challenges of today's international business are huge. The internal need for standardisation, simplification and reduction of IT software solutions, consolidation of business reporting lines and regulatory pressure are becoming more and more demanding in terms of audit readiness and availability of VAT relevant data etc.

Another important issue is the international trend in taxation over the last decade to reduce corporate income tax rates and income and to increase indirect tax/VAT rates and income.

Ever increasing complexities of business operations, the geographical spread thereof and the legal, international, structure(s) and often inconsistent regulatory demands by regulators are major challenges for senior management to meet compliance obligations for VAT in a variety of jurisdictions. Meeting these types of challenges is not only a concern for senior management but is considered to be a mutual challenge for both IT and indirect tax/VAT compliance officers too.

One example: according to Thomson Reuters,[2] in the US, businesses had to deal with over 580 indirect tax rate changes in 2012 only. Imagine the burden of these changes to the daily operations of IT departments. Since many companies have chosen to relocate large portions of in-house IT functions to 'IT outsourcing' services providers abroad, non-compliance risks are increasing. In times of budgetary constraints, politicians might decide to increase VAT rates or to adopt new Indirect Tax legislation overnight, whilst IT budgets are under budgetary pressure. This certainly creates a 'pressure cooker' scenario for Tax Assurance specialists.

One good 'VAT' example illustrating the impact of a 'minor'(?) operational change or event on IT:

A new ERP system implementation by a multinational company is led by a new, Indian ERP implementation steering team. This team had unfortunately never heard of European VAT legislation and was therefore given a 'webcast European VAT basics' training of two hours.

---

2   See: http://onesourceindirecttax.com

Many years after the implementation of the new ERP system, internal VAT compliance test investigations identified a compliance issue in the input VAT tax code design, as a result of which over-claimed input VAT[3] had been filed exceeding EUR 50,000,000. The automated purchase invoice approval procedures failed to test the Effective (input) VAT Rates, as a result of which input VAT numbers were calculated over the gross invoice amount(s) instead of the net invoice amounts.

11.2.4 Internal audit

In the two previous paragraphs I have discussed two operational functions impacted by VAT, Finance and IT. It would be a mistake to say that sales and purchases departments are not influenced or impacted by VAT, since obviously they are.

Yet, for the future Tax Assurance professional, I believe that Finance, IT, Tax and Internal audit are the most relevant departments. The reason for this is that, in my opinion, VAT related issues are only issues when measurable.

> *An issue is not an issue until it becomes a measurable issue.*

The fact that input VAT cannot be deducted by a company that is not executing VAT subject transactions is not an issue. It is merely a VAT relevant fact, but certainly not an Indirect Tax assurance relevant fact. It becomes relevant when the strategy of the company changes and management decides to start executing business transactions that are subject to VAT. Of course, input VAT deductibility also becomes an issue when a business that used to execute taxable transactions only, starts to execute VAT exempt transactions.

In general, VAT issues are subject to measurement, likelihood assessment and the business need to respond to an issue. A VAT issue response will only be effected when these are material to the business's financial performance or the business's reputation.

> *When you can't measure it, you can't assess it,*
> *when you can't assess it, you can't remediate it,*
> *when you can't remediate it, you can't control it,*
> *when you don't control it....*

The main difference between the Tax (read: VAT) and Internal Audit roles when compared to the Finance and IT roles is that Tax and Internal Audit are supposed to

---

3 Input VAT: VAT on purchases charged by suppliers.
  Output VAT: VAT on sales charged by sellers.

challenge and judge underlying facts and circumstances of business transactions executed, whereas Finance and IT roles are supposed to *support and document* these.

The Tax department will challenge the business from a 'tax legal' point of view considering VAT related financial exposures risk, whereas the internal audit department will do so from an internal controls effectiveness and financial reporting point of view. Connectivity between these two roles is crucial.

11.2.5   The role of the tax administration

The importance of the role of the tax administration is, in my opinion, often undervalued. The tax administration does play an important part 'within' the tax function. External review and supervision that frequently tests the effectiveness of tax controls will be beneficiary to the tax and finance functions performance and the tax payers' reputation of a taxable person.[4]

Assuming that companies are acting as compliant indirect tax payers, i.e. as tax payers that file the complete volume of VAT subject transactions and subsequently pay the VAT on time, there is no reason to fear the tax auditor. On the contrary, transparency, open mindedness and constructive consultation with tax administration representatives can substantially reduce a taxable person's Indirect Tax risk profile and is beneficiary for a taxable person's reputation.

I believe that companies that communicate with regulators with comfort, will demonstrate trustworthiness in a non-verbal fashion which is immediately 'recognised and appreciated' by twenty first century tax administration professionals.

Unfortunately, this 'dream scenario' is not usually a daily scenario. In reality, tax payers in the small and medium markets area still fear the tax inspector, whereas many tax departments of larger multinational companies often believe that they are excused for not being in control of their ('international' and 'more difficult') VAT accounting and reporting obligations.

Sometimes finance and IT complexities that 'colour' the tax risks' profiles of a multinational company are used as an excuse, arguing that effective internal tax controls investments are costlier than bearing a tax related financial risk, especially when considering the (fair or unfair?) detection risk of non-compliant behaviour.

An effective Indirect Tax control framework involves internal and external audit roles in a rotational tax audit execution plan. Demonstrating effective tax risks and opportunity management also requires external supervision, review and confirmation.

---

4   A 'VAT' taxable person is anyone (company or individual) who executes VAT subject transactions.

Even more important:

Tax functions that do not manage opportunities well, will certainly not manage their tax exposures either...

11.3 Paradoxes and misunderstandings

11.3.1 The paradox: 'VAT is paid by companies that are exempt from VAT'

The essence of the Value Added Tax is the right of deduction of input tax by non-consumers.

Suppliers issue sales invoices for the goods or services delivered, adding VAT to the net invoice price(s). This VAT number is the Output VAT. The VAT number added on to the net invoice amount is paid to the government.

European VAT law (VAT Directive 2006/112/EC) dictates that a taxable person is entitled to reclaim the VAT that has been invoiced to him by his suppliers. The recipient, acting as a taxable person, of the invoice is entitled to reclaim the VAT charged to him as Input VAT, assuming that the invoices comply with the VAT Directive's invoice requirements.[5]

The VAT amount/Input VAT numbers can be reclaimed by the taxable person as from the invoice day, i.e. the day as from which the VAT has been invoiced to him by his supplier(s).

An important condition, other than meeting the VAT invoice requirements, is that input VAT reclaims are not allowed for goods and services that are not used for taxable transactions. Accordingly, no input VAT deduction is granted to companies that supply goods and services that are exempt from VAT.

A brief example to illustrate the financial impact hereof:

Company A is a company that sells office furniture in country X only.
Company B is a trading company selling only products subject to VAT.
Company C is an insurance company that only provides VAT-exempt services.

A, B and C are companies that execute all of their business operations inside the same EU Member State.

Company A sells the same type and model of an office chair to both company B and company C for EUR 1,000 ex VAT. The VAT rate is 20%. For the sake of comparison, please see the following cost comparison in table 1:

---

5 Article 178(e) VAT Directive

	Invoice amount	Income	Purchase price	Output VAT	Input VAT
A	EUR 2,400 (receivable)	EUR 2,000		EUR 400	
B	EUR 1,200 (payable)		EUR 1,000		EUR 200
C	EUR 1,200 (payable)		EUR 1,200		0

Table 1. Purchase price comparison of company A, B and C

Explanatory comments
Company A issues two invoices of EUR 1,200 each. Both invoices are including EUR 200 VAT. The VAT is filed on the VAT return and paid to the tax administration. The income amount, as a result of this sale to B and/or to C, is total: EUR 2,000.

Company B receives the invoice of EUR 1,200 and pays supplier A EUR 1,200. B reclaims the input VAT on its VAT return from the tax administration, the VAT is repaid by the tax administration. The purchase price of the office chair for B is now EUR 1,000, i.e. the 'net' invoice amount excluding VAT.

Company C cannot reclaim the input on its VAT return since he is not using the office chair for any taxable transaction. As a result, the purchase price of the office chair for C is now EUR 1,200, i.e. the 'gross' invoice amount. In essence, VAT has become a cost, making the cost price/purchase price of the chair for C 20% higher than for B. ((EUR 1,200/EUR 1,000) – 1)%

As you can see, the company that provides VAT exempt supplies 'pays' for the VAT, since both company A and B are VAT payers *and* VAT collector(s). Unfortunately, C cannot reclaim and recollect the VAT that he has paid to his supplier. As a result, C, i.e. the VAT exempt service provider, is the only 'VAT payer *not* VAT collector'.

11.3.2 'VAT is not a cost'

VAT is not hitting the profit and loss statement, so why bother about indirect tax, *especially for the Tax Assurance profession*, at all?

11.3.2.1 The European VAT GAP

Certainly for Europe, VAT is not only a source of income but a cost as well. Budgetary deficits are bothering many politicians all over Europe. The fact that large numbers of expected/projected VAT incomes are not collected has been food for thought to the European Commission for many years.

Many VAT fraud combatting initiatives, legislative changes, a variety of studies and the standardisation of European tax audit file requirements and auditing techniques have, unfortunately, not contributed in closing the gap between expected/projected VAT income and the collection thereof. The latest VAT GAP studies by the European Commission show that the VAT GAP in 2011 has been estimated at almost EUR 200,000,000.00.[6] (EUR 192,957,000,000 EURO).

This VAT GAP number(1), the fact that the European Commission puts a lot of energy into trying to change legislation to combat VAT fraud(2) and the search for new cross border tax auditing techniques and methods(3), in itself should be a wake-up-call for the tax function.

As mentioned before, a lot of research has been done to find explanations and to identify the root causes for the VAT gap. Some studies indicate that carrousel fraud and tax evasion are the main factors. Other commentators are challenging the data quality and integrity used by the compilers of the VAT GAP reports. Politicians, for obvious reasons, have challenged the effectiveness of tax compliance monitoring policies and tax audit execution(s).

11.3.2.2 The 'VAT dogma'

Let us step away from Europe's VAT GAP concerns to that of a Chief Financial Officer's VAT GAP concerns.

One of the biggest dogmas in taxation today is still that VAT is not a cost. 'VAT is not a cost', in a few words, tells the story of the hidden tax. VAT is hidden, by the fact that it does not appear in the financial statements as a cost or as an income line. As a result, little attention is paid to VAT related risks because VAT simply is not there.

Since we have seen that each year a large amount of expected VAT income is not collected in the European Union,[7] and because of the fact that we also know that VAT is not a cost for VAT entrepreneurs, there seems to be little reason to discuss the costs of VAT. VAT persons can reclaim the input VAT charged to them, the VAT charged to customers is collected on behalf of the government and subsequently the balance of the output VAT and input VAT numbers is paid to the government.

Even in VAT exempt businesses the costs of VAT does not appear separately in the financial statements.[8]

Some valid and unanswered questions to ask, in my opinion, are:
1. Where is the missing part?[9] (i.e. the EUR 200 billion VAT that is missing according to the EC VAT GAP report; see section 8.3.2.1)

---

6   Source: http://ec.europa.eu/taxation_customs/common/publications/studies/index_en.htm
7   Underpaid VAT assessment periods usually cover a five (or more) years span, penalties excluded.
8   Other than the VAT payable number in the year-end balance.

2. Who is bearing the financial risk of the missing part? Who is going to be assessed for underpayments of these VAT numbers?
3. What is the impact on the cost/income ratio's on equity and/or profitability of a company when being assessed for five years of underpaid VAT, interest charges and penalties?
4. Who is liable in case a company's financial statements are audited and the auditor has failed to recognize major VAT risks?

Before attempting to answer these questions, I will discuss the economic neutrality concept of VAT.

Basically, VAT does not impact a company's business decision in terms of allocation of means of production. This is only partly true, as we all know that many consumers living near the borders know their way to petrol pump shops on the other side of the border, where excise duty rates and VAT rates are low(er). The impact of increasing excise duties and VAT rates is undoubtedly an economic factor for both pump shop owners and consumers to consider.

Another 'economic reality' is the public's interest. Serving the public is what governments should do. In essence, the public is the most important stakeholder for the government. Now it is clear that a vast amount of VAT paid by consumers is collected but not paid to governments by the collectors/VAT persons, a VAT GAP of tens of billions of EURO's per year jeopardize faith in governmental regulators and supervisors and as a result might be harming the public's trust.

I am convinced that the public's willingness to accept and comply with higher income taxes might be under pressure when governments fail to collect large amounts of VAT. There is no doubt in my mind that the public's natural response, both in less developed countries as well as in developed countries, will be to increasingly become and act more tax evasively (why should I pay more whilst the other(s) pay less?).

This brings us to politicians. Economic neutrality is often challenged by politicians and political commentators discussing the impact of VAT rate differentiation, especially when lower VAT rate application is *not* applied to the 'necessities of life'. Discussions about zero VAT rate, low VAT rate or normal VAT rate application, on cultural and recreational services and even on chocolate teacakes,[10] are impacting consumer prices, business operations, profitability and competitiveness every day.

Yet, we all agree that such 'minor' details do not harm the economic neutrality concept 'as a conceptual framework'. Under normal, i.e. 'VAT subject' business to business conditions, VAT does *not* have a lot of influence on 'normal-economics-based' business decisions.

---

9   See: http://ec.europa.eu/missing-part
10 See: Marks & Spencer C-309/06

I am convinced that the dogma of economic neutrality and similar to that, of the so called 'absolute VAT' truths, have made professionals, regardless of whether they are engaged by regulators, audit firms, tax administrations or tax advisory firms – lazy, opportunistic and negligent.

> 'VAT DOGMA'S' AND 'VAT- ABSOLUTE TRUTHS'
> HAVE MADE US LAZY, OPPORTUNISTIC
> AND NEGLIGENT

Let us return to the questions and try to answer these:

Ad 1. Where is the missing part?
The answer is: nobody knows. Fact is: I believe, and I certainly hope, that we will all agree that the number of non-collected VAT is too high. VAT that consumers have paid to VAT persons is not paid by the latter to the EU Member State government(s). Assuming that EU Member States have implemented VAT legislation that enables them to assess VAT persons for a five year period, the total cost at stake is EUR 1,000,000,000,000 (EUR 1 trillion !?).[11]

In the meantime, budget deficits all over Europe are impacting on the daily lives of European citizens. I believe that reducing the VAT GAP and celebrating cross border VAT fraud combatting successes will be an important step in restoring trust in regulators and governments. If EU governments do not succeed in reducing the VAT GAP, the willingness of European citizens to pay VAT and income taxes is at risk and might even widen existing tax gaps in the near future.

Ad 2. Who is bearing the financial risk of the missing part?
Value Added Tax is paid to and collected by VAT persons. VAT is charged on each transaction carried out as an economic activity, whatever the purpose or result of that activity. The most crucial element is to understand that the invoice reflecting the details of the transactions must meet invoicing requirements to other VAT persons/ buyers to substantiate their right of Input VAT deduction. For the seller, an invoice serves as a piece of evidence detailing the transactional details and illustrating the reasoning behind the VAT rate applied.

Even transactions that are not invoiced, but for which a consideration is paid, are subject to VAT. VAT legislation demands that companies issue (VAT compliant) invoices, file periodic VAT income statements detailing their income per VAT rate on periodic VAT returns and pay the VAT in line with the VAT income statement filed to the government. In the case a VAT person fails to issue a VAT invoice, VAT is still due. In cases whereby a VAT person issues an invoice that mentions a VAT number that is too high, this 'higher' VAT number is still payable.[12]

---

11   i.e. an average 5-year assessment period multiplied with the VAT GAP number of EUR 200 billion.
12   The logic is that governments will not bear the risk of non-detection of over claimed input VAT.

Specific issues indirect taxes **11.3.2**

Summary: transactions, not invoices are subject to VAT. Considerations paid by consumers are supposed to include VAT. VAT persons, or more commonly 'companies', are collecting the VAT on behalf of the government(s) and therefore are the bearers of the financial risks of the VAT GAP as part of 'the missing part'. Consumers/ private individuals and tax persons/non VAT persons are not liable for not paying VAT in the ordinary cause of business operations.[13]

Ad 3. What is the impact on the cost/income ratio's, on equity and/or profitability of a company when being assessed for five years of underpaid VAT, interest charges and penalties?
VAT is an 'above the line' tax. This means that VAT assessments have a direct impact on profits before taxes of tax persons/companies. VAT assessment charges cannot be offset against future VAT receivable balances. VAT assessments as a result of over claimed input VAT, or underpaid output VAT, are levied on transactions executed during a VAT return filing period. In reality, a VAT return filing period is either a calendar month, a quarter or a calendar year.

Interest charges and penalties also impact the profits before taxes. Moreover, penalties can be (extremely) high, exceeding the underpaid output VAT or over claimed input VAT numbers by far, depending on the type of non-compliance. Penalties are often not deductible for the calculation of corporate income taxes.

VAT is levied on business transactions. Business transactions are often considered daily routines without major VAT compliance concerns. Business concerns, like Days of Sales Outstanding (DSO) management, and bad debt ratio management concerns are more popular and are considered by many to be easier to comprehend. Unfortunately, failing to comply with VAT legislation puts a VAT person/company at major[14] financial risk that cannot be offset against future VAT income statements filed or previous VAT income statements filed. VAT assessments, penalties and interest charges are thus impacting the above-the-line income statements. The financial impact of non-compliance risks are underestimated by many. 'Luckily' for them, regulators and tax administrations also fail to recognize the importance of VAT, as a result of which the detection risk, in reality, is small.

I believe that the answer to question 3 is:

In the past the risk for a VAT person/company to be assessed for underpaid VAT, interest charges and penalties over a five year period has been extremely low. The non-compliance detection risks while under tax audit(s) has been close to 0%. Today, the European Union, member states' governments, regulators and tax administrations are recognising that they have been failing in their role(s) as regulators/supervisors and will respond to the 'political' pressure as a result of publications like the VAT GAP studies. Governments must and will increase their performances and will soon

---

13   Tax persons always are VAT persons when they issue invoices with VAT.
14   'major'; VAT is due on *every* sale and can be assessed over multiple years (NL: five years).

celebrate VAT audit successes that will have a major financial impact on cost/income ratio's, equity, competitiveness and profitability of companies, thus contributing to tax persons' awareness of increasing VAT audits detection risks and exposures.

Ad 4. Who is liable in case a company's financial statements are audited and the auditor has failed to recognize major VAT risks?
This largely depends on the circumstances and typically is a question that not many like to ask and, even less, like to answer. In a few cases, companies have tried to blame auditors or have held directors liable for the financial consequences of unidentified and non-disclosed VAT risks that resulted in a VAT assessment that was impacting a company's financial performance and/or equity. In September 2012 a court of justice in Arnhem in the Netherlands ruled that an auditor who had failed to recognize VAT exposures, as a result of a lack of evidence supporting the 0% rate application on Intra Community Sales executed, was liable to pay for most, i.e. 80% of the underpaid VAT.[15]

11.3.2.3 The tax assurance professional's response

Indirect tax assurance specialists 'as if by nature' dislike dogmas. The standard reflex to a statement made like 'VAT is not a cost' by an indirect tax assurance specialist is:

'Are you telling me that VAT is 'income' to you?' (1) and/or 'I can't believe it, please tell me why, please show me?'(2); or in other words: please prove that to me...

That VAT is not a cost dogma has already been discussed. Yet, I would like to restate my belief that the only 'professional attitude' with respect to all dogmas and 'absolute truths' is to challenge them. I will do so by discussing the tax function's risk assessment function in section 8.4. and by providing examples of cases that I have been confronted with in section 8.5.

11.4 The (indirect) tax function's risk assessment function

11.4.1 Introduction

Before discussing indirect tax issues related realistic cases in section 11.5., it is important to spend a little time elaborating on the risk environment of the indirect tax function.

Assessing this risk environment requires adequate risk assessment techniques, since assessments without measurement of likelihood(s) and exposures, in my opinion, are not useful or effective and therefore meaningless. The first step towards adequate risk and opportunity management is finding more appropriate assessment technique(s) that provide quantitative results.

---

15   Court of Arnhem, September 19. 2012. Case number: 182198 / HA ZA 09-440.

Specific issues indirect taxes **11.4.2**

The majority of assessment techniques applied to the compilation of the tax risks exposure report are, foolishly, interview/questionnaire based techniques, failing to meet the demand for the quantification of risks and opportunities.

Without quantification, the professional judgement assessment about the need for disclosure(s) of exposures fails. Regardless of this, the fact that the likelihood of future cash payments is high, disclosing-of-exposures-rules, as we all know, requires not only likelihood assessments but also quantification.

Another weak element of this type of assessment technique is that VAT legislation is the starting point from which these 'VAT technical' interview/questionnaires are initiated. Especially when the VAT technical questions are misunderstood by the interviewees and answers are not validated, checked and/or audited, the usefulness of this type of assessment technique is extremely poor.

The assessment of the likelihood of future materialisation[16] of indirect tax related exposures can be executed by a (indirect) tax risk assessment concept that includes not only 'VAT legal' exposures to risks, but includes operational exposures to risks too. An appropriate equation or function for (indirect) tax risk assessment identification methodologies could be illustrated as follows:

$$TR = f(ITR, OTR, TCR, TDR)^{17}$$

In general: TR will be low (0%) when the tax function's design, operations and internal control execution meet all international tax auditing, tax accounting and reporting standards. TR will be high (100%), if the tax function fails to meet any of these standards.

I will explain the elements of the TR-function in the following pages.

11.4.2   ITR: Inherent Tax Risk (ITR)

Inherent Tax Risks are risks that result from an assessment of 'general VAT compliance and VAT controls' influencing factors of the tax function of a VAT person/company. Examples of the ITR influencing factors are:

National/international operations
The ITR factor is influenced by a variety of factors, of which complex international financial accounting /management accounting reporting environment is an important element. Other factors, like the design of the roles and responsibilities set up within the global tax function and the way global VAT relevant business operations and functions are organized are as important. The number of jurisdictions and (endless)

---

16   'materialisation' means the cash payment execution related to non-disputed tax assessments.
17   Similar to the theory of audit risk assessments: ACR = f(IR, ICR, DR)

varieties of VAT compliance obligations a company faces in these jurisdictions are typical ITR risks factors to consider.

IT and data
Also, the IT blueprint and the often complex and inconsistent tax and regulators landscape(s) are well known elements that influence the ITR factor assessment. Accessibility of IT systems' demands, and the storage and recovery needs with respect to underlying data, are often extremely demanding.

Tax department's connectivity
Connectivity or non-connectivity with global tax team(s) is a very relevant inherent tax risk reducing/increasing element. Since many tax management teams are relying on the professionalism of local tax teams and because of the fact that internal Tax Quality Review (I-TQR) is rarely institutionalised within tax functions, ITR is usually significantly impacted.

Soft controls, like 'professional judgement' (whatever that may be....), periodic meetings and/or interviews held, telephone calls discussing common and 'known' tax exposure areas are supposed to contribute to *the feeling or the perception* that acceptable tax assurance/comfort levels are reducing the ITR profile of tax payers/VAT persons.

'Feelings' or 'perceptions', when discussing tax assurance, are not enough, therefore, without further valid reasons for ITR reductions, ITR for 'connectivity' is set at 100%.

An ITR assessment outcome provides an answer to the demand of (large) numbers of detailed testing of (soft) controls executions, illustrates the need and potential volume(s) of repetitive VAT income reporting and compliance processes testing and may provide insights into the need for detailed investigations about the existence and materiality of known and unknown VAT exposures.

Mitigating ITR risk factors
- A reduction of the ITR seems to be fair when companies have demonstrated that no material tax assessments resulted out of tax audit execution in any jurisdiction for a longer period of time.
- Another ITR mitigating factor is often the governance, controls and compliance policies.
- In cases where these policies are solely 'risk adverse, highly aware/conscious of reputational damage risks' etc., ITR can be reduced.

Comments
In recent years many companies (especially multinational companies) are aiming to standardise accounting and reporting processes and procedures. Reduction of standardised IT solutions is often part of this type of so-called finance transformation programmes. I believe that ITR levels are reduced as a result of these programs, since

many of the IT and reporting landscape's complexities will be simplified. Simplifications will certainly contribute to a reduced ITR.

11.4.3 OTR: Operational Tax Risks

Operational Tax Risks (OTR) impact the performance of the tax department. A widespread misunderstanding is that the tax department is the tax function. The tax function includes all the roles and functions within a tax payer's organisation that influences the compliance and controls around a company's risks and opportunities profile.

OTR is influenced by a variety of both internal and external factors of which some are listed below (in random order):

External OTR influencing factors
- Cultural differences in the acceptance of tax evasion;
- Underpayment of government officials;
- Increasing numbers of VAT controversy discussions in increasing numbers of EU member states as a result of which resource availability is under pressure;
- Regional inconsistencies in tax authorities' compliance and controls supervision and auditing method application;[18]
- Increasing cross border automation of tax audit processes by tax authorities;
- Inconsistencies in techniques applied during tax audits as a result of which resource needs differ per region/country;[19]
- Governments putting pressure on tax administrations as a result of budget deficits leading to conflicting interpretations of international tax legislation and subsequent increased double taxation exposures;[20]
- Regional and international differences in discretionary power execution by tax inspectors;
- Differences in interpretation of materiality;
- Poor harmonisation of indirect tax/VAT legislation;
- Lengthy and costly court case procedures leading to uncertainties in tax positions;
- Inconsistent views by tax administrations on 'auditability' and tax books' requirements;
- other

Internal OTR influencing factors
- Limited availability of tax auditing and tax accounting resources capable of truly partnering with other functions;
- No ownership of tax controls per tax area;

---

[18] For example: differences in 'styles' such as: 'horizontal' monitoring versus 'vertical' monitoring audit styles.
[19] Ref: Horizontal Monitoring publications by the Dutch Ministry of Finance (see: www.belastingdienst.nl – Horizontaal Toezicht)
[20] Source: page 1 of the second report of EY's global 2014 Tax Risk and Controversy Survey

- Lacking of continuous controls monitoring technology for taxes;
- Search for cost savings within finance function operations, potentially contradicting the need for reputational risks management controls improvement needs;
- Lack of meaningful connectivity between tax, finance, internal audit and IT functions;
- Knowledge gaps leading to poor communications between previously mentioned functions/departments:
- Data quality and data integrity levels are not tested and therefore 'unknown';
- Lacking of a tax technology strategy or roadmap;
- Unclear definition of tax team(s) performance measurements and monitoring thereof;
- other

Comments
Especially in the area of VAT risk assessments, the OTR rate is set high.

The main, or most common, reasoning behind this is that VAT compliance is considered to be a 'delegated' responsibility of local finance functions and sometimes even of 'outsourced' functions, like external accounts payable services providers.

Another important reason for increased OTR rates is that VAT persons/companies tend to believe that VAT compliance levels are strongly impacted by their capability of meeting the EU Directive's invoice requirements. The latter are 'obviously' met, since buyers will challenge 'our' level of invoice requirements compliance too, safeguarding that they will not endanger their right of input VAT deduction too... etc.

Unfortunately these considerations, although understandable, are obviously not assurance-proof and can only lead to high(er) OTR ratings.

11.4.4 TCR: Tax Controls Risk

TCR is perhaps the most complex element of a tax risk assessment (TR) function.

The Tax Controls Risk for VAT is the risk that a VAT person/company bears as a result of insufficient internal tax controls design, failing automated and semi-automated VAT exemption reporting and lacking internal VAT controls execution.

VAT controls execution is often a delegated responsibility for business unit leaders. Unfortunately, instructions for the execution of automated and/or manual VAT controls are unclear, do not make sense, or do not exceed 'VAT controls for Dummies'[21] levels. Monitoring instruments, automated VAT treatment inconsistency tests and supporting the need to challenge the effectiveness of tax controls execution by the tax department at head office barely exist. Repetitive VAT audit execution by an Internal

---

21 An example: when a country increases the standard VAT rate, the tax code must be 'adjusted'.

Specific issues indirect taxes   **11.5.1**

Audit department is almost never institutionalised in an effective way[22] and even worse: regular internal tax audit execution is often not even part of the 'general' tax control framework.

Mitigating TCR risk factors
- Tax compliance processes and procedures documentation and web-based workflow solutions, thus reducing the chances of late filing risks related exposures to penalties;
- Tax-engines implementation that provide 'daily' inconsistency reports about input VAT accounting and reporting execution

Additional comments
See ITR

11.4.5   TDR: Tax Detection Risk

The Tax Detection Risk (TDR) is the risk that a company fails to disclose financially material tax exposures, with respect to either unknown tax risks and/or known tax risks of which the likelihood of being challenged during an audit is unrealistically understated. Unknown tax risks may exist when ineffective internal tax controls and internal tax audit execution(s) come together.

Twenty first century governance standards all meet modern tax exposure disclosing standards, thus meeting the need of shareholders for reduced risks of 'financially unpleasant' surprises originating from (many) years back. As a result, tax risk management policies, with respect to Tax Detection Risks, are usually set at 100% due to the fact that it is commonly accepted to believe that tax risk can be disclosed without any reluctance from stakeholders, including tax administrations.

Comments
The TDR is set at 100

11.5   Indirect tax issues

11.5.1   Introduction

In this section I will discuss a few common, realistic, VAT issues that can influence (VAT-) accounting and reporting and that are often overlooked by auditors/tax auditors and regulators. I will *not* provide any judgment or comment on the question of whether these issues, in my personal opinion, are evasive or fraudulent.

---

22   Meaning: real tax audit execution instead of annual questionnaires type of reporting.

11.5.2 Direct debits and credits

The execution of business transactions is part of the daily routine for VAT persons/companies. Often, especially in Business to Consumer trade activities and in cases whereby the recipients of services or goods supplied are not allowed to reclaim input VAT, the legal obligation to meet standard invoice requirements for VAT is not perceived as an important issue.

Identification and scrutiny of direct debits and credits in the VAT compliance processes is often overseen in these situations.

Case
A health insurance company repays health care expenses claimed by individuals and collects its health insurance premiums income from a large population of private individuals.

Health insurance transactions are exempt from VAT.[23] VAT is therefore not accounted for by insurance companies, since VAT is always considered a cost. Disregarding input VAT numbers in healthcare expense-claims accounting has resulted in an inconsistent VAT cost element risk for many insurance companies. The following case illustrates that.

Company A sells medical products to private individuals and charges the normal VAT rate of 20% on its invoices. Company B 'sells' the same medical products and charges 6% VAT on its invoices. The gross price, i.e. the price including VAT is EUR 100.

A private *individual* (Mrs. C.) has bought two products of the same brand (product X), one product from company A, one product from company B. The costs of the products are claimed back from the insurance company which agrees to repay Mrs. C.

Table 2 shows the impact of the different VAT rates applied.

	Mrs C.	Net income: (ex VAT)	VAT paid:	Cost for insurance company	VAT income (+) Loss (-):
	EUR	EUR	EUR	EUR	EUR
Health care expenses	200.00	–	–	200.00	–
Company A	n.a.	83.33	16.67	100.00	0
Company B	n.a.	94.34	5.66	100.00	10.99
Paid by health insurance company	–200.00			–	
Balance:	0.00	177.67	23.33	200.00	10.99

Table 2. Impact of different VAT rates

At first sight the only party that suffers a (VAT income) loss is the tax administration.

---

23 Article 135 to 137 VAT Directive

Assuming that the product is indeed subject to the standard VAT rate of 20%, an additional 'income win' by company B of EUR 10.99 is made, whereas a VAT income loss of EUR 10.99 of underpaid output VAT is the financial impact for the tax administration.

When we assume that company B is charging the correct VAT rate of 6% on the net sale amount of the product, company B has gained a much better 'competitive pricing' position compared to A. Assuming that A has 'failed' to recognise the 'opportunity' to apply the 6% VAT rate, B can reduce his sales price to EUR 88.33 without harming his net income compared to A (EUR 88.33/1.06 = EUR 83.33).

Notes
The likelihood of tax administrations executing VAT audits with VAT exempt companies, as I have experienced in the Netherlands, is remote. I have discussed this phenomenon with a variety of tax audit professionals engaged by the Dutch Ministry of Finance, of which many responded to me in disbelief and/or denial, telling me that incorrect VAT rate application in a business to business environment is non-material and VAT never hits the P&L…

As a matter of fact, the reality is that VAT is an important part of the cost price for both VAT subject (timing!?) and VAT exempt services and/or product sales. As a result, suppliers will always and automatically seek opportunities to 'compete' with VAT rates and VAT exemptions. It is foolish to deny that this is not the case.

Returning to this case: I hope it clearly shows that company B 'benefits' from a reduced VAT audit risk detection opportunity.[24]

Comment:
I believe that VAT exempt companies, like health insurance companies, are not to blame for not challenging VAT invoice requirements by their suppliers. Yet tax administrations that consider executing a VAT audit at companies that do not account for VAT might obtain valuable insights that can be financially rewarding to them (and to the public).

11.5.3 Foreign VAT

In a business to business trading situation between taxpayers, input VAT can be reclaimed by the customer.

When VAT is charged on services or goods purchased by an EU taxpayer in another EU member state, articles 170 and 171 of the VAT Directive provide for the refund of VAT in accordance with the Eighth Directive, i.e. Directive 79/1072/EEC. The refund of VAT paid by non EU Member State taxpayers is facilitated via the Thirteenth Directive, i.e. Directive 86/560/EEC.

---

24 See section 8.4.3. 'External OTR influencing factors' on page 13.

A scenario that might be overseen by accounts payable departments is a scenario whereby non EU Member State taxpayers charge 'local, i.e. the recipient's country' VAT.

Case
A supplier from a less developed country, 'culturally' known for less developed tax compliance standards',[25] ships goods to the EU. As a service, the supplier issues two *non identical* copies of the invoice to the customer. One copy of the invoice is sent to the customs agent in the country of arrival of the goods, a second copy of the invoice is sent to the shared services center of the customer, which is based in Manilla.

The first copy of the invoice that is used by the customs agent for declaring the goods for importation into the EU does not show a VAT number. The second copy of the invoice shows the following VAT line: 'Subject to 20% VAT'. The net invoice amount on both copies is EUR 1,000,000, the VAT on the first copy of the invoice is EUR nil, the VAT on the second copy invoice is EUR 200,000.

The result of the 'friendly service' by the supplier for issuing two *non identical* copies of the invoices (as requested by the customer?) you can see in table 3.

	Income	Purchase Price	Input VAT reclaimed by buyer:	Output VAT paid by supplier:	Tax income loss:
	EUR	EUR	EUR	EUR	EUR
Supplier	1,200,000			0	
Customer		1,000,000	200,000		200,000

Table 3. Tax result as a result of issuing two non identical copies of invoices by a non EU VAT compliant vendor

Note: a variety of factors influencing the VAT risks profile of a company have led to a tax income like this.
− Cultural differences: the supplier believes he is 'helping' his customer
− The supplier, of course, also helps himself, since he will not pay the VAT to the government as he is not a European VAT person/company. The supplier apparently assumes that the EU Member State's tax authorities will not audit his books...
− Outsourcing of finance functions/cost reduction programs. Question should be: is an account payable clerk in the Far East capable of understanding or interpreting incorrect European VAT invoicing? The processing time of purchase invoices is usually less than 10 seconds...

---

25 See 11.3, Operational Tax Risks – 'cultural differences in acceptance of tax evasion' on page 293.

Comment:

The books of this EU company have been audited by the tax authorities. The invoices that show 'local'[26] European VAT charged on import transactions which are not subject to local VAT have been reviewed and approved by the auditor(s) that have executed the tax audit on behalf of the tax administration.

The unanswered question to me is: is the supplier the only partner in this 'deal' that financially benefits from the tax income loss?

11.5.4   Supplier/customer transactions

Some services, like hospital and medical care services as defined by member states, are exempt from VAT. In these cases, no right to deduction of input VAT charges exist.

When one party in a supply chain is *not* allowed to reclaim input VAT, business partners might be willing to discuss or negotiate pricing arrangements.

Case
A doctor is negotiating the purchase price of a piece of medical equipment with a supplier. Medical equipment can be quite expensive, as a result of which non-deductible VAT is an important cost factor. The sales company is willing to offer the doctor a special fee arrangement. If the doctor is willing to promote the piece of equipment to his fellow-doctors, a marketing fee arrangement can be arranged.

The purchase agreement is signed. The sales price of the equipment is EUR 500,000 excluding EUR 100,000 VAT. Annually, the doctor receives a marketing/promotion fee of EUR 100,000 excluding EUR 20,000 VAT (marketing fees are subject to VAT). Payment of the sales price is 'netted' with an advance payment for the marketing fee services.

Table 4 shows the financial exposure for a VAT income loss for the government.

	Sales price equipment minus marketing expenses:	Balance of VAT paid minus VAT reclaimed for company A:	Marketing fee income	VAT paid/ reclaimed by the Doctor
	EUR	EUR	EUR	EUR
Company A	400,000	80,000		
Doctor			100,000	–
Tax income effect (loss):		20,000		

Table 4. Tax income loss

---

26   Transactions normally are subject to 'local' VAT, when executed within one EU Member State.

Note: The sales company is liable to pay EUR 100,000 VAT, since the sale of the equipment is subject to the standard VAT rate of 20%. The doctor is liable to pay EUR 20,000 VAT. Marketing services are also subject to the standard VAT rate of 20%. Assuming that marketing services have been provided to company A, company A is entitled to reclaim the VAT charged by the doctor.

Doctors provide VAT exempt services. The non-compliance risk increases when doctors are not listed as VAT payers. VAT charged on invoices issued by doctors that are not listed as VAT persons, and therefore do not file VAT income statements, will most likely not be collected by the Government. An accounts payable clerk located in the Far East, at an outsourced accounts payable services center of company A, will probably post the VAT charged on the marketing invoices routinely as reclaimable input VAT.

As a result, company A 'by mistake and by routine' reclaims the VAT charged on the marketing fees and the 'unpaid VAT payable' charge of EUR 20,000 that the doctor has added to his marketing fee invoice has become an additional income for the doctor. The government/the public pays the bill.

Comment:
Supplier/customer transactions come in all kinds of scenarios. I like to emphasise that, in standard VAT subject trade transactions, VAT compliance scenario planning can also be financially rewarding to tax payers. Especially payment settlements, as part of invoice netting arrangements are subject to increased VAT risk profiles. I will demonstrate this by the next casus in section 11.5.5.

11.5.5 Netting

Company A is a retail organisation that sells fashionable consumer products in the Business to Consumers Industry (B2C). A seeks opportunities to reduce its financial exposures with respect to unsold products. It has therefore decided to redesign its Triple A located shops to 'Fashion Experience Centres' whereby producers can rent 'Brand Experience Centre (BEC)' sales locations in a number of cities. Monthly BEC rent installments are calculated by A as a percentage of sales. Daily product sales reports are monitored by A's automated cashier registration system(s), enabling A to monitor itemized BEC stock levels.

Company B, a supplier, signs an agreement with A, agreeing to accept monthly netting invoices whereby A pays out the total sales numbers, whilst reducing that number with the rent installments (the VAT rate is 20%).

A's invoice mentions the following (see table 5).

	Invoice totals	VAT paid by A	Risk of over claimed input VAT collected by B	Risk of underpaid output VAT by B	VAT GAP
	EUR	EUR	EUR	EUR	EUR
Products sold and cashed by A on B's behalf:	1,200,000	200,000			0
Rent installment (25% of products sold) netted:	–300,000	–50,000		*50,000*	50,000
Paid to B (including 20% VAT) by A:	900,000		*150,000*		150,000
			Total (loss):		200,000

Table 5. VAT GAP risk as a result of netting

B files its monthly VAT statements showing a net sale volume of EUR 1,000.000. As a result, B pays EUR 200,000 output VAT to the Government. B believes that he is still 'entitled' to reclaim the VAT on the rent installment which would be EUR 50,000 (EUR 300,000 * 20/120).

B's right of input VAT deduction can only be effected when B is capable of showing an Invoice that meets European VAT Directive's invoicing requirements. Unfortunately, B is unable to show such an invoice and therefore consults his VAT advisor. Supported by the VAT advisor's explanatory notes and comments, B obtains a VAT ruling that allows him to reclaim EUR 50,000 input VAT on his monthly VAT statement.

A pays EUR 900,000, 'including EUR 150,000 VAT' to B. Rather than paying EUR 50,000 on its rent income, there is a chance that B 'by mistake?' reclaims EUR 150,000 on its payment to A. As a result, the government suffers a VAT income loss of EUR 200,000 which is calculated as follows: EUR 50,000 (underpaid output VAT on the rent installment) plus EUR 150,000 (over claimed 'input VAT' on the outgoing payment to A).

Note: Netting, similar to 'intense' customer/supplier relationships and contracts, as I have discussed in previous cases, often leads to high risk VAT compliance exposure levels that are often overlooked. Yet, I believe that netting, as such, is not the real VAT compliance issue. In my opinion, the real issue is a lack of skills by professionals that leads to failures in recognising and detecting this type of VAT risk. At the same time, tax inspectors that are often trained as corporate Tax specialists, do not always oversee the financial impact and consequences of VAT invoicing and VAT accounting. As a result, netting often results in VAT GAPs.

Not much creative thinking is required to understand that financially rewarding strategy changes could surface when almost nobody recognises VAT exposures related to netting…

11.5.6 Bad debt accounting

A mistake that is very often made is VAT accounting as a result of bad debt provision accounting.

Unfortunately, many accountants annually assess the number of outstanding bad debt for bad debt provisioning without considering the fact that VAT in the account receivable numbers will always be recollected, either from the debtor or the tax administration.

Case
A total of EUR 120,000 of the accounts receivable balance at year end is considered to be subject to bad debt provisioning-policies. The VAT rate is 20%. The following journal entry is posted by the AR accountant (see table 6).

1.	EUR	EUR
Contribution to the bad debts provision	120,000	
a/ Provision for bad debts		120,000

Table 6. Journal entry for bad debts

As a result of this entry, income before taxes is incorrectly impacted by EUR 20,000 VAT. ((20/120) * EUR 120,000 = EUR 20,000). Since VAT was never posted as income at first instance, now suddenly VAT has become a 'non-deductible' loss. As a result the balance sheet's Tax receivable number is understated with the same number, since VAT will become 're-claimable' when debtors go bankrupt.

Accountants often argue that this scenario, in reality, does not happen. Unfortunately, it happens daily. Alternative entries posted *are* excluding VAT and show the profile in table 7.

2.	EUR	EUR
Contribution to the bad debts provision (ex VAT)	100,000	
a/ Provision for bad debts		100,000

Table 7. Journal entry for bad debts excluding VAT

The negative impact of this entry on income before taxes is correct, VAT is no longer considered an income factor. Unfortunately, the VAT number is still remaining as an

Specific issues indirect taxes **11.6**

outstanding accounts receivable balance. The net income impact is right, but the balance sheet still does not show a VAT reclaimable number of EUR 20,000. In case of bankruptcy, VAT in most EU member states can be reclaimed from the tax administrations and therefore must be accounted for as a tax receivable.

To ensure that VAT and Corporate Income Tax accounting rules are obeyed, the journal entry in this casus should be (see table 8) as follows.

3.	EUR	EUR
Contribution to the bad debts provision	100,000	
Reclaimable Output VAT	20,000	
a/ Provision for bad debts		120,000

Table 8. Correct journal entry for bad debts

11.6 Conclusive remarks

The most common VAT issues relate to risks that can be allocated to:
- Lack of VAT accounting and VAT auditing education programmes;
- Negligence of the financial impact of VAT related, non-compliance risks by legislators, tax administrations and regulators;
- 'Unexplainable' VAT rate differences;[27]
- Negligence of cultural differences with respect to fairness of taxation (our Prime Minister is accused of tax evasion and of tax fraud, so why 'blame' us if we 'act' the same..?[28]);
- Netting or 'strategic' VAT invoicing, aiming to increase net income;
- VAT charged by VAT exempt tax payers to VAT persons that *are* allowed to deduct input VAT, aimed to increase the income of VAT exempt tax payers;
- Political tendencies to increase VAT rates as a way to close budgetary deficits without paying attention to TAX/VAT GAP's;

In brief: in my opinion, VAT issues related risk identification, VAT risk accounting, VAT risk reporting and VAT risk management is about understanding the economics of VAT and about the willingness to challenge absolute truths and dogmas.

Risks related to VAT issues are NOT raised to (complex) VAT legislation.
   Risks related to VAT issues are raised by economics.[29]

Often the idea has crossed my mind that VAT is an 'EU-wide, generally accepted, money making machine for VAT entrepreneurs with an increased risk profile'. Will-

---

27 Why are Hungarians paying 27% VAT on consumer goods whereas others pay 'only' 20%?
28 In 2014, former Italian Prime Minister Silvio Berlusconi was sentenced to community services for tax fraud.
29 Bill Clinton's most often quoted phrase (Presidential Campaign 1992): 'It is the Economy Stupid.'

ingness to accept a very small risk of detection whilst benefiting from a high chance of 'collecting' taxes paid by EU citizens, for some tax payers, has proven to be an attractive, financially rewarding, business case. I hope that some of the realistic cases that I have discussed in section 8.5 illustrate this statement.

A minor change in the essence of the VAT Directive, which might be changing the wording relating to the right of deduction into *paid* input VAT, rather than *all, i.e. paid and unpaid*, input VAT by VAT persons might be effective. This offers tax administrations the opportunity to validate output VAT payment by the suppliers/vendors simultaneously.

Whatever our politicians will decide, new VAT Directives will come to us. Enjoy it, study them, but never 'believe' them, because VAT risks issues are 'VAT economics' i.e. 'financial' issues.

EELCO VAN DER ENDEN
ERIC VAN DER STROOM

12. Specific issues corporate income taxes

12.1 Introduction: Why is it difficult to manage CIT?

First of all, we have to admit that in continental Europe tax has been a legal profession in the past and managing tax relevant data never got the attention it deserved. So managing Corporate Income Taxes (hereafter: CIT) was deemed filing a return and waiting on any challenges of a tax administration, if any. Now days most companies will accept that more is needed than a passive reactive approach. However, in our experience CIT is still not a boardroom topic outside issues relating to the effective tax rate (ETR) and possibly some reputational issues. The problem is that CIT is often regarded as a 'stand-alone topic' whereby the necessity for cooperation and interaction between the various functions within the organisation is neglected. It is exactly the interdependency between the various (mostly finance related) functions within the organisation that is key for enabling a company to rightfully claim it is indeed in control of CIT.

In this chapter we would like to take you on a theoretical and practical journey on what we deem good tax governance around CIT. Theoretical because we believe that without a solid scientific foundation one cannot manage (tax) risks in a professional way. Why should CIT risk management be different from generic and financial risk management methodologies? Practical because novices in the field of risk management find it difficult to comprehend on the basis of mere theory what good tax governance means. Needless to say in this context that we do not believe that managing CIT consists simply of a check the box list with a top 5 legal CIT risks whatever they may be.

Managing CIT is in essence being able to follow transactions, extract proper data and report them in the required format to the relevant stakeholders following tax laws, regulations, international accepted accounting standards and statutory financial regulations. All starts with getting the relevant facts (and data) out of the organisation. Unfortunately for tax practitioners, management accounts and internal reporting standards of companies seldom follow the lines of tax. We see this mostly in the field of CIT with transfer pricing where late adjustments at local level (far) after the

closing of the month or even of the financial year is quite common. But also arbitration issues on debt or equity resulting in discussions on (deductible) interest or (non-deductible) dividends. If CIT is not embedded within the administration of the organisation, risky (late) adjustments need to be made. Managing after closing adjustments with prior year financial and tax effects is quite difficult. We often see tax risk management for CIT consisting of:
- Drafting a report or an advice justifying a position;
- Legal documentation.

However important these actions may be, they do not translate the CIT policy into business economic reality and is therefore an easy target to challenge not only for competent authorities with a divergent view, but also for external and internal auditors and NGO's.

Quite new is that under pressure of policy makers and public opinion rulings or special agreements with tax administrations are under scrutiny. 'Sweetheart deals' between big business and tax administrations are being deemed 'too close for comfort' or even worse 'illegal state aid'. The days that tax directors with their counterparts of the tax administration could play the game of CIT according to their rules within their comfortable closed inner circle are gone with the introduction of concepts like 'transparency' and 'fair share'.

Although we know that many companies have special arrangements with tax administrations it does not mean, in our opinion, that one is in control of CIT. It merely reflects the 'would be' (or could be) behaviour of the tax administration regarding a certain transaction, but only then if properly reflected in the company's administration. In other words, if the intended tax effects are resting on the sound pillars of economic reality and a proper administration. Tax risk management of CIT means embedding tax into the business administration and reporting cycles of the organisation. It should not be an incidental, stand alone, ex ante exercise.

12.2 The model

To enable the organisation to be in control on CIT, the organisation should have a Tax Control Framework (hereafter: TCF) in place. A TCF can be defined as:

"... the internal control of all processes and transactions with possible tax consequences. This means that the specific requirement to be "in control" of all tax issues – able to detect, document and report any relevant tax risks to the revenue body in a timely way - needs to extend to all processes in scope of the ICF (Internal Control Framework)."[1]

With this definition, the OECD makes a distinct link between being in control on taxes and an organisations Internal Control Framework. We embroider on this by dealing

---

1   Co-operative Compliance: A Framework – From Enhances Relationship to Co-operative Compliance, OECD 2013, page 59.

Specific issues corporate income taxes   **12.2.1**

with specific CIT issues in this chapter by means of a COSO based approach for tax, the Tax Management Maturity Model[2] (hereafter: T3M). We look at tax risk management by dealing with the following building blocks:
1. Business and tax environment
2. Business operations
3. Tax operations
4. Tax risk management
5. Monitoring and testing
6. Tax Assurance

All these elements should be taken into account when looking at the tax risk management of an organisation. We will go through these elements giving examples on what this specifically means for the organisation with respect to CIT. The CIT risks we come across in the chapter relate on the one hand to CIT technical risks and on the other to CIT risks with respect to processes, people and systems.

To name just a few:
- CIT technical risks:
  - Participation exemption and CFC;
  - Substance requirements;
  - General anti abuse regulation.
- CIT process, people and systems risks:
  - Timing and due dates of CIT return and CIT payment;
  - Data input of the CIT return;
  - Governance of an audit by the tax authorities.

These risks are seen throughout the chapter and are specifically dealt with in the paragraph Tax Risk Management

We will go through the six above mentioned building blocks of tax risk management based on the following case:

Assume you are responsible for the CIT in a multinational operating company. Your CFO wants to make sure CIT exposures are reduced to a minimum. How would you approach this, taking into account the fact that the tax department cannot manage tax by itself but needs to mobilise various functions within the organisation enabling you to get in control of the CIT.

12.2.1 Business and tax environment

The responsible tax manager needs to understand the context where he is working in. If you want to reach out to your organisation you first must know the organisation and secondly think of a process of effective communication. And above all you must

---
2   The Tax Management Maturity Model was developed by PwC and Nyenrode Business University.

understand the business. Elements belonging to the core of the tax environment in relation to the business, organisation and administrative functions are:
1. the tax strategy;
2. roles and responsibilities with respect to tax;
3. tax awareness of the organisation;
4. the system of hard and soft controls.

12.2.1.1 Tax strategy

Determining a tax strategy is not just a compulsory vision of the tax department.[3] This, since the tax strategy has an impact on the entire tax operation. The tax strategy, as determined by the Board with input from the tax department, is the magnetic north of the tax function of the company. It is the essence of how it wants to be perceived with respect to taxation and what it wants to achieve in that field. Therefore, the organisation and its operations must be set-up in such a way that the tax strategy can indeed be executed.

In general, the tax strategy of every organisation will/ should include the vision of being compliant with (tax) law and regulation. This seems a basic premise; have you ever seen a company stating that it has the strategy not to comply with laws and regulations? However, we do not often see how the company thinks it's going to achieve these obvious objectives. In a multinational dynamic environment this is easier said than done.

Four aspects can be distinguished in respect of tax compliance[4]:
1. (justifiably) register to pay tax;
2. file the applicable returns (in time);
3. file correct and complete returns;
4. pay its due tax (in time).

This strategy therefore has an impact on:
- The business and tax operations, as the organisation needs to set-up its business and tax processes in such a way that it is able to comply;
- Its risk management responsible department to enable it to discover issues, remediate or escalate and setting up tax controls to enable proper tax risk management;
- Monitoring and testing to check if the above is properly executed by means of (for example) sampling and controls testing;
- Tax assurance and the relation with the tax authorities;
- Key performance indicators and a performance measurement system. Are set objectives achieved?;
- A vison with respect to the company's reputation. Are we for minimization of the CIT burden or do we take 'the spirit of the law' into account? How do we communicate with third parties like NGO's, tax administrations and the public?

---

3 See also chapters 3.2.4. and 5.2.1.
4 Netherlands Tax and Customs Administration, Supervision Large Business in the Netherlands, April 2013, page 4.

Specific issues corporate income taxes 12.2.1

You see that the tax strategy should really be the basis for tax management, and more specifically form the foundation of the tax risk management infrastructure of the organisation.

The tax strategy should be fully supported by the Board and Executive Board. It is the essence of what the organisation wants to achieve in the field of tax. It is the 'raison d'être' of the tax department. It is the tax departments' license to operate and therefore a powerful communication tool. Do not underestimate its psychological effect. One of the biggest risks is that the drafting of a tax strategy is not taken seriously or the strategy is not executed. This will seriously undermine the credibility of the tax department and the company as a whole.

12.2.1.2 Tax roles and responsibilities

When looking at the tax strategy, the organisation also needs to determine the roles and responsibilities of the various departments and people with respect to CIT. For the group tax department in relation to other headquarter departments, these could be:
- Finance (data and reporting);
- Treasury (cash tax);
- Procurement (service providers);
- IT (process and technology);
- Internal Audit (control and monitoring) and
- HR (people and key performance indicators).

The organisation needs a clear vision on the division of roles with respect to CIT between group tax department and the (local) operating companies: who is doing what and who is ultimately responsible for data, local CIT compliance and local CIT risk management. The times that a head of tax could say 'we are a decentralised organisation, local compliance and statutory accounts are not my concern' are over.

In picture 1, you will find a suggested approach for the division of the roles and responsibilities

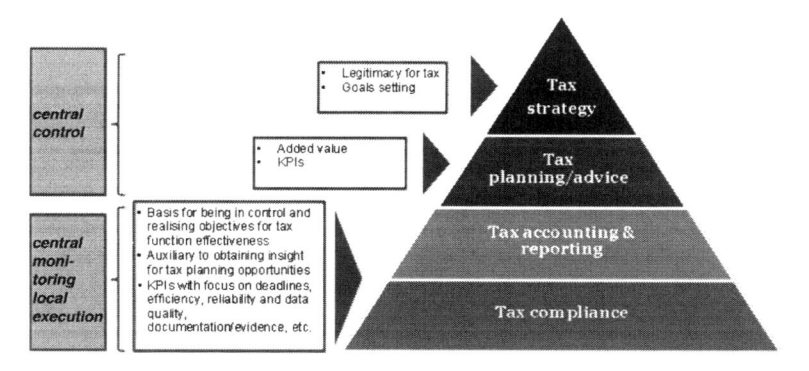

Picture 1: approach for roles and responsibilities with respect to tax for Group tax and local operational companies.

In our view the group tax department should be responsible for the tax strategy and tax planning activities throughout the organisation. With respect to tax accounting & reporting and tax compliance, local operating companies should be responsible since they 'sit' close to the source of relevant data for the preparation of tax compliance and reconciliation of commercial data with tax data.

However at Headquarters (hereafter: HQ) level, group tax needs to *monitor* if the operational companies are in control and executing the tax policies properly. More specific for CIT, this means that group tax drafts the tax strategy (e.g. in our example above: be compliant with tax law and regulations). Next to this, group tax does the overall tax planning for the organisation and can provide advice to its operating companies. Operating companies are responsible to execute their own respective CIT compliance, given the group tax strategy, and perform their tax accounting and reporting responsibilities. Group tax has to monitor by means of on sight visits and/or by means of testing the key tax controls if the operating companies have executed the tax policies and compliance. Most likely, group tax will do this in a joint effort with Finance and Internal Audit.

In order to make things work it could be considered to set clear objectives for local finance management with clear Key Performance Indicators (hereafter: KPI's) that can be measured. For example:

Objective	Efficient quality CIT filing process. Three months after closing local financial book years, CIT returns have to be filed.
Time	Achieved within 2 years from now <date>.
Monitoring process	Reconcile book-to-tax accounts on a half year basis. Mistakes to be remedied.

12.2.1.3   Tax awareness

As stated above, group tax has to interact with several other departments within the organisation such as Finance and Internal Audit. With respect to CIT, we note that a crucial element for ensuring complete and correct numbers in the tax return is that all relevant matters with a possible material CIT impact are communicated to the tax department or local CIT responsible person. In other words, is the tax function aware of all developments within the organisation that might have a possible material CIT impact? This requires basic tax awareness at the level of other departments. Not everybody needs to be a tax expert, it just simply means they need to understand when to contact the tax department. Depending the impact and materiality of a transaction this might also mean a process whereby sign-off by group tax is required, for example with respect to mergers and acquisitions, divestures or transactions with a certain impact on the company's effective tax rate (ETR). This may seem very basic, but in practice we see a lack of processes and structure in the field of CIT, resulting in errors in the CIT return and surprises with serious impact on the ETR.

In our case it means that at a local level a sustainable function is created that is responsible for executing the CIT policy and see that adjustments are properly booked and commercial data and tax data are reconcilable, stored and proper documentation is in place (service level agreements, required legal documentation and access to the transfer pricing justification reports and legal tax opinions). People tend to leave companies. See to it that CIT knowledge is retained in the organisation and not only dependent on (the minds and memories) of certain people.

12.2.1.4 Soft controls

Every organisation has its own culture with respect to compliance. An airline company will for example have a zero tolerance policy with respect to flight safety and maintenance. This kind of compliance culture is set in stone for the entire company. An important aspect within soft controls is the tone at the top within an organisation. With respect to CIT, we see growing attention in the Board and Executive bodies. Boards seem to focus mostly on the tax strategy in relation to the organisations reputation management and it's ETR. However, in the field of tax it should be about more. It is about the intrinsic will of the Board and the employees of the organisation to do what is right. Do I follow the tax policies because I have to in order to keep my job or do I follow the policies because I see paying the proper amount of tax as a part of our corporate responsibility and reputation. Do I feel pride in what I do or am I just working for a living. The better motivated your workforce, the more compliant behaviour you will see. Leading by example, setting the tone at the top and putting the money where the mouth is, is crucial in this respect. We came across many occasions were the tax policy objectives could not be reached due to the lack of a proper budget and/or mandate for the group tax department. This brings the tax function into an impossible position.

All the above items are part of the business and tax environment of the organisation and thus form part of the first basic building block for CIT risk management. If one is missed and not taken into consideration there is a serious missing link in the CIT control chain.

12.2.2 Business operations

This paragraph deals with the operating units within the organisation. As we have seen tax relates to many operations throughout the entire company, e.g. finance, treasury, procurement, sales, research & development (intellectual property), and human resources. Therefore, tax cannot be dealt with in splendid isolation by the tax department alone. The tax department needs to interact with the rest of the organisation and as such, it should be included in existing business, reporting and risk management processes. When looking at tax risk management in general, and CIT risk management specifically, within the business operations building block, we need to take a closer look at business processes from a tax perspective. Below we have set out an example.

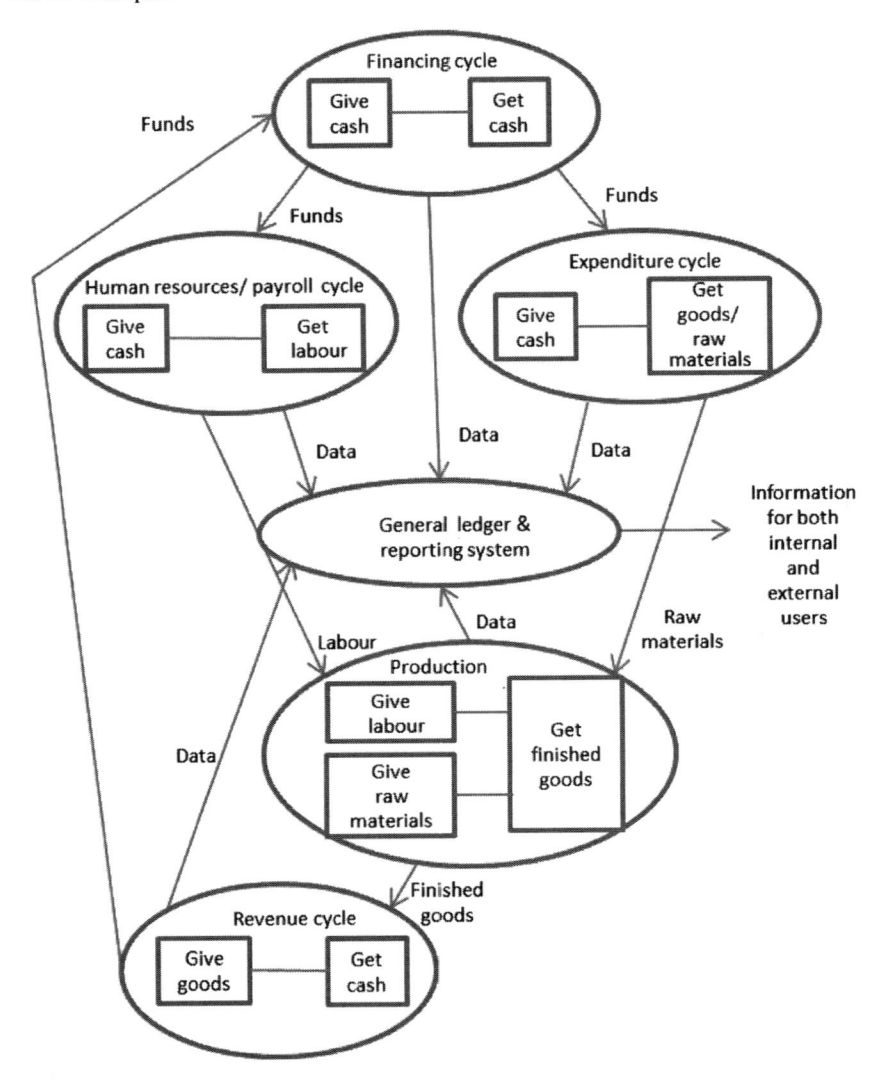

Figure 2: the primary business processes (Romney and Steinbart[5]).

As figure 2 shows, several primary business processes can be observed when looking at the organisation as a whole. These are the financing cycle, expenditure cycle, production cycle, revenue cycle, and the human resources cycle. These cycles feed

---

5   Romney M.B. and P.J. Steinbart, Accounting Information Systems, 12th edition, Pearson Education Limited, 2012, page 27.

data into the general ledger and reporting system which provides information for both internal and external users. Information from all these business cycles is key as it is the input for all output documents the organisation is (legally) obliged to provide, e.g. the CIT return. The information needs to be complete, accurate, provided timely, which all should occur in the most efficient way. However, as input is divers, transformation occurs and regulations with respect to the different output requirements are different, there is an information deviation ('delta') between most of the information flows. The Delta-model as included in figure 3 gives a simplified overview of the information flows within a company and all possible delta's that occur.

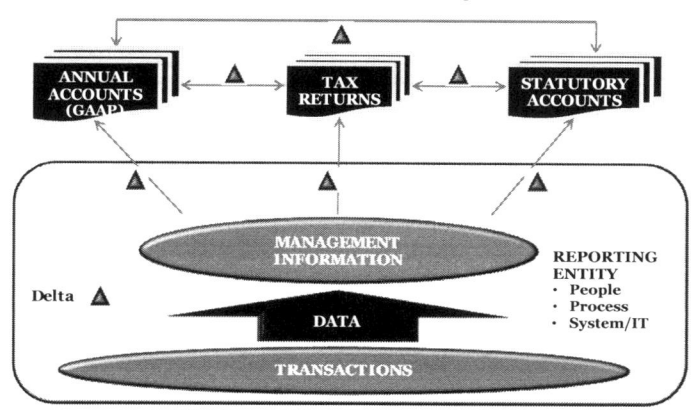

Figure 3: The Delta-Model, Eelco van der Enden.

The output the organisation needs to deliver consist of its annual accounts, tax returns and statutory accounts. This information is derived from the management information within the organisation. The management information is ultimately based on the transactions by (and within) the organisation and is stored in the general ledger. Between all the laws, rules and regulations (internal and external) related to the various reporting requirements (output formats) there are delta's (GAPS).

Within the business operations building block, the organisation needs to take a closer look at the CIT impact in the different business cycles. Following this, if there is a delta between the information the cycles provide and the data which is required with respect to CIT, the impact on the organizations administration should be measured and a plan of approach should be drafted on how to embed CIT into the systems. For example the concept of commercial profit and tax profit will differ in many jurisdictions since CIT has many (tax) exempted and non-deductible items that are not followed from a book or statutory accounting point of view.

The closer one is to the general ledger, the more easy it is to see the information is properly stored and ready for use. If not it will be an ex post data hunting exercise that is both time consuming, low value and high risk. For CIT this means that a proper taxonomy is to be developed that enables the organization to track deviations between local book-statutory financial-tax legal regulations and embed this taxonomy in the reporting cycles at the local level. An automated process is preferred since it will lead to more efficiency and less (manual) mistakes. This will be a joint effort between finance, IT and group tax, followed by a thorough training programme for local controllers on how to work with the new systems and understanding the transfer pricing policy. The fact that a policy is available on the intranet of the company does not mean it will be followed automatically.

12.2.3   Tax operations

From the business operations, we will now specifically zoom in on the tax operations in the organisation with respect to CIT. Elements of interest here are the business/ tax structure of the organisation, tax planning, tax compliance and more specifically the CIT return, and tax accounting. In fact, the CIT return is where it all comes together. Always begin with the end in mind.

The tax structure and tax planning are usually the responsibility of group tax. We have indicated that we prefer local tax accounting and local tax compliance to be executed by operating companies and to be monitored by group tax. In figure 4 we have included a high level example overview of all CIT relevant processes for the Tax Department.

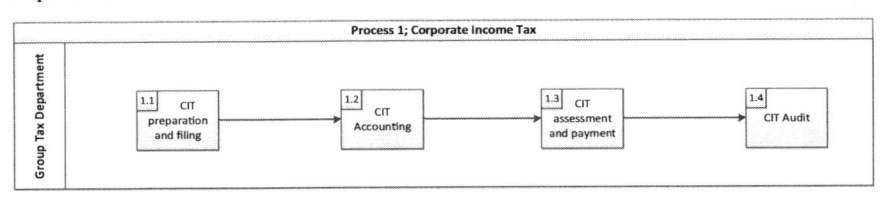

Figure 4: example overview of CIT processes within the Tax Department.

In order to dive into the specific risks within the CIT process, we will go into the following basic CIT processes in a bit more detail:
- CIT preparation and filing (1.1);
- CIT accounting process (1.2);
- CIT assessment and payment (1.3); and,
- a possible CIT audit by Tax Authorities (1.4).

We have included example flowcharts for these processes in the following paragraphs. A flowchart will provide the organisation with clarity on the roles and responsibilities in the process, can give insight in possible GAPS/ risks within the process, and the required controls to remediate these risks. This will form a sound basis for the organisations CIT risk management platform. The same approach will be maintained in the Risk Management paragraph, to dive into the specific risks within these CIT processes that should be reflected in the tax return.

Specific issues corporate income taxes   **12.2.3**

12.2.3.1 CIT preparation and filing

The CIT preparation and filing process basically drills down to the input of relevant information for the CIT return, the preparation of the CIT return and filing the CIT return.

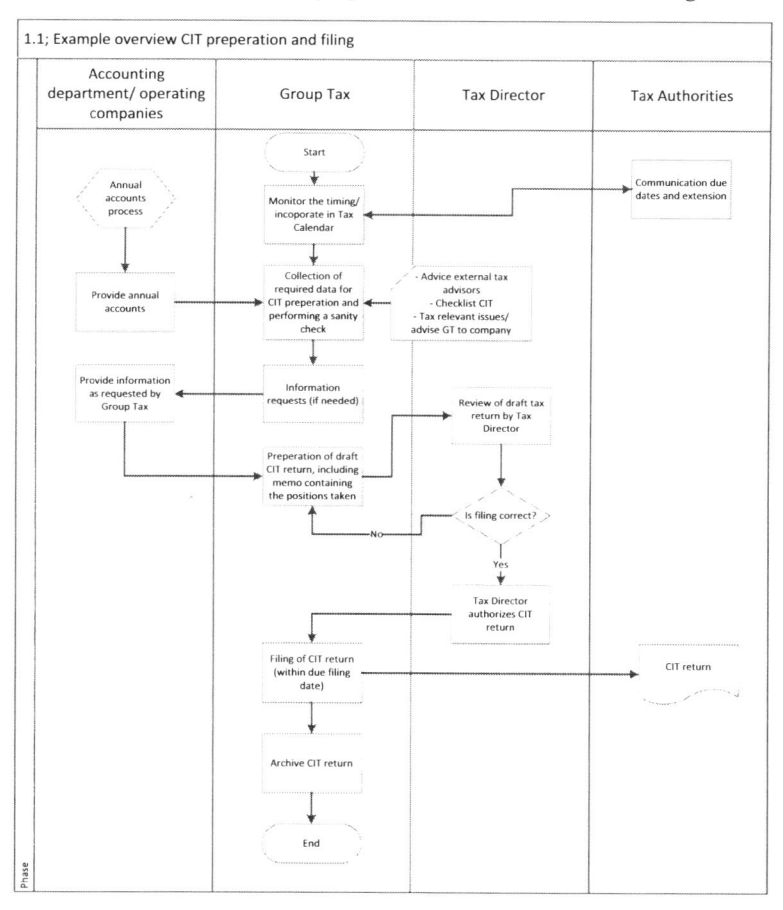

[Figure: 1.1; Example overview CIT preparation and filing — swimlane flowchart with columns: Accounting department/operating companies; Group Tax; Tax Director; Tax Authorities. Group Tax flow: Start → Monitor the timing/incorporate in Tax Calendar → Collection of required data for CIT preparation and performing a sanity check → Information requests (if needed) → Preparation of draft CIT return, including memo containing the positions taken → (decision: Is filing correct? — No loops back; Yes continues) → Tax Director authorizes CIT return → Filing of CIT return (within due filing date) → Archive CIT return → End. Accounting department provides: Annual accounts process → Provide annual accounts; Provide information as requested by Group Tax. Tax Director: Advice external tax advisors / Checklist CIT / Tax relevant issues advise GT to company; Review of draft tax return by Tax Director. Tax Authorities: Communication due dates and extension; CIT return.]

Figure 5: example flowchart CIT preparation and filing.

The flowchart makes clear that group tax is dependent on group finance for the input of raw data (the annual accounts). Group tax is also fed relevant CIT information to get insight in the relevant tax issues throughout the organisation. This is crucial since you cannot take into account what you are not aware of. We need to be sure of the facts and circumstances of the tax positions in the annual accounts and local CIT returns. This process can be copied to the local level for local CIT compliance purposes.

Cooperative compliance, an enhanced relationship with Tax Authorities is a relatively new phenomenon which is based on co-operation with the purpose of assuring compliance.[6] It could have a serious impact on the CIT compliance process. The basic premises for cooperative compliance is that tax payers provide timely and correct information to Tax Authorities, who in their turn provide (upfront) certainty on the tax payers tax positions. Therefore, communication with the Tax Authorities needs to be conducted on possible tax issues before the CIT return is filed. The organisation should adjust its CIT preparation and filing process in such a way that it has a transparent, auditable and functional internal tax data validation process in place. In practice, a cooperative compliance arrangement should mean that the filed tax return will correspond to the tax assessment of the tax authorities, thus decreasing any uncertainty with respect to the CIT return.

12.2.3.2 CIT Accounting process

Next to the CIT return, the organisation also has to incorporate tax numbers in the annual accounts.[7]

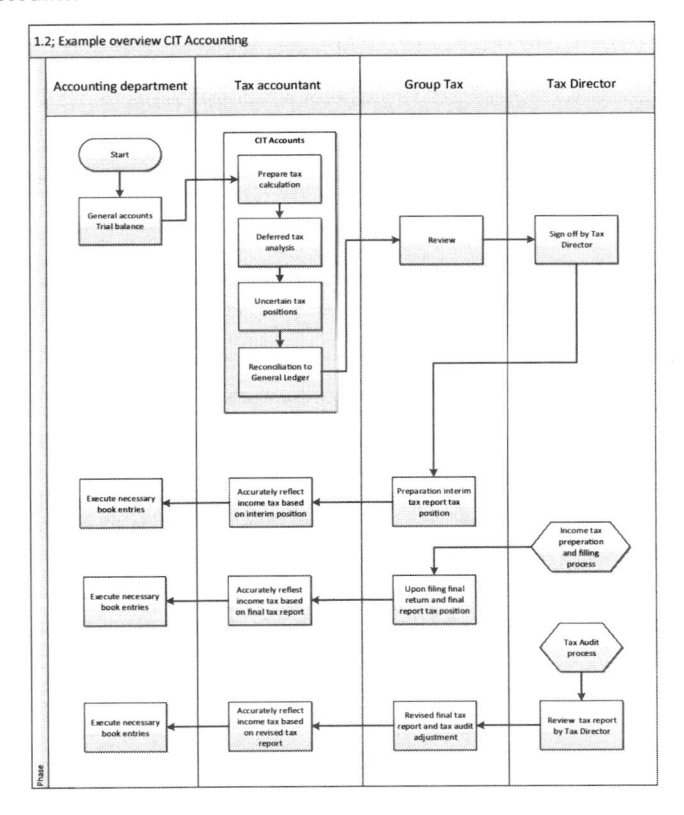

Figure 6: example flowchart CIT Accounting.

---

6   Co-operative Compliance: A Framework – From Enhances Relationship to Co-operative Compliance, OECD 2013.
7   See chapter 9 on Tax Accounting for more detail.

Specific issues corporate income taxes   **12.2.3**

The Tax Accounting process basically drills down into input of information from the accounting department and the assessment by group tax on the CIT specific elements. The tax position in the annual accounts is influenced not only by the current tax position of the organisation based on local tax law, but also deferred tax assets and liabilities according to whatever accounting standard you must report under (IAS 12, ASC 740). Over the past years tax accounting became a science by itself. Reconciling book and tax data and reporting in the applicable format within a multinational environment is not easy (see the delta-model).

The annual accounting process does normally not correspond to the timing of the filing of the CIT return and a possible tax audit by Tax Authorities. Both will occur after year end closing. However, when preparing the CIT return or after a CIT tax audit, the organisation can come to new insights with respect to the CIT position in the annual accounts. This should be reflected in new book entries. This process is also known as 'thru-ing up' the tax position. As will be appreciated, the more closely the return is prepared and filed to the end of the financial year the less risk on mistakes in the tax position in the annual accounts are likely to happen. As an example, late transfer pricing adjustments form a risk for every organisation since retroactive (tax) book keeping puts a lot of strain on the finance and tax organisation and could damage the reputation and credibility of the organisation seriously.

12.2.3.3 CIT assessment and payment

After receiving the temporary or final CIT assessment from the Tax Authorities, the organisation needs to evaluate if this corresponds with its own provision. If it does, the organisation needs to assure that the CIT payment is done in time. If it does not, the difference should be analysed and, if desired, the organisation could file an appeal and plead for an extension for payment with the tax administration. This again links to the tax strategy as set out in the business and tax environment building block: the organisation wants to comply with tax laws and regulations and thus wants to pay its due tax in time.

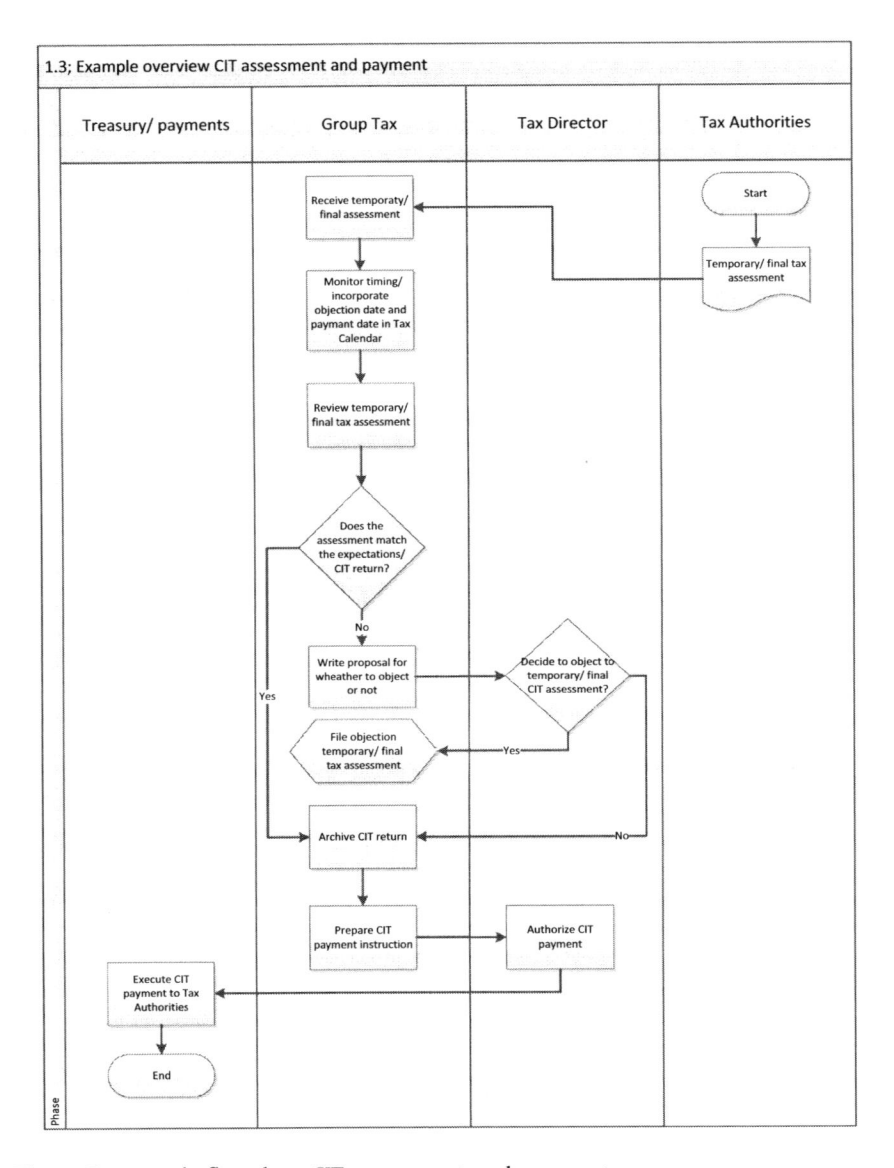

Figure 7: example flowchart CIT assessment and payment.

12.2.3.4 A possible CIT audit by Tax Authorities

The organisation should have a basic procedure in place in case Tax Authorities announce a tax audit.[8] The question to start with is: how much autonomy do operational companies have in these issues? This should already have been made

---

8   See chapter 15 for more detail on tax audit.

Specific issues corporate income taxes 12.2.3

very clear in the overview of roles and responsibilities as outlined in the business and tax environment. Generally, we see that operating companies have the obligation to inform and consult group tax if the monetary risk exceeds a certain amount. However, with ongoing discussion on fair tax, even if the risk is not material, a tax audit may form a reputational risk as well. Depending on the risk analysis of group tax and the local company it can determine who is in the lead in dealing with the audit, and whether or not an external advisor should be involved.

The international element of CIT and the negative reputation it has with tax administrations as a tool for aggressive tax planning, combined with the ever growing exchange of information between tax administrations in our view makes it necessary to monitor and control all CIT related audits at the central tax group level to safeguard the uniformity of the approach.

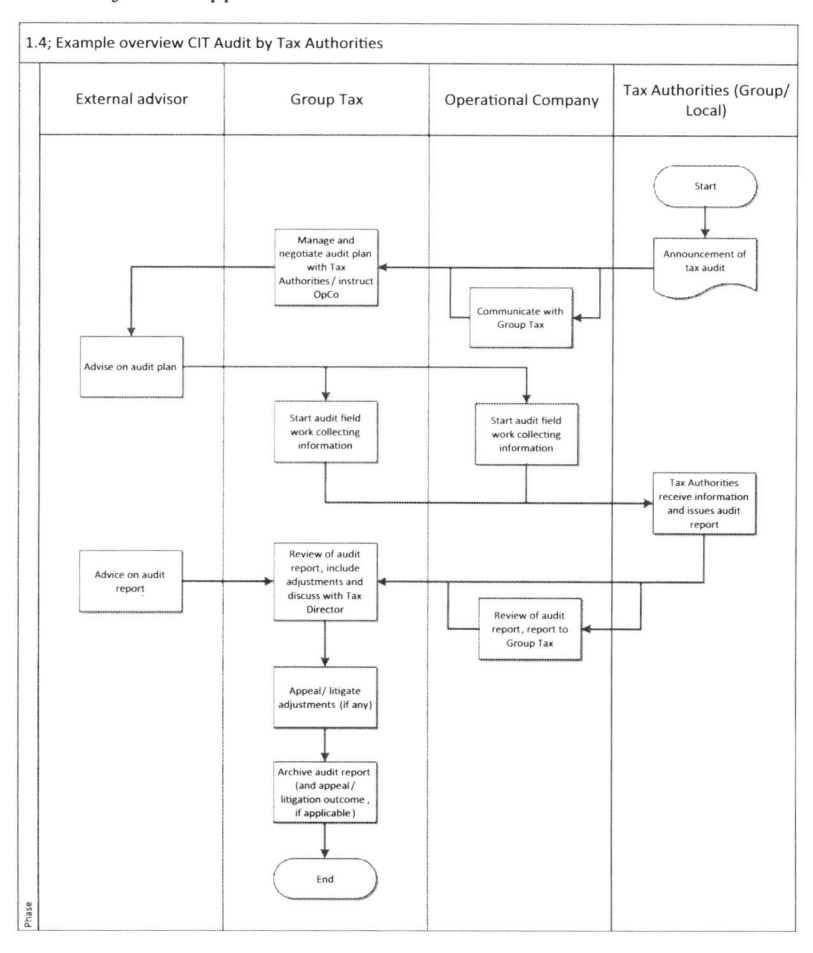

Figure 8: example flowchart CIT Audit by Tax Authorities.

319

The CIT Audit process can be affected by several broader developments in society. On the one hand, as mentioned earlier, we see cooperative compliance arrangements in which organisations should inform and attune possible tax issues upfront. This means that all uncertainties should be dealt with in the CIT preparation and filing process. On the other hand we see tax authorities increasing their audit appetite and aggressiveness, among others due to the economic downturn. Especially the latter will have a serious impact on the tax operations of the organisation and on this process specifically. A broad vision on this should therefore be included in the tax strategy/ tax policy.

12.2.4 Tax risk management

At this point, the organisation has a clear view on its business and tax environment (including a tax strategy and policy) and the general processes in which tax is included and the specific CIT processes are drawn-up. The next step is to have a look at the tax risk management approach. When looking at (tax) risk management, the organisation should have a risk appetite process, risk identification and risk response process and control activities in place.

The first step in every risk management approach is determining the risk appetite. This should be directly linked to the tax strategy/ tax policy as determined in the business and tax environment building block. The organisation needs to determine how much risk it is willing to take. When looking at companies' risk report in the annual report, we can generally identify risks of the following nature: strategic, operational, financial, reporting, and compliance.[9] When looking at risk reporting for tax in the annual report, the financial, reporting and compliance risk are (especially from a monetary perspective) dominant. However, when looking at the CIT tax risk appetite, the organisation should have a vision within all these risk categories. Some risks, like for example reputational risk within the strategic category, may not seem to have a direct monetary effect, we have seen organisations being confronted with customer boycotts due to their alleged CIT structures.[10]

Group tax should also have a vision on the responsibility of identifying tax and more specifically CIT risks. Generally, group tax is confident that Risk Management, Internal Control and/ or Internal Audit have tax risks in scope. More than often it occurs that these departments do not have the tax expertise to be able to take CIT risks in scope and are therefore (rightly or wrongly) confident that group tax is monitoring it. This should therefore be made clear in the roles and responsibilities of the tax function. When group tax is responsible for Tax Risk management and more specifically the

---

9   Groot, de, J.I., Op weg naar een raamwerk voor risicoverslaglegging, Tijdschrift voor Jaarrekeningenrecht, nr. 1/2, April 2010.
10 We refer for example to Starbucks (Lucas L., B. Jopson and V. Houlder, Starbucks ground down, Financial Times, December 7, 2012 (http://www.ft.com/cms/s/0/8640ad26-4069-11e2-8e04-00144feabdc0.html#axzz3LVnTX5tN) and Vodafone (Bergin, T., Insight: Vodafone in new 1 billion pounds tax "scandal", Reuters, June 26, 2012 (http://uk.reuters.com/article/2012/06/26/uk-vodafone-tax-idUKBRE85P0GO20120626).

Specific issues corporate income taxes **12.2.4**

identification of tax risks, it should assure it is closely linked to those departments and business transactions that could carry a possible issue with CIT impact.

The organisation should have risk response and control activities in place. Depending on the likelihood and impact of a CIT risk in relation to the risk appetite, the organisation can implement risk mitigating actions. These are: acceptance of the risk, stopping the activities that cause the risk, transfer the risk to third parties (e.g. insurance), or to implement control measures.

12.2.4.1 Main CIT risks

In general, when looking at CIT risks, a distinction can be made between tax technical risks, and risks that relate to processes, people and systems. For the latter, we can define some standard, generic CIT issues and risks and the (key) tax controls to remediate these in line with the CIT processes as defined in the tax operations building block.

With respect to CIT technical risks, it is more complicated to define a generic set of risks, as these more than the other category depend on the CIT laws and regulations of each country individually.

In the subparagraphs below, for both categories examples of potential risks and a suggestion for a possible control activity are included. The purpose of a control activity is to prevent and/ or detect and correct misstatements that may arise in a process timely. Controls are therefore used as a defence that a risk is materialising or manage the risk when it occurs. Also, for each risk a possible KPI for the tax department is included.

12.2.4.1.1 Tax technical risks[11]

Participation exemption and CFC	
Risk:	If requirements with respect to participation exemption and CFC (Controlled Foreign Company) are not complied with, the company can be subject to taxation on the profits realized by foreign subsidiaries. This could result in double taxation and possible penalties.
Explanation:	Ascertain that the participation exemption applies/CFC rules do not apply is essential to avoid taxation of profits of subsidiaries held. However, given the complexity of the rules, companies may not always be aware of the possible issues and may not always monitor these rules on a continuous basis.

---

11   With special thanks to Jeroen Schmitz and Eric Schiffer, PwC the Netherlands.

Participation exemption and CFC	
Possible control:	Before a transaction is carried out, review the participation exemption/CFC position and prepare a write-up (prepared or reviewed by tax advisor)/conclude ruling with the tax authorities if possible. Further, monitor the accurateness of the write-up on the facts at hand on an ongoing basis.
Possible KPI:	Availability of write-up and ongoing monitoring.

Treatment of interest expenses	
Risk:	If interest expenses are dealt with in an incorrect way, this may result in tax adjustments and a possible penalty.
Explanation:	Almost all countries have rules regarding the limitation of the deductibility of interest costs for tax purposes. Over time, these rules have become more complex and therefore may have an impact in unexpected situations.
Possible control:	Before a transaction is carried out, review the deductibility of interest costs and prepare a write-up (prepared or reviewed by tax advisor)/conclude ruling with the tax authorities if possible. Further, monitor the accurateness of the write-up on the facts at hand on an ongoing basis.
Possible KPI:	Availability of write-up and ongoing monitoring.

Tax Grouping	
Risk:	If the organisation does not comply with the relevant conditions for tax grouping, the tax group may dissolve resulting in individual tax compliance requirements of the relevant entities which may have an adverse tax impact.
Explanation:	Several entities may apply a tax grouping regime for CIT purposes. This e.g. means that all entities are consolidated into the (parent) entity for tax purposes and/or that taxable profits and tax losses between group members can be offset. Tax grouping requires that is complied with specific requirements. If requirements are not met, the tax grouping regime may be no longer apply/challenged by the tax authorities
Possible control:	The organisation should monitor that the application for the grouping regime is filed in line with the tax requirements and within the deadline. Further, it should be monitored that the specific requirements of the Tax Grouping are complied with on a yearly basis. Adjustments of any kind in the legal, economic and tax structure have to be signed off by Group Tax.

Tax Grouping	
Possible KPI:	Monitoring of Tax Grouping requirements is performed on an annual basis.

Substance requirements	
Risk:	If the Group/company does not comply with the relevant substance requirements in a specific country it could result in adverse tax consequences, including a penalty risk. It may also have a negative impact on the relation with the tax authorities.
Explanation:	Companies are required to have appropriate substance in the countries in which they operate for tax purposes. This may for example mean that organisations need to have the employees in that country to which the relevant functions and related risks can be allocated to substantiate that these functions are actually performed in that jurisdiction. For multinational enterprises operating around the world with a flexible and constant traveling workforce, this may be very complicated in practice.
Possible control:	The company should have a functional overview of the location of (key) employees and what the functions of these employees are, including the related risks. This overview should be updated on a yearly basis and subsequently compared with (and brought in accordance to) the substance requirements.
Possible KPI:	The functional overview of the location of (key) employees is updated on an annual basis, adjustments are documented.

General anti-abuse regulation (abuse of law doctrine)	
Risk:	Application of abuse of law doctrine typically results in the relevant transactions being disregarded.
Explanation:	If transactions are structured in such a way that e.g. the aim is to avoid tax and/or are in contradict with the purpose of the tax law, it could result in tax due and penalties, (criminal) indictment, an impact on the relation with the tax authorities and a reputational risk.
Possible control:	Business purpose should be the overriding reason for entering into a transaction. Further, such business reasons should be documented.
Possible KPI:	The Tax Department has documented the business reason for all relevant transactions.

Correct implementation and monitoring of tax advice and rulings	
Risk:	If tax advice or a ruling with the tax authorities is not or incorrectly implemented by the company, this could lead to an adverse tax impact due to non-applicability of the tax advice/ ruling. It could also result in penalties and may have a negative impact on the relationship with the tax authorities.
Explanation:	A ruling or tax advice only has value to the extent it is correctly implemented and monitored to comply with all requirements. Furthermore, the organisation must monitor retrospectively that implementation has been executed properly.
Possible control:	Tax Department, Internal Control or Internal Audit includes implementation and monitoring in their internal audit plan. When testing this, the requirements with respect to tax rulings / tax advice should be included as the standard to which the outcome is compared.
Possible KPI:	Group Tax could be held accountable if Internal Control/ Internal Audit find any deviations in their monitoring and testing activities.

Ongoing monitoring of changes in tax law and regulations	
Risk:	The company does not comply with tax laws and regulations due to unawareness of changes in tax laws and regulations or wrong interpretations of tax laws and regulations. This can result in a penalty, reputational damage and can have a negative impact on the relation with the tax authorities.
Explanation:	Changes in tax rules and regulations may have an impact on the tax affairs of the organisation. If these changes are not duly noted, the completeness and correctness of the CIT return may be compromised.

Ongoing monitoring of changes in tax law and regulations	
Possible control:	* The company has a responsible person for monitoring changes in tax law and regulations. This person has to follow regular update training sessions on CIT, ascertain that is receives regular update newsletters on law changes from e.g. tax advisor; * Changes in tax law and regulations are communicated with the relevant tax department (e.g. in a monthly tax technical session) and other stakeholders within the organisation; * The company is provided with tax updates by a tax advisor and discusses possible tax issues due to changing laws and regulations with them; * The tax department takes appropriate action if needed.
Possible KPI:	The tax responsible person or group tax as a whole participates at least in one CIT update training annually.

State aid	
Risk:	Tax regulations or agreements with the tax authorities can be considered unlawful state aid, resulting in repayment of such benefit and reputational damages.
Explanation:	The European Committee is investigating tax regulations and agreements with tax authorities in different European countries to determine whether these can be considered unlawful state-aid. State aid must be repaid by the company who obtained such benefit (including interest). Furthermore, being subject to a State Aid investigation can also have reputational damages as it draws a lot of media attention.
Possible control:	Have regular checks with an independent tax advisor to determine whether state aid can be considered to have an adverse impact.
Possible KPI:	The organisation has reviewed all its tax regulations and agreements with respect to state aid within a period of three years from <date>.

12.2.4.1.2 Risks relating to processes, people and systems

12.2.4.1.2.1 CIT preparation and filing

Timing, due dates of the CIT return	
Risk:	The CIT return is not filled in time, resulting in a penalty. This can have a negative impact on the relation with the tax authorities.
Explanation:	Looking at the tax strategy as described in the business and tax environment building block, we stated that, among others, the tax return must be filled in time. However, organisations regularly do not have a clear overview of what the due dates of their CIT return(s) is/ are.
Possible control:	A basic control measure for this is to set-up and implement a tax calendar. This tax calendar will include information regarding due dates for filing the CIT return, status of the return, due dates for appeals, and due dates for payment. This information is recorded for each entity on a per country level. Tax compliance providers can provide IT applications that include a tax calendar and a dashboard overview of the status its tax compliance per entity.
Possible KPI:	Organisations that have tax compliance as a high strategic priority sometimes link Key Performance Indicators of Group Tax and operational companies to the compliance with due dates.

Data input CIT return	
Risk:	The input data is inaccurate or incomplete leading to an incorrect CIT return, incorrect CIT payments, reputational damage and/ or tax penalties.
Explanation:	Data relevant for CIT and the preparation of the CIT return can be received from other departments then (Group) Tax. CIT knowledge and awareness may not be sufficient to secure the quality of the data provided. Data provided should be reviewed based on checks included in the CIT return Tax Manual.

Specific issues corporate income taxes   **12.2.4**

Data input CIT return	
Possible control:	* 'Sanity' check on input, i.e. review financial information from annual accounts/additional information and check with other sources (e.g. information from systems) based on experience and/or variance analysis. * Communication with and training of staff members providing CIT relevant data with the purpose of increasing knowledge and awareness.
Possible KPI:	The relevant staff members participate in a CIT training on an annual basis.

12.2.4.1.2.2 CIT Accounting process

Tax calculations and tax reporting packages	
Risk:	Tax calculations contain errors, leading to incorrect current and deferred corporate income tax provisions.
Explanation:	Current and deferred CIT provisions need to be calculated accurately. For a multinational operating organisation, local entities need to report the relevant data by using tax reporting packages. These are mostly based on excel, which are prone for error in itself. Also, persons completing the tax reporting packs need to have knowledge on what is required from them and have some general tax accounting knowledge, to enable them to provide correct and complete data.
Possible control:	* Excel based tax reporting packages are used for calculating and monitoring the current and deferred CIT provision on local and group level. * Before consolidating the local tax reporting packages, these are reviewed by local Finance staff. The group Tax Accountant reviews and approves the accuracy of effective tax rates, current and deferred tax positions and uncertain tax positions. * Local staff is trained in completing the tax reporting package annually.
Possible KPI:	Local staff needs to follow training on completing the tax reporting package annually.

12.2.4.1.2.3 CIT assessment and payment

Review of CIT assessment	
Risk:	It remains unnoted that CIT assessments are not correct, resulting in an inaccurate amount of tax payable or receivable.
Explanation:	(Group) tax should assess the CIT assessment imposed by the tax authorities to review if it corresponds with the CIT assessment/return of the organisation. Deviations should be analysed and documented and thus provide input for the decision if the organisation will appeal or not.
Possible control:	Review and sign-off of the CIT assessment imposed by group tax. Deviations are analysed and the tax advisor is consulted if the deviation is significant.
Possible KPI:	All CIT assessments are signed-off. All CIT due is paid in time. The organisation does not incur any fines relating to exceeding the payment due dates.

Timing of CIT payment and/ or appeal due dates	
Risk:	The CIT payment and/ or appeal is not done in time, resulting in a penalty.
Explanation:	Looking at the tax strategy as described in the business and tax environment building block, we stated that, among others, the CIT payment must be done in time. However, organisations regularly do not have a clear overview of what the due dates of their CIT payments and or appeals are.
Possible control:	As with the timing of the filing of the CIT return, a basic control measure for the monitoring of due dates for payments and/ or appeal to CIT assessments is to set-up and implement a tax calendar.
Possible KPI:	Organisations that have tax compliance as a high strategic priority can link Key Performance Indicators of Group Tax and operational companies to the compliance with due dates.

12.2.4.1.2.4 A possible CIT audit by Tax Authorities

Tax audit	
Risk:	Tax audits are not adequately governed, coordinated and/ or followed-up, leading to reputational damage and/ or penalties.

Specific issues corporate income taxes

Tax audit	
Explanation:	A CIT audit conducted by the Tax Authorities should be accurately managed. If it is unclear who is in the lead or who is authorised to communicate with the Tax Authorities regarding the audit, lack of clarity may arise or Tax Authorities can be misinformed.
Possible control:	* Appointment of responsible person ('single point of contact') for CIT audits conducted by Tax Authorities at Group Tax but also at the level of operational companies. * Group Tax periodically reviews the status of each tax audit and reviews and approves measures that are taken to remediate issues noted.
Possible KPI:	Operational companies have a CIT audit procedure in place. All tax audits are reported to the Group Tax department.

12.2.5 Monitoring and testing

The organisation has a tax policy, has fitted its business and tax processes accordingly and has implemented a tax risk management process. Thus, the design and existence of its tax (risk) management is in place. The question that remains now is: is the CIT risk management system working, is the organisation actually in control of CIT? To be able to gain comfort on its CIT risk management system, the organisation should implement a monitoring and testing function in order to demonstrate the functioning of its tax management system to internal and external stakeholders like audit committee, tax administrations or external auditors. This should lead to two activities we call monitoring and testing.

1. On the one hand, this means the organisation needs to test if all controls are implemented and functioning as they were set-up.
2. On the other hand, the organisation should test if the set-up itself is effective. In other words, do the implemented controls (as tested under 1.) cover all (major) CIT risks or is the CIT risk management process incomplete and should other tax controls be added.

Monitoring and testing can be conducted in several ways. On the one hand, this can be done by means of testing the (key) CIT controls of which some examples where provided in the previous chapter. On the other hand, the organisation can conduct sampling testing to test whether items were dealt with in a correct way from a tax perspective. We will elaborate on both in a bit more detail below.

12.2.5.1 Controls testing

In the set-up of the processes and linked to the tax risk management, the organisation has identified several (key) tax controls with respect to CIT. The organisation can test their efficiency by means of controls testing. One of the most familiar obligatory testing of tax controls is performed under the Sarbanes-Oxley regulation (SOx).[12] Here, the external accountant has to test the key controls, including the CIT controls. As outcome of this way of monitoring, the organisation (or its assurance provider) is able to give comfort on the proper functioning of the (key) CIT controls.

12.2.5.2 Substantive testing

Substantive testing is an efficient, objective and transparent way to conduct monitoring of the tax management function of an organisation. Basically, transactions in the organisation are extracted based on statistical sampling testing. Next it is tested if these transactions are treated in the correct tax way for tax purposes (correct tax legal judgement took place), and ultimately are correctly processed in the CIT return.

One variation on substantive testing is a dual purpose substantive test. This test combines a substantive test with controls testing. Dual purpose substantive testing:
1. Provides insight if the selected key (CIT) controls have functioned as designed;
2. The outcome gives insight in to which degree the selected transactions are treated in the correct tax way. Has the tax item been processed in the right way (from registration, tax interpretation till recording in the CIT return).

If irregularities or defects in the tax risk management system of the organisation are detected by the monitoring and testing activities, the organisation should remediate these in the processes and controls. The organisation should, in our view, have a continuous improvement cycle in place in line with the Deming cycle.[13] The Deming cycle consist of the phases: *plan – do – check – act* (or adjust). By incorporating these phases in its tax risk management, the organisation continuously monitors its control environment and makes adjustments to improve the environment, thus the term continuous improvement.[14]

---

12 Under the SOx regulation, and specifically section 404, the management of an organisation must provide an assessment on the effectiveness of the internal controls structure and procedures for financial reporting. This must be attested by the Auditor.
13 Named after William Edwards Deming.
14 Kerklaan, L, De PDCA cirkel is springlevend, SIGMA, nr. 2, April 2014.

The organisation needs to determine who/ which part of the organisation is responsible for monitoring and testing activities for CIT. When looking at the roles and responsibilities outline in the business and tax environment building block, it was setout that group tax monitors activities of the operational companies. However, who monitors group tax? A notable development is that monitoring and testing of CIT is getting more and more in scope of Internal Control and Internal Audit departments. These departments have the knowledge and expertise with respect to monitoring and testing that tax departments generally do not have (looking at their legal background). A combination of Internal Audit and Group Tax, with its tax technical knowledge (input), is a very suitable one to conduct the monitoring and testing activities with respect to CIT.

A notable development is that we see organisations communicating the outcome of monitoring and testing activities with Tax Authorities. This can mostly be attributed to the increase of cooperative compliance arrangement throughout the world. We will get back to this in a bit more detail in the next paragraph.

12.2.6   Tax Assurance

The final element of the CIT risk management system of an organisation is to provide internal, and if required external, assurance.

12.2.6.1   Internal Assurance

Corporate governance codes or regulations generally require organisations to state in their annual report that the organisation is 'in control' and that its internal risk management and control systems functioned properly. An example of this is the Dutch Corporate Governance Code which states:

"As regards financial reporting risks the management board states in the annual report that the internal risk management and control systems provide a reasonable assurance that the financial reporting does not contain any errors of material importance and that the risk management and control systems worked properly in the year under review. The management board shall provide clear substantiation of this."[15]

As we have seen throughout the previous paragraphs, tax is part of the financial reporting function of an organisation, thus is included in the broader in control statement of the organisation. To enable the Board of an organisation to provide an in control statement that includes (corporate income) tax, a tax risk management system including monitoring and testing should be in place. Next to this, the organisation must have a reporting structure in place to allow group tax to communicate significant CIT risks to the management board.

---

15   Article II.1.5 of Dutch Corporate Governance Code as enacted on January 1st 2009.

We see a development of organisations incorporating a 'Tax In-control' (hereafter: TIC) statement in their (tax) risk management set-up. In line with other in control statements used throughout organisations, the TIC should be provided by senior tax employees in the operating companies and senior tax employees in group tax. A basis for in control statements are Control Self Assessments performed by lower management. These are generally already part of the broader risk management approach of the organisation. Installing these for tax risk management purposes will therefore be more of a supplementary nature, hence this will not seriously impact the risk management activities of the organisation. The Control Self Assessment should however include all CIT risk management elements as described in the previous paragraphs, starting with and coming from the tax strategy.

12.2.6.2 External Assurance

Within external assurance, we can distinguish between broader general tax assurance, e.g. in the annual accounts, and tax assurance towards Tax Authorities.

Depending on the scope and materiality, CIT may be in scope for the accountant by means of an audit of tax. This means CIT is incorporated in the year end assurance process and thus some comfort on this process and the data outcome is provided.

Tax assurance towards Tax Authorities can be compulsory or on the tax payers own initiative. An example of the first can be found in the United Kingdom. Here, the Senior Accounting Officer (SAO) of large companies are required to report on the adequacy of their tax accounting systems for the production of an accurate tax return. In other words, the SAO is required to provide HMRC with a sort of external TIC statement.[16]

We also see regulated self-assessment developments, where (tax) auditors are required to audit and sign-off on the CIT return of large companies. In these systems, Tax Authorities are provided with assurance on the CIT return by an external service provider.[17]

External assurance on tax on behalf of Tax Authorities on the initiative of tax payers was the other option. The relationship an organisation has with Tax Authorities is a relevant tailpiece in the tax risk management process. Developments like increasing aggressiveness by Tax Authorities on the one hand and cooperative compliance developments on the other have been noted in the previous paragraphs. Cooperative compliance in most cases requires some sort of external assurance on tax towards Tax Authorities on the initiative of tax payers.

---

16 Enden van der E., J. de Groot and E. van der Stroom, Tax Risk Management, from risk to opportunity, chapter 12 "The Netherlands", IBFD, edited by A. Bakker and S. Kloosterhof, 2010, page 350.
17 Towell, N. Business tax free-for-all, The Sidney Morning Herald, January 16 2014, http://www.smh.com.au/national/business-tax-freeforall-20140115-30veg.html#ixzz2qeLfUbdS.

Numerous countries have implemented cooperative compliance arrangements. These differ in the details. However, gaining insight in and comfort on the TCF of taxpayers is most of the time an integrated part of these arrangements. Therefore, Tax assurance towards Tax Authorities within cooperative compliance, can be arranged in several ways:
- The organisation can give insight in its TCF, for example in the processes, the internal controls and the audit plan;
- The organisation can communicate the outcome of monitoring and testing activities such as the results of (dual purpose) sampling exercises;
- The organisations can provide the Tax Authorities with an Agreed Upon Procedure (hereafter AUP) on the CIT process performed by an assurance provider. In an AUP, the aspects the accountant provides comfort on are clearly defined in the audit protocol. Therefore, an AUP is not a general statement for the entire internal tax risk management and control systems, but only on predefined processes, in our case for example the CIT preparation and filing process including transfer pricing reconciliation.

By providing one or more of the above, the organisation can substantiate it is in control on tax, and can thus provide tax assurance to Tax Authorities.

12.3 Concluding

CIT risk management can never be dealt with just by looking at specific tax technical risks. CIT risk management starts with a tax policy, business and tax processes that have been fitted to comply with the strategy, a tax risk management system to secure proper CIT risk management, monitoring and testing that the above actually works, and ends with being able to communicate this with internal and external stakeholder, such as Tax Authorities.

We have looked at the field of CIT risk management in the past to much as a legal issue or question of proper documentation. If we have given food for thought that CIT risk management means more, the authors have succeeded in their mission.

IRENE BURGERS
JELTJE VAN DER MEER-KOOISTRA

13. Control Frameworks for Cross-Border Internal Transactions: the Tax perspective versus the Management Control perspective

13.1 Introduction

According to the 2013 EY Transfer Pricing Survey - an industry benchmark chronicling taxpayer views on transfer pricing - 66% of respondents[1] identified risk management as their highest priority in transfer pricing (an increase of 32% compared with 2010).[2] Moreover 47% of parent companies reported experiencing double taxation as a result of a transfer pricing audit. According to a 2012 survey of Alvarez & Marsal Taxand LLC, a tax-advisory affiliate of the U.S. management consulting firm Alvarez & Marsal, among 60 CFOs of companies with more than $1 billion in annual revenue, 18 CFOs (30%) said transfer pricing was their chief tax risk and, in total, transfer pricing was the No. 2 risk just behind global compliance.[3] According to the 2013 EY Transfer Pricing Survey, the growing willingness of tax administrations in rapid-growth markets to challenge transactions, as well as broad and intense focus by the media and social justice organisations, have amplified the pressure on prioritising tax risk management in transfer pricing.[4]

Nevertheless, only four of the CFOs (7%) in the Alvarez & Marsal survey said that transfer pricing was the tax area where they spent the most time and money.[5] This is remarkable as research by Zinn, Riedel and Spengel[6] shows that more than 80% of

---

1 878 executives of the world's leading companies across 26 markets. EY Transfer Pricing Survey 2013, p. 2, http://www.ey.com/GL/en/Services/Tax/2013-Global-Transfer-Pricing-Survey.
2 In comparison, the percentage of companies identifying cash tax or effective tax rate optimisation as their highest priority fell by nearly one-third to 17% since 2010. EY Transfer Pricing Survey 2013.
3 Murphy, M. (2012). CFOs See Tax Risk in Transfer Pricing. *The Wall Street Journal* online, May 29, 2012, http://mobile.blogs.wsj.com/cfo/2012/05/29/cfos-see-tax-risk-in-transfer-pricing/
4 http://www.ey.com/GL/en/Services/Tax/2013-Global-Transfer-Pricing-Survey.
5 Murphy, M. (2012). CFOs See Tax Risk in Transfer Pricing. *The Wall Street Journal* online, May 29, 2012, http://mobile.blogs.wsj.com/cfo/2012/05/29/cfos-see-tax-risk-in-transfer-pricing/
6 Zinn, Th., Riedel, N. & Spengel, Ch. (2014). The Increasing Importance of Transfer Pricing Regulations: A Worldwide Overview. *Intertax*, Volume 42, Issue 6 & 7, p. 368.

states in North America, South America, Asia and Australia require documentation in national tax law and short or long disclosure is required,[7] while in 10% of these states, although a documentation requirement is not introduced in national tax law, it exists in practice (especially in the course of an audit) and in 5% no documentation requirement exists. In respect to Europe, their research shows transfer pricing requirements are posed in many states but on a less strict basis: in 32% of states documentation requirements are introduced in national tax law requiring short disclosure; in another 32% of states full documentation must be available upon request. In approximately 30% of states a documentation requirement, although not introduced in national tax law, exists in practice and in 8% of the countries surveyed no documentation requirement exists.

In its 30 July 2013 White Paper on Transfer Pricing Documentation the OECD acknowledges 'the growing compliance burden on business as more and more countries adopt transfer pricing documentation rules, increasing costs for MNEs in an area of activity that may be largely viewed by business as having few benefits beyond penalty avoidance, or gives rise to decisions to simply not comply in the time and manner desired by the governments promulgating the documentation rules. Ad hoc materiality and risk screens are applied by businesses, largely as a matter of self-preservation, given the burden of complying with the rules as written.' The OECD aims at improving documentation rules in such a way that the intended purposes are reached in the most efficient possible manner. These purposes are to the OECD as follows:
- to provide governments with the information necessary to conduct an informed transfer pricing risk assessment at the commencement of a tax audit;
- to assure that taxpayers have given appropriate consideration to transfer pricing requirements in establishing prices and other conditions for related party transactions and in reporting the income derived from such transactions in their tax returns;
- to provide governments with all of the information that they require in order to conduct an appropriately thorough audit of the transfer pricing practices of entities subject to tax in their jurisdiction.

In order to reach these goals the OECD proposes a Coordinated Approach to Documentation in which the taxpayer provides the tax administration with a master file and country files. The master file portion of the documentation would seek to elicit a reasonably complete picture of the global business, financial reporting, debt structure and tax situation of the MNE to enable tax authorities to identify the presence of significant transfer pricing risks. In particular, the information requested in the master file can be grouped in five categories:
- information on the MNE group;
- description of the MNE's business or businesses;

---

7   The authors use the following definitions for these terms. 'A short content is assumed to exist if only a summary or overview of transactions is necessary for disclosure, while a long content is assumed if (almost) full documentation (also called a transfer pricing study) is required.' See p. 359 of the article referred to in footnote

- information on the MNE's intangibles;
- information on the MNE's intercompany financial activities;
- information on the MNE's financial and tax positions.[8]

The country files focus on specific transfer pricing analyses related to material transactions taking place between a local country affiliate and associated enterprises in different countries. Country files should supplement the master file and help to meet the objective of assuring that the taxpayer has complied with the arm's length principle in its material transfer pricing positions. This implies that where 'conditions are made or imposed between the two enterprises in their commercial or financial relations which differ from those which would be made between independent enterprises, then any profits which would, but for those conditions, have accrued to one of the enterprises, but by reason of those conditions, have not so accrued, may be included in the profits of that enterprise and taxed accordingly'.[9]

Besides documentation required by the tax legislators/tax administrations, an adequate tax assurance to the stakeholders in respect of transfer pricing governance requires the design of a transfer pricing strategy and a tax control framework as well as the implementation of such a strategy and framework in the business. The tax control framework should provide for, amongst others, tools to monitor:
- that the right information will be provided in time by the work floor to the department responsible for tax issues;
- legislative requirements and legislative changes;
- requests for rulings and advance pricing request;
- dispute resolutions and legal proceedings.

Companies use some form of control framework on internal transactions for tax purposes. Companies also use a control framework, called management control system, for managing and controlling their activities. The managers of companies want to ensure 'that the behaviours and decisions of their employees are consistent with the organisation's objectives and strategies'.[10] With the controls included in the management control system, managers can influence the decisions and behaviours of their employees.

The management control system is also used for the management and control of internal transactions.[11] We call the whole of controls used for managing and controlling internal transactions the management control framework of internal transactions. The controls included in this framework partly depend on the decision-making

---

8   OECD (2013). *White Paper on Transfer Pricing Documentation*, par. 80.
9   OECD (2010). *Glossary OECD Transfer Pricing Guidelines 2010*.
10 Merchant, K.A. & Van der Stede, W.A. (2012). *Management Control Systems: Performance Measurement, Evaluation and Incentives*, third edition. London: Prentice Hall.
11 We use the term of management control framework for the controls that focus on the management and control of internal transactions. This framework is part of the management control system of the enterprise.

structure of a company. Companies can have a centralized or a more or less decentralized decision-making (or organisational) structure. In companies with a centralized decision-making structure, the central management takes all decisions, including the decisions about how to manage the internal transactions. In companies with a decentralized decision-making structure, decision-making authority is portioned out to the managers of organisational units, e.g. business units, divisions or service units. If these organisational units are related to each other by means of transactions of goods or services, the managers of these units have to manage their internal transactions.

The transactional relationships between the transacting organisational units can be very complex. For example, the production capacities of the internal supplier and the internal buyer need to be geared to each other, the internal parties have to pay attention to technological and market developments and they need to co-ordinate their activities on a daily basis. The more complex the transactional relationship is between the internal parties, the more difficult it is for the central management to manage the internal transactions. Then it is likely that the managers of the organisational units manage the internal transactions as they are better informed about the characteristics of the internal transactions and the market they operate in than the central management. Decentralization of the management of the internal transactions enhances the quality of the decisions and accelerates the decision-making process. Informing the central management will take time and, moreover, will overload them with information.

In order to make the managers of the organisational units responsible for their decisions, the (financial) results of these decisions have to be measured. Therefore, the financial boundaries between the transacting organisational units have to be determined, as well as their responsibilities with respect to the quality and the timeliness of the internal transactions. Furthermore, the (financial) results of each organisational unit have to be measured in a transparent way.

The way internal transactions are managed and controlled is influenced by various factors. Van der Meer-Kooistra[12] refers to the following factors: characteristics of the organisational context in which the internal transactions take place (e.g. the portioning out of authority and responsibility); characteristics of the internal transactions (e.g. level of uncertainty of the transaction environment, degree of asset specificity, size and frequency of the internal transactions); and characteristics of the internal transacting parties (e.g. level of information asymmetry between the transacting parties and possibility of opportunistic behaviour). Information needs to be collected about these factors in order to set up a management control framework of internal transactions.

---

12   Van der Meer-Kooistra, J. (1994). The co-ordination of internal transactions: the functioning of transfer pricing systems in the organizational context. *Management Accounting Research*, 5(2), p. 123-152; Van der Meer-Kooistra, J. (2004). A model for making qualitative transfer pricing adjustments. *International Transfer Pricing Journal*, 11(5), pp. 190-195.

The effectiveness and efficiency of collecting information and storing it in a company's transfer pricing documentation could be enhanced if the tax control framework and the management control framework of internal transactions can be integrated. Moreover, tax risks could be reduced, as tax administrations may find information that is also used for management control purposes more reliable than information that is only used for tax purposes. If the information is used for both purposes, it is less likely that the taxpayer included information in its fiscal documentation concerning certain transactions in order to reduce the tax burden without any valid business reason for the transaction. However, there are several reasons why it may be difficult to integrate both frameworks in one control framework as suggested in the literature.[13]

The aim of this Chapter is to investigate whether the principles underlying the tax control framework and the management control framework as set up for cross border internal transactions allow an integration of both frameworks. Therefore, we will analyse the background of both the tax perspective and the management control perspective on cross border internal transactions and discuss the differences between both perspectives. In addition, we will point out the implications of these differences for managing and controlling cross border internal transactions in practice by using an integrated tax and management control framework.

The structure of this Chapter is as follows. The background of the tax perspective will be described in section 13.2 and the background of the management control perspective in section 13.3. In section 13.4 the most important differences between the tax and the management control perspective will be presented. Section 13.5 will discuss the implications of using one integrated tax and management control framework and in section 9.6 we draw conclusions.

---

13 Baldenius, T., Melumad, N.D. & Reichelstein, S. (2004). Integrating managerial and tax objectives in transfer pricing. *The Accounting Review*, 79(3), p. 591-615; Cools, M. (2002). *International transfer pricing: tensions between tax compliance and management control in multinational enterprises*, dissertation. Antwerp: University of Antwerp; Cools, M., Emmanuel, C.R. & Jorissen, A. (2008). Management control in the transfer pricing tax compliant multinational enterprise. *Accounting, Organizations and Society*, 33(6), p. 603 – 638; Van Egdom, J.T. (2011). *Verrekenprijzen; de verdeling van de winst van een multinational*. Deventer: Kluwer, p. 280 and pp. 284-287. As to Van Egdom the differences between both systems can only be minor, as both for management control purposes and for tax purposes the starting point of the analysis is that value creation should be rewarded and both for management control purposes and for tax purposes, the distinction between key activities and routine functions is made. He is of the opinion that as long as a company does not use its transfer pricing system to minimise the tax burden, the gap between the tax perspective and the management control perspective can be bridged. Companies should build a transfer pricing system on the basis of principles developed in the management control literature. The methods prescribed by the OECD should be used to test if the transfer pricing systems developed by companies result in arm's length results. Both tax administration and taxpayer should be flexible. The tax administrations must understand that in certain cases the arm's length principle used by the company may be in conflict with the requirements of the management control system. The company should take into account that the arm's length standard is the international standard for tax purposes.

13.2 The tax perspective

13.2.1 Introduction

Domestic tax laws of most countries contain rules requiring companies to fulfil the arm's length principle in respect of internal transactions both for intercompany transactions (for tax purposes defined as transactions between two or more related legal entities with common control) and intracompany transactions (for tax purposes defined as transactions between two or more entities within the same legal entity).[14] This rule is also codified in most tax treaties. Most tax treaties contain the same rules as laid down in art. 9 OECD-Model and art. 9 UN Model for intercompany transactions and in art. 7 OECD-Model and art. 7 UN-Model for intracompany transactions. The OECD provides guidance on how to interpret these rules in their Transfer Pricing Guidelines 1979, 1995 and 2010 and in the Reports on the Allocation of Profits to Permanent Establishments 2008 and 2010. In this section we elaborate on the standard for both intercompany and intracompany internationally accepted arm's length principle and on the guidance of the OECD in interpreting this principle both for intercompany and intracompany transactions (sections 13.2.1-13.2.5). The OECD also provides guidance in respect of transfer pricing documentation in its Transfer Pricing Guidelines and Reports on the Allocation of Profits to Permanent Establishment (section 13.2.6). In its 2013 White Paper on Transfer Pricing Documentation, the OECD presented a new approach – that is also recommended by the EU Transfer Pricing Forum – consisting of a master file and country files. In section 13.2.7 we will provide an overview of this approach. Moreover, in 2013 the OECD published a draft of a Transfer Pricing Risk Assessment Handbook for tax administrations. This Handbook will enable tax administrations to focus on effective risk identification and taxpayers to determine their tax compliance risk. Section 13.2.8 provides some more information on this. The aim and scope of a Tax Control Framework is discussed in section 13.2.9.

13.2.2 Arm's length principle

For tax purposes, if internal transactions take place cross border, the international standard agreed by both OECD and UN Member States is the arm's length principle. The aim of this principle is to reconcile the legitimate right of states to tax the profits of a taxpayer based upon income and expenses, that can reasonably be considered to arise within their territory, with the need to avoid double taxation and thus create a

---

14 See http://www.businessdictionary.com/definition/intracompany-trade.html#ixzz3Civl5Pb2; http://davidhaimes.wordpress.com/2007/11/26/intercompany-vs-intracompany/.
In the fields of Finance and Accounting the term intracompany trade may in the same way as for tax purposes refer to transactions within the legal entity (Simkiss, Th.J. & Briggs, L. (2012). *Intercompany and Intracompany in R12 – A deep dive*. BizTech. http://www.eprentise.com/wp-content/uploads/2013/10/9038_tsimkiss_wp_1.pdf), but it may also refer to a transaction that occurs between two subsidiaries of the same parent company (http://financial-dictionary.thefreedictionary.com/Intracompany+Transaction) or to transactions between divisions (Caplan, D. (2010). *Management accounting concepts and techniques*. Albany: University at Albany (New York). http://denniscaplan.fatcow.com/Chapter22.htm).

level playing field between (groups of) companies that operate locally and internationally operating (groups of) companies, and thus to contribute to the expansion of world trade on a multilateral, non-discriminatory basis and to achieve higher sustainable economic growth.[15]

13.2.3 Codification in Art. 9 OECD Model and Art. 9 UN Model for intercompany transactions (parent-subsidiary)

This standard is codified in the domestic legislation of numerous states, as well as in tax treaties, for *intercompany transactions* – between different *entities* that are or are treated as body corporate that are part of the same group - generally based on the provisions included in art. 9 OECD Model and art. 9 UN Model both reading (with a slight deviation indicated below in italics) for associated companies:

'Where
a. An enterprise of a Contracting State participates directly or indirectly in the management, control or capital of an enterprise of a Contracting State, or
b. the same persons participate directly or indirectly in the management, control or capital of an enterprise of a Contracting State and an enterprise of the other Contracting State,

and in either case conditions are made or imposed between the two enterprises in their commercial or financial relations which differ from those which would be made between independent enterprises, then any profits which would, *(OECD:) but for those conditions, have accrued to one of the enterprises, but, by reason of those conditions, have not so accrued, may be included in the profits of that enterprise and taxed accordingly/ (UN:) but for those conditions have not so accrued, may be included in the profits of that enterprise and taxed accordingly.*'

In the OECD Commentary on this article it is explained that tax authorities of a Contracting State may, for the purpose of calculating tax liabilities of associated enterprises, re-write the accounts of the enterprises if, as a result of the special relations between the enterprises, the accounts do not show the true taxable profits arising in that State. The OECD Commentary furthermore clarifies that re-writing of the accounts of associated enterprises is not authorised if the transactions between such enterprises have taken place on normal open market commercial terms - that is on an arm's length basis.[16] In order to prevent double taxation Art. 9 (2) OECD Model (and most bilateral tax treaties) provides that: in the case that state A re-writes transactions between associated enterprises, state B should provide for a corresponding adjustment if state B considers that the figure of adjusted profits correctly reflects what the profits would have been if the transactions had been at arm's length. However, as par. 6 of the Commentary to this article clarifies, the adjustment is due only if state B considers that the figure of adjusted profits correctly reflects what the profits would have been if the transactions had been at arm's length.

---

15   OECD (2010). *Transfer Pricing Guidelines 2010*, Preface, par. 4 and 7.
16   Par. 2 Commentary to Art. 9, OECD, *OECD Model Tax Convention*.

13.2.4 Codification in Art. 7 OECD Model and Art. 7 UN Model for intracompany transactions (PEs)

For transactions between *parts of the same company* situated in different countries (*intracompany transactions* between head office and permanent establishment or between two permanent establishments) the arm's length principle is laid down in art. 7 (2) OECD Model and art. 7 UN Model (2) determining that:

'For the purposes of this Article and Article (23A) (23 B)' (providing for the methods to prevent double taxation: IJJB and JvdM-K), 'the profits attributable in each Contracting State to the permanent establishment referred to in paragraph 1 are the profits it might be expected to make, in particular in its dealings with other parts of the enterprise, if it were a separate and independent enterprise engaged in the same or similar activities under the same or similar conditions, (OECD:) *taking into account the functions performed, assets used and risks assumed by the enterprise through the permanent establishment and through the other parts of the enterprise.*' (italics added by IJJB and JvdM-K).

The words '*taking into account the functions performed, assets used and risks assumed by the enterprise through the permanent establishment and through the other parts of the enterprise*' have been added in the 2010 revision of the Commentary[17] to the OECD Model in order to express that the 'functionally separate entity approach' is the international standard for the interpretation of Art. 7 OECD Model. This approach was developed in the 2008 OECD Report 'Attribution of Income to Permanent Establishments' in order to prevent the problem of inconsistent interpretation of earlier versions of Art. 7 OECD in which these words were not added. These earlier versions did not sufficiently make clear that all *internal dealings* (dealings between the permanent establishment and other parts of the company) should be remunerated at arm's length. The wording left room for an interpretation that internal dealings should not be rewarded at arm's length at all, which would imply that only third party gross income derived by transactions of the permanent establishment with third parties and related third party costs should be allocated to the permanent establishment (e.g. sales of products). But on the other end of the spectrum, it also leaves room for an interpretation that the permanent establishment should be deemed to be a fully independent enterprise and thus all internal transactions should be rewarded at arm's length (allowing internal royalties and internal interest payments). The latter interpretation would also imply that the permanent establishment should be deemed to have its own Board of Management and Shareholdings Meeting (shareholder costs

---

17 Revision of the 2008 Report was required as the OECD in 2010 adopted a new Art. 7 OECD in order to accommodate for the fact that there were differences between some of the conclusions of the 2008 Report and the interpretation of Article 7 previously given in the Commentary to Art. 7 OECD. Report on the Attribution of Profits to Permanent Establishments, par. 6. E.g. the new OECD approach allows for internal services to be taken into account on an arm's length basis no matter whether these services are part of a service or transaction performed for third parties (and thus there is Aussenumsätz) or whether there is just the internal transaction.

are not deductible), as well as a (minimum) endowment capital (implying that financing costs related to this fictitious endowment capital are not tax deductible).

The 'functionally separate entity approach' does not transform a permanent establishment into a fully independent enterprise but merely states that *all internal transactions* (transfer of goods, services, financing, use of know-how, management) should be rewarded at arm's length and that the permanent establishment should be allocated part of the capital of the worldwide enterprise, as a certain amount of funding made up of 'free' capital and interest-bearing debt is required to carry out the activities of the permanent establishment.

As is the case regarding intercompany transactions, states are entitled to make an adjustment where the taxpayer has not determined the profits attributable to a permanent establishment in conformity with an article in a bilateral tax treaty reading similar to Art 7 (2) OECD Model. The other State may, to the extent necessary to eliminate double taxation on the profits, make a corresponding adjustment in order to avoid double taxation (Art. 7 (3) OECD).

13.2.5 Transfer Pricing Guidelines and Reports on the Allocation of Profits to Permanent Establishments

The OECD, to a great extent, influences the interpretation of these rules and the transfer pricing documentation obligations to be fulfilled for tax purposes. This organisation drafted 'Transfer Pricing Guidelines' in 1979 for the tax authorities of the OECD Member States and then revised versions in 1995 and 2010.

The aim of these Guidelines is to encourage the acceptance of common interpretations of the Model Articles, thereby reducing 'the risk of inappropriate taxation and providing satisfactory means of resolving problems arising from the interaction of the laws and practices of different countries'.[18] In the 2008 Report on the Allocation of Profits to Permanent Establishments the OECD, for the first time, stated that the principles for attributing losses and profits laid down in the Transfer Pricing Guidelines for legally distinct and separate enterprises (*intercompany transactions*) also apply to permanent establishments (*intracompany transactions*). This remark is also made in the 2010 Report.

The Transfer Pricing Guidelines and Reports on the Allocation of Profits to Permanent Establishment show that, both for intercompany and intracompany transactions, a *functional analysis* and a *comparability analysis* have to be made.

---

18 OECD (2010). *OECD Transfer Pricing Guidelines 2010*, Preface, par. 10. The OECD does not clarify the term 'inappropriate'. It only gives some examples of what should be considered as 'inappropriate'. For example, the OECD states in par. 7.35 of the Guidelines that, if the controlled transaction has a higher proportion of overhead costs to direct costs than the otherwise comparable, it may be inappropriate to apply the mark-up received in that transaction without a mark-up adjusting the cost base or the associated company to make a valid comparison.

A *functional analysis* is an analysis of the functions performed (taking into account assets used and risks assumed) in controlled transactions of associated companies or in internal dealings between a permanent establishment and its head office or between two permanent establishments of the same company. Controlled transactions are transactions between two enterprises that are associated enterprises with respect to each other. Internal dealings are transactions between a head office and a permanent establishment or between two permanent establishments.

A comparability analysis is a comparison of a controlled transaction/internal dealing with an uncontrolled transaction or transactions. Controlled and uncontrolled transactions are comparable if none of the differences between the transactions could materially affect the factor being examined in the transfer pricing methodology, or if reasonably accurate adjustments can be made to eliminate the material effects of any such differences.[19]

For *intercompany transactions* the functional analysis is part of the comparability analysis and aims to identify and compare the economically significant activities and responsibilities undertaken, assets used and risks assumed by the parties to the transaction. Adjustments should be made for any material differences from the functions undertaken by any independent enterprises with which that party is being compared. Assumption is that, in transactions between two independent enterprises, compensation will usually reflect the functions that each enterprise performs taking into account assets used and risks assumed.

For *intracompany transactions* a functional analysis should take place before the comparability analysis can be executed, as the functional analysis removes the difficulty that – different from intercompany transactions – contracts are not available in intracompany dealings. For intracompany transactions the functional analysis will lead to:
- the attribution to the permanent establishment of *the rights and obligations* arising out of transactions between the enterprise of which the permanent establishment is a part and separate enterprises;
- the identification of *significant people functions* relevant to the attribution of economic ownership of assets and the attribution of economic ownership of assets to the permanent establishment;
- the identification of *significant people functions* relevant to the assumption of risks and the attribution of risks to the permanent establishment;
- the recognition and determination of *the nature of those dealings* between the permanent establishment and other parts of the same enterprise that can appropriately be recognised;
- the attribution of *capital* based on the assets and risks attributed to the permanent establishment.[20]

---

19 OECD (2010). *OECD Transfer Pricing Guidelines 2010 Glossary.*
20 OECD (2010). *Report on the Attribution of Profits to Permanent Establishment 2010*, par. 59.

The OECD uses the term *significant people function* only in the context of intracompany transactions. The term *significant people functions* is not defined. But the OECD does provide for examples. For instance, for R&D programmes, the term implies taking the initial decision to develop the intangible or carrying out the active management of the R&D programme. Significant people functions are, amongst others, designing the testing specifications and processes within which the research is conducted, reviewing and evaluating the data produced by the tests, setting the stage posts at which decisions are taken and actually taking the decisions on whether to commit further resources to the project or abandon it. No assets or risks should be allocated if no significant people functions are performed.

The use of the term 'significant people functions' does not imply that functions other than significant people functions *(routine functions)* should not be remunerated at arm's length. Moreover, the OECD stresses that a *permanent establishment is not the same as a subsidiary* and is not, in fact, legally or economically separate from the rest of the enterprise of which it is a part. Thus:
– save for exceptional circumstances, all parts of the enterprise have the same *creditworthiness* and thus dealings between a permanent establishment and the rest of the enterprise of which it is a part should be priced on the basis that both share the same creditworthiness;
– there is no scope for the rest of the enterprise to guarantee the permanent establishment's creditworthiness or for the PE to guarantee the creditworthiness of the rest of the enterprise;
– dealings between a permanent establishment and the rest of the enterprise require a greater need for *scrutiny*, as these dealings do not have legal consequences for the enterprise as a whole. A threshold needs to be passed before a dealing is accepted as equivalent to that of a transaction that would have taken place between independent enterprises acting arm's length: the functional and factual analysis should determine whether a real and identifiable event has occurred that should be taken into account as a dealing of economic significance between the permanent establishment and another part of the enterprise.[21]

The functional analysis for both intercompany and intracompany transactions should consider the *type of asset used* and the *nature of the assets used*. Moreover, the *material risks* assumed by each party have been considered, as the assumption or allocation of risks would influence the conditions of transactions between the associated enterprises. The *types of risk* include market risk, risk of loss associated with the investment in and use of property, plant and equipment, risk of the success or failure of investment in research and development, interest rate variability, credit risk and so on.[22]

---

21 OECD (2010). *Report on the Attribution of Profits to Permanent Establishments 2010*, par. 33 – 36.
22 OECD (2010). *Report on the Attribution of Profits of Profits to Permanent Establishments 2010*, par. 145.

Regarding the *comparability analysis*, the TP Guidelines identify five factors determining comparability between controlled and uncontrolled transactions:
- characteristics of property or services;
- functional analysis;
- contractual terms;
- economic circumstances;
- business strategies.

The OECD underlines that all these factors, with the exception of contractual terms, are also applied to evaluate internal dealings, as they are essentially based on facts.[23] We want to emphasise that this implies that, in PE situations, a functional analysis is relevant twice: once in order to adapt internal dealings to arm's length dealings and once in order to determine the correct arm's length price.

13.2.6 Transfer Pricing Methods

The OECD Transfer Pricing Guidelines distinguishes traditional transaction methods (Comparable Uncontrolled Pricing Method, Cost-plus and Resale-minus) and transactional profit methods (profit split and the transactional net margin method (TNMM)). As for the 2010 TP Guidelines, there is no hierarchy between these methods as no one method is suitable for every possible situation. However, where the CUP method and another transfer pricing method can be applied in an equally reliable manner, the CUP method is to be preferred.[24]

In short the methods have the following characteristics:[25]
- the Comparable Uncontrolled Price Method compares the price charged for property or services transferred in a controlled transaction to the price charged for property or services transferred in a comparable uncontrolled transaction in comparable circumstances. A price is comparable if one of two conditions is met:
  - None of the differences (if any) between the transactions being compared or between the enterprises undertaking those transactions could materially affect the price in the open market; or
  - Reasonably accurate adjustments can be made to eliminate the material effects of such differences;
- the Cost Plus Method adds an appropriate cost plus mark up to the costs incurred by the supplier of property (or services) in a controlled transaction for property transferred or services provided to an associated purchaser;
- the Resale Price Method reduces the price at which a product that has been purchased from an associated enterprise is resold to an independent enterprise by an appropriate gross margin on this price. This gross margin represents the amount out of which the reseller would seek to cover its selling expenses and

---

23   OECD (2010). *Report on the Attribution of Profits 2010*, par. 189.
24   OECD (2010). *OECD Transfer Pricing Guidelines 2010*, par. 22 and 23.
25   See for more detailed info a.o. Wittendorf, J. (2010). *Transfer pricing and the arm's length principle in international tax law*. Deventer: Kluwer.

other operating expenses and, in the light of the functions performed (taking into account assets used and risks assumed), make an appropriate profit;
- the Profit Split method seeks to eliminate the effect on profits of special conditions in a controlled transaction by determining the division of profits that independent enterprises would have expected to realise from engaging in the transaction or transactions.[26] It first identifies the profits to be split for the associated enterprises from the controlled transactions in which the associated enterprises are engaged in (the 'combined profit'). Next, the combined profits would be divided between the associated enterprises based upon the relative value of the contribution, being a reasonable approximation of the division of profits that independent enterprises would have been expected to realise from engaging in comparable transactions (contribution analysis). Alternatively, each participant is first allocated an arm's length remuneration for its non-unique contributions in relation to the controlled transactions in which it is engaged by applying one of the traditional transaction methods or TNMM. Any residual profits (or loss) remaining after this stage would be allocated among the parties based on an analysis of the facts and circumstances (residual analysis). The profit split method is not adequate if one party to the transaction performs only simple functions and does not make any significant unique contribution;
- the Transactional Net Margin Method seeks to eliminate the effect on profits of special conditions in a controlled transaction by determining the division of profits that independent enterprises would have expected to realise from engaging in the transaction or transactions.[27] The net profit (instead of the gross profit as is the case in respect of cost plus or resale-minus) relative to an appropriate basis (e.g. costs, sales, assets) that a taxpayer realises from a controlled transaction is examined. TNMM is a one-sided method and is used for the determination of the profit of the 'least complex entity', the part of the enterprise that performs routine functions. The residual part of the profit is allocated to the other part of the company. Fully loaded costs are often used, including all the direct and indirect costs attributable to the activity or transaction, together with an appropriate allocation in respect of the overheads of the business. As is the case regarding the cost plus method, depending on the facts and circumstances of the case, actual costs, as well as standard or budgeted costs, may be appropriate to use as the cost base. Net-operating items such as interest income and expenses and income taxes should be excluded from the determination of the net profit indicator.[28]

Other methods may be acceptable, e.g. in par. 2.56 of the Transfer Pricing Guidelines, the OECD mentions, without further explanation, that the Comparable Profit-method (CPM), as developed under U.S. Transfer Pricing Law, Section 1.482-5 IRC, may be acceptable if it is consistent with the Guidelines. This method is, to a great extent, similar to TNMM, but instead of comparing the net profitability of controlled and uncontrolled particular transactions of the same taxpayer by making use of profit

---

26 OECD (2010). *OECD Transfer Pricing Guidelines 2010*, par. 2.108.
27 OECD (2010). *OECD Transfer Pricing Guidelines 2010*, par. 2.85.
28 OECD (2010). *OECD Transfer Pricing Guidelines 2010*, par. 2.80, 2.93 and 2.95.

level indicators, the determination of an arm's length result is based on the amount of operating profit that the tested party would have earned on related party transactions if its profit level indicator were equal to that of an uncontrolled comparable (comparable operating profit).[29] The determination of an arm's length result is based on the amount of operating profit that the tested party would have earned on related party transactions if its profit level indicator were equal to that of an uncontrolled comparable party (comparable operating profit). As to Section 1.482-5 IRC, comparable operating profit is calculated by determining a profit level indicator for an uncontrolled comparable, and applying the profit level indicator to the financial data related to the tested party's most narrowly identifiable business activity, for which data incorporating the controlled transaction is available (relevant business activity). The tested party will be the participant in the controlled transaction whose operating profit attributable to the controlled transactions can be verified using the most reliable data and requiring the fewest and most reliable adjustments, and for which reliable data regarding uncontrolled comparables can be located. In most cases the tested party will be the least complex of the controlled taxpayers and will not own valuable intangible property or unique assets that distinguish it from potential uncontrolled comparables.

The OECD acknowledges that often, instead of one single figure, a range of figures, all of which are relatively, equally reliable, were produced (an *arm's length range*). The taxpayer may select from this range the most appropriate point in the range or, if that proves to be impossible, the OECD suggests using measures of central tendency to determine this point (for instance, the median, the mean or weighted averages, etc., depending on the specific characteristics of the data set).[30]

Moreover, the OECD allows the use of *more than one method* as long as this will result in the best estimation of an arm's length price (par. 2.11 Transfer Pricing Guidelines).

One of the benefits of forming a group of companies is the *synergy effect*: teamwork will enable the group to outperform even its best individual member. As to the OECD's Working Party that drafted the Transfer Pricing Guidelines 2010, 'the incidental benefits caused by synergy effects, ordinarily, would not cause these other group members to be treated as receiving an intra-group service because the activities producing the benefits would not be ones for which an independent enterprise ordinarily would be willing to pay' (par. 7.12). Par. 9.63 and par. 9.84 of the Transfer Pricing Guidelines 2010 reconfirm that the tax perspective approaches transfer pricing from the perspective of that of the individual companies rather than that of the group:

---

29 Amerkhail, V. (2006). Functional analysis and choosing the best method, par. 12.06, http://www.transferpricing.com/pdf/Functional%20Analysis.pdf, reprint from Cole, R.T. (2006). *Practical guide to U.S. Transfer Pricing*, Third Edition. Washington: Matthew Bender & Company Inc.
30 OECD (2010). *OECD Transfer Pricing Guidelines 2010*, par. 3.62. Not all OESO Member States agree. E.g. the Dutch Secretary of State for Finance in a Decree on Transfer Pricing of 14 November 2013, IFZ 2013/184M indicates the Netherlands will use the median if no specific point can be pinpointed at.

'9.63. The arm's length principle requires an evaluation of the conditions made or imposed between associated enterprises, at the level of each of them. The fact that the cross-border redeployment of functions, assets and/or risks may be motivated by sound commercial reasons at the level of the MNE group, e.g. in order to try to derive synergies at a group level, does not answer the question whether it is arm's length from the perspectives of each of the restructured entities', and

'9.84. The fact that centralisation of intangible property rights may be motivated by sound commercial reasons at the level of the MNE group does not answer the question whether the disposal is arm's length from the perspectives of both the transferor and the transferee'.

This does not imply that the synergy effects should not be taken into account at all. However, if the synergy effects benefit the individual associated company, they should be taken into account. Regarding business restructurings, the OECD argues that it is relevant 'whether a third party would have been willing to acquire the loss-making activity (e.g. because of possible synergies with its own activities) and if so under what conditions'.

For intracompany transactions the OECD gives the example of the creditworthiness of a company and its permanent establishment situated in another country. The OECD is of the view that it would be inconsistent to grant all the benefits of synergy to the head office... as 'the authorised OECD approach is based on the factual situation of the enterprise, which is that the capital, risks, etc. are fungible'. And also regarding the allocation of capital to the permanent establishment, synergy effects are taken into account:

'Since the capital allocation approach seeks to attribute the actual capital of the enterprise, in theory it distributes the benefits of synergy around the enterprise in a way that minimises the likelihood of double taxation (par. 123)'. Again, not the perspective of the group but that of, in this case, the permanent establishment is decisive.

Finally, it should be mentioned that the OECD in its 2010 Transfer Pricing Guidelines introduced two new concepts: *'control over risk'* and *'commercially rational behaviour'*. The OECD introduces the concept of 'control over risk' in Section D.1.2.2 of the Guidelines where the OECD provides guidance on the use of the functional analysis. As to par. 1.49:

'there are many risks, such as general business cycle risks, over which typically neither party has significant control and which at arm's length could therefore be allocated to one or the other party to a transaction. Analysis is required to determine to what extent each party bears such risks in practice'.

The concept of 'commercially rational behaviour' is used to provide evidence whether or not tax evasion is at stake. In par. 1.65 the OECD describes that there are two particular circumstances in which it may, exceptionally, be both appropriate and legitimate for a tax administration to consider disregarding the structure adopted by a taxpayer in entering into a controlled transaction. The first circumstance arises where the economic substance of a transaction differs from its form. In such a case, the tax administration may disregard the parties' characterisation of the transaction and re-characterise it in accordance with its substance. The second circumstance arises where the form and substance of the transaction are the same but the arrangements made in relation to the transaction, viewed in their totality, may differ from those which would have been adopted by independent enterprises behaving in a commercially rational manner. Moreover, practically speaking, the actual structure should impede the tax administration from determining an appropriate transfer price.

The concept of 'control over risk' is also used in the context of tax evasion. As to par. 21 of the OECD Transfer Pricing Guidelines 2010:

'In the absence of comparables evidencing the consistency with the arm's length principle of the risk allocation in a controlled transaction, the examination of which party has greater control over the risk can be a relevant factor to assist in the determination of whether a similar risk allocation would have been agreed between independent parties in comparable circumstances. In such situations, if risks are allocated to the party to the controlled transaction that has relatively less control over them, the tax administration may decide to challenge the arm's length nature of such risk allocation'.

Par. 9.23 provides for a definition of 'control':

'In the context of paragraph 1.49, 'control' should be understood as the capacity to make decisions to take on the risk (decision to put the capital at risk) and decisions on whether and how to manage the risk, internally or using an external provider'.

13.2.7 Documentation requirements

The Transfer Pricing Guidelines not only give guidance in respect to the use of the five transfer pricing methods mentioned above but also in respect to documentation.

Most countries have adopted transfer pricing documentation requirements since the time the U.S. introduced strict requirements together with severe penalties in 1994. The OECD Transfer Pricing Guidelines Chapter V provides general guidance for tax administrations to take into account in developing rules and/or procedures on documentation to be obtained from taxpayers in connection with a transfer pricing inquiry. These Guidelines also provide assistance to taxpayers on how to identify documentation that will show that their controlled transactions satisfy the arm's length principle. Globalisation severely increased the amount of documentation requirements. The 2013 OECD Transfer Pricing Documentation White Paper gives an example of a multinational producing around ten documentation studies per year in the early 1990s to approximately two thousand separate transfer pricing studies by

2007.[31] The OECD acknowledges that 'the proliferation of transfer pricing documentation requirements, combined with a dramatic increase in the volume and complexity of international intra group trade and the heightened scrutiny of transfer pricing issues by tax authorities, makes transfer pricing documentation one of the top tax compliance priorities on the agendas of both tax authorities and businesses'. International co-ordination may 'simplify and consolidate the compliance obligations of business, while at the same time assuring that tax authorities have ready access to the information necessary to efficiently enforce their transfer pricing laws'.[32]

An internal review of the transfer pricing documentation of 25 countries organized by OECD Working Party 6 revealed that transfer pricing documentation requirements amongst countries vary widely, the purposes are not always clear, the requirements are addressed at a domestic level and focus on the domestic side, timing requirements of documentation disclosure varies and the documentation does not always yield a complete understanding of the global business context of the individual transactions. Most countries ask for information on the legal and organisational context, a description of the internal transaction and explanation of the transfer pricing methods used and a functional and comparability analysis, but only a few ask, for example, for information on the business strategy, the supply chain or the price negotiation process, financial or accounting data. The survey does not reveal to what extent companies use the same information for both tax purposes and management control issues.

The OECD, in its White Paper on Transfer Pricing Documentation, points out that tax authorities need ready access to sufficient information at the early stages of an audit. Transfer Pricing Documentation rules should be designed in such a way that the risk assessment can be carried out efficiently and with the right kinds of reliable information.[33] As for the OECD, businesses may provide, without undue burden, individual country data based on either management accounts, consolidating income statements and balance sheets, and/or tax returns that would provide tax administrators with a general sense as to how their global income is allocated and where pressure points in the transfer pricing arrangements might lie. Such information would likely not be a sufficient basis for a detailed transfer pricing analysis of individual transactions and prices, nor would it provide a substitute for a full functional analysis.[34]

The OECD acknowledges that the past few years' enterprises developed 'sound tax risk assessment and management systems for purposes of administering and com-

---

31   The OECD refers to McWilliams, R. (2014). GE Counsel Details Transfer Pricing Documentation Challenges. In: *Tax Management Transfer Pricing report*, BNA (April 2007).
32   OECD (2013). *OECD White Paper on Transfer Pricing Documentation*, 30 June 2013, p.4, http://www.oecd.org/ctp/transfer-pricing/white-paper-transfer-pricing-documentation.pdf, par. 2
33   OECD (2013). *OECD White Paper on Transfer Pricing Documentation*, 30 June 2013, p.4, http://www.oecd.org/ctp/transfer-pricing/white-paper-transfer-pricing-documentation.pdf, par 50.
34   OECD (2013). *OECD White Paper on Transfer Pricing Documentation*, 30 June 2013, p.4, http://www.oecd.org/ctp/transfer-pricing/white-paper-transfer-pricing-documentation.pdf, par. 72.

plying with transfer pricing rules', but costs, time constraints and competing demands for the attention of relevant personnel can undermine these objectives.[35] Therefore the OECD recommends that the transfer pricing documentation should focus on significant transfer pricing risks. The OECD proposes a 'Co-ordinated Approach to Documentation' and a two-tier structure similar to that proposed by the EU documentation package. Taxpayers provide master file information either on a company wide basis or by line of business, depending on which would provide the most relevant transfer pricing information to tax authorities. This master file should provide a complete picture of the 'global business, financial reporting, debt structure and tax situation of the multinational enterprise. Specific transfer pricing analyses related to individual transactions could be reserved to local country documentation. The aim of the documentation requirement is 'to enable tax authorities to identify the presence of significant transfer pricing risks'. The master file 'would seek to elicit a reasonably complete picture of the global business, financial reporting, debt structure and tax situation of the MNE to enable tax authorities to identify the presence of significant transfer pricing risks'. The OECD divides the information that should be included in the master file into the following groups:

- information on the MNEs business, including a description of value drivers, supply chain, main markets for material products and services, competitors and important business restructuring transactions occurring during the last 5 years;
- a description of the MNEs organisational and legal structure;
- information on the immaterial assets of the MNE;
- information on financial intercompany activities of the MNE;
- information on the financial and tax positions of the MNE.

The country files should provide for information on the organisational and management structure of the local entity and for a functional and comparability analysis with respect to each documented category of internal transactions. These files should also contain the annual local entity financial accounts for the previous (x number of) years, audited if they exist, as well as information and allocation schedules showing how the financial data used in applying the transfer pricing method may be tied to the annual financial statements.

13.2.8 OECD Transfer Pricing Risk Assessment Handbook

In order to encourage early collaboration between tax administrations and taxpayers and to avoid protracted transfer pricing disputes, the OECD published a Draft Transfer Pricing Risk Assessment Handbook on its website on 30 April 2013 and asked the public for comments.[36] The aim of the Handbook is to provide tax administrations information on how to select the right transfer pricing cases for tax audits, as effective risk identification and assessment are critical if tax administrations are to select the right transfer pricing cases for audit. It also enables the actual audit to be more

---

35 OECD (2013). *OECD White Paper on Transfer Pricing Documentation*, 30 June 2013, p.4, http://www.oecd.org/ctp/transfer-pricing/white-paper-transfer-pricing-documentation.pdf, par. 47.
36 http://www.oecd.org/tax/transfer-pricing/Draft-Handbook-TP-Risk-Assessment-ENG.pdf

focused, shorter and more effective. Thus, both the resources of the tax administration and that of the taxpayer may be used in the most efficient way. The Handbook provides information on recent country procedures, transfer pricing methods and practices. Tax administrations can use this information to design their own risk assessment approaches and to select transfer pricing issues for audit. The Handbook also discusses the exchange of information under tax treaties between governments.

Of course, this Handbook also gives taxpayers insight into the many different approaches used by tax administrations, which will enable them to determine their tax compliance risk.

At the time of writing this Chapter (December 2014), the OECD is working on the final version of the Handbook.

13.2.9   Tax Control Framework

In the previous subsections, an overview of the hard law and soft law requirements posed in the domestic statutory law of states, the OECD Transfer Pricing Guidelines and the EU documentation package has been provided. The information collected by companies about their internal transactions for calculating taxes due and for the purpose of providing evidence to tax administrations that the profits assessed are at arm's length, is part of the Tax Control Framework of companies. However, Tax Control Frameworks have a wider scope, as these Frameworks are set up to identify and monitor tax risks. Tax Control Frameworks, amongst others, contain information about the organisation of the company and its business process, the tax strategy of a company and its execution, the tax process (such as timing issues), the tax accounting process, tasks and responsibilities related to the tax process (including information on what to do in case of conflict between the tax authorities and the company) and tax accounting process, and the IT-systems used.[37]

In its 'Tax Control Framework' Memorandum, the Dutch Tax Administration defines a Tax Control Framework as an internal tax control system in which businesses establish their tax processes, that is part of the companies' Management Control System that is set up to control business processes.[38] Thus, management control tools such as risk maps, responsibility matrixes, flow charts and dashboards are also used for the Tax Control Framework. For more detailed information on Tax Control Framework see chapters 2, 5 and 6.

---

37 Hoyng, R., Kloosterhof, S. & Macpherson, A. (2010). Tax Control Framework, Chapter 2. In: Bakker, A. & Kloosterhof, S., *Tax Risk Management*. Amsterdam: IBFD, electronic publication, first published as book in 2010.
38 Belastingdienst (2008). *Thinking differently Behaving differently, working differently*. http://download.belastingdienst.nl/belastingdienst/docs/thinking_differently_behaving_differently_working_differently_dv4001z1pleng.pdf

13.3 The management control perspective

13.3.1 Introduction

In order to manage and control internal transactions we need to know why transactions are wound up within a company and not on the market. We use the ideas of Transaction Cost Theory to answer this question. Williamson,[39] the most prominent advocate of Transaction Cost Theory, argues that transactions will take place within a company (he talks about the hierarchy) if winding up these transactions on the market leads to higher transaction costs. The management control framework of internal transactions has to reap the benefits (i.e. lower transaction costs) of winding up the transactions within the company. To be able to reap these benefits, the management control framework of internal transactions has to support the decision-making over internal transactions by the central management and the managers of the transacting organisational units in such a way that the goals of the company are achieved. Both aims of the management control framework of internal transactions, i.e. reaping the benefits of internal transactions, and effectively supporting the decision-making by the central management and the management of the transacting organisational units, will be discussed in more detail below in the sections 9.3.2 and 9.3.3. In section 9.3.4, we will present the key elements of the management control framework of internal transactions.

13.3.2 Benefits of internal transactions: lower transaction costs

The first aim of the management control framework of internal transactions is to realise the benefits of winding up transactions within the company, i.e. lower transaction costs.

Transaction cost theory claims that the following three dimensions of transactions influence the level of transaction costs:
- *the degree and character of asset specificity*; i.e. the specificity of the investments made in assets (tangible and intangible assets, and human knowledge) needed for the production of the goods or services being exchanged;
- *the frequency and volume of the transactions*: if the transactions are more frequent and have a higher volume the connection between the transacting parties is closer;
- *the level of environmental and behavioural uncertainty*: if the level of environmental and behavioural uncertainty is high, the risk of opportunistic behaviour by one of the transacting parties is high.

Transaction cost theory argues that if the degree of asset specificity and the level of uncertainty are high, and the transactions are frequent and have a high volume, winding up the transactions on the market could lead to high transaction costs as the

---

39　Williamson, O.E. (1985). *The economic institutions of capitalism: firms, markets, relational contracting*. New York: The Free Press; Williamson, O.E. (2008). Outsourcing, transaction cost economics and supply chain management. *Journal of Supply Chain Management*, 44(2), p. 5-16.

risk of opportunistic behaviour by one of the parties is high. The party that has invested in specific assets connected to the transactions runs the risk that when changing market conditions require renegotiation of the transaction terms, the partner could take advantage of this situation by insisting on a lower price. The party is forced to accept the lower price as terminating the relationship prematurely strongly decreases the value of the investments made in specific assets. The risk of opportunistic behaviour can be mitigated by winding up the transactions within the hierarchy (instead of on the market), within which management controls can be developed to influence the behaviour of the transacting parties.

Transaction costs related to transactions on the market are: costs of looking for a suitable partner, costs related to negotiating contractual arrangements and monitoring whether the partner complies with these arrangements, costs of renegotiating the contractual arrangements, and missed revenues due to opportunistic behaviour of the partner. These costs will not be made if the transactions are wound up internally. However, winding up transactions within the company also involves transaction costs such as: costs of setting up and using a management control framework of internal transactions, arbitration costs in case of conflicts between the transacting organisational units and costs of information processing. Nevertheless, the costs of information processing could be lower by winding up transactions within the company. Furthermore, the exchange of technological and market knowledge between the internal parties will be easier, which enhances the quality and co-ordination of the internal parties' production activities.

13.3.3 Supporting the decision-making process

The second aim of the management control framework of internal transactions is related to the way the decision-making process is structured. The larger companies are and the more different products they produce and sell on the market, the more complex their decision-making processes are. To take decisions, information is required. In large companies the required information is available at different organisational levels. If all decisions are taken by the central management, information that is available at lower organisational levels needs to be passed on to the central management. This increases the cost of information processing but it also slows down the decision-making process. Moreover, all information cannot easily be passed on to a higher management level. Specifically, tacit knowledge, i.e. knowledge an individual gets from personal experience, which is difficult to transfer to other individuals by means of writing it down or verbalising it. In order to prevent loss of information and/or a slow decision-making process, decision rights can be decentralised to lower management levels.[40] Decentralising decision rights implies that responsibilities are apportioned to lower management levels.

---

40 Galbraith, J.R. (1973). *Designing complex organizations*. Reading, Massachusetts: Addisson-Wesley Publishing Company.

The degree of decentralising decision rights and responsibilities can differ. In the management control literature various types of responsibility centres are distinguished: investment centres, profit centres, cost centres, and revenue centres.[41] The management of an *investment centre* is held responsible for both the centre's profits (revenues minus costs) and the investments made to generate those profits, whereas the management of a *profit centre* is held responsible for the centre's profits but not for the investments made. The management of a *cost centre* is held responsible for the costs made within the centre. The management of a *revenue centre* is held responsible for the revenues generated by the centre. The management of an investment centre has the highest level of autonomy. Less autonomy is given to the management of a profit centre, as this management is not allowed to decide about the centre's investments, but it can influence the costs and revenues of the centre. The management of a cost centre can only influence the efficiency of the production process and the purchase of materials and intermediates. The management of a revenue centre can only influence the revenues and not the costs of the goods or services sold by the centre (except some expenses, such as the salaries and travel expenses of the sales people).

The differences in apportioning responsibilities to the management of responsibility centres also have consequences for their level of autonomy with respect to the management of internal transactions.[42] In line with its high level of autonomy in general, the management of an investment centre decides about the management of its internal transactions. The management has significant decision-making authority over the sourcing of its transactions (i.e. the selection of the buyer and seller of goods and services) and over the transaction terms. The management of a profit centre has authority over the transaction terms of the internal transactions (price, quality, etcetera), but it may have limited authority over the sourcing of its transactions, specifically if the profit centre has made highly specific investments. The management of a cost centre has no authority over the sourcing decisions and most of the transaction terms. Instead, the internal transactions and most of the transaction terms are prescribed by the central management. The management of a cost centre determines the quality and efficiency of the production of internal goods or services. The management of a revenue centre is held responsible for the centre's revenues and therefore it has authority over its sales of goods or services bought internally.

The degree of decentralisation of decision rights partly determines the design of the overall management control system of a company (see chapter 3.2.6.3. for the

---

41 Vosselman, E.G.J. (1999). *Management accounting en control.* Utrecht: Lemma; Merchant, K.A. & Van der Stede, W.A. (2012). *Management Control Systems: Performance Measurement, Evaluation and Incentives*, third edition. London: Prentice Hall.
42 Van Helden, G.J., Van der Meer-Kooistra, J. & Scapens, R.W. (2001). Co-ordination of internal transactions at Hoogovens Steel: struggling with the tension between performance-oriented business units and the concept of an integrated company. *Management Accounting Research*, 12, 357-386; Cools, M. (2002). *International transfer pricing: tensions between tax compliance and management control in multinational enterprises.* Ac. Diss, Antwerpen; Merchant, K.A. & Van der Stede, W.A. (2012). *Management Control Systems: Performance Measurement, Evaluation and Incentives*, third edition. London: Prentice Hall.

corporate governance aspects of (de)centralisation). The management control framework of internal transactions is part of the overall management control system. Therefore, the management control framework of internal transactions has to be geared to the overall management control system. In this way, the behaviour of the lower level managers can be influenced in a consistent way.[43]

13.3.4 Key elements of the management control framework of internal transactions

Research[44] shows that a management control framework of internal transactions consists of the following key elements:
- application area: which internal transactions the rules are applied to;
- general starting points: for example, the aim is to stimulate market-oriented relationships between the transacting parties;
- apportioning of authority:
  o who is involved in the development of the system?
  o who determines the choice of the internal supplier or internal buyer?
  o who determines the transfer price?
  o who determines the other transaction terms, such as terms of delivery, product specifications, quality requirements and control?
  o who determines the investments in production capacity?
- transfer price basis and the definition of this basis;
- transaction terms i.e. terms under which the internal transactions take place;
- consultation structure: consultations about the management of internal transactions between the internal supplier and internal buyer as well as between the transacting parties and the central management;
- administrative support: processing of orders, recording of internal transactions, information processing to the transacting parties;
- arbitration process in case of conflicts between the internal parties;
- conditions that may require adjustment of the management control framework of internal transactions;
- the process of developing adjustments: who is involved in this process, who decides about the adjustments, and how are the adjustments communicated.

These elements determine how internal transactions are prepared, concluded and wound up and to what extent the authority, with respect to internal transactions, is decentralised.

---

[43] Emmanuel, C.R. & Mehafdi, M. (1994). *Transfer pricing*. London: Academic Press; Van Helden, G.J., Van der Meer-Kooistra, J. & Scapens, R.W. (2001). Co-ordination of internal transactions at Hoogovens Steel: struggling with the tension between performance-oriented business units and the concept of an integrated company. *Management Accounting Research*, 12, 35-386.

[44] Van der Meer-Kooistra, J. (1994). The co-ordination of internal transactions: the functioning of transfer pricing systems in the organizational context. *Management Accounting Research*, 5(2), 123-152; Van Helden, G.J., Van der Meer-Kooistra, J. & Scapens, R.W. (2001). Co-ordination of internal transactions at Hoogovens Steel: struggling with the tension between performance-oriented business units and the concept of an integrated company. *Management Accounting Research*, 12, 35-386.

The financial boundaries between the transacting organisational units are determined by the transfer price. This price can be based on the market price or the costs of the goods or services. As the management of investment centres and profit centres are held responsible for their profits, they are allowed to determine the transfer price of their goods or services themselves. The transfer price used by investment centres and profit centres can be the outcome of negotiations between the transacting parties. The transfer price used by cost centres and revenue centres will be prescribed. The transfer price used by cost centres will be based on the costs of the goods or services. By using the standard cost price of the goods or services, the management of a cost centre is stimulated to produce in a cost efficient manner.

The transfer price used by revenue centres will be based on the market price of the goods or services. In specific circumstances, dual pricing can be applied which implies that the internal supplier receives a higher price for the goods or services sold than the (lower) price paid by the internal buyer. The higher price received by the internal supplier consists of the (lower) price paid by the internal buyer and a budget supplied by the central management. In this way the internal buyer is stimulated to buy the goods or services internally. Dual pricing can be applied to stimulate the introduction of new products or services on the market. In this way the sales department gets motivated to sell the new products or services on the market.

The management control framework of internal transactions needs to be adjusted if the characteristics of the internal transactions, the transacting parties and/or the organisational context change.[45] Therefore, this management control framework indicates when adjustments are allowed and who has to be consulted about the development of adjustments.

13.4 Differences between the tax perspective and the management control perspective

A comparison of the tax perspective and the management control perspective, described in section 9.2 and section 9.3 respectively, allows us to indicate the main differences between these perspectives. Below, we will elaborate on these differences.

13.4.1 Goal of the perspective: preventing double taxation and profit shifting versus influencing behaviour within the company

The aim of transfer pricing rules for tax purposes is to prevent both double taxation and profit shifting between different organisational units of internationally operating companies: the profit that is allocated to the different organisational units should

---

[45] Van der Meer-Kooistra, J. (1994). The co-ordination of internal transactions: the functioning of transfer pricing systems in the organizational context. *Management Accounting Research*, 5(2), 12-152; Van Helden, G.J., Van der Meer-Kooistra, J. & Scapens, R.W. (2001). Co-ordination of internal transactions at Hoogovens Steel: struggling with the tension between performance-oriented business units and the concept of an integrated company. *Management Accounting Research*, 12, 357-386

reflect the profit that uncontrolled companies would make. The tax perspective's aim is to allocate legal entities being part of a group within or outside of the state of residence of the other entities that are part of the group, on an arm's length basis (intercompany transactions), and to allocate profits to permanent establishments on an arm's length basis taking into account the functions performed, assets used and risks assumed by the enterprise through the permanent establishment and through the other parts of the enterprise (intracompany transactions).

The aim of the management control perspective is to realise the benefits of winding up transactions within the company as well as to support the (centralised and decentralised) decision-making related to internal transactions in such a way that the goals of the company are achieved. The management control perspective focuses on the conditions of winding up internal transactions such as quantity, quality, price, delivery date, payment methods, administrative support and apportioning of authority with respect to internal transactions to the organisational units (who decides about the sourcing of goods and services, the transfer price and the other terms of delivery?). These conditions influence the behaviour of the parties involved in the internal transactions.

13.4.2 Goal of the perspective: focus on significant transfer pricing risks versus risks in general

Risk management is a relevant element of the overall management control framework. Risk management identifies all types of risk a company faces and develops measures to prevent or reduce these risks, including the tax risk, but also other legislative and non-legislative risks. To be able to manage the risks connected to internal transactions, these risks need to be identified. An internationally operating company has to comply with the tax rules of the countries it operates in. By taking adequate management control measures, the company can reduce this tax compliance risk.

Identifying transfer pricing risks is not only important for companies but also for tax administrations. In its 2010 White Paper on Transfer Pricing Documentation the OECD suggests companies should provide a master file that will allow tax authorities to identify the presence of significant transfer pricing risks, in particular in respect to financial transactions and transfer of immaterial assets.

However, risks connected to the transactions of goods and services in general are not limited to the significant transfer pricing risks. The OECD 2010 White Paper on Transfer Pricing Documentation focuses on; i.e. the risks related to financial transactions and transfer of immaterial assets. Management control measures should also prevent or reduce general risks. The focus of the OECD relating to significant transfer pricing risks may result in companies neglecting other risks connected to internal transactions that may be relevant for the management control perspective. For example, if a company uses one control framework that focuses on reducing tax compliance risks and does not take into account the overall management control perspective, this may lead to tensions between the transacting parties and suboptimal decisions.[46]

13.4.3 Point of departure: legal entities versus organisational units

Tax law uses the arm's length principle both for intercompany transactions and intracompany transactions. For intercompany transactions the *contract* is the starting point, whereas the functional analysis is used for intracompany transactions to determine which functions, assets and risks should be allocated to which part of the company and which *internal* dealings should be rewarded with an arm's length price. Both for domestic law and tax treaty law, purposes tax law considers the different organisational units of a (group of) company(ies) – whether or not a separate legal entity - as independent parties. The profit that should be allocated for tax purposes to these different organisational units should reflect the profits independent parties would make. For this purpose, analysis of functions performed, assets used and risks assumed is part of the comparability analysis. Such analysis is also needed for intracompany transactions as a proxy for the contracts that would have been signed if the transaction would not have taken place within the legal entity but between third parties.

The management control perspective does not take into account the legal structure of a company but it focuses on the company's organisational structure. The organisational structure recognises organisational units, no matter whether these units are separate legal entities or not. Moreover, the management control perspective does not use the concepts of functional analysis and comparability analysis.

13.4.4 Point of departure: country-by-country versus organisational unit-by-organisational unit

The tax perspective by its very nature focuses on the profits per country. Thus, it is logical that the OECD in its 2013 Transfer Pricing Documentation White Paper suggests that, besides a master file, the company should draft country specific files.[47]

For the management control perspective, country specific information processing will be less relevant if the company's activities are not structured per country but, for example, per group of countries (e.g., Europe or Southeast Asia) or per product group. Then the company is interested in information about the profitability of its activities in, for example, Europe and Southeast Asia or the profitability of each of the product

---

46 Cools, M. & Slagmulder, R. (2009). Tax-compliant transfer pricing and responsibility accounting. *Journal of Management Accounting Research*, 21, 151-178.
47 The OECD, in this, follows the EU Code of Conduct on Transfer Pricing Documentation for associated enterprises which gives guidance for a two-tier documentation structure consisting of an MNE Master file and country-specific documentation. Resolution of the Council and of the representatives of the governments of the Member States, meeting within the Council, of 27 June 2006 on a code of conduct on transfer pricing documentation for associated enterprises in the European Union (2006/C 176/01).

groups distinguished. Hence, the company with such an organisational structure is not interested in the profits per country.

13.4.5 Point of departure: transfer pricing documentation requirements that may differ from country to country versus transfer pricing documentation determined by the (group of) company(ies)

The transfer pricing documentation requirements prescribed by tax law vary from country to country. Whereas some countries, such as the U.S. and Germany, make use of extensive and detailed rules, other countries, such as the Netherlands, use a general rule. Moreover, the rules may vary depending on whether the state uses a system of taxation that is residence based (worldwide income is taxed in the state of residence), source based (only income having its source in the state is taxed in that state) or both. These differences in rules result in high tax compliance risks and in complex transfer pricing administrations.

For management control purposes the administration supports the processing of orders, the recording of internal transactions and the processing of information about the internal transactions (such as production costs, overhead, etc.) to the transacting parties. Usually, companies strive for administrative tasks being as simple as possible. Companies are not bound by any rules on documentation for management control purposes.

13.4.6 Synergy effects versus transaction costs

The comparison with independent parties as prescribed by tax law, in principle, takes into account synergy effects for the existence of internal transactions. Tax law looks at synergy effects from the perspective of the individual parts of the group and not from the perspective of the group as a whole, as is illustrated by quotes from the OECD Transfer Pricing Guidelines 2010 and the 2010 Report on the Attribution of Profits to Permanent Establishments referred to in par. 2.

The management control perspective does not only pay attention to synergy effects and other effects (such as: effects of scale and scope) which could decrease the costs of internal transactions but it also takes into account the transaction costs of internal transactions. Apportioning authority over the internal transactions to the transacting parties, whereby their knowledge of the characteristics of the internal transactions can be used, and adequately informing them about the internal transactions, are management control measures which allow the company to reap the transaction cost benefits of internal transactions.

13.4.7 Aim of transfer pricing methods used: arm's length result versus desired degree of decentralisation

The arm's length principle used for tax law purposes is not used for management control purposes. For management control purposes the transfer pricing method used should fit in with the decision-making structure of the company (i.e. the degree of decentralisation of authority and responsibilities). Nevertheless, transfer pricing methods used for tax law purposes such as CUP (for management control purposes referred to as market price) and the cost plus method are used for management control purposes too. Using an arm's length price could satisfy both tax and management control purposes if a company has not portioned out authority to lower level managers. Then the central management takes all relevant decisions and prescribes the internal transactions' terms to the lower level managers. Such a centralised, organisational structure assumes that the central management possesses all the information and, hence, can make the best decisions. However, processing all information to the central management is costly and in this process relevant information may get lost. Therefore, companies decide to portion out authority to lower level managers who can use their local knowledge and experience. By decentralising the decision making, companies are able to save on transaction costs and to reap the benefits of internal transactions. The more authority is portioned out to the lower level managers the more they influence the management of the internal transactions. Hence, it may be expected that the managers of investment centres, who are held responsible for the investments made in their centres' production capacity and the profits of their centres' output, decide about all the terms of their internal transactions, i.e. the sourcing of their transactions, the transfer price (which can be based on the market price, the costs, or can be the result of negotiations) and the other transaction terms. It may also be expected that the managers of profit centres, who are held responsible for the profits of their centres (they are not held responsible for the investments in their centres' production capacity), decide about the sourcing of their transactions, the transfer price (which can be based on the market price, the costs, or can be the result of negotiations), and the other transaction terms. As the managers of cost centres are only held responsible for the costs of their inputs and resources consumed, these managers decide about the efficiency of their activities, but they cannot decide about the sourcing of their transactions and the transfer price. To make the managers of cost centres responsible for the efficiency of their activities, the standard cost price will be used as transfer price. However, the standard cost price generally will not be the arm's length price required by the tax authorities. The managers of revenue centres are held responsible for the revenues of their centres. Therefore, they determine how to operate on the market (selection of customers, development of customer relationships, setting of selling prices). The transfer price of the internal deliveries of goods or services to the revenue centres will be prescribed.

13.4.8 Determination of costs: what costs would be used by third parties versus what costs would influence the behaviour of the transacting parties

The management control perspective can use different concepts of costs when it uses transfer prices based on cost, such as variable costs, fixed costs, direct costs, indirect costs etc. In the case of a cost centre, the concept of standard cost will be used in order to be able to identify inefficiencies in the cost centre's activities and to hold the cost centre accountable for its inefficiencies (see also the next difference). Standard costs are the costs of the inputs and resources that should have been consumed in producing the products or services. Inefficiencies are the differences between the costs that were actually incurred minus the standard costs.

The OECD Transfer Pricing Guidelines also refer to variable and fixed costs, to direct and indirect costs, to the internal and external costs and pass-through costs. However, the concept of standard cost price, which is an important concept for management control purposes, is not referred to in these Guidelines. By using the standard cost price as transfer price and not the actual costs, the cost centre cannot pass through inefficiencies to the internal buyer. This will encourage the cost centre to produce its products or services as efficiently as possible.

As the OECD Transfer Pricing Guidelines do not refer to the standard cost price, tax administrations may require companies to use the actual costs.

13.4.9 Bargaining as transfer pricing method

For management control purposes, the transfer price could be determined in negotiations between the transacting parties. As managers of investment centres and profit centres are responsible for the profits made within their centre, allowing them to negotiate over the transfer price fits in with their responsibility.

The OECD acknowledges in par. 1.5 of the Transfer Pricing Guidelines 2010 that bargaining may be used to determine the transfer price but at the same time warns tax administrations that the relationship between the associated enterprises may influence the outcome of the bargaining: 'Therefore, evidence of hard bargaining alone is not sufficient to establish that the transactions are at arm's length'.

13.4.10 Acceptance of simultaneous use of two or more transfer pricing methods

For management control purposes, in order to stimulate the managers of organisational units to buy specific products or services internally, companies could simultaneously use two or more transfer pricing methods, called dual pricing. For example, to stimulate the sales of newly developed products or services, the sales department pays a lower price than the price received by the production department. By so doing, the sales department is prepared to sell products on the market which have a lower profit margin.

The use of more than one method is allowed for tax purposes though the OECD, in par. 2.11 of its Transfer Pricing Guidelines 2011, remarks that, generally, it will be possible to select one method that is apt to provide the best estimation of an arm's length price. In difficult cases, where no one approach is conclusive, the OECD recommends a flexible approach, as long as 'a conclusion will be reached that is consistent with the arm's length principle that is satisfactory from a practical viewpoint to all the parties involved, taking into account the facts and circumstances of the case, the mix of evidence available and the relative reliability of the various methods under consideration'.

13.4.11 Timing issues: 'no hindsight' versus 'making use of up-to-date information'

For tax purposes 'hindsight' is not allowed. This implies that changes in the economic and market factors that occur after the date of the transaction should not be taken into account when determining the transfer price, and information from the years following the transaction can only be taken into account to the extent that it does not take into account subsequent events. Data from years following the year of the transaction may be used for determining the comparable transactions, e.g. subsequent conduct may be relevant for tax purposes in ascertaining the terms and conditions that operate between the parties and data from later years may be useful in determining the comparable transactions (e.g. similar life cycles).[48] For management control purposes the information used should be 'up to date'; in other words, changes in the economic and market situation have to be taken into account. Decisions related to internal transactions have to be based on the actual situation.

13.4.12 Relation of transfer pricing systems with the overall Management Control System

The management control framework of internal transactions is an element of the overall management control system, which may – but not necessarily has to - include a tax control framework. The overall management control system is only effective if all its elements match and do not lead to opposite signals. As already mentioned, the requirement that an arm's length price including a profit mark up should be used for tax purposes may lead to such opposite signals. Thus, as we have discussed above, if one control framework is used for both management control purposes and tax purposes, in particular cost centres cannot adequately be managed. This may cause tensions between the transacting parties and lead to suboptimal decisions.

13.5 Consequences of using one framework for controlling internal transactions for both the tax perspective and the management control perspective

In section 13.4, we have described the main differences between the tax perspective and the management control perspective on internal transactions. This description shows that the differences are of a fundamental nature. The aims of both perspectives differ in such a way that it is hardly possible to fully align them. If companies use one framework, we observe that this framework focuses primarily on one perspective. As indicated in section 13.4, this may cause tensions between the transacting parties and lead to suboptimal decisions. On the other hand, being able to use one control framework for both perspectives would decrease the administrative costs of internal

---

48 Definition provided by: EU Joint Transfer Pricing Forum (2013). *Supplementary Discussion Paper on Compensation Year-End Adjustments*, meeting of 14 February 2013, http://ec.europa.eu/taxation_customs/resources/documents/taxation/company_tax/transfer_pricing/forum/jtpf/2013/jtpf_004_2013_en.pdf. The OECD, up to the time of writing of this Chapter (December 2014), did not provide for a definition of the term.

transactions. In addition, using one control framework might convince the tax authorities that the company does not strive for shifting profits between countries. Lately, the OECD has an even keener eye for the management control perspective and the fact that using two control frameworks increases the administrative costs of internal transactions. The OECD's proposal to introduce a master file and separate country files can be viewed in that light. The introduction of the concepts 'commercial rational acting independent parties' and 'level of control' in the TP Guidelines 2010 can stimulate the use of one control framework. However, until now the OECD has not clearly defined these concepts, which hinders their use. Moreover, the elements that have to be included in the master file and the country specific files proposed by the OECD in the White Paper on Transfer Pricing Documentation are described in general terms, which complicates their use.

Cools & Slagmulder[49] have investigated the problems caused by using one control framework. They have studied the control framework of a multinational enterprise (MNE) which decided to focus its control framework on the tax perspective. The study of Cools & Slagmulder indicates that using one control framework that focuses on the tax perspective causes problems, as this framework does not fit in with the apportioning of authority. This misalignment does not adequately stimulate the behaviour of the lower level managers. In addition, the control framework of internal transactions does not fit in with the overall management control system, which creates tensions between the central management and the lower level managers leading to sub optimal decisions. Cools & Slagmulder conclude that, as for tax purposes the internal transacting parties were not allowed to negotiate about the transfer price, the perceived level of autonomy has strongly been decreased and the loss of bargaining power has led to suboptimal decisions. [50] In order to comply with the tax rules, the MNE has implemented uniform profit margins for all similar stages in its value chain. This has caused suboptimal decisions. Moreover, by using profit margins, cost centres and revenue centres were treated as profit centres. In the first instance, the MNE tried to find a solution by evaluating the cost centres and the revenue centres according to their responsibility whilst, from the tax perspective, these centres were treated as profit centres. In a later stage, the MNE decided to evaluate these pro forma profit centres as real profit centres.

The differences we mapped in this chapter confirm, from a theoretical perspective, Cools & Slagmulder's finding. If an internationally operating company uses a control framework that focuses on the management control perspective, there is a risk that this framework does not comply with the tax rules. This tax compliance risk will be high if the management control framework distinguishes cost centres and revenue centres, as in these centres the transfer price does not include a profit mark up. If the management control framework recognises investment centres and profit centres,

---

49 Cools, M. & Slagmulder, R. (2009). Tax-compliant transfer pricing and responsibility accounting. *Journal of Management Accounting Research*, 21, 151-178.
50 Note that other than the 2010 OECD Transfer Pricing Guidelines, the 1995 OECD Transfer Pricing Guidelines did not accept a negotiated transfer price.

then the compliance risk will be lower as a profit mark up is included in the transfer price.

As mentioned, since 2010 the OECD Transfer Pricing Guidelines do allow a negotiated transfer price, the research of Cools and Slagmulder is, to some extent, outdated. If the transfer price is negotiated, the compliance risk will be low as it may be expected that the transacting parties base their negotiated transfer price on the market price, if available. If a market price is not available because of the specific characteristics of the internal transactions, the negotiated transfer price will be based on the costs of the goods or services. Moreover, the managers of the investment and profit centres will mark up the costs by a profit margin, since these managers are held responsible for the profits made by their centre. Nevertheless, as illustrated by par. 1.5 of the OECD TP Guidelines, there is a risk that the tax authorities do not accept the negotiated transfer price even though this price is based on the market price or the costs. The negotiated transfer price may differ from the arm's length price as the bargaining power of the transacting parties plays a role in the negotiations, and the bargaining power of internal parties can differ from the bargaining power of independent parties.

Another reason why the management control framework and the tax control framework of internal transactions may differ, results from the fact that the tax perspective takes separate legal entities and profits that should be determined per country as a starting point, whereas the management control framework takes business units or divisions into account that are not organised per country. If the internationally operating company uses a management control framework that does not pay any attention to the profits made in the separate countries in which the company operates facilities, the company is not able to provide the country information required by the tax rules. Hence, the company needs to collect this information separately.

A solution to the problems caused by the differences in perspective may be the use of 'hybrid transfer pricing systems' as evidenced by the research of Boeltjes, De Vries and Steens. These authors describe the transfer pricing system of the centrally managed purchase organisation Liz Claiborne/Mexx that starts from the management control perspective and contains adjustments for the tax perspective.[51] However, as argued in section 13.4, it will be easier for companies with a centralised decision-making structure to integrate the tax control framework and the management control framework. Such an integration will be much more complicated for companies with a decentralised decision-making structure.

13.6 Conclusions: one or two control frameworks of internal transactions?

For tax assurance purposes, a tax control framework that is able to identify, monitor and mitigate transfer pricing risks is of utmost relevance as the transfer pricing risk, as

---

[51] Boeltjes de Vries, Y.R.Chr. & Steens, H.B.A. (2011). Transfer pricing als instrument van management control: casus Liz Claiborne/Mexx. In: *Handboek Management Accounting*, www.finance-control.nl, visited 14 October, 2014.

is shown in section 13.1, is considered to be one of the most important types of tax risks. In order to mitigate compliance risks, companies, amongst others, should take care that their transfer pricing documentation fulfills the requirements of the tax administrations. New developments, such as country-by-country reporting requirements proposed by the OECD, could increase compliance burdens and risks. Thus, administrative costs may rise. As to the OECD White Paper on Transfer Pricing Documentation par. 72, businesses may provide, without undue burden, individual country data based on, amongst others, management accounts, consolidating income statements and balance sheets and/or tax returns. This seems a logical statement, but up to our knowledge evidence that in practice this will indeed be possible without limitations in all cases is not available.

It also seems not more than logical to integrate the tax control framework into the management control framework as suggested in the literature and regarded as self-evident by the Dutch tax administration. The analysis in this Chapter focused on the question as to why it may be difficult to integrate both perspectives in one control framework/documentation set. The analysis showed that there are fundamental differences between both perspectives: whereas the tax perspective focuses on the most appropriate allocation of taxation rights between countries and on preventing double taxation and tax evasion, the management control perspective focuses on managing the behaviour of the transacting parties and reaping the benefits of internal transactions. The point of departure is also different. The tax perspective starts from the perspective of intercompany transactions (transactions between associated enterprises) and internal dealings (transactions between a permanent establishment and its head office or between two permanent establishments of the same company). Such transactions should be rewarded the same profits as independent companies would have derived in similar circumstances. The management control perspective perceives the organisational units as dependent parties and takes into account that the organisation has deliberately chosen for internal transactions, instead of transactions through the market, in order to reduce transaction costs.

Moreover, the tax perspective does not take into account the degree of decentralisation of authority and accompanying responsibilities desired for managing the internal transactions. In addition, the tax perspective does not take into account the consequences of different transfer pricing methods for the behaviour of the transacting parties. Country specific information is required for tax purposes. Such information may not be available in the accounts if the management control perspective focuses on organisational units instead of countries.

We investigated the consequences of making use of one framework for both perspectives. If companies use the tax control framework for both perspectives this may lead to suboptimal decision-making for companies with a decentralised organisational structure. On the contrary, using a control framework that takes the management control perspective as a starting point, requires adjustments for tax purposes, the extent of which will depend not only on whether or not the company controls the behaviour of the parties in the internal transaction from a country perspective but also on deviations between what type of risks should be documented and monitored between the tax perspective and the management control perspective. Van Egdom[52] argues that the differences between both control frameworks can only be minor, as both frameworks take value creation as a starting point, and as long as a company does not use its control framework to minimise the tax burden. As the comparison made in section 9.4 shows, this seems to be an oversimplification.

Two separate control frameworks may result in compliance risks as tax inspectors may not understand why the transfer price used for tax purposes deviates from the price used for management control purposes. Moreover, two control frameworks are more costly. Therefore, making use of one framework for both perspectives is to be favoured. A survey amongst a few companies shows that, indeed, companies located in the Netherlands make use of the management control framework, but that the use of hybrid frameworks may be required in order to take into account the differences between the two perspectives, as is evidenced, amongst others, by Boeltjes, De Vries and Steens in their description of the transfer pricing system of Liz Claiborne/Mexx aiming at a centralised management for their purchasing organisation.[53]

Further research is needed to investigate which information – given the degree of decentralisation of the company - can be used for both perspectives, which information is needed for only one of the two perspectives and how and to what extent interactive ICT-systems, such as SAP, enables companies to integrate both perspectives.[54]

---

52 Van Egdom, J.T. (2011). *Verrekenprijzen; de verdeling van de winst van een multinational*. Deventer: Kluwer, p. 280 and pp. 284-287.
53 Boeltjes de Vries, Y.R.Chr. & Steens, H.B.A. (2011). Transfer pricing als instrument van management control: casus Liz Claiborne/Mexx. In: *Handboek Management Accounting*, www.finance-control.nl, visited 14 October, 2014.
54 Robert Kremlacsek argues material ledger offers the option to show intercompany profits both from a legal and a management perspective. PowerPoint presentation PWC Transfer Pricing. Framework and SAP Scenarios, http://www.sapevent.ch/landingpagesfr/manager/uploads/1369/pwc.pdf

LEEN WESDORP

14. Audit of tax

14.1 Introduction

In this chapter I will discuss the main topics of the audit process of the income tax position in the consolidated financial statements of multinationals. Fist I will discuss the general objective of an audit and the meaning of an unqualified opinion including the concept of materiality. Also the general audit methodology will be discussed from a high level perspective. This audit methodology is based on the International Standards on Auditing (ISA)[1] and also on guidance (non-public) that is available within EY. Subsequently in the second section (14.2), I will discuss the application of this general audit methodology to the income tax position in the consolidated financial statements. Also a short summary and conclusions are included in this section. Finally, in the last section (14.3), I will discuss the main differences between an audit as conducted by a public auditor and by a Tax Authority.

14.1.1 General purpose of an audit

The purpose of an audit is to enhance the degree of confidence of intended users in the financial statements. This is achieved by the expression of an opinion by the auditor on whether the financial statements are prepared, in all material respects, in accordance with an applicable financial reporting framework.[2] In the case of the IFRS and the US GAAP framework, that opinion is on whether the financial statements are presented fairly, in all material respects, and give a true and fair view in accordance with the framework.

An unqualified opinion of an auditor means that the auditor is of the opinion that the financial statement are free of material misstatements. An unqualified opinion does therefore not mean that the auditor is of the opinion that the financial statements are free of any error or misstatement. As long as the misstatements on an individual and at an aggregate level are not material there will be no hindrance to

---

[1] International Standards on Auditing 200 (hereafter "ISA xxx.x"), issued by the International Federation of Accountants (IFAC) through the International Auditing and Assurance Standard Board, www.ifac.org/.../a008-2010-iaasb-handbook-isa-200.
[2] ISA 200.3

provide an unqualified opinion. The question arises what is exactly meant by a material misstatement or error.

In general, misstatements, including omissions, are considered to be material if, individually or in the aggregate, they could reasonably be expected to influence the economic decisions of users taken on the basis of the financial statements. Judgments about materiality are made in the light of surrounding circumstances, and are affected by the auditor's perception of the financial information needs of users of the financial statements, and by the size or nature of a misstatement, or a combination of both.[3] The auditor's opinion deals with the financial statements as a whole and therefore the auditor is not responsible for the detection of misstatements that are not material to the financial statements as a whole. I will discuss the determination of the materiality in more detail in paragraph 14.1.3.1.1.

14.1.1.1 Objective of an auditor

Given the role and responsibility of an auditor, the two objectives[4] of the audit to be conducted by an auditor are:
1) To obtain reasonable assurance about whether the financial statements as a whole are free from material misstatement, whether due to fraud or error, thereby enabling the auditor to express an opinion on whether the financial statements are prepared, in all material respects, in accordance with an applicable financial reporting framework; and
2) To report on the financial statements and communicate in accordance with the auditor's findings.

14.1.1.2 Reasonable Assurance

Reasonable assurance is a high level of assurance. However, this is not the same as an absolute level of assurance.[5] There are several inherent limitations of an audit. These limitations result from factors such as:
- the use of sampling;
- the inherent limitations of internal control (for example, the possibility of management override or collusion);
- the fact that audit evidence is typically persuasive rather than conclusive;
- the need for the audit to be conducted within a reasonable period of time and at a reasonable cost.

Audit evidence[6] is information that an auditor uses in arriving at the conclusions on which he bases his audit opinion. Audit evidence is cumulative in nature and is primarily obtained from audit procedures performed throughout the audit. Audit evidence may include information obtained from sources such as:

---

3 ISA 200.6
4 ISA 200.11
5 ISA 200.5
6 ISA 200.13b and ISA 200 A28

Audit of tax   **14.1.2**

- the entity's accounting records;
- previous audits (assuming the auditor has determined it is still relevant to the current audit);
- the firm's quality control procedures for client acceptance and continuance;
- an expert employed or engaged by the entity;
- industry and market data.

Audit evidence comprises information that supports and corroborates management's assertions and any information that contradicts such assertions. The absence of information (for example, management's refusal to provide a requested representation) also constitutes audit evidence.

Sufficiency[7] is the measure of the quantity of audit evidence. The quantity of audit evidence required is affected by the combined risk assessment (CRA), (the higher the CRA, the more audit evidence is likely to be required, see also paragraph 14.1.3.2.2) and also by the quality of audit evidence (the higher the quality, the less audit evidence may be required). Obtaining more audit evidence, however, may not necessarily compensate for its poor quality.

Appropriateness[8] is the measure of the quality of audit evidence, that is, its relevance and its reliability in providing support for the conclusions on which the auditor bases his audit opinion. The reliability of evidence is influenced by its source and by its nature, and is dependent on the individual circumstances under which the evidence is obtained.

An auditor should obtain sufficient appropriate audit evidence to reduce audit risk[9] to an acceptably low level, and allow drawing reasonable conclusions on which to base an audit opinion. Determining whether the auditor has obtained sufficient appropriate audit evidence is a matter of professional judgment.[10]

14.1.2 Risk based methodology (audit risk model)

The audit risk model demonstrates the relationship between inherent risk and control risk and the level of detection risk that an auditor is are willing to accept when performing his audit procedures. The objective of an audit is to limit audit risk to an acceptably low level (i.e., 5%). This level of audit risk is generally accepted in the profession as an acceptable level of audit risk and recognizes that an auditor performs an audit to obtain reasonable, not absolute, assurance that the financial statements as a whole are not materially misstated.

Inherent risk and control risk are the entity's risks and exist independently of the audit. Inherent risk and control risk arise from many factors including, but not limited to, the nature of the entity's business and the strategies that the entity undertakes, and can be increased or reduced by management's attitude to risk. Some businesses

---

7   ISA 200 A29
8   ISA 200 A30
9   ISA 200.13
10 ISA 200 A31

and strategies are inherently more (or less) risky than others and result in higher (or lower) risks that material misstatements of the financial statements may occur.

Management can mitigate inherent risk by implementing effective internal control; however, inherent risk cannot be totally eliminated due to the limitations of controls arising from the realities that human judgment in decision-making can be faulty and that breakdowns in internal control can occur because of human error.

Detection risk is directly influenced by the procedures performed and judgments made by the auditor throughout the audit process.

14.1.2.1 Risks of material misstatement at the financial statement level

Risks of material misstatement at the financial statement level[11] refer to risks that relate pervasively to the financial statements as a whole and potentially affect many assertions. Risks of this nature are typically not associated with specific assertions. Rather, they represent circumstances that may increase the risks of material misstatement across many assertions, for example, through management override of internal control. When an auditor identifies risks of material misstatement at the financial statement level he determines his overall response to those risks, such as including professionals in the engagement team with relevant knowledge and experience.

14.1.2.2 Risk of material misstatement at the assertion level

An auditor assesses risks of material misstatement at the assertion level[12] in order to determine the nature, timing and extent of any additional audit procedures at the assertion level that are necessary to obtain sufficient appropriate audit evidence. For more details with respect to the relevant assertions (occurrence, completeness, measurement, existence, right and obligations and valuation) I refer to paragraph 14.1.3.1.7. An auditor determines relevant assertions at the significant account and disclosure level.

Risks of material misstatement at the assertion level consist of inherent risk and control risk. Therefore, the combined risk assessments (CRA) represent the assessed risks of material misstatement at the assertion level. The nature, timing and extent of the audit procedures are a direct result of the combined risk assessments made. Making the appropriate combined risk assessments and then reflecting them in the audit strategy contributes significantly to executing an effective and efficient audit.

14.1.2.3 Risk assessment procedures

Risk assessment procedures are those procedures performed to obtain an understanding of the entity and its environment, including the entity's internal control, to identify and assess the risks of material misstatement, whether due to fraud or error, at the financial statement and assertion levels and include:[13]

---

11 ISA 315.25.a
12 ISA 315.25.b
13 ISA 315.6

- Inquiries of management, of appropriate individuals within the internal audit function and of others within the entity;
- Analytical procedures;
- Observation and inspection.

The risk assessment procedures provide a basis for designing and executing audit procedures to respond to the assessed risks of material misstatement. Risk assessment procedures by themselves, however, do not provide sufficient appropriate audit evidence on which to base the audit opinion.[14] In other words, an auditor performs tests of controls and substantive procedures in addition to risk assessment procedures to obtain sufficient appropriate audit evidence to conclude whether the financial statements are presented fairly, in all material respects.

Professional standards require an auditor to use his judgment in assessing risks of material misstatement and in determining what tests of controls, if any, and substantive procedures to perform to obtain sufficient appropriate audit evidence. This concept is referred to in the standards as the audit risk model and forms the foundation of the audit methodology.

The audit risk model allows the auditor to take a variety of circumstances into account in selecting the most effective and efficient audit approach to reduce audit risk to an acceptably low level. An auditor makes judgments about the level of inherent risk related to an account balance or disclosure and decides whether to rely or not to rely on internal controls. These judgments have a direct effect on the nature, timing and extent of the substantive procedures an auditor performs.

For example, if controls over sales and accounts receivable are effective and an auditor intends to rely on them, he will be able to reduce the number of accounts receivable confirmation requests that he will send at an interim date. Conversely, if controls are not effective, he may send a larger number of accounts receivable confirmations at period end as he perceives there is greater risk of material misstatement because he has not obtained evidence about the operating effectiveness of the controls.

The audit risk model is described as:

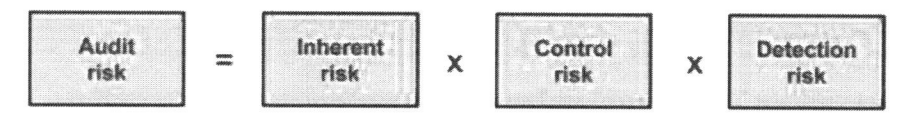

$$\text{Audit risk} = \text{Inherent risk} \times \text{Control risk} \times \text{Detection risk}$$

Where:
Audit risk: The risk that the auditor expresses an inappropriate audit opinion, for example, expressing an unmodified opinion when the financial statements are materially misstated.

---

14   ISA 315.5

Inherent risk: The susceptibility of an assertion about a class of transactions, account balance or disclosure to a misstatement that could be material, either individually or when aggregated with other misstatements, before consideration of any related controls.

Control risk: The risk that a misstatement, which could occur in an assertion about a class of transactions, account balance or disclosure and that could be material, either individually or when aggregated with other misstatements, will not be prevented, or detected and corrected, on a timely basis by the entity's internal control.

Detection risk: The risk that the procedures the auditor performs to reduce audit risk to an acceptably low level will not detect a misstatement that exists and that could be material, either individually or when aggregated with other misstatements.

Detection risk is the risk that a material misstatement would not be detected by the substantive procedures. The substantive procedures include Primary Substantive Procedures (PSPs) and Other

Substantive Procedures (OSPs) as appropriate. PSPs and OSPs comprise:
- Substantive analytical procedures
- Test of details, which may include testing of key items and/or representative samples

The audit risk model and the combined risk assessment can be depicted as follows:

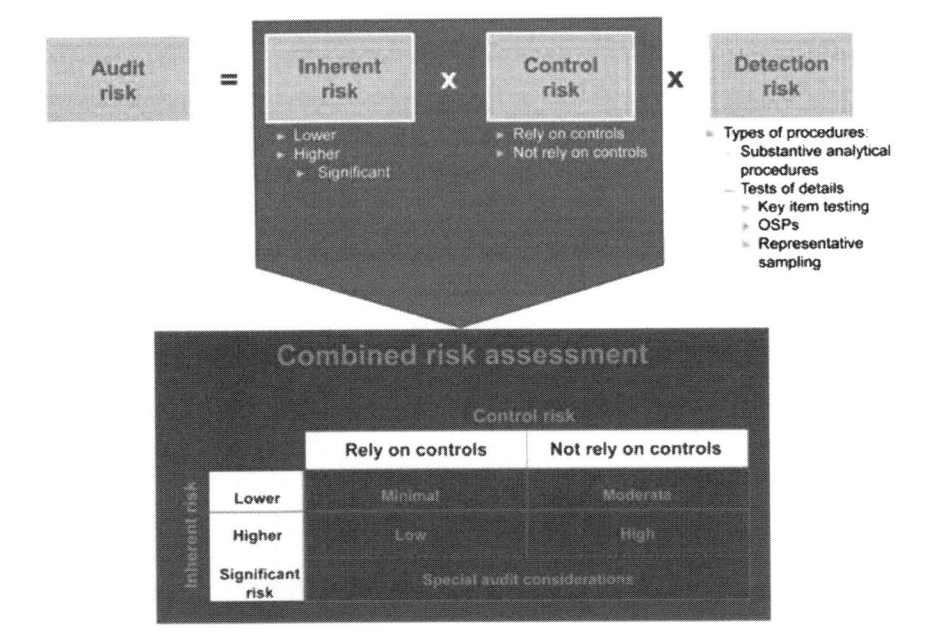

Audit risk = Inherent risk × Control risk × Detection risk

Inherent risk:
- Lower
- Higher
- Significant

Control risk:
- Rely on controls
- Not rely on controls

Detection risk:
- Types of procedures:
  - Substantive analytical procedures
  - Tests of details
    - Key item testing
    - OSPs
    - Representative sampling

Combined risk assessment

Inherent risk	Control risk	
	Rely on controls	Not rely on controls
Lower	Minimal	Moderate
Higher	Low	High
Significant risk	Special audit considerations	

14.1.3 High level summary of the audit process

The audit process can be divided in four broad phases[15]; planning and risk identification (paragraph 14.1.3.1), strategy and risk assessment (paragraph 14.1.3.2), execution (paragraph 14.1.3.3) and conclusion and reporting (paragraph 14.1.3.4). In this paragraph I will briefly discuss the main activities of these phases.

14.1.3.1 Planning and risk identification

In this phase the auditor obtains a broad understanding of the entity, including the nature of the business and its environment and the risks that the entity faces. Based on this understanding, the auditor determines the need for specialized skills on the team. The auditor identifies the risks of material misstatement due to fraud or error and relates these risks to the financial statements as a whole and to relevant assertions for significant accounts and disclosures. Furthermore, he determines the materiality and what accounts and disclosures are significant.

As described in paragraph 14.1.1, the materiality is defined as the magnitude of an omission or misstatement that, individually or in the aggregate, in light of the surrounding circumstances, could reasonably be expected to influence the economic decisions of the users of the financial statements.

The auditor applies the concept of materiality in planning and performing the audit, in evaluating the effect of identified misstatements on the audit and in forming his audit opinion. The auditor determines the materiality at the overall level (i.e., planning materiality) and at the individual account level (i.e., performance materiality).[16] This performance materiality is also known as tolerable error, hereafter "TE[17]".

If, in specific circumstances of the entity, the auditor identifies specific accounts or disclosures for which misstatements of a lesser amount than planning materiality (PM) could reasonably be expected to influence the economic decision of the users of the financial statements, he develops his audit strategy at the significant account or disclosure level using a lower level of materiality to be responsive to those expectations rather than modifying PM.

Planning Materiality (PM) is the overall materiality level for the financial statements taken as a whole. The TE relates to the application of planning materiality at the individual account or balance level. It is set to reduce to an appropriately low level the probability that the aggregate of uncorrected and undetected misstatements exceeds planning materiality.

In addition to determining PM and TE, the auditor also determines the amount below which identified misstatements are considered as being clearly trivial, called the SAD nominal amount. These audit differences are reported to the management of the entity and to those charged with governance. However, if the sum of the audit

---

15 www.unifr.ch/ses/.../Audit_methodology_FS_10.pdf
16 ISA 320.10-11 and ISA 320 A2-A12
17 www.unifr.ch/ses/.../Audit_methodology_FS_10.pdf

differences is not material, the auditor can still provide an unqualified opinion, even if these audit differences are not adjusted.

14.1.3.1.1 Determination Planning Materiality

Determining PM requires the exercise of professional judgment and, though influenced by many factors, is driven by the following:
- The perspectives and expectations of the users of the financial statements in the context of the auditors understanding of the entity and the environment in which it operates;
- The appropriate measurement basis;
- The appropriate percentage to apply to the measurement basis;

Note that the materiality for the financial statements as a whole (and, if applicable, the materiality level or levels for particular classes of transactions, account balances or disclosures) may need to be revised as a result of a change in circumstances that occurred during the audit[18] (for example, a decision to dispose of a major part of the entity's business or other new information). This revision will also have an impact on the determination of the TE and SAD nominal amount.

14.1.3.1.2 The perspectives and expectations of the users of the financial statements

Primary users of the financial statements may include one or more of:
- The owners of the entity (shareholders, investors, the owner in a privately owned business or the parent company when the entity is a subsidiary of a group);
- Major lenders or bond holders;
- Regulators of the entity or the industry in which the entity operates;
- Analysts for listed entities or entities in a regulated industry;
- Other stakeholders in some jurisdictions such as employees, suppliers or customers;
- Tax or legal authorities.

For example, in the case of a privately-held entity which publishes financial statements – expected users of the financial statements may include industry sector analysts, government regulators, tax authorities, employees and creditors of the entity . In the case an entity listed on a local stock exchange – expected users of the financial statements may in addition include shareholders, analysts, and regulators of the stock exchange.

After the auditor has identified the primary users of the financial statements, he considers what he believes could be material to them in the context of the financial statements. In doing this, he assumes that users of the financial statements have reasonable knowledge of business and economic activities and accounting, and understand that the financial statements are prepared, presented and audited to a

---

18 ISA 320.12-13

certain materiality level. As a result, the perception of what is material may differ between users.

The expectation of the users of the financial statements of a listed entity probably differ from those of a non-listed entity. This also applies with respect to entities within a regulated industry (e.g. bank institutions).

Although not a primary consideration, also the expectations of those charged with governance of the entity may impact the level of materiality (for instance, reporting misstatements at a lower level).

14.1.3.1.3 The appropriate measurement basis

The first appropriate measurement basis of the materiality can be the pretax income of the entity. However, there are circumstances that the pretax income cannot be considered as appropriate, for instance if the entity is a non-profit organization. Furthermore, if an entity operates at or near breakeven the pretax income is probably not the appropriate measurement basis. The most appropriate measurement basis in this respect may be gross margin, revenue, ebitda or operation income. When liquidity or solvency is critical, the most appropriate measurement basis is probably equity.

14.1.3.1.4 The appropriate percentage to apply to the measurement basis

Although the international standards do not prescribe certain percentages for the determination of the materiality, in practice the international audit firms have developed global audit policy in this respect. General speaking, for listed entities the materiality is set at a lower level than for privately held entities. The ranges for the other measurement bases may vary depending on the circumstances and also specific country practices may have an impact on these percentages. Within international audit firms there is internal guidance for the determination of the range of percentages for each measurement basis. However, this is not public information.

14.1.3.1.5 Determination Tolerable Error (TE)

TE is the application of planning materiality at the individual account or balance level.[19] Planning the audit solely to detect individually material misstatements overlooks the fact that the aggregate of individually immaterial misstatements may cause the financial statements to be materially misstated, and leaves no margin for possible undetected misstatements. TE is set to reduce to an appropriately low level the probability that the aggregate of uncorrected and undetected misstatements exceeds PM.

The determination of TE affects:
- accounts that are considered to be significant
- sample sizes

---

19   ISA 320.11 and A12

- the starting point for identifying key items and setting testing scopes and thresholds
- the starting point for determining the variance threshold when performing substantive analytical procedures

If the TE is set at a higher level, the size of the misstatements that may go undetected increases. It is therefore important that the TE is set at an amount that recognizes the expectation of misstatements, including the potential for undetected misstatements, to appropriately design the audit procedures.

The following considerations are taken into account for the determination of the TE:
- Expectation about misstatements and risk assessment;
- Understanding of the entity and of the industry in which the entity operates;
- Audit findings of the past / new engagement;
- Observations of the entity's control environment.

Based on the above considerations, the TE is set at a certain percentage of the PM. TE is set at a lower percentage of the PM if the auditor considers the risk of material misstatements in the financial statements as high or at a higher percentage if the auditor considers the risk as low. For the execution of the audit procedures at the level of an individual account often a threshold is applied of 5%-25% (high – low risk) of the TE.

14.1.3.1.6 Determination SAD nominal amount

The SAD nominal amount is designated at an amount below which misstatements, whether individually or accumulated with other misstatements, would not have a material effect on the financial statements. In other words, amounts below the SAD nominal amount, judged by any criteria of size, nature or circumstances, are clearly trivial and, in the aggregate such amounts are not considered in the overall evaluation of misstatements.[20] The audit differences above the SAD amount are communicated with the management of the entity and with those charged with governance.

The SAD is set at a certain percentage of the PM depending on the level of the TE and on the expectations of those charged with governance. The amount selected for the SAD nominal amount neither has an effect on nor is to be used for setting scopes and thresholds; rather, it merely sets the threshold at which the auditor accumulates and communicates misstatements.

14.1.3.1.7 Identification of significant accounts and disclosures and determination of relevant assertions

The auditor identifies (including evaluating during the audit) significant and not significant accounts and disclosures.[21] A significant account is an account that could

---
20 ISA 450.5
21 ISA 315.25

contain a material misstatement based upon its size (i.e., materiality of the account to the financial statements as a whole) and/or that has an identified risk of material misstatement associated with it. Generally, all disclosures are significant, including amounts being disclosed and the related disclosure narrative.

For these accounts and disclosures the auditor develops an audit strategy regarding the inherent risk identified related to the account and disclosures and also regarding the nature, timing and the extent of the substantive procedures.

For a not significant account (account with balances approaching or exceeding TE that have limited or no risk of material misstatement), the auditor should obtain a brief understanding of the nature and purpose of the account.

For an insignificant account (account with balance less than TE), the auditor should assess whether the account is susceptible to material misstatement.

After the auditor has identified the significant account and disclosures, he determines which financial statement assertions are relevant to the significant account and disclosures. The assertions can relate to a significant account that accumulates over the period (e.g. revenue), or to a significant balance sheet account or to a disclosure item. For significant accounts that accumulate over the period under audit, the following assertions are relevant:[22]

- Occurrence; a recorded transaction or event that pertains to the entity actually took place during the period;
- Completeness; there are no unrecorded transactions or events, or undisclosed items;
- Measurement; a transaction or event is recorded at the appropriate amount and in the appropriate accounts.

For significant accounts associated with account balances at the period end, the following assertions are relevant:[23]

- Existence; an asset, liability, or equity interest exists at a given date;
- Rights and Obligations; an asset or a liability pertains to the entity at a given date;
- Completeness; there are no unrecorded assets, liabilities, equity interests, transactions or events, or undisclosed items;
- Valuation; an asset, liability, or equity interest are recorded at an appropriate carrying value.

For disclosures the assertion is that an item is classified, described and disclosed in accordance with the applicable financial reporting framework.[24] The significant accounts and disclosures and relevant assertions are documented including the rationale for why an account is not significant.

---

22   ISA 315 A124.a
23   ISA 315 A124.b
24   ISA 315 A124.c

14.1.3.2 Strategy and risk assessment

In this phase the audit strategy and audit plan is determined. The strategy and risk assessment consists of the following activities:
- Identification of the significant class of transactions (SCOT), significant disclosure processes (SDP) & related IT applications;
- Understanding of the SCOT and SDP
- Performing of walkthroughs;
- Understanding and evaluation of the financial statement close process (FSCP);
- Selection of the controls to test;
- Understanding of the IT general controls (ITGC), design and execution of tests regarding ITGC and evaluation of ITGC;
- Performing the combined risk assessment;
- Designing test of controls, journal entry tests and substantive procedures and general audit procedures;
- Preparation of an audit strategy memorandum.

Although the above audit procedures are highly relevant for audit of the profit before tax and of all assets and liabilities, I will not discuss these procedures in detail because a significant part relates to the audit of non-income tax balances. The procedures relating to income taxes in this respect are discussed in section 14.2.2.

14.1.3.2.1 The identification and understanding of the SCOT, SDP and FSCP, performing walkthroughs and testing of manual and IT controls

A significant class of transactions (SCOT) is a class of transactions that materially affects a significant account and its relevant assertions, either directly through entries in the general ledger or indirectly through the creation of rights or obligations that may not be reported in the general ledger. It includes significant routine, non-routine and estimation transactions from initiation, recording, processing, correcting as necessary and reporting to the financial statements.

A significant disclosure process (SDP) is a process by which transactions, events, or conditions required to be disclosed by the applicable financial reporting framework are accumulated, recorded, processed, summarized and appropriately reported in the financial statements.

The auditor identifies SCOTs and SDP that affect the relevant assertion for each significant account and disclosure including the relevant IT applications.

By performing walkthroughs for the SCOTS the auditor makes an evaluation of the effectiveness of the relevant controls. Based on this evaluation the auditor decides whether a control reliance strategy is still appropriate. If not, the substantive strategy is required.

For each identified control (IT or manual) it should be concluded whether the control is effective or ineffective. A control is effective if based on the walkthroughs performed the auditor concludes that the control has been designed effectively to mitigate the WCGWs[25] (what can go wrong) identified, has been implemented and is operating as designed.

A control is ineffective if the control has not been implemented as understood and/or the design does not mitigate the WCGWs identified.

14.1.3.2.2 Performing the combined risk assessment

In order to develop an audit strategy that is responsive to the entity's risks of material misstatement, the auditor makes a combined risk assessment (CRA) for each relevant assertion for each significant account and disclosure.[26] This is achieved by:
- Assessing inherent risk;
- Assessing preliminary control risk;
- Combining the assessment of inherent risk and control risk to arrive at a CRA for each relevant assertion for each significant account and disclosure.

Once the auditor has determined the combined risk assessment for a relevant assertion, the remaining audit risk (i.e., detection risk) is addressed by designing substantive procedures that are responsive to the CRA.

Assessment inherent risk
Based on the planning procedures as described in paragraph 14.1.3.1 the auditor identifies risk factors, including business risks that may give rise to material misstatements. The following overall factors may affect relevant assertions for may accounts and disclosures:
- Integrity of management;
- Unusual pressure on management;
- Nature of the business;
- Factors effecting the industry;
- Stakeholder influences;
- Risks of material misstatement due to fraud;
- Management's experience and knowledge;
- Complexity of the organization.

The following account –specific factors may only affect the accounts and disclosures for which the assessment is made:
- Susceptibility to material misstatement;
- Size and composition;
- Variations from expected amounts;
- Effects of external factors;
- Competence and experience of personnel;
- Degree of subjectivity;
- Completion of unusual or complex transactions at or near period-end;

---

25 www.unifr.ch/ses/.../Audit_methodology_FS_10.pdf
26 ISA 315.25

- Transactions not subjected to routine processing;
- Existence of related parties

The inherent risk assessment is a matter of professional judgment taking above factors into account. The inherent risk is assessed as higher when the assertion is affected by a significant risk or by a specific risks that may result in a higher likelihood of a material misstatement.[27]

Significant risks are inherent risks with both a higher likelihood of occurrence and a higher magnitude of potential misstatement. The auditor assesses assertions affected by a significant risk as higher inherent risk.[28] The following risks are significant risks:[29]
- Risks of material misstatement due to fraud ;
- Significant transactions with related parties that are outside the normal course of business for the entity.

Significant risks are identified in order to determine the special audit considerations. The relation between the magnitude of potential misstatements and the likelihood of occurrence can be depicted as follows:

Inherent risks

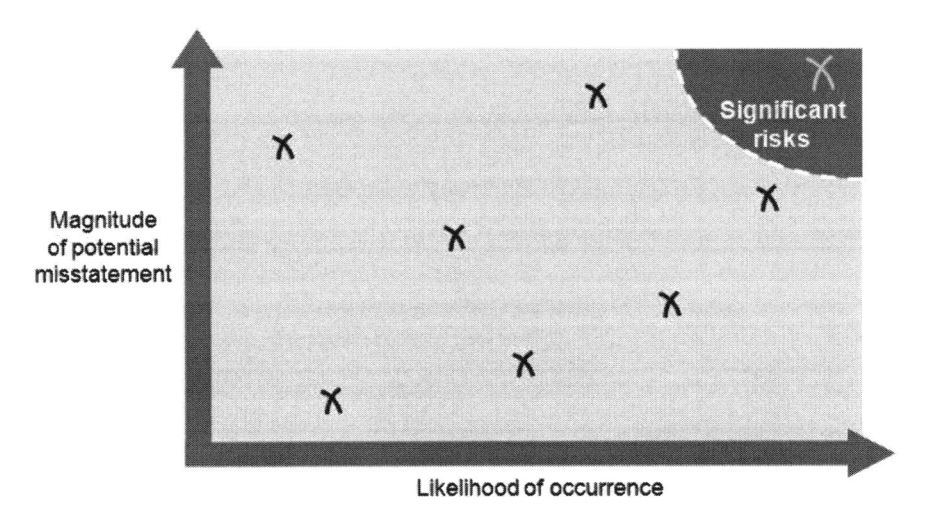

The auditor exercises professional judgment as to which risks are significant risks and considers at least the following when assessing the likelihood and magnitude of the significant risk:[30]

---

27 ISA 315.27
28 ISA 315.26
29 ISA 315.28
30 ISA 315.28

- Whether the risk is related to recent significant economic, accounting or other developments and, therefore, requires special audit considerations;
- The complexity of transactions
- Whether the risk involves significant transactions with related parties within the normal course of business
- The degree of subjectivity in the measurement of financial information related to the risk, especially those measurements involving a wide range of measurement uncertainty
- Whether the risk involves significant transactions that are outside the normal course of business for the entity, or that otherwise appear to be unusual

Risks of material misstatement may be greater for significant non-routine transactions, when there is:
- Greater management involvement in the accounting treatments
- Greater manual involvement in the data collection and processing
- Complex calculations or accounting issues
- Difficulty implementing effective controls over the risks
- Significant related-party transactions
- Similarly, risks of material misstatement may be greater when accounting estimates are developed in areas subject to differing interpretations or requiring subjective or complex judgments or assumptions about future events.

Preliminary assessment of the control risk
The auditor assesses the control risk for each relevant assertion for each significant account and disclosure by evaluating the effectiveness of the design and operation of individual controls. The auditor assesses the control risk as either - rely on controls- or – not rely on controls- for each relevant assertion.

The auditor preliminary concludes to rely on controls if controls have been designed and are operating effectively throughout the period of reliance. The assessment to 'rely on controls' at this stage in the audit is a preliminary assessment.

The auditor concludes not rely on controls when after gaining the necessary understanding of the entity's SCOTs or significant disclosure processes:
- The controls have not been designed appropriately, implemented effectively, or are unlikely to operate effectively throughout the period of reliance, and therefore the auditor has decided not to test controls;
- Substantive procedures are identified that will provide the evidence necessary to support the related account balances or disclosure;
- The testing controls would be inefficient.

Combined risk assessment
Based upon the assessments of inherent and control risk for each relevant assertion, the auditor makes his combined risk assessments for each relevant assertion for each significant account and disclosure.

The table below shows how the auditor combines the assessment of inherent and control risks into one combined risk assessment.

Inherent risk assessment		Control risk assessment	
		Rely on controls	Not rely on controls
	Lower	Minimal	Moderate
	Higher	Low	High
	Significant risk	Special audit considerations	

The auditor designs and performs additional substantive procedures that factor in the results of the tests of controls and are responsive to the significant risk (rely on controls).

Special audit considerations for a significant risk when the auditor does 'not rely on controls' are:
- Obtain an understanding of the controls relevant to the identified significant risk and confirm those controls have been implemented;
- Design and perform additional substantive procedures that are responsive to the significant risk, recognizing that the auditor does 'not rely on controls'.

In other words, regardless of whether the auditor tests controls intended to mitigate the significant risk, he identifies controls over significant risks and obtains audit evidence that these controls have been implemented. The auditor designs substantive procedures, considering whether or not he decided to rely on controls to respond to the significant risk and the increased risk that a material misstatement may occur.

The relation between the combined risk assessment and the performance of procedures (test of controls or substantive) can be depicted as follows:

Combination of procedures dependant on CRA

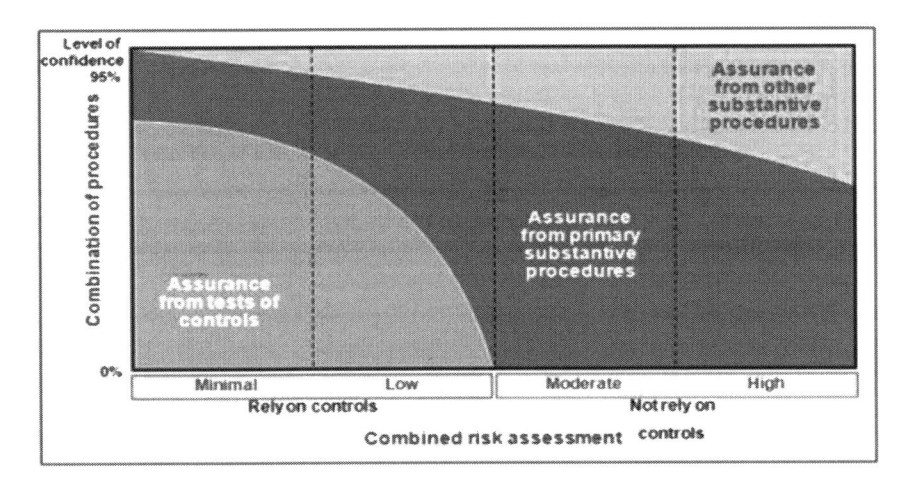

Audit of tax   14.1.3

The table below shows the risk conclusion and the effect on the substantive procedures:

CRA	Risk Conclusion	Effect On Our Substantive Procedures
Minimal	Sufficient evidence is available to conclude that controls are effective at preventing or detecting and correcting risks of material misstatement from occurring	Designed to confirm that material misstatements have not occurred
Low	Sufficient evidence is available to conclude that controls are effective at preventing or detecting and correcting risks of material misstatement from occurring. However, the auditor assesses there is a higher likelihood that risks of material misstatements will occur	Designed to confirm that the risks that have created a higher likelihood of misstatements occurring have not resulted in a material misstatement
Moderate	The auditor has insufficient evidence to conclude that controls operated effectively and will prevent or detect and correct misstatements from occurring	Designed to detect and evaluate misstatements that may not have been prevented or detected and corrected by controls
High	Insufficient evidence is available to conclude that controls operate effectively and will prevent or detect and correct misstatements from occurring and the auditor assesses there is a higher likelihood that risks of material misstatements will occur	Designed to detect whether risks of material misstatement have resulted in a material misstatement

14.1.3.2.3 Designing test of controls including journal entry tests, substantive and general audit procedures

The auditor designs the nature, timing and extent of the tests of controls to obtain sufficient appropriate audit evidence that the controls selected for testing operate effectively as designed throughout the period of reliance to prevent or detect and correct material misstatements at the assertion level.

The nature of the procedures applied during the test of controls can be:
- Inquiry (seeking information from persons within or outside the company);
- Observations (watching processes or procedures being performed by the entity's personnel;
- Inspections (examination of documents, internal or external and physical examinations);
- Recalculations (checking the mathematical accuracy of documents and records);

- Re-performance (re-performance and independent execution of internal control procedures);
- Data analysis (application of data analysis techniques).

The journal entry testing consists of:
- Obtaining understanding of the types of journal entries;
- Consideration of the management override;
- Making inquiries relating to unusual entries and other adjustments;
- Determination of population for and method of testing including assessment of completeness of the population.

The auditor designs substantive procedures so that the combination of the procedures (including tests of controls) provides sufficient appropriate audit evidence to reduce audit risk to an acceptably low level and enables the auditor to draw reasonable conclusions on which to base our opinion. This can be achieved by:
- Designing overall responses to risks of material misstatement at the financial statement level;
- Customizing primary substantive procedures (PSPs) for significant accounts and disclosures;
- Designing other substantive procedures (OSPs) for significant accounts and disclosures;
- Planning the timing of substantive procedures;
- Designing roll-forward procedures;
- Designing procedures for 'not significant' and insignificant accounts;
- Determining information required from the entity;
- Reviewing and approving planned substantive procedures.

The general audit procedures are procedures relating to area's notwithstanding the combined risk assessment. These procedures are applicable for every audit. The procedures relate to:
- Compliance with laws and regulations (written representation from management);
- Litigations and claims (audit inquiry letter regarding litigation and claims);
- Minutes and contract (audit committee meetings, board meetings, shareholders meetings and significant contracts);
- Going concern considerations;
- Related party relationships and transactions;
- Written representation of management.

14.1.3.2.4 Preparation of audit strategy memorandum

The auditor prepares an audit strategy memorandum (ASM) that contains the overall audit strategy and the audit plan. I will not discuss the content in detail.

Audit of tax

14.1.3.3 Execution

The auditor performs the tests of controls and substantive procedures as planned in the strategy and risk assessment phase. The combined risk assessments will be reassessed throughout the audit and the auditor determines whether changes are necessary to the audit strategy in response to a change in the combined risk assessments. The execution phase consist of the following steps:
- Execution of the test of controls;
- Journal entry testing and fraud procedures;
- Performing substantive audit procedures;
- Performing general audit procedures.

14.1.3.3.1 Execution of the test of controls

The testing procedures are performed in order to obtain sufficient and appropriate audit evidence relating to the operating effectiveness of the relevant controls.[31] Based on the audit evidence obtained the auditor concludes whether the controls are effective. The reliability of the information to be used as audit evidence depends on the source and nature under which the information is obtained.[32]
- The reliability of audit evidence is increased when it is obtained from independent sources outside the entity
- The reliability of audit evidence that is generated internally is increased when the related controls imposed by the entity are effective
- Audit evidence obtained directly is more reliable than audit evidence obtained indirectly or by inference
- Audit evidence in documentary form, whether paper, electronic, or other medium, is more reliable than audit evidence obtained orally
- Audit evidence provided by original documents is more reliable than audit evidence provided by photocopies.

If the auditor identifies an control exception (control does not operate as designed or is not implemented) he investigates the nature and cause of the exception and evaluates its effect on the planned audit procedures.[33] A control exception can be systematic or random. In case the exception is systematic the exception will occur in every similar circumstance. In this case the auditor concludes "not to rely on controls". In this case the CRA will be reassessed. This may result in additional audit procedures.

For random exceptions additional tests (e.g. extend sampling size) need to be performed. If further exceptions are identified the auditor concludes "not to rely on controls" The auditor concludes to "rely on controls" if no further exceptions are identified or if other compensating controls are effective.

---

31 ISA 330.8
32 ISA 500.7 and ISA 500 A26-A33
33 ISA 330.17 and ISA 530.12

Deficiencies in internal controls occur when the design or operation of a control does not allow management or employees in the normal course of performing their assigned functions, to prevent or detect misstatements on a timely basis. Significant deficiencies are reported to those charged with governance.

14.1.3.3.2 Journal entry testing and fraud procedures.

For the sample of journal entries and other adjustments selected for testing, the auditor reviews supporting documentation and discusses the purpose of the entries and other adjustments with management. If unusual items are discovered he considers whether the misstatement may be a result of fraud. For each selected journal entry the auditor assesses whether the entry is;[34]
- Supported by an appropriate, underlying business rationale;
- Properly authorized ;
- Accounted for correctly;
- Properly recorded.

14.1.3.3.3 Performing substantive and general audit procedures

The auditor performs substantive and general audit procedures so that the combination of the procedures (including tests of controls) provides sufficient appropriate audit evidence to reduce audit risk to an acceptably low level and enable the auditor to draw reasonable conclusions on which to base his opinion.[35] A misstatement is a difference between the amount, classification, presentation or disclosure of a reported financial statement item and the amount, classification, presentation or disclosure that is required for the item to be in accordance with the applicable financial reporting framework.

The misstatements are classified as reclassification, factual, projected or judgmental misstatements in order to evaluate the effect of misstatements accumulated during the audit.[36] The misstatement may result in reassessment of the materiality and of the CRA.

14.1.3.4 Conclusion and reporting

The auditor performs the procedures to complete the audit. The most important procedures are:
- Preparation of the summary of audit differences and of the summary of review memorandum;
- Execution of financial statement procedures (determine whether the financial statements meet the requirements of the applicable framework);

---

34 ISA 240.32
35 ISA 500.16 and ISA 200.17
36 ISA 530.12

- Evaluation whether sufficient appropriate audit evidence has been obtained that provides the auditor with reasonable assurance about whether the financial statements as a whole are free from material misstatement, whether due to fraud or error;
- Evaluation of all identified audit differences and communication with those charged with governance;
- Completion of documentation.

14.2 Application of the audit methodology to income taxes

14.2.1 Specific characteristics of the income tax positions in the consolidated financial statements

14.2.1.1 Introduction

Accounting for, and auditing of income taxation in financial statements must begin with some consideration of the nature of taxation. Taxation on income[37] has certain characteristics which set it apart from other business expenses, and which may justify a different treatment. Before discussing the application of general audit methodology on income taxes, I will first elaborate on some specific characteristics of income taxes on the basis of the picture as depicted below.[38] These characteristics have an impact on the inherent risk assessment and ultimately on the audit approach.

Note that I will not discuss the audit procedures for other (non-income) taxes. Within the IFRS and USGAAP frameworks there is a separate standard for income taxes (IFRS: IAS 12 and US GAAP: ASC 740). For other taxes, IAS 37 and ASC 450 are applicable. Because the standards for income taxes differ from the standard for other taxes a correct qualification of the nature of a taxation is relevant.

---

37 International Financial Reporting Standards (IFRSs) together with their accompanying documents are issued by the International Accounting Standards Board (IASB) , www.ifrs.org here after "IFRS or IAS" IFRS standard IAS 12.2 and the Financial Accounting Standard Board (FASB) US GAAP standard ASC 740-10-15 hereafter ASC 740. https://asc.fasb.org/

38 Tax accounting in general is the subject of Chapter 9.

Current and deferred tax positions X Inc

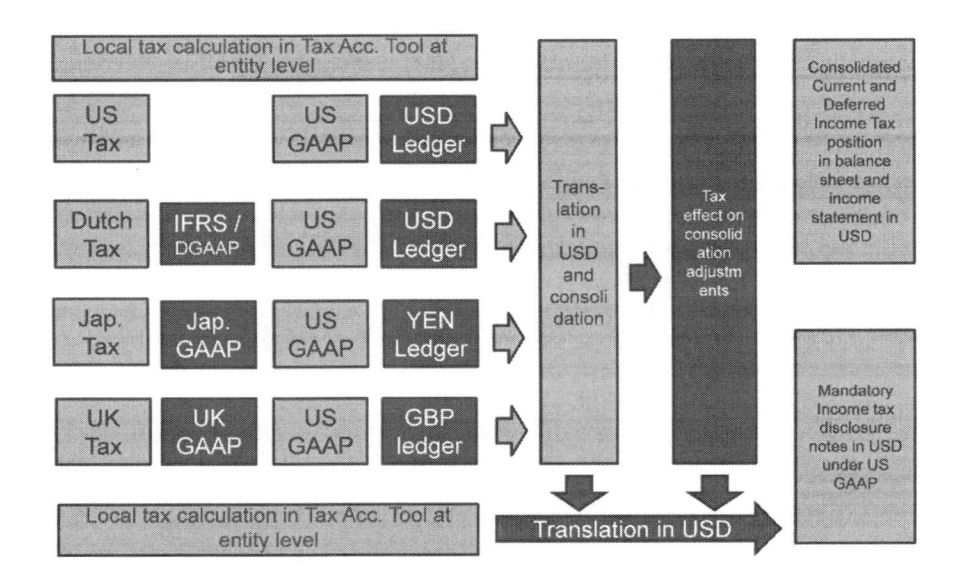

[Figure: Diagram showing local tax calculation in Tax Acc. Tool at entity level for four jurisdictions:
- US Tax → US GAAP → USD Ledger
- Dutch Tax → IFRS / DGAAP → US GAAP → USD Ledger
- Jap. Tax → Jap. GAAP → US GAAP → YEN Ledger
- UK Tax → UK GAAP → US GAAP → GBP ledger

Arrows lead to Translation in USD and consolidation → Tax effect on consolidation adjustments → Consolidated Current and Deferred Income Tax position in balance sheet and income statement in USD; and Mandatory Income tax disclosure notes in USD under US GAAP.]

14.2.1.2 Jurisdictions and different frameworks and currencies

A US multinational enterprise (hereafter "X Inc Group") operates in four different jurisdictions (for the sake of simplicity) and prepares its consolidated financial statements (USD as reporting currency) under the US GAAP framework. The US entity is the parent company of the group and performs manufacturing and trade activities. The Dutch entity has an intermediate holding function and the Japanese and the UK entities also perform trade activities. Goods are purchased from the US parent entity.

All transactions are recorded in the local general ledgers and in the local functional currency. The functional currency is the currency of the primary economic environment in which the entity operates.[39] For the Japanese entity the functional currency is the YEN, for the UK entity the GBP, and the US and the Dutch entities apply the USD as their functional currency. Based on local requirements all entities must file their stand-alone financial statements based on local GAAP. Each entity needs to file a corporate income tax return based on the local income tax law. For consolidation purposes all entities must also meet the US GAAP requirements. Therefore, within the X Inc Group the following tax laws and frameworks (and functional currency) need to be applied:
- UK income tax law (GBP)
- UK GAAP (GBP)

---

39 IAS 21.8-14

- Japanese income tax law (YEN)
- Japanese GAAP (YEN)
- Dutch income tax law (USD)
- IFRS or Dutch GAAP (USD)
- US income tax law (USD)
- US GAAP (all entities in functional currency and consolidated in reporting currency USD)

Besides the above frameworks and tax laws, the tax treaties between the above mentioned jurisdictions and European directives will have an impact on the total income tax expense of the X Inc Group.

14.2.1.3 Current income tax

The income taxes to be paid or to be received (current income tax) are based on the applicable local income tax laws and also on the available case law in each jurisdiction. Income tax laws can be (very) complex and may be open to different interpretations. This can result in uncertain tax positions. For these uncertainties it needs to be assessed whether a liability should be recorded. The income tax risks also depend on the nature of the group's business. For example, the income tax environment of an oil production company is totally different from the income tax environment of a real estate investment company.

The current income tax due (YEN) in Japan depends on the results derived from the Japanese activities and on the Japanese income tax law. The current income taxes due in the other jurisdictions (UK in GBP, the Netherlands in EURO and the US in USD) depend on the local results and on the local income tax laws. Intercompany transactions have an impact on the stand alone results of the local entities and therefore on the current taxes to be paid. The arm's length nature of the transactions within the group are often subject of discussion.

The current tax expense can relate to the results of the current year but also to the results of prior years. Tax authorities can issue additional assessments for prior years (depending on the statute of limitations), or adjust the taxable income as reported in a tax return filed. Therefore, for each jurisdiction the total current tax expense to be recorded should consist of the estimated current year tax expense and also of the estimated or final prior year tax expense.

Besides tax rates, there are many other differences between the income tax laws of countries. For instance, in the Netherlands dividends and capital gains derived from group companies are tax exempt based on the assumption that the participation exemption is applicable. In the US, similar types of income are fully taxed taking into account a tax credit for the income taxes paid at the level of the respective subsidiary. The income tax laws in the various jurisdictions may change every year. Therefore, multinationals are facing increased challenges in keeping up with changes in the global tax legislative and regulatory environment. Many of these changes can significantly affect a company's accounting for income taxes, tax return preparation, and identification and monitoring of tax risk.

Within an international environment tax treaties between different jurisdictions are relevant. Tax treaties decide (amongst others) which state is allowed to levy tax and to which extent. This is especially relevant for withholding taxes on dividends, royalties and interest and for taxation of capital gains. There may also be interpretation differences regarding the application of tax treaties.

The consolidated current income tax position consists of the sum of the income tax positions in functional currency of all entities converted into USD.

14.2.1.4 Deferred income tax

The overall income tax position in the consolidated financial statements consist of current and deferred taxes. The consolidated deferred income tax position consists of the sum of all local deferred income tax positions in local functional currency converted into USD and of the deferred income tax positions due to consolidation adjustments.

The recognition of assets, liabilities, equity, revenue and costs in the consolidated financial statements is governed by the US GAAP framework. The standalone financial statement are governed by the local GAAP requirements. For income tax purposes the recognition is governed by the application of the tax law taking also the case law into account. Therefore difference may arise between the income and equity under US GAAP versus local GAAP versus local tax laws. As discussed in chapter 9.4, deferred tax positions should be recorded for temporary differences between the above frameworks (besides a few exceptions). Also, consolidation adjustments (for instance intercompany profit elimination) may result in deferred tax positions. The total deferred income tax position can be depicted as follows:

Deferred tax positions X Inc

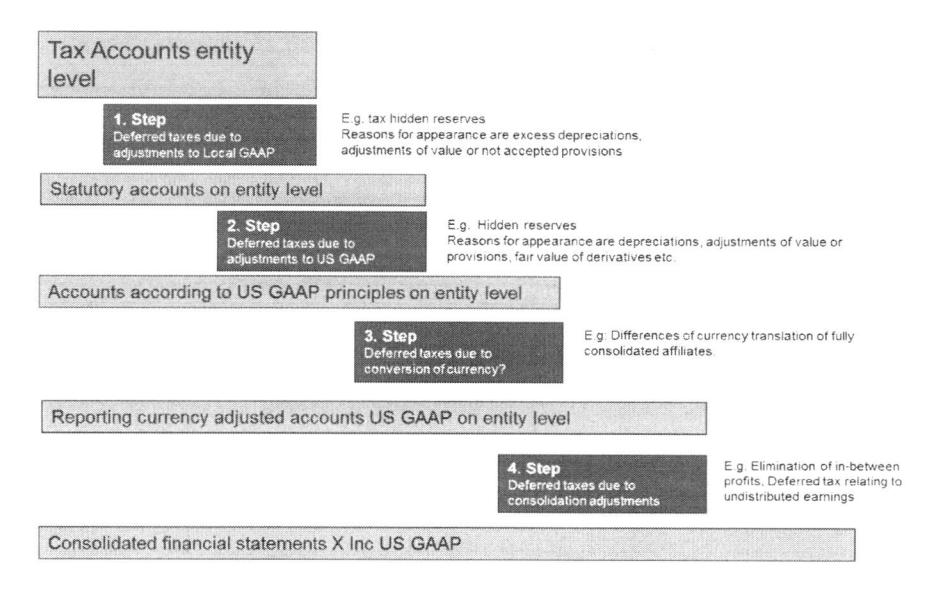

Tax Accounts entity level

1. Step — Deferred taxes due to adjustments to Local GAAP
E.g. tax hidden reserves. Reasons for appearance are excess depreciations, adjustments of value or not accepted provisions

Statutory accounts on entity level

2. Step — Deferred taxes due to adjustments to US GAAP
E.g. Hidden reserves. Reasons for appearance are depreciations, adjustments of value or provisions, fair value of derivatives etc.

Accounts according to US GAAP principles on entity level

3. Step — Deferred taxes due to conversion of currency?
E.g. Differences of currency translation of fully consolidated affiliates.

Reporting currency adjusted accounts US GAAP on entity level

4. Step — Deferred taxes due to consolidation adjustments
E.g. Elimination of in-between profits. Deferred tax relating to undistributed earnings

Consolidated financial statements X Inc US GAAP

14.2.1.5 Disclosure requirements and tax accounting tools

Under US GAAP (and also under IFRS) there are a number of mandatory disclosure requirements. For more details in this respect refer to chapter 9.5. The consolidated tax footnotes contain information of all the local income tax positions in the local functional currency converted into the reporting currency. This information is recorded at a local level in a tax accounting tool (often excel files). A tax accounting tool should at least contain the following information:
- Calculation of the current tax expense based on the reconciliation of US GAAP profit before tax to local GAAP income before tax to taxable income with a split between permanent and temporary differences;
- Deferred tax calculation based on the differences in the valuation between the US GAAP assets and liabilities, the local GAAP assets and liabilities and the valuation for tax purposes;
- Deferred tax calculation for losses carried forward and for other tax credits carried forward;
- Roll forward of the current and deferred income tax position, including movements recorded in income statement and into equity;
- Comparison of the tax calculation with the tax return filed (true up or return to provisioning)
- Roll forward of the liability for uncertain tax positions;
- Reconciliation of the effective tax rate.

The translation of all income tax positions from functional currency into reporting currency is an automated process. However, the consolidation and translation of the disclosure note information is often a manual process and therefore error prone.

14.2.1.6 Restatements procedures and income taxes

When an error is material[40] to the prior-period(s) financial statements, a company is required to revise previously issued financial statements and correct the error. The audit opinion is also revised to disclose the restatement.

When an error is immaterial to the prior-period(s) financial statements, but correcting it in the current period would materially misstate the current-period income statement or statement of comprehensive income, the error is corrected in the current-period financial statements by adjusting the prior-period information. The company does not need to amend the previously filed financial statements and the audit opinion is not revised. This type of restatement often occurs when an immaterial error remains uncorrected for several periods and aggregates to a material number.

When an error is immaterial to the prior-period(s) financial statements and correcting it in the current period is not material to the current-period financial statements, the error is simply corrected in the current period. Financial statements for the prior period(s) are not restated.

Based on analyses of the restatements in 2010 and 2011 in the US,[41] accounting for income taxes is one of the leading causes of restatements. The main errors in accounting for income taxes relate to:
- the deferred tax position (difference between book and tax bases of assets and liabilities);
- recognition of deferred tax assets
- tax effect on intercompany transactions (specific US GAAP rules)

The main reason for errors are:
- complex accounting standards (ASC 740)
- complex tax laws
- lack of the combination of tax law skills and accounting skills at single individual or department level;

---

40 ASC 250, Accounting Changes and Error Corrections, SEC Staff Accounting Bulletin Topic 1-M, Materiality, and SEC Staff Accounting Bulletin Topic 1-N, Considering the Effects of Prior Year Misstatements when Quantifying Misstatements in Current Year Financial Statements.
41 Technical Line, Financial reporting development , No 2012 21, 7 August 2012, Lessons learned from our review of restatements, Ernst & Young, www.ey.com/

14.2.1.7 Impact on inherent risk assessment

Based on the above observations, the current and deferred income tax position in the consolidated financial statements depend on a lot of complex elements. Therefore the inherent risks relating to the income tax position is often assessed as high.

14.2.2 Audit methodology and income taxes

In this paragraph I will discuss the application of the ISA audit methodology for income taxes. Note that the specific additional US audit requirements will not be discussed. I will use the X Inc. Group as an example to explain the audit procedures in more detail. I will not discuss the other audit procedures regarding the other balance sheet and income statement items. Hence the profit before tax per entity, the planning materiality, tolerable error and the nominal amount are the starting point of the audit procedures regarding the income tax position.

14.2.2.1 Planning and risk identification

The procedures performed in the planning and risk identification phase with respect to income taxes relate to the following elements:
- Obtaining a broad understanding of the business per entity and the complexity of the applicable income tax law(s). The current and deferred income tax position of a trading company like the entities in Japan and in the UK is driven by other factors than the income tax position of the Dutch intermediate holding company. The current and deferred income tax position of the parent company in the US may also be influenced by consolidation adjustments.
- Obtaining information about related party transactions that may give rise to uncertain tax positions and therefore may result in a risk of material misstatement.
- Obtaining a detailed understanding of the organization of the tax function[42] (roles and responsibilities) of X Inc Group at parent level, and at entity level.
- Obtaining a broad understanding of the IT tools used for the calculation of the income tax positions. Which tax accounting tool is used and how is this tool implemented in the overall reporting system?
- Obtaining understanding of the IT tools used for monitoring the impact of tax law changes and for the monitoring of the income tax risks per jurisdictions.
- Obtaining a broad understanding of the policies, processes and the design of the internal control with respect to the income tax position per entity and also at consolidated level.
- Obtaining understanding of management's attitude with respect to income taxes (prudent versus aggressive).

---

42 See Chapter 5 in more detail on the tax function.

For a multinational company like X Inc. Group, the starting point is that the inherent risk regarding income taxes can be considered as high. This risk can also be considered as a significant risk because income tax risks are risks with both a higher likelihood of occurrence and a higher magnitude of potential misstatement. The income tax accounts and disclosures are considered to be significant and therefore tax (accounting) specialists are needed for the audit of the income tax position. The relevant assertions with respect to the *current* income tax account balances are:

- Existence; a current income tax asset or liability exists at a given date based on the local income tax law taking into account the applicable case law and also the application of tax treaties or other directives;
- Rights and Obligations; the current income tax asset or a liability pertains to the entity at a given date based on the local income tax law taking into account the applicable case law and also the application of tax treaties or other directives;
- Completeness; there are no unrecorded current income tax assets and liabilities (based on the local income tax law taking into account the applicable case law and also the application of tax treaties of other directives) and there are no undisclosed income tax items (based on the applicable framework; US GAAP ASC 740);
- Valuation; the current income asset or liability is recorded at an appropriate carrying value based on the US GAAP framework;
- Presentation and disclosure; the current income tax asset or liability is classified, described and disclosed in accordance with the US GAAP framework.

The relevant assertions with respect to the *deferred* income tax account balances are:
- Existence; a deferred income tax asset or liability exists at a given date due to a temporary difference for which a deferred tax position should be recorded based on the applicable framework. . A temporary difference is a result of a different treatment between the US GAAP framework and the local income tax law (taking into account the applicable case law and also the application of tax treaties or other directives);
- Rights and Obligations; the deferred income tax asset or a liability pertains to the entity at a given date based on the applicable US GAAP framework and local income tax law (taking into account the applicable case law and also the application of tax treaties or other directives);
- Completeness; there are no unrecorded deferred income tax assets and liabilities based on the applicable US GAAP framework and local income tax law (taking into account the applicable case law and also the application of tax treaties or other directives);
- Valuation; the deferred income tax asset or liability is recorded at an appropriate carrying value based on the US GAAP framework;
- Presentation and disclosure; the deferred income tax asset or liability is classified, described and disclosed in accordance with the US GAAP framework.

The current and deferred income tax expense or benefit are based on the movement of the income tax account balances (balance sheet approach as applied under US GAAP and IFRS). The relevant assertions are:

- Occurrence: the current and deferred income tax expense or benefit are based on the transactions and events that took place during the period and that pertain to the entity;
- Completeness; there are no unrecorded current or deferred income taxes in the income statement for this period and there are no undisclosed current and deferred income tax items;
- Measurement; the current and deferred income taxes are recorded at the appropriate amount in the income statement (some current and deferred tax movements should be recorded into equity);
- Presentation and disclosure: the current and deferred income tax expense or benefit is classified, described and disclosed in accordance with the US GAAP framework.

14.2.2.2 Strategy and risk assessment

In this phase of the audit process the auditor obtains an understanding of the income tax closing and disclosure process. As discussed in paragraph 14.2.1.3 the current and deferred income tax position consists of the total of all local income tax positions taking into account translation into reporting currency, and the tax effect on consolidation entries. The local income tax positions are calculated in a tax accounting tool and are recorded in the local general ledger. The auditor obtains an understanding of the tax accounting tool used and tests whether the tax accounting tool provides the correct outcome by using fictive numbers.

The auditor assesses 'What Can Go Wrong' (WCGW) with respect to the current and deferred income tax calculations per entity and at consolidated level. The following WCGW are applicable for income taxes:
- Not all tax law changes have been identified and the impact of these changes has not been taken into account in the tax calculations;
- The profit before tax number used for the tax calculations does not tie with the profit before tax as reported in the general ledger;
- Not all permanent differences between the US GAAP income before tax and the Local GAAP profit before tax and the taxable income are identified;
- Not all temporary differences between the US GAAP income before tax and the Local GAAP profit before tax and the taxable income are identified;
- The utilization of losses carried forward is not correct;
- The utilization of tax credits carried forward is not correct;
- The current year tax rate is not correct;
- The differences between the current and deferred tax expense based on the tax return filed for a certain year and the provisioning of that respective year are not recorded (return to provision adjustments, also known as true up calculations);
- The temporary differences (differences between US GAAP book base, Local GAAP book base and tax base of assets and liabilities) are not correct or cannot be substantiated based on the tax return filed in prior years;
- The tax rate used for the calculation of the deferred taxes is not correct;
- The losses carried forward at balance sheet date are not correct;
- The tax credits carried forward at balance sheet date are not correct;

- The deferred taxes to be recorded outside the income statement (equity) are not properly identified;
- The recognition of the deferred tax assets cannot be substantiated with the four sources of income as described in the US GAAP (or IFRS see chapter 9) framework, or the four sources of income have not been evaluated properly;
- The deferred tax liability regarding the undistributed earnings is not correct;
- The deferred tax impact on the consolidation adjustments are not recorded properly;
- The current and deferred income tax positions are not converted properly from the functional currency into the reporting currency;
- The current and deferred income tax positions do not tie to the underlying trail balances;
- The uncertain tax positions (including state aid risk) for the years for which the tax authorities (or EU authority) can issue additional assessment or can adjust the taxable income are not identified properly;
- The uncertain tax positions identified are not measured properly;
- Mutual agreement procedures regarding transfer pricing (uncertain tax positions) are not properly taken into account (tax effect of compensating adjustments);
- Interest and penalties relating to uncertain tax positions are not correct;
- The current taxes are not set off properly;
- The deferred taxes are not set off properly;
- The disclosure notes are incomplete or are not in accordance with the US GAAP disclosure note requirements.

Based on the above WCGWs and the judgmental character income taxes the auditor will apply a substantive audit strategy because the operational effectiveness of the internal controls regarding income taxes can only (in many cases) be determined by performing primary and other substantive audit procedures.

14.2.2.2.1 Combined risk assessment relating to income taxes

The general basics of the combined risk assessment are discussed in paragraph 14.1.3.2.2. In this paragraph I will discuss the combined risk assessment in more detail with respect to income taxes. The inherent risk regarding income taxes is the risk on a material misstatement relating to income taxes either individually or when aggregated with other misstatements before consideration of any related controls. The following items / indicators are relevant for the assessment of the inherent risk:
- Nature of the business (each industry has its own specific tax risks);
- Number of jurisdictions in which the Group operates;
- Complexity of the applicable income tax laws;
- Significant tax law changes;
- Number of intercompany transactions;
- Complex tax planning undertaken;
- Tax driven intercompany financing;
- Tax rulings with specific income tax benefits that may constitute state aid;

- Advance Tax Rulings and Advance Price Agreements concluded with tax authorities;
- Horizontal monitoring agreements;[43]
- Number of differences in profit between before tax and equity between US GAAP, local GAAP and tax;
- Acquisitions (purchase price accounting often results in deferred tax positions);
- Disposals;
- Weak tax department with lack of tax accounting experience or significant changes in staff;
- No clear description of roles and responsibilities regarding tax accounting;
- No clear description of processes;
- Use of unprotected excel files for tax calculations;
- Income tax disclosure notes are not generated automatically;
- Significant outstanding queries with tax authorities or lengthy tax audits;
- Backlog in corporate income tax filing;

The inherent risk assessment will take place at consolidated level and also at entity level because there can be significant differences between the level of the inherent risk per entity. For instance, the most relevant issue for the Dutch income tax position relates to the participation exemption. The inherent risk in this respect is limited due to the fact that the UK and Japanese subsidiaries perform trading activities that cannot be considered as passive. Furthermore, these subsidiaries are taxed against relatively high tax rates (UK (2014) 21-23%, Japan at least 28.5%). Therefore it is likely that the participation exemption will be applicable. Hence, the audit procedures to be performed for the Dutch entity will differ from the audit procedures to be performed for the other entities.

Due to the judgmental character of the income tax calculations in a multi-jurisdictional environment the design of the substantive audit procedures will mainly depend on the inherent risk assessment.

14.2.2.2.2 Design of primary and other substantive audit procedures relating to income taxes

Depending on the tolerable error (performance materiality) and the nominal amount (paragraph 14.1.5.1.5 and 14.1.5.1.6), the relevant assertions (paragraph 14.1.5.1.7), the WCGWs identified (paragraph 14.2.2.2) and on the combined risk assessment the following primary substantive audit procedures (PSP) may need to be performed:
1) Testing of the reconciliation of US GAAP profit before tax to local GAAP profit before tax to Taxable income and the calculation of the current tax due;
2) Testing of the provision for current and deferred income taxes;
3) Testing of the need for impairment of deferred tax assets;
4) Testing the movement of the current and deferred account balance from opening balance to ending balance;

---

43 See Chapter 6 for more information on horizontal monitoring for multinational companies.

5) Testing whether the provision for uncertain tax positions is in accordance with the US GAAP framework;
6) Testing the at arms' length nature of the intercompany transactions.

The other substantive procedures (OSP) relating to income taxes are:
7) Reconciling the current and deferred income tax balances from the trial balances to the financial statements including evaluation whether the income tax are correctly classified;
8) Testing whether the income tax disclosure notes meet the US GAAP requirement;
9) Determine the tax effect on other adjustments and determine whether the overall audit difference relating to income tax is above the tolerable error;
10) Obtain management representation relating to income taxes.

As explained above the procedures to be performed may differ per entity depending on the TE, WCGW per assertion and the combined risk assessment.

14.2.2.3 Execution of the substantive procedures

In this paragraph I will discuss the execution of the substantive audit procedures. Because X Inc. prepares its consolidated financial statements under US GAAP, reference is made in this paragraph to this framework. If IFRS was applied, references would be made to IFRS. For the audit procedures to be performed there is no difference.

14.2.2.3.1 Testing of the reconciliation of US GAAP profit before tax to Local GAAP profit before tax to Taxable income

The starting point of a corporate income tax calculation of each entity is the profit before tax based on the US GAAP framework. Often there are differences between the US GAAP profit before tax and the profit before tax under the local GAAP framework and the taxable income. The reconciliation of the income and the calculation of the current tax to be paid for the current period can be depicted as follows:

Audit of tax

Reconciliation of US GAAP profit before tax to taxable income

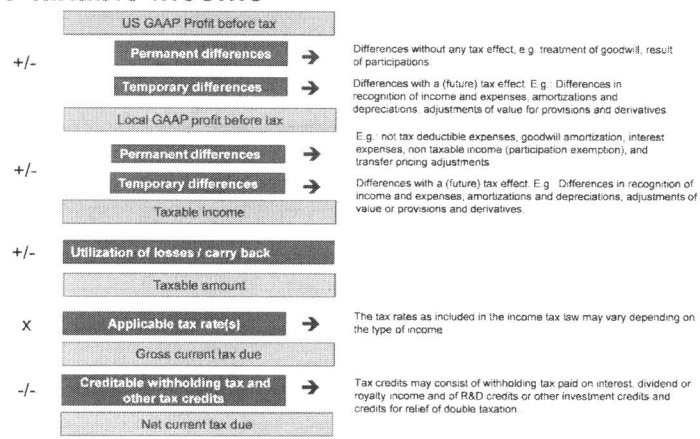

	US GAAP Profit before tax	
+/−	Permanent differences →	Differences without any tax effect, e.g. treatment of goodwill, result of participations
	Temporary differences →	Differences with a (future) tax effect. E.g.: Differences in recognition of income and expenses, amortizations and depreciations, adjustments of value for provisions and derivatives
	Local GAAP profit before tax	
+/−	Permanent differences →	E.g.: not tax deductible expenses, goodwill amortization, interest expenses, non taxable income (participation exemption), and transfer pricing adjustments
	Temporary differences →	Differences with a (future) tax effect. E.g.: Differences in recognition of income and expenses, amortizations and depreciations, adjustments of value or provisions and derivatives
	Taxable income	
+/−	Utilization of losses / carry back	
	Taxable amount	
×	Applicable tax rate(s) →	The tax rates as included in the income tax law may vary depending on the type of income
	Gross current tax due	
−/−	Creditable withholding tax and other tax credits →	Tax credits may consist of withholding tax paid on interest, dividend or royalty income and of R&D credits or other investment credits and credits for relief of double taxation
	Net current tax due	

The differences in income can be permanent or temporary. A deferred tax position should be recorded only for temporary differences. Therefore, this distinction is highly relevant. The review of this reconciliation includes reviewing the treatment of differences identified by the entity (occurrence and correctness), as well as considering whether any additional differences should have been identified (completeness).

The auditor takes the following into consideration for the review of the reconciliation of the income:
- Can the tax be considered as an income tax as defined in the framework?
- Does the US GAAP profit before tax as presented in the tax calculation tie with the US GAAP general ledger (are all late time adjustments taken into account)?
- What are the expected differences based on the business activities and on an analytical review of the assets and liabilities of the entity?
- What are the differences identified based on the corporate income tax returns filed for the past years?
- Are the differences challenged by the tax authorities during an audit or during another review of the tax return in the past?
- Are the differences in accordance with the Local GAAP framework and with the local income tax law including the applicable case law?
- Is the classification between permanent and temporary correct?

The auditor documents all audit evidence obtained for the determination that the differences are correct and complete. Furthermore, the auditor reviews the utilization of the losses carried by determining whether these losses exist based on the tax returns filed and on the calculation of the taxable income for the period for which the tax returns have not been filed yet. Besides this, the auditor also reviews whether any limitation may be applicable for the utilization of the losses.

The auditor verifies whether the tax rate(s) used are correct. In case different tax rates are applicable for different types of income, the auditor also verifies whether the amounts of these types of income are calculated in accordance with the local income tax law.

In case the gross current tax due is decreased by withholding taxes the auditors verifies whether these withholding taxes are withheld and whether these taxes can be taken into account as a credit. For other tax credits the auditor verifies whether these credits are calculated in accordance with the local income tax law.

14.2.2.3.2 Testing of the provision for current and deferred income taxes

The total tax expense (provision) consists of the current and deferred tax expense. The effective tax rate (ETR) is the result of the total tax expense divided by the profit before tax. A proper and detailed explanation of the ETR is a very important indicator whether the income tax expense is recorded appropriately. If there are no (permanent) differences between the US GAAP income before tax and the taxable income, the ETR will equal the statutory tax rate. There are a number of items that can have an impact on the ETR. The most common and relevant differences at entity level are:
- Non-taxable income (e.g. participation exemption, non-taxable capital gains or tax holidays);
- Non-deductible expenses (e.g. meals and entertainment and non-deductible interest);
- Changes in income tax rates (different deferred income positions due to tax rate changes);
- Prior year adjustments;
- Utilization of unrecognized tax losses / credits;
- Unrecognized deferred taxes for the current year and changes in the recognition of deferred taxes of prior years;
- Non-creditable withholding taxes;
- Additional local tax based on income (state taxes etc.);
- Changes in the liability for uncertain tax positions.

The auditor reviews each deviation of the ETR compared to the statutory tax rate. In fact the review of almost all items is covered by performing the other substantive procedures relating to income taxes. One of the exception is the review of prior year adjustments. The determination of the tax liability for an entity should relate to all years that are open for review by the tax authority. It may be several years after the end of a reporting period before the tax liability for that period is finally agreed with the tax authorities and settled. Therefore, the tax liability initially recorded at the end of the reporting period to which it relates is no more than a best estimate at that time, which will typically require revision in subsequent periods. For instance, in case the final tax return deviates from the provisioning or in case the liability is finally settled (final / additional assessment or even after legislation). Deviations between the best estimate of the tax liability at the end of a reporting period and the tax liability based on the tax return or final settlement are called prior year adjustments because there is no relation with the profit before tax of the current year. These adjustments (expense or benefit) are a separate line item in the reconciliation of the effective tax rate. Note that for financial reporting purposes the nature of any revision to a previously stated tax balance should be considered to determine whether the revision represents a correction of a prior period *error* or a *refinement* in the current period of an estimate made in a previous period (in which case it should be accounted for in the current period). In case of an error the auditor assesses whether this error is material. For material errors the financial statements of prior years should be restated.

In some cases the distinction between error and change in measurement (refinement) is clear. If, for example, the entity used an incorrect substantively enacted tax rate to calculate the liability in a previous period, the correction of that rate would – subject to materiality – be a prior year adjustment. A more difficult area is the treatment of accounting changes to reflect the resolution of uncertain tax positions. These are in practice almost always treated as measurement adjustments in the current period. However, a view could be taken that the eventual denial, or acceptance, by the tax authorities of a position taken by an entity indicates that one or the other party (or both of them) were previously taking an erroneous view of the tax law. As with other aspects of accounting for uncertain tax positions, this is an area where considerable judgment may be required.

Another item reviewed by the auditor is the allocation of the current and deferred income tax expense. Current and deferred tax expenses / benefits are recorded in the income statement unless they relate to items that are recorded outside the income statement. Examples are movements recorded in the other comprehensive income, certain tax effects of share based payments and deferred taxes relating to business combinations.

14.2.2.3.3 Testing the need for impairment of deferred tax assets

A deferred tax asset can relate to losses/ tax credits carried forward and to deductible temporary differences. As discussed in chapter 9.4, deferred tax assets can only be recognized to the extent that it is probable that these assets will be recovered. Based on the IFRS and US GAAP frame work the company should take the following into consideration:
- Are there sufficient taxable temporary differences relating to the same taxation authority and the same taxable entity (reversals of deferred tax liabilities in the period in which the losses and deductible temporary differences can be realized;
- Are there sufficient carry back possibilities to utilize the deductible temporary differences in the next years;
- Are there sufficient taxable profits in the period before the losses will expire
- Are there tax planning opportunities.

The first two sources of income are more or less straight forward calculations and are free of judgmental measurement issues. The auditor reviews the scheduling of the reversal of deductible and taxable temporary differences and checks whether the losses will be utilized before they expire.

However, the estimated future taxable income should be based on the management's best estimate and therefore this forecast is highly judgmental. The auditor reviews the management's estimate of the future taxable income taking the following into account:
- What is the reason for the net deferred tax asset position (net operation losses or deductible temporary differences, is the origin of the tax losses identifiable and is it unlikely to recur)?
- Are the losses and tax credits available in accordance with the tax returns filed and with the assessments received (existence of the losses and tax credits)?
- Are there any limitation regarding the utilization of the losses and tax credits?
- Is the forecast of the taxable income in line with the numbers that are used for the impairment testing of fix assets?
- What are the reasons for any deviation between the forecast of last year and the current year realization?
- Is the forecast in line with other representations of management (press releases etc.)?
- Is the forecast in line with other available market information, are the results of the market in which the entity operates volatile?
- Are all future differences between the profit before tax and the taxable income taken into account?

Tax planning strategies are transactions (or elections) that create or accelerate future taxable income. If management makes use of a tax planning strategy for the recognition of deferred tax assets the auditor reviews the following aspects of the tax planning strategy:
- The tax planning should be prudent and feasible. Implementation of the strategy must be primarily within the control of management. Management must have the ability to implement the strategy and expect to do so unless the need is eliminated in future years. If the action is not considered prudent, management probably would not undertake it, and if the action is considered not feasible, management would not have the ability to do it;
- It should be probable that the tax planning results in a realization of the deferred tax assets and therefore the risk that a tax planning may be successfully challenged by the tax authorities should be limited (lower than 50%)

The auditor takes all positive and negative evidence into consideration and concludes whether he agrees with the position taken by the management. If he does not agree the auditor will discuss the different point of view with the management and when no agreement at this point will be achieved the auditor reports an audit difference (judgmental).

14.2.2.3.4 Reviewing the movement of the current and deferred account balance from opening balance to ending balance

The movement of the current and deferred taxes can be depicted as follows:

Movement of current and deferred income tax balances

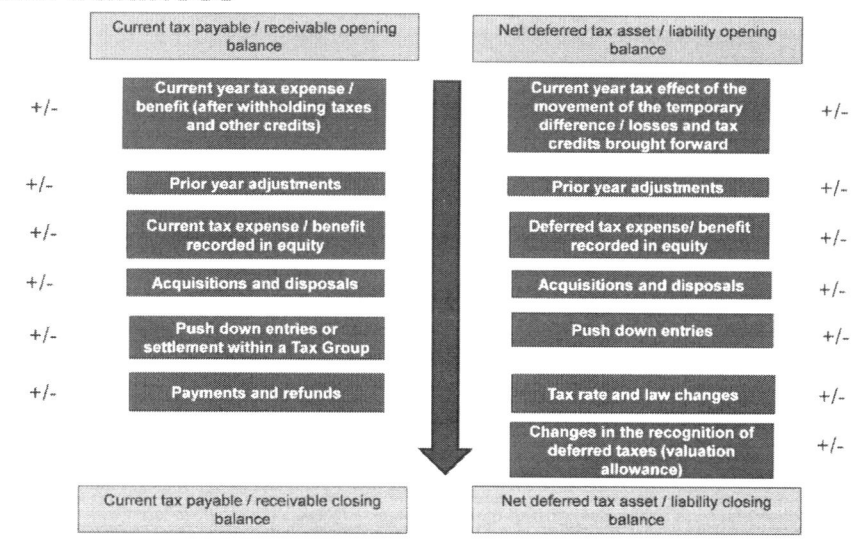

	Current tax		Deferred tax	
	Current tax payable / receivable opening balance		Net deferred tax asset / liability opening balance	
+/-	Current year tax expense / benefit (after withholding taxes and other credits)		Current year tax effect of the movement of the temporary difference / losses and tax credits brought forward	+/-
+/-	Prior year adjustments		Prior year adjustments	+/-
+/-	Current tax expense / benefit recorded in equity		Deferred tax expense/ benefit recorded in equity	+/-
+/-	Acquisitions and disposals		Acquisitions and disposals	+/-
+/-	Push down entries or settlement within a Tax Group		Push down entries	+/-
+/-	Payments and refunds		Tax rate and law changes	+/-
			Changes in the recognition of deferred taxes (valuation allowance)	+/-
	Current tax payable / receivable closing balance		Net deferred tax asset / liability closing balance	

Current tax

Based on the above depicted movement schedule, the following procedures are performed.
- The auditor reconciles the opening balances of the current taxes with the prior year closing balances. The movement of the current year tax expense is tied with tax expense as calculated based on the reconciliation of the profit before tax to taxable income (see PSP1 paragraph 14.2.2.3.1). The review of the prior year adjustments is part of the testing of the income tax provision (see PSP2 paragraph 14.2.2.3.2). The auditor identifies the items that are recorded outside the income statement for financial statements purposes (i.e. Other Comprehensive Income entries like: cost of issuance of share or foreign exchange results on intercompany loans) and obtain evidence that the tax effect (if any) is recorded in the same manner as the underlying movement.
- The additional current taxes due to acquisitions/disposal are reconciled with the current taxes in the opening balance of the acquired company or with the ending balance of the disposed company.
- In case an entity forms part of a tax group or fiscal unity, the auditor reviews whether the settlement is in accordance with the underlying agreement and whether all entries at fiscal unity level balance to nil. Furthermore the auditor reviews all payments and refunds of the current income taxes by obtaining all

bank details of the payments and refunds and reviews whether these are in line with the final and preliminary assessments. For each fiscal year that is still open for review by the tax authorities (statute of limitations) the auditor reviews whether the assessments issued by the authorities are paid or determines that the amount due or to be received is in accordance with assessments, payments and refunds.

Deferred tax
Deferred tax positions can relate to temporary difference, losses carried forward and tax credits carried forward. For more details in this respect I refer to chapter 9.4.

There are some similarities with the current income tax procedures to be performed. However, there are also significant differences. An important difference relates to the fact for current income taxes annual assessments are issued by the tax authorities. Therefore any difference between the estimated current tax expense as recorded in the financial statements for a certain period and the final assessment for that respective period will automatically come to the surface. This mechanism is not applicable for deferred taxes.

The temporary differences at a reporting date are a result of the differences between the book and tax base of the assets and liabilities. The existence and completeness of the temporary differences are reviewed by the auditor by analyzing the temporary differences based on the latest tax return filed. Based on the tax return, the auditor reviews each difference between the book and tax base of the assets and liabilities and he assesses whether the difference is permanent or temporary of nature. The auditor reviews whether the temporary differences identified (including the roll forward of the temporary differences for the years for which the tax return has not been filed yet) reconcile to the temporary differences as included in the deferred tax calculation of the company. The auditor reviews whether for each temporary difference a deferred tax position has been recorded (unless an exception is applicable.) against the correct income tax rate.

The losses carried forward and the unused tax credits are reconciled with the latest tax return filed and with the movements of the losses and tax credit for the years for which no tax return has been filed yet. The auditor reviews whether a deferred tax position has been recorded for the losses and tax credits against the correct income tax rate.

Additionally, the auditor reconciles the opening balances of the deferred tax position with the prior year closing balance. The movement of the current year deferred tax expense are tied with deferred tax expense as calculated based on the reconciliation of the profit before tax to taxable income (see PSP1). The review of the prior year adjustments is part of the testing of the income tax provision (see PSP2). The auditor identifies the items that are recorded outside the income statement for financial statements purposes (i.e. Other Comprehensive Income entries like movements of the pension asset or liability) and obtain evidence that the tax effect (if any) is recorded in the same manner as the underlying movement.

Acquisitions often result in additional deferred tax positions due to the US GAAP (and IFRS) acquisition accounting rules.[44] The auditor reviews each temporary difference that are a result of the acquisition (business combination) and reviews that the movement of these taxes are recorded via goodwill. The movement of the deferred tax position due to disposals are reconciled with the deferred tax position in the ending balance of the disposed company at the moment of disposal. Furthermore, the auditors reviews whether the push down entry (journal entry to transfer tax positions from parent level to subsidiary level) balances to nil at consolidated level.

The auditor determines whether tax rate and law changes have been properly taken into account and he reconciles the changes in the recognition of the deferred taxes (valuation concept under US GAAP) based on PSP3 (paragraph 14.2.2.3.3)

14.2.2.3.5 Testing whether the provision for uncertain tax positions is in accordance with the US GAAP framework

The provision in ASC 740(for the accounting for uncertainty in income taxes utilizes a two-step approach for evaluating income tax positions. Recognition (step 1) occurs when an entity concludes that a tax position, based solely on its technical merits, is more likely than not to be sustained upon examination. Measurement (step 2) is only addressed if step 1 has been satisfied (i.e., the position is more likely than not to be sustained). Under step 2, the tax benefit is measured as the largest amount of benefit, determined on a cumulative probability basis, that is more likely than not to be realized upon ultimate settlement. If step 1 has not been satisfied a provision should be recorded for the full amount. Hence, no tax benefit can be taken into account. Irrespective the applicable framework, due to the judgmental character (accounting estimates) of the application of the recognition and measurement rules, accounting for income taxes is a complex area, also from an audit perspective. First the auditor reviews (recognition and measurement) the uncertain tax position identified by the company. Secondly he reviews whether all potential uncertainties have been taken into account (completeness).

Uncertain tax positions identified by the company
During the planning and risk assessment phase, the auditor obtains a detailed understanding of the design of the Tax Control Frame work, especially with respect to the tax risk monitoring procedures. For each uncertain tax position identified by the company the auditor reviews the tax technical merits of the uncertainty. If necessary a subject matter tax specialist will be involved. Management's view should be laid down in tax position paper (per unit or account). This paper should contain:
- a description of the tax uncertainty;
- the years open for review to which this uncertainty relates;
- assessment whether the recognition threshold is met and the measurement of the provision;

---

44 See Chapter 9.4.1.3.1.

- assessment whether interest and/or penalties are due;
- calculation of the provision including interest and penalties.

For the evaluation of the assessment and the use of accounting estimates by management the auditor takes the following into consideration:[45]
- Determining whether events occurring up to the date of the auditor's report provides audit evidence regarding the accounting estimate (i.e. settlement with tax authorities or new case law);
- Testing how management made the accounting estimate and reviewing the accuracy, completeness and relevance of the data on which it is based. This includes an evaluation of whether the method of measurement used is appropriate in the circumstances and whether the assumptions used by management are reasonable given the measurement requirements of ASC 740 (i.e. is the assessment of management (including estimates) supported by:
    o tax opinion(s);
    o tax advice;
    o authoritative literature;
    o transfer pricing studies;
    o case law or resolutions and decrees of the tax authorities.
- Evaluate management's estimates based on the audit evidence available and assess whether the outcomes are reasonable/professional judgment of the auditor (in liaison whit tax subject matter specialist);
- Reviewing management judgment of tax uncertainties and assumptions related to accounting estimates included in the prior period financial statements or any subsequent reassessments in the current period.

Completeness of the tax uncertainties
One of the most difficult aspects of auditing income taxes relates to the determination whether all uncertainties that may exist have been taken into consideration. For the determination of the completeness of the uncertain tax liabilities the auditor takes the following into consideration:
- Are there any adjustments made by the tax authorities in the past that were not identified as an uncertainty by the management of the company and what was the reason that the underlying tax position was not identified as an uncertainty?
- Has the tax impact of all significant transactions been assessed by the tax department of the company?
- Which potential uncertain tax positions are described in the accompanying letter of the corporate tax return filed?
- What are the expected uncertain tax positions based on the activities of the entity?
- Are all tax driven transactions and structures agreed upfront with the tax authorities or provided with tax opinions/advice?

---

45 ISA 540.14

- Have all tax rulings (within the EU) been assessed for the risk that these ruling may constitute state aid?

Taking the audit threshold into account, the auditor will assess in detail each potential uncertain tax position. If necessary a subject matter tax specialist will be involved.

14.2.2.3.6 Testing the at arms' length nature of the intercompany transactions.

Within a multinational group there can be a variety of intercompany transactions. Based on almost all local income tax laws, the transfer pricing of these transactions is generally based on the (OECD) at arms' length principles.[46] However, the applications of these principles can vary between tax authorities.

Often the transfer pricing (supply chain) model is designed to decrease (or defer) the overall consolidated tax expense by allocating income to low taxed jurisdictions. These transactions are often concluded in the normal course of business. Within a multinational environment, companies may also benefit from a different tax treatment in jurisdictions of certain transactions or benefit from a different qualification of entities (transparent or not). These transactions (or structures) are often outside the normal course of business.

Note that intercompany transactions are eliminated for consolidated purposes. However, the tax effect of these transactions will not be eliminated unless the tax effect relates to an intercompany transfer of an asset. At the end the differences in tax rates and/or a different income tax treatment of transactions or entities in the respective jurisdictions will have an impact on the net tax expense at consolidated level. Therefore the risk of a material misstatement relating to the tax effect on intercompany transactions will increase if the tax rates of the entities involved deviate significantly (i.e. transfer of goods from the US (tax rate 40%) to the UK (tax rate 21%) or vice versa. The risk on a material misstatement will also increase if a group makes use of a different qualification for income tax purposes of certain transactions (for instance in the Netherland interest income on hybrid loans can be tax exempt under the participation exemption if certain conditions are met and the corresponding interest expense can be tax deductible in another jurisdiction).

A transfer pricing dispute (other than qualification differences) in one jurisdiction may result in a compensating adjustment in another jurisdiction. Within the European Union the tax authorities should agree upon the compensating adjustment based on the EU Arbitration Convention. In a lot of tax treaties a mutual agreement procedure has been included for transfer pricing disputes. The result should be the same as under the EU Arbitration Convention. However, in contrary to the EU Arbitration Convention, it is not mandatory for the taxation authorities to agree

---

46 See Chapter 13 for more details on transfer pricing.

upon the adjustments, but practically speaking they often do. For more details on transfer pricing see chapter 13.

Based on the above, the net impact on the tax expense in the consolidated financial statements may therefore be limited to tax rate differences, interest expenses and penalties if applicable. However, companies do not always want to make use of mutual agreement procedures or to a lesser extent of the EU Arbitration Convention because these procedures can be time consuming and therefore (too) expensive. Furthermore, the tax authority that needs to decrease the taxable amount often conducts an audit as a result of the mutual agreement procedure. This can also be an argument for a company not to start up such a procedure.

The following steps apply regarding the testing of the at arms' length nature of the intercompany transactions:
- Identification of the intercompany transactions within the group that can have a tax impact above the audit threshold;
- Obtaining information relating to the identified transactions;
- Assessing whether the documentation and transfer pricing applied meet the income tax law requirements in this respect;
- Conclusions and reporting.

Identification of the intercompany transactions
The auditor obtains understanding of the legal structure and all related parties. He also obtains an understanding of the controls that management has put in place to identify, account for, disclose and authorize related party relationships and transactions. Based on an overview of all intercompany transactions of the entities involved, classified per type of transaction including volumes (sale or purchase of goods, providing services, manufacturing, licensing, cost contribution agreements, loan agreements etc.) the auditor assesses which transactions may have a risk of misstatement above the audit threshold taking into account the applicable tax rates, the volume of the transactions and unrecognized losses and tax credits per entity.

Obtaining information
For all selected intercompany transactions the auditor obtains all available evidence regarding the substantiation of the transfer pricing method and transfer price applied. The following information per transaction or class of transactions is relevant in this respect:
- Intercompany agreements with all conditions etc., including loan agreements;
- Substantiation of transfer pricing method(s) applied;
- Transfer pricing studies or other comparable third party transactions;
- Valuation models applied for the determination of the transfer price of intangibles (if applicable);
- Applicable rulings (Advance Price Agreements and Advance Tax Rulings);
- Announced or pending transfer pricing audits;

Assessment

Based on all available information the auditor (if necessary assisted by a subject matter tax specialist) assesses whether the transfer pricing documentation meets the applicable income tax law demands per entity. Furthermore, he assesses whether the transfer pricing applied is within the at arms' length range as described in the transfer pricing study or based on comparable third party transactions.

Conclusions and reporting

Based on the assessment performed the auditor concludes whether there are any additional transfer pricing risks (compared to the risks already identified by the company) and estimates the range of the potential outflow of sources. He also reviews the potential compensating impact of a mutual agreement procedure or of the application of the EU Arbitration Convention. If management does not agree with the findings of the auditor (after discussing the different views with those charged with governance) the auditor will record the estimated difference in the tax expense and liability/receivable as an audit difference (often as judgmental). Furthermore, the auditor will, besides audit differences, also communicate recommendations and potential areas of improvement relating to transfer pricing

14.2.2.3.7 Reconciling the current and deferred income tax balances from the trial balances to the financial statements including evaluation whether the income taxes are correctly classified

As part of the financial statement procedures, the auditor reconciles all income tax positions as recorded in the trial balances of all entities, including adjustment entities, to the financial statements. He also reviews whether the income tax balance sheet accounts are properly offset and whether a correct classification between non-current and current income tax balance sheet positions has been applied under US GAAP.

14.2.2.3.8 Assessment tax effect of other audit adjustments

The starting point of the audit of the income taxes is the US GAAP profit before tax and the US GAAP equity as recorded by each reporting entity. Any difference compared to the recorded US GAAP profit before tax and equity may have an current or deferred income tax effect. Therefore, for all non-income tax related audit differences identified, the current or deferred income tax impact should be assessed. Based on the summary of audit differences the auditor assesses whether this difference has a current, deferred or no income tax effect. Any potential income tax effect will also be recorded as an audit difference.

14.2.2.3.9 Testing whether the income tax disclosure notes meet the US GAAP requirement

Based on ASC 740 there are a number of mandatory income tax disclosure requirements. The IFRS income tax disclosure requirements are more or less the same. The main difference relates to the disclosure of uncertain tax positions. Under US GAAP detailed disclosures are required and under IFRS only possible tax risks should be disclosed (see Chapter 9.5 for more detail).

The auditor uses a disclosure note checklist and reviews whether all required income tax related disclosures are included in the financial statements

14.2.2.3.10 Obtain management representation relating to income taxes.

There are a number of income tax positions of which the recognition and measurement depend on the intention of the management or on estimates used by management. The most common examples are:
- Recognition of deferred tax assets based on future taxable income or tax planning (see paragraph 14.2.2.3.3);
- Identification, recognition and measurement of uncertain tax positions (see paragraph 14.2.2.3.5);
- Whether undistributed earnings will be distributed or whether other temporary differences on investments will reverse in the future (see paragraph 14.2.2.3.11).

The auditor obtains written confirmation from management with respect to these estimates and intentions. Furthermore, management will be asked to confirm that all known uncertain tax positions are disclosed and that all available evidence in this respect (tax opinions, advice and correspondence with the tax authorities) has been provided to the auditor.

14.2.2.3.11 Specific tax accounting topics at consolidated level

As depicted in paragraph 14.2.1.1 the consolidated accounts consist of all numbers of the entities that are part of the consolidation process. In the consolidated accounts. all transactions within a group are eliminated for financial statement purposes. These journal entries and other top level adjustments are often processed in an adjustment or in a consolidation reporting entity (often not a legal entity). Generally speaking the following types of journal entries can be recorded at top level:
(1) Elimination of intercompany income statement items without any net impact on the profit before tax (i.e. elimination of intercompany revenue/purchases and intercompany charges like licensing fees and cost contribution agreements);
(2) Elimination of investments and the corresponding equity elements of the consolidated subsidiaries;
(3) Elimination of intercompany balance sheet items without any impact on the net equity (i.e. elimination of intra group loans, receivables and payables;
(4) Elimination of balance sheet items with an impact on the profit before tax and on the equity (i.e. elimination of intercompany profits on inventory via revenue and purchases or elimination of intra group profits or earnings due to transfer of intangibles or other fixed assets);
(5) Top level adjustments (provisions for reorganizations for subsidiaries and other (tax) liabilities.

For each journal entry the potential income tax impact should be assessed. Therefore, the auditor performs the same substantive and other procedures (see paragraph 14.2.2.3) for the adjustment entity as for all other legal entities. The entries that can be categorized under 1,2 and 3 should not have a current or deferred tax impact because the book base of the assets and liabilities will not change. The consolidation entries under 4 will likely have an income tax impact because the book base of the assets will change and therefore also the deferred tax position. Furthermore, the auditor reviews whether the specific tax accounting rules under US GAAP for intra group transfer of assets has been applied properly.

Furthermore, it is common practice to record provisions for reorganizations or other sensitive liabilities at consolidated level (top level adjustments under 5). For these liabilities a deferred tax impact should be recorded in case the corresponding expenditures will be tax deductible in the future. Any change in the deferred tax position results also in a re-assessments of the recognition of deferred taxes and in the netting.

In case future distribution of un-remitted earnings of subsidiaries will result in additional withholding taxes or corporate income taxes a deferred tax liability should be recorded unless the foreign earnings are permanently invested abroad. Let's assume that the earnings of the Dutch entity will not be permanently invested in the Netherlands or lower level and that these earnings will be taxed at US parent level upon distribution. In this case the future US tax liability (net off qualifying foreign tax credits) in this respect should be recorded as a deferred tax liability for all Dutch undistributed earnings that exist at balance sheet date. The auditor reviews whether this liability has been recorded properly or obtains written confirmation of management that the earnings will be permanently invested abroad.

14.2.2.4 Conclusions and reporting

The auditor prepares a tax review memorandum containing all significant income tax related items and a summary of the results of the execution of the substantive audit procedures including the identified audit differences relating to income taxes.

The income tax related audit differences are part of the overall assessment of all audit differences. The auditor evaluates whether the audit differences at an aggregate and at individual level are considered to be material. Also the audit differences of prior years will be reviewed on the current year impact.

The audit differences are also evaluated with respect to the nature of the misstatement. The misstatement can be factual, projected, judgmental or can relate to a reclassification. Factual misstatements are misstatements about which there is no doubt, and generally relate to non-judgmental issues, such as the misapplication of accounting principles / tax laws/ tax rates or mathematical errors.

Projected misstatements relate to the exploration of misstatements identified during sample testing. This type of misstatement often does not relate to income taxes.

Judgmental misstatements are differences arising from the entity's judgments concerning accounting estimates that the auditor considers unreasonable. These type of misstatement can relate to income taxes, i.e. valuation of deferred tax asset or recognition and measurement of uncertain tax positions.

Reclassification misstatements can for example relate to changes in current and deferred taxes. There is no net impact on the tax expense in the income statement and on the equity. However, there is a difference between the current tax and deferred tax liability and between the current and deferred tax expense in the income tax disclosure notes.

All audit differences are evaluated with respect to the impact on the auditors opinion taking the applicable materiality into account. Furthermore, all income tax related audit differences and the findings regarding the operational effectiveness of the internal controls relating to income taxes are communicated with those charged with governance.

14.2.3 Summary and Conclusions

Auditing income taxes in the consolidated financial statements of an international group is often a very complex exercise. The current and deferred income tax positions depend on the applicable frame work (US GAAP / IFRS), local income tax laws including available case law, tax treaties and if applicable EU directives including EU case law. The application of income tax laws is often open for different interpretations and therefore uncertain tax positions may arise. It is often necessary to involve subject matter tax and tax accounting specialists to make a proper assessment from an audit perspective. Besides the complexity of income tax laws, the application of the tax accounting rules under the US GAAP and IFRS frameworks can also be very complex.

As described in the Internal Standards on Auditing (ISA) an auditor applies a risk based approach. The audit procedures to be performed depend on the combined risk assessment (combination of inherent risk, control risk and detection risk). Due to the complexity of income tax calculations the auditor will often not rely on controls and apply a substantive approach (performing primary and other substantive audit procedures).

Furthermore, the auditor takes a planning materiality (PM) into account. Materiality is defined as the magnitude of an omission or misstatement that, individually or in the aggregate, in light of the surrounding circumstances, could reasonably be expected to influence the economic decisions of the users of the financial statements. The PM is often a percentage of the profit before tax but can also depend on another basis that can be considered as appropriate (gross margin, equity or revenue etc.).

The performance materiality, also known as tolerable error (TE) is the application of planning materiality at the individual account or balance level. The TE (percentage of PM) is set to reduce to an appropriately low level the probability that the aggregate of uncorrected and undetected misstatements exceeds PM. The overall tax expense and tax balances in the consolidated accounts consist of a variety of underlying

Audit of tax   14.3.1

amounts. In the execution of the audit procedures the auditor applies a threshold for each underlying amount. This threshold is often set at 5%-25% of the TE.

The SAD is set at a percentage of PM depending on the level of the TE and on the expectations of those charged with governance. The audit differences above the SAD amount are evaluated with respect to the impact on the auditors opinion taking the applicable materiality into account. These audit differences are also communicated with the management of the entity and with those charged with governance.

14.3 Comparison with tax audits performed by Tax Authorities

When we compare the tax audit performed by a tax authority (as discussed in more detail in chapter 15) with the audit of the income tax position in the consolidated financial statements far more differences will be identified than similarities. The main similarity is that both audits have the objective (amongst others) to determine whether the local income law has been applied correctly for the years under review. In other words, is the calculated current tax to be paid to tax authorities determined in accordance with the income tax law taking into account the applicable case law and the application of tax treaties. Another similarity is that both audits are based on a risk approach.

Regarding the following area's the audit of the income tax position in the financial statements differs from the audit performed by a tax authority;
- Level of materiality, tolerable error and nominal amount;
- Nature of the audits;
- Compensating effect of current and deferred taxes;
- Liability for uncertain tax positions and current tax payable/receivable accounts;
- Tax effect on compensating adjustments relating to mutual agreement procedures;
- Deferred tax positions;
- Disclosure note requirements;
- Communication regarding the operational effectiveness of the internal controls and audit differences.

14.3.1 Level of materiality, tolerable error and nominal amount

For both audits certain thresholds are applied to plan and design the audit procedures. However, the materiality and the tolerable error as applied for the audit of the income tax position is often significantly higher than the materiality as applied by the tax authorities. Some tax authorities apply no or a very low audit threshold. Note that the tolerable error for financial statement audit purposes can be for example USD 30 million and the audit threshold applied by the tax authorities for example USD 50,000.

The audit differences identified by the auditor (income tax audit differences and the tax effect on other audit differences) below the tolerable error may not be adjusted as long as on an aggregate level the sum of all audit differences are below the materiality threshold for the financial statements as a whole. The audit differences below the nominal amount are even not reported. Hence, an unqualified opinion of the auditor does not mean that no adjustments will be made during the audit performed by a tax authority during the same period.

14.3.2 Nature of the audits

The audit of the income tax position in the consolidated financial statements is a recurring annual process for all entities that are part of the consolidated process. Hence, the auditor obtains audit evidence and concludes on an annual basis with respect to the income tax position taking the audit threshold into account. For the year under review, no corporate income tax return has been filed yet. The audit is based on an engagement between the audit firm and the company. The company provides the auditor with all necessary information and confirms in a letter of representation that all relevant issues are included in the financial statements.

An audit performed by the tax authorities is often not an annual process because it is limited to certain years for which the corporate income tax returns are already filed. Furthermore, an audit performed by tax authorities relates (generally speaking) to one jurisdiction. The rules regarding the information to be provided to the tax auditor is laid down in local income tax law and in tax treaties.

14.3.3 Compensating effect of current and deferred taxes

The income tax expense in the consolidated income statement consists of the balance of the current and deferred income tax expense. Under US GAAP and under IFRS it is prohibited to discount deferred taxes. Therefore, deferred taxes are recorded at the nominal amount. Hence, for the determination of the tax expense in the income statement and of the net equity amount, the timing of the taxation of income is less relevant because there is a compensating effect between current and deferred taxes. In some cases the distinction between current and deferred is relevant when a company suffers problems of liquidity. Also when the potential interest and or penalty component on this position will exceed the nominal amount the auditor will assess in detail whether the deferral of income is acceptable under the income tax law.

The timing of the taxation is relevant for the audit performed by a tax authority because the audit is primarily focused on current tax to be paid for the period under review.

14.3.4 Liability for uncertain tax positions and current tax payable/receivable accounts

For the audit of the consolidated financial statements the auditor needs to assess (amongst others) whether the current income tax position is in accordance with local income tax law and with the applicable framework. Besides the compensating effect of deferred taxes as discussed above, there can also be a compensating effect of a liability for uncertain tax positions.

In case a company takes the position that certain income should be considered as tax exempt, no current tax liability will be recorded. However, the company considers this position as uncertain and records therefore a liability for uncertain tax positions (including potential penalty due). From a financial statement perspective the income tax expense and the related tax liability regarding to that specific income has been recorded in accordance with the framework, Hence, there is no audit difference.

The above tax position (tax exempt income) will be recorded in the corporate income tax return. When the tax authority will conduct an audit relating to the above income tax position the auditor will probably (depending on the nature of the uncertainty) identify an audit difference. Whether or not the current tax liability or the liability for uncertain tax position has been recorded in the financial statements is not relevant in this respect. This may only have an impact on the assessment whether a penalty may be due.

Certain tax rulings may constitute state aid. For the audit of the financial statements the auditor should assess whether the company has recognized and measured the uncertainties in this respect in accordance with the applicable framework. Whether certain tax rulings may constitute state aid is not part of the scope of an tax audit as performed by a tax authority.

14.3.5 Tax effect on compensating adjustments as a result of mutual agreement procedures

A transfer pricing adjustment in one jurisdiction may result in a compensating adjustment in another jurisdiction. Within the EU, the tax authorities should agree upon the compensating adjustment based on the EU Arbitration Convention. Therefore, there should be no double taxation within the EU regarding transfer pricing adjustments. In this case the auditor of the financial statements takes both tax effects of these adjustments into account and the net impact on the income statement is equal to the tax rate difference between the jurisdictions and eventually the interest and penalties due. In the balance sheet the tax receivable and payable in this respect should be recorded separately because they relate to different jurisdictions.

Outside the EU the tax treaty (if applicable) provides rules how to deal with transfer pricing adjustments. Generally speaking, these rules should have the same result as within the EU. However, it is not mandatory for the tax authorities to agree upon the compensating adjustment. Therefore, in practice there is still a risk that a transfer pricing adjustment in one jurisdiction may not result in a compensation adjustment in another jurisdiction. Furthermore, a mutual agreement procedure is a very time consuming and expensive process. This is also the reason why companies do not always start a mutual agreement procedure. In this case double taxation will occur. The impact on the income statement will therefore be higher.

14.3.6 Deferred tax positions

As discussed in paragraph 14.2.1.4 deferred tax positions can arise on different levels. For the audit of the financial statements these positions are often significant and are therefore covered by the audit procedures. The deferred taxes can be the result of differences relating to the recognition of income or expenses and to losses/tax credits carried forward but also to differences relating to fair value adjustments based on acquisition accounting rules.

The audit performed by a tax authority only relate to current taxes and not to deferred taxes.

14.3.7 Disclosure note requirements and communication regarding the operational effectiveness of the internal controls and audit differences

As discussed in paragraph 14.2.1.5 the preparation of the income tax disclosure notes in a multinational environment is a cumbersome process. The income tax disclosure notes in the financial statements should meet the requirements of the applicable accounting framework. Therefore, separate audit procedures are performed in this respect. For the audit as performed by a tax authority, the disclosure notes are covered by audit procedures.

14.3.8 Communication regarding the operational effectiveness of the internal controls and audit differences

During the audit the operational effectiveness of the internal controls relating to income taxes are tested by performing substantive audit procedures. The findings in this respect and also the audit differences identified above the nominal amount are communicated with those who are charged with governance. As long as the audit difference are not material (individual or on an aggregated level) the audit will still provide an unqualified opinion.

The audit differences identified during an audit performed by the tax authorities will result in additional assessments and eventually the company can take the matter to court.

JOOST ENGELMOER

15. Tax audit[1]

15.1 Introduction

In Chapter 14 'Audit of tax' an overview of general audit principles is provided, including the purpose of an audit, objectives of an auditor and the risk based audit methodology. In section 14.1. a brief summary of the audit process is given. In this Chapter, I will give a general and high level overview of the principles and process of a tax audit. I will furthermore discuss the interaction with a *Tax Control Framework* and cooperative compliance or horizontal monitoring. This Chapter is based on a Dutch point of view.

15.2 Tax risk management process

The strategic goal of the Netherlands' Tax and Customs Administration (hereinafter: NTCA) is to strengthen the compliance, defined as the willingness of taxpayers, either businesses or individuals, to fulfill their tax obligations by reporting relevant facts correctly, on time, and in full.[2] To achieve this objective, the NTCA uses a risk management based approach, based upon taxpayers' characteristics, their behaviour and available capacity of the NTCA. These factors determine which enforcement actions have to be undertaken.

The NTCA aims to be as effective and efficient as possible. Therefore the NTCA uses various enforcement tools. These tools can be divided into preventive measures, such as an upfront communication campaign, and repressive measures, for example the assessments of tax returns after tax returns are filed.

Tax audit is another enforcement tool that can be applied by the tax authority. The tax risk management process can be illustrated as follows (see figure 15.1).

---

1 This contribution is personal and does not necessarily reflect the views of my employer.
2 Hornstra, J. (2011). *The Netherlands*. In: Khwaja, M., Awasthi, R. & Loeprick, J. *Risk-Based Tax Audits Approaches and Country Experiences*. Washington, D.C.: The International Bank for Reconstruction and Development / The World Bank, p. 83.

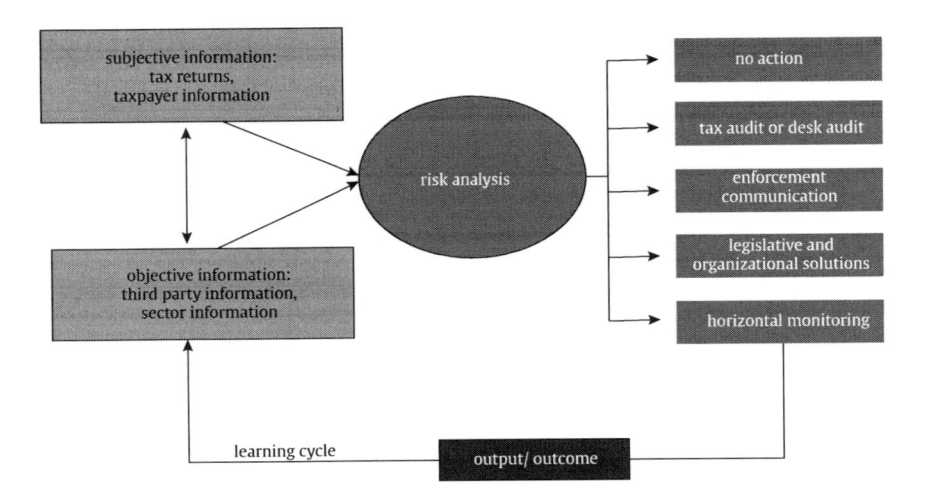

Figure 15.1. Tax risk management model[3]

The Dutch tax approach aims to stimulate voluntary compliance as much as possible. This approach is based on the concept of responsive regulations. In this concept, enforcement is progressively related to the behaviour of the subject, in this case the taxpayer. The concept can be illustrated as follows (see figure 15.2).

---

3   Hornstra, J. (2011). *The Netherlands*. In: Khwaja, M., Awasthi, R. & Loeprick, J. *Risk-Based Tax Audits Approaches and Country Experiences*. Washington, D.C.: The International Bank for Reconstruction and Development / The World Bank, p. 85.

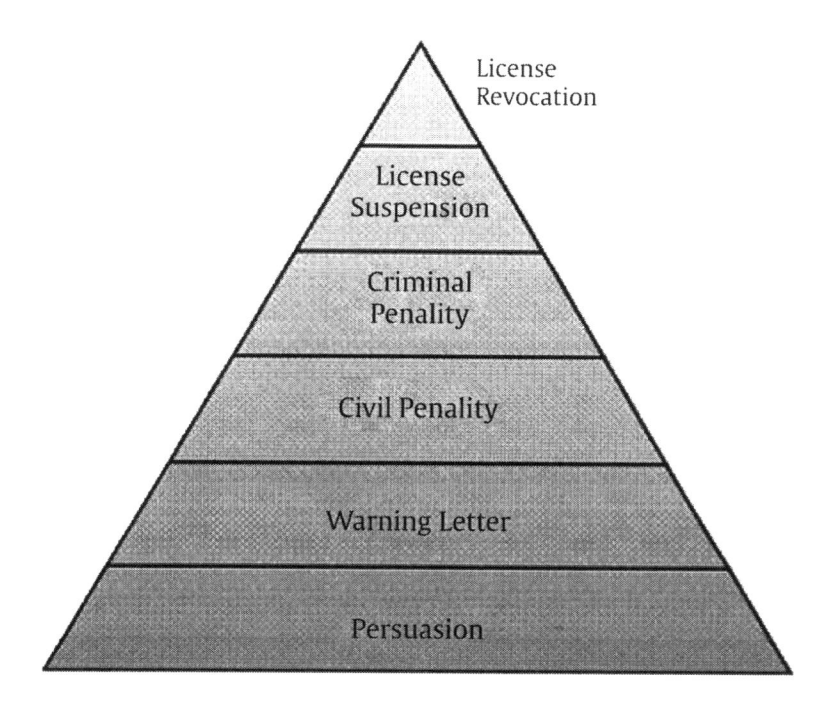

```
        License
        Revocation
      License
      Suspension
    Criminal
    Penality
   Civil Penality
   Warning Letter
    Persuasion
```

Figure 15.2. Pyramid of regulations[4]

15.3 Tax audit related law and legislation

Despite the differences in legislation per jurisdiction, law and regulations often contain two significant principles. To understand the context of the tax audit, these principles are addressed in this section. Firstly, taxpayers are often responsible to provide information to the tax authority. Secondly, taxpayers are often responsible to keep an adequate administration. As auditing mainly consists of gathering audit evidence, these requirements are highly important to the tax auditor. To illustrate such regulatory requirements, two important articles of Dutch tax legislation are discussed.

Article 47 of the Dutch General Tax Act ('*Algemene wet inzake rijksbelastingen*') states that a taxpayer has to inform the tax inspector on his request, within a reasonable

---

[4] Ayres, I. & Braithwaite, J. (1992). *Responsive Regulation Transcending the Deregulation Debate.* Oxford: Oxford University Press, p. 35.

period of time.[5] Thereby the tax inspector has the power to prescribe the form in which manner requested information has to be delivered.

In principle, all requested information has to be delivered, unless it is restricted by law. The General Tax Law states, for instance, that information from lawyers and solicitors does not have to be provided. In addition to this, the Dutch Supreme Court ruled in 2005 that information to enlighten a taxpayer's tax position – tax advices for instance – also does not have to be given to the tax authority.[6]

Article 52 of the Dutch General Tax Act ('*Algemene wet inzake rijksbelastingen*') contains the obligation for certain taxpayers to keep an adequate administration. Those taxpayers must also retain all relevant data for at least seven years.[7] Furthermore, this article prescribes that a taxpayer should administrate in a way that a tax audit can be performed in a reasonable period of time.

To meet this obligation a *Tax Control Framework* (hereinafter: *TCF*) can be very helpful, if not crucial. A *TCF* forms an integral part of a company's *Business* or *Internal Control Framework*. A *TCF* refers to all elements of control relevant to tax, whereby the term 'tax' covers all types of taxes.[8] A *TCF* often consists, amongst other things, of tax policies, roles and responsibilities related to tax, an overview of tax risks and tax related measures of internal controls.

15.4 Principles of the tax auditing approach

A tax audit has to be effective and efficient.[9] Therefore the tax auditor gathers sufficient audit evidence – not less or not more – to achieve reasonable assurance, necessary to complete his assignment. Audit evidence can also be obtained by using information that is already available, for example, in the company itself. Although this sounds obvious, this reasoning is one of the fundamentals of the Dutch tax auditing approach. In this section I describe the 'transactional model' and the 'audit layer model' to illustrate the above principles.

15.4.1 Transaction model

To comply with tax legislation, all transactions, estimates and relevant information must first be recorded properly, accurately and timely into the taxpayer's administration. Next, all relevant information has to be recorded into the tax return. In addition, all specific tax laws and regulations have to be applied correctly.

---

5   Article 47 of the General Tax Act ('*Algemene wet inzake rijksbelastingen*'). In some cases a taxpayer has to inform the tax inspector not only on request, see for instance article 10a of the General Tax Act.
6   Decisions of the Dutch Supreme Court (HR) of 23 September 2005, no. 38 810, BNB 2006/21.
7   Article 52 of the General Tax Act ('*Algemene wet inzake rijksbelastingen*').
8   Belastingdienst (NTCA) (2008). *Tax Control Framework. From a focus on risks to being in control: a different approach*, p.4.
9   Belastingdienst (NTCA) (2013). *Controleaanpak Belastingdienst (CAB), De CAB en zijn modellen toegepast in toezicht*, p. 2-11 (only available in Dutch).

These principles can be visualised as follows (see figure 15.3).

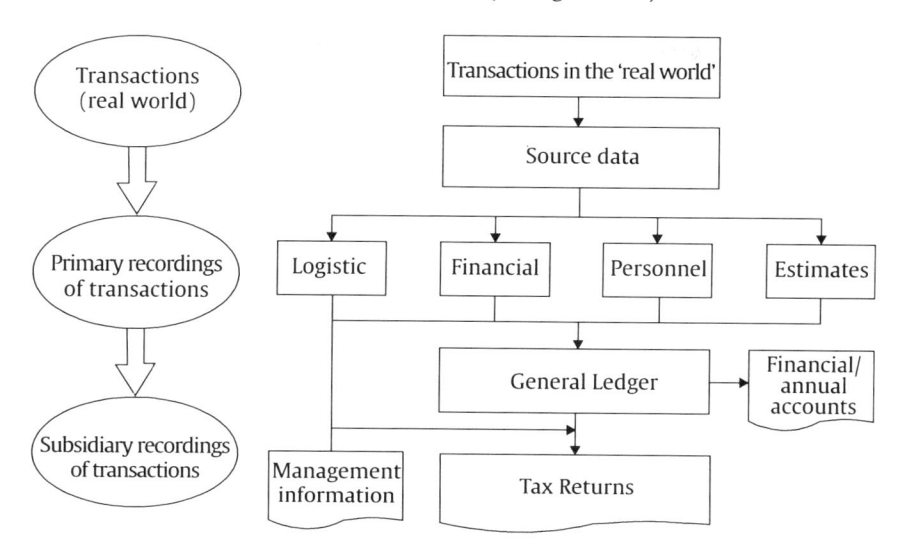

Figure 15.3. Transaction model[10]

15.4.2 Audit layer model

It is not necessary for the tax auditor to collect all the audit evidence himself. This fundamental principle is described as the 'audit layer model' and can be illustrated as follows (see figure 15.4).[11]

---

10   Extracted form: Belastingdienst (NTCA) (2013). *Controleaanpak Belastingdienst (CAB), De CAB en zijn modellen toegepast in toezicht*, p. 12 (only available in Dutch).
11   Sometimes also referred to as the 'onion skin' (layer) model.

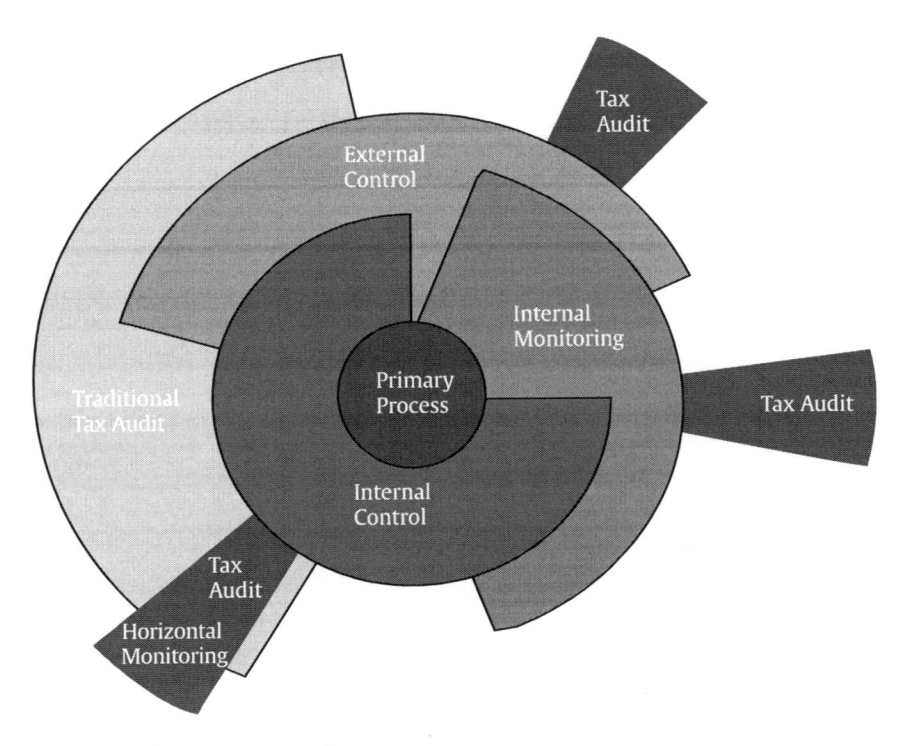

Figure 15.4. Audit layer model[12]

This audit layer model is based on the idea that every entrepreneur needs reliable information in order to run their business. Therefore, the entrepreneur has taken measures of internal control to assure reliability of information.[13] In figure 15.4, this is represented in the first layer ('internal control'), whereas the inner circle presents the business activities of the entrepreneur. The measures of internal control designed and implemented for taxes, are a significant part of a TCF. Other parties also provide assurance on the quality of information, for example, the external auditor or the tax assurance provider ('external audit').[14] The nature and extent of activities already performed (internally or externally) affect the audit procedures the tax auditor has to perform himself.

---

12   Belastingdienst (NTCA) (2013). *Controleaanpak Belastingdienst (CAB), De CAB en zijn modellen toegepast in toezicht*, p. 7-11 (only available in Dutch). Translated into English by author. See also: Kloosterman, H.H.W. (1991). *Schillenmodel*. De Accountant, no. 7, p. 403-406 (only available in Dutch).
13   Often referred to as business or internal control framework.
14   See section 15.12.

15.5 Traditional tax auditing approach

A tax audit is based on risk analysis.[15] By analysing the *'accounting organisation and measures of internal control'* (hereinafter also referred to as AO/IC) the tax auditor finds himself able to assess the risks that need to be covered with sufficient audit procedures.

Audit procedures always consist of a combination of various audit techniques, including analytical reviews and (comprehensive) coherence tests. Audit procedures are always a mix of tests of controls and substantive testing. In this section, a traditional tax audit auditing approach is described as used in the Netherlands.[16] This methodology is based upon the International Standards of Auditing and specially adapted for tax audit.

15.5.1 Definition of tax audit

'A tax audit is an audit whereby an auditor checks or assesses the object of the audit for which another party is responsible on the basis of criteria and about which the tax auditor forms an opinion which provides the intended user with a certain degree of assurance.'[17]

A tax audit can cover one or more private or legal persons and can focus on one or more tax returns, such as corporate income tax (CIT) or value added taxes (VAT). It is also possible to audit only a specific part of a tax return, e.g. a specific account. The applicable criteria are recorded in tax laws. The intended user will often be the tax inspector. In general, a tax audit qualifies as an assurance engagement.[18]

15.6 Stages of a tax audit

A tax audit consists of four stages, successively – 'pre-planning', 'completeness checks', 'accuracy checks' and 'overall evaluation and reporting'. Each step begins with planning of the intended activities and is finalised with – after all planned audit activities are performed – an evaluation. The process can be displayed as follows (see figure 15.5).

---

15 See also: AICPA (2012). *Evolution of Auditing: From the Traditional Approach to the Future Audit*, p. 1-9. New York: American Institute of Certified Public Accountants Inc.
16 As described in: Jonker, B. & Snippe, M. (2013). *Tax audit guide International edition*. Utrecht: NTCA. See for a more broader perspective of tax audit: Hell, L. van der (2011). *Intra-Community Tax Audit*. Amsterdam: IBFD and Kamerling, R.N.J. (1999-2003). *The International Guide on Tax Auditing*. Amsterdam: IBFD.
17 Jonker, B. & Snippe, M. (2013). *Tax audit guide International edition*. Utrecht: NTCA, p. 34.
18 See: International Federation of Accountants (2012). *International Framework for Assurance Engagement*. In: *Handbook Of International Quality Control, Auditing, Review, Other Assurance, And Related Services Pronouncements Part II*. New York: International Federation of Accountants, p. 1-24.

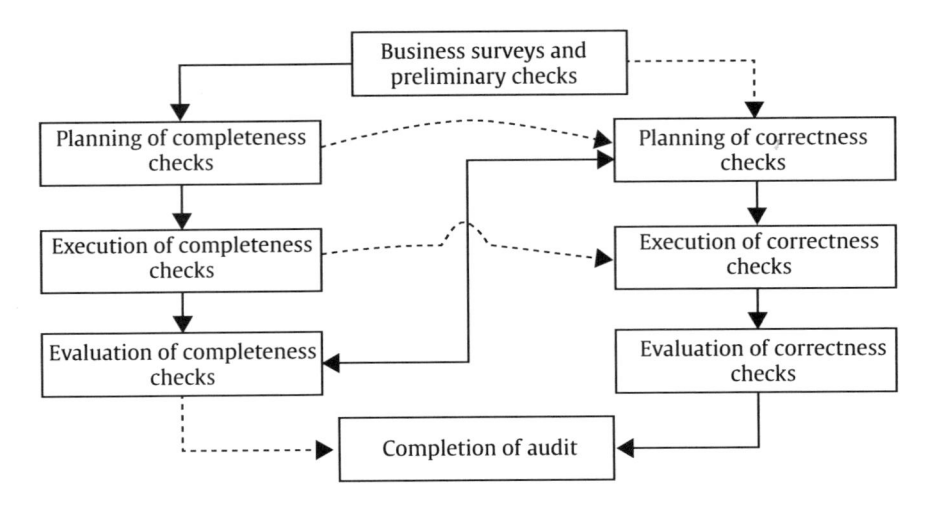

Figure 15.5. Workflow model[19]

The stages of a tax audit will be described in the following sections.

15.7 Pre-planning

After the assignment is given and the tax auditor considers himself able to perform his assignment, the tax auditor starts the tax audit with the pre-planning. In this step, the tax auditor tries to get a full and complete view of both audit subject and object. This step is highly important and defines the context in which the tax audit is performed. As part of the risk based approach, the tax auditor focuses on the *'accounting organisation and measures of internal control'* (AO/IC).

15.7.1 Gathering information about the company

The first step in pre-planning is to collect general information about the company. The tax auditor therefore uses internal and external sources to determine:
- the nature and size of the company (such as amount of revenues, profit, number of staff members etc.);
- the (legal) organisational structure of the company;
- the nature of the business (products, type of transactions);
- the market in which the company operates (including the most important competitors);
- the internal processes and systems used within the organisation;

---

19 Belastingdienst (NTCA) (2005). *Tax auditing special No. 2 – Tax Auditing Approach of the Tax Administration in the Netherlands.* p. 7.
See also: Kloosterman, H.H.W. (2004). *Wat is eigenlijk risicoanalyse in de accountantscontrole?* Maandblad voor Accountancy en Bedrijfseconomie, December, p. 570-578 (only available in Dutch).

- parties the company is depending upon (financers, suppliers, related parties);
- the (most important) tax regulations the company has to deal with.

The tax auditor mainly uses interviews with staff members and inspection of documents to collect this information. In many cases, the tax auditor also uses an on-site observation to observe the company's activities himself.

15.7.2 Preliminary risk analysis

Based on recent annual reports, tax returns (e.g. VAT, CIT) and other financial information, the tax auditor performs initial analytical audit procedures to determine potential risks. The number and nature of risks that are identified is often related to the type and complexity of the organisation involved.

The tax auditor can perform several kinds of analytical reviews, such as:
- comparison of actual and historical (numerical) data;
- comparison of ratios (e.g. liquidity ratio, gross margins);
- comparison of performance indicators with branch averages.

In order to be efficient, the tax auditor will use audit automation techniques, for example, the (standard) audit file. This file contains all journal entries made into a company's general ledger.[20] Nowadays this feature is provided by standard accounting software.[21]

In this phase of the tax audit, the tax auditor also concentrates on the reconciliation between the annual report and tax returns. There are different types of relations between financial and tax accounting as they differ per jurisdiction.[22] Relations between both can be divided between formal and material (in)dependence.[23] If the tax return is based on the annual report and specific tax adjustments have to be made, the tax auditor will assess those adjustments.[24]

---

20 OECD (2005). *Guidance for the Standard Audit File – Tax*. OECD/Centre for Tax Policy and Administration.
21 OECD (2005). *Guidance on Tax Compliance for Business and Accounting Software*. OECD/Centre for Tax Policy and Administration.
22 See also: Chapter 9 on tax accounting.
23 Essers, P. & Russo, R. (2009). *The precious relationship between IAS/IFRS, National Tax Accounting Systems and the CCCTB*. In: Essers, P., et al, *The Influence of IAS/IFRS on the CCCTB, Tax Accounting, Disclosure, and Corporate Law Accounting Concepts, A Clash of Cultures*. Alphen aan de Rijn: Kluwer Law International, p. 31-38.
    Also: Russo, R. (2010). *Risk management in taxation*. In: Dealen, M. van & Elst, C. van der, *Risk Management and Corporate Governance, Interconnections in Law, Accounting and Tax*. Cheltenham: Edward Elgar Publishing, p. 166-170.
24 Also: Zeng, T. (2000). *Taxpayers' Tax and Financial Reporting and Auditing in a Game Theoretical Model*. Waterloo: Wilfrid Laurier University.

Due to recent initiatives, such as country-by-country (Cbc) reporting, annual reports will contain even more tax relevant information.[25] Cbc reporting will, for instance, provide valuable information to the tax auditor to detect transfer pricing events.

15.7.3 Materiality

At this stage the tax auditor also sets the amount of materiality. A tax audit is set up with a certain margin of error, which is indicated by the amount of materiality. To assure a level playing field in the Netherlands, the amount of materiality is based upon a fixed table whereby materiality is related to a company's turnover. Due to differences in scope, nature and extent, the amount of materiality used for tax audit often diverge from the amount of materiality used in the external audit of the annual report. Another major difference compared to the external audit is that normally all detected and known misstatements, negative and positive, above a certain amount, are to be corrected, even though misstatements aren't material.

15.7.4 Critical internal processes

The next step in pre-planning is to determine a company's most critical internal processes. A critical process has material effects on the outcome, i.e. the tax returns. A critical process is related to the object of audit. If, for example, the object of audit is wage tax, HRM and payment processes are likely to be indicated as critical. If, on the other hand, the object of audit is corporate income tax (CIT), the revenue process is often indicated as critical. The tax auditor determines all steps taken in all individual critical processes. He thereby focuses on the input and output of each process step. Process mapping is a useful model to capture data streams (primary records) for each individual process step. This phase of pre-planning is not only necessary to understand the nature of the company's business in a more detailed manner, it is also necessary to determine a company's compliance with data retention regulations, since tax law generally demands, for instance, that certain information is recorded and is maintained for a certain period of time.

After these audit activities, the tax auditor will determine the expected – minimum – *'accounting organisation and measures of internal control' (AO/IC)*.[26] This expectation is referred to as the 'SOLL' position. In the next steps of pre-planning, the tax auditor will compare this 'SOLL' position with the actual *'accounting organisation and measures of internal control'(AO/IC)* ('IST' position). Deviations will have a further impact on tax audit procedures.

---

25 OECD (2014). *Discussion Draft On Transfer Pricing Documentation And Cbc Reporting.* OECD. Also: Murphy, R. (2012). *Country-by-Country Reporting.* Richard Murphy/Tax Justice Network.
26 Often the *AO/IC* that is related to a tax position is referred to as *Tax Control Framework (TCF)*.

15.7.5 Design of the AO/IC

The next step is to determine the administrative context. Therefore the tax auditor first analyses the design of the AO/IC. The AO/IC is generally documented formally into plans, procedures, instructions, regulations of power, job descriptions and process manuals. As referred to earlier, the AO/IC related to critical processes will be analysed in more detail because of its impact on the tax return(s). Important shortcomings in the design of the AO/IC will have consequences for the further tax audit.

15.7.6 Existence of the AO/IC

Preceding his audit, the tax auditor now needs to determine the existence of the AO/IC. It is possible that measures of internal control are not or not correctly implemented in the organisation. It is also possible that controls de facto are in place, but haven't been formally documented. The tax auditor may not have noticed them when analysing the design of the AO/IC.

Normally, an auditor uses direct audit techniques to determine the existence of the AO/IC, such as walk-through tests, on-site observations and interviews with staff members. During a walk-through test an auditor follows all relevant processes of a transaction in order to assess the procedures to which the transaction is subject to.[27] A walk-through test can be performed in two ways. The auditor can start with the recorded transaction, in order to follow it back to its initial primary document, or in reverse, from initial document up to the point of administration. The first approach is commonly referred to as the grave-to-cradle test, the latter as the cradle-to-grave test.

A tax audit often concerns historical instead of actual positions. Therefore direct audit techniques aren't always possible. Only in situations where the actual processes haven't (largely) changed compared to the year of the tax audit, these direct audit techniques can be applied. In other situations, the tax auditor should consider other audit techniques. He could, for instance, rely on the findings of the external auditor.

15.7.7 Residual risk for the management

After the above audit procedures have been performed, the tax auditor evaluates the AO/IC. He estimates the risks that could still remain, in spite of all the measures of internal control. He qualifies the remaining risk by using three types of qualifications: 'high', 'moderate' and 'low'. If the tax auditor qualifies the remaining risks as 'low', he will normally choose a system-based auditing approach by performing tests of controls.

---

27 Jonker, B. & Snippe, M. (2013). *Tax audit guide International edition*. Utrecht, NTCA, p. 213.

If, on the other hand, the remaining risks are qualified as 'high' it is likely that the management cannot control the risks themselves, because of absent or inadequate measures of internal control. In this situation, the tax auditor cannot rely on the *AO/IC* and so he will have to perform substantive tests to obtain sufficient audit evidence. Substantive testing could be labour intensive and time consuming.

15.7.8   Preliminary audit tests

To determine a taxpayer's compliance with specific administrative regulatory requirements, the tax auditor analyses documents to ensure that:
- books and records are kept according to applicable (tax) law and regulations;
- books and records can be verified in a reasonable period of time;
- necessary reconciliations can be made.

The latter is also referred to as the 'audit trail'. This means that there has to be a connection between transactions as recorded into the company's general ledger and the tax returns. If those requirements are not met, the tax auditor has to rely on other kinds of information (i.e. third party information).

15.7.9   Effectiveness of the AO/IC

The last step regarding the *AO/IC* is to determine the effectiveness of the measures of internal control. To do so, the tax auditor uses a combination of interviews with staff members, on-site observations, repeating of procedures and verification and inspection of documents to assure the measures of internal control function as designed and are effective. To increase efficiency, these activities can be combined with substantive testing (referred to as dual purpose tests).

Not all controls have to be tested. The tax auditor will generally focus on key controls. If the controls are IT related (e.g. application controls), the tax auditor will be assisted by an EDP or IT-auditor. The number of tests that have to be performed is a case of professional judgment. The NTCA has set a table, based upon the nature and frequency of the control, to give the tax auditor guidance in doing so.[28] If, for example, a control is conducted several times a day, the tax auditor has to test at least 25 controls. If, on the other hand, a control is conducted once a year (for example general IT controls), this control should be tested by the tax auditor. If any imperfections are found, the tax auditor should consider the impact on the further audit. Detailed examination of imperfections will always be necessary. Depending on the situation, tests of controls could be extended.

Often, the organisation tests its own internal controls periodically. This activity is described as (internal) monitoring. Monitoring is also an important part of a *TCF*. In

---

28   Jonker, B. & Snippe, M. (2013). *Tax audit guide International edition.* Utrecht: NTCA, p. 227. Compare: Chambers, A. & Rand, G. (2010). *The Operational Auditing Handbook.* Chichester: John Wiley and Sons, p. 169.

such situations, the tax auditor performs analytical reviews on these internal monitoring tests, by analysing the way they are set up and performed. The tax auditor will also repeat some tests to ensure the quality of the (internal) assessments.

15.7.10 Residual risk for the tax auditor

The last step in pre-planning is to plan substantive audit procedures. The extent and scope of these activities is deeply related to the tax auditor's judgment of the *AO/IC*. If the tax auditor finds the *AO/IC* reliable, substantive testing can be reduced to a minimum. It is worth noting that substantive tests cannot be reduced completely. Some substantive tests (such as reconciliation checks) will always be necessary.

If the tax auditor finds the *AO/IC* not or not fully reliable, the tax auditor has to consider which, and to what extent, substantive tests should be performed, in order to obtain the necessary audit evidence. As mentioned earlier, substantive testing could be labour intensive and time consuming.

Imperfections in the *AO/IC* can sometimes be restored or compensated by performing (additional) substantive tests.[29] Not all imperfections in the *AO/IC* can be restored or compensated sufficiently.[30] In some cases, this can lead to the situation whereby the tax authority estimates the amount of tax that should have been paid and shifts the burden of proof towards the taxpayer.[31] The scope and extent of substantive testing can be summarised as follows:

AO/IC	Completeness checks	Accuracy checks
Sufficient	Limited to a minimum	Limitations possible and allowed
Insufficient	No limitations possible	No limitations possible

Table 15.1. Summary of substantive testing[32]

15.8 Completeness checks

After the pre-planning, the tax auditor performs audit procedures to confirm the completeness of transactions and statements. The nature and the extent of the activities that need to be performed are highly related to the tax auditor's judgment on the quality of the *AO/IC*. As stated earlier, an effective *AO/IC* means that completeness checks can be reduced to a minimum.

---

29 The tax auditor – unlike the external auditor – could, for instance, perform third party audits, on site observations and third party information requests. It is possible that those audit activities would not lead to sufficient audit evidence.
30 Sometimes referred to as irreplaceable procedures of internal control.
31 See also: Gleason, C.A. Pincus, M. & Rego, S.O. (2012). *Consequences of Material Weaknesses in Tax-Related Internal Controls for Financial Reporting and Earnings Management.*
32 Based on: Jonker, B. & Snippe, M. (2013). *Tax audit guide International edition.* Utrecht: NTCA, p. 235.

If completeness checks have to be performed, the tax auditor normally uses detailed analytical reviews and (comprehensive) coherence tests to gather sufficient audit evidence. In some cases the tax auditor performs additional substantive tests such as third party investigations or detailed analysis of cash accounts. The first includes investigations of the documents of others, apart from the taxpayer himself, i.e. a debtor, to determine the completeness of reported revenue. In the case of a detailed analysis of cash accounts, the tax auditor aims to find irregularities. These audit procedures could include different kinds of mathematical methods such as a Chi-square test or Benford's law test.

15.8.1   Minimum procedures

The tax auditor always performs substantive tests, such as reconciliation checks between annual accounts, administration and tax returns. He thereby also focuses on preliminary account adjustments, because of the possibilities for a company's management to (easily) adjust figures.

15.9   Accuracy checks[33]

The next stage in the tax audit process is to perform checks to determine whether records, transactions and statements are accounted accurately. To achieve this objective, the tax auditor performs substantive tests, often detailed analytical reviews combined with verification and inspection of documents.

The tax auditor can use numerous approaches to select transactions for detailed analysis. The first approach is based on non-statistical sampling. The tax auditor can use partial observation, whereby the tax auditor can select the most critical or largest transaction in order to assess them in more detail. He could also use a block sampling method, where documents for a specific period, for example a month, are selected. Another method is based on the theory of Pareto, which states that approximately 20% of transactions cover 80% of the corresponding value of all transactions.[34] Although the above methods are easily applied, it is difficult to extrapolate (partial) findings to the population as a whole.

The use of a statistical approach pre-empts those shortcomings. Monetary unit sampling, used by the NTCA, is an example of a statistical method. Transactions are selected based on their amount, so each amount has an equal chance to be selected. The sample can consist of a company's costs or expenses, depending on the tax auditor's objectives. The sample is based on the size of the population, the materiality and requested statistical reliability (set at 95%). The sample is set up with the expectation that no errors will be found. At least 60 units have to be selected.[35] All

---

33   Also referred to as correctness checks.
34   Compare: Parmenter, D. (2007). *Pareto's 80/20 rule for corporate accountants*. Hoboken: John Wiley & Sons, p. XV.
35   $n = R / pk$. $R = 3$ (zero error expectation) and $pk = 0.05$; $n = 3/0.05 = 60$.

selected transactions will be audited in detail by verification and inspection of documents. If the *AO/IC* works effectively, the sample can be reduced.[36] These possibilities will be discussed in section 15.11 ('Tax audit and Tax Control Framework').

The tax auditor evaluates his findings using statistics. Because of the complexity of this (mathematical) evaluation, I will not discuss this evaluation. If the maximum error exceeds the amount of materiality, the tax auditor cannot approve the examined population. As part of the burden of proof, the tax auditor then first enables the taxpayer to do further research into the population. If this is not applicable or not sufficient, the tax auditor will suggest a correction based on the best estimate of expected errors.

15.10   Overall evaluation

To finalise the tax audit, the tax auditor performs an overall evaluation. The tax auditor accumulates all of his findings and considers corrections to be made. A major difference compared to the external audit is that normally all detected and known misstatements, negative and positive, above a certain amount, are to be corrected, even though misstatements aren't material. Auditor's findings are always discussed with the company's management. The tax auditor will document all of his findings in a report.

15.11   Tax audit and Tax Control Framework

As described in section 15.4 ('Principles of the tax auditing approach'), the tax auditing approach aims to be as efficient as possible. Due to inadequate internal control substantive testing is often necessary. This can be labour intensive and time consuming. An adequate *AO/IC*, as a significant part of a *TCF*, will normally lead to reduced tax audit procedures. Although reduction is always a made to measure consideration, certain general guidelines apply.

15.11.1   *Monitoring as a part of a Tax Control Framework*

As described in section 15.7 ('Pre-planning') and section 15.8 ('Completeness checks'), the tax auditor should perform numerous tests of controls to assure effectiveness of tax related internal (key) controls. Monitoring is part of a fully designed and implemented control framework. Monitoring activities can be performed internally or externally and are set up to ensure adequate performance of the measures of internal control. In situations where monitoring is in place, the tax auditor will mainly review performed activities, instead of performing all tests of controls himself. He will

---

36 To determine the effectiveness of the *AO/IC*, generally twenty-five tests of controls have to be performed. Those tests are often dual purpose tests. They are used simultaneously for testing the applicable control as well as substantive testing.

only repeat a couple of tested controls. In this situation the tax auditor shifts to a more review-based, less labour intensive, auditing approach.

15.11.2 Reduction of completeness checks

If the *AO/IC* is set up adequately and is working effectively, the tax auditor only needs to perform minor activities such as reconciliation checks and analysis of preliminary account adjustments.[37]

15.11.3 Reduction of accuracy checks

The accuracy checks, if based upon a statistical approach, can also be reduced significantly. The levels of reduction differ per situation.[38]

If the *AO/IC* is adequately designed and existing, the substantive tests can be reduced by 75% in relation to the original sample size. To assure the adequate design and existence of the *AO/IC*, the tax auditor will perform 25 tests of controls. Those tests are conducted simultaneously with the substantive testing (referred to as dual purpose tests).

If the *AO/IC* functions effectively and also includes adequate monitoring, substantive testing can be reduced by 87.5%. In addition to the dual purpose tests, the tax auditor now also reviews and discusses the monitoring activities.

In cases where monitoring is fully aligned with the tax auditing approach, substantive testing can be fully reduced. The tax auditor will only review (10% of the monitoring activities) and discuss the monitoring activities with the company.

In table 15.2 the reductions that apply in different scenarios are presented.

---

37 See section 15.8.1
38 Belastingdienst (NTCA) (2013). Controleaanpak Belastingdienst (CAB), De CAB en zijn modellen toegepast in toezicht, p. 24 (only available in Dutch).

Tax audit

Stage of audit:	Type or qualification:		
	'Traditional' AO/IC	AO/IC includes monitoring	
Preplanning			
To assure effectiveness of AO/IC	Full tests of (key)controls. Extent of testing depends on nature of the control	Focus on monitoring function, (analytical) review of performed activities, repeat a couple of tests.	
	No or ineffective AO/IC	Effective AO/IC	
Completeness checks			
Worked to be performed by the tax auditor	Nature and extent of audit procedures to be performed depends on tax auditors judgment	Reduced to a minimum (such as: reconciliation checks, examination of preliminary account adjustments)	

Accuracy checks	No or ineffective AO/IC	Adequately designed and existing AO/IC	Effective AO/IC, including a form of (internal) monitoring	(Internal) Monitoring aligned with the tax auditing approach (based on statistical sampling) with the same scope and reliability (95%))
Worked to be performed by the tax auditor	Based on statistical sampling with a full sample size. At least 60 units to be tested substantively.	75% reduction of sample size and 25 dual purpose tests (combination of test of control and substantive testing)	87,5% reduction of sample size. 25 dual purpose tests (combination of test of control and substantive testing) and review/discuss performed monitoring activities.	100% reduction of sample size. Review/discuss performed monitoring activities (10%).

Table 15.2. Summary of reductions in different scenarios

15.12 Tax audit in relation to the external auditor and tax assurance provider

The audit layer model implies that the tax auditor tries to use information gathered by others as much as possible. As explained earlier, these activities can be performed as part of the external audit. If applicable, the tax auditor now shifts to a more review-based approach instead of performing audit activities himself. In this section, two situations are discussed briefly.

15.12.1 External auditor

As part of the annual external audit, the external auditor gathers a lot of information related to the *AO/IC* of a company. And as stated in Chapter 14 'Audit of Tax' the external auditor also performs specific audit procedures related to the fiscal positions recorded in the annual accounts. Although a fiscal position often consists of various jurisdictions and not only those relevant to the tax auditor, the work performed by the external auditor can be relevant to the tax auditor.

Under certain conditions the tax auditor can take this information into account by reviewing and discussing dossiers of the external auditor.[39] Information to enlighten a taxpayer's tax position, which includes tax advice, is exempted.[40]

15.12.2 Tax assurance provider

The above also applies when a tax assurance provider has performed activities related to taxpayers' fiscal positions. Depending on the scope and quality of work performed by the tax assurance provider, tax audit procedures can be reduced.

As both (external) parties gather relevant information, the tax auditor will normally be able to reduce his own audit procedures. The tax auditor will always have to review and discuss third party services. Reduction is always a made to measure consideration, depending on the specific situation.

15.13 Tax audit and cooperative compliance or horizontal monitoring

In section 15.11, I described the benefits of a *TCF* in relation to tax audit. If an *AO/IC*, as part of a *TCF*, is designed adequately, works effectively and includes monitoring, tax audit procedures can be reduced to a minimum. In the case of cooperative compliance or horizontal monitoring, additional reductions can be made.[41] These are discussed in this section.

---

[39] NIVRA/NOvAA (2010). *Praktijkhandreiking 1113. Praktijkhandreiking inzage in de controledossiers van de openbaar accountant door de Belastingdienst.* Amsterdam: NIVRA/NOvAA (only available in Dutch).
[40] Decisions of the Dutch Supreme Court (HR) of 23 September 2005, no. 38 810, BNB 2006/21.
[41] See Chapter 6 (large entities) and Chapter 7 (small and medium sized entities) for a more detailed discussion of the concept of cooperative compliance, the requirements and benefits of this concept.

15.13.1 Pre-planning

As described in section 15.7, the pre-planning of a traditional tax audit requires a considerable amount of work to be performed. In situations of cooperative compliance or horizontal monitoring, much of the needed information will already have been provided, so numerous steps of pre-planning should not have to be repeated or at least not in full.

Furthermore, information about the design and existence of the *AO/IC* will already be discussed during compliance checks that are performed as part of the horizontal monitoring process.[42] This reduces tax auditor's activities in advance.

15.13.2 Preliminary consultations

One of the requirements of cooperative compliance is to inform the tax authority of tax relevant situations, for instance the taxpayer's point of view relating to an uncertain tax position. These issues are addressed before the tax returns are filed. By discussing these situations upfront, tax authority and taxpayer can reach mutual agreement on how to take these (uncertain) issues into account. The tax auditor now only has to determine that those issues have been taken into account accordingly. This also applies to situations of uncertainties regarding the explanation of tax law and regulations. Due to transparency on both sides all of the needed facts have been gathered already, so discussion will focus on the interpretation of (tax) laws. The tax authority benefits from this concept by reduced complexity of the tax audit. The taxpayer benefits by getting assurance in a fast and efficient way.

15.13.3 Non-routine (tax) events

The above especially applies to non-routine (tax) events, such as mergers and acquisitions. Because of their nature, these situations are often not covered by any type of internal control. Upfront discussion reduces conflicts with a tax authority.

15.14 Conclusions

It is the taxpayer's responsibility to comply with the law. Because of increasing complexity of the law, it is a challenge to be fully compliant. A *TCF* is a helpful, if not crucial, instrument to be and stay compliant.

A tax audit is one of many instruments for the tax authority to determine taxpayers' compliance. Because of its nature and extent, a tax audit can be labour intensive and time consuming. An adequate and effective *AO/IC*, as a significant part of a *TCF*, as well as third party services, for instance, performed by the external auditor or tax

---

42 See for a detailed description of this process: Belastingdienst (NTCA) (2013). *Supervision Large Business in the Netherlands*.

assurance provider, will lead to reduction of tax audit procedures. Ultimately, this should lead to the reduction of the costs of governmental supervision.

Increased attention towards tax compliance will strengthen professional development of a *TCF*. Positive evolution of the concept of cooperative compliance is to be expected.

In section 14.3 the audit of tax and tax audit are compared. Overlap in numerous areas is detected. Differences between both can also be found. Differences are possible due to the nature of the audit, the effects of certain annual accounts (especially in relation to deferred tax positions) and due to different disclosure requirements. Another difference is the amount of materiality used for both audits. Despite these differences I find that the work performed by the external auditor is (still) relevant to the tax auditor.

About the authors

Nathan Andrews (1969) is a partner and national practice leader for Deloitte's Tax Management Consulting practice in the United States. As a tax transformation specialist, Nathan has worked with corporate tax departments of all sizes across multiple industries and countries in the areas of organizational design, data management, process design and technology change for tax departments. Nathan also serves on Deloitte's Global Tax Management Consulting leadership team.

Irene Burgers (1962) holds a double-appointment at the University of Groningen, the Netherlands as Professor of International and European Tax Law at the Faculty of Law and Professor of Economics of Taxation at the Faculty of Economics and Business. She took her doctorate at this University with a dissertation entitled "The allocation of fiscal profits to branches of internationally operating banking enterprises". For this dissertation she was awarded the Mitchell. B Carroll Prize 1992, an award granted by the International Fiscal Association for the best work devoted to international tax law. She practiced tax law as tax adviser with PricewaterhouseCoopers. Furthermore she was one of the independent persons for the EU Arbitration Committee (1995 – 2013). Irene Burgers interests focus on tax aspects of doing international business from an International Tax Law, European Tax law, Tax Policy, and Tax Risk Management perspective.

Eelco van der Enden has been a partner within PwC since 2007. He leads PwC's global Tax Function Effectiveness and Tax Administration Consulting practices. Eelco has over 25 years' experience in his field. Before joining PwC in 2007 he worked for various multinationals as head of tax, treasury, risk management and cfo. Eelco is lecturer at Nyenrode Business University Centre for Tax Management and Tax Assurance and guest lecturer at many European universities. He was co-founder of the Tax Assurance Academy. He published more than 25 articles on tax governance and is chief-editor of the Tax Assurance Magazine.

Joost Engelmoer (1984) is a Charted Accountant (RA) and works at the Netherlands' Tax and Customs Administration (Financial Institution Unit, a Large Case division). Joost studied Accountancy at Nyenrode Business University and Tax Law at Vrije Universiteit van Amsterdam (Cum Laude). He is a guest lecturer on Tax Assurance at Tilburg University. Joost's contribution to this tax assurance book is written in his personal capacity.

Eveline Gerrits (1966) started her career as an auditor at Arthur Young (currently EY) in 1988. From 1992 up till and including 2003 she has been working with the Dutch

Tax Authorities as a tax auditor for the banking group. Since 2003 she is working for Meijburg & Co as a tax lawyer, specialized in tax accounting and the tax control framework. This period includes working for Nuon Energy NV as an internal tax accountant from 2009 until 2011. Furthermore Eveline is working on a PhD regarding the mutual influence of tax accounting rules and legislation on tax policy, tax advice and tax compliance at the Tilburg University (Netherlands).

Hans Gribnau is a Professor of Tax Law at the Fiscal Institute and the Centre for Company Law at Tilburg University and at Leiden University; e-mail: J.L.M.Gribnau@tilburguniversity.edu.

He teaches methodology of tax law, procedural tax law and research skills. His current research interests lie in the quality of tax regulation, the regulatory use of tax law, governance and tax ethics. He has extensively published in these research fields as well as on procedural tax law, tax theory, legal principles, trust & compliance theory, and Spinoza. For some English publications, see: http://ssrn.com/author=441648.

Richard Happé (1946) is an emeritus professor of tax law. Before, he was a professor at the Fiscal Institute Tilburg of Tilburg University in the Netherlands from 1997 till 2011. His specializations are procedural tax law, methodology of tax law. His field of expertise also includes ethics of taxation and tax assurance.

He is also a deputy judge at the Courts of Appeals of Amsterdam and 's-Hertogenbosch. After obtaining his law degree from Leiden University in 1971, he also obtained his philosophy degree in 1988. From 1991 until the end of 1997 he was a part time teacher and researcher at the Leiden University.

In 1997 he obtained a doctorate in law. Before he was appointed as a professor, he had worked for the Dutch Tax Administration for 25 years. Among other things, he was a corporate tax inspector and head of the education of tax inspectors at the former Education Institute of the Ministry of Finance.

Bas Herrijgers (1983) works at the Netherlands Tax and Customs Aministration (Segment Large Entities). Bas studied Accountancy at Nyenrode Business University and Tax Law at Vrije Universiteit van Amsterdam. He is a guest lecturer Tax Assurance at Tilburg University. Furthermore Bas is working on a PhD regarding the audit of tax in the financial statements and the influence of this audit on the compliance strategy of Tax Authorities at the Nyenrode Business University. His contribution to this book is personal and does not necessarily reflect the views of his employer.

Robbert Hoyng (1968) is a senior tax partner, leading Deloitte's Tax Management Consulting Group (TMC) in the Netherlands and member of the Global TMC leadership team. Robbert has been working for both Deloitte Consulting and the Tax function. His background is on strategy and change management and since 1998 Robbert has applied this knowledge in the tax arena. Robbert is visiting lecturer at Tilburg University.

About the authors

Mark Kennedy (1975) is a tax partner within Deloitte's Tax Management Consulting (TMC) group in the UK. Mark leads the UK's Tax Strategy, Risk and Operations team and specialises in helping multinational clients address their most significant tax management challenges. Mark leads Deloitte's engagement with the UK tax authority on compliance issues and regularly presents and is published around the themes of tax strategy, governance and control

Elmer van Lienen has over 16 years of experience in advising international and national clients with respect to the (inter)national payroll taxes position. He is part of the Employee Benefits Tax Consultancy team of PwC in the Netherlands. Mr. van Lienen developed best practice methods for and with clients with respect to becoming in control for payroll taxes. He is very well-experienced in implementing control frameworks with clients. Mr. van Lienen is guest lecturer at the University of Tilburg with respect to the Tax Assurance program. Further, Mr. van Lienen is registered at the Register for *Tax Assurance Providers (in Dutch: RTAP).*

Edwin van Loon (1966) started working as a tax auditor trainee (1985-1987) and subsequently joined BIG 4 audit firms as an auditor in The Netherlands and The Dutch Antilles (1987-2004). Before joining ING Bank N.V. as Tax Control Framework Project leader, Edwin has lead an international team of Indirect Tax advisors, Technology and IT specialists, focusing on the design and implementation of Indirect Tax risks and opportunity assessment techniques and technology, Indirect Tax Function performance measurement methods and Indirect Tax auditing.

Edwin is a Chartered Tax Assurance Provider and tax assurance trainer at a number of Universities in The Netherlands. Edwin is a frequent speaker on conferences and seminars in The Netherlands and abroad for a variety of International Institutions, lecturing about Indirect Tax Auditing and Indirect Tax Assurance.

Marieke Louwen has almost 7 years of experience in advising clients on (inter) national payroll taxes related issues. She is part of the Employee Benefits Tax Consultancy team of PwC in the Netherlands. Mrs. Louwen is very well-experienced in assisting (international) clients to become more in control for payroll taxes, in identifying the payroll taxes risks and the implementation of the control measures which can be taken in this respect. Further, she is specialized in the designing and implementing of payroll taxes processes. Mrs. Louwen is a member of The Dutch Association Of Tax Advisers (in Dutch: NOB).

Jeltje van der Meer-Kooistra is emeritus Professor of Financial Management at the Faculty of Economics and Business, University of Groningen. Until 2010 she was director of the Management Accounting Research Institute and director of the BSc and MSc Accountancy & Controlling. Her research focuses on the management and control of intra-firm and inter-firm transactional relationships. Her current research projects include the following topics: the governance of product development projects, the role of learning processes in developing control of inter-firm relationships, dynamics in joint venture relationships, and the management and control of intra-firm transactions. She is a member of the editorial board of the journals *Management*

Accounting Research, Qualitative Research in Accounting & Management and *MAB*, a Dutch scientific journal.

Ronald Russo (1963) started work as a tax inspector in 1985 and switched to tax consultancy in 1990. From 2006 he works for the Fiscal Institute of Tilburg University (Netherlands), currently as academic director of tax economics and responsible for the Tax Assurance program. Prior to this he has worked for the universities of Utrecht and Leiden combining this with his work as a tax inspector and tax consultant. He holds a PhD in (tax) law (1992). His current research includes the concept of profit for taxation purposes and the interactions with the profit for commercial purposes, nationally but also in a European perspective as well as tax assurance in its broadest sense.

Eric van der Stroom is specialised on advising organisations to be in control for tax. He works for the Tax Reporting & Strategy practice at PwC in the Netherlands. Eric advises international and national clients on improving their Tax Control Framework, including the set-up of their tax policy and tax department, process descriptions, tax controls and implementing monitoring and testing activities. He also advises organisations on cooperative compliance arrangements between tax authorities and tax payers. Eric has written several publications and regularly provides guest lectures on these topics.

Jan van Trigt is a senior partner in The Netherlands' tax practice of Deloitte. He has a wide range of experience during a 25 years career in tax which started with Dutch Revenue Service and continued since 1989 with the current firm.
The clients for which Jan is working are active in an international field. Type of work is related to: strategy, risk management, governance, efficiencies in tax accounting and compliance processes, technology and data analytics.

Robbert Veldhuizen (1965) is a Chartered Accountant (RA) and Certified IT auditor. Until 2013 he was technical coordinator Tax Audit and member of the Tax Compliance Expert Team of the National Office of the Netherlands Tax and Customs Administration (NTCA). Since 2007 Robbert is involved with the development of the Horizontal Monitoring programme of the NTCA. He is co-author of several policy documents and guidelines on supervision of the NTCA. With Ronald Russo he started the Tax Assurance program in the masters programs Tax Law and Tax Economics, at Tilburg University in the Netherlands in 2011. In 2013 he started as the project leader of a study into the individual account management for large businesses by the NTCA. The objective of this study is to get a better understanding of the impact of the treatment strategy on the tax compliance of large businesses. Robbert is PhD student at Tilburg University. His research is on internal control and compliance management systems. He provides lectures at Tilburg University, Delft University of Technology and Nyenrode Business University in the Netherlands. Any views expressed, in his contribution to this book, are those of the author and do not necessarily reflect those of the NTCA.

About the authors

Arco van de Ven is a full professor Accounting Information Systems at Tias – school for business and society at Tilburg University. His research focuses on risk management, the controlling profession and internal control. He is a chartered accountant (RA) by education and did his PhD at Erasmus University Rotterdam. As a practitioner Arco fulfilled a number of positions as a (interim) CFO, Controller and consultant. He was program director of different post-initial master educations, the Executive Master of Finance & Control (Register Controller) and Certified Public Controlling at the Erasmus University Rotterdam and the Financial Controller education of the Open University of the Netherlands. Currently Arco is a member of different supervisory and advisory boards, and member of the examination board of Tias.

Leen Wesdorp (1966) is a certified public accountant and also graduated with a Master Degree in Information Management at Nyenrode University. Before joining Ernst & Young in 2006, Leen worked in the Dutch tax administration for more than 17 years as a tax inspector, tax auditor and member of the APA/ATR team. Leen is an Executive Director in EY's Rotterdam office. He is a specialist in Dutch corporate taxation and tax accounting. Since joining EY in 2006, Leen has focused on corporate tax advice and tax accounting. His clients mainly consist of quoted multinationals. Leen acts as a lector at Nyenrode University and at the University of Tilburg and also as an instructor for IFRS and US GAAP tax accounting courses within EY (EMEA) and also facilitates accounting trainings and workshops for clients. Leen's contribution to the this tax assurance book is written in his personal capacity.